Debt Capital Markets in China

Founded in 1807, John Wiley & Sons is the oldest independent publishing company in the United States. With offices in North America, Europe, Australia, and Asia, Wiley is globally committed to developing and marketing print and electronic products and services for our customers' professional and personal knowledge and understanding.

The Wiley Finance series contains books written specifically for finance and investment professionals as well as sophisticated individual investors and their financial advisors. Book topics range from portfolio management to e-commerce, risk management, financial engineering, valuation and financial instrument analysis, as well as much more.

For a list of available titles, visit our Web site at www.WileyFinance.com.

Debt Capital Markets in China

DR. JIAN GAO

John Wiley & Sons, Inc.

Published by John Wiley & Sons, Inc., Hoboken, New Jersey.
Published simultaneously in Canada.

Wiley Bicentennial logo: Richard J. Pacifico.

For general information on our other products and services or for technical support, please contact our Customer Care Department within the United States at (800) 762-2974, outside the United States at (317) 572-3993 or fax (317) 572-4002.

Wiley also publishes its books in a variety of electronic formats. Some content that appears in print may not be available in electronic books. For more information about Wiley products, visit our Web site at www.wiley.com.

Library of Congress Cataloging-in-Publication Data:

Gao, Jian.
   Debt capital markets in China / Jian Gao.
     p. cm. — (Wiley finance series)
   Includes bibliographical references and index.
   ISBN-13: 978-0-471-75120-5 (cloth)
   ISBN-10: 0-471-75120-0 (cloth)
1. Government securities–China. 2. Bond market–China. 3. Debts, Public–China. I. Title.
   HG5785.G35 2007
   332'.04150951–dc22

                                                                 2006026721

Printed in the United States of America.

10 9 8 7 6 5 4 3 2 1

Contents

v

Foreword

The stunning transformation of the Chinese economy over the past 28 years is, by far, the most remarkable chapter the world has ever seen in the modern-day saga of economic development. The breakthroughs have been especially dramatic since the early 1990s. As recently as 1991, China and India stood at parity in terms of gross domestic product per capita—around US$350 per person. In 2006, China's living standard as measured by this gauge was about $2,000 per capita—more than double the $800 level in India. It is not that India fared poorly on the road to economic development—to the contrary, its improved state of economic prosperity has been most impressive. But India's accomplishments pale in comparison. In the past 15 years, China has rewritten all that we once thought we knew about economic development.

China's extraordinary journey has revealed its strengths but also unmasked some if its weaknesses. China's strength can be boiled down to one simple concept—reform—and by the willingness of its leadership and people to push ahead on reforms at all costs. In doing so, China is engineering a truly remarkable transformation from a state-owned system controlled by central planners to a privately owned system ruled by the marketplace. Today, China is close to midway in this transformation—essentially a blended economy that straddles both state and private ownership regimes. Market forces are evident in many areas of economic activity but glaringly absent in others. But China is now past the point of no return—its commitments to a market-based system have now taken on a life of their own, and there is no turning back.

That places China at a critical juncture in its transformation to a modern economy. It has pushed its current growth model to the limit—a model dominated by exports and by investments in infrastructure and manufacturing capacity that support export production. In fact, China may well have taken this model too far. It has become overly reliant on becoming a supplier to the rest of the rest of the world and has neglected the development of its internal demand. Collectively, exports and fixed asset investment now make up about 80 percent of Chinese GDP. By contrast, private consumption fell to a record low of 38 percent of Chinese GDP in 2005. The result is an unprecedented—and unsustainable—state of internal imbalance in China's booming economy. As indicated in the newly enacted eleventh Five-Year Plan adopted by the National People's Congress in March 2006, the Chinese government is committed to an important rebalancing of its economy, with focus aimed at correcting the imbalance between excess supply and inadequate internal demand by reining in a runaway investment boom while at the same time taking actions to boost the emergence of a strong and vibrant consumer culture.

Chinese is missing one key piece in its development model that is essential in order to engineer a successful rebalancing: capital markets reform. In particular, the allocation of capital remains very much in the hands of an inefficient, fragmented, and antiquated banking system. In 2005, for example, China's domestic capital markets—equity and bonds, combined—accounted for only about 15 percent of the total funds raised by the business sector. Banks, however, accounted for fully 85 percent of total credit intermediation. Yet China's banking system is ill-equipped to handle the bulk of the capital allocation process. There is a veritable absence of risk-adjusted commercial lending practices—an important mainstay of modern market-based financial systems. With a fragmented banking system long focused on funding China's vast network of inefficient and largely unprofitable state-owned enterprises, the Chinese banking system has become encumbered by a massive buildup of nonperforming loans. In the meantime, the projects those loans have funded have left the real side of the Chinese economy with an equally serious problem of excess capacity in many key industries and sectors. especially aluminum, cement, steel, coal, autos, and, of course, residential property.

A fragmented banking system, with lending practices dominated at the local level by the employment and social stability objectives of local Communist Party officials—is a recipe for a chronic misallocation of capital and a further buildup of excess capacity. Putting bank lending on a sound, risk-adjusted commercial basis through accelerated banking reform is an increasingly urgent challenge facing China in its next phase of economic development. The good news is that Beijing is very focused on this task. The bad news is that it has only just begun. Two of the four major policy banks have been publicly listed in world equity markets, and the remaining two should follow suit shortly. But the initial public offering is only the first step in a long reform process that must, in the end, lead to the establishment of a centralized, commercially sound lending culture—a far cry from the legacy of policy-based lending that has long plagued Chinese banks. Nor can banks be expected to do the job alone. The market-driven allocation of well-developed equity and bond markets are two additional and very important legs of the stool that must be added to the Chinese capital allocation process. The sooner China pushes ahead on such capital markets reforms, the better.

Dr. Gao Jian offers an important prescription on how that task can be accomplished. There is no practitioner better qualified than Dr. Gao, who is known to insiders as the father of the Chinese bond market, to lay the groundwork for what could well end up being the most rapidly growing corporate bond market in the world. *Debt Capital Markets in China* is a living testament of the genesis of the Chinese bond market. It is actually Dr. Gao's third book on the Chinese bond market but the first such effort ever published in English. But it is far more than a history book—it is a bible of a market at the dawn of creation. It offers the reader a detailed assessment of what it will take for the Chinese bond market to grow and prosper.

Gao Jian does not underestimate the daunting task that lies ahead for China in the establishment of a fully functioning corporate bond market. But he is equally insistent that China has no choice other than to move quickly down that path. He argues forcefully that it is not only an essential piece of the efficient capital allocation process but that it is equally important to ensure the efficacy of monetary and financing policies of the central government. As the experience in the West has long demonstrated, bond markets are linchpins of well-developed financial systems. They also provide important benchmarks for international investors to value one economy relative to others—in this case, offering China an international scorecard on its accomplishments. Given the heavy lifting that lies ahead in the next stage of Chinese reforms and development, Dr. Gao argues that it is hard to envision success without a well-developed bond market. I couldn't agree more.

This book is, by far, the most complete reference document I have ever seen on the subject. From the history and legal framework of the Chinese bond market to its interface with China's treasury market and public policy, *Debt Capital Markets in China* leaves few stones unturned. I took away three lessons from this masterful text: First, the development of the Chinese bond market cannot occur in a vacuum. As Dr. Gao stresses, the establishment of the rule of law and private ownership rights go hand in hand with a fully functioning bond market. The development of market-driven currency and monetary policies are equally important byproducts of the capital-market reform equation. Second, China cannot hope to establish a thriving business sector without the assistance of a robust domestic bond market. China has the most "open" development model I have ever seen, stressing cross-border connectivity to a vast network of suppliers and end markets. Yet an increasingly market-based Chinese economy will not succeed in pushing ahead on the next leg of its development journey unless the financial underpinnings of such a corporate structure are, as Dr. Gao notes, deep and balanced. Third, China's bond market will not spring to life overnight. Dr. Gao underscores the painstaking efforts that have been required to get this far on the journey. Given the complexity of Chinese regulatory and bureaucratic oversight, capital markets reform, in general—and the development of the bond market, in particular—is a process that could easily take another five to ten years.

In recent years, the world has been stunned by the emergence of China as a major economic power. So far, however, this emergence has been quite lopsided: concentrated more on the production side of the real economy than on the financial side of its capital markets. That imbalance needs to be rectified in the years ahead. China is now the fourth largest economy in the world. Yet, adjusted for its size, it has the smallest bond market in the world. That bond market must grow to a size that is commensurate with the scale of its business sector and real economy. Such growth is now under way, but it is only a glimmer of what to expect in the years to come. In fact, I can't imagine a more exciting growth story for any financial market. For English-speaking market participants who are on the outside looking in, Dr. Gao Jian's *Debt Capital Markets in China* is both a handbook and a guide of what to expect along the way. It is a reference manual that I am confident will stand the test of history for years to come.

STEPHEN S. ROACH
Chief Economist, Morgan Stanley
New York
September 2006

Preface

*D*ebt Capital Markets in China is a book about the history and development of China's contemporary debt capital market. It is the culmination of my 15 years' experience in, as well as my research into, China's treasury and banking systems. In it, I hope to introduce readers to China's debt capital market, which is essential for an understanding of its financial market and the economic reform occurring throughout China today.

The bond market is part of my life—it is the focus of my devotion and dedication. I belong to a generation whose destiny was randomly governed by various political movements. Prior to the reform, I was sent to the countryside for reeducation, a movement that reshaped the lives of at least two generations. Next, I served in the armed forces. Later, I stepped into a public securities bureau. Such experiences were typical at that time. Like a small boat adrift on the tide of political movements, I had little freedom to select a job in which I might really be interested. However, I was fortunate and always landed in the forefront of the times. Although my early life contributed very little to my academic career, it had a positive impact on building my character, and, as the rest of my life demonstrates, I have benefited a great deal from those experiences.

After the reform, I had an opportunity to study in university, and I graduated from Beijing College of Political Science and Law in 1982. I immediately went to work in the Ministry of Finance. I began in the comprehensive planning department, first in the Division of General Financial Planning and then in the Statistical Division. I spent one year with the Legal Department before stepping into the State Debt Department in 1990, which was the beginning of my career in the bond market.

China's financial market is becoming increasingly integrated with the world's financial markets. As a result, there has been a growing interest in understanding China's economic development. On the eve of World Trade Organization participation, China is pressing ahead with its commitment to open its capital markets to foreign competition by 2007. It is therefore essential that those outside China understand its bond market. This book is intended for a wide audience, including investors, academics, and others generally interested in Chinese contemporary economic development.

WHY I WROTE THIS BOOK

As Norman Chan, the deputy chief executive of the Hong Kong Monetary Authority pointed out during the discussion at the UNESCO roundtable conference in April 2000:

> *There are numerous studies and literature about the bond market in Asia explaining why it is relatively underdeveloped. There has been little disagreement amongst the policymakers and regulators in Asia on the desirability of developing their domestic bond markets. The advantages have become even more self-evident after the latest Asian financial crisis. Yet, despite this consensus, the question still remains: why is it that domestic bond markets are still developing at a rather disappointingly slow pace notwithstanding the benefits an economy can gain from them?*

This is a very good question indeed. It is my hope that China's experiences can provide some insight into the question. In my view, bond market development in China rests on four pillars:

1. Innovative ideas
2. Institutional evolution
3. The role of agencies
4. Technological progress

This view later evolved into the IEEN (institutional economic engineering) framework, reinforced and transfixed throughout this book. However, most of the comments thus far on this issue emphasized only on the importance of market structure and regulatory framework without a consistent theoretical framework to reveal the essence of the debt capital market, which I would set as my task.

LEARNING FROM HISTORY: SHARING EXPERIENCES, DRAWING LESSONS

Although Asia's bond capital markets are generally underdeveloped, and China's is no exception, the reasons behind this underdevelopment are manifold. The case in China is unique. China is a large country, and its debt capital market in particular is built on an inefficient financial market at a nascent stage in the development of its market economy; that is, China is in the process of transforming itself from a planned economy into a market economy.

Using historical development as our road map, we must gain insights and draw lessons from this important period, so that we can further improve China's market mechanisms. As Victor Hugo stated, "If a writer wrote merely for his time, I would have to break my pen and throw it away." In this book, therefore, I summarize the experience of China's bond market in order to achieve a better understanding that will help us improve it.

First, it is apparent that an appropriate strategy is essential to the development of China's bond market. The reasons for establishing a sound bond market need to be very well defined. The lesson we can draw from the past is clear: If a bond market is built only for the purpose of financing, the bond market will inevitably fail. China's stock market around the turn of this century was an example of this failure.

It is also apparent that the strategy used has to be consistent with Chinese characteristics. Government agencies need to understand that if the objective is financing, first a financial market must be established. To build a financial market, there must be a clearly delineated institutional framework.

Second, the establishment of an institutional framework for the bond market is crucial to the market. Institutional investors, financial intermediaries, a bond dealers' association, and a settlement and clearance company are all interconnected and critical to the overall success of the bond market.

China's experience shows that without a sound institutional investor base, it is impossible to establish a liquid and cost-effective bond market. Institutional investors are market experts who tend to participate in the primary market and trade bond instruments frequently.

A financial intermediary whose function is to reduce trading costs is essential to the smooth functioning of the market. For a long time, China's financial intermediary industry did not exist; financial intermediaries were thought of as a "merchants," people who earned money without incurring cost, which in China has a negative connotation. This prevailing view hindered the thinking of government debt managers and eventually dragged down the development of China's financial intermediary industry. Today the role of the financial intermediary is recognized, and this led to the first step of market-oriented reform (i.e., the 1991 underwriting syndication program).

For many years prior to bond market reform, bond distribution (placement) was very costly. For example, the expenses incurred in printing, transporting, and safeguarding paper securities were extremely high, creating a large financial burden for the government. Thus, it is in the government's interest to reduce these costs. Therefore, a paperless bond trading system (book-entry form) is a prerequisite for a cost-effective bond market. The government realized that it was necessary to eliminate the costs associated with paper securities; however, this is possible only if institutional investors and financial intermediaries are part of the system.

Third, the rational sequencing of any reform program is very important. A well-prepared reform program has to include every step of the reform program. China's bond market reform followed a rational sequence.

Institutional investors and financial intermediaries were introduced first, so that paperless securities could be instituted. Before 1991, bonds were sold mainly to individuals through an administrative network, so there was no need for institutional investors. Individuals, each of whom held a small number of bonds, preferred paper securities because they were easy to store at home and could be seen and touched, which made individual investors feel safer.

In 1991, when the underwriting syndication was introduced, syndicate members included both financial intermediaries and institutional investors, who preferred the convenience of book-entry form securities, which were introduced in 1993. (As newly issued securities become paperless, the stock exchange can use its electronic transmission system to trade securities.)

Following the introduction of the book-entry form for newly issued securities in the primary market, the Shanghai Stock Exchange in collaboration with the Ministry of Finance set up a special section for trading government securities; however, the coupon or rate of interest of newly issued government bonds was still determined by the State Council. As a consequence, the primary issues were not market based, and there was no de facto primary market at all.

The need for market-based pricing of the primary issue soon became evident. In 1995, the Ministry established the settlement date auction, creating a market-based primary market that continues to this day. However, existing bearer bonds remained untradable at the time.

The Ministry next set in motion a series of programs to establish a settlement and clearance system that was designed to eliminate paper securities—specifically, to create paperless book-entry form securities that are traded electronically. In 1996, the Ministry, in collaboration with the People's Bank of China, officially established the China Government Securities Depository Trust Company. Financial innovation, including the China Development Bank's (CDB) endeavors in the post-reform era, started to flourish. In 1996, 10-year bonds, which were the longest-maturing bond in China at that time, were introduced. Their creation was possible because pension and insurance funds had developed and become the mainstay of institutional investors.

In only five years, China had established a framework for its contemporary bond market, an achievement that has as much to do with its strategy, implementation sequence, and institution-based efforts as it does to its vision and courage.

Fourth, without a sound money market and sound financial market, a bond market cannot be developed. As China's debt capital market developed faster than other components of its financial market, the weaknesses of the money market have become problematic. In Hong Kong, it is noted, the Hong Kong Monetary Authority (HKMA) is always able to stimulate bond market development, but the government bond market there is small because the government has been running a fiscal surplus for many years. Hence, there is little need to issue government bonds. Therefore, the HKMA has to issue short-term commercial paper to absorb liquidity. As Hong Kong's money market has been put in place, should conditions permit (as is present the case), the HKMA is ready to develop a sound bond market.

Unlike Hong Kong, China has a growing government deficit since reform, which it must finance by issuing government bonds. This requires that government bonds be issued on a regular basis. Thereby it is possible to provide a benchmark for China's bond market. However, although the bond market is developing, the slow pace of money market development has held the bond market back. The recent development of money market instruments is reassuring and should activate and energize the interbank bond market. Although the central bank's move is driven by its desire to streamline its monetary policy instruments, it is also conducive to the bond market.

SPECIAL CHARACTERISTICS OF CHINA'S BOND MARKET

Admittedly, the reform of the bond market has benefited from the experiences of Western countries, especially the United States. Working in the Ministry, I have had many chances to learn from my experiences abroad. I benefited tremendously from the study and training I received in the United States and Europe. I studied debt management at the World Bank program at the Economic Development Institute in 1989 and 1990 and the banking business in Italy in 1983. Three years later, I spent a few months attending a program in the Japan Economic Planning Agency on macroeconomic planning, followed by the International Monetary Fund program on financial programming. Later, working in the Government Bond Management Department, I attended seminars sponsored by JP Morgan, Credit Suisse First Boston, Lehman Brothers, Chase, and Salomon Brothers on fixed-income and derivative instruments. These experiences and on-the-job training acquainted me with advanced financial theory and fresh ideas, which I have used as I formulate and apply the latest ideas to the reform of China's bond market.

It is important to understand, however, that the reform of China's bond market is by no means a copy of the Western system. The Western tree cannot be transplanted on China's soil without grafting. This is true for every reform program. For example, the United States uses an auction system to sell government bonds; syndicates are available only for selling corporate bonds. In China, the Ministry of Finance holds syndicate members liable for subscribing government bonds because without this requirement, syndicate members have no incentive to bid in the auction process. Furthermore, Chinese bond auctions use both the multiple-price (American) auction and uniform-price (Dutch) auction systems while the United States and the United Kingdom use only multiple-price auctions.

In China, the financial intermediary industry remains underdeveloped. Moreover, since there are not enough instruments traded in the secondary market and there is no when-issued short selling before the offering, bidders cannot be certain what the "right" price bid should be. Therefore, changing price differentials were designed to narrow the bidding range. This practice is also unique to China.

Combining the latest innovations in the West with China's specific situation is a difficult task. Symmetrical bonds, for example, were a Chinese invention. China issues the same amount, same maturity, fixed-rate bonds as floating-rate notes, and, after one year, investors can swap one with the other. China Development Bank recently launched a securitization program. It is not, however, a simple replica of the U.S. practice in which an asset-backed security or mortgage-backed security is issued via a special-purpose vehicle (SPV). Although use of SPVs is against China Securities Act and Corporate Act, the CDB instead pursues its securitization program via a trust institution.

All these synthesized instruments are China-specific. I resist the temptation to assert that this universally applicable, but it fits well on an ad hoc basis in China presently. Using innovative ideas and considering successful experiences around the globe, China has been able to create its own version of financial market development; indeed, China's fertile soil will undoubtedly engender fresh models as a legacy for the rest of the world.

FOREIGN INTEREST IN CHINA'S BOND MARKET

Foreign interest in China's domestic market can be traced back to 1993, when executives from Morgan Stanley started to talk to me about how to open China's market to the outside world. Subsequently, many efforts were made to position China's market on the world stage. Clearly, it is in our interests to integrate our market with those of the rest of the world.

I am frequently asked about the timetable for opening China's bond market. Actually, the gradual process is already underway. There are a number of joint ventures between foreign banks and their Chinese counterparts (domestic securities firms). Recently qualified foreign institutional investors were introduced to participate in the secondary bond market, though at the early stage, some restrictions have been imposed. The CDB wishes to see foreign participation in its syndicate and, better still, foreign bank participation in China's primary bond market. Foreign banks still need to obtain the licenses from the China Banking Regulatory Commission.

As China's financial market is increasingly integrated with those of the rest of the world, it is essential that investors and financial institutions alike gain a greater understanding of this market in order to pave the way for future participation in it.

The growing importance of the bond market to developing a sound financial market and facilitating economic development stimulated government officials and researchers to consider the main weakness of China's current economy. Many books have been devoted to the stock market, but so far relatively little attention has been paid to the problems in the bond market. Yet we have seen a growing need for a thorough inspection and review of the bond market in order to convince the decision makers of the need for a fundamental change. I have written several books on the subject in Chinese since the mid-1990s, which I have modified over time to reflect the changes that have occurred in the bond market as well as the evolving economic environment.

From my experience with bond market reform and the concomitant financial innovations, I realized I had to address two kinds of problems:

1. The growing need to improve awareness of market participants—for example, securities firms—of the positive implementation of reforms.
2. The need to educate market participants, especially individual investors, about how to calculate bond yield.

The need to educate investors and even bank depositors stimulated my thinking about initiating an investor education program, and the books I wrote were part of these efforts. I hope that they are useful for those who are engaged in bond investment and trading, researchers, and others who are interested in China's bond market. My first book, written in 1993, is a research paper named *The Issues on China's Government Debt*. The second book is a descriptive introduction to China's bond market and covers its historical development, the functional and operational aspects of the primary and secondary markets, settlement of bonds, and market participants and financial intermediaries. Its original title was *China's Government Bonds*, and it was published in 1996. After I wrote that book, I moved to the China Development Bank, where my focus has been on the bond market. The CDB is one of the major bond issuers in China, with an issuing volume second only to the Ministry of Finance. Thus my knowledge of the bond market was no longer confined to government bonds, and therefore, in 2000, I updated the book and renamed it *China's Bond Market*.

At the CDB, my devotion to the bond market remains unchanged. Moreover, CDB governor Chen Yuan, a reform-minded former central bank governor, is fully supportive of my innovative endeavors and academic pursuits. After several years, the CDB became the pioneer in bond market innovations. Furthermore, since 2002, the CDB has been one of the largest underwriters of corporate bonds. During this time, I have had several opportunities to participate in seminars and conferences on bond market development in China.

My third book, *Government Bond Market*, is a technical introduction to the bond market in China. Its focus is on the time value of money and the calculation of the yield of different bond instruments. I also introduced derivative markets to give the reader some idea of how derivative instruments, such as swaps, options, and futures, are priced in China.

Debt Capital Markets in China is based on *China's Bond Market*, but with four major changes. First, a theoretical framework is established to give a full explanation of debt capital market development in China. Second, it is a translation of a more up-to-date, not-yet-published Chinese version. Third, it provides more background information to make it easier for non-Chinese readers to understand the evolving processes of the market. Fourth, it provides greater focus on the operational aspects to reflect the fact that technical progress played an important role in the development of China's bond market.

HOW TO USE THIS BOOK

This book, which provides a comprehensive introduction to China's debt capital market based on a theoretical framework, is divided into eight principal parts:

Part One provides a sketch of the overall financial market in China from a theoretical and practical perspective. To highlight the main features of the bond market in China, comparisons are made between the bond market there with that in the rest of world.

Part Two provides a historical perspective and offers a description of the development of the primary market in China.

Part Three focuses on the bond market's status and the historical development of the secondary bond market in China as well as the relationship between the primary market and secondary market. Special attention is paid to the operational aspects of the bond market, including how to open an account in a securities firm, delivery versus payment trading, and the development of financial intermediaries in China.

Part Four focuses on policy issues.

Part Five is devoted to the organization and legal structure of China's bond market.

Part Six looks at the international market and considerations affecting market entry, covering the history of international bond offerings. The legal process is described in detail to give practitioners a road map to how to conduct an international bond offering for Chinese issuers. This part also highlights the market strategy of the issuers; Chinese borrowers always misunderstand this strategy when they enter the international capital market.

Part Seven delves into non-governmental bond instruments. The corporate bond market and the financial debenture bond market, among others, are described in detail, as are innovations of the CDB.

Part Eight emphasizes the relationship between the economy and the bond market. Special attention is paid to the size of government debt calculated as a debt to gross domestic product ratio.

In order to be faithful to the original framework, which I believe is sound, I have primarily used the writings and source materials developed for the Chinese version of this book. However, the English version is designed to meet the needs and preferences of English-language readers who are interested in China's bond market. Therefore, sections that are of interest only to Chinese readers have been eliminated. Every effort has been made to facilitate the understanding of the bond market for those who do not live in China. International practices and experiences have been introduced only for comparison, and to the extent necessary; therefore, they are discussed as briefly as possible.

Acknowledgments

Although the original book is basically a result of my own effort, my intellectual debt is to the schools, the international organizations and financial institutions where I learned about finance banking and the securities market. This book would not have been possible without inspiration from many people. My deepest gratitude goes to each and every one of them. My largest debt goes to those who support my work and encourage me to go ahead with the reform efforts. First I want to acknowledge former minister of finance Liu Zhong Li and Vice Minister Liu Ji Bin, whose understanding and support were invaluable. Their appreciation of the idea that I proposed for the reform program served as the main impetus to support my academic endeavors. Second I must acknowledge the numerous men and women who worked with me in designing the bond market reform program and innovative financial instruments, and those who encouraged me and gave me the confidence to press ahead with the bond market reform in China. I am deeply indebted to each and every one of you.

This book could not have borne fruit without the kind and generous support of my colleagues at the Ministry of Finance and the China Development Bank, and many other financial institutions, to whom I would express my profoundest gratitude. Jing Zhao Jeme, Jin Jing and Mark Fang, who have remained longtime, loyal friends, and have firmly supported me in my endeavors. Their frequent discussions with me on many subjects concerning the economy and bond market have been critical. Special thanks to my colleagues working in the Debt Department of the Ministry and the National Association of Government Securities Dealers and Treasury Department of the CDB, who participated in the landmark events in China's bond market development. A special thank you goes to Mr. Zhu Fu Lin and Mr. Zhang Jia Lun, who supported the 1991 underwriting syndication.

I would also like to thank all my students who have helped me to gather data and information to update the statistics. Among them are Nin and Yang, Guangjin Teng, and Zhiping Zhou. My students have also shared their insights and views with me. Their assistance and support were valuable and crucial to the book. I am also indebted to my secretary, Jianming Liu, Tenshan Men who arranged the translation and many logistical issues, without whom this book could not have been prepared in time for publication. Windy Liu, who contributed to the first-round editing work, deserves many thanks. Without her, the manuscript would not have been ready for submission to the publisher.

At Wiley, special thanks to developmental editors Ellen Coleman and Emilie Herman, senior editor Bill Falloon, and senior production editor Stacey A. Fischkelta. I am grateful to these people and many others at Wiley who contributed to the production of the book.

The book would not have been possible without the help and inspiration from my family. My sister and brothers generously shouldered my part of family responsibilities while I studied and worked in Beijing. Finally, I want to thank my wife, Like Wang, and my daughter, Weishan Gao, from the bottom of my heart. Their love and care light up my world and provide a constant source of joy.

Introduction: Bond Market Reform and Financial Innovations, A Historical Perspective

I keep some paper securities as a reminder of a bygone era. They call to mind many episodes related to that special period when bond market reform was in progress. It is not the reform itself but the way in which the reform was carried out that is most important to an understanding of China's financial market and economic development as it exists today.

The reform of the bond market was an agency-initiated program, something unprecedented at the time.

The debt capital market in China had experienced profound changes, yet the path in the 1990s was rocky and labyrinthine. Reform triggered a debate over whether the placement of treasury bonds (T-bonds) should be targeted to individual or institutional investors. Of course, this is no longer the subject of debate since bond market reform, which focused on institutional investors, turned out to be hugely successful, especially when it is compared with the stock market and corporate markets, both of which suffer from either cyclical or placement problems.

In some sense, I, as one of the major designers, was at the heart of the bond market reform. However, it is the collective efforts that made it possible, and I am proud of being part of this process.

In the second half of 1990, when I transferred to the Government Bonds Management Department (now the Treasury Department) from the Comprehensive Planning Department in the Ministry of Finance as a deputy director general, treasury bonds were still distributed through administrative placement. The Finance Department set the quota and arranged with local financial departments to distribute the bonds to government agencies, institutions, and state-owned enterprises (SOEs). At that time, the public demonstrated little enthusiasm for this practice.

Although the first few transactions, in the early 1980s, were smoothly placed to SOEs and individuals, this was mainly because buying T-bonds was thought to be a patriotic deed, helping tide the central government over its financial difficulties. However, the administrative placement method aroused unease and complaints from unwilling individual buyers. Among other things, individual buyers complained about the bonds' long time to maturity and the fact that they were not redeemable prior to maturity. For these reasons, it was increasingly difficult to distribute the bonds, and promoting their sale gradually became a major task for the department.

The government, therefore, sought to reinforce the marketing organization. One measure taken was the creation of a T-bond promotion committee directly affiliated to the State Council, which had its working office at the Ministry. Another was to set up the Treasury Bond Service Department to promote the sale and redemption of treasury bonds. These departments were affiliated with the local finance departments.

When I moved to the Government Debt Management Department, I knew little about the debt market. Some of my knowledge was related to the practices in the Comprehensive Planning Department; debt management was only one of its divisions that was involved in issuing government bonds before 1989. During that time, I also participated in China's first international borrowing of DM (Deutsche Mark) 300 million in 1987.

In my endeavor to reforming China's bond market, I wished we could have followed the conventional international model, but we realized it would not work. Instead, we decided that the first step was to create an underwriting syndicate. We did not go directly to an auction system because, at the time, the coupon rate was set by the State Council and the Ministry could not change any major term—neither the face value (par) value nor the coupon rate. The Ministry, however, could change the settlement date, and, as was usually the case when the government forced individuals to buy bonds, postponing the settlement date was quite common. I therefore believed that syndication was an easier first step for the Ministry.

In 1991, market interest dropped due to rectification program initiated by the central government, and the market situation became very favorable. As a matter of fact, the coupon rate set by the State Council was close to the market rate—that is, the yield in the secondary market. I talked with people at the Stock Exchange Executive Council (SEEC), a private organization affiliated with the State Economic Restructure Commission (SERC). SEEC called together a group of young students who graduated from schools in the United States and was then actively pushing for securities market reform. Our conversation was quite friendly and we reached an agreement on the underwriting syndication program.

Everything seemed to be going well, until April 1991 when the People's Bank of China (PBOC) formally told the Ministry to cancel the signing ceremony on the agreement of the underwriters' syndication. The PBOC indicated that any move away from the then-prevailing practices had to receive its consent and that it remain at the service of the Ministry of

Finance for the sale of T-bonds. If the PBOC was not cooperative regarding this matter, the underwriting syndication program would be stillborn.

The situation was extremely urgent, and the SEEC referred this matter to Chen Jin Hua, the chairman of the SERC, who then called Wang Bing Qian, the minister of finance, to suggest that some compromise needed to be made. The minister convened a meeting and agreed that we could proceed with the program but should invite the PBOC to participate in it. He called the vice governor offering a compromise whereby the Ministry would allocate a portion of the bonds to the PBOC to keep the original channel for bond securities distribution, so that the vested interests were secured. Fortunately, in the end, the underwriting syndication program was saved.

Auction selling was instituted on trial basis in 1995. That August, an RMB1 billion offering was about to launch in Shanghai. As usual, the Ministry convened a meeting with underwriters and discussed the terms of the new issue with them. Apparently, the underwriters had no incentive to buy at the government-set coupon, and the negotiation between the Ministry and the syndicate failed to achieve the full amount that the government had intended to sell, because the parties failed to reach a consensus on the offering price. As a matter of fact, at that time, the Ministry was not in a position to change the coupon and selling price set by the State Council. The transaction was running into a stalemate.

I called Liu Jinbin, then the vice minister of finance, to report the failure of the negotiations with the underwriters and the possible shortfall in the issuing amount, and asked if it was possible to postpone the settlement date and increase the commission fees. To my surprise, Mr. Liu agreed to both my suggestions.

Based on my calculations, the range of autonomy that I was given to move settlement dates and fees were sufficient to make the bond's yield to maturity consistent with the underlying market yield. I realized that this was an opportunity to attempt a new selling method—tender—something that had been put on our reform agenda but had never been formally practiced. Encouraged by my assistants, I decided to risk using the auction method, although we were not fully prepared to do so.

We rushed through the preparatory work: first, we worked out a rule for tender. Then we used a Hongtashan cigarette paper box to hold the handwritten paper bids that the bidders were to submit at a specified time. According to the auction rule, the underwriters elected a supervisor and notary to ensure the fairness of the bidding process. Bidders were permitted to select a settlement date for the repayment of the proceeds of the issue. The closest settlement date was set for those who did not want to bid but who had to subscribe the quarto. Successful bidders were subject to the settlement date they selected, which was applicable to the quarto as well. In the end, the underwriters realized that it was better to bid than not, and, therefore, they all participated in the bidding process, which made it more competitive. The tender turned out to be a success, as it created competitiveness, and the successful bidding volume met the issuing target.

Inspired by the successful debut tender issue, the new issue technique was formally endorsed at the Ministry of Finance. Our next step was to develop a timetable for engineering electronic bidding software. In the interim, 1996's auction was conducted in a room that housed all the bidders—it was China's first formal bond auction. To avoid conspiracy and manipulation, the Ministry set a ceiling and floor for the bidding price, within a range of one-half of 1 percent. Some banks conspired to undercut the price but failed in bidding. The year 1996 was eventful; many new reform programs—for example, the 10-year T-bond and the tender selling—were carried out and resulted in satisfactory performances. Between 1997 and 1998, the auction had no bidding range. Since 1998 the bidding range was reinstituted because the State Council wanted to keep the selling yield at no more than 1 percent of the deposit rate at the same maturity.

At that moment, it seemed to me that the bond market had embarked on a market-based approach that would lead to smooth progress, but the later events proved that this would not be the case. In the second half of 1996, some individual investors complained about the problems they had in buying T-bonds. As institutions started to participate in the bond primary market, individuals were squeezed out and lost access to the primary issue. In addition, the soaring bond price in the secondary market after 1996 further stimulated individual investors' desire to buy T-bonds in the primary market.

In meeting retail investors' demands for T-bonds, the Ministry was faced with a great challenge. In 1994, savings bonds that were tailor-made for risk-averse retail investors were introduced into the market. The idea hitherto developed for introducing savings bonds was that if the individual appetite for government bonds were satisfied with savings bonds, there would be little opposition to the ongoing bond market reform, and the majority of government bonds could still be targeting to institutional investors.

We soon realized that although the individual investors needed to be protected, it was important not to lose sight of the fundamentals of the bond market, which, as we understood it, is largely a market for institutions. As the participation of the institutional investors in the primary bond market is the necessary condition for a market-based bond market and individual investors are mainly buy-and-holders, targeting just individuals would have a negative effect on market liquidity and efficiency.

Educating investors was crucial in China. Two examples prove this.

First, when I visited a Government Securities Service Department in Xuanwu District in 1993, I met a group of people waiting in a line for their turn to buy T-bonds. There were two counters, one for selling new bonds at the face value of RMB100 and the other for selling secondary bonds at a discounted value of RMB98. The two bonds had exactly the same date to maturity and coupon rate; the only difference was that the discounted bond had been issued two months earlier. All the people were waiting in the line for new bonds; no one showed any interest in the discounted bonds. I was curious, and asked one person why this was so. The answer was "The new bonds can be trusted. The discounted bonds are worthless. Their price is low because people don't want them—so they sell them." I was shocked at their ignorance.

The second example occurred just after the execution of a transaction via the administrative method. I inspected the sales records to see how individual investors responded and if there were any problems—very routine work at that time. I was accosted by a bondholder who had just bought the newly issued bond and discovered that the price in the secondary market had gone down to RMB98. He was disappointed and angry with me; he said he was cheated, and accused me of being a liar; my minister, he said, was a liar as well. I asked why. He roared, "Your ministry said this was a gilt-edged bond [presumably he meant risk free], but I have already suffered some losses!"

Understanding that he confused market risk with credit risk, I explained that we were not liars and that the bond carried a coupon and the Ministry would definitely repay the coupon and principal. He wanted the Ministry to buy back the bond at par value immediately. I explained that this was impossible because, under the rules, the bond could not be redeemed before maturity, though it could be traded on the secondary market at the market price. The next day he called to say he sold the bond at a price of RMB98. "If you don't need the money," I asked, "why not keep the bond to maturity?" He replied that he felt uncomfortable with the discounted price.

The price of this bond went up substantially over par value as the market yield went down, and I am sure this man regretted selling the bond in the secondary market.

I mention these things not to boast about my personal contributions. Rather these historical examples illustrate how the process of bond market reform was driven by the interest structure and the degree of people's awareness of the market. Without an understanding of these driving forces behind the market, it is not possible to comprehend China's challenges on the road to reform.

The agency's own interest is an important factor that also needs to be considered when we consider the reform program, and I will elaborate on this later.

INSTITUTIONAL VERSUS INDIVIDUAL INVESTORS: A PROLONGED DEBATE

While bond market reform promoted distribution efficiencies, it also triggered a prolonged debate over the issue of targeting investors. On one side were the individuals and some government agencies that favored exclusively targeting the individual; on the other side were the Ministry of Finance, local finance departments, some SOEs, and the financial intermediaries who favored targeting institutional investors and financial intermediaries.

The Ministry of Finance was criticized for neglecting the needs of individual investors. The pricing power that had been delegated—at least the ministry itself thought it had been delegated as there was no such legislation on the delegation—to the ministry was withdrawn and the coupon of government bonds was once again set by the central government and pegged to the deposit rate, which at that time was about 1 percent higher than the bank deposit rate. Between 1998 and 2002, the Ministry increased the number of savings bonds, which were first introduced in 1994, it issued in a bid to meet individual demand for T-bond investment.

Before bond market reform, individual investors were reluctant to buy T-bonds, which were distributed through administrative measures; now they changed their minds. Why? The answer is simple. There are two types of individual investors: active market players and those who buy and hold. After bond market reform, the active market players soon discovered that they could earn money from bond trading. This was especially true after 1996. As interest rates kept declining, bondholders were able to make quick capital gains. After bond market reform, financial intermediaries, including primary dealers and syndicate members, were able to directly access primary issues, while active individual players could only buy T-bonds in the secondary market. Seeing that the securities firms could get the premium of primary issue made these individual investors very unhappy.

The buy-and-hold investor perceived T-bonds as a kind of savings vehicle because of their high yield relative to deposit rates. Therefore, as is always the case, these individual investors will stand in a long lines for savings bonds.

The No. 696 transaction was the first marketable 10-year government bond. It was made possible only in the aftermath of the institution-based bond market. For a long time (1981 to 1991), government bonds were received coolly by the public because of the absence of a market; short-term government bonds—under three years' maturity—were merely acceptable. Longer-term bonds—over five years—were not salable because of the lack of a sound and liquid secondary market.

Minister Liu Zhong-Li openly expressed his concern over the increasing cost of refinancing that resulted from short-term nature of the bonds. The 10-year No. 696 bond was an experiment to see whether an auction of such a bond could be conducted successfully. As it turned out, the market perception of the bond was very positive and a sign of solid institutional participation.

The dispute culminated when the No. 696 transaction concluded and started to trade in the secondary market in June 1996. As rumors spread that the central bank was likely to lift interest rates soon, the market responded quickly, and the price went up to over RMB127, or a 27 percent increase in one month. Some individual investors who were not able to buy the bond in the primary market directed their resentment and anger onto the Ministry.

In the second half of 1996, soon after the No. 696 auction, a research institution submitted a proposal to the State Council, suggesting another new issue aimed exclusively at individual investors. Since there was no financing need, the Ministry did not want to go forward with it. In addition, it did not have approval from the National People's Council. What is more, there was the issue of how to price the new bond: Should it be at the original RMB100, or at the then market price of RMB127? If the issue were priced at RMB100, everyone would profit; if it were priced at the market price, no one would be interested.

I drew six important lessons from these incidents:

1. People's awareness of markets and government agencies' own interests are intertwined, which complicates bond market reform. Therefore, these factors must be taken into consideration.
2. Institutional change is an evolutionary, not revolutionary, process. Therefore, institutional evolution, such as the emergence of financial intermediaries and institutional investors, provides the necessary institutional framework required for changes. Without institutional change, reform would not be possible.
3. Government's role is to define property rights and provide financial infrastructure, not direct participation in market activities.
4. Organizations such as banks have the incentive to improve and build institutions. They therefore will come up with innovative ideas to stimulate their evolution.
5. The design and introduction of new financial instruments with diverse maturity profiles make the market more efficient.

6. Technological developments are catalysts for institutional change; auction selling and book-entry systems were made possible by advances in computer technology and software design.

These lessons were reinforced by my later experiences in the China Development Bank.

CHINA DEVELOPMENT BANK'S CONTRIBUTIONS TO BOND MARKET REFORM

Bond market development slowed down and was sidelined toward the end of the 1990s, as the interaction among groups with competing interests led to compromise rather than advances with the ongoing reform.

In 1999, when I joined the China Development Bank (CDB), where I hoped to continue my efforts in financial market development, I was assigned to the Treasury Department, which was responsible for financing and managing the bank's cash position.

Chen Yuan, the governor of the CDB and the former vice governor of the central bank, is a reform-minded man. Before he took the position as the governor of the CDB, the bank financed its investments by issuing financial debentures (FDs) through administrative distribution. FDs targeted mainly state-owned commercial banks as the potential investor base. From time to time, the CDB also borrowed money from the central bank. To address the liquidity issue in the banking system, it is common for the PBOC to lend money to state-owned banks through the so-called reloan facility, and reloan rates tended to be low to reflect the central bank's policy.

As early as 1996, the Treasury Department of the CDB wanted to follow the Ministry and float its securities in the market. With the arrival of Governor Yuan, their dream came true. Governor Chen permitted FDs to become a market instrument in early 1999 (before I moved to the bank), and they were placed through auction using the same electronic transmission system in the Government Securities Depository Trust Company the Ministry of Finance used. Since the market was already there, the CDB's market-oriented reform proceeded smoothly. The CDB achieved more cost-effective funding than through administrative placement.

In the 1990s, the central bank relied primarily on its reloan facility to manipulate the money supply. It soon realized how inefficient this method was and decided to improve the market environment, so that it could carry out open market operations. Part of the PBOC's efforts were to revitalize the inter-bank bond market (IBBM) in which, beginning in 1998, the CDB had become an active player. Therefore, the central bank supported, or at least gave its consent to, the CDB's market-oriented reform. In the following years, the CDB concentrated on adding to the number of bonds it issued while reducing the number of bonds via administrative placement.

As a banker, I was no longer in a position to carry out cross-institutional reform programs as I had at the Ministry of Finance. The only thing that I could do was promote financial innovation. I applied the lessons I learned from my participation in bond market reform and tried to refrain from being in the public eye, or taking credit. I encouraged my colleagues to keep low profile as well—no interviews, no TV appearances—and keep the CDB out of the spotlight.

Every time we introduced new instruments, we held a meeting with representatives of investors and financial intermediaries in order to notify them and educate them the in advance of the issuance. We explained why we designed this instrument, what its features were, and how the yield was calculated. As a rule, I also published an article to introduce the technical features of the new bond, explaining how to price it.[1] These communications and the mutual understanding they provided were essential to the diversification of bond market instruments and our other financial innovations.

The first few years of the new century witnessed a rapid development of the IBBM, as banks became the main subscribers of government bonds and FDs. In an effort to help the banks manage their assets and liabilities, in 2000, the CDB introduced floating-rate notes to the market. The notes were pegged to a one-year maturity bank deposit rate, and bids were based on the spread over one-year deposit rate, since there was no LIBOR (London inter-bank offer rate) or similar indicator in China. The instrument was very well received by the market because most investors and other market participants believed that interest rates had bottomed and would shortly rise. This instrument was soon used by many other corporate bond issuers, including the Ministry of Finance and the Export-Import Bank.

To meet the hopes of investors to hedge their risk, the CDB developed put-able bonds, which gave buyers an option to exercise the bond before maturity.

Zero-coupon bonds are popular in many countries; they were introduced for tax reasons or for creating a spot yield curve. The CDB introduced STRIPS (separate trading of registered interest and principal of securities) in 2001, which allowed the coupons to be traded separately. This contributed to the increased number of zero-coupon bonds and helped price the coupon-bearing bond instruments as the latter can be seen as a sum of the former.

The CDB was also a pioneer in issuing subdebt, which banks used to increase their tier two capital to comply with Basel II requirements. In

2002, the CDB issued the first of its kind of subdebt: a 10-year maturity, call 5, with step-up in the second 5 years, a format that is typical in the international capital market. The bond was callable; the issuer had the right, but not the liability, to exercise the option.

The market fluctuated greatly during the first few years of the decade. To stabilize it, the CDB designed a future where the price is determined by two bids. The first bid defines the rate, the second the price at settlement. If interest rates go up when the future is settled, then the second price is applicable; if interest rates go down and the second price results in a lower yield, then the initial rate applies. This future is China specific and very popular in China's bond market.

The CDB's financial innovations are not limited to bond market instruments; its financial innovations extend to asset management as well. To make bank loans, since 1999 the CDB has been exploring a securitization program. That effort bore fruit when the State Council formally endorsed the program early in 2005. Platforms for selling bank assets have been established at financial hubs, such as Beijing, Shanghai, and Shenzhen. The active participation and rising prices are evidence that these loan-selling platforms are successful financial innovations.

The success of the CDB's financial innovations is partly attributable to the PBOC's policy of supporting the IBBM, its deliberate focus on institution building, the low profile it kept in an effort not to draw public attention to itself, the persistent support of Governor Chen Yuan, and internal understanding. Although many of the instruments we introduced to China are not new elsewhere in the world, they were modified to suit China's context and its current institutional framework. For example, in China the category 1 floating-rate note is benchmarked on the one-year deposit rate rather than on a proxy of LIBOR, which, as mentioned, does not exist in China. In addition, a number of instruments created are China-specific. Among them are the auction with descending and consecutive bidding price intervals, the swap auction (in the primary market), and the securitization program without special-purpose vehicles.

Crucial to the CDB's reform efforts are the lessons that we learned from bond market reform:

- Bond market reform and financial innovations are technically simple but institutionally complex.
- To succeed, you must convince the agencies affected of the positive implications of the reform program and financial innovations, select the right time, and avoid sensitive issues.

The contribution of financial market reform, which created the institutional framework for a market-based economy, cannot be overestimated.

As J.J. and G.J. Jime pointed out in 2004, "The reforms themselves did not...cause growth and structural change, but rather created...incentives and institutions absent in the socialist planned economy, which were necessary preconditions for rapid growth and structural change to occur."[2]

I carefully considered the important lessons of both the Ministry of Finance and the CDB in my mind before I created a new theoretical framework.

Bond Market: Theory and Practice

CHAPTER 1

Theory of Institutional Economic Engineering in China

My initial intention is to describe, not theorize, about China's economic reform program. However, a proper theoretical framework is necessary in order to understand the issues and problems China faces and, more important, the possible solution to these problems.

It is my deep conviction that China will have a prosperous future as long as it chooses innovative strategies, such as market-driven reforms in the financial sector, rather than conventional wisdom as part of its economic development program.

For many years, my focus has been on economic development and China's financial and debt capital markets. In the course of my study, I have come to these conclusions:

- China will sustain relatively high rate of growth in the long term because of investment sustained by a higher savings rate, cheap labor, the evolution of its institutional framework, its ability to innovate, and so on. There will be economic fluctuations because of structural issues relating to China's financial and industrial framework.
- Governmental improvements to management and encouragement of financial innovation and evolution of institutions can help minimize the fluctuations. The debt capital market is located right at the center of the financial system. Equally important is integrating the debt capital market into the financial market. A sound legal framework, well-defined corporate governance, deregulation, the evolution of institutions, increased financial awareness, and technological progress are solutions to the debt capital market problems that China faces today.
- The crucial factor is education, education, and, again, education. The first education stands for the knowledge-based education, such as the study of economics, technology, and the like. The second type

of education is competition- or innovation-based education—mainly management science, which will help raise our competitive advantages. The third is incentive-driven, institution-based education, which will help to ensure the continued development of education. Therefore, education that fosters the creation of ideas generally and sharpens our competitive edge should be high on China's list of priorities.

I base these observations on my study of the key issues in the financial and bond markets in China, and am motivated by two fundamental questions: (1) why has mainstream economics failed to explain the phenomenon of China's financial and bond markets? and (2) why are constraints, which neoinstitutionalists[1] perceived as inherent in institutions, not a solution to China's debt capital market development? I was also inspired by recent developments in economic theory, such as information economics, game theory, and neoinstitutionalist economics,[2] which shed light on how to interpret and identify the issues in financial markets, especially the bond market in China. This exploration motivated me to develop a new theoretical framework.

First I will give a brief introduction of the institutional economic engineering (IEEN) theory. For a theory to be precise and sound, it has to be consistent with a philosophical proposition. Here I review briefly the methodological debates on economic theories and discuss the mission of all sciences: seeking for truth. Truth can be divided into relative truth and absolute truth. Absolute truth contains all relative truth insofar as conditionality and applicability are concerned. Sciences have different tranches, and the more basic sciences contain more specific and concrete science. Therefore, economics has to be built on sociological propositions, which focus on the human exchange, the principal category of sociology. By the same token, financial science is based on economic science; the theory of the debt capital market is based on financial theory.

From absolute-relative truth framework, we move along two different lines: conditionality and applicability. As basic science is less conditional than concrete science, we specify the sciences orderly in terms of conditionality and indicating the more basic science contains the more concrete science.

Institutions first can be viewed as people's social relationships; the movement of institutions is based on an interaction between incentives and constraints. Within the IEEN framework, a rhombus paradigm is used to explain the process of institution formation. IEEN aims to achieve economic development through social, socioeconomic, and economic exchange in an endogenously driven, evolutionary process. The economic exchange is accomplished mainly through markets whereas social and socioeconomic exchanges basically are achieved through means other than markets. IEEN is distinct from other theories because of its emphasis on the internal nature of driving forces behind the evolution of institutions.

Based on rhombus theory, we make a distinction between the primary exchange and the secondary exchange. The primary exchange is a mandate, or a derivative, from the secondary exchange to save exogenous transaction costs. The secondary exchange functions to reduce endogenous transaction costs. The primary political exchange deals with the relationship between the public and other actors; the secondary political exchange deals with the relationship among parties. The primary administrative exchange deals with the relationship between government and government agencies; the secondary administrative exchange deals with the relationship among the government agencies.

Similarly, the primary economic exchange deals with the relationship between government and market participants; the secondary economic exchange deals with the relationship among market participants. The primary financial exchange covers the relationship between government financial authority and financial market participants whereas secondary financial exchange covers the relationship between financial market participants. The primary bond exchange deals with the relationship between the government and bond market participants; the secondary bond exchange deals with the relationship among bond market participants. In this book, we focus on the primary and secondary economic exchange, the financial exchange, and bond exchange.

In recognition of IEEN as an applied economic science, we posit three fundamental factors underlying the path-dependent nature of institutions. This trilogy—the base-value-path (BVP) framework—is useful for creating this new methodology for the analysis of economic, financial, and capital market issues in China. Here we redefine the function of government in the economy. In light of the evolutionary nature of institutions, it is suggested that the government's role should be limited to facilitating the reduction of transaction costs, for example, by defining property rights, creating the legal framework in which markets operate, promoting innovative ideas, supporting education, and pursuing market-based macroeconomic policies.

Therefore, it is crucial that we first define what we mean by the financial system and then review current theory on the subject. Problems with the theory will be explored later. We begin by putting economic, financial, and capital market issues in a new perspective. With respect to financial markets, the new view suggests that transaction costs can be economized by institutional and technological progress. Later, in the summary of the primary market and secondary market development, I highlight the importance of institutional progress to the bond market development. There has to be an incentive to each party so that institutional progresses can be made. Parties have to reduce transaction costs to achieve a win-win arrangement. Technological progress only helps to reduce the transaction costs so that institutional progress is possible via exchange. (Please see "The Nature of Finance and the Financial Structure.")

We begin with a brief overview of financial theory, especially those that China has in common with many of the "less developed countries" (LDC; a United Nations designation). At the same time, we must remember that financial theory does have a number of drawbacks.

We then focus on the path to financial reform. Here we emphasize the importance of the initial condition of financial markets and the factors on which the government and market participants judge the condition, goal, and path the reform program takes. We also redefine the goal of financial market reform and provide several key checkpoints along the road toward achieving the goal of financial market reform. (See "A New Methodology for the Analysis of Financial Issues.")

We next examine how institutional and technological progress drive economic growth. Here we emphasize that, more often than not, the institutional revolution may not necessarily be accompanied by technological revolution. In fact, they alternate to reflect the transaction costs, or transformation cost, of the revolution. Whichever is less expensive comes first. Similarly, financial revolution precludes economic growth, and vice versa. Finally, the interaction between incentives and constraints works to make economic movement gradual. (See "The Role of the Government in the Economy.")

INSTITUTIONAL ECONOMIC ENGINEERING

The new theory on which the book is based is built on the achievements of neoclassical economic theory, especially the A-D framework, game theory, and information theory as well as the achievements of neoinstitutionalists. We will approach the new theory along three different lines.

To Douglass North, institution is the rules of game; to Masahiko Aoki, institution is the finale of game play, or an equilibrium state. In the IEED framework, both rules of game and game play are elements of institution. However, rules of game and game play are not interdependent; rather they are closely related and unified in one complex institutional arrangement. Both rules of the game and game play are engendered via exchanges. As a game-playing process, the secondary exchange, a principal exchange, will come up with an equilibrium state (the institution in Aoki's framework). The participants of the game, or exchange, are the game players or exchange participants. In most case, the rules of game are worked out by the participants or game players, and they are engendered by the secondary exchange. But the rules are likely to favor of the party who has more comparative advantages. This legitimizes the primary exchange, the exchange between the rule maker and the participants of secondary exchange. In the modern economy, primary exchange implies the exchange between government and market participants. It is reasonable to suppose that rules are not exogenously made but endogenously made via exchange. Viewed in this light, it is fair to say that the IEEN framework fundamentally deviates from the basic framework of neoinstitutionlists.

Let us look at the issues from a different perspective, in which institutions and institutional arrangements are the focus. On the face of it, institutional issues (or transaction costs) involve only information asymmetry and the enforcement of contracts and laws, but, in fact, they go far beyond this narrow definition. Institutions comprise the entire social structure (social arrangement); that is when social activities (game playing) are in equilibrium. Different pillars—internal driving forces—underlie the evolution of institutions. Internal force drives the movement of institutions while external force lays out the conditions for that movement.

Institution and technological progress can reduce transaction costs, as neoinstitutionalists point out. Therefore, the only role that the government can play is to create the conditions in which institution building and technological progress can be made. Thus, it is necessary to distinguish between government policies that reduce transaction costs and those that would increase them. This distinction can serve as a criterion by which to judge government policy. However, within the current segmented and inconsistent theoretical framework, how to address financial issues remains problematic.

Here we regard the institution as the core factor behind this economic issue and redefine it based on the new theory. The driver of evolutionary development of institutions is interpreted as an interaction between incentives and constraints.

Then we conceptualize institutions as an internal force driving the interaction between incentives and constraints. The implication is that the nature of the interaction between incentives and constraints reveals the essence of incentive structure, something that is only implied in the Douglass North's seminal work, *Institution, Institutional Change, and Economic Performance*. According to North, "Institutions are the rules of the game in a society or, more formally, are the humanly devised constraints that shape human interaction. In consequence they structure incentives in human exchange, whether political, social, or economic. Institutional change shapes the way societies evolve through time and hence is the key to understanding historical change."[3]

In addition, we want to prove that institutional progress in any society is a win-win solution. People enter a transaction with knowledge as well as certain advantages and disadvantages. The incentive of each party to a transaction is to realize the advantages and eliminate the disadvantages. This is accomplished through an exchange in much the same way as comparative advantage is negotiated in trade agreements between two countries.

It is my hope that by redefining the meaning of institution and providing an understanding of the drivers of institutional evolution, IEEN theory can provide the groundwork of the institutional architecture. My other goal is to establish the link between, or among, the different analyses of institutional development in order to make the theoretical framework more consistent and coherent.

We also highlight the importance of competitive advantages and the necessity to reduce endogenous transaction costs, but this in no way implies that comparative advantages are not important or not as important as competitive advantages. In fact, efforts are usually made either to reduce the exogenous transaction cost to sharpen the comparative advantage or to reduce the endogenous transaction cost to sharpen the competitive advantages. The one that is less painful to achieve will be used first. Note, however, that sometimes the reduction of endogenous transaction costs is achieved by the reduction of exogenous transaction costs. Comparative advantages are transferable to competitive advantage, and vice versa; the same is true of exogenous transaction costs.

By recognizing the homogenous nature of human behavior and the ubiquity of exchange, it is possible to blur the dividing line between economics and sociology and rebuild the economic groundwork so that public selection theory, game theory, information theory, and all other schools of economic theory would be a consistent part of the economic system. The common ground of such a system has yet to be established. Institutional economic engineering is an attempt to do just that.

What Is Institutional Economic Engineering?

We define institutional economic engineering as a socioeconomic science for the designing of institutions.

Nowadays financial engineering is believed, especially in China's financial sector, to be at the top of economic theory. Although the idea of introducing engineering into social economics is stimulating, the purpose of institutional economic engineering is not to pander to fashion; rather it is to extend the thinking behind the design of financial products to the design of an institutional arrangement. This philosophy fundamentally affects economic theory and has long been debated among the different economic schools, insofar as the methodology of economics is concerned.

Nowadays, it is recognized that "falsifiability" is a necessary test of any theory. Eugene Kelly puts it this way:

> *A theory, on a standard account of science, must meet at least three requirements. First, it must contain some general statements that describe relationships among phenomena or mechanisms within phenomena, in terms of which an event or a series of events can be explained. These general statements account for the known facts. Second, the account must lead us to expect as yet unobserved phenomena. It must suggest new avenues for future research. Third, it must be falsifiable, that is, it must be possible to state some observable conditions, which, if they were met, would force the alteration or abandonment of the theory. In short, the theory must explain something about the world, must suggest new ways of exploring phenomena, and must tell us what it would be like for its explanations to be wrong.*[4]

Absolute-Relative Truth Framework

However, this definition still leaves some confusion. To clarify, it is necessary to define the truth, theory and knowledge in a new framework, so that the Institutional Economic Engineering could encompass all academic contributions so far.

Max Weber's last words were: "The true is the truth."[5] I don't know what Weber implied at the moment, but I believe truth has no conditions. In existentialism, this is called "being of itself."[6]

Something unquestionably true is called *absolute* truth, or gospel; something conditionally true is called *relative* truth. Absolute truth is universally and eternally applicable; relative truth is applicable only under certain circumstances. Both absolute truth and relative truth exist in the real world, but only relative truth is observable. Absolute truth encompasses relative truth; therefore, countless relative truths are components of absolute truth. Relative truth can approach being an absolute truth but can never equal the absolute truth.

It is worthless to argue whether the conditions and assumptions of a relative truth are true or false. The condition or assumption may not be reasonable, realistic, practical, or likely to happen in a certain period of time or under certain circumstances. But this only implies that it has lower applicability at the moment; it in no way means that it is not truth, or a relative truth. Relative truth is also subject to "falsifiability" when conditions or assumptions are changed.

However, it is important to note that truth can vary in its ability to withstand time, universality, and applicability. The more durable, comprehensive, or extensive it is, the closer it comes to being an absolute truth. Therefore, the basic natural sciences, such as mathematics, physics, and chemistry, may contain within them the social sciences, such as sociology, philosophy, law, and economics. Similarly, within the social sciences, sociology contains economics.

The more a theory approaches absolute truth, the more likely it is to achieve its completeness and integrity. Therefore, it is reasonable to suppose that what is wrong with the approach taken by neoclassical economics is not its comprehensive use of mathematics but its lack of a base in sociology, philosophy, and law, which are necessary links in economic theory. The lack of these links makes the theory incomplete.

In short, neoclassical economics offers a very narrow explanation of a very large problem or set of problems for an institution. For this reason IEEN is more precise and comprehensive in its analysis.

Figure 1.1 illustrates the relationship between absolute truth and relative truth and demonstrates why the truth is falsifiable as experience and practice increase. The horizontal axis stands for the absolute truth, and the curves represent relative truths. The lower level of curve represents the more widely applicable truth, which contains the more relative level of truth. Below the curve, each point is truth, but above the curve, each point is false. As more research is done, the theory may be found to be false.

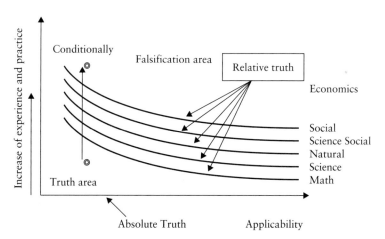

FIGURE 1.1 Relationship between Absolute Truth and Relative Truth

The vertical axis represents conditionality, which demonstrates that all relative truths are conditional. However, conditionality includes three different categories: (1) conditions related to time and space; (2) conditions related to value and culture that people attach to reality; and (3) conditions related to ad hoc objectives. Max Weber shed light on the meaning of sciences when he argued that "science in itself is neutral."[7] Elsewhere he stated, "While the meanings that people attach to various phenomena play no role in the natural sciences, they are absolutely crucial to the social sciences, including economics." Like most economists, Weber regarded scarcity as central to the constitution of economic phenomena, but he also emphasized that what ultimately mattered is the meaning that people attach to reality.[8] The truth is something that the theory is intended to reveal and to make applicable; knowledge is created from both theory and practice. The sources of knowledge are:

- Our own experiences and from learning by doing
- Others' experiences; what we hear and what we observe
- Books and education
- Induction and deduction from above-mentioned sources of knowledge

Knowledge may be divided into three categories: descriptive knowledge, judgmental knowledge, and knowledge of resolutions.

Economics is by nature a social science and an applied science. The IEEN framework contemplates to bridge the gap between math and economics, so that it can provide the knowledge of resolution. In IEEN theory, the extensively used math of neoclassical economic theory can be justified by the containment principle.

So far we know that natural sciences are used in four different areas:

1. *Deduction.* Math is a useful instrument for syllogistic deduction. In mathematics, a logical statement involves three propositions: the major premise, a minor premise, and a conclusion. The conclusion is necessarily true if the premises are true.
2. *Simulation.* Simulation is creating a parallel situation that is comparable to something found in the real world. For example, the random walk in finance theory is comparable to the movement of chemical molecules.
3. *Technological progress.* As functions become more automated, costs tend to be reduced by increases in productivity. For example, the introduction of computers led to a reduction in transaction costs.
4. *Environment.* Changes in the physical environment may affect cost positively or negatively. Scarcity of resources would reduce competition and diminish the rate of return.

As more dominant science (the law of which has more extensive coverage) contains less dominant science (the law of which has less extensive coverage), natural science contains social science, economics contains finance theory, and finance theory contains the theory of debt capital market. But social science has its own laws. Mark Gertler and Andrew Rose wrote: "Insofar as scientists are aware, air molecules have no incentive to deceive observers as to their natural properties. Unfortunately, life is not so straightforward in the world of banking, nor for that matter, in much of economics."[9]

Sociological Base of Economics

Social engineering has to do with sociology because it involves human behavior. It also reaches into the domain of game theory, information theory, and financial engineering in that it attempts to design an institutional arrangement that will lead to the realization of comparative advantage. Since advantage can be realized through exchange, as long as the transaction costs can be minimized, a new institution can be built, and since the law of institutional evolution is identifiable, designing institutions and institutional arrangement is possible. In line with the formulation of international trade theory by Adam Smith and David Ricardo, and analogous to principles of international trade theory, institutions based on comparative advantage can achieve mutually beneficial solutions; in other words, they can achieve a win-win outcome.

According to IEEN, institutions (finance is one form of institution) are essential to the economy. Other factors, such as government, organizations, and legal systems, can all be addressed by institutional arrangements, and are secondary when compared with institutions per se. These systems are endogenously created by institutions and nevertheless play an important role in the evolution of institutions.

IEEN theory combines mainstream economics, such as information economics and game theory, with social economics. Social economics was originated by Max Weber. Influenced by both old histology and new histology, Weber established the foundation of economic sociology. "What basically motivated Weber to pursue economic sociology was a realization, shared by many economists and sociologists today, that it is absolutely imperative to take the social dimension into account when one analyzes economic phenomena."[10]

Integration of Sociology into Economic, Financial, and Bond Market–Related Theory   Each of us has some relationship with others in the society. There are person-to-person relationships, person-to-group relationships, and group-to-group relationships. The person-to-person relationship is composed of two categories: direct contact and indirect contact. Weber first differentiates the social relationship. According to Weber, personal action in a society can be driven by economic motivation, material motivation, and sociological motivation; accordingly these actions can be classified as economic action, economic social action, and social action.[11] As institutions develop, economic social action—the economic action that is oriented to the behavior of others—becomes the predominant form of social relationship. This, according to Weber, is the subject of economic sociology. The parties to the economic social action are driven by material interests, habit, and emotions.[12] This classification, though heuristic, is subject to debate.

According to institutional economic engineering theory, people can have direct relationships and indirect relationships. In a direct relationship—whether it is a social or economic action, whether it is competitive or cooperative—the parties reach an equilibrium state through exchange. In a competitive relationship, the parties reduce endogenous transaction costs to achieve the exchange of comparative advantages. In an indirect relationship, there is no exchange.

In addition, there are group-to-group relationships and person-to-group relationships. People in a group are basically in cooperative relationships, but sometimes they also have a competitive relationship (e.g., competition for promotion in a bureaucratic system). Group-to-group relationships, like person-to-person relationships, include direct and indirect relationships. In direct relationships, the exchange occurs between groups; in indirect relationships, exchange does not happen.

The person-to-group relationship, while similar to the person-to-person relationship and the group-to-group relationship as far as direct and indirect relationships are concerned, may occur with a person either inside or outside the group. The former can be seen in individual-to-government relationships, the latter can be seen in worker-to-company relationship. When they are in a direct relationship, exchange can occur. This concept was first articulated by Robert Putnam in his analysis of social capital and how societies revolve around this informal system.[13]

Social relationships are constantly changing. Direct relationships can become indirect relationships, and vice versa.

Sociology and Economics Sociology is about people-to-people relationships while technology is about the human-to-nature relationship. Human relationships can be maintained through exchanges. It is not what is to be exchanged that divides society into different categories, but the nature of the interaction between the incentive structure and constraint structure that separates one society from another.

The exchange of comparative advantage, the equilibrium reached through game play, and the competitive struggle for existence through the removal of internal transaction costs are essentially part of the same process and realized simultaneously. Marx referred this process in a narrow sense as class struggle. Weber used the notion of struggle to describe competition, indicating the role that struggle (*Kampf*) plays in the economy.[14]

Incentive has been conceptualized as the opposite of constraint. It contains the assumption of the rational or somewhat rational human behavior to reconcile neoclassical and neoinstitutional economics. Incentive can be motivated by both utilitarianism and value-based judgments.

Institutions may be optimal or suboptimal. By what yardstick are we to judge their worth? According to North, there are two different kinds of government: violated and predatory. Modern theory has revealed that this is due to principal agent issue, which incentive theory addresses. Our view is that the principal agent issue is due to incomplete primary exchanges; we discuss this further later on.

Essence of Human Relationships: The Exchange   Broadly speaking, all human social behavior, such as making choices, selecting one thing over another, and decision making, are by their nature exchanges or transactions. A transaction is the act of possessing something by paying something for it. Simply put, to produce a material product is one thing, but to obtain it if one has not produced it is quite another.

A transaction in an economic sense is called a trade or an exchange. To realize a transaction, one has to sharpen one's comparative and competitive advantages by paying an exogenous as well as an endogenous transaction cost. In terms of the realization of a transaction, competitive advantage is more crucial than comparative advantage.

There are times—ranging from mundane theft by individuals or groups of people to extraordinary actions such as war between tribes or nations—when people get something for nothing. In reality, however, these actions are not cost-free; there is a transaction cost. For example, throughout history, endless blood has been shed in wars and battles; the aggressors obtain the land, material goods, natural resources, and other things, and they pay with the lives of their soldiers as well as the cost of the goods and services needed to conduct the war. The defenders, too, pay with the loss of life and cost of logistical material. These then are the transaction costs. The cost of materiel is the exogenous transaction cost, whereas the cost of training soldiers and commanders for reconnaissance and fighting the war are endogenous transaction costs.

During times of peace, economic activities tend to be confined to the exchange of goods for goods or goods for money transactions because the exogenous and endogenous transaction costs of trade is less and, therefore, preferable to war. There is a corollary in game theory, the "prisoner's dilemma," where participants tend to choose cooperation because there are more winners than losers. However, for a number of reasons, including lack of information, participants do not always choose cooperation.

In the field of economics, the same principle applies: How something is possessed through trade is more important than how it is produced. In other words, the terms of trade between two people or two nations are more important than the production of trade.

Here the inclusion of human behavior would remedy the deficiency of neoinstitutionalist theory with respect to choices that lead to a transaction or exchange in economic activities.

Incentives and Constraints: The Dialectic of Institutions

The Dialectic of Institutions   An institution is a union of opposites: incentives and constraints. It is an equilibrium state created from the interaction between the two. North noticed this dichotomy as it affected an institution's stability and changeability, saying: "The major role of institutions in a society is to reduce uncertainty by establishing a stable (but not necessarily efficient) structure to human interaction. But the stability of institutions in no way gainsays the fact that they are changing."[15]

North also gives a representational definition: "Institutions provide the basic structure by which human beings throughout history have created order and attempted to reduce uncertainty in exchange. Together with the technology employed, they determine transaction and transformation costs and hence the profitability and feasibility of engaging in economic activity."[16] Still, to North, institutions represent only constraint.[17]

However, it is important to note that if institutions evolve, it is hard to imagine that any prime mover outside the institution drives them; instead, they are driven by an internal force: the institution's sinew. Without incentives, institutions will not move forward; similarly, without constraints, institutions will not move either. It is reasonable to suppose that it is the contradictory movement, or interplay, between the incentive structure and the constraint structure that drives the institutional movement.

Greif defined an institution as a system of social factors—such as rules, beliefs, norms, and organizations—that "guide, enable, and constrain the actions of individuals."[18] To Greif, as it to North, an institution is a kind of constraint, having nothing to do with incentives. Although the word "enable" may appear to be an "incentive structure," that is not how Greif means it. Moreover, he confuses institution with organization. North argues that institution is different from organization. Institutions impose constraints on human behavior. However, an organization is a group of people functioning within an institutional framework, created, in North's words, to take advantage of the opportunities provided.[19]

According to Rodrik: "Institutions that provide dependable property rights, manage conflict, maintain law and order, and align economic incentives with social costs and benefits are the foundation of long-term growth.... State institutions are not the only ones that matter. Social arrangements can have equally important and lasting consequences.... Modest changes in institutional arrangements...can produce large growth payoffs... [but] the required changes can be highly specific to the context."[20] Although Rodrik does not regard institutions as an interaction between incentives and constraints, he nevertheless touches on both, albeit separately. Schotter defined "institution" as "a regularity in social behavior that is agreed to by all members of society, specifies behavior in specific recurrent situations, and is either self-policed or police by some external authority."[21] To him, an institution is not only a game, but also a rule of the game. Calvert, like Masahiko Aoki, perceives of an institution as a state of equilibrium.[22]

About the interactive nature of the two elements, incentive and constraint, within institutions, Coase says:

> *If rights to perform certain actions can be bought and sold, they will tend to be acquired by those for whom they are most valuable for either production or enjoyment. In this process, rights will be acquired, subdivided, and combined to allow those actions to be carried out which bring about that outcome which has the greatest value on the market. Exercise of the rights by one person inevitably denies opportunities for production or enjoyment by others, for whom the price of acquiring the rights would be too high. Of course, in the process of acquisition, subdivision, and combination, the increase in the value of the outcome which a new constellation of rights allows has to be matched against the costs of carrying out the transactions needed to achieve that new constellation, and such a rearrangement of rights will only be undertaken if the cost of the transactions needed to achieve it is less than the increase in value which such a rearrangement makes possible.[23]*

A property right is the right of one party but the constraint of the other. The protection of innovation and invention is the incentive for one group of people but a constraint on another group of people who use the innovation and invention without paying anything.

Why do institutions move from one arrangement to another? To apply Marxist philosophical theory (i.e., dialectical materialism), an institution is a union of opposites. Depending on the circumstances, they provide both incentives and constraints. Incentives are the positive factor in the union of opposites. When constraints encumber incentives, tension emerges between them. In the end, constraints change in response to changed incentives. Thus, their relationship is in equilibrium when constraints are consistent with incentives and in disequilibrium when constraints no longer cater to incentives. At this point, a new equilibrium needs to be established, which, when it happens, constitutes institutional change.

A union of opposites has three outstanding characteristics:

1. Incentive and constraint are interdependent; in other words, the existence of one is the precondition of the other. There is no incentive without constraint, and vice versa.
2. Incentives become constraints and constraints become incentives as conditions change. As one party's incentive is his or her counterpart's constraint, one party's constraint is his or her counterpart's incentive.
3. Incentives are positive and inconstant; constraints are relatively passive and stable.

IEEN would serve as a new theoretical instrument to explain institutional change. It is different from information theory in that social engineers believe that equilibrium in information theory is not readily achievable, as a transaction cost always exists. From IEEN's point of view, equilibrium occurs when the unity of opposites is in place; transformation takes place when there is disequilibrium. Information theory would provide mathematical proof for the condition of the equilibrium and transformation from incentive to constraints and vice versa; IEEN focuses on the behavior of human beings or organizations, applying the logic of game theory to show how institutions evolved in the midst of contradictory movement between incentives and constraints.

IEEN differentiates itself from neoinstitutional theory, which posits transaction cost as the key to explaining institutional evolution and focuses only on the constraints side of institutions. Evolutionary economists put great emphasis on innovative idea generation but fail to show that institutional change can be evolutionary and revolutionary, gradual and radical. A win-win outcome can be achieved when the movement is evolutionary; a win-loss outcome, or interest redistribution, occurs when institutional movement is revolutionary.

It is important to note that incentives and constraints can change individually, concurrently, and sequentially.

How Incentives and Constraints Work Incentives occurs when the participants in a transaction can benefit from the exchange of their comparative advantages, and there is a way both parties can realize these advantages by the exchange of a material or social commodity (which represents their comparative advantages) to achieve a win-win solution. Here, the social commodity is defined as a social relationship, which is exchangeable in the formation of institutions. Exchange here has a broad meaning; it is not necessarily confined to commodity exchange. In a broad sense, choice is, by its nature, an exchange; for example, when a person selects one thing, he or she gives up another.

Constraints are related to both external and internal transaction costs. The external transaction cost is the price paid to increase one's advantage. Internal transaction costs are those incurred in the process of competing: for example, negotiation cost, lost opportunity cost in the process of achieving equilibrium, and the cost incurred in seeking opportunities and finding counterparts, including the cost for information. Reducing endogenous transaction costs will create more value added.

Incentive is an active factor compared with constraint. The changing nature of incentive is North's central argument: "incentives have varied immensely over time and still do."[24] The key is that the constraint apparatus should go hand in hand with the incentive apparatus. The interaction between them drives institutional change.

Marx was the first to reveal the dialectical nature of institutional change. To him, the contradictory movement between productive force and productive relationships drives the social change that brings about institutional revolution. Productive force is more active than productive relationships. However, the productive force cannot replace the incentive apparatus, nor is the productive relationship a proxy for the constraint apparatus. It is difficult to calculate the change in productive force, in terms of total capital or total output, or to what extent the productive relationship can contain the productive force. However, the incentive structure can be established based on the incentive theory.[25] Incentive theory is based on the principle of optimization, equilibrium, lack of arbitrage, and game theory; it reveals the true nature of the principal-agent relationship[26]

Neoclassical economists construct their models without considering transaction costs. Neoinstitutitionlists developed a concept of transaction cost and indicate that as long as transaction cost can be removed, equilibrium can be reached (this is the Coase theorem).[27] According to game theory, the endogenous transaction cost is paid to achieve the equilibrium. What IEEN contributes is the idea that comparative advantage can be realized through exchange to achieve a win-win outcome in which both parties have an incentive to reduce transaction costs; as a result, institutions can evolve. When comparative advantage is realized through exchange, the two parties reach the game theory equilibrium where the constraint structure can better contain incentive structure. This process is better illustrated using rhombus theory.

Rhombus Theory and the Formation of Institutions

Rhombus theory, which is based on an IEEN framework, is concerned with the formation of institutions. At the outset, institutions are in a state of equilibrium because of the interaction between incentives and constraints. The incentives and constraints reach equilibrium as the institution achieves its comparative advantage. The process has two stages: The first stage has to do with transforming the institution's assets into comparative advantages. This can be done only under certain conditions, and the price paid for this transformation is an exogenous transaction cost. Because of this cost, incentives and constraints may also change, together or individually. If the incentive structure changes while constraints remain unchanged, there is conflict between them. In the end, either constraint relaxes or both incentives and constraints move forward in a coordinated fashion.

The second stage has to do with the transition from comparative advantage to competitive advantage, a result of the successful exchange of advantages with a counterpart. In this case, the cost incurred is an endogenous transaction cost. Figure 1.2 illustrates the process.

The formation of an institution can now be seen from two different dimensions. The establishment of a financial system (or "financial structure") is a process of institution building. It is also an interaction between incentives and constraints. Participants in a financial system have the incentive when opportunities come to change their status quo as well as constraints. The interaction between incentive and constraint is also reflected in the games played by the parties. In the end, a state of equilibrium can be achieved. This equilibrium marks the formation of a new institution or a new institutional arrangement. During the interaction between incentive and constraint, transaction costs can be reduced.

Thus, there are two categories of transaction costs. The first, the exogenous transaction cost, has to do with the cost of improving the institution's assets or alleviating constraints by, for example, circumventing laws and regulations, legally evading taxes, or avoiding other legal constraints. The second, the endogenous transaction cost, is the cost incurred in realizing the institution's comparative advantages, such as the cost of the negotiating with a counterpart, information cost, or the cost of uncovering opportunities.

Understanding this two-stage process helps us define the role of government. It is reasonable to presume that the government's role is to reduce exogenous rather than endogenous transaction costs. Laws and regulations should be limited to such things as defining the property rights, establishing the legal framework, setting rules, and encouraging innovative ideas.

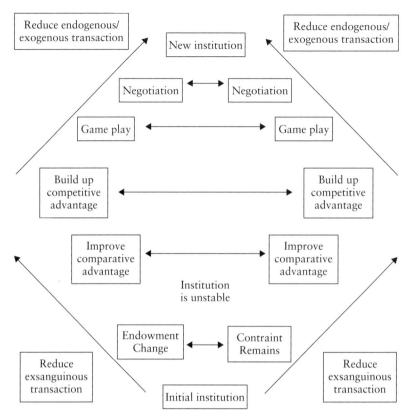

FIGURE 1.2 Rhombus-shape Graph Illustrating the Process from Initial to New Institution

These are the rules of game; anything that goes beyond that will be counterproductive. In fact, the legal framework should help to reduce rather than increase transaction costs; therefore, at times deregulation will help to reduce exogenous transaction costs and thereby expedite the process of institutional movement.

The participants themselves (the game players) can deal with endogenous transaction costs without government intervention. It is important to bear in mind that the formation of institutions is game play. Laws and regulations are the rules of game. In most cases, government is not player but a referee. The players themselves determine who wins the game; that is, it is the players who determine which institution to form.

Endogenous transaction costs are more rewarding than exogenous transaction costs, which are harder to reduce because they are riskier, more uncertain, and require more work. Due to the nature of endogenous transaction costs, innovative ideas are essential to the realization of exchange. In the second stage of the institution formation process, achieving comparative advantage, reducing endogenous transaction costs and game play are essentially the same. They both reveal the nature of institutional movement from a different perspective.

A good example of the game play process is table tennis. The players' degree of skill is their comparative advantages. The exogenous transaction cost is the cost of training to qualify for the game. The cost incurred by the players to learn the playing strategy and to pay their coaches is the endogenous transaction cost.

The wisdom to win the game is the competitive advantage. Professional players know well that winning mainly depends on their competitive advantage rather than comparative advantage, as the skill of qualified players is more or less at the same level. Rhombus theory reveals how institutions move from one state to another. It exposes the nature of institutions, which is essentially revolutionary. When the market can play a role, there is little role for the government to play.

Assets, Comparative Advantages, Competitive Advantages, Competitive Capability, and Idea Generation   Assets are the conditions under which participants are going to form a new social arrangement. Since institutions evolve because of the interaction between incentive and constraint, this process is based on the assets, what each party brings to the new arrangement.

Depending on the institution, these assets may vary. For individuals, assets include social endowments, such as family background, parents' social status, and so on, as well as natural endowments, such as gender, health, and the like. For a firm or a country, assets are the condition for competition. Joseph R. D'Cruz in his lecture on international competitiveness distinguished between basic and advanced factors and generalized and specialized factors. Basic factors include natural resources and unskilled labor; advanced factors include human capital and infrastructure. Generalized factors include capital pool, infrastructure, public facilities, and public products while specialized factors are principally industry specific.[28] (See Figure 1.2, which illustrates the real structure.)

The rhombus theory provides a clue to the right role that government on one hand and the organization and individuals on the other can play. For the economic system as a whole, the government's role is related to reducing exogenous transaction costs, which occur mainly in the first stage of the dynamic process; the role of organizations and individuals is related to reducing endogenous transaction costs, which occur in the second stage of the dynamic process. (Both are reflected in Figure 1.2.)

Rhombus theory also helps us understand the two basic exchanges in the economic area. The first stage represents the primary economic exchange, which is the exchange between government and market participants. The second stage represents the secondary economic exchange, where market participants exchange their assets and comparative advantages. This is how we traditionally perceive the market. Transactions in the primary economic exchange are not public exchanges; they are made through an implicit market; the secondary economic exchange is accomplished through an explicit market.[29]

There are different schools of economic thought about competitiveness: Environmentalists believe structural features determine a country's or firm's competitiveness while reconstructionalists favor endogenously determined competitiveness. The IEEN framework is an endogenous model and therefore is consistent with the reconstructionalist view.

The steps toward the creation of an institution can be seen as the transaction cost chain, a dynamic process of serial institutional arrangements to reduce transaction costs. A number of transaction costs need to be addressed to compare the neoclassic Arrow-Debreu framework with the behavior of the person who engages in institution formation. For example, to realize an exchange or a transaction, we need to create a market if it does not exist. To do this, we need an organization or a firm that is in a position to build up the market. To motivate the organization or the firm, we need to set up an incentive structure. To set up an efficient incentive structure, we first need to learn how to set one up. It is important to note that transaction costs connect to each other to form a chain.

Idea Generation: The Essence of Competition   Without incentives and innovative ideas, progress in the evolution of institutions would not be possible. Institutional equilibrium results from three types of games: lose-win games, zero-sum games, and win-win games. Only win-win games can help the social system progress. A person, a country, or an organization can achieve its goals through institutional arrangements, which, in many cases, are win-win games, and result in cooperation between the parties.

A successful win-win game relies on innovative ideas, which are different from normal thinking based on conventional wisdom. Four different ways of thinking can result in the creation of innovative ideas. The first is what is called "exchanging shoes" thinking. Using this mode of thinking, one party sees the issue from the perspective of the other (i.e., a competitor or an enemy).

The second way of thinking is "shift dimension" thinking (i.e., seeing an issue from a different perspective). The third way of thinking is "blue sky" thinking. Blue-sky thinkers seek alternative ways to address a problem. The fourth way is "shift order thinking." For example, Premier Wen Jiabao said that any small figure multiplied by 1.3 billion becomes a big number; any large figure divided by 1.3 billion becomes a very small number.

There is a Chinese saying that if you want to see a panoramic view, stand at a higher level. Mathematically, shifting thinking from the first order of magnitude to the second order of magnitude gives a broader perspective. Thus, shifting order enhances imagination.

It is useful to distinguish innovation from invention. Invention is predominantly a product-focused idea while innovation is primarily an institution-focused idea.

How do new ideas influence the government? "Ideas and ideology shape the subjective mental constructs that individuals use to interpret the world around them, and make choices."[30] Government's key role is its economic policy; the quality of that policy is determined by its new ideas.

Competitive Competence According to the IEEN theory, competitive competence is crucial to the economy, and requires innovative institutional arrangements and the deepening of the market, among other things. As the most sophisticated marketplace, the soundness of financial market represents the competitive edge of a country, and the capital market sits at the top of the financial market. Given the sophistication of capital market, it is impossible to build a sound debt capital market without well-developed institutional arrangements, such as institutional investors and financial intermediaries, and technological processes, which change the comparative advantages and make the formation of a new institutional arrangement possible.

IEEN can help us trace the trajectory of social and economic development and point the way to future development. Through exchange, each person, organization, institution, and country can realize its comparative advantage, and all related costs are internal transaction costs. These endogenous transaction costs can be reduced in four ways:

1. *Make comparative advantage readily exchangeable.* Commercialization is a way to turn products into tradable goods, or commodities. The first step is to set up a market, a place for concentrated exchange, such as a supermarket. This substantially reduces transaction costs. The second is to standardize in order to meet a specific need, which makes it easy for the seller and buyer to make decisions. Most of our daily necessities are made this way. The third is to diversify goods and services to meet the different needs of consumers. A supermarket is an example of this.

The fourth step is to agglomerate the marketplaces. Shopping malls and streets of small boutiques reflect this idea.

2. *Develop industries that help reduce transaction costs.* These include the entire tertiary sector, where every industry's purpose is to reduce transaction costs, as well as specialized industries, such as communications, transportation, logistics, commerce, service, and finance, that make the tertiary sector more efficient.

3. *Internalize, liberalize, and innovate.* The three traits—internalization, liberalization, and innovation—characterize contemporary government policy and legal systems. Internalization implies the efforts to incorporate outside ideas and practices and thereby better define the property rights.[31] Deregulation is a way to liberalize the economy and give it more incentive and vitality. Innovation is the government policy to encourage new ideas and creative ideas. These ideas are not limited to technological progress; they also include those things that lead to the evolution of institutions. China has come a long way toward realizing this important point and reaching its goal of becoming an innovative country.[32]

4. *Translate technological progress into an exchangeable commodity.* This can be done by combining functions, finding practical applications for these advances, accelerating the process, and encouraging innovation through incentives. For example, technical research is combined with the production process. Research and development is part of the business function, which, in turn, fosters the invention of practical ways to use the new technology. In the area of technological progress, government should encourage innovation through favorable tax treatment, subsidies, and other incentives. The final impact and cost on society is not always directly reflected in the supply and demand curves. Society receives other benefits from research and development that are not always properly reflected in the gross domestic product of an economy.

It is important to note that exogenous transaction costs and endogenous transaction costs are mutually transferable, and the ability to reduce internal transaction costs is a competitive advantage. As the economy develops, knowledge-intensive industries (the fourth-level industries)—education, management science, consulting, law, accounting, and others—that can help reduce endogenous transaction costs become the leading industries.

As endogenous transaction costs come down, comparative advantages become exchangeable and a win-win outcome can be achieved. As a result, the economy develops, and social wealth is increased.

Ideology versus Reality

The basic elements of institutions—government, individuals, organizations, leaders, and technology—are all strongly influenced by ideas (see Figure 1.3).

The controversy over ideology and reality (i.e., what actually happens in the "real" world), and which one determines the other, has been the subject of debate throughout human history. Marx argued that reality determines ideology. At the same time, he recognized the inherent conflict between ideology and the reality. Weber, however, focused on the role of ideology although he also emphasized that reality influenced ideology. This egg-chicken argument is still undecided, yet at its heart, we will doubtless discover the essence of the revolution of new ideas. The confusion stems from conventional thinking on the subject, as Figures 1.4 and 1.5 illustrate.

Both egg and chicken change as they interact. Heraclitus's famous remark that "you cannot step into the same river twice, for the water (or the river) is constantly new"[33] illuminates this view.

Similarly, the relationship between ideology and reality is conventionally conceived as a one-to-one relationship, as shown in Figure 1.6, when, in

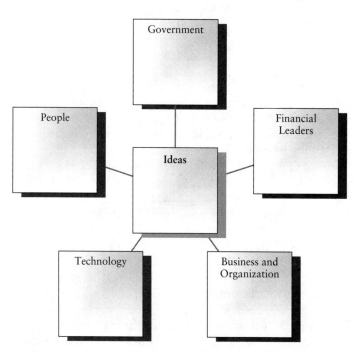

FIGURE 1.3 Basic Elements of Institutions Influenced by Ideas

FIGURE 1.4 Simple Model:
Egg-Chicken Argument

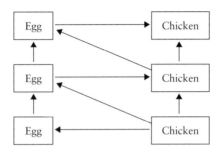

FIGURE 1.5 Standard Model:
Egg-Chicken Argument

FIGURE 1.6 Simple Model:
Ideology-Reality Argument

fact, the relationship between ideology and reality is nothing like that. Both ideology and reality have their own history, and it is in the dynamic movement between them that ideology and reality interact (see Figure 1.7).

If we assume that the relationship between egg and chicken, reality and ideology, is evolutionary, then reality will reflect changes in ideology. This implies that ideology itself is revolutionary. Changes in ideology go hand in hand with changes in reality. Similarly, the interaction between incentives and constraints drives institutional movements. This reality is naturally reflected in the evolution of new ideas.[34]

Economic and financial theory works in the same way. For example, John Maynard Keynes's theory (Keynesian economics)[35] that proposes the need for government intervention follows the constraint requirement ideology, and classical and neoclassical theory, which posit a free economy, follow the incentives requirement ideology. It is reasonable to suppose that reality, which features the movement of institutions driven by the interaction between incentives and constraints, is consistent with the history of the ideology, which is characterized by the interaction between the

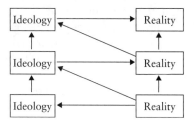

FIGURE 1.7 Standard Model:
Ideology-Reality Argument

incentive requirement ideology and the constraint requirement ideology. Here the implication is that the endless debate over which comes first, egg or chicken, ideology or reality, is meaningless and can never be conclusive. What matters are the innovative ideas rooted in the evolution of new ideas.

Reducing Transaction Costs

The efforts to reduce transaction costs are made primarily through technological progress. However, transaction costs can be reduced in three ways in addition to advances in technology: exchange, abstain, and hedging.

Exchange The cost paid for access to information is a transaction cost. Due to information asymmetry, each party has advantages in its access to information access relating to the good or service it wishes to trade through exchange. Transaction costs caused by information asymmetry can be reduced through the exchange of information between the parties. As the owner of information has comparative advantages, the exchange of information would reduce the transaction cost and thereby benefit both parties.

Abstain Transaction cost can be also reduced by avoiding certain transactions. A good example is the vertical or horizontal integration of corporations, which can eliminate transactions with suppliers or competitors and thereby save the transaction costs.

Hedging Hedging also is a way to offset transaction costs. When one category of transaction cost is negatively correlated with another category of transaction cost, the two categories can offset one another. As one increases, the other decreases. Hedging, a sophisticated tool, is extensively used in the financial sector, such as in the futures markets. It creates stability in the proper functioning of the mature capital market. For example, if a company wins a contract for equipment that requires rare metals which fluctuate in price, the company may adopt a hedging strategy with rare metals supplier to lock in the price today for materials that will be delivered in the future. This hedging provides not only stability but reduces transaction costs for both supplier and customer.

In attempting to reduce any transaction cost, the benefits and losses must always be compared. In certain circumstances, equilibrium can be reached through actions based on game theory that will benefit both parties.

In reality, the Nash equilibrium theory is based on the constraint incentives of both parties.[36]

Transaction costs can also be reduced as a result, or in the process, of abating other transaction costs, creating in effect a chain of transaction costs. The principal-agent relationship, which is created by exchange and realized through transaction, is designed to help the principal more efficiently abate transaction costs. In this case, incentive theory[37] creates equilibrium conditions for the principal-agent relationship, just as game theory does for the exchange parties.

It is important to note that game theory and incentive theory can work only in certain circumstances—only when the transaction cost is zero. Where there are diverse and multidimensional transactions costs, their dynamic nature makes it difficult to achieve competitive advantage and realize the transaction. Thus, innovative ideas reflected in the evolution of institutions are closely related to finding new ways to abate transaction costs.

PRIMARY EXCHANGE AND SECONDARY EXCHANGE

Many works have touched on issues associated with the primary exchange and the secondary exchange. Some have great insight into this fundamental public choice issue and shed light to the primary–secondary-exchange framework. Buchanan, for example, distinguished constitutional and post-constitutional choice, indicating their different institutional functions.

> *Public choice analysis, which has as one of its central elements, the critical distinction between constitutional and post constitutional choice, strongly implies that reform or improvement in political outcomes or results is to be sought through possible changes in the set of constraints within which political decisions are made... and not in changes in day to day policy that temporary politicians may somehow be persuaded to follow.*[38]

Coase recognized the complexity of the relationship between legal system and economic system, saying: "The interrelationships between the economic system and the legal system are extremely complex, and many of the effects of changes in the law on the working of the economic system (the very stuff of economic policy) are still hidden from us."[39] Specifically, Buchanan and his associates have paid much attention to the economic constitutions, for example, fiscal constitutions, which is close to one of the element of the primary financial exchange.

However, public choice theory failed to position its arguments in a consistent framework. This is because the theory is not grounded in the nature of the person-to-person relationship, which, to our way of thinking, is the exchange through which people are able to come up with a win-win outcome driven by incentive apparatuses. In addition, public choice also failed to make all factors in political exchange to be explained (endogenously) within its theoretical framework. Institutional movement comprises two stages: reduce exogenous transaction costs and reduce endogenous transaction costs.

Ideally, the IEEN will address the problems that underlie public choice theory: lack of consistency and endogeneity via its framework focuses on human exchanges.

Foundation of Primary and Secondary Exchange

Market is the place where market participants exchange their advantages and endowments. These advantages are transformed or embodied as products in commodity market, or as power in political market. Here the exchanges are made between or among market participants.

Economists perceive imperfect market from different perspective. Neo-classical economists list a number of reasons for the imperfection of market. For example, to a neoinstitutionalist, exchange is a game play (Aoki) or rule of game (North). From IEEN perspective, the market is complete when rule play is based on rule of game. When there is only game play, we say the market is confined to secondary exchange; when there are both game play and rule of game, the primary exchange, we say the institution is complete. Therefore it is reasonable to suppose that the imperfect market is due to incompletion of institution, or lack of primary exchange.

However, most institutions and institutional arrangements are incomplete. When there is no primary exchange, contracts tend to favor the party who has a comparative advantage or endowments. Without rules of the game, game play can also reach equilibrium. In such circumstance, the equilibrium is reached through *private ordering*.[40] This is different from when there is a rule of game engendered by primary exchange. According to Dixit:

Observable information can be the basis for contracts that are enforced by extralegal or private methods, because the two parties can know fully well whether a breach has occurred. Such extralegal methods of enforcement come in two broad types. One is enforcement by insiders, third parties with specialized knowledge that enables them to verify information that consider general courts of law cannot; arbitrators in industry associations are the most prominent enforcers of this kind. The second is based on a relationship or ongoing interaction between the parties; a breakup of this relationship constitutes the punishment that may deter one of the parties from breaching. This covers many possibilities. The same two parties may meet repeatedly; the two may not have a direct repeated interaction with each other, but each may interact with others in a group or network that transmits information about any breach to all members and collectively sanctions the miscreant, using ostracism in business interactions or social relationship or both.[41]

The social and economic activities are driven both endogenously and exogenously within an institutional framework. The rhombus theory is a way to understand the two basic exchanges in the economic area. The first stage represents the primary economic exchange (PEE), which is the exchange between government and market participants. The second stage represents the secondary economic exchange (SEE), where markets participants exchange their assets and comparative advantages. This is what we consider the market in the usual sense. Transactions in the PEE are not public exchanges; they are made through the implicit market. The SEE is accomplished through the explicit market.[42]

In the same way, in the political system, there is political exchange (PE), which can be divided into primary political exchange (PPE), the exchange between public and political parties, and secondary political exchange (SPE), the exchange among political parties. Analogously, between political exchange and economic exchange there is administrative exchange (AE), which contains the primary administrative exchange and secondary administrative exchange. The political system and government are important to the primary exchange; however, it is important not to lose sight of intermediate linkages, such administrative exchange, economic exchange, financial exchange, when attempting to explain the capital market, especially the bond market.

In principle, the PPE determines the PEE. However, the people's political will is passed on through a chain of primary and secondary exchanges. Compared with economic exchange, political exchange is more complicated than economic exchange. "The problem of the distribution of power is a more difficult one than the problem of the distribution of wealth."[43]

The lower layer of the primary exchange is the derivative of secondary exchange at a higher layer. The lower layer of exchange will improve the function of the primary exchange at a higher layer. For example, the primary financial exchange is the derivative of the secondary economic exchange; however, the primary financial and secondary financial exchange will help to improve the function of primary economic exchange.

Primary and secondary exchange at a higher layer influence primary and secondary exchange at a lower layer. However, the more orderly and efficient social structure is that the primary exchange only governs the secondary exchange, and it is the secondary exchange that governs lower layer primary exchange. Secondary exchange cannot proceed efficiently and sustain without the primary exchange.

There are two important distinctions with respect to the primary–secondary-exchange framework: primary exchange versus primary exchange and primary exchange versus secondary exchange. It is meaningless to argue which of the primary exchanges came first. For example, is it economic exchange or political exchange? As we mentioned earlier, this is an egg-chicken problem. One thing is certain: They are interacting. But the way one acts to the other may be different. For example, the PEE may act on political exchange via the SEE. The changed economic status will require changed of political status, and give rise to a political exchange. However, the political exchange does not exert direct influence on the PEE, but rather works through the primary and secondary administrative exchange.

Long ago, economists and sociologists noticed that public choice deviated from individual choice and tried to find the answer.[44] "Can it [public choice] introduce into the public discussion upsetting or surprising perspectives on political phenomena of the kind that economics has done so successfully for economic phenomena?"[45]

Surely public choice has not yet done as well as economics in this respect. From the point of view of IEEN, this may be due to a number of reasons: first, economic exchanges are getting more and more quantifiable as a result of commoditization, specialization, and standardization processes of the SEE. Second, the PPE, SPE/PAE, SAE transactions are not fully realized due to monopolistic nature of one party (Williamson referred as "assets specificity"[46]). For example, PPE confined to a certain group of people due to indirect voting. Third, there are transaction costs for the exchanges. For example, group-to-group exchange and group member–to–group exchange all have transaction costs, such as information costs, learning and education costs, and others.

PPE is achieved through the political marketplace. Public choice economists have been studying this marketplace for many years.

It is important to note that the economic policy is not determined by the government but by SAE, as was indicated by Rupert Pennant-Rea: "The charge of being unrealistic comes so easily and so often to the lips of policymakers that the rest of us ought to be instantly suspicious. In many areas of public policy, proposal for innovation and reform are judged by the standards of perfection. If they fall short, then they are marginalized."[47]

PPE is a place of exchange where basic law, such as constitutions and political system is determined. SPE is a place where parties struggle in the parliament. PPE/SPE is also referred as political market. PAE is where the administrative system or government structure is determined. The SAE is the interdepartmental exchange. However, in the real world, this sequence of exchanges is not necessarily applied. In some countries, PAE is the same as PPE and PPE directly governs of SAE, the parliament, government, and judiciary system. Then the PPE directly influences the SPE and the SAE. In many cases the government has more power than parliament; this is because government is in a better position to influence the PPE. As Rowley noted, "Although Parliament technically is supreme in a system in which there is no formal separation of power, much of the power is actually wielded by external agencies located in the executive branch are loosely labeled the government."[48]

To summarize, in a modern political system there are in principle two levels of rule of game: PPE and PEE vis-à-vis one level of game play, SEE. The PPE governs SPE and PAE. SPE formulates constitutions and political system. Legislature and judiciary system is relatively stable vis-à-vis administration which is more changeable; this legitimized the PAE to govern the administration, the government. The SAE is governed by PAE and has external function and internal function, which in turn govern the SEE (see Figure 1.8).

For the SEE to work, there have to be both a PAE and a SAE. The PAE represents the exchange between political groups, which governs the arrangement of cabinet. The SAE stands for the exchange between government agencies, or cabinet members. The SAE has been mostly neglected by neoclassical and public choice economists. "Different agencies have their own agenda; the transactions costs of negotiating between the different agencies are high and many externalities are no longer internalised."[49] As "bureaucrats do not benefit personally from cost reductions, there are only weak incentives to reduce costs."[50] The agent problems came as a result of the fact that the government makes decisions based on the consensus opinion of different government agencies, therefore principal-agent paradigm does not follow. For example, often the agency division chiefs make decisions.

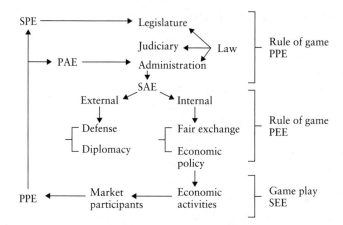

FIGURE 1.8 The Work Flow of Primary and Secondary Exchange

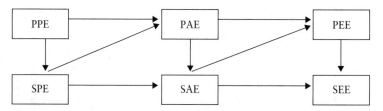

FIGURE 1.9 Relationship of Different Exchanges with Respect to Institution Formulations

This upside-down principal-agent (P-A) issue necessitates the research of PAE and SAE framework.

In summary, institutions can be built both exogenously via primary exchange and endogenously via secondary exchange. Social progress can be made and social activities are more efficient if every layer of exchange is functional and the transfer of social function from primary exchange to secondary exchange is efficient and orderly. This process can be better illustrated by Figure 1.9. If a society is based on a sound institutional framework, the function of governs shall pass on via the order of PPE-SPE-PAE-SAE-PEE-SEE whereas public delegation shall pass on the other way round, that is, SEE-PEE-SAE-PAE-SPE-PPE.

The primary and secondary exchange can be also visualized from group actions perspective. A group action underlies two different exchanges: group-to-group exchange and the exchange among group members. The former is a primary exchange while the latter is the secondary exchange.

Function of the Primary Exchange

As was indicated earlier in this chapter, the exchanges that underlie human relationships are the drivers of institutional movement. The institution is, in the language of neoinstitutionalists, a game. While North defines institution as the rule of game, Aoki defines institution as game play (or equilibrium of game play to be more precise) from the IEEN's point of view. These two definitions are not mutually exclusive, but complementary. IEEN defines the rule of game as PE, and the game play as SE. Both are functional component of institution with PE as a reducer of exogenous transaction costs and SE as a reducer of endogenous transaction costs.

This new view will help to explain the arguments on this important subject. The yardstick to judge the PE is whether it brings about an effective rule of game and equality. Rupert compared the United Kingdom and the United States and concluded that the rule-based institution is superior to discretion-based institutions. "An emphasis on transparency in policy matters, and on rules rather than discretion, would certainly curb the power of sectional interests in the political marketplace, and require them to seek economic advantage in the commercial market instead."[51]

However, in SPE (i.e., the political market are not characterized by market clearing equilibrium), as was indicated by Charles K. Rowley, "although the political markets are viewed as competitive, the prices at which individuals agree to transact are not modeled as universally market-clearing, nor are they assumed necessarily to reflect full information even though all individuals are assumed to engage in optimal search in political markets."[52] As SPE is by governed by PPE, therefore, the better organized PPE is in place, the more efficient SPE is going to be.

Equality Function in Primary Exchange Is Conducive to Economic Performance

Insofar as equality is concerned, people's social relationships are established and maintained via the exchange of their comparative advantages. Equality is required first to ensure a win-win outcome as opposed to a win-lose or lose-lose outcome.

In most cases the exchange ends up with a win-win outcome; however, how much the disadvantageous party can win also matters. If the win is too much in favor of one side, the incentive from the other side is very limited and the likelihood of the exchange becomes slim. Therefore, equality is positive to economic efficiency if it gives the disadvantageous party more incentive to participate in the exchange. In this sense, equality is not a moral requirement but an economic requirement, as it can mitigate the disparity between those who enjoy so few comparative advantages that they do not have an incentive to compete and those who have far more comparative advantages. Therefore, equality can help to establish sound institutions or, in the language of IEEN, achieve a win-win outcome. This can help to explain why evidences indicate that less income disparity would lead to better economic performance.

A graphical representation of this idea is shown in Figure 1.10. The points on iso-curve 1and 2 is the possible combination of advantages of party A and B. The initial point *a* in iso-curve 1, reflects the initial distribution of advantages between party A and B represented by vertical axis and horizontal axis. The PEE can equalize the advantage between A and B, this can be achieved by the movement from initial point *a* along the curve to point *c*, which is the intersection between radial 1 and iso-cure 1. The radial that partitions the panel at 45 degrees represents the equal distribution of advantage. The equalization of advantages will give disadvantageous party B more incentive; as a result of this, an exchange is more likely to realize and a win-win outcome can be achieved represented by point *b* in iso-curve 2.

There are two options to realizing social progress in an institutional movement. To make a win-win outcome:, move from the initial point *a* to point *d* in the higher indifference curve, or move from initial point *a* to point *c*, along the same curve. The win-win outcome is not always achievable, although it is preferable. The win-lose outcome is conducive to the exchange insofar as it can boost the incentive to one party without much disincentive to the other. Under such circumstances, although the optimal point is located between initial point *a* and the intersection point *c* in a

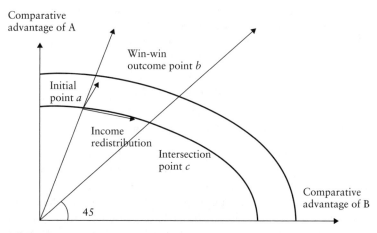

FIGURE 1.10 Graphical Representation of Income Redistribution and Win-Win Outcome

win-lose framework (i.e., along the lower indifference curve), whether the optimal point can be reached or not depends on the primary exchange. Because the exchange always has transaction costs, the optimal point is rarely achieved in practice.

Therefore, neither egalitarianism nor absolute liberalism is preferable from the perspective of IEEN, which judges economic policy based on how conducive it is to the incentive system.

A society is stable if it is configured with ranked classes, such as nobility, middle class and third estate—where the middle class dominates as its incentive is to become nobility, while the third estate has incentive to become middle class. This new framework helps explain why the hierarchy defined above is conducive to economic performance and social stability.

Evolutionary versus Revolutionary

Evolution takes place in both institutional movement and technological progress. However, insofar as institutional movement is concerned, revolution takes place only in primary exchanges as opposed to the secondary exchange. When exchanges come up with a win-lose outcome, revolution take place, whereas when a win-win outcome is reached, evolution would take place with respect to the primary exchange. In other words, primary exchange can have either a win-win aftermath and result in evolution or a win-lose aftermath and result in revolution.

The revolutionary change in the primary exchange will fundamentally change the rules and equality requirements whereby secondary exchange can be carried out. It is reasonable to suppose that a revolutionary institutional change that marked social progress would improve the secondary exchange. If the consequences of revolution in the primary exchange turn out to be the opposite, it is still a win-win exchange due to, for example, externality, then the revolution cannot lead to social progress. Therefore, revolution does not (as it is usually believed) bring about more advanced society insofar as the role of revolution to the social progress is concerned.

Issues Peculiar to the Primary Exchanges in China

The PAE in China is more independent from the PPE. The party system goes across administrative system, there is some overlapping governance. For example, in each state-owned enterprise (SOE) and local provinces, party and administrative body have overlapping jurisdiction. As the SAE has been more discretion based than rule based for a long time, it is more biased toward the National Development Reform Commission. This has a number of implications for debt capital market development. In the PEE, it is easy to understand that a more discretion-based than rule-based PEE would in favor of government agencies as they would thus possess more power so that it is possible for them to seek rent to compensate the underpaid wages. As low wages and salary could attract only less sophisticated people, the management would become increasingly less effective and hence less efficient. Therefore, in the early time of reform, less efficient PEE slowed down the financial market reform process.

What the PEE ends up with is also attributable to which of the pressure group is stronger. This helps explain why only issuers, listed companies, or banks and not investors and depositors have been concerned. Obviously, this is due to the influence the former has as a *pressure group*.[53] Agencies also tend to protect SOEs rather than investors, which is why the stock market collapsed.

The outcome of PAE is a strong central bank and a weak Ministry of Finance in power in early 1990s. The two agencies made many compromises in bond market reform; for example, the interbank bond market (IBBM) became the main bond marketplace due to the influence of market participants. The outcome of PAE was the rising of a strong National Development and Reform Commission (NDRC), which is in a position to work out corporate bond policies.

There are a number of issues and problems insofar as primary exchange is concerned. For example, regarding rule versus discretion, agencies are always in favor of discretion; regulations tend to be biased toward constraint, not incentives. In addition, policy orientation is always biased to SOEs because SOEs have more bargaining power. That the bond market can be developed at the initiative is due to the fact that the Ministry of Finance can establish a market on its own. Later, the market-based reform suspension is because within the primary financial exchange framework, the central bank (the People's Bank of China) has become more powerful than the Ministry.

Relationships between Exchanges

Insofar as economic exchange is concerned, financial exchange is a derivative of economic exchange, and bond exchange is a derivative of financial exchange. It is clear, both from history and from logic, that economic exchange came first followed by financial exchange; similarly, financial exchange came first followed by bond exchange. How did the derivative exchange come about? The derivative exchange may come from the secondary exchange at higher levels. When a new, but less cost-effective commodity emerges in the market, a new primary exchange comes into being to help economize the exogenous transaction costs. Likewise, the derivative exchange may come from the primary exchange at higher levels, when institution building is more costly in terms of reducing transaction costs.

The financial exchange derived from the primary economic exchange when the money circulation was seen as an important area to create value added and there was a strong requirement to promote related exchange through reducing transaction cost. In the same way, the bond exchange came from the secondary financial exchange.

The features of primary bond market and secondary bond market can be also seen in the relationship between the primary and the secondary exchange.

PRIMARY ECONOMIC EXCHANGE AND ANATOMY OF ECONOMIES IN TRANSITION

According to conventional wisdom, the perfect market economy implies that everything is exchanged through the market. However, economists have finally discovered that this is not true. Neoclassical economists assume it's an imperfect market. The market here is confined to what we referred to as secondary economic exchange (SEE). As mentioned earlier in the chapter, the distinction between PEE and SEE is derived primarily from the rhombus theory.

Consistent with the distinction between the stage of reduction of exogenous and endogenous transaction costs in the formulation of a new institutions, the PEE concentrates on issues related to the government in its capacity to reduce exogenous transaction costs in the economy, while the SEE concentrates on the issues related to the market participants in their capacity to reduce endogenous transaction costs in the economy in question. However, the PEE is not necessarily realized through the market.

Primary Economic Exchange

The mission of PEE is to establish a condition for the SEE, which is the market exchange for allocation of resources. The objectives of PEE are to ensure the equality (i.e., fair exchange) to realized institutional arrangement for incentive structure (for example, the defining of property right, a proper legal framework, or the enforcement system). In addition, the PEE is also designed to improve macroefficiency, such as infrastructure, specialization, and cluster efficiency.

The process of PEE in a market economy can be considered from two different perspectives:

1. PEE functions to reduce exogenous transaction costs vis-à-vis the function of SEE, which is to reduce endogenous transaction costs.
2. PEE is driven by the interaction between government or government agencies, and market participants. However, PEE works only when the performance of government employees is evaluated based on the P-A principle. In other words, if government employees improve their service, the benefit is reflected in their wages and salaries, which are set based on game theoretical logic.

As was indicated, the administrative system should be the agent of the congress. Their principal-agent relationship should be built on the incentive theoretical framework; that is, should comply with the two basic requirements: participation constraint, and compatibility constraint.[54] The relationship between congress and administration should help to prevent moral hazard and adverse selection.[55]

The relationship between government and its administrative or bureaucratic system is essentially a principal and agent relationship. With the development of principal-gent (P-A) theory,[56] the essence of this relationship has been revealed. According to P-A theory, the principal has to pay the information costs in exchange for the agent's trustworthy efforts—no cheating, moral hazards, or adverse selection. Although the theory actually discusses the conditions for the equilibrium, in our view, what it revealed is essentially applicable to the exchange between government and its administrative or bureaucratic system.

However, in China, these two conditions have not been fully met yet. The exchange between principal and agent may be made with some implied income from the business sector, "power in exchange for money" can be seen from time to time. This is referred to as rents seeking, illegally abusing power for personal interest. The status quo is obviously counterproductive to the development of a transparent PEE.

The SAE also affects the PEE. For example, most laws and regulations related to economic issues are legislated by government agencies. Agencies shall get consensus view via exchange (here the exchange may be dialogue, or power struggle) before an economic law or regulation is made. However, there is no direct influence from market participants to SAE. Market participants wield influence via a chains of exchange, PPE-SPE-PAE-SAE, to the PEE.

In the primary exchange, government has to pay the transaction cost in exchange for an intended incentive system, such as contract responsibility system policies to farmers, bonus and welfare system to workers, retain profit to SOEs, and sharing tax systems between central government and local government in 1980s. These preferential and decentralization policies were made at the expense of the state budget (transaction cost). It reduced central government revenue in the short run, but would pay off in the long run to the state budget. Normally government has to raise employee wages and salaries in exchange for their power to seek for rents.

Here the government is a decisive element. Marx and Engels have pointed out the government may lead in a right or a wrong direction. North also differentiates the good and bad actions of government. The behavior of government depends on the ways in which institutions are formulated: an exchange ended up with a win-win outcome and an exchange with win-lose outcome. The yardstick to measure the PEE is, in principle, whether the exchanges result in win-win outcome in the SEE. However, it is in no way means that a win-lose outcome is never necessary. Under circumstances of income disparity, a win-lose ending in favor of the poor would, as an income redistribution, help to establish equality and thereby improve incentives of the SEE.

The function of the PEE is to build up the institutional framework for the markets. As in the PEE, the institutions are exogenously arranged other than endogenously formulated. It is important to ensure that all participants in the SEE only have defined property rights, and within an institutional framework. The PEE, which is equivalent to the exogenously arranged institutions, should guarantee the fair exchange of endowments and comparative advantages of persons and organizations. As indicated, the PEE in the economy is the exchange between government and market participants. For the property right, the government has to ensure the externality is internalized, and therefore it has to pay the transaction costs, i.e., the costs related to define the property right.

The importance of PEE has been proved by historical experience. The goverance of the economy is driven by PEE, on one hand, and SEE on the other. It is recognized that the transition to the market economy in the West has been going through for almost two centuries, and the process was full of political, social, and economic exchange.

Primary Political Exchange

IEEN overlaps in many areas with political science and public choice-theory.

Unlike public choice, IEEN contains the neoclassical theoretical framework rather than based on it. IEEN covers the political science, but to IEEN, political arena as human exchange is functioning to reduce transaction cost of property right, rule of exchange, and enforcement type. The primary exchange is derived from SEE; the administrative exchange (AE) is derived from PEE. However, as AE is group to group exchange, and its function shall be carried out through collective action rather than personal action, the SAE shall help to pursue its function in a democratic way. The PAE, derived from SAE, was to set the rule and engage in the enforcement of the rule. Similarly, AE necessitates the need for a political exchange (PE), the exchange between political institutions.

For public choice, there is no distinction between PPE and PAE. There is no explanation of what the social function of PPE is. Public choice does not reveal the essence of social relationships, which is the exchange between people.

Much of the PPE has been explained by public choice theory. "It does not represent some huge mistake on the part of experts or politicians but can be explained as the result of rational self-interested behavior on the part of citizens in their various capacities as legislators, voter, bureaucrats, and so forth."[57]

The nature of the transaction cost may transfer from exogenous to endogenous and vice versa. For example, when attention is focused on group-to-group exchange, transaction costs incurred in the exchange within a group is exogenous while those incurred in the exchange among different groups are endogenous, as the objective is to achieve win-win outcome between groups. Alternatively, if the objective is to secure a win-win outcome within the group, the transaction costs between groups is exogenous while the transaction costs to achieve exchanges within the group would be endogenous.

Administrative exchange exists for three reasons:

1. Group action needs to be balanced.
2. Group consensus-based decision making is essentially rule based.
3. The need to have administrative exchange depends on whether exogenous transaction costs are in excess of the administrative costs. However, the efficiency of SAE would help to economize the endogenous transaction cost for the work out of agency regulations and government policies.

To reinforce administration, government tends to add more agencies and departments. As a result, decisions would be made based on a consensus among different agencies. The hierarchy tends to stifle the reform program. As reform per se is a public good, like other public goods, it has externality; therefore, government stuffs have no incentive initiate reform programs. Therefore, often policy initiatives come from grassroots units rather than from government agencies.

Macroeconomic Policy

As indicated, the PEE functions to establish rules for the SEE and to guarantee fair exchange. The macroeconomic policy as a product of PEE is derived from equality principle specified in PEE. When government derived its function for printing money, it has to ensure the money printed provided equal to the money demanded. The consequence of the oversupply of money is inflation, and inflation would give rise to income redistributions. Therefore, it comes as no surprise that monetary function is for equality.

The fiscal policy is also focused on equality. Tax cuts and rebates are good examples. The progressive tax rate is designed specifically for income redistribution. The government only provides public goods when it increases expenditures, which is used as a substitute for market failure. It is therefore reasonable to assume that all macroeconomic policies are functional for equality. The government often pursues fiscal policy to stimulate economic development. However, for fiscal policy to work, the exchange rate has to be fixed; this means currencies are not tradable. For a market economy, this is not the case.

Transition

In the transitional economy, the institutional movements have two different stages: the exogenous development stage (similar to the PEE) and the endogenous development stage (similar to the SEE). At the first stage, before the market has been established, the institutional arrangement is carried out through the administrative or bureaucratic system. This function is carried out via PAE and SAE. The purposes of this stage are to transform government allocation of resources to market allocation of resources and establish a sound legal framework and enforcement system.

At the same time, competitiveness and fairness in the market, or SEE, have to be ensured so that the endowment and comparative advantage of market participants can be adjusted so that each market participant has an incentive to participate in the market activities through tax policy. As a rule setter, the government should never be a game player; therefore, it is necessary to restrict the ability of government employees to engage in business. To this end, government has to build up a sound institutional infrastructure, such as defining property rights, setting laws and regulations, establishing an enforcement system, and creating market participants.

Economists tend to take government economic policies as exogenous variables; however, in our view, they are endogenously determined via PEE (i.e., through the exchange of comparative advantage between government and the business sector). There are many exchanges between these parties, such as the exchange between government and its bureaucratic administrative system and between the administrative system and business sector. It is important to note that PEE may be accomplished through the market or through other modes of exchange, such as dialogue.

Here the transition of economy means the directory of compulsory plan transfer to the fiscal and monetary policies, the constraint-oriented institution-building transfer to incentive-based institution building and macroefficiency transfers to microefficiency.

Many economies in transition have a sound SEE (market system), whether it was created by a colonial regime or evolved on its own, but do not have a sound PEE. As a result, income disparity becomes a problem due to the lack of an equality policy in the PEE.

In comparison with former socialist countries, which are good at equality in PEE but not good at SEE, many economies in Africa have good market system but an unequal distribution of income. Therefore, each country must follow a different path to achieve its economic development objectives.

Socialist countries need to improve their incentive-based institutional arrangements and macroallocation of resources in their PEE framework. Other emerging economies need to improve the equality in their income distribution.

The success of China's economic reform lies in the artful arrangement of the sequence of reform programs. For example, China maintains macroefficiency to make the majority of people feel comfortable and happy. It may also boost financial revenue, so that the government can assist the poor regions through transfer payments. At the first stage of economic reform, the compulsory plan is not abundant but reinforced. At the same time institution development is underway. Gradually, the incentive system is established.

In many transitioning economies, the PEE results in an interest redistribution, or win-lose outcome, although SEE are almost in place. Obviously, this triggers social instability and prevents SEE development and eventually hinders economic growth. PEE is driven by political exchange. In a top-down political system, the winners and losers are often chosen by bureaucratic and politicians exogenously rather than via markets endogenously.

When the former Soviet Union collapsed and Russia embarked on an economic transition, the PEE for this process did not formulate. Instead, it made this transition through an erroneously implemented policy economist Jefffrey Sachs called "shock therapy." In hindsight, it became clear that without PEE, the Russian economy would face recession for many years.

To realize a smooth transition to PEE, government must consider social stability and economic viability. Social stability has to be ensured through equal competition. Equality is an important factor underpinning the smooth transition to the market economy. There are two categories of equalities: equality prior to the SEE and equality in the aftermath of the SEE exchange. The ex ante equality should ensure that only given, as opposed to derived, endowments and comparative advantages are legally guaranteed. To achieve this, government has to restrict the abuse of power by the administrative system, such as corruption and seeking rent, and restrict the opportunities to take advantage, such as smuggling. The ex post equality should be achieved by the government's tax policy. Progressive tax rates would help to ensure the equality and reduce the income disparity. These two aspects have to go hand in hand to make the transition smooth.

Therefore, the government has to balance economic efficiency with equality and balance the way financial resources are allocated through administrative means vis-à-vis through the market.

The gradualism (as opposed to radicalism) that China has followed so far in its market-oriented reform program is essentially a win-win arrangement in the PEE. The government's unique economic power, stable policy, win-win arrangement, macroeconomic allocation efficiency, and juste-milieu (middle-of-the-road) culture remain the key factors that contribute to successful economic reform in China.

The achievements are evident as far as market developments are concerned. In 2004, 96 percent of commodities were subject to market demand and supply. The factor market has developed as well; the labor market is basically in place. Finally, a number of developments have been made in the capital market; it is driven by increasing the number of market and international participants (as opposed to government participants) with concomitant reform being implemented at the same time.

However, in this stage, market efficiency has yet to be accomplished; therefore, economic growth has to be maintained through so called macroallocation efficiency: infrastructure, cluster, and specialization efficiency. It is through macroallocation efficiency that China balances the social stability vis-à-vis market development.

For the market infrastructure, after many years' efforts, China has established a legal framework that is compatible with the development of the advanced market economy. Most recently, the draft bankruptcy law has been adopted. Since reform and opening up, building up the legal system has been the main focus. In the early stage of reform, more rules were drafted and enacted; later on, enforcement has been emphasized. A civil servants act was promulgated to regulate the conduct of government employees.

The formal rules, as the mainstay of the legal system and as part of constraint structure, have to be modified from time to time to cater to the changing incentive systems. This is not only due to the fact that formal rules tend to be more restrictive at the beginning, but also due to the changing nature of incentive structure. As the market system gradually takes shape, the call for deregulation is increasing.

In addition, to formulate the market system, diversified ownership has to be established to make transactions possible and active. This is a problem that any planned economy has to face. Direct privatization has been proven unsuccessful as it gives rise to income redistribution and triggers social disability. China followed a gradual process for the diversification of ownership. The first stage is to provide sufficient room for the private ownership to survive; then implement privatization of SOEs; and finally, encourage the private sector to thrive. This step-by-step process will help to secure a smooth transition without many social repercussions.

The PEE has four basic aspects: instructions for economic actions, institution developments, allocation of resources, and transaction through the market.

The economies differ in the PEE. Market economies differ from transition economies in four ways. (See Table 1.1.)

The four components of primary exchange are reenforceable and complementary, rather than substitutes for one another. There were tendencies when institutions have not been put in places, in the absence of PEE, curtail administrative control would trigger market chaos. However, it is tempting but wrong to say that administrative control should be resumed. On the contrary, institutional movement should be accelerated. On many occasions in China, administrative control over economic activities resumed in the aftermath of economic overheating. These actions should be avoided as administrative control only serves to hinder the proper development of a mature market.

TABLE 1.1 Differences in Primary Exchange between the Economy in Transition and the Market Economy

Economy	Instruction	Institution	Allocation	Transaction
Economy in transition	Directory or compulsory planning	Constraint oriented	Macro-efficiency	Government procurement, government spending
Market economy	Fiscal and monetary policy; Tax and interest policies	Incentive oriented	Micro-efficiency	Government procurement, government spending

From a historical perspective, the PE moves toward a more institution-centered framework. In the market economy—for example, in the United States—administrative functions have gradually been replaced by the rule-based institutional framework.

Although both PEE and SEE are path dependent, the PEE determines the SEE insofar as its capability to reduce the exogenous transaction costs are concerned.

Primary Financial Exchange

Analogous to the PEE, the task of the primary financial exchange (PFE) is related to the establishment of financial market, the secondary financial exchange (SFE). (See Table 1.2.)

In the planned economy, there were more administrative means, as opposed to economic means, insofar as central government's instruction is concerned. Credit plans were extensively used rather than the financial market with respect to the allocation of resources. Financial markets were regulated rigorously at early stage of financial market reform. Analogous to the primary economic exchange/secondary economic exchange, primary financial exchange should go hand in hand with secondary financial exchange.

This view is not followed properly in China in the early stage of financial market reform. Evidence from financial markets indicates that administrative action was frequently resumed in later 1990s. It is noted the more administrative measures that were retained, the great amount of power bureaucrats possess. As a result reform process slowed down.

For financial market reform to proceed smoothly, incentives from both market participants and government agencies have to be ensured. North makes this argument when he states that rules of the game are changed only

TABLE 1.2 Differences in Primary Exchange between the Planned Economy and the Market Economy

Economy	Instruction	Institution	Allocation	Transaction
Planned economy	Directory or re-loan facility, or credit ceilings	Constraint oriented	Credit plan across region or across industries	
Market economy	Monetary policy Government credit enhance-ment	Incentive oriented	Financial market	OMO

when the benefits to the player are evident and any positive effect of the new rule change to society is of secondary importance.[58]

The PFE is determined by the PEE. As a financial system is essentially an institutional arrangement, and the weak point of the PEE is the institutional development, the financial market reform at early stage is relatively slow. However, as we will see in the bond market reform, it provides a successful example of reform through institutional building to boost the lending to the real sector.

Primary Bond Market

Analogous to PEE and PFE, primary bond exchange (PBE) as a governance of secondary bond exchange aims to provide conditions for a successful secondary bond market. The PBE is realized through both market and non-market approaches. The market approach is through so-called primary bond market, which is the direct exchange between the government and market participants. The non-market approach is related to the dictates and instructions from government agencies on bond market, institution building, and allocation of resources by government agencies. (See Table 1.3.)

Interactions between Exchanges

The PEE and the PFE influence the PBE. In turn, the PBE determines the secondary bond exchange (SBE, the bond market). Figure 1.11 illustrates the relationship between PEE, PFE, and PBE on one hand, and the relationship between SEE, SFE, and SBE, on the other; and also the relationship between the PE and the SE.

In summary, the primary exchange is not confined only to the market. As Figure 1.11 shows, it comprises four different aspects; we call it the instruction-institution-allocation-transaction quadrinomial paradigm. It covers all the function and attributes of primary exchanges and includes the

TABLE 1.3 Differences in the Primary Bond Exchange between China prior to Reform and in the Market Economy

Era	Instruction	Institution	Allocation	Transaction
China prior to the reform	Patriotic propaganda	Constraint oriented	Administrative allocation	Over-the-counter sale to individuals
Market economy	Issuance schedule	Incentive oriented	Primary dealer system	Primary bond market

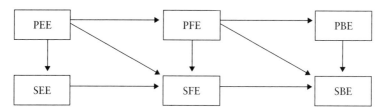

FIGURE 1.11   Relationships of Primary and Secondary Exchange

PEE, PFE, and PBE. It is important to observe the anatomy of the exchanges so that the question of why reform was successful in some economies and not in others can be understood. The microscopic view of exchange helps to reveal the reasonable sequence of reform in a given condition of the economy in question prior or to the reform. It postulates that there is a division of function between PE and SE. PE should be confined to defining property rights, rules of game setting, and incentive promotion. Some functions are transitory and fade gradually. For example, government-directed participation in the market gave way to market-based and rule-based primary exchange.

The PE helps to build up institutions exogenously, whereas the SE builds up institutions endogenously. However, the SE cannot substitute for the PE as the latter can help to define property rights and set up the rules of game for the SE. It seem to be fair to suppose that the PE only engages in defining property rights and setting the rules of the game while leaving all other things to the SE. However, if the PE can help to set up incentive apparatuses or promote the interaction of the incentive and constraint structure, institution development would be accelerated.

Note that in the PEE, a win-win institutional arrangement is evolutionary and path dependent, and a win-lose institutional arrangement is revolutionary. Obviously, revolutionary change may take place when cumulative evolutionary change is strong enough to make a fundamental change. However, evolutionary change would have fewer social repercussions than revolutionary changes. Therefore, it is preferable to have evolution rather than revolution as far as institution development is concerned.

Another tendency is for resources allocation and transaction in primary exchange to become more rule or institution based. For example, open market operation (OMO) by the central bank become more rule based and transparent in the United States[59] (see the quiet evolution). The questions here are why the primary exchange may result in both market-based instruments (such as primary bond market) and non-market-based instruments (such as administrative placement in selling government bonds), and why China took administrative measures to control the economy when economy was overheating. The answer is that if an economy is transforming from planed economy, it is transaction cost-effective to use non-market-based instrument first before the market-based instrument can be utilized.

We believe the weakness of the primary economic exchange in China is related to the defining of property rights. In addition, it is recognized that for a long time more rules have been designed from the constraint perspective rather than from incentive perspective. It is important to confine the primary exchange to the property right defining, make rules of game and design incentive mechanism for secondary exchange.

The virtue of China's PEE is its allocation of resources. This allocation of resources is mostly conducted through government administration as opposed to the market, and, it is important to note, allocation of resources in the PEE creates macroeconomic efficiency.

The primary bond exchange is, as it turns out to be, successful in China as it helps to set up the incentive structure. Here, the incentive structure refers to the policies to attract institution to participate in bond market. Later, we will see, primary dealer status and reasonable return give great incentive to the institutional investors and financial intermediaries in bond market. On contrary, the administrative allocation took great effort of government, yet, proved to be unsuccessful.

The change of technology and productive force would change the comparative advantage and competitive advantage as well as the incentive structure and thereby alter the outcome of exchange, but technology does not directly change the institution.

Win-Win–Based Incentive and Equality-Based Incentive

Although people or groups can benefit from a win-win type of exchange, if their comparative advantage is insignificant, they do not have the incentive to realize their comparative advantages. They may wish to seek more equalized comparative advantages. For example, they can join in a group that can help them to lobby in parliament. Their choice depends on the comparison of transaction cost between prior equalization exchange and post equalization exchange.

APPLICABILITY OF TRUTH AND THE BVP TRILOGY

The absolute-relative truth framework can be also viewed along the line of applicability wherefrom we induce the base-value-path paradigm, or BVP paradigm. Base, value, and path are the three overlapping components required for the evolution of institutions (see Figure 1.12). Each leg contains three elements.

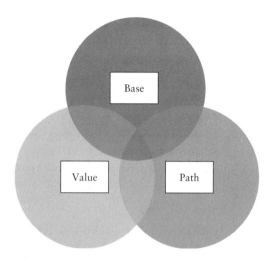

FIGURE 1.12   Base, Value, and Path Trilogy

Base: The Initial Condition

The base is the starting point for the creation of an institutional movement. For a person, the base is personal endowments, both natural and social. For a country, the base is the natural, social, and economic conditions on which the economy grows or reform is initiated. The base of a financial system is the status quo at the time reform was initiated. The base serves as a precondition for financial system development or reform, including China's reform program.

As Gerard Caprio Jr., Izak Atiyas, and James A. Hanson put it, "Initial conditions in finance—the portfolios of banks, their 'information capital,' their human capital, and their internal incentive system—play a key role in determining the success of reform efforts, and implicitly offer a blueprint for the design of reform programs."[60]

The base is the history. As North concluded, "History matters; it matters not because we can learn from the past, but because the present and future are connected to the past by the continuity of a society's institutions. Today and tomorrow's choices are shaped by the past. And the past can only be made intelligible as a story of institutional revolution."[61]

The base is composed of three parts: (1) natural and social endowments, (2) social environment, and (3) social relationships. The social environment includes the legal and social system; the social relationship contains all the social connections and network.

By saying that base matters, we are saying that history matters or that institutions are path dependent. Thus, if we copy a model from outside

China, we need to take into account China-specific issues as well as the preconditions that the model requires in order to function.

Value: The Guide to Human Behavior

Value is based on culture and tradition, and is used to determine objectives and make judgments about the way to achieve those objectives (what actions and behaviors are appropriate).

In one way or another, philosophy, which is the search for a better way of life, is also close to our notion of value. According to Eugene Kelly, "Our minds are fallible, and prone to error. We often jump to conclusions without having examined the evidence, for example. We have all accepted many ideas as true that have turned out instead to be false, or confused, or we find ourselves unable to give an adequate account of them."[62]

The behavior of human beings is primarily a conditioned reflex against actions that cause irritation or pain. Ideas are important to guide human behavior, but fostering a culture of creativity and receptiveness to innovation can take as much time as developing the ideas themselves.

The conditioned reflexes of adults may differ from those of infants, who rely on instinct; an adult's response depends on many factors, including past experience, tradition, culture, and values. Adults normally follow rules, but what rules they follow depends on their standards, or values. The rules may be based on self-interest, utility, or moral standards or idealism. Figure 1.13 is a graphical representation of how this operates.

Rationality originates in "reinforcement," which is thought to stimulate the idea that it is probable that an event will repeat itself. As to the outcome of reinforcement, there are several explanations. Herrnstein[63] argues that it is the result of a matching law. This idea has drawn academic attention but fails to explain what motivates selection in animals.

Optimization theory, as developed by Rachlin, Green, and Battalio,[64] attempts to interpret how individuals make choices based on matching law. Herrnstein and Vaughan[65] apply optimization theory to the behavior of the individual.

It is essential to define the terms "rationality" and "irrationality" properly. The dividing line between rationality and irrationality is whether people have a so-called consistent preference and whether their motivation is driven by "maximum utility." Individuals have rational thinking only if they can understand the information and the uncertainty of their external environment. If their behavior relies only on the supernatural perception and external stimulus, they are irrational. Behavioral economists believe social cognition is subjective probability and that it is the crucial variable of human behavior. Given the importance of social cognition on decision making, the

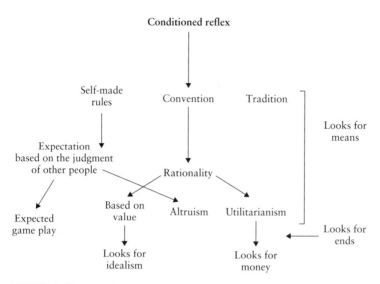

FIGURE 1.13   Conditioned Reflex: Human Behavior

value function eventually replaced traditional utility as the value yardstick for decision making. However, once a spontaneous irrational reaction is combined with optimization, confusion between rationality and irrationality arises.

In mainstream economics, rational selection theory is related to individuals' "maximum utility" behavior; a person operating at that level is thought to be a "rational person." However, behavioral economics focuses on physical reactions and the process of action regardless of its utility.

Behavioral economics, which is based on positivism and zoological experimental theory, is a natural science of animal and human behavior. For example, Kahneman and Tversky[66] predict that in reaction to the stimulus of external reinforcement, individuals will respond, depending on their experience, differently. Their reactions may be either rational or irrational.

It becomes widespread belief among many different economic schools that human behavior is based on bounded rationality, i.e., human rational thinking only constrained by their ability to access information. To reconcile the discoveries of different economic schools, it is logical to assume that rationality and irrationality interrelate; that a human being's choice is an exchange within his or her mind. (See Figure 1.14.)

Simon divides rationality into material rationalism and process rationalism. Material rationalism examines the rational person from an instrumental perspective. It reflects the values of Benthamism and utilitarianism.

FIGURE 1.14 Interrelationship of Rationality and Irrationality

The rational expectation of neoclassical economic theory follows this tradition. Von Neumann and Morgenstern[67] established this utility theory based on expectation, and later, Arrow and Debreu[68] added it to their equilibrium analysis framework. Prospect theory concludes that when the return is certain, human beings are risk averse; when loss is certain, they are risk friendly.

Homo Economics and Public Choice

The human exchange covers the exchange of any material (for example, commodities) or nonmaterial endowments and comparative advantages (such as political power), as well as the exchange inside human mind, i.e., human choice. Human choice, in a sense, is an exchange as well. When people make choices, they forgo one thing in exchange for another. The "transaction costs" of this type of exchange is the energy expended in making the decision. People make mistakes not because they are irrational, but because they have incurred transaction costs in the choice.

The theory of human choice and public choice has been around for 100 years. The prevailing view on the homo economics (human beings are economic animals), whether rational or irrational, is that it focuses on the driving force of human behavior.

Rationality means three things: It is interest driven, actions are based on logical thinking, and decisions are cost effective. By "decisions are cost effective," we mean that people make the choice that would cost less energy. In our view, when people make comparisons, calculation is a kind exchange within human being as opposed to the person-to-person exchange, the intra-human exchange need to consume energy as well, therefore is a kind of transaction costs.

"'Public Choice' is the name given to an approach to the analysis of the behavior of policymakers, especially economic policymakers, and the context in which those policy choices are made."[69] In our view, public choice is made through personal choice. Public choice is also made via the exchange between persons and groups and among group members.

The three parts of value are tradition, culture, and level of cognition. The meaning of each component is self-evident. Culture and tradition shape the path that we follow. How this path is determined requires several value-based social choices. Experience provides a conduit through which the base influences value and innovative ideas.

The initial condition of the financial system and the initial ideology regarding financial and debt issues are essential to the reform. For example, China's mentality at the outset of reform was the outcome of a multilevel process of social exchanges that had attached a strong sense of debt phobia. In other words, at that time China regarded debt as evil and feared it, especially national debt.

Path: The Road to Action

The path is the approach to achieving the objectives; it can also be seen as a strategy.

Like base and value, path includes three components: goal, methodology, and means, which, in turn, are determined by base and value. For example, one's standards determine one's goal, which may be based on ends or means. Value influences the methodology, which may be structurally based or reconstructionally based (i.e., the methodology may depend on comparative or competitive advantage). The means is affected by whether it is government or institution based.

These three components constitute the dimensions of the evolution of institutions. It is evident that this BVP approach is different from the state-structure-performance (SSP) approach, as the former is process based while the latter is end based. It is important to note that for BVP, the end is the starting point of the next institutional arrangement, in the end of prior institutional arrangement, the new base is formulated; for SSP, the goal in the path will counteract the base and value; there is no endogenous and dynamic movement.

Impact on the Reform Movement

One of the fatal drawbacks of institutionalism is its lack of theoretical soundness and consistency. Although it recognizes that transaction cost is not limited to commodity exchange and is a component of political and social exchange, it does not extend the exchange and transaction cost to the social behavior of individuals, although their social behavior essentially encompasses all choices and decisions and therefore comes with opportunity as well as lost opportunity costs. Extending exchanges to include the social behavior of individuals has important implications on the pioneering work of North and other neoinstitutionalists.

As international trade theory demonstrates, comparative advantages can be realized through trade to achieve a win-win outcome. Since everything can be traded, even social and natural advantages can be realized through exchange. The significance is that institutional movements are endogenously determined and therefore are evolutionary.

Comparative advantages are realized through the competitive process designed to reduce endogenous transaction cost (whereas, as we have seen, the effort to improve comparative advantages is to reduce exogenous transaction costs). The reduction of endogenous transaction costs is far more important than reducing exogenous transaction costs, which helps explain why competitive advantages are far more important. Reducing endogenous transaction costs demands more innovative ideas, which provide the foundation for consistent, up-to-date thinking, such as blue-sky theory.

The interaction between incentives and constraints drives the evolution of institutions, which progresses through the realization of comparative advantages. The main driver of the evolution of institutions is the incentive apparatus. This process can be graphically manifested as a rhombus shape, so this theory is dubbed rhombus theory.

Based on this theory, the interrelationship and interaction of all the endogenous factors can be illustrated as a triangular relationship, which provides the philosophical base for the methodology by which the goals can be achieved.

Goals are important to those who are motivated. There are value-based and calculus-based people. Value-based people have preferences, whereas calculus-based people have goals. It is noted that the calculus-based people are more readily motivated by incentive apparatus than value-based people.

Base is the precondition for financial market reform. Gerard Caprio Jr. indicated the importance of preconditions when financial reform commenced.[70] Some people believe that present-day China's financial market was started from scratch. This is not true. China had a financial system, even before reform, although it was characterized by financial repression, which is why the 1980s bond offerings were mainly accomplished through administrative placements.

The recent controversy over the privatization of the big four state-owned commercial banks—Industrial and Commercial Bank of China, China Construction Bank, Bank of China, and Agricultural Bank of China—triggered much debate about the path of financial market reform in China, especially banking-sector reform. The essence of that debate is this question: Should China transplant a model from outside and graft it onto China's base, or should China remold itself and replace its own model through an evolutionary process?

There are many examples of what happens when a country attempts to copy foreign models directly. In those that were successful, the key is that the constraint structure of the domestic institutional and legal frameworks must cater to the incentive structure of the foreign models. It is therefore advisable to accelerate the improvement of the domestic country's legal framework, giving more room for the institution to maneuver, and thereby permitting the whole system to evolve and the new institutional framework to be established.

Government therefore needs to set priorities for the whole program. In our view, the sequence of reform should be first to liberalize the legal framework, which should then be followed by institutional evolution. Less legal control by government facilitates the establishment of the incentive structure, making it easier to apply foreign models.

It is useful, therefore, to identify the differences between the financial system in a market economy and in developing countries and what the issues in developed countries are, because even after China becomes a market economy, we will still face a number of issues. Part of this analysis is to differentiate between the problems specific to underdeveloped countries and those specific to China.

The other category is issues that are specific to China, for example, the fact that the government controls the interest rate and can therefore manipulate the financial market. China first has to deal with China-specific issues (which, in our view, are deeply rooted in China's institutional framework), but with an eye on the specific issues in developed countries. Due to differences in the initial conditions in China and developed countries, China should not slavishly follow the models of developed countries but draw lessons from their experiences. For example, for many years, the U.S. banking industry was prohibited from entering the brokerage business, but this is no longer the case in the U.S., and China can learn from this experience but not follow in the U.S.'s footsteps.

China's financial market cannot be fully understood without recognizing several issues that underlie its current institutional framework.

REPRESSION OF FINANCIAL INSTITUTIONS AND ECONOMIC DEVELOPMENT

The financial market movement has much to do with China's industrial policy and economic growth strategy. Recent literature indicates that China's industrial development has been accompanied by so-called financial repression.[71] Financial repression occurs in the early stage of economic development. The British philosopher John Stuart Mill, writing in the nineteenth century, noted: "Policymakers have viewed the financial sector as irrelevant, except in times of crises, and hence have tried to repress finance and use it for the convenience of government."[72] Financial repression has been seen in some newly emerged newly industrialized countries as well and is well established in the economic literature.

The rationale behind a policy characterized by financial repression is that in order to accelerate economic development, the government directly controls and allocates all resources in order to pursue industrialization. The financial market is the only source of financial resources. Therefore, to channel money to the industrial sector, the government has to maintain a relatively low interest rate to make investment money affordable. Banks act only as money providers. A capital market becomes a major conduit of financing only when it has been proved to be able to provide a convenient source of money.

For a policy of financial repression to function, financial resources made possible by huge individual savings are needed. Savings are easier to allocate when there are fewer financial instruments available. The affordability of state-owned enterprises provides a base price for interest rates. As their rates of return tend to be very low, the interest rate should be kept low as well.

Administrative System Accountability for Mobilizing Financial Resources

The nature of subordination of the financial sector to the industrial sector is the main characteristic of the economic structure in developing countries. This nature is dubbed by economists as financial repression. When industrialization policy is pursued under circumstance of underdeveloped financial system, the financial sector is only a money provider for the country's industrialization program.

Therefore, make the financial resources cheaper and expediency is government's priority, so low interest rates, fewer financial instruments, and an underdeveloped capital market are always byproducts of the financial repression. These features all helped to shape China's economic policy landscape prior to reform of the financial structure.

Although the 1990s showed signs of a "financial revolution," the practice of repressing institutional development remains unchanged to this day.

Impact of the Ideology of Material Production on Financial Reform

In Marxist theory, output is material production; services are not included as output. Based on this theory, the economic achievements are material goods, such as the concrete buildings, factories, and machinery, all of which are state assets. The erosion of state assets means the machines are rusty.

The pricing of the assets is not based on the discounted value of future cash flow; rather it is based on the book value, or reproduction value. In this macroeconomy, the manager always runs the economy through the National Planning Commission (NPC, the former National Development and Reform Commission) rather than through the Ministry of Finance or PBOC. This ideology, which easily gives rise to a pro-planning economy management format, is deeply rooted in the thinking of many who have been managing China's economy since the reform. Banks are regarded as money providers or essentially glorified cashiers; the capital market is considered the place to finance government or corporate deficits; and the stock market is a place recoup the losses of SOEs. When bonds, for example, were introduced, they were used only to finance government deficits rather than as market instruments.

CHINA'S FINANCIAL MARKET TODAY

Today's market structure grows out of the policy to separate the China's banking system from the stock market.

The second half of the 1990s was marked by a financial contraction. In order to control the overheated stock market, the central government decided to cut the link between the banking system and stock market to isolate them from one another (as had been done in the United States). In 1997, the central government issued a circular requiring all the banks to withdraw from the stock exchange.

As the banks still held government bonds, they had to trade among themselves, which gave rise to interbank trading of bond securities. Subsequently, the PBOC set up the interbank bond market.

Today there are two marketplaces: the stock exchange, which trades government bonds and corporate bonds, and the IBBM, where government bond and financial debentures are traded.

Because it is administratively easier for regulators to supervise individual financial sectors than a more integrated financial market, it is tempting but wrong to say that this institutional arrangement is productive.

Primary Economic Exchange

Historical Perspective: Technology, Population, and the Growth of Institutions
China's economy after reform has fluctuated substantially, constrained not by capital and labor but by demand, resources, and, more than anything else, institutional constraints. Institutions can alleviate both consumption and resources constraints.[73] The internal driver is the interaction between incentives and constraints.

However, there also are interactions between institutions and technology and between institutions and the population. Economic historians Rondo Cameron and Larry Neal noticed that population growth is in principle subject to the logistic curve (see Figure 1.15), an S shape curve, which reflects the three stages of population change: growing slowly, growing rapidly, and stagnating.

> *The modern economic system has taken its shape in the west since medieval time and the process took many centuries.*
>
> *During the eleventh, twelfth, and thirteenth centuries, European civilization expanded from the heartland of feudalism between the Loire and Rhine rivers to the British Isles, the Iberian peninsula, Sicily, and southern Italy, into central and eastern Europe, and even to Palestine and eastern Mediterranean temporarily during the Crusades. In each locale, the institutions of feudalism were adapted to local conditions and customs, creating a variety of economic systems. In the late fifteenth and sixteenth centuries maritime exploration, discovery, and conquest took Europeans to Africa, the Indian Ocean, and the Western Hemisphere. . . . By the seventeenth century, however, the variety of institutional arrangements in Europe created some pockets of prosperity in the midst of overall decline; for example, cities grew rapidly in the Low Countries and northern Italy.*[74]

The fourteenth century and the first half of the seventeenth century witnessed a slowdown in population growth, which led to stagnation in per capita income. This, in turn, stimulated the incentive for technological and institutional progress. In the nineteenth century, the institutional arrangement in Europe had undergone profound changes.

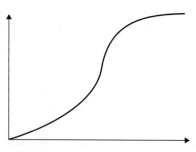

FIGURE 1.15 Logistic Curve of Population Growth

Therefore, it is reasonable to suppose that the evolution of institutions and the growth of population are the driver of economic development. Having said this, we should note that there are correlations between population growth and economic development. As was pointed out by Cameron and Neal, "The hypothesis of economic growth accompanying the growth of population is strongly supported by the unquestioned evidence of both physical and economic expansion of European civilization during each of the accelerating phases of population growth."[75] The corollary is clear: Logic and history demonstrate that it is technological and institutional progress that facilitates economic growth, thereby stimulating population growth.

Thus, when institutional transaction cost is greater than technological transformation cost, there is a strong incentive to improve technological progress. Conversely, as medieval history illustrates, when technological transformation cost is greater than institutional transaction cost, there is a strong incentive to drive institutional progress.

Industrialization led to capitalist institutions. In this process technological progress reduced institutional transaction cost, thereby promoting institutional progress. In the case of China's bond market reform, institutional progress reduced technological transformation cost, thereby promoting technological progress.

History also shows that when an institution is evolving, technology advances rapidly; when technology is progressing, institutions evolve or revolve rapidly. As Richard Sylla explained, "Past and current differences in development around the world can be explained by historical differences in the spread of modern financial systems, which serve to facilitate the acquisition and application of both nonhuman and human capital, new production techniques and mass schooling."[76]

Public Awareness and Understanding of the Government's Role   Heritage, custom, and path are three interrelated factors that affect the public's perception of institutional change.

Heritage includes comparative advantage, competitive advantage, and competitive competence. Competitive competence has more weight than competitive advantage, and competitive advantage has greater weight than comparative advantage. Heritage is the foundation for incentives that can be achieved.

Custom includes values, conventions, and rules as well as rational thinking. It is the reference by which people judge actions and make choices.

Path is the process by which comparative advantage can be realized. It includes the efforts made to convert comparative advantages into competitive advantages. A successful person always has competitive competence (vision and insight) and the ability to find and seize opportunities; he or she must also have perseverance and persistence.

Competitive competence derives from idea generation, in particular the generation of innovative ideas. In Chapter 3, we will see how the public's lack of awareness of the market in China led to its failure in 1993.

Innovative ideas also influence the thinking of government officials, organizations, and even the nation. As Robert Merton points out, the development of finance theory plays an important role in the financial market development.[77]

In China's case, the public's lack of cognition of financial markets dragged down financial market development. The old planned economic development theory hindered their way of thinking about market development and stifled innovative ideas. The lack of financial knowledge combined with the self-interest of agencies diminished their vision, passion, and courage. It is therefore no accident that reform initiatives were suspended several times as a result of Asian financial crises. Indeed, liberalization or deregulation shall, as a change of constraint apparatus, go hand in hand with the change of incentive apparatus. Therefore, unilateral liberalization would not work. As Gertler and Rose put it: "Liberalization alone is not a panacea."[78]

Role of Government Agencies   Most people assume that government agencies will behave as people do, but this perception has been challenged. First, principal-agent theory and incentive theory view the relationship between government and government agencies as a principal-agent relationship. Government is the principal while government agencies are agents. When there is information asymmetry between them, government agencies do not act as the government would like. In addition, if the payoff to the agencies does not satisfy the incentive theory, or if the constraints are not compatible with the incentives, then the incentive apparatus will not work. As indicated before, when this happens, government agencies tend to seek "rent" in compensation. This happened in China, especially in the 1990s, when most government employees were underpaid.

Public choice theory perceives public service, especially reform programs, as public goods, which have externalities. Due to free-ride problems, government employees are unwilling to initiate reform programs.

Although governments at various levels in China have increasingly come to recognize that many activities can be carried out more efficiently and with greater cost effectiveness by the private sector, there is little sign that the government will walk away from financial involvement and suspend direct intervention in the financial market. Therefore, relatively little attention has been paid to institution building and encouragement of innovation in this area.

China's government has paid more attention to the formal rules of organizations and little attention to the informal rules. Intervention turns out to be counterproductive. Informal rules and personal relationships work as constraints on incentives.

These characteristics of China's financial system have great implications for its bond market. First, the corporate bond market is small vis-à-vis the government bond market due to the government's preference to raise capital to finance its economic development program rather than to use the financial sector as an institution to promote the program. Second, banks are the main investors in capital market instruments, especially bonds.

In China, as elsewhere, government agencies try to protect their own interests. This affects the function of economic and financial development as well, which has great implications for agency. We discuss this topic further in Chapter 3.

Collective Actions

Introduction to Collective Actions   My argument is that people in the group or organization do not necessarily share the same interests. The historic work on this subject is, of course, by Mancur Olson. Olson argues simply that collective action is very difficult to achieve because interests among individuals are so varied. Often individuals or groups choose not to act because they know that someone else will on their behalf. This dilemma is called the "free-rider" effect. Only when individuals and groups value the achievement of a certain goal more than the value they place on their own time does successful collection action ensue.[79]

All human exchanges are, in our view, subject to the law of rhombus theory, where institutions are perceived as an equilibrium state by which comparative advantages are realized. That is to say, when people enter into kind of relationship with other people, they are in a state of exchange. Essentially, when the new member enters a group, a relationship is established. This relationship is maintained via person-to-group exchange, which follows the same logic is followed as the person-to-person relationship where exchange between persons takes place. What is exchanged between one person and another group member, or the group as a whole, is not confined to the material commodities but their natural and social endowments and the comparative advantages that arise from them.

This exchange is reflected in the fact that new members pay membership fees and make effort to contribute to the group, and get their share of the benefits when group efforts turn out to be a success. Although human beings as individuals have different comparative advantages, they can nevertheless end up with a win-win outcome based on the same principle as of trade theory. During person to group relationship, as a result of exchange of comparative advantages, both the new member and the rest of group end up with a win-win result. This institutional arrangement gives rise to social progress if there is no negative externality incurred to the people outside of the group.

However, there are other kind social arrangements regarding the person to group relationship which end with a win-lose or lose-lose outcome where the person leaves the group. Therefore, it is reasonably to assume that collective action is also made within an institutional framework and the way to set up a person-to-group relationship is essentially the same as to set up a person-to-person relationship under different circumstances.

What differs is that collective action may have more additive effects than individual efforts, for three reasons. First, collective actions are guided by the collective wisdom, which is far more sophisticated than individual wisdom. Second, the people in group can enjoy the cluster effect and create a kind of synergy. When people live and work together, they have easier access to information and thereby they save transaction costs. As they have common concerns, they discuss and share views more frequently and thereby save transaction costs. Third, members enjoy community facilities, which is free of charge. Therefore, the group has more power to help new members to achieve their goal, which the individual may not be able to achieve on his or her own.

However, there are a number of disadvantages when people are in groups or organizations. As has been explained by many economists, groups or organizations have an externality problem. Internalizing the externality (i.e., eliminating the effect of externality) would incur transaction cost. In addition, big groups or organizations incur more management costs. Supervisory costs occur as well. Therefore, the bigger the group or organization, the larger the transaction costs would be. Individuals should do cost-benefit analyses and compare the cost and benefit when they are in the group with when they are outside the group.

All human relationships have the same characteristics. People do not share common interests insofar as collective action is concerned; they share common concern. However, in the case of a person-to-person relationship, people may have different concerns. Under such circumstances, people address others' concern, and the benefits are shared between them.

Role of the Organization Who is the main player in institutional building? To North it is the institution. If an institution were formed outside of an existing institution, it would mean that institutions are not built from within. Further, it would mean that the institution is not evolutionary. It is important to note that institutions are indeed endogenously built and evolutionary, which means that all the participants are in a position to shape the institutions.

Remember, based on rhombus theory, institutions are formulated at the second stage of the rhombus framework (refer back to Figure 1.2), where the participants, or game players, are trying to achieve their goals by reducing the endogenous transaction cost. Because the participants have an incentive to reach an agreement so that all parties can benefit, institutions can move on automatically. Organizations and financial institutions can help to build new institutions and make institutional arrangements. By doing so, transaction costs can be reduced, issues and disputes can be addressed, and solutions can be framed. As time goes by, a new system is established. It is now clear that organizations, if they are the game players, have incentives to foster innovative ideas to build up institutions. If they are not the players, they are generally not in a position to build up institutions. The exception is associations and arbitrage institutions that play a role similar to that of government; that is, they set the rules of games and supervise the enforcement of those rules.

It is suggested, therefore, that the government's role be restricted only to those areas where the government can assist organizations and institutions to function (e.g., by encouraging innovation and reducing the obstacles for the institutions to innovate and by creating the legal framework needed to reduce transaction costs). Here the role of government is not clear-cut. Many emphasize the legal environment for financial reform, but the legal environment—North's formal rules—provide constraints and is antithetical to the general trend toward deregulation.

In China, for instance, most laws tend to constrain financial activities, especially innovative ones. In my view, the legal system should foster financial innovation, defining property rights rather than prohibiting them. This view is supported by Gertler and Rose, who assert that government policies must be selective.

Relying on self-regulatory organizations to regulate the market has proven to be one of the most successful institutional arrangements.

Primary Financial Exchange

Although it is commonly recognized that finance is the linchpin of a modern economy, as Deng Xiaoping stated in 1990, in China, little that is convincing has been said about why it is important to the economy. Is it important because it provides financial resources? Alternatively, is it important because it is the engine of economic growth? According to Ronald Coase's theory, if property rights are well defined, there is no transaction cost.[80] In that case, resources will move automatically to those places where they can be used most efficiently, and the economy can grow to its full potential. Put another way, if an economy cannot achieve its maximum potential, it is due either to ill-defined property rights or the existence of some transaction cost. It follows that the financial market can be an engine of the economy only if it is efficient. However, an efficient market is not a given. In China's case, the idea of the firm (or company) is a new development, as is the idea of a market. Therefore, it is logical, then, that the law is the last frontier in which development and reforms should take place, thus reducing but not removing transaction costs in China.

As indicated, the function of primary financial exchange is to achieve more efficient secondary financial exchange by means of reduction of exogenous transition costs. The secondary financial exchange can be better performed within the Arrow-Debreu (A-D) framework. However, without an efficient primary financial exchange, the A-D framework would not be in place.

Finance Theory: An Overview

Puzzle of the Arrow-Debreu Framework   Before we get into the details of the new theoretical framework, let us briefly review mainstream financial theory, which is based on the A-D paradigm. The A-D framework has been challenged recently by many different schools of economics; however, it offers a perfect starting point and frame of reference through which to detect the difference between the theory and reality.

Let us suppose we are in an A-D universe. There are no transaction costs, there is a perfect competition, information is freely available, and the financial market performs flawlessly and without friction. Because of the absence of informational friction, individuals can make credible commitments to honor their agreements and contracting parties are able to make credible promises, which implies that everyone could lend and borrow freely at a risk-corrected rate of interest.

Under this assumption, savers are able to search over the entire world capital market for the best possible risk-corrected returns. In an A-D framework, with perfect markets, the financial system washes a considerable quantity of risk out of the economy. What is left is the systematic risk. Borrowers and lenders are able to make fully contingent arrangements to ensure against unanticipated short-term needs for funds, and there is no need for government participation in the market. Institutions here are unimportant since there are no transaction costs.

Once you enter the real world, however, incentive problems arise because of limited information and lack of sufficient enforcement. However, transaction costs can bridge the gap between theory and practice.

Defects of Finance Theory   In an A-D universe, with no transaction costs, there is no credit risk, no market risk, no liquidity problems, no government role, and no need for contracts or institutions. However, this ideal universe does not exist. Even in the United States, the nation whose financial system is considered the most advanced in the world, the market is not perfect.

Mainstream finance theory has several pitfalls. Mainstream financial theorists regard finance as a money machine or a consumption plan. Institutions play no part in this theory. Institution is the missing link in their theoretical framework. Conversely, neoinstitutionalists fail to point out the interplay between incentives and constraints, which drives the evolution of institutions. Although traditional economic theory has focused on transaction cost issues and provided great insight into the role of institutions and their evolution, it is segmented and internally inconsistent, and therefore vulnerable to theoretical criticism.

Nature of Finance and the Financial Structure

How to Redefine the Financial System   The financial market is not as complicated as many people think. Still, the nature of finance has been much debated among the various schools of economic theory. Early economists viewed money as a machine. As John Stuart Mill put it, "Money...is a machine for doing quickly and commodiously what would be done, though less quickly and commodiously, without it; and like many other kinds of machinery, it exerts a distinct and independent influence of its own only when it gets out of order."[81] Finance, too, is a machine.

Money can function as a machine only in an institutional framework. Marx reiterated that credit as a way to use money can work as a lever, to accumulate money to achieve economies of scale. According to mainstream economics, finance is a consumption plan. The main contribution of mainstream financial theory is the A-D and Modigliani-Miller[82] methodology for pricing financial instruments.

A new development in finance theory is the recognition of finance as an evolutionary institution and institutional arrangement. As was indicated by Charles P. Kindleberger, author of *A Financial History of Western Europe*, "One can easily exaggerate the importance of finance, both when it is skilfully conducted and when it is not, but the suggestion that it usually falls into line and accommodates real forces—discoveries, inventions, population change, and the like—stretches belief."[83]

North believed that institutions were created to reduce the uncertainty. Ross Levine[84] studied the relationship between finance and economic growth and concluded that a financial system is created to reduce transaction costs *and* uncertainty, or in his words, to ease exchange. Finance enables savings to transfer into investment more efficiently than barter, for example. However, Levine does not examine the motivation for reducing transaction costs or what the incentives are for the individual or organization.

Greenwood and Smith[85] set up a model based on the relationship among exchange, specialization, and innovation. Like me, they believe that financial systems are created to reduce transaction costs.

> *More specialization requires more transactions. Since each transaction is costly, financial arrangements that lower transaction costs will facilitate greater specialization. In this way, markets that promote exchange encourage productivity gains. There may also be feedback from these productivity gains to financial market development. [Therefore] economic development can spur the development of financial markets.*[86, 87]

Neoinstitutionalism has made great contributions in uncovering the essence of finance. However, the work so far leaves open the question of how to distinguish financial institutions from other institutional arrangements. If finance is defined only as an institutional arrangement, how do we differentiate finance from other institutional arrangements? Institutional arrangements and reduced transaction costs are not unique to finance; they have existed throughout the history of human beings, while finance only emerged in the eighteenth century.

However, these questions can be better clarified via primary–secondary-exchange framework. Financial exchange is derived from economic exchange. When economic exchange becomes more sophisticated along the line of commoditization and securitization, new financial products are derived, such as bonds, the commoditized and securitized loan; futures, the commoditized and securitized forward contract; share the commoditized and securitized equity. When the new financial products come into being and become exchangeable, new markets—such as capital market and derivative market—emerged. Finance differentiates itself from other economic activities by sophistication of exchange, which is characterized by commoditization and securitization.

Institutional Economic Engineering and a Redefinition of the Nature of Finance   After its creation in the so-called financial revolution, China's financial sector, along with the functions that enable it, has developed along evolutionary lines. In this way, the institutional framework of a financial system has been created. For example, to stabilize the financial system, a new function—speculation—emerges, because its counterparts—hedgers—need to minimize their risk. As a result, another group of people become speculative specialists. Here again, the incentive of speculation encounters the constraints of hedgers. The specialist function is necessary because the efforts of specialists move the market from disequilibrium to equilibrium.

A financial system is comprised of many such interrelated functions, which, in turn, constitute sociological chains. A missing link in one chain can give rise to a socioecological problem, just as it does in natural ecology.

As the IEEN theory demonstrates, the function of institutions is not just constraint; rather, it is incentive. IEEN highlights the crucial role of the incentive structure and the interplay between incentive and constraint. Finance should contain these elements:

- The ability to transfer money and reduce transaction costs
- An incentive structure with cost benefit consideration
- An institutional arrangement with win-win outcome
- The opportunity to get value added via exchange

With this in mind, we define finance as an institutional arrangement designed to achieve the most augmented value added through an incentive structure to reduce endogenous transaction costs.

Evolutionary Development of Financial Systems   Nowadays the financial sector, which is an outgrowth of the economic system, is located at the end of the value chain. Historically, financial systems around the world become evolutionary after revolution. After the financial sector experiences a period of development, it changes its focus from facilitating money flow to the financial market, which includes the money, equity, bond, and derivative markets, and finally to knowledge-based services, such as consulting.

Throughout history, whoever possessed competitive advantage and competitive competence controlled the direction of economic and institutional movement. Institutional movement can be both revolutionary and evolutionary. Both types of movement are driven by the interaction between incentive structures and constraint structures: When incentives change and constraints remain unchanged, revolution will occur. When both the incentive structure and constraint structure change, or change their form (e.g., when there are more informal rules than formal rules), evolution takes place. As indicated, the changing incentive structure requires the new constraint structure to adapt, and vice versa. The relaxation of the regulatory framework, among other things, stimulates the incentive for financial innovation. "The stimulus for financial innovations is strong, arising from the interaction of a changing regulatory environment, expanding technology, volatile markets, shifting current-account balances, and growing competition among financial institutions."[88]

Financial markets are formed mainly to reduce risk and uncertainty, which incur transaction costs. Transaction costs in a financial system are both exogenous and endogenous. Endogenous costs include, among others, those that arise from fraud, opportunism, moral hazard, adverse selection, and the like, which occur in the process of making a transaction. Because of the change in the value of money over time, both exogenous and endogenous transaction costs change. As the value of money changes constantly, exogenous transaction costs may increase or decrease, changing comparative advantages and the incentive structure. In turn, the constraint structure must change to cater to the new incentive structure. As a result, the institution evolves. Thus, the financial market is always in a state of disequilibrium.

One of the important functions of any financial market is reducing risk and uncertainty. By institution formation, risk can be neutralized, hedged, or diversified, which means it first has to be priced so that a transaction can occur. The price of an asset is adversely related to its risk, or uncertainty. As North says, "The greater the uncertainty of the buyer, the lower the value of the asset."[89] Neoclassical finance theory contributes a great deal to financial asset pricing, thereby facilitating the development of the derivative, stock, and commodities markets.

The development of an institutional framework is, as we said earlier, one of the underlying elements of the financial structure. Financial institutions played an important role in this respect. However, this development is not driven by government; rather it is a spontaneous process. In China, financial institutions mushroomed in the early 1990s. This was primarily a natural process; there was no government intervention.

The modern financial system, as we have seen, benefited from technological progress, the development of financial theory, and the institutional revolution. As Merton has indicated, "Those financial innovations came about in part because of a wide array of new security designs, in part because of the advances in computer and telecommunications technology and in part because of important advances in the theory of finance."[90] Rapid advances in computer technology facilitate the electronic transmission system, simplifying the book-entry form of securities trading. The development of China's bond market has also benefited from this technological progress. For example, China used paper bond securities for only about 12 years, while Europe used paper securities for over 100 years.

As finance is an institutional arrangement and institutional change is evolutionary, financial systems are evolutionary as well. This implies that financial movement is endogenously driven. "Financial system is endogenous after all, and they change over time. Required is an understanding of what determines the relative efficiency of a country's financial system, and how this efficiency may evolve."[91]

It is desirable to establish a financial system by creating an institution rather than an administrative system.

Incentive Structure and the "Value Chain" To build a sound financial system, an institution must achieve a certain level, which, as indicated, is driven by the interaction between the incentive and the constraint structure. The incentive is the opportunity to obtain added value, which is the result of a win-win outcome through the exchange of comparative advantages. Similarly, the incentive structure is engineered by the constraint structure to realize a comparative advantage of the person or organization in its pursuit of added value.

Throughout history, economic scale has played a very important role in the efficiency of an economy. "A production activity displays increasing returns to scale if an expansion in the scale lowers the unit costs of operation. Equivalently, a proportionate increase in the variable inputs of production leads to a greater-than-proportionate increase in the output from the activity."[92] This is also true of specialization, by which I mean the division of labor. There are two types of specialization: horizontal division of labor, which facilitates the creation of different types of products, and vertical division of labor, which facilitates the production and marketing functions.

History has witnessed the transition of economies from agricultural to manufacturing and, ultimately, to the specialized manufacturing process, where the division of labor reduces transaction costs. As a result, tertiary industries, such as communications, transportation, logistics, commerce, and finance, have emerged. These sectors all serve to reduce exogenous transaction costs.

It is important to note that the sole purpose of industries such as commerce, finance, consulting, and other management sectors is the reduction of transaction costs, and therefore these should be classified in a new sector, the fourth-level industries. It is therefore reasonable to assume that these sectors or products, which augment (increase) value added, represent *the direction of productive force*. They offer greater payoff and less cost. The result, therefore, is that the technological progress they contribute reduces transformation costs, while institutional evolution works to reduce the transaction costs and augment value added. If we further divide transaction costs into exogenous and endogenous ones, we recognize that the former can be reduced by both technological progress and institutional evolution, whereas endogenous transaction costs can be scaled down only by the evolution of institutions.

Thus, it is at the end of the value-added chain that greater value added is cultivated. The initial sectors are full of competition. However, as the opportunity to cultivate new area of value added is revealed demand tends to be high, and the production cost, or transaction cost, tend to be lower.

As the area develops, technological progress and institutional evolution, both of which rely on innovation, work to augment value added.

The economic sector is divided into three sectors:

1. *Value-augmenting industries.* Industries that increase value added, mainly manufacturing
2. *Transformation-cost-reduction industries.* The industries that reduce the material costs, mainly tertiary industries
3. *Transaction-cost-reduction industries.* Finance information industries, education, consulting

All three can create value added. The third group, in which finance is the leading industry, is created to reduce exogenous transaction and endogenous transaction costs.

How Financial Structure Is Determined   Based on the IEEN framework, the force driving a financial system is no longer only government. Rather, there are five different forces: government, institutions, new ideas, technological progress, and financial leaders. (See Figure 1.16.)

FIGURE 1.16   Determinants of Financial Structure

Financial infrastructure includes accounting, auditing, and related functions. The role of the other factors is self-evident. It is important to be cognizant of financial leaders and their role in financial market development. As Richard Sylla, an economic historian, has stated, "Financial leaders can matter a lot. Such leaders know and understand what I have called the key institutional components of good financial systems; how these components function, interact, and reinforce each other in financial networks; and how they serve the needs of governments and the economy."[93] Sylla offers a number of examples of successful financial leaders including Alexander Hamilton, in the eighteenth-century United States, and Masayoshi Matsukata, the Japanese finance minister during the 1890s. In each of these periods of reform, the government undertook serious measures to make the marketplace driven by market forces. This condition led to increasing economic strength for these countries, and eventually they became worldwide economic powerhouses.

In summary, the financial system in China has much in common with that of most less-developed countries, but, of course, there are many China-specific issues as well. Its ingrained administrative system and obsolete way of thinking, which had its origins in a planned economy, are two examples that work to alienate China from a market economy. However, it is important not to lose sight of those things from which China benefits. For instance, local governments in China have a lot of power to allocate resources, which saves a great deal in transaction costs. In addition, the generations who grew up guided by a philosophy of altruism have now become the managers of the economy.

NEW METHODOLOGY FOR THE ANALYSIS OF FINANCIAL ISSUES

Using the base-value-path paradigm, we will define the financial issues facing China and examine their solutions from three different perspectives. To guide our exploration, we can identify three questions:

1. Viewed from the base dimension, what is the condition on which China's current financial system is located? As "initial conditions matter a great deal in determining the impact of economic reforms on a given system,"[94] as demonstrated by the BVP paradigm, the answer to this questions provides the base on which the financial system will develop.
2. Based on the value dimension, what kind financial system is China going to establish, a market-based system or a bank-based system?
3. Based on the path dimension, how can China achieve its goal of setting up a modern financial system?

Effect of Overlapping Jurisdictions and Division of Labor

This separation of the banking business from the stock market and insurance industry tripled the number of agencies needed to supervise the financial industry: the China Securities Regulatory Commission oversees the stock market, the China Banking Regulatory Commission supervises the banking sector, and the China Insurance Regulatory Commission monitors the insurance industry.

On the face of it, the division of labor is clear-cut, and concentration in one sector would seem to make supervision more efficient. While this may appear to be a positive step, in practice, its efficiency is hardly proven. Most of the banks in the world are in a consolidation phase—the abolition of Glass-Steagall Act (which forbids banks to engage in both banking business and securities business) in the United States reflects this worldwide tendency—financial services are in the forefront of most bank organizations, and bond markets are interrelated with the bank lending market, the stock market, and the insurance industry. Based on the experience of other countries, it would seem that the separation of banking from other parts of financial market is counterproductive to China's financial market reform and innovations.

Drivers of Bond Market Reform and Financial Innovation

China's institutional framework, characterized by an administrative hierarchy, an economic system derived from a planned economy, and underdeveloped financial markets, is the major factor influencing its bond market development. Still, why did the central government prefer administrative placement of bonds for so long, and why did it return to a regulated coupon rate after the auction method had been successfully introduced and managed? The answers lie in the current regulatory system.

Bureaucratic government agencies are another factor contributing to the slow response to reform. Ideas for changing the status quo originated either from the grassroots units or from agencies of the central government, and, when the ideas come from the bottom up, they tend to be ignored.

China's contemporary financial market is very much influenced by ideology and institutions that had their origins in the planned economy. The conventional wisdom about financial market reform is that the agencies in charge of the financial industry are advised or educated by international experts or domestic think tanks on how to put into practice the latest ideas or programs, and, therefore, these agencies are going to carry out the reform program. In fact, this has rarely happened in China.

We can gain some insight into the reason for this from the recently developed public selection theory and institutional theory, which highlight the importance of the interest of the agency itself. Recent research on public selection by James Buchanan[95] has provided great insight into the behavior of organizations.

According to the theory, agencies are interest groups that are playing games in the political market. Reform is a kind of public good. Like other public goods, it has so-called externalities: The reformers would take the risk, reduce their power, and potentially be blamed for failure by others from their own group; conversely, those who enjoy the benefits are freeloaders. As a result, the theory says, agencies have little incentive to push ahead the reform program.

Setting Goals for China's Financial System

There are two categories of goals: the repression of financial institutions and financial restructuring. The observation that a market-based financial system is superior to one that is administratively based is hardly controversial; however, the proposition that a bank-based or capital market–based financial system is superior is among the most debated subjects. By applying IEEN theory, which evaluates institutions according to their incentive structures and transaction costs (the system with the higher-level incentive structure and lower transaction cost is superior) as a yardstick, it is easier to evaluate the institutions. (See Table 1.4.)

Looking at Table 1.4, we can see that a capital market based on a financial system is superior to a bank-based financial system, because it has

TABLE 1.4 Capital Market-Based versus Bank-Based Financial Systems

Goals	Methods	Means	Features of Financial Market	Incentive Structure	Category of Transaction Cost
Repression of financial institutions	Intervention	Administrative		Lower	More exogenous
Financial restructuring	Evolution	Market based	Bank based	Middle	More exogenous, less endogenous
			Capital-market based	Higher	More endogenous

a higher-level incentive system. This is consistent with the experience of other countries. As Ross Levine correctly noted:

> *For over a century, economists and policy makers have debated the relative merits of bank-based versus market-based financial systems. Recent research, however, argues that classifying countries as bank-based or market based is not a very fruitful way to distinguish financial systems. The results indicate that although overall financial development is robustly linked with economic growth, there is no support for either the bank-based or market-based view.*[96]

The yardstick by which the financial system is judged is how convenient it is to the exchange of comparative advantages, or whether it reduces endogenous transaction costs or promotes transactions.

Sylla outlines the key institutional components of a modern financial system: "They are: sound public finances and public debt management; stable monetary and payments arrangements; sound banking system (more, generally, institutional lenders); an effective central bank; good securities market for debt, equity, and money-market instruments; and sound insurance companies (more generally, institutional investors)."[97]

Judged by these criteria, a modern financial system should focus on the discovery of a new dimension of value creation. In other words, financial systems should be creative and innovative; there is no fixed model.

From the IEEN perspective, the financial system should include both primary and secondary financial exchanges. A primary financial exchange is an exchange between government agencies and market players. It may use either a market (e.g., open market, which is an exchange between monetary authority and market player) or non-market approach (e.g., the state budget, legislation, and enforcement, which are exchanges between legislative and supervisory bodies and market participants). These exchanges are conducted through dialogue, which helps to maintain a balance between stable policies and market development or, in the language of IEEN, help achieve equilibrium between the incentive and constraint structures.

The secondary financial exchange is market exchange; market participants, financial institutions, and individuals conduct transactions to achieve market exchange. It can function only if the markets are in place and all the market rules are public and enforceable, which is the task of the primary financial exchange. Therefore, a primary financial exchange is the precondition for a secondary financial exchange.

As an economy in transition, China's primary financial exchange must also balance economic efficiency (both macroefficiency and microefficiency) and equality (e.g., fairness and transparency).

Path toward Financial Restructuring

The importance of the financial market, specifically the bond market, in economic growth is universally recognized, but how the financial system should function is widely debated. One view is that the financial system can contribute to the efficiency of the transformation from savings to investment. "The financial system contributes to growth and development by mobilizing saving and then efficiently allocating this savings across investment projects."[98] Another school favors institutions, and argues that a pure market does not exist, even in the United States, and, therefore, the A-D paradigm does not work. In the real world, A-D cannot work unless the institutions are in place.

There are two ways to achieve goals once they've been established: institutionally or administratively. The principal difference between the two is the incentive and constraint structure. As institutions and institutional arrangements are a result of an evolutionary process that resulted in a win-win outcome, the incentive structure must conform to the principles of participation and incentive compatibility. However, the administrative system is organized artificially, using promotion and job security as its incentive structure. As a result, in China, government employees generally are underpaid.

An economy in transition, such as China's, should take advantage of the government's ability to allocate resources to achieve macroefficiency to maintain growth momentum so that everyone can benefit from the reform. This can also help alleviate the tension between different interest groups. However, the government should not revert to the administrative approach to allocate financial resources, which would be counterproductive to market efficiency. It should limit its function to reducing exogenous transaction costs, and as soon as the market is in place, the government should leave that area.

Since an institutional system is superior to an administrative one in many ways, it would seem that government would be as small as possible, yet in China the size of government is growing rather than shrinking. Hierarchical bureaucratic systems tend to expand. The more one relies on administrative measures, the more one needs to increase the size of government. The more one needs to increase the number of organizations, the more one needs to coordinate the relationships among institutions. It is also true that the more government organizations there are, the more the government intervenes in business activities, which leads to higher transaction costs because of red tape and other inefficiencies.

Although an administrative system is not an efficient method in the overall scheme, it is easier (i.e., more cost effective to the administration itself) to operate. Therefore, it is still widely used as an instrument to achieve economic goals, although most of the arguments favoring an administrative system are losing strength in China. Institution formation, while the more advanced method, is in some respects more difficult to carry out (actually, it is easier as long as the participants in the institution have incentives to achieve win-win outcome), and it needs a more sophisticated government legal framework, more room for the innovative ideas, and more educated people.

However, what kinds of institutions should be established and how they would work is hotly debated as well. There are two types of institutional arrangements: administratively arranged and organizationally arranged institutions. To facilitate institution formation, the government must set up an appropriate legal environment and understand what goals, methods, and means must be pursued in order to achieve a desired institutional arrangement.

There are two different policy orientations a government can adopt vis-à-vis the formation of institutions: containment and engagement. A policy of containment includes more regulations so that the development of financial markets can be well controlled. A policy of engagement means that some guidelines are given, then the financial market is left to develop on its own (i.e., by evolution). We recommend that China follow a policy of engagement.

There is also discussion on rule-based versus power-based management. Rule-based management is predicated on set rules; power-based management is predicated on power. It is recognized that China's macroeconomic efficiency has benefited from its management based on administrative power, but it is also recognized that this is only transitional.

Another argument is the reliability-based versus validity-based system. Martin expressed the dichotomy: "Validity and reliability anchor down opposite ends of a spectrum that defines how systems are conceived and solutions are framed."[99] In his view, "reliability drives the exclusion of variables and judgment-free measurement, while validity drives the inclusion of variables and judgmental measurement."[100] In this sense, management is an art rather than a science (engineering). Overall, we favor a view that balances both a reliability-oriented approach and a validity-oriented approach.

In summary, the primary financial exchange is far more complicated than the secondary financial exchange. As North put it, "The institutions necessary to accomplish economic exchange vary in their complexity, from those that solve simple exchange problems to ones that extend across space and time and numerous individuals. The degree of complexity in economic exchange is a function of the level of contracts necessary to undertake exchange in economies of various degrees of specialization."[101] Here we use the term "primary financial exchange versus secondary financial exchange" as a proxy for North's economic exchange versus simple exchange. Due to the path-dependent nature of institutional evolution, and given the initial condition of China's planned economy, we believe China must focus its reform efforts on the primary financial exchange in order to accomplish its goals in the financial sector.

Deregulation and Liberalization versus Regulation and Enforcement

IEEN explains that deregulation is a policy used by government to stimulate incentives to produce financial innovation and pursued in the process of financial market reform. The key to designing an incentive apparatus is innovative ideas or, in the language of evolutionary economics, idea generation. This means that the evolution of institutions cannot been explained solely by constraints, as North indicated.

How the Financial Sector Evolves

Base of the Financial Sector   It is important to note that the "base" has a natural inclination to evolve in a certain direction. In the financial field, the base is a given, but it cannot be taken for granted. As Caprio indicates:

> *An appreciation of the various initial conditions in banking and their importance to the evolution of this sector suggests a strategy for reform that differs from the usual choice of pursuing either real or financial sector reform first. Instead, it would appear sensible to begin with those elements—often dubbed institution building—that are crucial for the development of banking and other financial institutions and without which higher profile reforms, such as interest-rate deregulation or bank privatization will possibly lead to a loss of financial stability.*[102]

The institutional framework of the financial sector, which we call the financial structure, determines the functions of the financial system. We can see the financial structure from two different perspectives:

In the first, the hierarchical structure is viewed vertically, illustrating the layers of financial deepening. This allows us to see the functions performed at different levels of institutional hierarchy (see Table 1.5).

In the second, the functions of financial activities and the layers of financial deepening are viewed vertically, demonstrating the functions of different institutions (see Table 1.6).

TABLE 1.5 Functions at Different Levels of Institutional Hierarchy

	Credit	Bond Market	Stock Market	Derivatives Market	Securitization
Government	Supervision	Supervision	Supervision	Supervision	Supervision
Intermediary	Loans	Underwriting	IPO	Swaps, options, futures	
Infrastructure	Legal, technical support	Legal, technical support	Legal, technical support	Legal, technical support	Legal, technical support

TABLE 1.6 Functions of Different Institutions

	Credit	Bond Market	Stock Market	Derivatives Market
Issuer	Business firms	Government, corporate	Corporate	
Intermediary	Banks	Underwriters		Risk takers
Investor	Depositors	Bond investor		

Institutions evolve out of function; thereafter, the interaction of all of the members of a society or participants in a financial system shape institutions.

The choice of methodology is determined by tradition, culture, and understanding of the value trinity. Obviously, the more highly educated the participants are, the higher the methodology.

Institution Formation in the Financial Sector   One might imagine that there would be little to argue about the role of government in economic growth, yet this is fertile ground for debate among economic analysts. Gertler and Rose have specified policies that are positive to economic growth, which include providing for and enforcing the legal framework:

> *The most direct way a government can contribute to this process is by offering an efficient judicial/regulatory system, one that facilitates the enforcement of private contracts and punishes fraud effectively. There is also a role for some kind of public safety net to guard against a disruptive liquidity crisis, as we have discussed. But this objective must be balanced against the efficiency costs of providing public insurance.*[103]

However, judged by the transaction cost standard, the policies should also include those that facilitate defining property rights and encouraging financial innovation—that is, policies that facilitate institution building and support economic growth.

Government's Role in the Economy   So far we have focused on institution formation, but this in no way implies that government is not important. The role of government in the economy is hardly controversial. Experience elsewhere in the world provides examples of governments' attempts to improve their management function, mainly by reducing direct participation in economic activities. Strictly speaking, government is not a player in the economy but a property right definer, rule maker, and enforcer. "Third-party enforcement means the development of the state as a coercive force able to monitor property rights and enforce contracts effectively."[104]

> *Adam Smith wrote in Wealth of Nations: It is not from the benevolence of the butcher, the brewer or the baker that we expect our dinner, but from their regard to their own self interest....[Every individual] intends only his own security, only his own gain. Moreover, he is led by an invisible hand to promote an end, which was no part of his intention. By pursuing his own interest, he frequently promotes that of society more effectually than when he really intends to promote it.[105]*

However, the invisible hand can only be applied to a limited extent. When resources are not subject to the market, and when price is artificially distorted, the invisible hand does not work.

> *According to Coase: In the medieval period in England, fairs and markets were organized by individuals under a franchise from the King. They not only provided the physical facilities for the fair or market but also were also responsible for security (important in such unsettled times with relatively weak government) and administered a court for settling disputes (the court of pie powder). Fairs and markets have continued to be provided in modern times.... Of course, their relative importance has tended to diminish.... With the government providing security and with a more developed legal system, proprietors of the old markets no longer had to assume a responsibility for providing security or to undertake legal functions, although some courts of firepower survived late into the nineteenth century.[106]*

The true function of government is to set up the market to help reduce transaction costs. In many countries, some of the functions of government have been outsourced to the private sector, which also reduces the strain on government budgets and heightens understanding and cooperation between the public and private sectors.

Public-private partnerships (PPPs) are one way to shift part of the government's burden to the private sector. In the last decade, projects such as the construction and operation of hospitals in the United Kingdom, construction and operation of federal prisons in the United States, and the construction and operation of Highway 407 in Ontario, Canada, are all examples of successful PPPs.

In each case, the respective governments were responsible for establishing the criteria, regulations, and guidelines under which these entities would operate, while the private sector operated the facilities. For example, the U.K. government set standards for private-sector hospital management, which included delivery of meals on time, prompt response to telephone queries, and high-quality medical care.

In every country, government provides the framework in which all businesses conduct their affairs: the legislation and regulations related to weights and measurement, unfair competition, foreign ownership, telecommunications, e-commerce standards, safety and labeling requirements, patent protection, recycling, taxation, financial reporting, land use, and environmental requirements, among many others.

Government should encourage the development of self-regulatory institutions, or associations, as they tend to have closer relationships with both government and the business sector and are more efficient than government operating directly. Thus, business associations and proprietary lobbyists represent various sectors (as well as subsectors), such as banking, manufacturing, insurance, forestry, and retailing.

Laws and regulations governing business and the financial sector should be monitored periodically with an eye toward deregulation, in order to minimize constraints and provide more incentives to the financial market.

Still, government should not adopt a completely hands-off policy. As Douglas C. North says:

> *Authorities now have come to recognize the need to nurture regional markets and to build necessary infrastructure. Some experts argue that markets should evolve spontaneously, without official intervention. Indeed, the Euro-Market developed without the endorsement of authorities; rather, it developed as a means to circumvent regulations that restricted market transactions. However, it is important to recognize that infrastructure was already in place.*[107]

TABLE 1.7 Evolutionary Characteristics of Institutions

Evolution of Institutions	Competitive Competence	Market Movement	Economic Efficiency	Organizational Structure	Technological Progress
Informal rules	Idea generation	Commodity market	Division of labor	Private firm	Labor
Formal rules		Financial market	Specialization	Partnership	Invention of steam engine
	Knowledge of management	Derivatives market	Economies of scale	Corporation	Electronics
Culture	Brand-based competitive edge	Function-based operators			
	Core technology	Safety-based operators		Banks	Information
				Financial institutions	
	Knowledge of competition			M&A	

As illustrated in Table 1.7, economic development is predicated on three dimensions: informal rules, formal rules, and culture. Government's role varies depending on the situation. In areas such as agriculture, mining, and energy exploitation, governments can legislate to ensure their effective use, protect the environment, and so on.

The government's role vis-à-vis technological progress is in such things as patent and copyright law. In terms of organizations, its role is to provide corporate laws that will promote small and medium enterprises; with respect to the division of labor, the government's role is to levy value-added tax; and insofar as market building is concerned, the government's role is to set up the market infrastructure, incentive apparatus, and, most important, rules.

Industrialization-Based Policy versus Finance-Driven Policy The classical economists did not overlook the issues of economic growth. As North pointed out:

> *Output is determined by the stock of capital, both physical and human, and we can increase the stock of capital in the neoclassical*

world by investing at whatever margins have the highest rate of return, there is no fixed factor. We can overcome resource scarcities by investing in new technologies and we can overcome any other scarcity by investing in new knowledge to overcome that potentially fixed factors.[108]

According to North, Marx was the first economist to highlight the role of institutions: "to the extent that these models convincingly related institution to incentive to choices to outcomes they are consistent with the argument of this study."[109]

As indicated, finance-driven policy is superior to the industrialization-based policy, which has always been accompanied by financial repression. The two different policy orientations are compared in Table 1.8.

What distinguishes an industrialization-based policy from a finance-driven policy is the way in which the whole economy is managed. Thus far, China has pursued an industrialization-based policy.

A finance-driven policy focuses on interest or exchange rates, through which the government pursues its macroeconomic policy. However, more than anything else, a finance-driven policy focuses on building institutions because without institutions in place, the interest rate policy cannot be carried out. Here the way institution creation is pursued is crucial, and the government's focus should be on setting up the regulatory framework and leaving the institutions to evolve on their own until everything has been put into place.

TABLE 1.8 Industrialization-Based Policy versus Finance-Driven Policy

	Industrialization-based Policy	Finance-driven Policy
Political orientation	Supports SOEs	Supports SMEs
Supervision orientation	Protects SOEs	Protects investors
Attitude toward failing companies	Bailouts	Bankruptcies
Attitude toward competition	Division of labor, against competition, discourages new entry	Encourages competition and new entries
Attitude toward consumption	Levies withholding tax	Increases disposable income
Policy instrument orientation	Fiscal policy	Monetary policy
Industrialization	Manufacturing	Third-level industries

SUMMARY OF IEEN

In summary, the IEEN is based on five important pillars (i.e., the arguments draw on five lines of thoughts), which related to each other:

1. The exchange underlies human relationships. Human beings keep their relationships, whether person to person, person to group, or group to group, via the exchange of their endowments and comparative advantages.
2. The exchange of comparative advantages can come up with a win-win finale or a win-lose aftermath. The outcome may run counter with their initial desires.

   The win-win type of game theoretical equilibrium or institutional arrangement is evolutionary, while the win-lose type of game theoretical equilibrium is revolutionary. If an institutional arrangement can reach a win-win outcome without triggering externality (the impact to other people), it is possible to lead to social progress. The win-lose outcome may have three different social consequences: a revolution that leads to social progress, income redistribution, and disfranchisement that leads to social regression.
3. Institutions underlying human relationships are dynamic and driven by the interaction between incentives and constraints.
4. Institutions are both the game per se and the rules of game. Institutional progress is achieved via the efforts to save the transaction costs, exogenous and endogenous. Setting the rules of game would help to reduce exogenous transaction costs, while game play would win by saving endogenous transaction costs.
5. A society is structured by primary exchange and secondary exchange to save exogenous transaction costs and endogenous transaction costs, respectively. The PE is a mandate by SE (i.e., the PE is derived from a mandate from the SE). That is to say, rules internally created, from secondary exchange, are internal rules; or from primary exchange, are external rules.

Without referring to the PE and SE, it is difficult to define social progress and regression. Insofar as the SEE is concerned, the win-win outcome marks progress, whereas the win-lose and lose-lose outcomes mark backsliding. However, the same is not necessarily true for political exchange, where the win-lose exchange may be a revolution that marks a social progress.

It is important to note that the more exchanges are carried out in the secondary exchange, the more benefits are engendered to the public. However, for the exchange to happen, property rights have to be defined first. In addition, these exchanges have to follow certain rules to ensure fair competition, and the rules have to be enforced effectively. This legitimizes the PE as a superstructure of the SE. There are two important points:

First, the rules here are also endogenously engendered. This is obviously contrary to the North's view that institutions are rules that are exogenously made. The primary exchange is also an exchange and therefore also has to follow rules, which necessities the higher level of primary exchange whereby rule for the exchange can be engendered. In this book, the administrative exchange is the superstructure of economic exchange and the political exchange is the superstructure of administrative exchange.

The exchanges, rather than those through economic market, are carried out through the so-called internal market, or political market. It is recognized there are many internal markets. The internal market, in our view, includes administers to bureaucratic, the exchange among agencies and the exchange between central and local government.

Unlike the United States and the United Kingdom, the tax bureau is at the same ministerial level in China. Therefore, the tax policy is formulated via the exchange between the Ministry of Finance and the National Tax Bureau. As in the United Kingdom, local governments are only agents of the central government; therefore, there are exchanges between central government and local governments.

Most exchanges in the political market are not related to commodities, but to power, promotion, and other incalculable or invisible benefits.

Much of the literature on political science and public choice relates to the government administrative system. However, these subjects are discussed in isolation; most fail to specify the role of the secondary administrative exchange, and therefore lack theoretical consistency.

Essentially, there are many exchanges in a hierarchical structure to facilitate the diminution of exogenous transaction costs. In classical and neoclassical economics, government is mainly an economic unit and a black box. But in the IEEN framework, it is one party of the exchange or game play through which government policies and economic rules are engendered.

If the discrepancy of endowed comparative advantages between each party engaged in an exchange are largish, then the incentive to participate in the exchange for the less advantageous party is slim. This is because, even based on the fair exchange, the win or benefit is far more weighted toward the party who has more comparative advantage. This requires the PE to pursue the principle of equality. This view, which highlights the consistency of equality and efficiency, supported by the evidences that discovered in China and elsewhere, runs contrary to the prevailing neoclassical equality-efficiency trade-off.

Unlike many contemporary economic theories, to which the different views of neoclassical and neoinstitutionalist are hard to reconcile, within the IEEN framework, achievements in economics, sociology, and mathematics get along in harmony.

All the social and economic issues can be ascribed, in one way or the other, to what I called incomplete primary exchange. Therefore, the mission of the IEEN framework is to remedy the incomplete PE. Although the external PE cannot make the best enforceable rules, the primary or secondary internal exchange, can fill the gap.

In this book, the bond market is not seen from market perspective but from an institutional perspective. It is intended to link the bond market to the economic and social fundamentals (i.e., to the institutional arrangement). Many missing links are presented. Although the theory of IEEN seems to trace back to the principal social and economic issues, it is my hope that it can generate discussions of contemporary China's economic issues. In essence, here the bond market is symbolic of China's economic reform and is the epitome of modern social and economic development in China.

The function of the PE, internal and external, is to spawn formal and informal rules. As the internal PE is created by the participants of the SE, it can achieve a higher level of equilibrium between incentives and constraints and therefore is more economically efficient. This theoretical discovery has important implications for understanding the role of institutions on economic growth, finance and capital market issues, among others.

Laws and rules can be introduced, but exchanges can never be introduced from the outside. By the same token, tradition and culture heritage can never be introduced.

Up-to-date ideas and technological progresses contribute to the institutional evolution and revolution insofar as it economizes transaction cost, both exogenous and endogenous. Although there is no clear division line, in general, innovative ideas save endogenous transaction costs whereas technological progress saves exogenous transaction costs.

There are five categories of constraints:

1. Laws and regulations, formal rules
2. Religions and philosophy
3. Convention
4. Contracts
5. Norms

North has categorized these constraints as informal rules and formal rules. To North, laws are formal rules, and all the rest are informal rules. However, he did not say how formal and informal rules are engendered.[110]

In the IEEN framework, rules, both formal and informal, are created via primary and secondary exchange, internal and external. The internal exchange spawns informal rules except religions, which are created by external exchange, while the external exchange spawns formal rules. "Internal" and "external" are relative terms. To the bond exchange, financial exchange is external. And to the SE, the PE is external. Internal exchange is between or among parties and participants who are engaged in a transaction. Exchanges, primary and secondary, are the genuine engine of institutional change.

We must not get carried away and imagine that development of institutions in China was always on the same scale as seen elsewhere. It is noted that only formal rules and religions can be introduced from outside; informal rules cannot be enacted in a China-specific environment as they are created directly from exchange, and exchange per se cannot be introduced.

Knowledge is a comparative advantage, whereas innovative ideas are a competitive advantage. One of the important conclusions in this regard is that foreign models or practices cannot be transplanted directly to the domestic environment, but they can learned as an idea to those who are the participants of primary exchanges.

Although the IEEN is intended to explain the driving force of debt capital market development in China, its theoretical framework is applicable to any social economic issues, not just debt capital ones.

CHAPTER 2

The Practice

STRUCTURAL ISSUES IN CHINA'S FINANCIAL MARKET

International evidence suggests that stock market performance is positively related to economic performance. However, in China, until very recently, it was just the opposite. While the economy has performed very well—averaging a 9 percent growth rate for the last five years—the stock market has been sluggish, many times plummeting to new lows. This inverse relationship has been the main subject of recent debate. Fundamental differences in institutional arrangements between the rest of the world and China account for this inverse relationship (see Table 2.1).

For many years, China's policy was biased toward state-owned enterprises (SOEs), not investors; pricing always favored issuers, and the market lacked transparency. The reform in 1979 was a win-win program. The government decentralized its power and gave more autonomy to the SOEs and local governments. An incentive structure was established, followed by a constraint structure characterized by the development of the legal system. As a result of the new incentive structure, individuals were winners, SOEs were winners, local governments were winners, and the central government gained political support, making it a winner as well, but not in a fiscal sense.

Government deficits were a byproduct of decentralization. If the SOE reform had been able to generate sufficient income for the central government, the government would have been able to reduce its borrowing program, and everything would have ended up very well for all concerned.

However, the shortfall of the SOEs was so huge that the central government had to make up for it by issuing more debt. In 1997, government revenue accounted for only 11 percent of gross domestic product (GDP), which triggered a debate on the size of government debt. Many suggested that the government could not afford the burden and should shift it to the banks. Between 1998 and 2000, this gave rise to a debt equity

TABLE 2.1 Comparison of Financial Market Institutions in China and the United States

	China	United States
Market objective	Initial financing for state owned enterprises	Stockholder liquidity
Supervisory objective	Formal protection of investors; de facto protection of issuers	Protection of investors
Price setting	Government involved	Market
Supervisory agency	Government agency	Independent institutions
Investor base	Individuals	Institutions
Market transparency	Relatively opaque	Transparent

swap program. This was no longer a win-win arrangement. The SOEs were winners; the banks, already encumbered by policy loans to SOEs and a heap of nonperforming loans (NPLs), were losers. Against this background, the state pinned its hopes on the stock market to bail out the sickly SOEs. From very beginning, this was a win-lose arrangement.

Failure of the Stock Market

An institutional arrangement that does not comply with incentive structures is not sustainable. China's stock market rested on the shaky legs of the illegal operation of securities firms and investors' irrational investment behavior. Fair value was not pursued; market participants sought only capital gains. For a time the market overheated. The stock market is essentially a game played by the government agencies and investors. In this case, equilibrium was to keep the market price growing. Government intervention combined with the SOE bailout eventually led to an overheated stock market (see Table 2.2). The table presents a representation of theoretical equilibrium where 1 stands for preference and 0 stands for the opposite.

TABLE 2.2 Game Theory: Government Agencies and Investors

Government Agencies	Investors	
	Bullish	Bearish
Bullish	1,1	1,0
Bearish	0,1	0,0

It is understandable that maintaining a bullish stock market is in the interest of both government and investors. However, the fair value of a stock market is determined by the future cash flow discounted by market interest rate. Once either of these conditions collapses (in this case, the result of the market's weak underpinnings), the market will fall and eventually find support for fair value. In 1997, the government reinforced the regulatory framework, readjusted securities firms, and stopped supporting the market. As a result, the market price index went down substantially. The chronically sluggish stock market sobered up investors, who became more rational. This fact clearly demonstrates that the incentive structure is the mainstay of institutions, and if it is built on unstable ground, neither the institutions nor the institutional arrangement is sustainable.

Rise of the Bond Market

It is clear why the government bond market first developed in the early 1990s. It ensured the government's smooth issuance of securities to meet its need for financing, one of the pillars on which the decentralization policy was based.

Throughout the decade, little progress was made in the money market, as banks were only providers, and therefore the central bank had no incentive to pursue monetary policy.

Until the early 2000s, accumulated reserves and fixed exchange rates caused the real money supply to go beyond what had been planned. This triggered the overheated economy of 2003, when the central bank had to reinforce its open market operation, in turn necessitating the development of a sound monetary market.

The financial repression and policy of expedience toward financial market reform definitely affected the sequence of the reform program, making China's path to financial reform unique in the world.

Bond market reform is a win-win arrangement, and it turned out to be both successful and sustainable, whereas stock market reform is unsustainable if the incentive structure is not fully established. Given the same amount of resources, if the government possesses more, investors will possess less. As is demonstrated in Figure 2.1, on each convex curve, a point represents the distribution of resources between investor and government. The higher the level on the curve, the more resources there are to be distributed between investors and government. In a win-win situation, both investors and government benefit. The movement from the initial point to a point located on the higher level of curve represents a win-win situation. A win-lose arrangement is represented by a movement from the initial point to a point located at the same level of the curve.

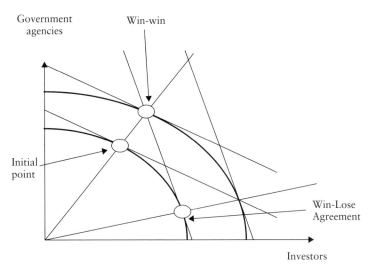

FIGURE 2.1   Effects of Financial Market Reform

Three sets of factors are crucial to the development of an efficient and liquid bond market. The first set has to do with culture and tradition—the informal rules. It includes such things as how people view the market and creditworthiness and how idea generation evolves. We will see later how these factors affect the thinking of investors and market participants.

The second set concerns laws and regulations as well as codes of conduct. These are the formal rules related to securities law, regulations, supervision, accounting rules, and tax policy. Giovanni Sabatini has noted that securities law depends on an appropriate legal framework for company law, commercial law, contract law, bankruptcy and insolvency law, competition law, and banking law as well as a dispute resolution system (e.g., arbitrage rules). Regulation is needed to ensure that markets are fair, efficient, and transparent, so that the interests of investors can be protected. The institutions should facilitate capital formation and economic growth. They should eliminate unnecessary barriers to entry and exit from markets and products, ensure that the market is open to the widest range of participants, consider economic effects, and ensure that market participants face equal regulatory burdens. Market supervision is needed to ensure market integrity by deterring insider trading, manipulation, and other abusive practices; it is also needed to examine market dynamics, for example, by continued monitoring of trading, large and concentrated positions, and anomalous market trends in specific securities.[1] This set of factors also includes what I call the rules of the game and market rules.

The third set of factors includes what Sabatini terms *market infrastructure*; that is, the infrastructure with respect to the primary market as it relates to the role of specialists, how auctions work, transparency issues, and the links with secondary markets. In the secondary market, issues include:

- Whether to use organized or over-the-counter markets
- What market microstructure is most appropriate
- What level of transparency is desirable
- Whether to allow an alternative trading system[2]

This set of factors has much to do with technological progress and market structure. We will see as we go along how these factors influence bond market development.

Role of Organizations in Institution Building

Institutions are not confined to informal and formal rules. Social arrangements also are a kind of institutional arrangement. Firms and organizations all have incentives to reduce transaction costs, and organizations can play a very important role in institution building. The activities of the China Development Bank in the financial sector provide a good example, and prove that China can create its own model of a successful bank.

Case Study: China Development Bank   Since 1998, the China Development Bank (CDB) has adhered to its own model of development in China. Although the reason behind the miracle of the CDB remains mysterious to its domestic peers, its financial statement, verified by PricewaterhouseCoopers (PWC), is convincing and impressive. The real reason for the CDB's success is institutional building.

Given the underdeveloped financial market, the CDB shifted its focus from financing policy to financing development, a concept put forward by Governor Chen Yuan. In practice, this means that the CDB relies on various institutional arrangements to reduce its financial risk, thereby achieving the best performance in China. Several of the CDB's institutional arrangements are worth mentioning:

1. The CDB used the financing platform as an instrument for local-government borrowing. In China, local governments cannot issue securities, such as local government or municipal bonds. They may not incur debt. Local governments must pay for construction with funds from their budgetary accounts. Most governments spend a quarter of their

total budget on capital (infrastructure) construction, which also includes spending for some manufacturing projects. Now the CDB requires that local governments assign a borrower on their behalf and use the amount budgeted for construction to repay the borrower. On this basis, the CDB agrees to lend around 10 times that amount to the local government. This institutional arrangement is reflected in agreements between the CDB and local governments that allow local governments to leverage their investment in infrastructure.

2. The CDB created an association of small and medium enterprises (SMEs) and a guarantee company to facilitate borrowing. For many years, SMEs were unable to access bank loans because of information asymmetry problems. Today any SME can join the association if it pays a small membership fee, currently RMB20,000 yuan. Other members are local government agencies and banks. A member conference convenes periodically to review loan applications. The local guarantee company is obliged to pay part or all of the bank's losses in the event of loan failure. Once these institutional arrangements are established, the CDB makes the loan at normal interest, currently 6.12 percent. Depending on its historical creditworthiness, an SME may also have to remit a formal bond. This social structure has been very successful in some provinces, such as Hainan and Sichuan.

To date, the CDB has 85 models of institutional arrangements that ensure loan repayment. The CDB recovers its loan by relying on these institutional arrangements rather than laws, regulations, and credit record (formal and informal rules). Table 2.3 demonstrates the CDB's track record.

TABLE 2.3   Size and Repayment History of the China Development Bank's Loans

	End of 2002	End of 2003	End of 2004	End of 2005
Number of loan failures	160	108	119	103
Number of loans recovered through legal remediation	68	38	44	28
Number of loans recovered by institutional arrangements	92	70	75	75
Percentage (%) of loans recovered by institutional arrangements	57.5	64.8	63.0	72.8

Source: CDB 2005 statistics.

Financial Market Development   A more detailed description goes beyond our needs for this book. Here it is important to point out that there is no one model for the financial market development.

In Chapter 1, we summarized the elements that determine the development of institutions. When all the elements are available or the necessary conditions are in place, all things being equal, revolution will take place; when only a few elements are available, all things being equal, evolution will take place. That is why the process of financial restructuring manifests itself as a process of revolution vis-à-vis evolution.

It is important to differentiate the government's role from other elements. In China, it is understood that the government is functioning in a more extensive area. Therefore, it is tempting but wrong to say that the financial revolution relies solely on a government's own efforts. In reality, innovative ideas play an even more important role.

The bond market experienced a *revolution* in the early and middle 1990s when all the major conditions were in place; the stock market, however, has been evolving; there has been no revolution. Although they were both the government's top priority, cognition of the role and function of the bond market was absent and the financial leaders are not available. Although they were both the government's top priority, we do not know how the financial leaders perceived each agency.

As Table 2.4 shows, the success of the government bond market, financial bond market, and money market reform results from the availability of innovative ideas and financial leaders. As we have seen, the constraint apparatus contains formal and informal rules. Formal rules and regulations should be established by government, but should be confined to those things that will reduce transaction costs, for example:

- Defining property rights and the rules of game play
- Formulating policies that encourage innovation and education
- Making more room for the evolution of institutions, which can then evolve on their own
- Encouraging organizations to promote financial innovation, thereby accelerating and guiding the evolution of institutions

INSTITUTIONAL ECONOMIC ENGINEERING THEORY AND BOND MARKET DEVELOPMENT IN CHINA

The bond market is an integral part of the financial, economic, and social systems. Understanding the interaction between the bond market and the financial market and the interaction between the financial system and the

TABLE 2.4 Institutional Characteristics of Various Financial Markets

	Outcome	Period when Market Was a Government Priority	Government's Policy: Hands on, or Hands off	Financial Leader	Institutional Evolution	Innovative Ideas	Technological Progress
Government bonds market	Successful	Early 1990s	Off	Available		Available	Available
Financial bonds market	Successful	Late 1990s	Off	Available	Available	Available	Available
Corporate bonds market		Early 2000s	On		Available		Available
Stock market		Late 1990s and early 2000s	On		Available		Available
Money market	Successful	2003–2005	On	Available		Available	

economic system is essential to understanding bond market development in China. The current condition of the bond market can be explained, at least in part, by the government's policy of financial repression, which, for example, favors the development of industry. However, this reason is not sufficient to explain certain issues in China's bond market.

Experience and theory demonstrate that six things are needed for a sound bond market to evolve:

1. *Less government intervention in the operation of the market.* In particular, the government should not manipulate market prices. Since reform, China has gradually embarked on a market economy and abnegated the notion of a planned economy. However, the legacy of macroeconomic management in the planned economy survived in the postreform era. The problem in the securities market continues to be too much government intervention, which gives the impression that there is a so-called iron (or policy) bottom for the price index. In comparing the bond market with the securities market, we can see that the pricing of bonds, especially government bonds and financial debentures, is through the tender system, where the price is completely subject to supply and demand; in contrast, the price of stocks is not solely determined by supply and demand of the market.

   It is essential that those playing the market—not the government—determine price through a mechanism that reflects the supply-demand relationship. In practice this means that the establishment of market itself is the government's proper role. Price should be determined by competition among issuers and investors through their efforts to reduce endogenous transaction costs.

   China's bond market provides a good example. Premature regulation is counterproductive to bond market development, as demonstrated in the less-regulated market environment of the early and middle 1990s, which led to the revolutionary changes in the bond market.

   China's experiences have important implications for the rest of the world. To develop a bond market, the government's role in establishing an institutional framework includes:

   - Creating the different levels of institutions that make the market functional
   - Establishing constraints—informal, formal, game playing, organizational, personal (conduct and/or philosophy), and market rules

2. *An incentive apparatus has to be established.* The creation of a sound bond capital market is not confined to building up a bond infrastructure

and institutional framework; it must also contain an incentive and constraint apparatus.

The focus shifts from time to time to reflect priorities of bond market development. For example, during the first stage of bond market reform in early 1990, the priority was to build up an incentive apparatus by setting up incentive devices, including the legal framework to protect property rights, reduce external and internal transaction costs, and ensure the positive evolution of the institution. Individuals and organizations tend to move spontaneously; for example, the current institution moves toward an institution that favors its development or a more cost-effective institution. As Deng Xiaoping said, "Encourage one group of people to become rich by making the effort."

3. *Financial liberalization, especially deregulation.* This undoubtedly is the right choice for countries that have experienced financial repression. It reduces exogenous transaction costs. However, it is the development of institutions that helps set up an institutional framework to generate greater disparity between incentives and constraints by reducing internal transaction costs.

   Deregulation became possible in the 1970s simply because the development of financial institutions makes some regulation unnecessary. In 1990 and 1991, the black market was rampant in China's major cities, but as soon as the primary government bond market was established, it disappeared.

   From a neoclassical point of view, interest and investment are negatively related. Developing countries keep interest relative low to finance their industrialization policy. The higher is the interest rate, the less incentive to make investment. In developing countries, the financial system is underdeveloped, and a rise in interest rates would increase investment. Only when real interest is over certain level will substitution work. When interest is higher, banks have an incentive to lend; when interest rates are low, banks have no incentive to lend. Reform raises the potential for profit of some new types of enterprises; however, these enterprises have no access to bank loans. Higher interest rates can attract more money for investment, thereby making more financial resources available. Money raised from the bond market carries a higher interest but attracts new types of enterprises. For this reason, after 2000, the bond market was able to step into spotlight of the financial market.

4. *Entrepreneurship and reform.* Public choice theory holds that the behavior of government agencies is not driven completely by the will of the people who delegate the power to those agencies; agencies have their own interest. In my view, their behavior is motivated by their values,

their interests consistent with the interests of people who delegate power to them, and their entrepreneurial spirit.

Members of the generation of the 1980s were all educated to believe in altruism and communist ideology, so their behavior was driven primarily by an entrepreneurial spirit. It was these entrepreneurial and reform ideas that drove the successful reform programs of the 1980s and 1990s. However, it was soon realized that reform came at the expense of the reformers' own interests. Subsequently, they kept away from bond market reform. In the late 1990s, the treasury bond market reform encountered a setback, and government employees soon realized that the less reform they carried out, the more power they would preserve.

Equilibrium is the point at which each participant concentrates on that which is in his or her own interest to pursue. Since the late 1990s, the bond market reform program has been characterized by market participant innovation. For this reason, we divide the bond market development into government-initiated reform and spontaneous market reform.

When market development can be justified as a government priority, then government agencies have the incentive to push market-oriented reform forward. After 2003, the central bank reinforced its effort to accelerate money market reform.

5. *Lower transaction costs.* Technological progress can reduce transaction costs automatically; government can reduce transaction costs through its effort to improve the market infrastructure; but mostly, market participants can reduce transaction costs. For example, often market players have different access to information because of information asymmetry; therefore, they have different transaction costs. Those who possess more information than the others can share information, so that every party can reduce transaction costs and eventually every party can share the benefits—a win-win result. A bond issuer, for example, can provide information to investors in order to clarify any uncertainty they may feel about the issue and to share the benefit with them. The CDB has used this principle extensively to lead its financial innovation.

6. *Provide standardization and specificity.* As a financial commodity, bonds are standardized and specific debt instruments, and therefore tradable. The better the standardization and specificity the bonds have, the more liquid and the better priced they will be, and the better served the interests of market participants will be. Because bonds are less risky and therefore more acceptable than stock instruments, I recommend that the bond market should be developed first, followed by the stock market.

Finally, it has to be emphasized that the institutional economic engineering theory does more than explain the bond and financial markets in China; its implications go well beyond this subject.

The Emergence of a Primary Market

CHAPTER 3

Primary Market for Treasury Bond Transactions

Overview

In 1953, faced with severe economic challenges, the central government set in motion a series economic restoration programs. One of these programs was a plan to finance the budget shortfall by issuing state construction bonds. The central government continued to do so until 1958; then it stopped issuing treasury bonds for the next 23 years. It was not until the early 1980s that the treasury bond market began to develop in any meaningful way. Between 1981 and the end of 2005, China issued bonds worth a total of RMB5268.7 billion, of which RMB2387.64 billion have been redeemed, leaving RMB2981.09 billion outstanding.

The description of bond market is intended to provide evidence in support of the institutional economic engineering (IEEN) framework.

BOND MARKET REFORM TIMELINE

Prior to 1991, as we have seen, treasury bonds were distributed through a combination of political mobilization and administrative allocation. Since 1991 onward, a new era of bond market reform has unfolded.

1991   A pilot underwriting syndication was successfully carried out by financial intermediaries, signaling the emergence of a primary market for treasury bonds. This, in turn, provided the central bank with the means to adjust the national economy by means of financial instruments.

1993	The book-entry form of government bond was introduced on a trial basis.
1994	Treasury bond certificates targeted at individual investors were introduced.
1996	Government securities issued through market-oriented auction method rather than by the State Council; scripless bonds gradually replaced paper securities.
1998–2001	The State Council resumed its power to set the coupon rate of government securities. Treasury bonds were issued mainly to banks, and the issuance of market-oriented treasury bond gradually decreased.

As a result, in 1999, banks left the exchange markets, and the inter-bank bond market (IBBM) was established. As the soaring increase in volume and creation of innovative financial products attests, this change had significant implications, both positive and negative, because the segmented market hindered further development of the financial market. Relative to the IBBM, the exchange market was shrinking, resulting in a less efficient, less active bond market.

As the history of China's bond market illustrates, an efficient and cost-effective treasury bond market should:

- Include a well-defined goal for market development (i.e., an efficient and cost-effective bond market). *Efficient* means a short and effective issuance period, while *cost effective* refers to the minimum cost acceptable to both issuers and investors.
- Be established in accordance with the requirements of a market economy.
- Offer market-oriented interest rates, scripless bonds, electronic trading, diversified products, and standardized procedures.
- Have a sound and advanced financial infrastructure including registration, custody, and settlement and clearing systems to ensure its healthy development.

In addition:

- A sound financial market should be established for the treasury bond market. In developing the money market, stock market, and IBBM, careful consideration must be given to their effect on the treasury bond market.

HISTORY OF CHINA'S TREASURY BOND MARKET

Chronology of Issues

The development of bond market in China can be divided into seven stages, outlined below.

Bond Market Prior to Reform: 1949 to 1980 Government-incurred debt in China can be traced back as far back as Qing Dynasty in 1846, when the government borrowed funds from the private sector to finance its war against an uprising of farmers and local warlords. The issuance of treasury bonds in the modern sense, however, can only be traced back to the establishment of People's Republic of China in 1949. At the end of 1949, the newly established People's Republic was faced with difficult economic conditions in the aftermath of the civil war. To finance its budgetary shortfall, the government decided to issue People's Victory Bonds. These bonds helped to alleviate the pressure of rising money demand.

China began implementing its first five-year plan for national economic and social development in 1953. Although the tasks for implementing national economic recovery were fulfilled successfully, productivity remained extremely low. At the end of 1953 the Central People's Government Committee began issuing the National Economic Development Bond. Through this bond, issued for five consecutive years, the state effectively achieved its funding program for economic reconstruction during the recovery period. However, in 1958 the government suspended issuing these bonds.

For the next 23 years, no treasury bonds were issued by the Chinese government, and in 1968, the state repaid all principal and interest on domestic and foreign debt. Hence, China had neither domestic nor foreign debt from 1968 to 1980.

In 1978, China began to carry out economic reform and opened its doors to the outside world to settle legacy problems, such as its underfunded social security system, and to speed up economic development, increase agricultural subsidies, expand enterprise, and gradually improve living standards.

After this initial phase, spanning 1949 to 1980, the history of the issuance of T-bonds since reform can be divided into four phases: administrative allocation (1981–1990), underwriting syndication (1991–1994), market taking shape (1995–1997), and diversification of instruments (1998–2006).

Administrative Allocation: 1981 to 1990 A significant budgetary deficit occurred in 1981, the result of the decline in general revenue over the previous three years, although income from foreign loans had been incorporated into general revenue. In order to ensure a balanced budget, the State Council, after a serious debate, decided to issue treasury bills and employ the local financial resources to make up the budgetary deficit. The legal basis for this move was *Regulations on the Treasury Bills of the People's Republic of China* adopted on January 16, 1981. Its primary objective was once again to collect the money at one time allocated to businesses to expand their autonomy. The treasury bills issued in 1981 were mainly targeted at state-owned enterprises (SOEs) and institutions.

Initially, it was understood that this was a one-time program. When, in 1982, economic conditions showed no sign of substantial improvement, the central government decided to continue issuing treasury bills to raise funds and ensure government spending programs. At the same time, thanks to reform and the policy of opening up, living standards in urban and rural areas had improved significantly, with private saving deposits increasing rapidly. Starting in 1982, treasury bond distribution was tilted toward individuals. During this year, while RMB1.8 billion of RMB4 billion treasury bills were allocated to SOEs and institutions, RMB2.2 billion went to individuals. Since 1982, the funds raised from the issuance of treasury bills have been deemed part of the government's general revenues.

From 1982 to 1984, the volume of treasury bill issuance had been kept at RMB4 billion; it was increased to RMB6 billion in 1985. In 1986, the offering price was raised to 10 percent annually for the individual tranche and 6 percent for the institutional tranche. In 1987, the government issued an RMB5.4 billion 6 percent key construction bond, which was earmarked for essential projects. Earmarked funding was used to integrate borrowing, use of proceeds, and repayment, so as to ensure repayment of the borrowed money by users.

Forced Selling: 1981 to 1988 At this time, most bonds were issued indirectly. Banks had the primary responsibility for providing loans to state-owned enterprises, since there was neither a securities market nor financial intermediaries or even institutional investors. Hence, treasury bonds were allocated to individuals. During this period:

- *The coupon rate of T-bonds was higher than the interest rate for savings deposits.* In the early 1980s, T-bonds were issued primarily to SOEs and had low coupon rates. No other bonds were available to them. Different interest rates applied to bonds issued to enterprises and to individuals, and bonds issued to individuals paid a higher rate than those issued to SOEs. For example, in the early 1980s, the coupon rate of bonds issued to state-owned enterprises was 4 percent, while the coupon to individuals was 8 percent. After the late 1980s, the coupon rate of the T-bonds was 1 to 2 percent higher than the interest rate for the bank deposits of the same term.

- *T-bonds issued in the 1950s and again in the 1980s went mainly to individuals for various reasons:*
  - T-bonds were issued for the purpose of economic construction, and the purchase of T-bonds by individuals was considered a patriotic act. Therefore, targeting individual investors was a policy decision.
  - Individuals were the leading holders of savings deposits and the major source of funds.
  - Because there were no market intermediaries or institutional investors, individual investors were the only potential purchasers for T-bonds.
- *The offering periods were comparatively long.* Because T-bonds were sold mainly to individuals, the execution involved many processes and procedures. In order to facilitate distribution as well as individual purchases and trading, physical bonds were issued, which created a time-consuming printing and delivery system. As a result, the offering period for issuing T-bonds prior to 1991 was at least six months. Without a change to direct issue to individuals, it was difficult to shorten the offering period.
- *Bonds were issued at their face value and one-time repayment of principal and interest at maturity.* T-bonds were issued at face value rather than at discounts or premiums due to the cash-basis financial accounting system used to calculate debt revenue. Issue by discount and premium would lead to accounting difficulties. The interest payment was calculated based on one-time simple interest at maturity, which was convenient for investors as well as for financial accounting. (The third issue of T-bonds in 1993 adopted the annual payment method for the first time, although, even then, most bonds utilized the one-time at-maturity interest payment method.)
- *Bonds held by individual investors traded over the counter (OTC), while those held by institutional investors and securities firms intermediaries traded at exchanges.* Because there were many bank counters and post offices in China, it was convenient for individual investors to trade T-bonds OTC. However, the intermediaries were not enthusiastic about participating in OTC transactions, and the spread between the selling and purchasing price set by securities firms was rather wide.

At the time the exchange market was underdeveloped, because most individual investors lacked knowledge of market and due to the complicated account-opening formalities, only a few individual investors entered into the on-exchange market. Given the active on-exchange transactions and tight trading spreads, securities firms and institutional investors mainly traded T-bonds on the floor.

- *Bearer bonds dominated the market.* Bearer bonds have been dominant since China began to issue T-bonds. These bonds are issued at various face values, are hard to alter, and are convenient to transfer.

Bond Transfer Open: 1988 to 1990   In 1988, treasury bills issuance increased from RMB6 billion to RMB9 billion. The Ministry of Finance was assigned the job of issuing a key construction bond. The objective was to fill the gap between the real expenditure due to an increase in capital construction and the original arrangement for budgetary expenditures plus borrowing from the People's Bank of China, the central bank. With a maturity of two years and a coupon of 9.5 percent, this key construction bond was issued OTC on a trial basis in a first attempt to reform the administrative allocation method that was then in use. The actual volume issued was only RMB3 billion (the projected issue was RMB7 billion) because the issue was poorly received by investors and because of inefficient issuing techniques.

In order to reduce and terminate its overdrafts and loans from the central bank, the Ministry of Finance decided to issue fiscal bonds to banks and non-bank financial institutions to replace the proceeds it received from direct borrowing from the central bank. Initially the idea was that the Ministry would repay the principal and interest on a more timely and formal basis, thereby establishing a more market-based relationship with the central bank.

Although the time to maturity and varieties of T-bonds had expanded to some extent, the lack of a secondary market had significantly restricted bond liquidity, which in turn greatly harmed the reputation of T-bonds. Therefore, in April and June 1988, China initiated two pilot reforms of treasury bill trading and transfer in 61 cities. However, bond transfer could only be done in compliance with relevant laws and regulations and on government-designated exchanges. As it turned out, the opening of the bond transfer market marked a milestone in the history of China's bond market.

In response to price increases in 1989, the state issued inflation-protected government bonds to safeguard the interest of investors. The Ministry of Finance also converted the institutional/corporate tranche into special T-bonds to differentiate them from the individual tranche. The idea behind the conversion was to ease the pressure of repayment of the principal and interest on T-bonds on the budget.

By 1990, interest rates on bank deposits and loans had increased considerably; as a result, the Ministry of Finance raised the coupon of treasury bills accordingly (three-year individual tranche to 14 percent, five-year special treasury bills to 15 percent). In 1989 and 1990, the secondary T-bond market witnessed an increased number of securities intermediaries focused on T-bonds trading.

Underwriting Syndication Introduced: 1991 to 1994   In 1991, the Ministry of Finance organized the first T-bond underwriting; 70 securities intermediaries participated in the underwriting syndicate. Underwriting syndication marked the emergence of a primary market (i.e., offering market) for the bond market.

Market Takes Shape: 1995 to 1997   At the beginning of 1995, the futures market for T-bonds was halted. This had a somewhat negative impact on the secondary market. The Ministry of Finance also conducted a T-bond auction experiment. Because it was required to keep the original coupon unchanged, the Ministry designed a settlement date auction (i.e., tenders were requested to bid settlement date; bids were selected as successful from most close-to-launch date bids until the cumulative amount up to the issuing amount). At the same time, the Ministry cancelled the value-preserving subsidies on tradable T-bonds and kept intact its value-preserving policy on non-tradable certificate T-bonds issued to individuals. Because of high value-preserving subsidies, the enthusiasm of individual investors created a higher demand for certificate savings bonds (CSBs), which led to a higher market share for non-tradable certificate bonds.

During 1996, the implementation of the auction method throughout the market was warmly welcomed. The Ministry of Finance tested three auction methods (i.e., price, yield, and settlement date auctions) separately on a variety of T-bonds, regulating discount, zero-coupon, and coupon T-bond transactions. In 1996, the 3-year bill, 7-year note, and 10-year bond were issued for the first time, which further helped diversify the maturity profile of T-bond issuance. The Ministry mainly targeted the sale of short-term bonds to banks, which paved the way for the central bank to carry out its experiment in open market operations in April of that year.

In 1997, the Ministry of Finance issued the 2-year zero-coupon T-bond via discount selling, which resulted in a rally in the secondary market. While the 10-year T-bond, with its low coupon rate, was issued through public auction, its yield after issue was in line with that of the secondary market. These two bonds became the best performers in the market. Thus, the method of issuing T-bonds transitioned smoothly to free public auctions with no restrictions on maturities and coupon rate, which further enhanced the selling efficiency in China.

Diversification of Instruments: 1998 to 2005   The Ministry of Finance increased certificate T-bond issues in 1998 and 1999, with treasury notes accounting for the largest proportion. The book-entry bond issuance was moved to the inter-bank bond market, which resulted in a further decrease in the number tradable bond varieties in the exchanges. Because of the difficulties in issuing long-term T-bonds in the IBBM and with the State Council's approval, the Ministry of Finance returned to that market. From 2000 to 2004, the Ministry began to issue T-bonds in the cross market (i.e., simultaneously in the stock exchange market and IBBM).

Changes in Issuing Techniques

Before 1991, because there was no primary market in T-bonds or institutional investors to purchase them, and because individual investors lacked sufficient financial awareness, T-bonds were issued mainly through administrative allocation combined with political mobilizations. The result was that fundraising demand was barely met, and key construction projects as well as a balanced budget was, however costly, secured.

Primary Market Emerges   China's T-bond primary market started to take its shape in 1991, when a T-bond was issued using an underwriting mechanism. This to some extent changed the administrative allocation system.

There were several unsuccessful attempts to reform the bond market before 1991's underwriting syndication. In 1985, the Ministry of Finance attempted to issue T-bonds through economic instruments (e.g., an RMB50 million T-bond transaction by institutional underwriters in Shanghai). In the following years, the Ministry attempted to issue treasury bills using OTC selling (e.g., the inflation-protected T-bond transaction in 1989). Apparently, the failures were due to the fact that coupon rates set were far lower than the real secondary market yield. In 1990, thanks to two interest rate cuts after the treasury pricing, T-bonds enjoyed conspicuous interest rate advantages. In order to take full advantage of this market window, the Ministry decided to issue an additional RMB2 billion treasury bills in OTC markets. These efforts were all in the direction of market-oriented T-bond issuance. However, it was not until 1991 that the conditions were ripe for T-bond underwriting.

The experiment in the secondary T-bond market in 1989 did help alleviate investors' discontent and the pressure of selling constraints. Perceived by the government as a success, this experiment was gradually expanded to other local cities. By 1990, the tradable T-bonds in the market had expanded from two to six categories, including treasury bills and fiscal bonds. By the end of 1990, the volume of transactions in the securities market totaled RMB12 billion, of which T-bonds accounted for more than 80 percent. In 1991, the pilot cities for T-bond issue had increased from 61 in 1988 to more than 400 cities and towns, and the secondary T-bond market had developed from a local market into a nationwide one.

Along with the development of the secondary market, the trading in T-bonds was gradually becoming robust, with the price rising and the yields of primary selling close to their theoretical levels. When the secondary market opened up in 1988, 80 percent of the bondholders sold off their holdings. After mid-1990, the decline in the interest rate for savings deposits resulted in a balanced supply and demand. Between then and the beginning of 1991, the T-bond market transformed from an oversupply to demand, which eventually led to a hard-to-buy problem for individual investors. As demand exceeded supply, the price of T-bonds rose rapidly, while the yield in the secondary T-bond market declined markedly. For example, between January and April 1991, the price of the treasury bill issued in 1990 increased nearly RMB3 yuan per month, with its yield dropping from 20 percent to about 10 percent—lower than that for two-year savings deposit. These developments in the secondary market created positive conditions for T-bond underwriting in the primary market.

Along with the establishment and development of the secondary T-bond market, securities intermediaries were also undergoing striking development. By the end of 1990, there were more than 300 securities companies and T-bond service companies in the financial and fiscal sector and more than 700 trust and investment and the securities companies in the banking sector. In addition, pension funds and other special-purpose fund industries had also taken shape.

Meanwhile, the central bank and the specialized banks began to divide along functional lines, at the same time as a number of shareholding banks (e.g., the Bank of Communications) emerged. In the wake of developments in the banking system, trust and investment companies, leasing companies, and similar enterprises came into being, and all of these non-bank financial institutions began to focus on T-bond investments.

In the process of market development, individual investors' financial awareness had been greatly enhanced; they began to transfer their knowledge of T-bonds, securities, and finance into the awareness of investment, risk, and protection strategies. At that time, the enthusiasm of individual and institutional investors for T-bonds was unprecedented, resulting in the so-called T-bond craze. With the trading spread narrowing, investors focused more on yields than on liquidity; with their rising awareness of risk, investors began to recognize the real value of T-bonds. This enhanced financial awareness was one of the critical factors that led to the successful transition to the underwriting method for issuing T-bonds.

Before going forward, the Ministry of Finance conducted a thorough feasibility study on underwriting mechanism. In order to meet underwriters' demand for direct institutional issuance, China created a series of new regulations about the transport and transfer of T-bonds, in order to guarantee that the new mechanism would have a sound legal framework.

On April 20, 1991, the Ministry of Finance signed the Underwriting Contract with ICBC Trust and Investment Co., Ltd., the lead manager of the underwriting syndicate. The total amount underwritten was RMB2.5 billion, which accounted for 25 percent of the planned volume. In accordance with the model of the central underwriting syndicate, the local finance departments and local banking systems each managed additional RMB2 billion, respectively. The Ministry of Finance mandated banks, post offices, and some securities companies to sell T-bonds via the OTC market to individual investors.

Thus, selling via underwriting syndication marked a step further away from the practice of administrative allocation.

Note that the transition from administrative allocation to the market-oriented issue was not accidental. It reflected the fact that institutional change had made the new selling technique possible. In other words, it is the development of institutional arrangements that created ready-made conditions for the emergence of T-bond primary market.

The emergence of the primary market for T-bonds had three significant implications for the overall financial market.

1. The formation of the primary market provided the conditions for further development of the secondary market, while the harmonious development of the primary and secondary markets led the way to overall market development.
2. The emergence of the primary market shifted the target market for T-bonds from individuals and SOEs to financial institutions, which greatly improved the market's efficiency and cost structure.
3. With the primary market in place, short-term treasury bill transactions could be executed. Such transactions were the precondition required for the central bank to carry out open market operations. In this sense, the emergence of the T-bond primary market laid a foundation for the central bank to adjust money supply by using these new financial instruments.

Move to Greater Market-Oriented Reform   The success of this experiment marked the emergence of the T-bond primary market in China, but it was only a preliminary trial because:

- The underwriting had only a small scope rather than affecting the whole nation.

- The basic terms and conditions in the underwriting contract and the coupon level were determined by the government rather than by direct negotiations between the issuer and underwriters.
- The underwriting contract was neither standardized nor implemented to the letter.
- The syndicate was incapable of managing all T-bonds, and, therefore, an interim issuing method combining central and local management and administrative allocation was adopted. Again, conflict of interests between the central departments and local authorities occurred.

To avoid these conflicts in the future, China implemented a local underwriting mechanism in 1992. However, the move from central to local underwriting was considered a setback, because it rested on a quota-task relationship between central and local governments, which was administrative in nature as well, although it did contain some market elements. In creating this underwriting mechanism, the central government and local authorities established a closer economic relationship.

In order to address the allocation conflicts between central and local underwriters, the Ministry of Finance in 1992 assigned all bond-issuing responsibilities to provinces, autonomous regions, and municipalities. The underwriting agreements for these bonds were signed by local financial bureaus and securities intermediaries within their jurisdictions. Although this method largely alleviated the conflicts between the central government and local authorities, the bond distribution channels from the central government to local authorities were still administrative in nature. At the end of 1992, an experimental T-bond futures market was introduced into the Shanghai Stock Exchange.

Once it had begun, the market-oriented progress should have been promoted and necessary measures should have been taken to create and develop favorable economic and financial environments to facilitate the development of the T-bond market, but in 1992, China had not yet made any substantial progress in this area. Consequently, beginning in the second half of 1992, the T-bond market deteriorated due to an overheated investment atmosphere, tightened funding, and rising interest rates. In the beginning, it was very difficult for brokers to distribute T-bonds to individual investors because of falling prices and rising interest rates in the secondary market. As the financially distressed brokers did not have sufficient access to short-term funding, they were forced to sell off T-bonds in the secondary market, which led to a sharp price decline and stirred a panic among institutional bondholders. In the end, price fluctuations in the secondary market had a direct negative impact on the 1993 issues.

China's vulnerable financial infrastructure could not stand the simultaneous shocks trigged by the investment craze, the real estate craze, and the stock market craze. Interest rates were out of control, fueled by a fundraising frenzy, which led to interest rate wars. The rising interest rate level further raised investors' expectations in the secondary market, and in the beginning of 1993, yields averaged around 20 percent.

As we have seen, although the underwriting system was adopted, the terms and conditions of the coupon were not created by negotiation between the issuer and the underwriters. Given the regulated interest rates in bank deposits and the "deposit rates plus" pricing mechanism, the T-bond's coupon rate inevitably deviated from the market level. Prior to the actual issue of T-bonds in 1993, the determined coupon rates for three- and five-year bonds were 9.5 percent and 10.5 percent respectively, a gap of 6 to 8 percent (600 to 800 basis points) compared to rates in the secondary market.

Under those circumstances, although it was originally determined that the 1993 T-bonds would be conducted via underwriting syndication, the securities intermediaries were reluctant to accept the issuing terms determined by the central government, which made central-local underwriting method unviable. Given the unfavorable conditions, after careful and thorough study, the Ministry of Finance resumed the OTC method, initiating various kinds of door-to-door services to market T-bonds, while maintaining the already launched market-oriented mechanism.

After the transaction was launched, however, local selling to end investors made very little progress. By the middle of the book-building process (a process in which the amount and yield of bond securities that each investor is willing to purchase are registered by the underwriters in a book during the marketing phase of issuance so that the demand can be calculated), only one-tenth of the volume was subscribed. In order to speed the sale, the State Council required local government at all levels to organize and mobilize various resources to boost demand and reinstituted the administrative allocation method. Local governments made their best efforts to complete the sale of the RMB30 billion issue.

The transaction of T-bonds in 1993 was eventually placed, and financing of the budgetary shortfall was secured. However, the resumption of the outdated administrative allocation mechanism had hindered the ongoing reform process, which greatly jeopardized the confidence of investors and financial intermediaries. In the history of T-bonds in China, one of the landmark events was the creation of the primary dealer system, with the objective of further developing primary and secondary markets and optimizing the intermediary structure. To this end, the Ministry of Finance and China Securities Regulatory Commission jointly formulated *The Interim Rules on the Primary Dealers of the Government Securities of the People's Republic of China*, according to which they approved 19 securities intermediaries and banks as the first group of primary dealers.

With a primary dealer system in place, the Ministry was able to maintain the central underwriting mechanism at the final stage of book-building period in order to secure selling via the central underwriting syndication. The central underwriters enjoyed annual interest payment and net price (excluding accrued interest) transactions. This process, although it took a lot of effort, did rekindle the movement for market-oriented reform. In fact, since 1991, the central underwriting system has been maintained. Along with this, scripless T-bonds, executed in the automated quotations system of the Department of Research and Development of China's Stock Exchange Executive Council (SEEC), were issued. In 1991, the scripless issues were collateralized by physical bonds; by 1992 and 1993, the physical bonds guarantee was no longer provided.

Reform of the Primary Market By the end of 1993, economic reform had entered a new stage. In the financial arena, the central bank focused on monetary policies, while the specialized banks no longer assumed any policy-related tasks. This reform has had three significant effects on market development.

1. The central bank, in a hope to retain its independence as a monetary authority, would no longer permit the Ministry of Finance to overdraw or borrow from it without its consent, which made issuing T-bonds the only viable method the Ministry could resort to make up fiscal deficits.
2. The central bank would pursue monetary policy through open market operations (OMOs); this would enable the commercial banks to hold and trade T-bonds.
3. The specialized banks, when they embarked on commercialization, preferred to hold T-bonds as their most liquid assets. Thus, on one hand, the reform of the banking system demanded further marketization of the T-bond sector; on the other hand, this reform of the banking system provided the conditions for market-based reform of the T-bond sector.

As the central bank prohibited fiscal overdraft, the Ministry of Finance had to seek alternative ways to finance its ever-increasing deficit. In 1993, the Ministry of Finance borrowed RMB68.8 billion from the central bank. In 1994, when the central bank barred the Ministry from direct borrowing, the gap between fiscal revenue and expenditure expanded further. In the fiscal budget in 1994, a fiscal deficit of RMB129 billion was to be financed by T-bond issuance; RMB102 billion was financed by domestic treasury bonds (twice as many as had been issued in 1993), with the remainder financed by foreign debt.

Given the difficulties encountered in 1993, the only funding choices were possible reinforced administrative placement or cracking down on further reform. After extensive debate, the Ministry decided to proceed with the ongoing reform program. These initiatives were specified:

- Focus T-bond distribution on banks and non-bank financial institutions. Modify the primary dealer system and require banks to participate in the primary dealers' organizations.
- Extend and diversify treasury products' maturity and varieties (i.e., half-year and one-year short-term treasury bills).
- Mandate that specialized banks underwrite short-term treasury bills, which was a precondition for the central bank to carry out its OMOs.
- Establish and develop the scripless book-entry system, with the Shanghai Stock Exchange as the temporary transaction and clearing center.
- Issue savings bonds to individual investors to meet their demands for T-bond investments.
- Continue distributing five-year treasury notes to pension funds and insurance companies via private placement.

These initiatives were very well designed and proved to be forward looking. However, at the beginning of 1994, a new factor appeared that affected the national economy: a soaring retail price index of around 20 percent in the first quarter. The emergence of inflation prompted China to curb the increase in the money supply. Fearing that the holdings of T-bonds by the specialized banks would increase the monetary supply, the central bank decided to issue the T-bonds directly to public investors or individual investors. A public offer of two-year 13 percent T-bonds as tradable bonds was launched on April 1 and closed on June 1, and the three-year certificate savings bond was targeted at public investors through the banking distribution system. Immediately after the closing of the transaction, these treasury bill certificates could be redeemed over the bank counters, with a yield to maturity of 13.96 percent annually.

Considering the risk exposure assumed by individuals and leveraging lessons learned from the experiences the United States had had in its years of issuing savings bonds, the Ministry of Finance decided to issue non-tradable savings bonds[1] to individuals, so that the target for the majority of government bonds could shift from individual investors to institutional investors. As a complement to tradable bonds, savings bonds provided individual investors with a new financial instrument free of market risk. Given the demands of individual investors, the savings bonds were designed as certificates, which are registered and could be recoursed if lost. Certificate savings bonds (CSBs) could be subscribed through the banking system.

Along with the reshaping of the T-bond primary market, new issuing methods were gradually established. However, because the terms of issuance were still pre-set by the government, new bond issues encountered problems in the volatile market. For instance, in 1993, at the time of issue the coupon was much lower than the yield in the secondary bond market; therefore, it was hard to find buyers. As a consequence, many municipalities actually reinstituted administrative allocation practices.

In the same year, China introduced the primary dealer system. Nineteen primary dealers were authorized to participate in underwriting the third transaction of T-bond issue in that year.

The year 1994 saw further expansion in both diversified maturity profiles and types of T-bond instruments. Also, China initiated a half-year and a one-year treasury bill and began to target individual investors for a non-tradable savings bonds issue. Meanwhile, the secondary market also witnessed rapid changes. The active futures market in 1994 fostered the development of the spot market, resulting in harmony between primary and secondary markets.

One landmark event of the T-bond market in 1994 was the launch of short-term treasury bills for the first time in China's history; these bills further enriched the bond categories.

Transition to Market-Oriented Issuance   Since the 1991 experiment with the underwriting method for issuing T-bonds, T-bonds have been underwritten by intermediaries and, by arrangement with financial authorities at different levels, resold to individuals over the counter and through national networks of intermediaries, banks, and postal savings desks.

During this period, various factors were driving the development of the T-bond market in China. Reform of various kinds—for example, new transportation vehicles and the establishment of custody and settlement systems, among others—provided many opportunities. However, development was constrained by the fact that the financial market was underdeveloped and banking reform lagged behind overall economic reform. Six trends characterized the primary market for T-bonds.

1. *Coexistence of short- and diversified term bonds.* Over the preceding decade, the term was decreasing. At the beginning of 1980s, T-bonds were issued for 10 years and 8 years. By the end of 1980s, most T-bonds had 8- and 5-year terms. From 1991 to 1993, the market was dominated by 5- and 3-year bonds, and, by 1994, by 3- and 2-year bonds along with some 12- and 6-month issues. The terms were becoming shorter and shorter for two reasons:
   a. Rising inflation rates leading to higher investment returns and low liquidity in the secondary market restrained investors' enthusiasm for long-term T-bonds.
   b. Along with the development of the T-bond market, the terms of T-bonds were expected to be longer in the future. Short-term T-bills

would develop into 3-, 6-, 9-, and 12-month bills and a complete series of medium-term bonds would arise. With the rising market liquidity, a variety of the long-term T-bonds would be added.

2. *Coexistence of market-oriented issuing methods and planned coupons.* The underwriting issuing method was first adopted in 1991, signifying the transformation from administrative allocation and apportioned purchases to a market-oriented distribution method. The subscription method for issuing T-bonds through dealers in the primary market was adopted in 1992, which led to further market-based reform of the primary market and facilitated the development and liquidity of the secondary market. However, before market-based reform of the interest rate on savings deposits in banks, the coupon rates for T-bonds had to change in accordance with the interest rates on bank deposits and loans.

3. *Coexistence of scripless bonds and physical bonds.* The development of scripless bond is an inexorable trend. The experiments with scripless T-bonds was conducted in China for four consecutive years and, in general, were successful, especially after the success of scripless stock markets. The scripless form of T-bonds was first adopted in the primary market after the development of the depository trust and the settlement system, which enabled the coexistence of physical and scripless bonds. Since T-bonds will be issued to individuals in China for a long time to come, paper T-bonds will no doubt continue for some time.

4. *Coexistence of diversified market instruments and the non-derivative market.* During this period, the lack of market instruments was the major contributor to low liquidity in the secondary market. In the future, it is anticipated that the number of market instruments will increase along with the development of the T-bond market and that the futures and repurchase markets will enjoy further development.

5. *Coexistence of standardized markets and non-standardized transactions.* Market development would be accompanied by healthier market organizations, enhanced market administration, more rules and regulations, as well as the increased development of self-disciplinary organizations, which would further regulate T-bond transactions. Before the market was well regulated, the development of derivative market was restricted, with the non-derivative market in a dominant position to prevent overspeculation. As it takes a long time to regulate trading procedures, the non-standardized transactions would continue to exist for some time.

6. *Coexistence of electronic settlement on the floor and paper settlement of OTC transactions.* By this time, T-bond transactions on the floor were settled electronically. It was anticipated that this type of settlement

would be further enhanced by the establishment of the institutions for depository trust and settlement. Integrated with T-bond custody and settlement procedures, various clearing and settlement systems would be interconnected to form a nationwide network. Due to technical limitations, the non-electronic settlement for the OTC transactions would remain for some period of time.

In 1995, the execution methods were in line with those employed in the previous year. However, due to the decline in demand for tradable bonds following the suspension of the futures market, the price of the T-bonds was below par for up to four months. Thanks to the increase in the subsidy rate for value-preserved bonds, the certificate bonds sold well, which made people temporarily forget their 1993 obsessions with selling.

Pricing T-bonds exclusively based on market conditions constitutes a decisive step forward in T-bonds reform. The landmark event that had a great impact on bond market development in 1995 was the auction experiment. The bid-tender method with manual inputting was used for the first time in a one-year T-bond issuance, and was a success.

Until 1995, the pricing and coupon had been set by the State Council on a case-by-case basis. The specific procedure started with a proposal (including the bond's coupon) by Ministry of Finance to the State Council for approval. The corollary was, as the interest rate was regulated by the People's Bank of China, the T-bond as a financial instrument should also be administrated by the government. Since individuals, who were the major investors, would compare coupon rates with bank deposit rates with the same maturity, T-bond pricing was benchmarked against the interest rate of bank deposits. The coupon rate was 1 percent higher than the interest on bank deposits to compensate for the inconvenience suffered by investors in selling those bonds, or the liquidity cost.

Whether individuals buy T-bonds depends on a comparison of the inconvenience of T-bonds and the opportunity costs of investing in other financial assets. Before 1995, most of the distribution work was so handicapped that, from time to time, the government had to resort to administrative measures. For years, the government authorities spent half a year on T-bond placement. However, the coupon rates set by government were not calculated on a market basis. Fortunately, the Ministry of Finance was in a position to decide on the settlement date and the issuing fees; therefore, it had more flexibility in adjusting bond yield. From 1991 to 1995, the Ministry frequently moved the yield to maturity (YTM) of government securities closer to the level in the secondary market by adjusting delivery date and expenses.

During this period, the Ministry often discussed the possibility of using the auction method for the sale of T-bonds. Willingness of underwriters and investors to buy is a precondition for an auction. At the time, this willingness did not exist. It was critical, therefore, to stimulate the underwriters' incentive to bid. It was suggested that a fixed volume of T-bonds be allocated to them as a compulsory subscription quota that had a return lower than the successful bidding yield, so that the underwriters would have an incentive to bid.

Development of the T-Bond Market   The year 1996 is significant in the history of T-bonds in China. In that year, the Ministry of Finance successfully issued RMB195.2 billion T-bonds using market-oriented issues. This issue successfully met budgetary targets and played a significant role in supporting the national economic reconstruction. The participation of the banks in the T-bond market did much to improve the management of banking assets and liabilities and facilitated the banking system's restructuring and commercialization efforts.

The principal framework of the bond market had been basically established by that year. A number of improvements marked the fundamental changes in the bond market in China. Since 1996, auctions have been extensively used for selling T-bonds.

Tender Issue Method Adopted   The tender issue method, by which issuing prices were settled through a bidding process, was fully implemented throughout the T-bond market in 1996. The price auction issuing method was used for discount bonds while the yield auction was employed for coupon bond offerings. For bearer bonds issued with fixed rate and terms, the method of settlement date auction was adopted. Meanwhile, in line with demand and supply, the single-price auction and the multiple-price auction were adopted separately. These flexible and diversified issuing methods are well in line with China's current market structure and the developmental level of its T-bond market.

As a consequence of the successful implementation of various auction methods, the T-bond issuing mechanism has fully transformed the market system. In only one year, 1996, the tender selling had diversified selling techniques, such as base subscription, range restriction, and surplus distribution into a full-volume tendering mechanism without compulsory quotas and restrictions on the bidding range. In line with the specific context in China, the multiple-price tender of changeable bidding price intervals and quadratic weighting was adopted based on the universally accepted method of secret tender in descending order.

Market Transformed from a Retail Market to a Wholesale Market   This transformation raised issuing efficiencies of T-bonds. In 1994 and 1995, the retail market accounted for two-thirds of the total volume, while in 1996, it accounted for only one-seventh. While the volume of bonds sold to the public through the retail market in 1996 declined, the proportion sold to institutional investors through the primary dealers greatly increased. At the same time, the offering period was reduced to 1.5 days from two to six months, and the time between settlement date and launch date was reduced to 10 to 20 days from two months.

Maturity Profile and Variety of T-Bonds Diversified Seven varieties of T-bonds were issued in 1996 (3-month, 6-month, 12-month, 3-year, 5-year, 7-year, and 10-year, among which the 3-month, 7-year, and 10-year bonds were newly issued benchmark T-bonds). After years of effort, China had basically achieved the diversification of the T-bond varieties, by which issuers could adjust their debt structure and arrange to issue in line with the terms and features of the funds needed. Diversification also helped attract investors and enriched the instruments available to market intermediaries. The bond market had begun to exercise the function of a capital market, which, to a certain degree, eased the debt service pressure on the Ministry of Finance.[2]

Central Bank's Open Market Operations Facilitated Beginning in 1994, the Ministry of Finance issued three T-bonds with terms less than 12 months. These issues were mainly focused on specialized and commercial banks, and their successful execution greatly facilitated the central bank's open market operations in April 1996.

Building Up the Market Infrastructure In 1997, under the leadership of the State Council and thanks to the concerted efforts made by the ministries and departments concerned, the issuing task was successfully fulfilled. This success was of critical significance in securing the national economic reconstruction and budgetary planning and in implementing the moderately tight fiscal and monetary policies.

In 1997, a total of RMB240.5 billion T-bonds were issued in the domestic market. Among these, RMB163.6 billion were certificate savings bonds, RMB39.5 billion were bearer bonds, RMB34.4 billion were book-entry bonds, and RMB3 billion were earmarked bonds.

The T-bond market developed smoothly in 1997. The majority of the T-bonds issued were non-tradable certificate bonds to meet the needs of the individual investors. RMB160 billion was issued, which marked a new high. In addition, RMB39.5 billion bearer bonds were issued exclusively to individuals. Individual investors' demand for purchasing T-bonds was then well met, which created a good foundation for meeting all of the issuing requirements for T-bonds that year.

Primary and Secondary T-Bond Markets Developed Harmoniously   As the primary market gradually improved, the bonds performed well in the secondary market. This made it possible to issue long-term coupon bonds. Although the price of T-bonds experienced some declines in the first half of 1997, it began to rally in the second half on rumors of an interest rate change, especially after the rate was increased on October 23. Thereafter, the market price of the T-bonds, especially the long-term coupon bond, grew rapidly, demonstrating both institutional and individual investors' enhanced confidence in the national economy as well as in the T-bond market in the long run.

Number of Institutional Investors in the T-Bond Market Increased Markedly   A number of pension funds expanded, and, in accordance with the regulations, 80 percent of the assets managed by these institutions were T-bonds. The participation of institutional investors in the T-bond market changed the composition of the T-bond market products.

Buildup of the Regulatory and Legal Framework   During this period, the Ministry of Finance promulgated the regulation of unified depository trust and warehouse management of T-bonds, which stipulates the registration, depository trust, clearing, and settlement methods, and further enhanced the construction of the T-bond market infrastructure.

In 1997, except for two transactions of book-entry bonds executed via the tender method, the coupon for T-bonds was determined by the State Council. However, the road to a market-based bond selling regime has been bumpy.

Bearer Bond Volume Declined   Again in 1997, the plan originally called for two issues, but only one was finally issued, because the first traded at a price lower than the face value. The second issue was converted into equivalent certificate bonds and were issued that same year.

Modern Market Starts to Take Shape   1995 to 1997 marked a stage of unprecedented development for the T-bond market. With the development of market-based interest rates, the coupons of T-bonds gradually went down. New issues were basically in line with the yield rate of the relevant bonds in the secondary market and only marginally higher than interest rates for bank deposits and loans. Scripless T-bonds were an accepted part of the system, and, beginning in 1996, bearer bonds were gradually phased out, with institutional tranches for the most part in scripless form. Thus, the T-bond market had been transformed from one dominated by individuals to one dominated by institutions and was gradually shifting from a retail to a wholesale market. With improved efficiency, the offering period had shortened from approximately half a year to half an hour.

Meanwhile, the issuing method was being transformed from underwriting to comprehensive auction. After 1996, the underwriting method had ceased but institutions still invested in T-bonds, largely because the rights-obligation relationship still existed between syndicates and the financial bond market. To ensure a balanced bond issue, syndicate members still enjoyed their basic underwriting quotas.

Bond Dematerialization As a step of bond dematerialization, bearer bonds were put in custody while trading was made via either OTC or securities intermediaries. Moreover, efforts were made to implement a special-purpose account system for T-bonds, which would make it easier for individuals and institutional investors to purchase the book-entry T-bonds. In the OTC selling, paper securities were held temporarily in the securities firms (which is called interim custody). At this time, new issues once again shifted to focus on individual investors. The fluctuation of the bond market cannot be ascribed solely to the changing macroeconomic climate; rather, it was mainly due to what I called the primary administrative exchange (PAE), especially the secondary administrative exchange (SAE), and the game play between agencies. As a matter of fact, bond market development elsewhere is also subject to this rule. To shorten the offering process and improve the efficiency of execution, more work had been done to optimize the issuing methods on certificate bonds. By employing (where appropriate) a multiple-phase interest rate calculation, issuing rates of certificate T-bonds had been kept in line with market rates as far as possible, which allowed them to adapt to changes in interest rates for deposits and loans.

Diversified Instruments Next, by diversifying the types of T-bonds and adjusting their terms to meet the needs of different investors (i.e., individual investors and various institutional investors [e.g., pension funds]), T-bond issues could meet different investor needs. Long-term bonds were targeted toward institutional investors, while short-term bonds were issued to coordinate with the central bank in its OMO transactions. The increased volume of short-term T-bonds was accompanied by the increase of longer-term T-bond deals to ease the debt repayment peaks. STRIPS (separate trading of registered interest and principal of securities) were also introduced on a trial basis in an effort to diversify market instruments.

Liquidity Enhanced More effort was made to establish a unified custody, settlement, and clearing system for the T-bonds market in an effort to eliminate market segmentation and to lower transaction costs, manage transaction risk, and create conditions for the central bank to conduct its open market operations smoothly. The integration of deal date and yield rate calculating methods was achieved by regulating the transaction modes and methods in the T-bond market. Meanwhile, liquidity in the T-bond market was enhanced by the development of the market maker mechanism.

Broker System Introduced   T-bond transactions in 1998 were characterized by significant changes in the investor base.

Non-Tradable Certificate Bonds Dominated the Public Market   Out of the originally approved RMB280 billion bonds, RMB220 billion were certificate T-bonds. They were issued mainly to individual investors, who resumed their dominant position in T-bond market and marked a change in the previous trend toward institutional investors.

Banks Permitted to Subscribe to T-Bonds   In the middle of 1990s, the central bank forbade banks from subscribing to T-bonds directly. According to Document No. 1996-45 by the State Council, commercial banks were required to sell all the T-bonds they held. In 1998, because of weak domestic demand, abundant liquidity in banks, and the negative effect on the bond market of the central bank's policy to contract the money supply, the State Council decided to distribute T-bonds directly to the banks in order to support its fiscal policy. As a result, banks resumed their leading position in the IBBM.

Special-Purpose T-Bond Transactions   In 1998, for the first time, T-bonds were designed to meet the needs of specific fiscal policies. To stimulate national economic growth, with the approval of the National People's Congress, RMB100 billion T-bonds were issued in mid-1998 with proceeds earmarked mainly for infrastructure construction.

Also with the approval of National People's Congress, a RMB270 billion bond issue was executed to replenish state commercial banks' capital so that they could meet Bank for International Settlements (BIS) standard capital adequacy ratio (CAR) of 8 percent.

In 1999, the government shifted its investment focus to the public sector as part of its macroeconomic policy. Government expenditure played an important role in achieving the economic growth rate of 7 percent. The National People's Congress approved an RMB60 billion bond transaction to invest in the infrastructure sector. As the government pursued its proactive fiscal policy and Go-West development strategies, the primary issue was expected to become more active.

The government's revenues grew 7.9 percent, to RMB690.4 billion, and expenditures grew to RMB920.3 billion, or 12.3 percent as of the end of

1999. As was the case in 1998, the majority of book-entry T-bonds was issued to banks in the IBBM, as the national savings rate was on rise. The banks, with an abundance of idle funds and no pressure to give loans to the business sector, considered buying T-bonds safer than lending to business.

During this period, the government further improved its regulatory framework on the bond market. Bonds, as a direct financing instruments, became important vehicles not only for government investment but also for corporate investment. The State Council revised its mandate on corporate bond management, and as a result, the regulatory authority for the corporate bond market was shifted from the People's Bank of China to the National Planning Commission to reduce managerial overlap.

To secure a stable financing conduit and ensure a smooth execution of bond issues, the Ministry signed underwriting agreements with banks and non-bank financial institutions. The primary bond market was extremely bullish in 2001 as a consequence of newly introduced innovative bond instruments and a record number of transactions. That year a total of RMB758.75 billion bonds were issued, including T-bonds, policy-related financial bonds, and corporate bonds, of which T-bonds were up by 4.86 percent over the previous year to RMB488.35 billion (certificate bonds rose to RMB180 billion and book-entry bonds to RMB308.35 billion), policy-related financial bonds to RMB269 billion, up by 57.45 percent year over year (yoy). The China Development Bank issued RMB210 billion bonds, up by 44.83 percent yoy, while the Export-Import (EX-IM) Bank of China issued RMB49 billion, up by 151.28 percent relative to the previous year. In 2001, contrary to the equity market, the bond market demonstrated strong momentum, with the total volume of transactions reaching RMB7 trillion.

In 2002, driven by the increasing domestic demand and the proactive fiscal policy, T-bond issuance maintained its rapid pace, with a volume of RMB946.13 billion issued, including T-bonds, policy-related financial bonds, and corporate bonds. Among these, book-entry T-bonds accounted for RMB446.13 billion (16 deals), up by 44.7 percent yoy, while certificate T-bonds accounted for RMB160 billion (4 deals). The book-entry bonds were RMB308.353 billion. Together RMB606.13 billion T-bonds were issued in 2002, an increase by 24.1 percent relative to 2001, surpassing the planned RMB592.9 billion. In addition, the China Development Bank issued RMB250 billion financial bonds to the financial institutions in the inter-bank market, an increase by 14.3 percent relative to 2001. The EX-IM Bank of China issued RMB57.5 billion financial bonds in the inter-bank market, up by 17.3 percent compared with 2001. Corporate bond transactions over the whole year totaled RMB32.5 billion.

In 2003, a total of RMB1.1158 trillion T-bonds, policy-related financial bonds, and corporate bonds were executed (excluding the five-year domestic

U.S. dollar bond of $500 million). T-bonds accounted for RMB628 billion, up by 5.9 percent yoy, certificate bonds for RMB250.46 billion, book-entry bonds RMB377.55 billion, and policy-related financial bonds RMB452 billion, up by 47 percent yoy. By issuer, the China Development Bank issued RMB410 billion policy-related financial bonds, up by 51.9 percent yoy, while the EX-IM Bank of China issued RMB32 billion, down by RMB25.5 billion yoy.

Market Decline and Downturn   Beginning in the second half of 2003, with the accelerated economic growth and rising Consumer Price Index (CPI), market expectations for the bond rates had changed. The turning point first began at the beginning of the second half of 2003, when the declining trend in offering rates for T-bonds began to turn. The yield curve of the T-bonds went from flat to steep, and the bond issues once again encountered challenges.

With further interest hikes looming, banks were hesitant to buy T-bonds, which made it difficult to issue the bonds. This turn of events also revealed problems in the primary and the secondary bond markets. The banks—the major investors in the inter-bank market—had similar reactions to policy changes due to the fact that banks are "buy and hold" by nature. From the banks' point of view, as long as deposit volume does not decline, they do not need to worry about solvency; therefore, they can choose to hold bonds even if bond prices are falling. That is not true for securities intermediaries who, one after another, had fallen into financial trouble. To make matters worse, the ability of those brokers to maintain their solvency was severely challenged by downturns in the equity market. Corporate bond issues were seriously affected, achieving only RMB10 billion in 2004, significantly lower than in 2003.

Changing Features of the Primary Bond Market

Individual Investors Resume Dominant Position in the T-Bond Market   In 1998, the central government set a three-year horizon for its financial reform program within a framework of a socialist financial system with Chinese characteristics. This was a landmark in the history of national economic development. The central bank ended its practice of controlling credit quotas and encouraged the banks to implement asset and liability management. It is recognized that high sustainable economic growth, well-contained inflation, and reform of state-owned enterprises aided the development of the T-bond market.

As originally planned, the objective for T-bond market development in 1998 was to execute the financing program in line with fiscal and monetary policy and to achieve a healthy, smooth, and well-disciplined market development in order to facilitate the development of the entire financial market.

An OTC trading system was developed while efforts to optimize on-exchange transactions went forward. In 1998, the Ministry of Finance issued a total of RMB550 billion T-bonds, which was a significant increase over previous years. Initially, with the approval from National People's Congress, RMB280 billion were to be issued to the public (including RMB220 billion certificate T-bonds) and RMB51.3 billion to commercial banks and insurance companies in the inter-bank market. RMB100 billion T-bonds were added to implement the government's proactive fiscal policy, and another RMB270 billion were issued for the replenishment of capital for the banks and were subscribed by the commercial banks. Of the total volume, RMB200 billion was used to finance the fiscal deficit and repay the interest and principal on the maturing bonds. However, because of the lack of new issues in the market, the variety of tradable bonds declined significantly. About one-third of the T-bonds were issued to the individuals in the form of savings bonds; book-entry bonds were issued in the IBBM. Only two bond transactions were executed on the Shanghai Stock Exchange. Because of the inconsistency between the coupon rates determined by the State Council and the yield rates in the secondary market, only one of them was successful.

In order to control the overheated stock market, the government asked the banks to withdraw from it and forbade bank funds to flow into the stock market in 1997. As a result, banks had to sell their bond holdings, which led to the formation of the inter-bank bond market in 1998.

The Ministry of Finance returned to the international capital market with a successful international bonds transaction. Because of three consecutive interest rate cuts, individual investors were very enthusiastic about savings bonds with a coupon rate 1 percent higher than the interest rate on bank deposits. The banks also demonstrated their enthusiasm for T-bonds designed to improve the quality of their assets. Along with the interest rate cuts, China's T-bond market saw several peaks by the end of 1998.

Emergence of Two Venues for T-Bond Transactions   As a result of shifting from targeting institutional investors to individual investors and shifting from exchange trading to IBBM trading, there emerged a number of problems. The certificate bonds issued to individuals were non-tradable bonds with no liquidity, while T-bonds issued to the banks were traded at the inter-bank market, which lacked liquidity due to the buy-and-hold nature of the banks.

By 1998, the exchange bond market and the inter-bank bond market had developed. Trading prices on the two markets were significantly different because of the different market participants.

Thus between 1996 and 1998, the T-bond's investor base had been transformed from an institution-dominated to an individual- and bank-dominated structure.

Nevertheless, due to the high liquidity of the bonds listed on the exchanges, the yields were low. In spite of this, however, the bond infrastructure was improving.

Resumption of T-Bond Pricing by the State Council and Shift in Focus to Individual Investors After 1998, the State Council resumed its role in pricing T-bonds. The number of certificate T-bonds issued to individuals increased, but T-bonds were issued mainly to banks. As a result, market-based T-bond issuance decreased gradually.

As the market-determined yield rates for T-bonds were different from the regulated interest rates for bank deposits and loans, there was concern that the coupon rates of the T-bonds would affect the state's policy on interest rates. With the issue of the two-year T-bond in 1997, the State Council reiterated its policy on treasury rates (i.e., treasury rates could be a little bit higher than the interest rate for underlying bank deposits, but shall not exceed 1 percent). After 1998, referencing this policy and the interest rate for underlying bank deposits, the Ministry of Finance submitted to the State Council its proposal for approval of its treasury bill's coupon rates.

Although more certificate bonds had been issued, individual investors still complained about the availability of these non-tradable treasury bills. Therefore, the State Council decided that T-bonds should be issued mainly to individuals.

Meanwhile, the T-bonds issued by Ministry of Finance entered the inter-bank bond market, which was established after the withdrawal of banks from the exchanges. As the state-owned commercial banks with abundant funds were major investors in the IBBM, the state encouraged them to buy T-bonds to offset the occurrence of nonperforming loans in these banks, and the IBBM became the primary venue for issuing T-bonds.

The China Development Bank (CDB) began its market-based issue of bonds in 1998; however, in compliance with relevant provisions of the People's Bank of China, the CDB was allowed to issue these bonds only in the IBBM. At the same time, the China EX-IM, another policy bank, also started its issue of the financial bonds at the IBBM.

During this period, the bond market witnessed the emergence of the IBBM and the trading decline of the exchange markets. The rapid development of the IBBM had significant implications for the rapid increase in the offering volume and innovations in T-bonds, while the coexistence of the two markets greatly constrained the bond market from developing further and the segregation of the two markets led to low market efficiency.

Role of the China Development Bank   Lack of liquidity is one of the major issues in the inter-bank bond market. As buy-and-hold investors, banks are reluctant to trade their bonds in the market. To increase market liquidity and reduce liquidity risks, the CDB has been active in promoting innovations in the bond market.

The CDB issued a floating-rate bond for the first time in 1999. Its issuing rate was based on the interest rate for a 12-month deposit, and helped banks lock in their interest rate exposure, which benefited their asset and liability management. Next, in quick succession, it introduced callable bonds, put-able bonds, and treasury STRIPS, all of which greatly enriched the instruments available in the IBBM and increased variety of investments and hedging instruments available to investors.

LESSONS LEARNED FROM CHINA'S TREASURY BOND EXPERIENCE

Although the Ministry of Finance successfully fulfilled the task of issuing T-bonds from 1981 to the present, the process was anything but smooth and stable. Between 1981 and 1990, the issues depended on administrative allocations, in 1991 and 1992 on underwriting, while in 1993 the administrative allocation method was resumed. In 1994, the issuance of T-bonds depended on bond futures; in 1995, on the inflation-protected bonds; in 1996, on auction; and in 1997, on ample funds from the banks. Each year was different from the next. Only in 1991 and 1996 did the offering really rely on the market; this was especially true in 1996, which represented a big step forward.

From 1996 to 2003, thanks to interest rate declines and rising bond prices, investors demonstrated high interest in T-bond investment. During this period, T-bond issue depended on the premium on bond principle, brought about by declining interest rates and bank enthusiasm for investing in T-bonds. Still, this does not mean that the bond market had entered a good cycle. Without a totally market-oriented issuing method, there cannot be a stable issuing mechanism.

Preconditions for Bond Market Reform

Based on our experience with bond market reform, we have learned that before an efficient and cost-effective market can be established, seven conditions must first be met. They include:

1. Clear objectives
2. Market economy

3. Solution to issuance difficulties
4. A full-fledged wholesale market
5. Market instruments
6. A favorable financial environment
7. An advanced financial infrastructure

Clear Objectives Essential for Designing a Phased Program The reasons for issuing T-bonds and the goals of T-bond market development are two different matters. T-bonds are issued for a variety of reasons, including:

- *Financing the shortfall between the central government's revenues and expenditures.* In other words, the direct aim of issuing the T-bonds is to make up the fiscal deficit.
- *Implementing the macroeconomic policies.* For example, bonds may be issued to adopt a tight or loose fiscal policy. Increasing T-bond volume means a loose fiscal policy to stimulate the economic growth, while reducing issuance means a tight fiscal policy to control the inflation rate. Usually T-bond issuance also aims at coordinating the fiscal policy and monetary policy. Therefore, motivation from the central government is the main driver of bond market development. And here again, the motivation was determined by what I referred as the secondary administrative exchange. After 1997, the auction selling was suspended and bonds were placed to individuals. Apparently, financing the government shortfall was no longer a problem, and individuals' concerns were priorities that the government needed to address. The design of the bond market development program had to take into account central government priorities.
- *Providing effective market instruments.* For example, T-bonds are financial commodities that trade in the market, and the number of financial commodities available can have an impact on supply and demand dynamics, which in turn can have an impact on the market price. The lack of diversified market instruments will eventually affect market transactions and lead to recessions. This is accomplished by the CDB's financial innovative efforts.
- *Providing the central bank with effective tools for open market operations.* T-bond issuance can be an effective means of macroeconomic control and regulation.
- *Providing banks with the means to manage assets and liabilities.* The commercially oriented specialized banks in China are required to hold part of their financial assets in T-bonds because of their high liquidity. In this sense, the T-bond is critical to bank management.

Thus, the issue of T-bonds plays an important role in banks' macromanagement and development. Therefore, future development of the T-bond market should have multifaceted rather than single-faceted objectives. It is one-dimensional to restrict the aim of issuing T-bonds and developing the market only to fundraising. The goal in developing the T-bond market should be to establish a market with high efficiency and low cost. On one hand, the offering process should be short and effective; on the other hand, the offering cost should be minimized and acceptable to both investors and issuers.

In the process of market-oriented reform, yield rates in the T-bond market were gradually declining and approaching secondary market yields. For example, the yield rate for No. 793 three-year T-notes in 1996 was only 0.16 percent higher than the interest rate for the bank deposit of the same term. From then on, the issuance cost was relatively low and the terms were rather long. The same was true of bonds issued to individuals, because the cost of issuing T-bonds to individuals was higher.

In 1994, to facilitate the market-based reform process and enable individual participation in the T-bond market, savings bonds were handled jointly by the Ministry of Finance and the People's Bank of China. Savings bonds accounted for a large part of the bond market in 1994 and 1996.

To further develop the T-bond market and meet the demand of individuals, China should:

- *Focus on the development of T-bond investment funds.* This can not only solve the problems individual investors face in purchasing T-bonds, but also improve investor structure and investment quality so as to enhance the in-depth development T-bond market.
- *Encourage individuals to enter the secondary T-bond market,* which means that the individuals will be able to enter both the exchange market and the OTC market. This can be done by:
  - Developing special accounts for individuals and letting individuals enter the exchange market. This is a way for individuals to participate in book-entry bonds. The experiment with these special accounts at the beginning of 1997 was successful, and they should be further developed in the future. At present, the Ministry of Finance is ready to expand this experiment to all large and medium-size cities.
  - Enlarging the OTC selling of T-bonds to include individuals. At present, securities intermediaries have fewer networks than the banks, but, at the appropriate time, the trading counters at banks could be allowed to buy and sell T-bonds to individuals. Currently the counters of banks only have access to secondary accounts for individual investors, which could lead to short selling; therefore, stricter regulation of these accounts would be required. The OTC transactions

of the securities intermediaries are inactive now. The exchange opens primary accounts for the securities firms, but the securities firms do not open primary accounts for individual investors.

In designing accounts for individuals to enter the secondary T-bond market, there were two primary considerations: (1) to expand the custodial accounts and (2) to open secondary accounts for the banks. The former is much safer but is inconvenient to individual investors, while the latter is convenient but not safe enough.

Market-Based Regime   During the 14th National Congress of the Communist Party of China, the notion of the market economy was identified as key to China's socialist economy and therefore became the goal of reform. On one hand, the formation of the T-bond issuing system should be based on the actual conditions in China and should fully reflect the history and characteristics of its financial and securities sectors; on the other hand, it should follow in the steps of the world's major economies.

The new selling technique marked a shift in the borrower-investor relationship from administrative to contractive. The underwriting syndication in 1991 was dubbed central underwriting as opposed to the local underwriting that prevailed in 1992. From 1992 onward, the Ministry granted local governments the mandate for selling government securities.

As the public placement by tender is consistent to the principle of high efficiency and low cost, it has been widely used by most of the advanced countries in the primary treasury market. In such a case, the interests of the investors will never be impaired. When subscription is by assignment, sometimes the interests of the issuers are compromised, sometimes the interests of the individual investors are compromised, and sometimes the interests of both issuers and investors are compromised and only the intermediaries profit. All these situations must be avoided in designing new issuing systems.

It is worth noting that the underwriting in 1991 was not actually an economic offering since the issuing terms were determined through administrative means. The transaction was a success only because the intermediaries were given favorable issuing terms. Clearly, the underwriting method is not ideal. Historically, many advanced countries once adopted the underwriting method; for example, the United States used underwriting, but then moved to the auction method. T-bonds are issued through underwriting in Japan today. The underwriting syndication in Japan is basically fixed, and the syndicate members focus on their long-term returns rather than the gain or loss during a given underwriting process. Moreover, in Japan, the coupon rate of T-bonds is affected by the interest rate level. However, some elements of the auction system are being integrated into the underwriting of the coupon bonds in Japan.

Without a market-based pricing mechanism, or the underwriters being forced to accept the price, they would have little incentive to underwrite all of the T-bonds and sell them to the end investors. Whatever method is adopted, it is critical that the issuing terms are determined by market supply and demand dynamics. Therefore, the way T-bonds are issued must evolve into an auction-dominated mechanism, that is, tendering. However, it is feasible only if the institution is in place. Viewed in this light, the selling of T-bonds by tender has to be based on an institutional framework.

Primary Dealer Regime   China initiated its primary dealer system in 1993. Since then the primary dealers have been in a position to subscribe in primary issues in book entry forms. The book entry form bonds are registered in the stock exchange trading system. The introduction of book entry bonds substanially increased the varieties of T-bonds available at that time. The primary dealer system is an important part of the financial infrastructure because primary dealers are obliged to underwrite and bid for T-bonds in the T-bond primary market, based on specific regulations. However, the 1997 primary dealer system has two important defects: (1) major commercial banks are not members of the primary dealers' organization; and (2) the system does not fully reflect the market-making and underwriting functions of primary dealers. The underwriting syndication regime that was put in place in 1991 has been gradually integrated with the auction selling system via syndicate, who bid in the primary issues since 1997.

In addition, the comprehensive tender and direct sale to individuals can be pursued simultaneously as an intermediate stage in market development.

Integrating Auction with Syndicate   As mentioned, the auction system was introduced and grafted onto the earlier underwriting syndication framework. The bidding process can be applied to some of the underwritten T-bonds, or the T-bonds might be tendered first and then underwritten in the sub-selling. As the primary dealers are obliged to underwrite a certain amount of bonds, the combination of the auction selling technique and underwriting syndication would help achieve the financing target during the transitional period of bond market development. In fact, T-bond issue in China has been carried out under the syndicate member bidding regime since 1997.

Two Conduits for Selling: Tender and OTC Selling   The MOF wished to combine the comprehensive tender and direct OTC sale to individuals. The idea, developed in 1997, was that after the scripless book-entry auction of the jumbo T-bonds, individual investors could purchase the tradable, already issued T-bonds or the savings bonds in the secondary market. Thus, there were conduits by which primary issue could be carried out: (1) through primary dealers and the intermediaries, and (2) by issuing T-bonds directly to individuals. The former is a direct channel and the latter is an indirect channel; they also differ in some other respects.

With the primary dealer regime and financial intermediaries in place, the selling of short- and midterm jumbo T-bonds by the Ministry of Finance via underwriting syndicate or tender has been substantially improved. Smaller-denominated T-bonds are better for OTC selling direct to individuals through the banking system, postal savings system, and the T-bond service system under local Departments of Finance.

When-Issued Market and Fixed Issuance Schedules When tender issue became predominant, the next step is to institute when-issued trading and fixed issuing schedules to improve selling efficiency. *When-issued trading* means distribution prior to the actual tendering process; the price is negotiated between the bidders and the investors, and the when-issued price becomes the basis for the bidders' offer. The advantage of this system is that the underwriters, as bidders, can get a better understanding of investors' appetite for the bond and the demand at a given price. The result is that the price at which the bond is tendered is closer to market realities. When-issued transactions, however, require a short-selling mechanism, but since the futures market was halted in 1995, no such mechanism exists. Forward bonds, which were issued for the first time by the China Development Bank in 2003, are similar to when-issued bonds, because the way they trade in the market definitely affects the pricing of on-the-run issues.

Starting in 2001, the Ministry of Finance and the CDB began to make public their planned issuing schedules, which is helpful for both underwriters and investors because it helps them to arrange their funds well in advance. Currently only medium- and long-term bonds are listed in the schedules, and more work needs to be done in this respect.

Move from Paperless to Book-Entry Securities As these institutional arrangements have gradually been put in place, the scripless book-entry form securities were introduced along with the emerging primary dealer system. The book-entry form helps save printing and transportation costs and facilitates transaction efficiency. However, at introduction, it was still a challenge for securities to trade outside the electronic trading system; therefore, paper securities were still being used in the manual OTC market for individuals, which resulted in different trading prices.

As banks became the major investors in China, to address this issue, it is essential to take into account the connection between the T-bond's trading system and the banks' payment system and the connections among their subpayment systems.

The most advanced and desirable settlement standard around the world, delivery versus payment (DVP) (i.e., bond securities delivery are made against payment at the same time), ensures that delivery and payment are made at the same time, which eliminates risk to both parties in a transaction. DVP can be achieved by integrating the debt instruments' settlement system with the real-time settlement function of the national payment system for transferring negotiable certificates. The full implementation of the real-time DVP requires three basic preconditions:

1. The central bank must fully implement the modern payment system. This enables securities companies to connect the delivery of paper bonds against money transfer
2. The linkage between the central securities book-entry system and the real-time settlement system in the central bank must be established.
3. Institutional arrangements for DVP must be made available. This includes real-time clearance by direct money transfer via central bank wire and the central bank payment system through designated settlement agents, and through current accounts in the central depositary.

On November 8, 2006, the treasury bond's entry and payment system at the CDC was connected to the payment system of the People's Bank of China, an important milestone in the development of China's financial infrastructures. This high-efficiency, low-risk settlement network has improved the infrastructure of China's bond market.

Diversified Instruments From 1981 to 1995, T-bonds in China were mostly three- and five-year bonds. From 1981 to 1984, a small number of five-year-plus T-bonds were issued. Thus, it is true to say that T-bond issues in China were once dominated by medium-term bonds. To rationalize the term structure, long- and short-term T-bonds should be increased. Pension funds and the rural unemployment insurance funds should be permitted to subscribe to a portion of 8- to 10-year T-bonds. Because pension funds must pay interest to beneficiaries at fixed time intervals, issues targeted to pension funds should be designed to pay interest annually.

Short-term T-bills should be targeted mainly to banks, to provide instruments the central bank can use in its open market operations and to serve as an important instrument for the treasury's cash management. These bonds can also provide a benchmark to facilitate development of the short-term money market and inter-bank market, which in turn will benefit the development of the treasury bond market.

Currently structural problems remain in the bond market. The inter-bank bond market is for financial institutions and the banks are leading underwriters and investors, although, as a matter of fact, banks cannot effectively distribute the bonds to individuals. For this reason, individuals still invest primarily in certificate T-bonds and other bonds issued at the exchanges. Over-the-counter selling to individuals in the IBBM began in 2000 but has never been active. To date, these issues have not been fully addressed.

Solution to Issuance Obsession   Before 1996, the coupon rate was set by the State Council, which issued the terms and conditions of treasury bond rates. As this was done without market basis, these terms and conditions usually diverged from the actual market yield.

Selling obsessions were the main problems between 1981 and 1996, even after the underwriting syndication regime was introduced. For example, in 1991, the selling was fairly easy this was not due to the fact that the transaction was carried out via underwriting syndication but due to the fact that bond coupon rate set was happen to be identical to the secondary market yield. However, the T-bond market became extremely volatile in the first half of 1992, similar to market in 1991. At that time, although the coupon rates of T-bonds were lowered in accordance with the lowering of the interest rates for bank deposits, they were still a little bit higher than market interest rates. In addition, institutional investors were optimistic about investment prospects, and the T-bonds sold well. As market conditions had changed by the time the bond offering was executed, the second issue of government bonds in 1992 encountered chilly market response, because the issuing terms had been determined and the underwriting contracts had been signed in the first half of the year; at the time of actual payment, the coupon rates greatly diverged from the market conditions.

In 1993, T-bond distribution encountered enormous difficulties. The transaction was handicapped early in the year, which legitimized the bond government's resumption of the administrative allocation method. The introduction of a new issuance technique in 1991, replacing the earlier assignment-based subscription method. Underwriting syndication did result in progress on the future market development. However, with the coupon rate regulated by the central government, the contractual relationship between the Ministry and syndicate members was not based on the market as it is understood. Underwriting should be a mechanism by which interest rates acceptable to both parties are determined through negotiation between the issuer and the underwriting syndicate.

When selling was handicapped, the views on future development were widely apart as to whether China should go forward to let the market price the bond transaction or whether China should resume the administrative allocation. It became clear that interest liberalization is the key for bond market reform, but, as it turned out, to turn the regulated bond issuing rate around would be an enormous undertaking.

It is also true that the chaotic financial environment was an important factor for the issuing obsession with T-bonds. High corporate coupon rates, interest rate wars, and rising yield rates for treasury bills in the secondary market were merely expressions of the rising interest rates in the financial, securities, and T-bond markets. In fact, the fundamental changes in the supply and demand dynamics led to rising interest rates. Therefore, the basic reason for the chaos lay in an overheated investment market, including a real estate craze and a stock craze that prevailed throughout the national economy.

The rising price index drives up the market's expectation on returns on investment, which inevitably leads to the decline of the coupon rate in the secondary market and rising yield rates. Fundraising costs grew due to the higher cost of capital. Given the inflationary environment, the interest rate level should be higher. As depreciation of repaid principal and interest on bonds at maturity exceeded the interest rate level, the real interest rate was negative. Other factors also contributed to the deterioration of treasury bond issue conditions, including an underdeveloped secondary market, insufficient derivatives, and intermediaries lacking sufficient counterparts for individual investors.

As a matter of fact, there were setbacks in issuing of the T-bonds during the second half of 1992 and 1993, so that some practices of administrative allocation were resumed. But this in no way implies that the new selling technique was not a success. Experience shows that the transition to tender selling should be made as soon as possible to avoid the juxtaposition of a dual selling system: underwriting and administrative placement. However, the tender selling technique requires the primary dealer system, book-entry form security, and an electronic transmission system for trading; apparently, these systems cannot be set up overnight.

When the tender selling technique is not in place, resumption of the old selling technique is likely. For example, tranches to individual investors were added in 1998 and 1999 transactions. At the same time, the public offer tranche via auction was suspended. Doubtless, this gave rise to a deficiency and added costs. Consequently, in 2000, the Ministry of Finance resumed the auction method, while the number of market-oriented registered T-bonds increased in size.

By following the market-oriented path, primary and secondary markets can develop harmoniously. Public offerings and an extensive investor base are important preconditions to a functional bond market. At the same time, however, the exclusive issue of T-bonds to the banks is essentially private placement. Although insurance and securities companies have already entered into the inter-bank bond market, it is still not open to other investors.

Currently, the interest deregulation is underway. If the bank deposit and loan rate is fully subject to the market demand and supply, then bank deposit rates tend to be higher than government bond rates. This would diminish banks' incentive to hold government bonds. Should banks reduce their T-bond holdings, it is questionable whether banks will remain the main investor in T-bonds and the IBBM will remain the main venue for bond selling and trading. To ensure a stable conduit for funding, the current IBBM needs to be restructured or, as many of the comments suggested, to be integrated with the stock exchange market.

Important Experiences Market-oriented reform has been a process of gradual development, one that includes a number of peculiarities:

- *Market-based interest rate.* The interest rate should be directly decided by supply and demand dynamics in the market, rather than by referencing other market instruments or being set administratively.
- *Tiered market.* The market should have a clear division of functions, for example, wholesale and retail selling; primary market and secondary market.
- *Scripless bonds.* The T-bonds should be issued by book entry, which reduces costs. Since 1996, except for certificate T-bonds, all tradable bonds have been issued in scripless form. However, some printed corporate bonds were issued to individual investors over the counter in 2004.
- *Electronic transactions.* On-exchange and off-exchange transactions should be carried out through computer systems, and information related to transactions should be transmitted electronically. Established in 1994, China Government Securities Depository Trust & Clearing Co., Ltd. is the primary venue for registration, depository trust, and clearing in the inter-bank bond market and the bill market.
- *Diversification.* There should be tradable and nontradable bonds, including book-entry bonds, bearer bonds, and registered bonds; there should be long-, medium-, and short-term T-bonds.[3]
- *Standardized procedures.* Fixed schedules and stable issuing methods should be adopted. Diversification of the terms and varieties of bonds requires that given varieties be issued at regular intervals and that a stable investor base be established. It is especially important to cultivate various kinds of pension funds and securities investment funds to assure stable demand for the long-term bonds.

As a matter of fact, there has been a significant development since 1996 in all these areas. In 2004, steps were taken toward a market-based interest rate. The determination of interest rates through auction became the primary issuing technique for subordinated bonds issued by financial institutions, as well as for T-bonds and financial bonds. However, to date, corporate bond issuance has to be approved by the National Development and Reform Commission on a case-by-case basis. In addition, most of the financial institutions offer their subordinated bonds through private placements.

Full-Fledged Wholesale Market Initially China's T-bond market was retail in nature because without a market-based interest rate mechanism, individual investors dominate the market, which, as we have seen, leads to issuing inefficiencies. If the primary market is a retail market, there will be no liquidity in the secondary market, which will adversely affect the T-bond primary market. The establishment of the primary dealer system in 1993 was actually aimed at transforming the T-bond market from a retail market into a wholesale market. The launch of savings (certificate) bonds in 1994 introduced marketable T-bonds into the market. With the creation of a wholesale primary market in 1996, T-bond transactions were essentially wholesaled out via the primary dealers.

Market Instruments A market never forms spontaneously. A complete and developed market should consist of a market institutional framework, instruments, and market players. When the secondary T-bond market was liberalized in 1987, there were only immature market players and under-developed market mechanisms. Most important, no market instruments were available. At present, there are hundreds of T-bonds on the run in circulation. Without these market-oriented bond varieties, the liquidity of the T-bond market would be severely impaired.

There must also be derivative instruments. The major functions of derivatives are to increase the liquidity and flexibility of the market and provide market players with effective hedging tools. Since China closed its T-bond futures market in 1995, repurchase has been the only derivative instrument available. Apparently, without derivative instruments, it is impossible for market participants to manage their risks through hedging. With the development of the T-bond market, the role of derivatives in setting prices and hedging tools will be further demonstrated.

Favorable Financial Environment The bond market is a component of the financial market, while the financial market is the basis for the bond market. The banks and other financial intermediaries are the major underwriters in the bond market; the development of insurance institutions has formed the investor base for treasury financial bonds. The financial market and the T-bonds market are related in these ways:

- Interest rates affect the coupon level of the T-bond market. At present, the interest rates for bank deposits and loans are still planned rates, which are inconsistent with the yield rates in the secondary T-bond market and therefore have an enormous negative impact on T-bond offerings. In China, banks purchase T-bonds because treasury rates are higher than the interest rates for bank deposits. Without a market-based interest rate, financial institutions are always willing to use their deposits to buy T-bonds thereby receiving risk-free returns.

- The participation of banks in the T-bond market affects the liquidity of the T-bonds. The banks' participation in the T-bond market and their investment in and holding of T-bonds are necessary preconditions for the commercialized management of the banks. T-bonds held by the banks are financial assets of the highest liquidity, and the banks must hold a certain amount of them for the purpose of asset and liability management.

    The T-bonds held by the banks are usually short-term bonds, and, therefore, the banks play a rather special role in the short-term T-bond market. The banks provide the T-bond repurchase or repo (buyback) market with funds and act as the major financing channel for the non-bank financial institutions. As the banks are relatively stable investors, they contribute to the stability of the T-bonds market.

- The equity and bond markets impact one another. The cash flows from one market to another leads to price hikes in one market and price declines in the other. Because of the intermediary role of the repo market, the two markets may be linked.

In short, in the process of developing the money market, the equity market, and the inter-bank market, the implications for the T-bond market must be taken into consideration. For instance, when the banks withdraw from the repo market, they should consider what impact that will have on the stability the T-bond market. In turn, maintaining a stable, highly liquid T-bond market is beneficial to the development of the whole financial market.

Advanced Financial Infrastructure   The financial infrastructure includes the systems for the registration, depository trust, and settlement and clearance of T-bonds, all of which are of vital importance to the development of the T-bond market. In recent years, implementing the use of scripless bonds in

China has been inextricably tied to the development of these systems. As we have seen, beginning in 2001, some steps have been taken to establish a more sophisticated transmission system and a more extensive national network.

CONCLUSION

In summary, the development of debt capital market in China as an institutional movement is driven by the primary exchange and secondary exchange. Primary exchange, internal and external, drives market development. It is reasonable to suppose that the bond market reform program should go hand in hand with social development.

The elements specified by economists and market professionals as important to debt capital market development have been pieced together into a theoretical framework: the IEEN paradigm. The driving force of bond market development can be viewed from two different perspectives:

- Bond exchange, both primary and secondary, is subject to financial exchange. By the same token, financial exchange, both primary and secondary, is subject to economic exchange. Similarly, economic exchange, both primary and secondary, is subject to political exchange.
- The secondary exchange is subject to the primary exchange at the same level, whereas the primary exchange is subject to the secondary exchange at a higher level.

Thus, bond market development can be perceived as a well-designed program for China's social and economic development, but the real trajectory was shaped by primary economic exchange and primary administrative exchanges, among others. Along this line, we can search for clues to understand the historical development of China's debt capital market. The primary bond market, as a most effective primary bond exchange, played very important role in China's market development as a whole.

CHAPTER 4

Issuing Methods and Practices Around the World

ISSUING METHODS IN DEVELOPED MARKET ECONOMIES

Drawing on extensive international experience, the treasury bond market in China has been adapted to meet the specific needs of the Chinese financial system.

Types of Treasury Bond Issuing Methods

At present, the developed countries employ four methods:

1. *Auction.* This method is very popular in most developed countries. Using this method, the issuer determines the price (or the interest rate) level by direct competitive bidding. More specifically, the issuer arranges the bids in descending order (or ascending order for interest rates). Then the issuer then sells to the bidder who offers the highest price (or who will accept the lowest interest rate) until the entire offering is distributed. Thus, the price determined by this method is equivalent to the market price determined by supply and demand.
2. *Underwriting.* Using this method, the issuer and the underwriting syndicate sign underwriting contracts whose terms are negotiated and agreed to by the both parties. As major securities companies and banks are very familiar with the market conditions, the syndicate members always require a relatively low price (or high interest rate) for T-bond distribution. However, the issuer always requires relatively high prices (or low interest rates) to reduce issuance costs. They reach a price (or interest rate) level close to the market level through negotiation and bargaining.
3. *Direct sale to individual investors.* Issuers directly contact investors, for instance, the sale of savings bonds over the counter of securities companies or banks through an agency servicing method.

4. *"Tap" issue.* Like a tap adjusting water volume, this method adjusts the offering volume subject to actual market conditions. Using this method, T-bonds are sold throughout the year. When the sales volume reaches a certain level or interest rates in the market have changed, the current issue stops being sold and the next issue follows once its interest rate is adjusted.

Auction Methods Compared

English Auction or Multiple-Price Sealed-Bid Auction   The U.S. Department of the Treasury currently uses this auction method. In the English auction,[1] bidders are required to submit their bidding form within a determined time frame. The content of the bid is confidential (known only to the bidder and the auctioneer). The bid includes the volume and price the bidder is willing to offer.

The seller sorts these bids (or relevant yield rate) in ascending order. The price the bidders are willing to offer reflects their bidding ability and market conditions. Since the successful bidder is the one who offers the highest bid price, this method is also called a first-price auction.

Using this auction method, in a sense, successful bidders are always at a disadvantage. Since some bidders are afraid they might bid too low and miss out on a good opportunity, they sometimes offer a price higher than what they might feel is appropriate; the higher their bidding price, the greater their possibility for loss if they win the bid—the so-called the winner's curse. For this reason, this auction method may dampen bidders' interest in participating.

The English method has two weaknesses as a way to determine the award cost in line with the actual bid prices: (1) a when-issued (WI) transaction tends to make the market price consistent with the bid price, which leads to reduced competition; (2) major bidders frequently exchange their views on market, which can result in a monopoly price favorable to the bidders. According to William Vickery, a leading authority on auctions, the best way to avoid this is to design an auction method where the result is consistent with the generally acknowledged market price.

Theoretically, the auction method employed by the U.S. Treasury for its bond offerings falls into the category of an English auction. Because it is representative, we will use it to explain the features of the English auction method. The U.S. Treasury realized the problems, such as winners' curse, inherent in this method, and replaced it with the Dutch auction method in the second half of the 1980s. In the middle of 1990s, Treasury officials told me that they had not reached a conclusion about the efficacy of the Dutch versus the English auction.

In the United States, all auctions of T-bonds use this tendering process, and every year, in 160 tender offers, the United States raises a total of US$1.5 trillion.

The Financial Management Service of the U.S. Department of the Treasury determines the size of each borrowing, and the deputy assistant secretary authorizes the Bureau of the Public Debt to perform the specific issues of the T-bonds. The procedure follows.

The first step is the offering quotation, which includes the type of T-bond, the issuing amount, auction date, and the offering periods.

In the case of a treasury bill auction, in the announcement, the issuer will require that the bidders provide their total bid amount based on the face value of the bills. According to the Uniform Offering Circular, the minimum bid amount shall not be less than US$10,000 and shall be multiples of US$5,000.

There are two categories of bidders: competitive and non-competitive bidders. Competitive bidders are required to express their desired yield rates. Non-competitive bidders are required not to exceed US$1 million in a single bid. The auctions of the regular 13- and 26-week treasury bills are usually conducted on Mondays (subject to postponement in case of a holiday). The offering announcement is made public through a press release on the last Tuesday, and these announcements are transmitted to the Federal Reserve Bank and their branches.

After receiving all the bidding materials, the officials with the Bureau of the Public Debt begin to identify the successful bidders based on English auction procedures, with all non-competitive bidders accepted according to an average yield rate, that is, a weighted average of all accepted competitive yield rates. The competitive auction will first satisfy the lowest yield rate bid and then the higher yield rate bids in succession, until the total offering is sold.

After the completion of its auction process, the Bureau of the Public Debt makes the results public through various news media and informs all bidders of the accepted amount. In the case of treasury bill issuance, the auction process often starts on 11:30 a.m. and closes at 1:00 p.m. Delivery date often follows the auction day.

Dutch Auction or Uniform-Price Sealed-Bid Auction   In this type of auction, the bidding documents are also sealed. At the end of the auction, the bonds are sold at a uniform price to all bidders. That final price is the second highest price offered, which is why this method is also called the second-price auction.

In a Dutch auction, the bidder who offers the highest price is sure of success and can still offer a price approaching the market price. The advantage of this method is that bidders are willing to participate directly in the bidding process rather through the primary dealers.

In 1959, the American scholar Milton Friedman suggested that the uniform-price sealed-bid auction (i.e., the so-called Dutch auction) for the sale of T-bonds. According to Friedman, this method eliminates the possibility of a bidder acquiring huge profits through market manipulation and reduces the possibility of a few bidders achieving a market monopoly. The uniform-price auction assures that the auction results reflect the true wishes of the investors in purchasing T-bonds and lets them bid directly and bypass intermediaries. According to Friedman, the uniform-price auction brings the demand curve at auction into line with that at the secondary market, and alignment between the primary and the secondary markets greatly reduces the possibility of speculation by intermediaries. This is because, if bids at auction are made without reference to the investors' anticipation, a successful bidder will encounter difficulties in distributing the T-bonds in the secondary market. Thus, if there is no potential return for the investors, there is no motive for bidders to manipulate the market.

French T-Bond Auction Techniques   Since 1985, the price auction is the primary method used for the sale of T-bonds. At present, in certain specific circumstances, the underwriting method by syndicates is employed.

In France, all companies registered with the clearing companies and the Banque de France are eligible to participate in the auction. Two working days before the auction date of treasury bills, the Ministry of Finance announces the offering amount as well as caps and floors for treasury notes and bonds. Different tendering methods apply to different bonds, but all auctions are conducted through real price or real interest rate rather than averages or marginal prices. Eligible companies submit their bids to Banque de France 10 minutes before the actual auction at latest.

Banque de France sequences the interest rates of the short-term bonds in ascending order; those of mid- and long-term T-bonds are sequenced in descending order. When the aggregate of the successful bids reaches the total offering volume, the auction process closes. Then Banque de France announces the auction results along with a list of the successful bidders. The Ministry of Finance carries out allocations according to the bid price and amount made by each bidder. For the mid- and long-term bonds, the total volume falls within the upper and lower limits (i.e., cap and floor). For the short-term treasury bills, the offering amount must be equivalent to the announced amount (with only a small amount of round-off). To ensure a precise issuing amount, the Ministry of Finance may reduce the offering size proportionally based on the minimum acceptable price.

Once the successful bids are examined, the auction results can be announced, and they appear on the computer screens of some of the agencies usually within an hour. Thanks to the advanced communications systems and the screen display data processing systems, the time between the delivery of the tendering documents and the auction results has been greatly shortened.

Issue-by-Tender This mechanism for issuing treasury bonds is based on the commodity auction system. Auction theory goes back as far as the early period of American history. More recently, William Vickery, Milton Friedman, and Paul Mitgrom have all made contributions to the field, particularly categorizing the different auction methods which to that point had been rather chaotic and contradictory. William Vickery was the first to employ standardized classification: Open or sealed tenders are categorized. In addition, he categorized auctions according to subjective–objective criteria (i.e., subjective bid and objective bid). A subjective bid is based on the bidder's personal assessment of the issue, while the objective bid is based on specific criteria. Vickery categorized the auction by biding direction (price going up or down) and by transparency (open biding or sealed bidding). Therefore, there are four kinds of auctions:

1. *Multiple Price Secret Bidding.* Bidders submit bids in a specified time. Bids are kept secret, and early time bids were put in sealed envelopes (currently, this is done through an electronic system). Successful bidders are selected from highest to lowest price (or from low to higher yield). The successful bidder's own bidding price is applied. In the market, this is called an American auction (Americans called it an English auction).
2. *Unified Price Secret Bidding.* Similar to multiple price secret bidding, bids are kept secret and submitted to the auctioneer at specified time, and bid selection runs from higher to lower price (if yield is bid, the order is opposite). Unlike multiple price secret bidding, though, unified price secret bidding applies one price (cutting price) to every successful bidder. This auction method is also called a Dutch auction.
3. *Descending Price-Open Bid Auction.* This method was once used in the Netherlands for the sale of flowers. The bidders were gathered at an auction venue, and the auctioneer asks for bids at a specific price—the highest he believes he can demand. If he receives no or few offers, he announces a new lower price. In the case of a single commodity or security, the auction ends when one of the bidders is willing to pay a competitive price. When numerous commodities or securities are auctioned, the auction continues until all of the commodities or

securities are sold at descending prices. In tendering T-bonds using this method, bidders enthusiastically exchange information and bid either collectively or through primary dealers.

4. *Ascending Price–Open Bid Auction.* Here the auctioneer asks prices in ascending orders. The bidders offer their different prices, and the auction closes when there are no further bids at a higher price. This method is usually applied in auctioning a single piece of artwork.

When selling multiple-unit securities, when the auctioneer states the first price, all bidders willing to buy at that price report how much they are willing to buy. The auctioneer then announces the demand at this price. Thereafter, the auctioneer raises the price and announces the demand at that price. The process continues; each time the auctioneer raises the price and announces the demand, until the total amount demanded is just below the total amount offered for sale. In this fashion, the price level is arrived at, and the auctioneer confirms that the second to last price is the highest price needed to complete the total offering amount. All bidders who offered the highest price and those who offered the second highest price are successful bidders. Those bidders who offered lower prices can also proportionately purchase at the amount they bid assuming there is anything left.

Since this is an open bid, the bidders know well the generally accepted value of the securities being auctioned. Therefore, from the bidders' perspective, this method reduces the dissatisfaction of the successful bidders because the price actually paid is at a point somewhere below the highest price offered.

Underwriting Methods Compared

As used in the securities market, the term "syndicate" or "syndicate underwriting" usually refers to a bond distribution method by which the issuer signs underwriting contracts with a group of banks or financial institutions to define relevant rights and obligations to ensure the successful execution of an offer. In China, this method is generally called underwriting.

There are two main features to consider in issuing T-bonds through underwriting:

1. The rights and obligations relationship between the issuer and the underwriters is defined by the underwriting contract, so insofar as determining the issuing terms and conditions is concerned, the issuer and the underwriters rank *pari passu*. This is different from the relationship between seller and buyer when administrative allocation and apportioned purchasing are used.

2. Underwriters are required to purchase the bond themselves if they fail to distribute all the bonds allocated to them. For this reason, the T-bond issue will close once the underwriting contract is signed.

In Germany and Japan, the underwriting mechanism is typically used in government securities offerings. In recent years, both countries have introduced the auction method for issuing their government securities, especially for the distribution of treasury bills. However, underwriting still remains one of the primary methods used.

In Japan, some indirect issuing methods, including mandated offering and subscribed offering, prevail for the sale of mid- and long-term government securities issues. In mandated offerings, securities intermediaries are assigned as sales agents and are not responsible for unsold securities. In subscribed offerings, the securities are distributed by securities intermediaries, and the undistributed securities are subscribed to by the intermediaries. The latter mechanism is widely used in issuing T-bonds since it ensures the success of executions.

Mid- and long-term government securities (10-year coupon bonds and 5-year discount bonds) in Japan are issued through this method to a group of banks, securities intermediaries, and other financial institutions, the so-called group subscription. Using the group subscription mechanism, the first step is the execution of the subscription contract between the Bank of Japan and the subscribing group. Then government securities are distributed to investors. The T-bond subscription group in Japan consists of 839 members (as of 1990), among which 38 members are industrial representatives, responsible for negotiating issuing terms and conditions as an agent, chamber or association, and for signing the underwriting agreement on behalf of other members of the subscription group.

Basic Methods for Underwriting Treasury Bonds   Usually the underwriting syndicate is composed of one lead underwriter, several co-lead underwriters and dozens of co-underwriters. Normally, the lead underwriter signs underwriting agreements with other syndicate members to define their relationship. The lead underwriter may undertake either unlimited liability or limited liability. Since China adopted underwriting mechanism in 1991, a limited liability system has used.

The subscription portion of the underwriting syndicate can be either fixed or variable. The fixed portion (a specific amount) is used in Japan, while a variable portion (a changing amount) is used in China. The reason for this difference is that Japan has a more stable financial system, under which the fixed portion can be applied. The strong point of this method is that the underwriters have a clear picture of the amount they should subscribe so that they can arrange funds as soon as possible. Due to the changes in issuing methods and the financial system in China, the variable portion method allows greater flexibility. Since the adoption of the primary dealer system in 1993, the subscription amount has been 1 percent of the total amount to be issued.

Tap Method   Government debt administrators when issuing non-tradable bonds to retail investors and depositors often adopt the tap method. In some market-oriented economies, the tap issue is integrated with the auction and underwriting methods to distribute mid- and long-term tradable T-bonds.

In cases where a country has volatile treasury rates and enormous funding requirements, authorities in charges of government debt management may adopt the tap method with a view to ensuring its continuity and flexibility. In applying this method, there are two alternative approaches. One is direct distribution by brokers in the secondary market, which requires that the brokers first underwrite the T-bonds on an exclusive basis. From an investor's point of view, there is no difference between subscribing in the primary or secondary market. The other approach is agent selling of T-bonds to investors through the distribution platforms of banks and post offices. There are substantial differences between these approaches in regard to keeping pricing in line with market conditions.

If there are a great number of sophisticated securities intermediaries and fund managers in the T-bond market, then direct distribution in the secondary market is a better choice. If a country possesses a full-fledged retail network for the sale of T-bonds, it may sell them to retail investors through banking and post office systems. The government's debt managers can also encourage the banks and the post offices to sell the T-bonds through retailing outlets by adopting flexible measures (e.g., increasing sales commission). If banks are required to sell the bonds at lower than market price, it is even more necessary to grant them some preferential treatment.

To ensure the smooth execution of the sale, the government debt manager should try to make the coupon rate of the debut issue in line with the yields of comparable bonds in the market. If the debt manager can frequently tap into the market through brokers or its own branches, it is better to adopt the method of selling T-bonds to individuals in the secondary market through brokers. In such case, the manager can adjust the issuing price at any time in the light of changes in the market. If there is indication that the T-bond supply exceeds demand, then the issuing price may be adjusted to make it a little bit lower than the yield rate in the secondary market. When the market rates are declining, the government debt managers may raise the issuing price to some extent to reduce the flotation cost. In general, however, government debt managers should be very prudent in adjusting the T-bond's issuing price in light of changes in the market as these changes might be transitory, and repeated adjustments of the issuing price may make investors lose confidence in the bond market.

Distribution through the banking system may not be as flexible through agents; an extensive banking network may make simultaneous changes of this kind impossible because the unified coupon rate and selling price cannot be guaranteed.

To address the issue of making price adjustments to stay in line with market changes when bonds are distributed using banks or post offices, government debt managers should employ one or several debt instruments; the terms of each of these debt instruments should be standardized to attract investment of small investors. This is especially important when government debt managers intend to promote T-bonds to an extensive and diversified investor base. Substandard or fragmented debt instruments would lead to the discontinuity of the selling process.

A high degree of flexibility on the issuing terms is not only conducive to the seamless execution, but also helpful in achieving other objectives. Using the tap method for issuing of T-bonds, government debt managers may adopt more flexible methods to secure the most favorable issuing terms. For instance, at a time of interest rate decline in the market, government debt managers may stop, or slow down, new offers and resume them once they have raised the issuing prices and adjusted the issuing terms. In the case of rising interest rates, debt managers may make the issuing terms in line with yield rates in the secondary market, transferring T-bonds from the primary market to the secondary market.

By halting bond issues to ease the pressure on the supply side or by maintaining the T-bond's interest rate to prevent the market rate from declining further, this high level of flexibility helps ensure supply-demand dynamics in the market and supports the interest rate policies of the government or central bank. Moreover, in the primary market, a yield rate higher than the secondary market level may encourage investors to purchase T-bonds directly in the primary market, thus easing the demand pressure in the secondary market. When the central bank intends to alter investors' anticipation of future interest rates by adjusting yield curves, debt managers may assist the central bank in achieving this objective by adjusting the maturities of the bonds it issues. Regardless, whether government debt managers can achieve flexibility by taking advantage of the discrepancies between the primary and the secondary markets will depend on the level of development and the availability of professionals on T-bond market (i.e., whether the primary dealers can exercise their roles as market makers).

Fixed Bond Issue Schedules At present, most of the world's market economies have adopted fixed schedules so investors know well in advance and can prepare for treasury bond issuance. For example, the U.S. Department of the Treasury currently applies this fixed auction schedule: 3-month and 6-month treasury bills are auctioned once a week, 52-week bills once a month, 3-year and 10-year treasury notes once a quarter, and 30-year T-bonds twice a year.

Methods that Attract Individual Investors Individual income minus consumption expenditure constitutes one of the major sources of investment money for T-bonds. Therefore, an important component of various government debt policies is how to attract the individual (retail) investors. For example, the U.S. government has specially formulated its policy to attract individuals to purchase government securities. Most other countries have their own unique policies to attract these investors. Among them are:

- *Specially designed bonds*, usually nontradable savings bonds, targeted to individual investors. The main purpose of issuing the savings bonds is to stimulate individual investors' enthusiasm, especially those buy-and-hold-to-maturity investors. As the savings bonds are usually non-tradable, they minimize the individual investors' risk exposure.
- *Participation in non-competitive biddings*. For example, individual investors may participate in the non-competitive bidding for U.S. government securities, and subscribe at the average price of the successful competitive bidders.
- *Facilitation of individual targeted distribution*. This might include encouraging such financial policies as tax exemptions, Treasury Inflation Protection Securities (TIPS), or swap opportunities with other bonds, and so on.

China has employed many investor-friendly approaches—among them converting long-term bonds into short-term bonds, converting old bonds into new ones, and door-to-door service—which have resulted in very positive results in T-bond promotion.

In general, meeting individuals' demand for T-bonds is contrary to the objective of establishing an efficient and cost-effective T-bond market. In China, however, individual investors have played a leading role in the T-bond market for a long time, and, therefore, they are one of the major components of the T-bond investor base. At present, because of a lack of investment channels, these individual investors remain enthusiastic about T-bond investment. A decline in interest rates has also contributed to the rising enthusiasm for the bond market.

FEATURES OF TREASURY BOND ISSUANCE WORLDWIDE

From a worldwide point of view, the objective is to create an efficient and cost-effective treasury bond market, characterized by:

- *Interest rates determined by and adjusted to market supply and demand.* Since the sufficiency of market capital is a relative concept, supply and demand can be adjusted based on the interest rate, which is represented by bond prices in the market. When the interest rate is high, bond prices become low, and vice versa. From an issuer's perspective, supply goes up with higher price and down with lower price; therefore, the supply curve is an upward sloping. By contrast, in the view of the investors, demand goes down with higher price and demand goes up with lowe prices; therefore, the demand curve is downward sloping. The point where the two curves intersect is the equilibrium point (A). (See Figure 4.1.)

   When the interest rate rests at the intersection of the two curves, maximum proceeds will be raised at the lowest cost. Therefore, so-called cost-efficient funding requires that interest rate terms be fixed in accordance with the precisely calculated supply and demand.
- *Wholesale rather than retail market.* Retail distribution involves excessive procedures, long periods, and high costs, and therefore is not suitable as a primary offering method. The only exception to this rule is savings bonds, which are issued in this way by most countries. In most cases, the underwriting group is typically composed of banks and other intermediary institutions and individuals represent buyers in the secondary market.

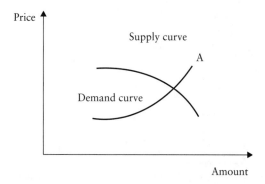

FIGURE 4.1 Equilibrium between Supply and Demand Curves

- *Participation of institutional investors.* Characterized by a stable capital base and long-term investment horizon, institutional investors are inherently perfect buyers of treasury bonds. Direct investments from institutional investors can help reduce costs and lengthen maturities.
- *Participation by foreign investors.* In developed market economies, treasury bonds held by foreign investors usually account for at least 15 percent of the total amount outstanding. Participation of foreign investors helps to create a reasonable holding structure and thereby increases the stability of the treasury bond market.

What China Can Learn from Issuing Patterns around the World

Developed countries typically adopt one or a combination of the issuing options described. Typically, they fall into these groups:

- U.S. and Italian pattern
- German, Japanese, and Canadian pattern
- British pattern

In the U.S. and Italian pattern, both countries apply a dominant or typical mode of public tender together with direct placement (see Figure 4.2).

In the German, Japanese, and Canadian pattern, there is dominant underwriting together with public tender (see Figure 4.3).

The British pattern is a combination of tap, public tender, and direct placement, characterized by tap (see Figure 4.4).

Because of differences in the various markets' historical development and specific conditions, issuance techniques adopted by various countries

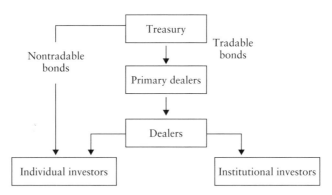

FIGURE 4.2 Public Tender with Direct Placement

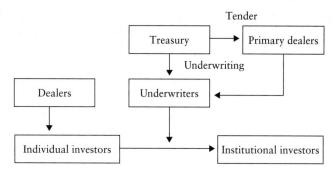

FIGURE 4.3   Underwriting with Public Tender

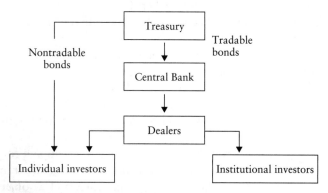

FIGURE 4.4   Tap Issue with Direct Placement

tend to be diversified. Figures 4.1 through 4.2 illustrate that, despite the existing diversity, primary markets for treasury bonds around the world exhibit quite a few properties in common.

Therefore, the development of China's treasury bond market should take into consideration the country's specific historic environment while following the path taken by most countries around the world.

From the study of issuance practices worldwide, we can conclude six things:

1. *The social, economic, and financial system has a great bearing on bond market development.* As was indicated in talking about theory, a financial system is built on a sophisticated institutional framework so that market participants can find value added in financial transactions. Lending money was not invented by capitalist societies, but it is only in modern societies that the institutional arrangement (the banking

industry, which is the intermediary between borrowers and investors) makes it possible to mobilize financial resources so effectively.

As indicated, comparative financial advantages can be realized only through exchange, and the market provides a cost-effective place for that exchange. Therefore, if a loan can be transacted in the market, financing will be more effective. Since a bond is a tradable loan, the bond market is a cost-effective place to trade loans. However, bond trading has to take place within an institutional framework, which includes, among other things, a legal, financial, and regulatory infrastructure, which needs to be created by through a primary financial exchange and primary bond market.

The United States experienced institutional evolution for many years in order to build up its bond market. Other countries, such as China, can develop a bond market through their primary financial exchange to accelerate this process. Government would play an important role in this process, but that role would be confined to the primary financial exchange and the primary bond market.

Ideally, a sound banking system and a developed money market are necessary preconditions of a sound bond market. When an economy in transition is building up its bond market, all these conditions are not necessarily met.

China's example convincingly proves that a developing country can develop its bond market even when not all its institutional arrangements have been put in place. Based on our experience, a clear objective and an appropriate sequence are important to a successful bond market. For example, China built up its institutional investor base and financial intermediary industry paving the way for the establishment of a primary bond market.

Insofar as the primary financial exchange is concern, the incentive system is important. When China built up its bond market, it was very committed to its incentive system; for example, the quote-based bidding method was used as was the combination of underwriting and auction to sell securities.

Beyond the primary exchange, the less government participation, the better. As was also indicated, the market participants themselves must diversify the market instruments through financial innovation. In this respect, financial deregulation is crucial for institutional evolution.

2. *Opening of the secondary bond market gave incentives to market participants*, and gradually the institutional investor base and financial intermediary industry was established, although when the bond market reform program was initiated, there was no money market and no

institutional investor base. Therefore, the transfer market, the preliminary stage of secondary market, was a necessary step in developing the bond market. However, without a primary market, the secondary market cannot be fully established. The process that followed was an interaction between the primary and secondary markets.

3. *The selling format may differ across countries.* Each country's issuance pattern is the result of its historical evolution, which contains that country's unique features; thus, no universally applicable models are available. The U.S. model relies on a primary dealer system while the United Kingdom relies on a central bank as its agent, through whose network the government securities are sold. The heterogeneous nature of the selling format was due to the historical institutional development of each country.

We believe the U.S. model is superior to the U.K. model as it gives more incentive to market participants, such as primary dealers. However, changing this system will incur transaction costs. Therefore, before deciding whether to make this change, marginal benefits and marginal transaction costs must be compared.

The selling format in China is similar to that in the United States in that both use the primary dealer system, but in China, for historical reasons, primary dealers are mainly banks, and banks are not as active as securities firms. The long-term syndicate contract functions as a supplement to the primary dealer system. The syndicate contract restricts the primary dealers' behavior, and primary dealers are asked to bid in each auction for both government securities and financial debentures.

4. *Nations tend to utilize a major form supplemented by other forms* rather than a single mode to meet the requirements of diversified financing and investment channels in the capital market. In the United States, savings bonds have been issued for many years to target the individual investors and encourage thrift. In China, similarly, certificate savings bonds are issued to tap individual savings.

5. *Diversified instruments.* While the marketable and non-marketable securities are issued to satisfy institutional investors and individual investors respectively, the diversified marketable securities mainly cater to the heterogeneous institutional investors. The specified timetable for the issuing bonds and the specificity of the bonds themselves are more convenient for investors and substantially reduce transaction costs.

6. *The more market participation, the more competitive and the fairer the pricing.* Public tender is becoming a major and increasingly dominant issuance mode. For instance, public tender has been accounting for

more and more shares in Japan's syndicate underwriting, based on the belief that public tender is the most efficient way to identify the interest rate determined by market supply and demand.

This analysis tells us that the development of China's treasury bond market should be directed toward public tender and that it should be implemented on a step-by-step basis, which is what most countries have done and are continuing to do. We should also bear in mind that reliance on any single mode is not advisable and that the specific circumstances of China's treasury bond market should be carefully examined. Although private placement was used on many different occasions, competitive biding turned out to be more efficient for selling and fairer for pricing.

CHAPTER 5

Path to a Cost-Efficient Treasury Bond Market

CHANGES IN CHINA'S TREASURY BOND ISSUING TECHNIQUES

Chapter 1 introduced China's debt capital market from a historical perspective. We've seen how the macro-economic environment changes, especially how institutional changes exert bearing on bond market. The primary exchange—the exchange between government and market participants—is the driver of market development. Innovative ideas and technological progress contribute to market development only to the extent that they help save the transaction cost, exogenous and endogenous, of the exchanges.

As indicated in Chapter 2, the experiences of international market development also provide evidence to underpin the institutional economic engineering (IEEN) framework. This chapter examines issuance techniques to illustrate how they have improved the primary bond market by facilitating transaction efficiency, and thereby benefit both issuers and investors, the main players of primary bond exchange.

Since 1981, China has seen four stages of treasury bond selling techniques (see Table 5.1):

1. Administrative allocation from 1981 to 1990
2. Underwriting from 1991 to 1993
3. Over-the-counter (OTC) sale in 1994 and 1995
4. Tender from 1996 on

Assignment-Based Subscription Method

After 1996, treasury bond issuance, at least in principle, took the form of OTC sales for certificate bonds and tenders for book-entry bonds. Policy-based financial bonds were offered on a book-entry and tender basis.

TABLE 5.1 Treasury Bond Issuance, 1981 to 2003

Year	Administrative Allocation	Underwriting	OTC Sale	Tender
1981–1990	Bearer			
1991		Bearer		
1992		Bearer		
1993	Bearer	Book-entry		
1994		Bearer	Certificate	
1995		Bearer	Certificate	Book entry
1996			Certificate	Book entry
1997			Certificate	Book entry
1998			Certificate	Book entry
1999			Certificate	Book entry
2000			Certificate	Book entry
2001			Certificate	Book entry
2002			Certificate	Book entry
2003			Certificate	Book entry

Administrative allocation issuances include assignment and assignment plus OTC sales. The former was applied from 1981 to 1985, at the early stage of T-bond issuance; the latter was applied from 1985 to 1990 and again in 1993. OTC sales were carried out through banks. Individual investors were not forced but encouraged to buy government bonds (see Table 5.2).

A quota-based administrative allocation, which had its roots in the planned economy of the 1950s, was adopted. Although it was simple, this method had five disadvantages.

TABLE 5.2 Administrative Allocation Issuances

1991	Central underwriting
1992	Local underwriting
1994	Central underwriting plus OTC sales of savings bonds
1991	Central underwriting
1992	Local underwriting
1994	Central underwriting plus OTC sales of savings bonds

1. *Bond distribution was incorrectly targeted.* Instead of focusing on financial institutions, the quota-based administrative allocations were mainly sold to state-owned enterprises (SOEs) and government institutions, many of which were in urgent need of funds rather than a source of surplus funds, as well as to individuals. Although individuals in both urban and rural areas had some savings, the lion's share of that money was held in bank deposits. Individuals usually used their cash in hand for emergencies; thus it was not available for investment in long-term T-bonds. Without a market-oriented interest rate system, the cash available to individuals generally was deposited into banks, not invested in T-bonds.

2. *The price of the T-bond was not being used as a benchmark for other securities in the capital market, as was the case in many developed countries, because its price was distorted by the administrative allocation.* Between 1981 and 1986, the disorderly fluctuation in T-bonds yields had a destructive effect on the established market mechanism. It is no surprise that when T-bonds were issued through administrative allocation, their purchase was seen as an obligation. As a result, rather than attaching any importance to the value of bonds, bondholders would sell them cheaply if they needed cash. In practice, this meant that individual investors would sell off their holdings as soon as the bonds were tradable, which usually led to sharp price declines in the secondary market. This, in turn, had a negative impact on the price at which new T-bonds could be issued. This phenomenon took place only in the early days of secondary market trading and was the result of the restriction on trading price and the limited number of markets. The sell-off by individuals during this period was mainly due to the fact that there had been no market for a long time. As the market gradually developed, individual investors became buyers and holders.

3. *The cost to issue the bonds increased.* Since individual investors were the targeted buyers of T-bonds, to meet their demand, the face value of a bond had be kept low, which raised the costs of printing, transporting, and storing each issue.

4. *Selling large amounts of T-bonds to individuals inevitably increases the administrative and selling expenses as well as the amount of time required to issue the bond.* Delays in issuing bonds made them vulnerable to changes in market conditions, which not only had negative effect on the funding needs of the National Treasury but also made it impossible to issue the bonds at the pre-set terms. Issuing scripless bonds to individuals was not feasible since at this time people most preferred to hold paper securities.

5. *Liquidity problems.* Most individual investors bought and held T-bonds for a long time, which is counterproductive to boosting bond liquidity. Throughout the 1980s, T-bonds were held until maturity rather than traded. Although in 1988 the T-bonds were negotiable in 62 cities, it was more a like redemption before maturity than a real trade in the bond market. This lack of liquidity brought complaints from institutional investors, which in turn led to higher selling costs: a vicious circle.

In the final analysis, administrative allocation had a negative effect on the treasury's reputation, increased the cost of issuing bonds, and diminished their inherent value. It was inevitable that the administrative allocation method would be transformed into the market-oriented method.

Figure 5.1 shows the straightforward techniques of administrative allocation.

Market-based Issuance Techniques: Overview

Since 1991, market-oriented reform has been under way. Underwriting syndication marked the start of this era. Underwriting was used from 1991 to 1994 (see Table 5.3).

Underwriting syndication is appropriate for unsophisticated issuers, underwriters, and investors, whereas tender makes more demands on both issuers and underwriters.

The 1996 tender issue had two forms: (1) The primary form featured a preset base quota and range to affect supply and demand; (2) the second is characterized by the absence of limitations and greater market orientation (see Table 5.4).

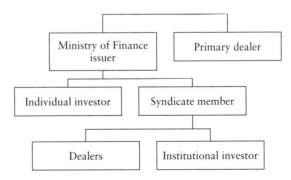

FIGURE 5.1   Administrative Allocation:
Organization Structure of Tender Issuance

TABLE 5.3 Underwriting Issuances

1981–1985	Assignment
1985–1990, 1993	Assignment plus OTC sales

Note: In central underwriting, the Ministry of Finance signs underwriting contracts directly with each financial institution; in local underwriting, local branches of the Ministry sign underwriting contracts with local financial institutions on its behalf.

Tender Issue Techniques

As used in China, tender issue techniques can be classified according to the bidding format, tender type, tender mode, subject matter, base quota/non-base quota, surplus/full, range/non-range, and pricing (see Table 5.5 for details).

As indicated in Figure 5.2, in the tender issuance of marketable government securities, the Ministry of Finance places its bond securities through two basic channels: primary dealer network that covers both stock exchange bond market and interbank bond market (the main institutions in the network are securities firms and insurance companies); and interbank syndicate network, which only covers interbank bond market (the main institutions are banks and insurance companies). Bonds have been distributed through both networks to the institutional and individual investors who engage in marketable government securities. In addition, the Ministry also placed its nonmarketable savings bonds via banks, post saving offices to the individual investors, such as older people and retired workers, who only contemplate their investment in nonmarketable bond securities.

Establishment of the Tender System

Bearer-form bonds are essentially only for administrative placement and targeting to individual investors, while book-entry bonds are tailored for tender selling techniques. The transaction instruments changed as China moved to market-based selling techniques.

TABLE 5.4 Tender Issuances

1st to 7th issues of 1996	Base-quota subscription, surplus tender, preset range, balance allocation
8th issue of 1996, 1st and 4th issues of 1997	No base quota, no range, variable price, quadratic weighting, full tender

TABLE 5.5 Tender Issue Techniques

Year	Bidding Format	Type of Bid	Tender Mode	Subject Matter	Base Quota/ Non-Base Quota	Surplus/ Full	Range/ Non-Range	Pricing
1-year bonds, 1995	Manual	Sealed bid/ descending order	Multiple price	Payment term	Base quota	Surplus	Preset range	Fixed
1-year bonds, 1996	Electronic	Sealed bid/ descending order	Single price	Price	Base quota	Surplus	Preset range	Fixed
6-month bonds, 1996	Electronic	Sealed bid/ descending order	Single price	Price	Base quota	Surplus	Preset range	Fixed
3-year bonds, 1996	Electronic	Sealed bid/ descending order	Single and multiple price	Payment term	Base quota	Surplus	Preset range	Fixed
1-year bonds, 1996	Electronic	Sealed bid/ descending order	Single price	Price	Base quota	Surplus	Preset range	Fixed
3-year bonds, 1996	Electronic	Sealed bid/ descending order	Single price	Price	Base quota	Surplus	Preset range	Fixed
10-year bonds, 1996	Electronic	Sealed bid/ descending order	Single price	Yield	Base quota	Surplus	Preset floor	Fixed
3-year bonds, 1996	Electronic	Sealed bid/ descending order	Single price	Yield	Base quota	Surplus	Preset floor	Fixed
7-year bonds, 1996	Electronic	Sealed bid/ descending order	Multiple price	Yield	Non-base quota	Full	Non-range	Variable
1st issue of 1997	Electronic	Sealed bid/ descending order	Multiple price	Price	Non-base quota	Full	Non-range	Variable
4th issue of 1997	Electronic	Sealed bid/ descending order	Multiple price	Yield	Non-base quota	Full	Non-range	Variable

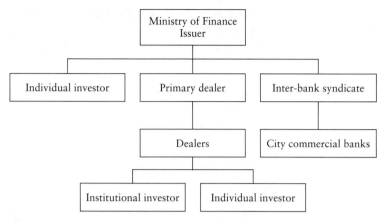

FIGURE 5.2 Organization Structure of Tender Issuance

Need for Ongoing Reform

Since underwriting syndication was introduced in 1991, T-bond issuing regimes have become increasingly market-oriented. However, as long as interest rates are not market-determined, the underwriting syndication technique represents only a change in the way T-bonds are distributed rather than a substantial transformation from administrative allocation to full-fledged market-oriented selling techniques. Therefore, it is possible, when prices derail from market yield, that selling would once again encounter setbacks. Under such circumstances, among the available selling methods, whichever is convenient is likely to be selected. As the administrative allocation is a ready-made method, it is more likely to be resumed. The return of administrative allocation in 1993 is a case in point.

Based on the experiences of most nations, the improvement of selling techniques is the key to ensuring a smooth and stable treasury bond market.

Tender Issues in China: Patterns and Features

Tender issue of treasury bonds breaks down into different types: multiple-price tender and single-price tender by award price; price tender, yield tender, and payment term tender classified by bidding objects; multiple-round tender and one-time tender by tender stages; and full tender and surplus tender by tender size.

Base Quota Subscription, Range Bidding, Surplus Tender, and Balance Allocation

In the early stages of China's T-bond market, the Ministry of Finance faced a difficult problem: There was little incentive for primary dealers to participate in the bidding. Differentiated base-quota allocation was imposed on primary dealers to force them to participate in bidding in the hopes of promoting demand for treasury bonds. In addition, a bidding range was also imposed. Because there was only limited number bond instruments, and because sophisticated bidders were lacking, a pre-set range set to keep the award price within reasonable limits was necessary. Also, since the early bidders tended to band together to manipulate the market, a pre-set range also prevented these tender issues from failing as the result of the manipulations.

Tender issues in 1996 were largely conceived as surplus tender (i.e., in excess of intended issue volume) (see Table 5.6).

Since 1996, surplus tender, which combines quota subscription plus tender (used in German T-bill issuance), and quota subscription plus tender (used in Japanese coupon treasury bond issuance) have been introduced, leveraging the pricing mechanisms of both the English and Dutch tender methods, but they are structured to reflect China's specific conditions as well as international practices.

Unlike tender modes adopted by United States and other developed nations (e.g., full tender in the United States), this surplus tender involves only part of the total issue. The underwriting part has no connection with the tender part in a Japanese issue; however, the two parts are closely combined in China (i.e., the quota part would depend on the tender result, which means that tender is used throughout the issuing process).

Discretionary Bidding, Variable Price, Quadratic Weighting, and Full Tender
During the trial period, base quota subscription, range bidding, surplus tender, and balance allocation proved successful in that they effectively boosted the demand for new issues. An undesirable outcome emerged: The intense competition for desirable price in the bidding process often resulted in an award price at the high end of the price range or the low end of yield range, and the lower-than-market-level yield depressed the enthusiasm of both underwriters and investors. Therefore, an optimized pattern of

TABLE 5.6 Tender Issuance Modes

Tender Mode	Multiple Price (American Style)		Single Price (Dutch Style)	
Subject Matter	Payment Term	Yield	Payment Term	Price
Full tender				
Surplus tender	1-year bonds, 1995	No. 5, 1996	No. 4, 1996	Nos. 1, 2, 3, 1996

discretionary bidding, variable price intervals, quadratic weighting, and full tender was introduced. It had four features and advantages:

1. *Abolition of the base quota.* Since a mandatory base quota was no longer necessary, this part was transformed into a noncompetitive tender to which primary dealers were entitled.
2. *Elimination of predetermined ranges.* Bidders could bid at their discretion, which supports the establishment of a pricing mechanism totally based on supply and demand as well as an enhanced market-oriented process.
3. *Adoption of variable-price interval method.* Using a discretionary bidding system, variable prices can ensure that the bid prices are within a reasonable range. Variable prices feature a wider spread on the upside and a tighter spread on the downside. Thus, bidders are reluctant to bid too high or too low, so that a moderate bidding range can be ensured. For example, the second issue of 10-year book-entry coupon bonds in 1997 resulted in the price variations listed in Table 5.7. In addition, continued price bidding was required, in which bidders have to bid in consecutive order.
4. *Elimination of contingent bids.* Quadratic weighting means to set a range after the initial calculation of the weighted average yield (e.g., a weighted average yield of $+/-$ 50 basis points). Bids falling out of this range are automatically removed and excluded from the secondary calculation of the weighted average yield. This method was applied in the issues of seven-year coupon treasury bonds of 1996 and two-year zero-coupon treasury bonds of 1997, both of which were proven successful by tender results to be completely in line with the market.

TABLE 5.7 Price Variations in the Second Issue of 10-Year Book-Entry Coupon Bonds,1997

Scales	Increments
Below 9.0	0.5
9.0~9.6	0.2
9.6~9.8	0.1
9.8~9.9	0.05
9.9~10.1	0.02
10.1 and above	0.01

The issuance of 10-year coupon treasury bonds of 1997 introduced variable ranges in quadratic weighting (i.e., the secondary weighting range is determined by the first weighting average award price). Thus, unreasonably low yields are eliminated in cases of relatively low weighted average yields, thereby ensuring that the tender results are in line with the real yields in the market.

This complicated structure, is peculiar to China, worked well in this context. Our experience indicates that the first pattern works well when demand is low while the second works when demand is strong.

Mixed Tender Following the Dutch auction and American auction models, the Ministry of Finance introduced a mixed tender in issuing book-entry treasury bonds (the third issue) in 2004. Integrating the qualities of Dutch auction and American auction, the mixed tender provided lower issuing costs, allowed bidders to better understand the movement of yield curve, and fully exploited the price discovery function in treasury bonds tender.

According to the tender scheme released by the Ministry for the interest rate tender, the overall weighted average award rate would be the coupon of the current issue. Award rates equivalent to or lower than the coupon would be executed at the coupon rate; award rates up to and including 10 percent higher than the coupon rate would be executed at their respective award prices; award rates exceeding 10 percent higher than the coupon rate would be deemed invalid.

Compared with the Dutch auction where the award rate is set by the highest bid to absorb the issue, mixed tender with the award rate fixed at the overall weighted average rate would further lower the issuance cost and avoid the winners' curse effect of a American auction. For example, assume a minimum bid of 3.01 percent and a final marginal award rate of 3.5 percent, using the Dutch auction (single-price) interest rate system, the finalized marginal award rate becomes the coupon of the current issue. However, using the mixed tender method, the finalized weighted average award would be below 3.5 percent, undoubtedly lowering the coupon. Even if some bidders colluded to pull down award prices to maximize the volume of bonds, the final price remained unchanged.

This initiative helped activate the syndicate to participate more accurately in the bidding. However, mixed tender also has its own constraints:

- *Negative impact on the performance in the secondary market.* Under the mixed tender regime, bidders with investment pressure will be forced to present high bids with a small margin. However, the successful bidders whose award rates are within 10 percent higher than the coupon rate can take profits on the secondary market, which will distort the secondary market price.

- *Vulnerability to market manipulation.* Experience indicates that, if a bidder can succeed at a price lower than others can, he or she will spare no effort to take the advantage.

  The Salomon Squeeze in the early 1990s can serve as an example to show that when there is a monopoly of major bidders and excessive bidding from individuals, manipulation and conspiracy can happen. In addition to bidding in the primary market, Salomon Brothers purchased bonds in the names of its clients and transferred them to its own account, without telling its clients. In this way, over the course of several auctions, Salomon Brothers bought large amounts of U.S. treasury bonds and managed to control 94 percent of the outstanding two-year U.S. treasury bonds. When this was ultimately disclosed, Salomon Brothers was penalized US$290 million and the U.S. Treasury resorted to the Dutch auction.

- *Deficiencies in the tender rules.* Should participants' opinions vary and aggregate bids significantly exceed the tender size, according to the "overall weighted average" rule, it is possible that only bids below the coupon will surpass the size of the planned issue. Even on a fully sub-scribed basis, the weighted average award rate is determined according to the highest bid; other bids will also be subject to this calculation, which results in a price that is inconsistent with the secondary market yield.

Therefore, although the mixed tender can reduce the issuance cost while encouraging rational bidding, given its constraints, it is advisable to revise the rules in order to mitigate issuance risks and further improve the market.

Dual Tender Process   In August 2004, the China Development Bank (CDB) first launched a dual tender to set the bond coupon in the issue of 04-CDB-13 bonds. On November 17, 2004, the CDB conducted the tender issue of another two-year floating rate note (FRN) with the same value date and payment date as the August issue. Should the award rate of the August issue be higher than that of the November 17 issue, the August issue would be repaid at its own award rate; otherwise, the average rate of the two issues would apply. Rolling tender, as an innovative solution to uncertain interest rate movement and a low rate of bidder participation, would give investors insurance against uncertainty and thereby secure the primary offering.

Analysis of issuance terms shows that the issue of 04-CDB-13 was essentially a tender at the two-year forward rate three months hence and that the tender result could be revised or updated in favor of investors with reference to that rate. Therefore, this tender of 04-CDB-13 bonds was actually compound pricing of a forward rate with an embedded reset option.

The thirteenth issue of financial bonds adopted a forward pricing strategy with an issue date of August 11, value date and payment date of November 23 (an interval of 104 days), and delivery date at November 23, which meant that investors should set a current yield and then purchase a two-year bond at this level three months later. To be free from arbitrage, bidders would execute these two operations with the same level yield-to-maturity:

Alternative A: Invest in a 2Y + 104d financial bond, assuming its yield is $R_{2.3Y}$.

Alternative B: Invest in a 104d (3m + 12d) bond, assuming its yield is R_{3m}; and upon maturity invest in another two-year financial bond, assuming its yield is R_{2Y}.

In a developed market where arbitrage can be made without cost, the terminal values of Alternative A and Alternative B will be the same (i.e., both satisfy $(1 + R_{2.3Y})^{2+104/365} = (1 + R_{3m} \times 104/365)(1 + R_{2Y})^2$).

Based on this assumption, a theoretical pricing of the thirteenth issue of financial bonds is applicable. Select the 2.3-year financial bond of 030229 with a higher liquidity in the inter-bank market and a current yield around 3.90 percent. Since the yield of three-month People's Bank of China (PBOC) notes was 2.85 percent, it follows that:

$$(1 + 3.9\%)^{2+104/365} = (1 + 2.85\% \times 104/365)(1 + R_{2Y})^2.$$

The calculation result is $R_{2Y} = 4.05$ percent, which is the theoretical award rate of the thirteenth issue of financial bonds.

In the real market, this is impractical, largely because participants rarely reference the capital returns 104 days prior to the pricing date. During the bidding process, institutions care more about the comparison among traded bonds with outstanding duration of about 2 years, namely financial debenture (FD) 040209 and FD 040212. According to the performance of the secondary market, the current yield of FD 040209 was around 3.79 percent, while that of FD 040212 was around 3.81 percent.

Viewed from the perspective of option pricing, the 04-CDB-13 bonds is actually a European-style option with an embedded forward rate of a two-year CDB bond, a strike price of the when-issued interest rate, a term of 3.1 months (from August 11 to November 17, 2004), an exercise direction of selling, and an option coverage ratio of 50 percent (the option is exercised by raising 50 percent of the when-issued interest rates to the real rate instead of 100 percent, i.e., averaging the real award rate).

Due to lack of option markets, the upcoming transactions for the putable and callable bonds faced uncertainty amid the changing future macroeconomic environment. Since the administrative policy package went into effect in April 2004, this round of macroeconomic policy achieved immediate slowdown of investment and credit. Investors preferred to wait and see in this changing market. However, policy makers were mindful of possible relapses because of uncertainties with respect to investment, producer prices, and consumer price index remain loomed, and the fourth quarter could foresee another period of proactive policy. In addition, the bond market environment in the next three months was unclear, and the intrinsic value of the forward rate option could be comparatively higher.

Taking both factors into account, the at-issue yield of the thirteenth issue of financial bonds was unlikely to reach its theoretical level of 4.05 percent, but it should definitely be much higher than 3.81 percent in the secondary market. Insofar as the actual tender result was 3.9 percent, the intrinsic value of the option had been reflected to some extent.

In conclusion, rolling forward bonds not only represent a breakthrough in issuance practice, but also provide a key driver for investments and transactions in the bond market, a market base for the development of rational investors, and tools for managing market risks. With this new instrument, the issuers can grasp market opportunities, lock in returns, and minimize the impact of interest hikes in the future. With the price discovery function of this newly designed bond, enrichment of forward bonds, and more frequent transactions, investors can draw up the yield curve as a pricing reference and hedge interest rate risk, thereby boosting the secondary bond market.

Tender Issue in China   Price tender was carried out mostly for the issuance of short-term treasury bills, as T-bills tend to be issued at a discount.

The single-price Dutch auction was used to create competitiveness for the pricing of the treasury bonds to encourage bidders to offer higher prices. This method was designed for relatively unsophisticated bidders; at that time, in China, most bidders lacked market information and were not skilled bidders.

In order to encourage primary dealers to take part in the bidding process and increase the demand for the treasury bonds, as an incentive, successful bidders, were permitted to change the underwriting terms of their base quotas.

The bidder base was expanded from primary dealers to include financial institutions with high credit quality that, in turn, were applying to become primary dealers. To ensure sufficient demand for the treasury bonds, a comprehensive underwriter base as direct participants in the tender would then be guaranteed.

Unlike most countries in the world, multiple-price tenders were used less frequently by the Ministry before 1997 and the CDB undertook it after 1999 in order to stabilize bidding prices within a preset range.

The issuing patterns that are currently used in China have proven to be effective and to prevent auction failure due to collusion. It is recognized that the tender issue in China is more diversified and innovative than that in other countries.

Basic Parameters of a Tender Issue   Three factors need considered when designing tender techniques:

1. *Base quota.* Base quota refers to the proportioned subscription to an issue by a primary dealer of treasury bonds. At present, the minimum base quota is 1 percent of the total size of the issue. This rule has been in effect since the second issue of treasury bonds in 1996. A base quota for banks was introduced with the third issue in 1996, but with the fifth issue in 1996, it was changed to 1 percent, just as it was for underwriters.
2. *Base price.* The base price has three implications: (1) the ceiling price, (2) the distribution price, and (3) the minimum price that underwriters can afford. The base prices of the first, second, and third issues of 1996 were determined by the Ministry of Finance with reference to market conditions. Taking into account the correlation between base price and tender result, American auction +RMB3 was introduced with the fifth issue of 1996, capped by the base price of the previous tender of the same term ± RMB0.05. Thus, not only is the correlation between market price determined by the base price and the tender result, which allows underwriters to have a certain spread, but the market price is prevented from deviating significantly from the previous issue, avoiding large fluctuations in the market.
3. *Minimum price.* Minimum price refers to the lowest price that bidders can bid, which is determined by the Ministry in line with the actual market conditions. In the complex tender of the fifth issue in 1996, the minimum price was set as the weighted award price of the American auction −RMB0.3, but no less than the level of previous tender.

Advantages of a Tender Issue   A tender issue creates pressure on the demand side. This pressure comes from the base quota as well as the single price. Pressure on the underwriters is created by the difference between the base price determined by base quota and the award price (see Figure 5.3).

Assume A represents a given demand curve and that the supply curve—representing the Ministry treasury bond supply—is a straight line (indicating that the Ministry supply is a constant RMB20 billion regardless

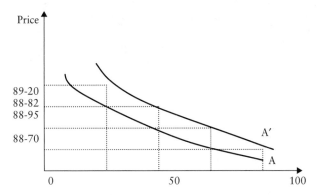

FIGURE 5.3 Case Study: Advantages of a Tender Issue

of the circumstances). As illustrated in Figure 5.3, the price at the intersection of the supply and demand curves is RMB88.7 (lower than the price range desired by the Ministry of RMB88.82 to 89.20), and market demand within this price range amounts to only RMB5 to 10 billion.

Since primary dealers are required to assume their base quotas, the demand curve should move up in tandem to form a new demand curve A'. The price at the intersection of the supply curve and the new demand curve is RMB88.95, within the approved price range of the Ministry. As a result, the total issue size of RMB20 billion is fully subscribed at an acceptable price.

The single-price mode encourages higher prices. Although the uniform price is determined by the minimum award price, that price is still higher than the weighted average price, which would be the outcome of multiple bid prices. As a higher bid is more likely to prevail, and the award price is not directly associated with that bidder's bid price, demand for T-bonds rises (see Figure 5.4).

With the preset base price and a minimum price, bid prices are contained within a specific range, thereby effectively controlling the award price.

TECHNICAL ISSUES

Supply and Demand Analysis of Tender Issues

Inherent in tender issuance of treasury bonds is a conflict of interest between issuers and underwriters. Issuers seek to reduce costs while underwriters pursue higher earnings. At the same time, the size of the offering desired by the issuers always correlates with the issuance cost, while the purchase

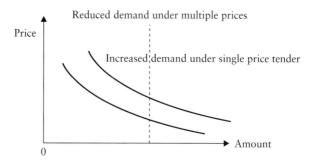

FIGURE 5.4   Advantages of a Tender Issue

volume desired by bidders is always linked to potential earnings. Issuers may vary the size of the offerings for different price levels, while underwriters may vary the amount they purchase at different price levels. The lower the price, the less the issuer wants to offer and the more the underwriters want to buy. The higher the price, the more issuers want to offer and the less the underwriters want to buy. In Figure 5.4, the price is the ordinate and the quantity is the abscissa. The two curves are derived by connecting all the points created by the price and quantity offered by the issuers and the underwriters respectively. Since the issuers are the suppliers of T-bonds, the issuer curve is also the supply curve. Similarly, since the underwriters are the purchasers of T-bonds, the underwriter curve is therefore the demand curve. From the issuers' point of view, the higher the price, the greater demand will be, so the supply curve is rising. From the underwriters' point of view, the higher the price, the less demand will be, so the demand curve slopes downward. As market participants are sensitive only to price in a certain range, both curves tend to be concave (see Figure 5.5).

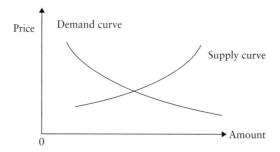

FIGURE 5.5   Supply and Demand Analysis of
Tender Issues

In practice, the Ministry of Finance, as the issuer of treasury bonds, faces a number of constraints; for example, the need to secure the budget; the supply and demand relationship; the size of the offering; the need to stabilize interest rates; and market affordability. When price is a priority, the issuer can find the desired price on the demand curve and then identify how much would be achieved through public offering versus how much could be achieved through in an alternative way. If public offering is the priority, the price at which the bonds are issued can be submissive; when price is the priority, the amount can be subsidiary.

Assume that the issuer pursues a policy where price is the priority and prices the proposed bond issue at RMB98. The corresponding point on the supply curve can be found and the corresponding amount on the abscissa axis can also be identified (RMB15 billion); this should be the amount that would have to be issued to secure the intended price. Conversely, if the issuer adopts a policy in which the amount is the priority and determines the desired offering size to be RMB20 billion, the corresponding point on the supply curve can be found and then the corresponding price (RMB96) on the ordinate axis can be decided (see Figure 5.6).

However, because of the limitations imposed by the National People's Congress of China and the rigidity of the government's budget, as a rule it is the amount of bonds to be issued that has to be secured. To this end, the government is forced to adopt a flexible price policy. Occasionally, in order to stabilize monetary and fiscal policies, the government must maintain the interest rate at a reasonable level. Thus provided with a less rigid amount constraint, a price priority policy may be applied.

At present, treasury bond issuance in China requires not only achieving the size of the issue, but also guaranteeing consistency between interest rates and the prevailing monetary policy. To meet this requirement, the base

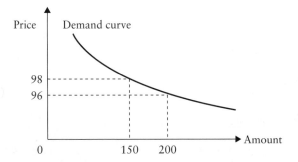

FIGURE 5.6 Case Study: Demand Analysis of Tender Issues

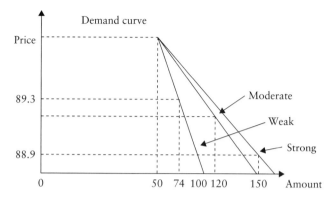

FIGURE 5.7   Application of the Base Quota Price and Price
Tender to Treasury Bond Issuance

quota subscription and price tender methods are currently used. As the base
quota price is fixed, the yield curve for this portion is flat, which maintains
the current interest level (see Figure 5.7).

Supply and demand analysis provides the basis for the formulation of
tender rules. Demand varies with the price, as illustrated in Figure 5.8(a). If
the supply is elastic and the curve is convex, then the supply curve can be
depicted as shown in Figure 5.8(b). Therefore, the Ministry must determine
the equilibrium point for the issue.

When an issue is contemplated, the Ministry may have two alternative
priorities for the offering—targeted amount and the level of price. The
supply curve is a straight line or horizontal in cases where price is the
priority and the supply curve is vertical when the amount is the priority.
If the government only wants to achieve a financing target regardless of
price, there is only a vertical supply curve. The demand curve is illustrated
in Figure 5.9.

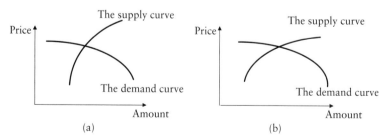

FIGURE 5.8   Equilibrium Analysis under Different Supply Elasticities

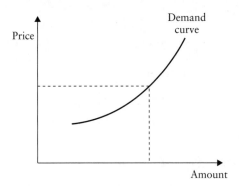

FIGURE 5.9 Demand Curve at Increasing
Levels of Fiscal Deficit Increase

When supply and demand are in disequilibria, the issuer has two choices:
(1) seek a new equilibrium price, or (2) adjust the issuing amount.

When the window for borrowing from the market is closed, the alternative way is confined to administrative allocation, which is based on an imbalance between supply and demand and therefore is not acceptable to investors, as illustrated in Figure 5.10(a). Seeking a new equilibrium can change the supply or the demand curve, even both of them simultaneously, as illustrated in Figure 5.10(b) and 5.10(c). The supply curve can be altered by reducing the bid amount or increasing the base quotas; the demand curve can be altered through varying the price.

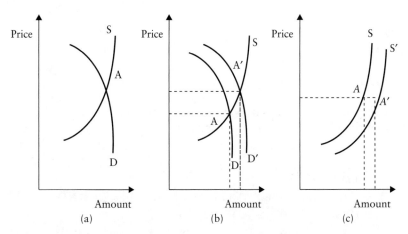

FIGURE 5.10 Administrative Adjustment on Disequilibria

Bond Market Math

Pricing T-Bills   Income is a key parameter to bond investors. Given the discount rate and the face value, the income of T-bills and discount bond can be calculated using this formula:

$$E = D \times F \times ND/360$$

where   E = income
        F = par value
       ND = remaining days to maturity

Calculating Price   For the issuer, when price is the primary consideration, it can be calculated using any of these formulas:

$$P = F - E$$
$$P = F(1 - D \times ND/360)$$
$$P = F/(1 + Y \times ND/360)$$
$$P = 1 - (D \times ND/360)$$

where   P = issuance price
        Y = yield
        D = discount rate
       ND = remaining days to maturity

Calculating the Discount Rate   Given the price, the discount rate can be computed with this formula:

$$D = (1/P)^{360/ND}$$

where   D = discount rate
        P = issuance price
       ND = remaining days to maturity

To compare the yield of coupon and zero-coupon bonds, the yield of the discount bond can be calculated using any of these formulas:

$$Y = (F/P - 1) \times 360/ND$$
$$Y = E/P365/ND$$
$$Y = (F \times D \times ND/360)/[F\,(1 - D \times ND/360)] \times 365/ND$$
$$= (D \times 365/360)/(1 - D \times ND/360)$$
$$= 365 \times D/(360 - ND \times D)$$

where   Y = yield
           F = par value
           P = issuance price
        ND = remaining days to maturity
           D = discount rate

Calculating the Relationship between Par Value and Price   The par value of discount treasury bonds equals the bond's future value at maturity, normally 100. In the event of prepayment, par value will deviate from 100, which can be calculated with this formula:

$$F = P\,(1 + Y \times ND/360)$$

where   F = par value
           P = issuance price
           Y = yield
        ND = remaining days to maturity

Calculating Yield in the Secondary Market   Assuming P1 is the purchase price and P2 is the selling price, the yield of discount bonds traded in the secondary market can be calculated like this:

$$[(P2 - P1)/P1] \times 360/ND$$

where ND = the remaining days to maturity

Calculating Allocation at the Final Award Price   If the bid amount at the finalized award price surpasses the offering size, the award amount is allocated pro rata. Let us assume an offering size of 10,000 and bid prices of 89.70, 89.69, 89.68, 89.67, 89.66, and so on. At 89.67, the aggregate bid amounts come to 9,000, still 1,000 short of the offering amount. If the bid amount at the next price level is 89.66 for 5,000, the award amount at this price level is equal to $500 \times 1000/5000 = 1000$. Therefore, each of the successful bidders at 89.66 shall be awarded at 20 percent of the amount for which they bid (see Table 5.8).

Calculating the Weighted Average Price in the Non-Competitive Tender   The weighted average price is applicable to investors participating in the non-competitive bidding for the discount treasury bonds. In a discount rate tender, the weighted average discount rate is calculated by the sum of each discount value, which is the product of par value and discount rate, divided by the aggregate par value. For example, bid prices for a par value of 10,000 are listed in the second column from left of the Table 5.9, the

TABLE 5.8   Calculating Allocation at the Final Award Price

Bid Price (RMB)	Bid Amount (RMB mm)	Award Amount (RMB mm)	Remarks
89.70	1000	1000	
89.69	1000	1000	
89.68	2000	2000	
89.67	5000	5000	
Subtotal	9000		Short of 1000
89.66	5000	5000 × 20% = 1000	1000/5000 = 20%, bidders at the finalized award price shall be awarded at a rate of 20%
Total	14,000	10,000	

TABLE 5.9   Calculating the Weighted Average Price in the Non-Competitive Tender

Price (RMB)	Discount Rate (%)	Yield (%)	Par Value of Bid (RMB mm)	Discount Value (RMB mm)	Remarks
979.6514	8.05		1000	8050	
979.6261	8.06		1000	8060	
959.2017	8.07		2000	16140	
897.8778	8.08		5000	40400	
979.5503	8.09		1000	8090	
Total			10000	80740	Weighted average price = 80740/10000
Minimum		8.05			
Maximum		8.09			
Weighted average yield		8.074			

derived discount rates are listed in the third column, par values of the bid are listed in the fourth column, discount values are listed in the fifth column, and the derived weighted average yield is 8.074.

Calculating Award Price in Yield Tender

The underwriting price = $100 \times (1 -$ coupon rate/award yield) $/(1 +$ award yield) $+ 100 \times$ coupon rate /award yield.

Calculating Bidder's Actual Cost and Yield To calculate bidder's actual cost, use this formula:

Bidder's actual cost = the underwriting price – commission – accrued interest

where Accrued interest = coupon $\times$ payment term/360

Assuming the coupon is 9.78 percent, the bidder's underwriting price is 100, and the commission is 0.38 percent, then the bidder's actual cost is RMB99.08.

To calculate the bidder's actual yield, use an HP12 Calculator, as illustrated in Table 5.10.

Calculating List Price With bidder's yield as the coupon and estimated market yield at listing as the yield, the listing price can be calculated using an HP12 calculator, as illustrated in Table 5.11.

TABLE 5.10 Calculating Bidder's Actual Cost and Yield

Keys	Function and Result
[CHS][PV]	Input bidder's actual cost = (99.08)
[PMT]	Input coupon = 9.78
[FV]	Input par value = 100
[n]	Input duration = 10
[i]	Calculated yield = 9.93%

TABLE 5.11   Calculating List Price

Keys	Function and Result
[PMT]	Input bidder's actual yield = 9.93
[I]	Input the estimated market yield = 9.6
[n]	Input duration = 10
[FV]	Input par value = 100
[PV]	Calculated present value (i.e., listing price) = RMB102.06

HOW TENDER ISSUES WORK IN CHINA

The first tender issue of the treasury bonds in 1996 was met with insignificant demand subject to the base quota. As the size of the offering increased, demand tended to diminish, creating an upside pressure on the issuance cost. Note that the base quota regime, in its early stages, was unique to China and is a transitory technique that made a great impact on the development of contemporary China's tender selling model. Figure 5.11 shows that, in the first four issues, supply and demand moved closer to each other as supply increased.

However, demand began to increase beginning with the fourth issue of 10-year book-entry treasury bonds, largely because it was properly priced. This and its excellent performance in the secondary market were the key drivers of demand for subsequent issues.

In 2000, the China Development Bank offered a total of 13 treasury bond issues. (The details of bids and awards are illustrated in Figure 5.12.)

In 2003, the CDB issued a total of 29 treasury bonds. (See Figure 5.13 for details.)

According to the data from 2000 through 2003, a relatively higher bid amount was recorded in the first half, but, in general, the trend was down.

Award Structure

In 1996, after the tender issue was fully implemented, the aggregate award of China's Big 5 banks [ICBC, CCB, BOC, ABC and Bank of Communication of China (BOCOC)] accounted for 26 percent of the total award; the remaining 74 percent was shared by other commercial banks and brokers (see Figures 5.14 and 5.15). Because the aggregate bid of the Big 5 represented only 21 percent, their success rate was evidently higher than that of other commercial banks and brokers throughout the year.

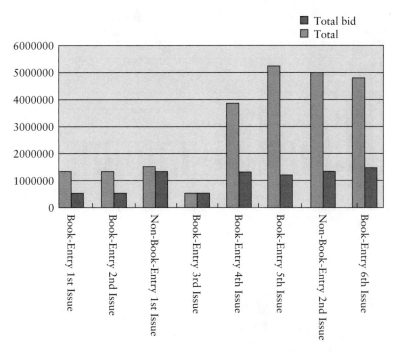

FIGURE 5.11   Tender Issues of Government Bonds, 1996

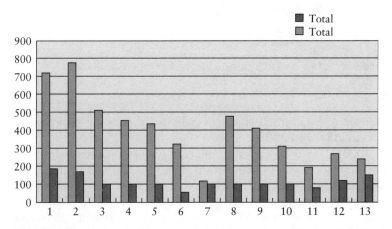

FIGURE 5.12   Bid and Award Details of CDB Financial Bonds Issued in 2000

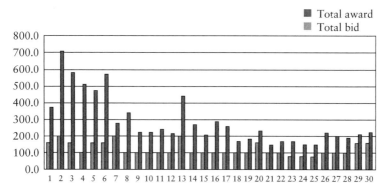

FIGURE 5.13 Bid and Award Details of CDB Financial Bonds Issued in 2003

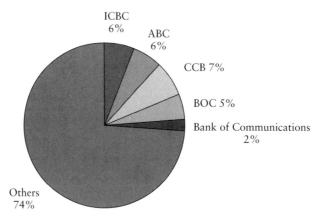

FIGURE 5.14 Award Structure by Investor of Tender Issue, 1996

Please refer to Figure 5.16 through 5.19 for the award structure of tender issues in 2000 and 2003.

As of 2000, the Big 5 banks accounted for 54 percent of the total award, an increase of 33 percent from 1996. In 2003, however, that number declined by 20 percent to 34 percent. (Figures 5.17a and 5.17b illustrate the award structure of CDB tender issues in 2000 and 2003.)

The Big 5 accounted for 44 percent of total award in 2000 and 33 percent in 2003. The drop of 11 percent demonstrates a lower investor concentration.

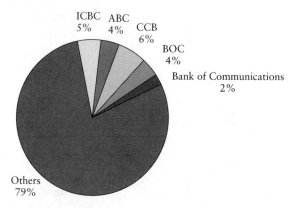

FIGURE 5.15 Bid Structure by Investor of Tender Issue, 1996

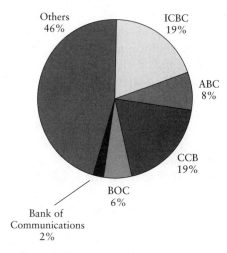

FIGURE 5.16 Award Structure by Investor of Tender Issue, 2000

Multiple- and Single-Price Combined Auction

One of the important innovations made by the Ministry of Finance since 1997 was its introduction, in April 2004, of the multiple- and single-price combined auction, or MSCA, as opposed to either the multiple-price or the single-price auction.

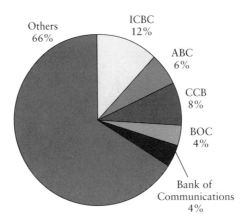

FIGURE 5.17   Award Structure by Investor
of Tender Issue, 2003

The MSCA is designed to take advantage of both the multiple-price American auction and the uniform-price Dutch auction. Based on the rule of MSCA, when yield is bid, the coupon rate is the weighted average bidding yield of all the bids. Different effective yield is applied to each bidders. The yields applied to the successful bids are based on how far their biding yield is from the calculated coupon rate. For those successful bidders whose bidding yield is equal to the coupon rate, the coupon rate is applied. For those whose bidding yield is 10 percent and below the calculated coupon rate, their own bidding yield is applied. Those whose bidding yield is above 10 percent of the calculated coupon rate fail in the auction.

Similarly, in case of bidding price, quantity weighted average price of all the bidding price is calculated as the issuer's selling price but bidders are subject to different prices depending on how far their biding price is from the selling price. For those whose bidding prices are higher or equal to the weighted average price, the weighted average price is applied. For those whose bidding prices are between 10 percent of the calculated weighted average and the calculated weighted average price, the successful bidding price is applied to each bidder in this category. Those whose bidding price is below 10 percent of the calculated weighted average bidding price fail for the auction.

Compared with single-price Dutch auction, MSCA can help to reduce the possibility of individual bidder winning a relatively larger share of successful bids. MSCA also takes advantage of the multiple American auction insofar as it stimulates rational bidding behaviour. For example,

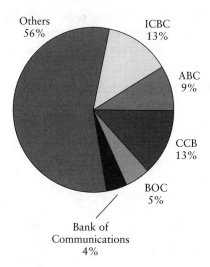

FIGURE 5.18 Award Structure by Investor of CDB Tender Issue, 2000

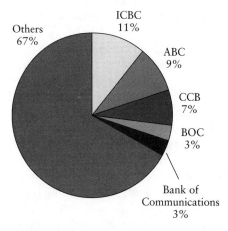

FIGURE 5.19 Award Structure by Investor of CDB Tender Issue, 2003

in the case of yield is bid, the successful bidding yield is applied if it is 10 percent and below the coupon rate (set based on the weighted average bidding yield), the bidders have incentive to bid for lower yield. To avoid failed bids, bidders tend to bid in a narrow range and the successful yields are closer to the weighted average yield. Under such circumstances, bidders are encouraged to improve their bidding techniques. However, if the views on the market are widely dispersed, the auction faces great challenges. Sometimes, in extreme cases, auction failure is possible.

Conditions Required before Implementation of the Tender Issue Method

The institutional development of China's treasury bond market over the past two decades has allowed it to achieve the conditions necessary for the introduction of the tender issue method. These preconditions include:

- *More sophisticated primary dealer system.* China established its primary dealer system for treasury bonds in 1993, when 13 banks and non-bank financial institutions were approved by Ministry of Finance and the China Securities Regulatory Commission (CSRC) to be the "first generation" of primary dealers in China. In 1995, another 50 primary dealers were approved by Ministry, the PBOC, and the CSRC, among them major specialized banks and commercial banks, which reinforce the foundation of the primary dealer system. Since 1993, primary dealers have been the dominant underwriters of treasury bonds in the primary market. After years of hard work, the legal rights and obligations of primary dealers are well defined, and today dealers represent financial institutions with high credit quality.
- *More participants, in-depth market expansion, and increased financial awareness.* Since 1995, more participants have been attracted to the treasury bond market, with both non-bank financial institutions, such as securities brokers and trust investment managers, and banks actively involved in the issuing and trading treasury bonds. At the same time, institutional investors and individual investors are all highly committed to the T-bond market. Along with a greater variety of treasury bonds and the introduction of new debt instruments, the T-bond market has grown in depth while most participants are becoming more sophisticated.
- *Comparatively well-developed secondary market with higher liquidity.* After eight years, the exchange market and the OTC market are now reasonably well established. More market instruments, better means for making transactions, and the enrichment of bond types, particularly the reform on the primary market, have resulted in increasingly higher liquidity of the treasury bond market.
- *Introduction of discount bonds.* Discount treasury bonds, whose yield was reflected in bond price, were issued for the first time in China in 1996.

- *Computerized systems to facilitate bidding process.* While not needed or useful for the administrative allocation or underwriting methods, computers are essential to the smooth operation of the tender system. Today, computerized electronic systems are widely used in treasury bond transactions and have greatly improved transaction efficiency and accuracy.

In short, after years of effort, the basic conditions were in place for a transition to the tender issue. As we have seen, the National Debt and Finance Department proactively was prepared for a theoretical framework of reform. In August 1995, the first trial of the tender issue method was conducted in Shanghai by the Ministry of Finance. However, interest rates in the primary market were still linked to the regulated deposit rate. Since bank deposit rates had yet to be liberalized, a market-oriented treasury bond market in the modern sense was not possible. As a result, all the treasury bond issuances in 1996 were based on the rates set by the State Council, and the final issuance price was determined based on the bids of primary dealers and other financial institutions.

CONSIDERATIONS FOR THE FUTURE

Theoretical Foundations for the Design of Tender Issue in China

In summary, the tender issue technique was designed to generate sufficient competition and thereby to achieve market cleared pricing. Demand can be boosted by means of a base quota or a smaller offering; a more non-competitive amount can cause a parallel movement of the demand curve, or it can be boosted by means of variable pricing to change the supply curve. The multiple-price auction can also keep the interest rate at a certain range or make it decline by increasing demand. Let us examine two possible scenarios.

Scenario 1 In the case of a multiple-price tender, the supply and demand curves move to the lower right, and the intersection of the two curves moves in parallel; therefore, the interest rate is unchanged and the offering size increases (see Figure 5.20). The effect of the variable price is that as the demand curve moves from D to D', the supply curve moves from S to S', and the intersection of two curves moves from A to A', with unchanged interest rate (r) and an increase in amount from Q to Q'.

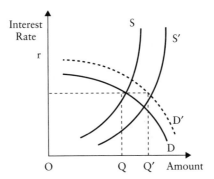

FIGURE 5.20 Supply Curve Moving with Demand Curve: Effect of the Variable Price

Scenario 2 The supply and demand curves change further, and the intersection moves to lower right, with a drop in interest rate and an increase in amount (see Figure 5.21).

As the demand curve moves from D to D′, the supply curve moves from S to S′, and the intersection moves from A to A′, resulting in a drop in interest rate from r to r′ and an increase in amount from Q to Q′.

Therefore, both variable price and base quota can alter supply and demand to lower the interest rate or raise the amount. Compared with base quota, the variable price approach is more market-oriented and effective. However, the combination of the two will generate market momentum and thereby help the issuer to achieve the intended target.

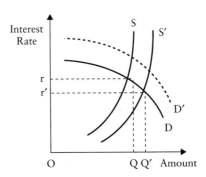

FIGURE 5.21 Supply Curve Moving with Demand Curve: Effect of Variable Interest Rate

Comparison of Issuing Techniques

Since the first test of the tender issue method on treasury bonds, innovations were added with each issue based on the knowledge gained from the previous transactions. Different selling techniques were tested during the mid-1990s, the early stage of tender selling.

- In the first issue, the Dutch, rather than the American, auction was introduced, along with a shift from administrative placement to price tender, and a capped bid amount.
- In the second issue, a minimum and a maximum amount for each bid were specified, and multiple price and consecutive price bidding were instituted. Also in the second issue of book-entry treasury bonds in 1997, quadratic weighting, variable correction range was tested.
- In the third issue, the bid amount was limited only by a floor; the ceiling was removed.
- The fourth issue introduced a two-stage complex tender that combined multiple-price with single-price tender.
- The fifth issue adopted the tender mode of nonrange, nonbase quota, variable price, and quadratic weighting.

As we have seen, the trial and application of various approaches led to huge successes in each issue. The next points remain to be determined as China moves forward.

Single-Price Tender versus Multiple-Price Tender   As mentioned, the multiple-price American auction is widely used worldwide. At present, both the United States and the United Kingdom have tested the single-price tender. Since the early 1990s, to get rid of the winners' curse, experiments on single-price tender have been carried out in the United States. Although the results of the experiments remain inconclusive, the single-price tender is supposed to help broaden the bidder base and boost demand, which is favorable to issuers; however, statistics on the test do not support this view. Therefore, although the single-price tender is theoretically preferable, its advantages are only partially demonstrated by the experiments.

Similarly, in the United Kingdom, the views regarding single-price versus multiple-price tender selling techniques are also widely divergent. The British government was awaiting the results of the U.S. government's single-price experiment. According to a survey conducted by the British government, end investors believe that single-price tender may motivate their participation in the tender; conversely, primary dealers (market makers) argued that the introduction of the single-price tender may lead to their curtailment of the total bid amount. For these reasons, to date the British government has no concrete plan to alter its routine issuance of gilt-edged bonds via multiple-price tender.

Preliminary indications in China show that the multiple-price tender works well when there is strong demand, while the single-price tender appears superior amid weak demand. However, it is premature to draw conclusions at this time.

Consecutive Bidding and Nonconsecutive Bidding   At present, consecutive bidding and nonconsecutive bidding are used concurrently in China. Consecutive bidding is used mainly by the China Development Bank, under which bidders can offer consecutive bids at specified price differentials (i.e., the price increment is set at 0.01 percent), and no price jump is allowed. In contrast, other issuers, such as the Ministry of Finance, prefer nonconsecutive bidding, where bidders can present random bids within a given range, without the consecutive requirement.

The major advantages of consecutive bidding is that concentrated allocation better reflects the consensus of investors in an uncertain market where investors hold different market views, and therefore it moderates the volatility of bidding price, especially in cases of successive issues. Conversely, nonconsecutive bidding tends to be more diversified, and therefore interest rates in successive issues are more volatile.

For this reason, nonconsecutive bidding is preferable when it comes to meeting the bidding requirements of financial institutions like banks and brokers who participate in bidding on behalf of their clients. Different requirements of bond yield by different clients of these financial institutions create a nonconsecutive yield range. When bidding on behalf of their clients, therefore, this method permits financial institutions to conveniently present nonconsecutive bids and avoids the need to compromise on bid range, which, in turn, helps them attract more clients.

From our point of view, it is best to apply consecutive bidding to short-term and other types of bond instruments with less diversified views on the market and nonconsecutive bidding to other bond instruments that are attractive to the more rational and sophisticated investor.

Supply and Demand Considerations   Tender issues should be designed to identify the price determined by supply and demand dynamics on a fully competitive basis. Excessive limitations are harmful to the result of tender offerings. However, under certain circumstances, a combination of tender and underwriting, together with the integration of base quota and variable biding interval, may be conducive to keep pricing in line with the market.

Insofar as the price bidding versus the yield bidding is concerned, practices in China indicate that price tender fits in well with discount treasury bonds and zero-coupon treasury bonds, while yield tender is preferable for coupon treasury bonds. If appropriate, when-issued trading can also be applied to provide market benchmarks. Given an underdeveloped and unstable treasury bond market in China, tender mode should be tailored to the specific supply and demand in each issue.

Variable Price and Quadratic Weighting　Driven by ambivalence, bidders normally hope to obtain a maximum quantity at the lowest price. Just as with the single-price tender, multiple-price tender increases bidders' ambivalence rather than leading them in a single direction, and entails a normal bidding price distribution, thereby ensuring a successful tender. Despite this, in case of multiple-yield tenders, the higher the yield the bidders offer, the less likely they are to succeed. This dilemma drives bidders to bid at a trade-off level.

Single-price tender may encourage bidders to bid at a higher price/lower yield, for the benefit of the issuers rather than the bidders. This would give rise to a disincentive to the bidders. Thus, the pros and cons of the two selling techniques are yet to be determined.

Multiple-price tender can capture the nature of bidding price distribution and narrow the bidding range, making the final weighted average price closer to the market price. Variable price may break down into four ranges: (1) sparse, (2) transitional, (3) dense, and (4) super dense. Given the relatively high marginal cost in the sparse range, bidders will try to avoid this bidding outcome. In spite of the lower marginal costs in the super-dense range, especially the small price increments, the chance of success is slim and therefore more competitive. This can not only ensure relatively low costs for issuers but also restrain bidders from bidding in a wide range. Consequently, multiple-price tenders help achieve fair pricing.

Quadratic weighting can be used to eliminate irrational bids. The inexperienced bidder's offer, which usually deviates from the average price, will be eliminated to ensure consistency between the tender yield and the real yield in the market.

To ensure a successful offering with tender techniques, these market infrastructures have to be specified as important institutional arrangements for the benefit of both issuers:

- *Gradually introduce a fixed tender issue schedule.* This would allow market participants to prearrange their market activities, including the raising and allocation of capital, among other financial needs.
- *Establish benchmarks for the T-bond market* for bonds of various terms and duration in order to provide extensive references for each issue. The successful issue of the 10-year coupon treasury bonds in 1997 owes much to the benchmarks set by the 10-year coupon treasury bonds and 7-year coupon treasury bonds issued in 1996.

How to Improve China's Tender Issue

There are four primary ways to improve China's program:

1. Set the tender date at the last Friday of every month.
2. After one year's trial, consider a single-price tender for discount treasury bonds and a multiple-price tender for coupon treasury bonds.
3. Proceed with nonrange, nonbase quota and variable-price tenders for coupon treasury bonds.
4. Combine competitive bidding with noncompetitive bidding, specifically 0.5 percent noncompetitive bidding for primary dealers and up to RMB5 million noncompetitive bidding for nonprimary dealers.

In light of the Chinese experience, the multiple-price tender should be integrated with when-issued trading. If when-issued transactions actually occur in China, the average-price tender might also be achieved more rapidly.

CHAPTER 6

Evaluation of Treasury Bond Issuance in China

ISSUING COST: COMPOSITION AND COMPARISON

In China, the issuing cost of the treasury bonds consists of interest cost and relevant offering expenses, including printing, marketing, offering costs, and settlement fees. "Printing expenses" refer to the costs incurred in the bond printing process, including plate making cost and physical bond printing cost. "Marketing expenses" refer to costs incurred by the Treasury Bill Promotion Committees and National Debt Service Bureau at different levels in promoting, instituting, and launching the issue. "Offering expenses" refer to service fees incurred in issuing the bonds and are paid to the syndicate members, or primary dealers. "Settlement expenses" refer to fees paid to the settlement banks.

From 1981 to 1990, issuing costs other than interest payments had been on an upward trend. Since the introduction of the underwriting system in 1991, the per-unit cost of noninterest payments substantially declined whereas interest payments increased to reflect direct or indirect market changes. However, expenses of this kind have been reduced gradually. After 1991, offering expenses of the treasury bonds in China has been kept to about 10 percent, due to the increased interest cost (see Table 6.1).

In analyzing the composition of offering expenses, it is necessary to consider the inflation rate. Since 1986, although nominal offering expenses have increased, given the inflation rate, the actual issuing cost has declined. Although the issuing cost of the treasury bonds in China has been rising in recent years, in general, its per-unit cost still remains low due to the general low deposit rate, which is perceived as a proxy of bond interest cost.

The efficiency of the primary treasury bond market in China has been improved greatly. Due to the growing savings rate and lower interest rates in the market, interest cost has declined significantly. In addition, service

TABLE 6.1 Issuing Costs of T-Bonds in China[1]

Type of Treasury Bonds	Issuing Cost Ratio (%)	Ratio of Issuing Cost	Settlement Fee (%)	Settlement Fee	Marketing Expense	Total Expenses[2]
T-bills 1981	0.5	0.2433	0.004	0.2647		0.508
T-bills 1982	0.5	0.21915	0.004	0.2668		0.48595
T-bills 1983	0.5	0.2079	0.004	0.2562	0.05	0.5141
T-bills 1984	0.5	0.21265	0.004	0.2632	0.05	0.52585
T-bills 1985	0.5	0.30305	0.004	0.3341	0.18	0.81715
T-bills 1986	0.5	0.31255	0.004	0.3567	0.36	1.02925
T-bills 1987	0.5	0.31435	0.004	0.3592	0.36	1.03355
T-bills 1988	0.5	0.4608	0.004	0.4625	0.36	1.2833
Subtotal in 1989						
T-bills	0.5	0.28035	0.004	0.3185	0.46	0.752183
Special treasury bonds	0.3	0.12852	0.003	0.2249		0.506753
Value-preserved treasury bonds	0.5	0.625	0.004	0.7121		1.490433
Subtotal in 1990						
T-bills	0.5	0.4673	0.004	0.5309	0.5	1.2482
Special treasury bonds	0.3	0.09804	0.003	0.1716		0.51964
Subtotal in 1991						
T-bills	0.5	0.99705	0.004	1.0369	0.48	2.27395
Special treasury bonds	0.3	0.05163	0.003	0.0749		0.36653
Subtotal in 1992						
Treasury bonds I	0.5	0.46075	0.004	0.5621	0.5	
Treasury bonds II						

Nonphysical treasury bonds	0.5	0.14125	0.004	0.1723		0.480217
Subtotal in 1993					0.5	
Treasury bonds I	0.5	0.36595	0.004	0.5429		1.057517
Treasury bonds II	0.5	1.13175	0.004	1.5573		2.855717
Nonphysical treasury bonds	0.5	0.07615	0.004	0.1092		0.352017
Subtotal in 1994					0.5	
6-month treasury bonds	0.3	0.15081	0.0006	0.0316		0.28241
1-year treasury bonds	0.3	0.24705	0.0006	0.0553		0.40235
2-year treasury bonds	0.5	1.42615	0.004	1.4376		2.96375
Certificate treasury bonds	0.5	3.50035	0.004	3.973		7.57335
Special treasury bonds	0.3	0.0588	0.003	0.1054		0.2642
Subtotal in 1995					0.5	
Bearer treasury bonds	0.5	1.25	0.004	1.435		2.785
Certificate treasury bonds I	0.5	5.2841	0.004	6.0027		11.3868
Book-entry treasury bonds	0.4	0.47556	0.0006	0.0799		0.65546
Special treasury bonds	0.5	0.1205	0.003	0.1296		0.3501
Certificate treasury bonds II	0.5	0.305	0.004	0.3465		0.7515
Subtotal in 1996					0.4	
Book-entry treasury bonds I	0.4	0.514711	0.0006	0.0869		0.646055
Book-entry treasury bonds II	0.3	0.62211	0.0006	0.1312		0.797754
Physical treasury bonds I	0.5	1.75	0.004	2.009		3.803444
Book-entry treasury bonds III	0.2	0.287973	0.0006	0.0887		0.421118
Book-entry treasury bonds IV	0.4	0.678121	0.0006	0.114		0.836566
Certificate treasury bonds	0.5	1.5	0.004	1.9836		3.528044
Book-entry treasury bonds V	0.4	1.0176	0.0006	0.3344		1.396444
Physical treasury bonds II	0.5	1.998186	0.004	2.1261		4.16873
Special treasury bonds	0.5	0.2	0.003	0.1728		0.417244

(continued)

TABLE 6.1 (*Continued*)

Type of Treasury Bonds	Issuing Cost Ratio (%)	Ratio of Issuing Cost	Settlement Fee (%)	Settlement Fee	Total Expense
Year 1997[3]					
Bearer treasury bonds	0.65	2.569385	0.4	1.58116	4.150545
Certificate treasury bonds (2-year maturity)	0.65	1.66647	0.4	1.02552	2.69199
Certificate treasury bonds (3-year maturity)	0.65	7.368725	0.4	4.5346	11.90333
Certificate treasury bonds (5-year maturity)	0.65	1.646385	0.4	1.01316	2.659545
Book-entry treasury bonds I	0.385	0.8232455	0.06	0.128298	0.951544
Book-entry treasury bonds II	0.385	0.5005	0.06	0.078	0.5785
Specially directional treasury bonds	0.57	0.167295	0.3	0.08805	0.255345
Year 1998[4]					
Certificate treasury bonds	0.65	7.928115	0.4	4.87884	12.80696
Certificate treasury bonds	0.65	6.372535	0.4	3.92156	10.2941
Special treasury bonds	0.18	0.7623	0.3	1.2705	2.0328
10-year coupon treasury bonds (I)	0.1	0.7	0.06	0.42	1.12
10-year coupon treasury bonds (II)	0.1	0.3	0.06	0.18	0.48
Book-entry treasury bonds	0.22	0.198	0.06	0.054	0.252
Specially directional treasury bonds	0.57	0.200469	0.3	0.10551	0.305979
Directional treasury bonds	0.4	0.24	0.3	0.18	0.42

Year 1999[5]

Certificate treasury bonds I	0.65	2.275	0.4	1.4	3.675
	0.65	0.975	0.4	0.6	1.575
Certificate treasury bonds II	0.65	2.275	0.4	1.4	3.675
	0.65	0.975	0.4	0.6	1.575
Certificate treasury bonds III	0.65	2.457	0.4	1.512	3.969
	0.65	0.9815	0.4	0.604	1.5855
Book-entry treasury bonds I	0.22	0.396	0.05	0.09	0.486
Book-entry treasury bonds II	0.22	0.352	0.05	0.08	0.432
Book-entry treasury bonds III	0.22	0.2068	0.05	0.047	0.2538
Book-entry treasury bonds IV	0.22	0.44	0.05	0.1	0.54
Book-entry treasury bonds V	0.22	0.3597	0.05	0.08175	0.44145
Book-entry treasury bonds VI	0.22	1.32	0.05	0.3	1.62
Book-entry treasury bonds VII	0.22	0.3586	0.05	0.0815	0.4401
Book-entry treasury bonds VIII	0.22	0.4257	0.05	0.09675	0.52245
Book-entry treasury bonds IX	0.22	0.33	0.05	0.075	0.405
Book-entry treasury bonds X	0.22	0.352	0.05	0.08	0.432
Book-entry treasury bonds XI	0.22	0.154	0.05	0.035	0.189
Book-entry treasury bonds XII	0.22	0.6424	0.05	0.146	0.7884
Directional treasury bonds (I)	0.4	0.08	0.05	0.01	0.09
Directional treasury bonds (II)	0.4	0.16	0.05	0.02	0.18

Year 2000[6]

Certificate treasury bonds I	0.65	0.702	0.4	0.432	1.134
	0.65	2.2295	0.4	1.372	3.6015
	0.65	0.3185	0.4	0.196	0.5145
Certificate treasury bonds II	0.65	0.78	0.4	0.48	1.26
Certificate treasury bonds III	0.65	3.12	0.4	1.92	5.04
	0.65	2.0735	0.4	1.276	3.3495
Book-entry treasury bonds I	0.22	0.44	0.05	0.1	0.54
Book-entry treasury bonds II	0.22	0.616	0.05	0.14	0.756

(*continued*)

TABLE 6.1 (*Continued*)

Type of Treasury Bonds	Issuing Cost Ratio (%)	Ratio of Issuing Cost	Settlement Fee (%)	Settlement Fee	Total Expense
Book-entry treasury bonds III	0.22	0.44	0.05	0.1	0.54
Book-entry treasury bonds IV	0.22	0.308	0.05	0.07	0.378
Book-entry treasury bonds V	0.22	0.44	0.05	0.1	0.54
Book-entry treasury bonds VI	0.22	0.2772	0.05	0.063	0.3402
Book-entry treasury bonds VII	0.22	0.44	0.05	0.1	0.54
Book-entry treasury bonds VIII	0.22	0.2244	0.05	0.051	0.2754
Book-entry treasury bonds IX	0.1	0.5	0.05	0.25	0.75
Book-entry treasury bonds X	0.22	0.264	0.05	0.06	0.324
Book-entry treasury bonds XI	0.1	0.2	0.05	0.1	0.3
Book-entry treasury bonds XII	0.22	0.5544	0.05	0.126	0.6804
Directional treasury bonds (I)	0.4	0.152	0.05	0.019	0.171
Directional treasury bonds (II)	0.4	0.8	0.05	0.1	0.9
Year 2001					
Certificate treasury bonds I	0.65	3.12	0.4	1.92	5.04
	0.65	2.08	0.4	1.28	3.36
Certificate treasury bonds II	0.65	2.275	0.4	1.4	3.675
	0.65	0.975	0.4	0.6	1.575
Certificate treasury bonds III	0.65	2.275	0.4	1.4	3.675
	0.65	0.975	0.4	0.6	1.575
Book-entry treasury bonds I	0.22	0.44	0.05	0.1	0.54
Book-entry treasury bonds II	0.22	0.44	0.05	0.1	0.54
Book-entry treasury bonds III	0.22	0.264	0.05	0.06	0.324
Book-entry treasury bonds IV	0.26	0.312	0.05	0.06	0.372
Book-entry treasury bonds V	0.22	0.396	0.05	0.09	0.486
Book-entry treasury bonds VI	0.22	0.44	0.05	0.1	

Book-entry treasury bonds VII	0.26	0.624	0.05	0.12	0.744
Book-entry treasury bonds VIII	0.18	0.36	0.05	0.1	0.46
Book-entry treasury bonds VIV	0.22	0.44	0.05	0.1	0.54
Book-entry treasury bonds X	0.22	0.44	0.05	0.1	0.54
Book-entry treasury bonds XI	0.26	0.416	0.05	0.08	0.496
Book-entry treasury bonds XII	0.22	0.44	0.05	0.1	0.54
Book-entry treasury bonds XIII	0.22	0.44	0.05	0.1	0.54
Book-entry treasury bonds XIV	0.22	0.44	0.05	0.1	0.54
Book-entry treasury bonds XV	0.22	0.44	0.05	0.1	0.54
Book-entry treasury bonds XVI	0.18	0.4752	0.05	0.132	0.6072
Year 2002[7]					
Certificate treasury bonds I	0.42	1.764	0.3	1.26	3.024
	0.42	0.756	0.3	0.54	1.296
Certificate treasury bonds II	0.42	0.63	0.3	0.45	1.08
	0.42	0.63	0.3	0.45	1.08
Certificate treasury bonds III	0.42	0.7035	0.3	0.5025	1.206
	0.42	0.7035	0.3	0.5025	1.206
Certificate treasury bonds IV	0.42	0.5166	0.3	0.369	0.8856
	0.42	0.483	0.3	0.345	0.828
Book-entry treasury bonds I	0.12	0.24	0	0	0.24
Book-entry treasury bonds II	0.12	0.432	0	0	0.432
Book-entry treasury bonds III	0.12	0.24	0	0	0.24
Book-entry treasury bonds IV	0.08	0.208	0	0	0.208
Book-entry treasury bonds V	0.16	0.416	0	0	0.416
Book-entry treasury bonds	0.12	0.552	0	0	0.552
Book-entry treasury bonds VII	0.08	0.208	0	0	0.208
Book-entry treasury bonds VIII	0.08	0.212	0	0	0.212
Book-entry treasury bonds IX	0.12	0.20796	0	0	0.20796
Book-entry treasury bonds X	0.12	0.24	0	0	0.24
Book-entry treasury bonds XI	0.12	0.24	0	0	0.24

(continued)

TABLE 6.1 (*Continued*)

Type of Treasury Bonds	Issuing Cost Ratio (%)	Ratio of Issuing Cost	Settlement Fee (%)	Settlement Fee	Total Expense
Book-entry treasury bonds XII	0.08	0.1528	0	0	0.1528
Book-entry treasury bonds XIII	0.16	0.384	0	0	0.384
Book-entry treasury bonds XIV	0.12	0.2688	0	0	0.2688
Book-entry treasury bonds XV	0.12	0.72	0	0	0.72
Book-entry treasury bonds XVI	0.08	0.2944	0	0	0.2944
Year 2003[8]					
Certificate treasury bonds I	0.42	1.26	0.3	0.9	2.16
	0.42	1.26	0.3	0.9	2.16
Certificate treasury bonds II	0.42	1.89	0.3	1.35	3.24
	0.42	1.89	0.3	1.35	3.24
Certificate treasury bonds III	0.42	1.05	0.3	0.75	1.8
	0.42	1.05	0.3	0.75	1.8
Certificate treasury bonds IV	0.42	0.85428	0.3	0.6102	1.46448
	0.42	1.26504	0.3	0.9036	2.16864
Book-entry treasury bonds I	0.1	0.35	0	0	0.35
Book-entry treasury bonds I (additional)	0.1	0.35	0	0	0.35
Book-entry treasury bonds II	0.1	0.26	0	0	0.26
Book-entry treasury bonds III	0.1	0.26	0	0	0.26
Book-entry treasury bonds IV	0.1	0.26	0	0	0.26

Book-entry treasury bonds V	0.05	0	0.13	0.13
Book-entry treasury bonds VI	0.1	0	0.26	0.26
Book-entry treasury bonds VII	0.1	0	0.46	0.46
Book-entry treasury bonds VIII	0.1	0	0.1638	0.1638
Book-entry treasury bonds IX	0.1	0	0.22	0.22
Book-entry treasury bonds X	0.05	0	0.11	0.11
Book-entry treasury bonds XI	0.1	0	0.31	0.31
Book-entry treasury bonds XII	0.05	0	0.1275	0.1275
Book-entry treasury bonds XIII	0	0	0	0

Notes:

[1] All figures, excluding ratio of settlement fees, are from Gao Jian, *China Bond* (1999), p. 71.

[2] Expenses include issuing costs, settlement fees, and marketing expenses, all of which are paid by the central government.

[3,4] Figures for 1997 and 1998 in the ratio of settlement fees column are derived from previous years' statistics.

[5,6] Data for certificate treasury bonds in 1999 and 2000 come mainly from financial statistics yearbooks. The figures on issuing cost ratio and ratio of settlement fees are derived from relevant statistics of previous years. Most of the data on book-entry treasury bonds in 1999 and 2000 are from www.chinabond.com and the official Web site of the National Debt Association of China. Other incomplete data on issuing cost ratio and ratio of settlement fees are derived from relevant statistics of previous years.

[7] After 2002, the Ministry of Finance cancelled the settlement fee for the book-entry treasury bonds. After 1999, the criteria for the issuing cost ratio has been standardized. The issuing cost ratio for the book-entry treasury bonds is 0 for those maturing within 12 months, 0.5 percent for those maturing in one to three years, and 1 percent for those maturing in five or more years.

[8] Data for 2003 are from www.chinabond.com and the official Web site of the National Debt Association of China. The issuing cost and settlement fee ratios are derived in accordance with relevant provisions (see preceding note).

fees have dropped gradually as well. In 2002, both the Ministry of Finance and China Development Bank cancelled service and settlement fees[1] to pull issuing costs down further. Compared with the United States and Japan, funding cost in China is indeed lower.

Issuing Costs of Treasury Bonds in the United States

The cost of issuing treasury bonds in the United States is usually higher than in China. Table 6.2 provides the details.

Issuing Costs of T-Bonds in Japan

Issuing expenses of T-bonds in Japan consist mainly of subscription placement, interest payment, and principal repayment fees, which make up a large proportion of the offering proceeds. Table 6.3 shows the cost of issuing every 100 Japanese yen treasury bond.

ANALYSIS OF TREASURY BOND ISSUING COSTS IN CHINA

In China, the issuing cost of treasury bonds consists of interest cost and issuing expense; interest cost accounts for a major proportion of the issuing cost. Table 6.4 provides the statistics on interest payment on T-bonds since 1981.

When treasury bonds were issued by means of administrative allocation, a certain part of the marketing expenses was paid by local governments.

TABLE 6.2 Proportion of Issuing Cost to Proceeds of T-Bonds in the United States (percent)

Offering Proceeds (US$mm)	Direct Selling			Public Offering		
	Underwriting Cost	Other Cost	Total	Underwriting Cost	Other Cost	Total
0.5 or below	1.7	1.1	2.8	7.3	2.9	10.2
0.5–0.99	1.4	0.9	2.3	5.5	3.2	8.7
1.0–2.99	0.9	0.5	1.4	3.5	2.1	5.6
3.0–4.99	0.6	0.4	1.0	1.4	1.3	2.7
5.0–9.99	0.6	0.3	0.9	0.9	1.0	1.9
10.0–24.99	0.3	0.3	0.6	1.0	0.7	1.7
25 or above	0.2	0.2	0.4	0.7	0.4	1.1

TABLE 6.3 Proportion of Issuing Cost to Proceeds of T-Bonds in Japan (percent)

Type of Cost	Coupon T-Bonds	Discount T-Bonds
General subscription fee	0.63	—
Placement fee	—	0.765
Other subscription fee	—	0.135
Interest payment fee	0.18	0.18
Principal repayment fee	0.09	0.09

(This sum is not included in this cost analysis.) Therefore, all interest and expenses paid by the central government constitute the issuing cost. The issuing cost ratio is the proportion of the issuing cost to the total offering proceeds (see Table 6.5 for these ratios for the years 1981 to 2003).

Based on the data shown in Table 6.5, the issuing cost ratios shown in Figure 6.1 can be derived.

Figure 6.1 shows that, at the beginning of 1980s, the issuing cost of treasury bonds in China was comparatively low. The cost increased gradually from that point until the end of 1980s and early 1990s, when it experienced two peak periods. Since 1993, the issuing cost of the T-bonds has been declining year by year.

The low issuing cost at the beginning of 1980s was due to (1) the low interest rate on bank deposits and (2) the use of the administrative allocation method for treasury bond issuance. The inflation China suffered at the end of 1980s and the beginning of 1990s is the major reason for the two peaks during this period. The decline in the issuing cost after 1993 resulted from the improved issuing methods, diversified bond types, and a more developed T-bond market. Furthermore, the lowered inflation rate and the cut in the interest rate for bank deposits and loans contributed to the decline.

Relationship between Interest Rates and Yields in the Secondary Market

Thanks to the improvement in market-based selling techniques, interest rates of China's bond securities have been approaching the bond yield in the secondary market since early 1996. This is demonstrated in Table 6.6.

The auction of the treasury bonds makes it possible for the primary and the secondary markets to be in line with one another. This is because the pricing of the new T-bonds is based on yield rates in the secondary market. This pricing principle not only ensures the smooth distribution of new issues, but also prevents new issues from negatively affecting the secondary market.

TABLE 6.4   Interest Payments of Treasury Bonds (Unit: RMB100 Million)[a]

Type of Treasury Bonds	Offering Size	Maturity (Years)	Interest Rate (%)	Interest Payment
T-bills 1981	48.66	9	4	17.5176
T-bills 1982	43.83	9	4, 8	22.8744
T-bills 1983	41.58	9	4, 8[b]	220.482
T-bills 1984	42.53	9	4, 8	23.2596
T-bills 1985	60.61	5	4, 8	22.9105
T-bills 1986	62.51	5	4, 8	26.677
T-bills 1987	62.87	5	4, 8	26.919
T-bills 1988	92.16	3	4, 8	23.4624
Subtotal in 1989	223.91			108.7044
T-bills	56.07	3	14	23.5494
Special treasury bonds	42.84	5	15	32.13
Value-preserved treasury bonds	125	3	14.14	53.025
Subtotal in 1990	126.14			63.7632
T-bills	93.46	3	14	39.2532
Special treasury bonds	32.68	5	15	24.51
Subtotal in 1991	216.62			67.5675
T-bills	199.41	3	10	59.823
Special treasury bonds	17.21	5	9	7.7445
Subtotal in 1992	367.19			211.284
Treasury bonds I	92.15	5	10.5	48.3787
Treasury bonds II	246.79	3	20	148.074
Nonphysical treasury bonds	28.25	5	10.5	14.8313
Subtotal in 1993	314.77			233.0891
Treasury bonds I	73.19	5	15.86	58.0397
Treasury bonds II	226.35	3	24	162.972
Nonphysical treasury bonds	15.23	5	15.86	12.0774
Subtotal in 1994	1137.52			395.2206
6-month treasury bonds	50.27	0.5	9.8	2.4632
1-year treasury bonds	82.35	1	11.98	9.8655
2-year treasury bonds	285.23	2	13	74.1598
Certificate treasury bonds	700.07	3	13.96	293.1893
Special treasury bonds	19.6	5	15.86	15.5428
Subtotal in 1995	1510.81			611.5887
Bearer treasury bonds	250	3	14.5	108.75
Certificate treasury bonds I	1056.82	3	14	443.8644

TABLE 6.4 (*Continued*)

Type of Treasury Bonds	Offering Size	Maturity (Years)	Interest Rate (%)	Interest Payment
Book-entry treasury bonds	118.89	1	11.98	14.243
Special treasury bonds	24.1	5	15.86	19.1113
Certificate treasury bonds II	61	3	14	25.62
Subtotal in 1996	2126.2			949.3524
Book-entry treasury bonds I	144.78	1	12.1	15.7421
Book-entry treasury bonds II	218.65	0.5	10.53	10.8459
Physical treasury bonds I	349	3	14.5	151.815
Book-entry treasury bonds III	142.7	0.25	9.9	3.531825
Book-entry treasury bonds IV	171.0	1	12.04	20.52
Certificate treasury bonds	349.0	5	13.06	196.8795
Book-entry treasury bonds V	255.8	10	11.83	302.6114
Physical treasury bonds I	325.3	3	10.96	106.9586
Special treasury bonds	33.6	5	8.8	14.784
Book-entry treasury bonds VI	211.2	7	8.5	125.664
Year 1997	2411.79			780.1501
Bearer treasury bonds	395.29	3	9.18	108.8656
Certificate treasury bonds	256.38	2	8.64	44.30592
	1133.65	3	9.18	312.1934
	253.29	5	10.17	128.8031
Book-entry treasury bonds I	213.8	2	10.69	
Book-entry treasury bonds II	130	10	9.78	127.3356
Special directional treasury bonds	29.35	5	8.8	12.936
Year 1998	3808.7			1424.352
Certificate treasury bonds	1219.71	3	7.11	260.162
Certificate treasury bonds	980.39	5	7.86	385.2972
Directional treasury bonds	423.5	7	6.8	201.586
Coupon treasury bonds	1000	10	5.5	550

(*continued*)

TABLE 6.4 (*Continued*)

Type of Treasury Bonds	Offering Size	Maturity (Years)	Interest Rate (%)	Interest Payment
Directional treasury bonds (I)	60	5	5.68	17.04
Directional treasury bonds (II)	35.1	5	5.85	10.26675
Book-entry treasury bonds	90	7	5.01	31.563
Year 1999	4015			906.4303
Certificate treasury bonds I	350	3	4.72	49.56
	150	5	5.23	39.225
Certificate treasury bonds II	350	3	3.02	31.71
	150	5	3.25	24.375
Certificate treasury bonds III	378	3	2.78	31.5252
	151	5	2.97	22.4235
Book-entry treasury bonds I	180	7	4.88	61.488
Book-entry treasury bonds II	160	10 (interest paid p.a.)	4.72	75.52
Book-entry treasury bonds III	94	7 (interest paid p.a.)	3.2	21.056
Book-entry treasury bonds IV	200	3 (interest paid p.a.)	2.72	16.32
Book-entry treasury bonds V	163.5	8 (interest paid p.a.)	3.28	42.9024
Book-entry treasury bonds VI	600	10 (interest paid p.a.)	5.22	313.2
Book-entry treasury bonds VII	163	2 (interest paid p.a.)	2.6	8.476
Book-entry treasury bonds VIII	193.5	10 (interest paid p.a.)	3.3	63.855
Book-entry treasury bonds IX	150	5 (interest paid p.a.)	3.31	24.825
Book-entry treasury bonds X	160	7 (interest paid p.a.)	2.85**	31.92
Book-entry treasury bonds XI	70	5 (interest paid p.a.)	3.32	11.62
Book-entry treasury bonds XII	292	3 (interest paid p.a.)	2.92	25.5792
Directional treasury bonds (I)	20	7 (interest paid p.a.)	2.75**	3.85
Directional treasury bonds (II)	40	5	3.5	7

TABLE 6.4 (*Continued*)

Type of Treasury Bonds	Offering Size	Maturity (Years)	Interest Rate (%)		Interest Payment
			Individuals	Institutions	
Year 2000	4657				7
					17.4741
Certificate treasury bonds I	108	2		2.55	5.508
	343	3		2.89	29.7381
	49	5		3.14	7.693
Certificate treasury bonds II	120	2		2.55	6.12
Issue certificate treasury bonds	480	3		2.89	41.616
	319	5		3.14	50.083
Book-entry treasury bonds I	200	7 (interest paid p.a.)	2.90**		40.6
Book-entry treasury bonds II	280	10 (interest paid p.a.)	2.80**		78.4
Book-entry treasury bonds III	200	2	2.44		9.76
Book-entry treasury bonds IV	140	10 (interest paid p.a.)	2.87**		40.18
Book-entry treasury bonds V	200	5 (interest paid p.a.)	3		30
	300	3		2.89	26.01
	180	5		3.14	28.26
Book-entry treasury bonds VI	126	7 (interest paid p.a.)	3.5		30.87
Book-entry treasury bonds VII	200	10 (interest paid p.a.)	2.72*		54.4
Book-entry treasury bonds VIII	102	5 (interest paid p.a.)	3.4		17.34
Book-entry treasury bonds IX	500	10 (interest paid p.a.)	2.55*		127.5
Book-entry treasury bonds X	120	7 (interest paid p.a.)	2.63*		22.092
Book-entry treasury bonds XI	200	1 (interest paid p.a.)	2.35		4.7
Book-entry treasury bonds XII	252	7 (interest paid p.a.)	2.85*		50.274
Directional treasury bonds (I)	38	5	3.5		6.65
Directional treasury bonds (II)	200	2	2.42		9.68

(*continued*)

TABLE 6.4 (*Continued*)

Type of Treasury Bonds	Offering Size	Maturity (Years)	Interest Rate (%)	Interest Payment
Year 2001	4884			1094.96
Certificate treasury bonds I	480	3	2.89	41.616
	320	5	3.14	50.24
Certificate treasury bonds II	350	3	2.89	30.345
	150	5	3.14	23.55
Certificate treasury bonds III	350	3	2.89	30.345
	150	5	3.14	23.55
Book-entry treasury bonds I	200	10 (interest paid p.a.)	2.82	65.4
Book-entry treasury bonds II	200	3 (interest paid p.a.)	2.88	17.28
Book-entry treasury bonds III	120	7 (interest paid p.a.)	3.27	27.468
Book-entry treasury bonds IV	120	15 (interest paid p.a.)	4.69	84.42
Book-entry treasury bonds V	180	7 (interest paid p.a.)	3.71	46.746
Book-entry treasury bonds VI	200	5 (interest paid p.a.)	3.36	33.6
Book-entry treasury bonds VII	240	20 (interest paid p.a.)	4.26	204.48
Book-entry treasury bonds VIII	200	2 (interest paid p.a.)	2.46	9.84
Book-entry treasury bonds IX	200	10 (interest paid p.a.)	2.77	55.4
Book-entry treasury bonds X	200	10 (interest paid p.a.)	2.95	59
Book-entry treasury bonds XI	160	20 (interest paid p.a.)	3.85	123.2
Book-entry treasury bonds XII	200	10 (interest paid p.a.)	3.05	61
Book-entry treasury bonds XIII	200	5 (interest paid p.a.)	2.86	22.88
Book-entry treasury bonds XIV	200	7 (interest paid p.a.)	2.9	36.54
Book-entry treasury bonds XV	200	7 (interest paid p.a.)	3	42
Book-entry treasury bonds XVI	264	3 (interest paid p.a.)	2.51	15.06
Year 2002				
Certificate treasury bonds I	420	3	2.42	30.492

TABLE 6.4 (*Continued*)

Type of Treasury Bonds	Offering Size	Maturity (Years)	Interest Rate (%)	Interest Payment
	180	5	2.74	24.66
Certificate treasury bonds II	150	3	2.07	9.315
	150	5	2.29	17.175
Certificate treasury bonds III	167.5	3	2.12	10.653
	167.5	5	2.36	19.765
Certificate treasury bonds IV	123	3	2.22	8.1918
	115	5	2.48	14.26
Book-entry treasury bonds I	200	10	2.7	54
Book-entry treasury bonds II	360	5	2.22	39.96
Book-entry treasury bonds III	200	10	2.54	50.8
Book-entry treasury bonds IV	260	2	1.9	9.88
Book-entry treasury bonds V	260	30	2.9	226.2
Book-entry treasury bonds VI	460	7	2	64.4
Book-entry treasury bonds VII	260	3	1.9	14.82
Book-entry treasury bonds VIII	265	1	1.91	5.0615
Book-entry treasury bonds IX	173.3	10	2.7	46.791
Book-entry treasury bonds X	200	7	2.39	33.46
Book-entry treasury bonds XI	200	12	2.64	63.36
Book-entry treasury bonds XII	191	3	2.3	13.179
Book-entry treasury bonds XIII	240	15	2.6	93.6
Book-entry treasury bonds XIV	224	5	2.65	29.68
Book-entry treasury bonds XV	600	7	2.93	123.06
Book-entry treasury bonds XVI	368	2	2.3	16.928

(*continued*)

TABLE 6.4 (*Continued*)

Type of Treasury Bonds	Offering Size	Maturity (Years)	Interest Rate (%)	Interest Payment
Year 2003				
Certificate treasury bonds I	300	3	2.32	20.88
	300	5	2.63	39.45
Certificate treasury bonds II	450	3	2.32	31.32
	450	5	2.63	59.175
Certificate treasury bonds III	250	3	2.32	17.4
	250	5	2.63	32.875
Certificate treasury bonds IV	203.4	1	1.98	4.02732
	301.2	2	2.25	13.554
Book-entry treasury bonds I	350	7	2.66	65.17
Book-entry treasury bonds I (Additional)	350	7	2.66	65.17
Book-entry treasury bonds II	260	10	2.8	72.8
Book-entry treasury bonds III	260	20	3.4	176.8
Book-entry treasury bonds IV	260	5	2.45	31.85
Book-entry treasury bonds V	260	3	2.32	18.096
Book-entry treasury bonds VI	260	5	2.53	32.89
Book-entry treasury bonds VII	460	7	2.66	85.652
Book-entry treasury bonds VIII	163.8	10	3.02	49.4676
Book-entry treasury bonds IX	220	15	4.18	137.94
Book-entry treasury bonds X	220	2	2.77	12.188
Book-entry treasury bonds XI	360	7	3.5	75.95
Book-entry treasury bonds XII	255	1	Offer price at 97.51 yuan	6.3495
Book-entry treasury bonds XIII	100	3-month	Offer price at 99.41 yuan	0.59

Notes:
[a]Figures are from *Finance Yearbook of China* and China Government Securities Depository Trust & Clearing Co., Ltd.
[b]The interest rate for institutional buyers is 4 percent, and the interest rate for individual buyers is 8 percent.

TABLE 6.5 Issuing Cost Ratios for Chinese T-Bonds, 1981 to 2003 (percent)

Year	Issuing Cost Ratio (%)	Year	Issuing Cost Ratio (%)
1981	4.116	1993	18.694
1982	5.922	1994	13.472
1983	6.145	1995	14.465
1984	6.214	1996	12.183
1985	7.830	1997	9.711
1986	8.865	1998	6.534
1987	8.892	1999	3.867
1988	8.950	2000	2.958
1989	14.74	2001	3.548
1990	14.882	2002	2.464
1991	9.903	2003	2.748
1992	14		

Note: "Cost" includes the offering cost and the settlement fee. The formula for calculating the annual cost ratio is annual cost ratio = (total cost/offering size) × 100%, in which the total cost equals the sum of the cost of each issuance/total maturity years. The offering size equals the sum of each issue's size in a particular year.

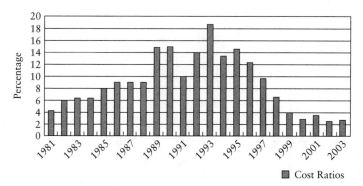

FIGURE 6.1 Issuing Cost Ratios of China's Treasury Bonds, 1981 to 2003

The two issues of treasury bonds executed by means of auction in 1997 maintained the close alignment of the primary market and the secondary market. Thanks to improvements in auction methods, the yield in the primary market and that in the secondary market had never been as consistent. For example, the yield of the 10-year TB-9704 issued in 1997

TABLE 6.6 Comparisons between the Interest Rates of T-Bonds Issued and the Interest Rate for Bank Deposits and Bond Yield Rates in the Secondary Market, 1996

Bond Type	Offering Date	Maturity	Issue Price (%)	Interest Rate for Bank Deposits with the Same Maturity (%)	Auction Date	91-day Repo Rate (%)	Yield Rate of Spot Bonds with Similar Maturities in Secondary Market (%)
Book-entry bonds (I)	01/08–01/30	1 year	12.11	1-year time deposit: 0.98	01/06	14	No T-bonds of similar maturity available
	02/12–02/16	6 month	10.53	6-month time deposit: 9.00	02/10	12.95	T-bonds I of 1995 with a residual maturity of 0.54-year: 9.88%
Registered bonds (I)	03/10–03/31	3 year	14.50	3-year time deposit: 12.24	03/03	13.2	3-year T-bonds of 1995 with a residual maturity of 1.99-year: 13.88%; value-preserved T-bonds issued in last February: 29%
Book-entry bonds (III)	03/15–03/20	3 month	9.92	3-month time deposit: 3.15	03/13	12.7	1-year T-bonds of 1995 with a residual maturity of 0.45-year: 11.19%
Book-entry bonds (IV)	04/02–04/18	1 year	12.04	1-year time deposit: 10.98	03/31	12.5	1-year T-bonds of 1996 with a residual maturity of 0.79-year: 11.88%

Certificate bonds (I)	05/15–06/30	5 year	13.06	5-year time deposit: 13.86; rate of 12.06 applied as of May 23			
Book-entry bonds (V)	6/14–07/11	10 year	11.83	8-year interest-drawing time deposit: 12.06	06/12	11.88	No T-bonds of similar maturity available
Registered bonds (II)	08/06–08/26	3 year	10.96	3-year time deposit: 10.80	07/16	12.5	3-year T-bonds of 1996 with a residual maturity of 2.65-year: 10.93%
Directional bonds	08/10–09/20	5 year	8.80	5-year interest-drawing time deposit: 10.08; rate of 8.28 applied as of August 23.			
Book-entry bonds (VI)	11/01–11/20	7 year	8.56	8-year interest-drawing time deposit: 9.00	10/30	11.52	696 T-bonds with a residual maturity of 9.62-year: 8.89%
Book-entry bonds (VII)	01/22–02/17	2 year	10.69	2-year interest-drawing time deposit: 7.92	01/09/97	13	396 T-bonds with a maturity of 2.18-year: 10.94%

was 9.57 percent, which was exactly the weekly average yield of the 10-year TB-696 issued in 1996.

The treasury bonds issued in 1998 were mainly certificate bonds issued to individuals and book-entry bonds issued to and traded in the inter-bank market. The interest rates of these bonds were determined by the State Council. For the first time, the level of the yield rate in the secondary market was lower than that of the primary market of the same year.

Both the absolute cost and the relative cost of the treasury bonds issued in 1998 were quite high. Although with an apparently low coupon, the real interest rates of these bonds were by no means low when the influence of deflation is taken into account. As result, the high real interest rate increased the absolute issuing cost of the bonds.

Since the yield rate of the treasury bonds in the secondary market was quite low, if the T-bonds of 1998 had been issued by means of auction, the issuing costs could have been reduced significantly. However, as the government-determined interest rates were higher than those in the secondary market, the relative issuing costs of these T-bonds increased significantly. Prior to the second adjustment of interest rates in 1998, the yield rate of the 10-year T-bonds in the market was around 5 percent, while the yield on the 3-year T-bonds issued to individuals was as high as 5.86 percent, and the interest rate of the 10-year T-bonds issued to banks was at 5.5 percent. All of them were higher than the yield of T-bonds in the secondary market.

From 1999 to 2001, treasury bond issuance was primarily market-oriented, and the Ministry of Finance based the yield rates on the secondary market when establishing price ranges for its bond auctions. It is obvious that the yield rate of the primary market was well aligned with those in the secondary market, although, in some cases, the price range was either too high or too low, which led to insufficient subscription. It is evident, therefore, that trying to control yields by establishing bidding ranges is the major cause for unsuccessful issuance of T-bonds.

Successful Low-Cost Treasury Bond Issuance　The issuing cost of the T-bonds dropped in 1996, which is demonstrated by the continuous decline in T-bond interest rates as the secondary market warmed up and the increasing liquidity of the treasury bonds. As illustrated in Table 6.6, in 1996 the primary T-bond market facilitated the development of the secondary market, while the active secondary market provided the primary market with conditions for further cuts in interest rates. As can be seen, for example:

- Interest rates of the first three issuances of T-bonds in 1996 were all 1.5 to 2.0 percent higher than the bank deposit rates and were fully consistent with the yield rate of T-bonds in the secondary market.

■ Bidding demand began to increase with the fourth issuance of T-bonds in 1996, which led to the decline of yield from 12.11 percent of the first issuance to 12.04 percent of the fourth issuance, only 1 percent higher than that of the bank deposit with same maturity. (Both the first and the fourth issuances were one-year treasury bonds).

Since the fourth issuance, the interest rate of T-bonds has been declining along with the market-oriented issuance of T-bonds. At the time of the seventh issuance of treasury bonds in 1996, the interest rate was merely 0.16 percent higher than that of bank deposit of same term, which was historically the narrowest spread between the interest rate of T-bonds and the interest rate for bank deposit.

In addition, the rate of decline in the interest rate for treasury bonds was higher than that of bank deposit rates. The interest on the seven-year coupon T-bonds of 1996 was 8 percent lower than that of the five-year coupon T-bonds of 1993, compared with the 2.5 percent decline for bank deposits during the same period (see Figures 6.2 and 6.3). From 2002 on, the yield of T-bonds was lower than the interest rate on bank deposits to reflect the credit differentials.[2]

Figure 6.2 illustrates the comparison between the yield rates of one-year treasury bonds with the favorable yield and higher liquidity, three-month

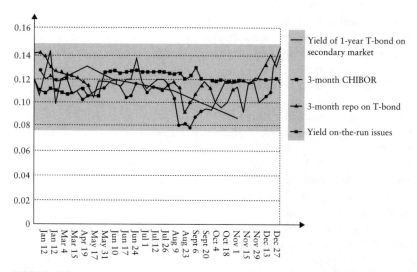

FIGURE 6.2 Comparison between the Yield of Government Bonds and the Interest Rate for Bank Deposits, 1996

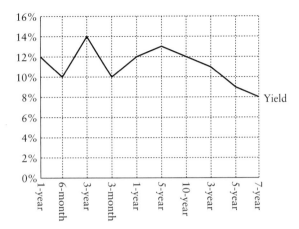

FIGURE 6.3 Award Yield Curve of the Government
Bond, 1996

China Interbank Offered Rate (CHIBOR) and three-month T-bond repurchases (repos) in 1996. We can see that, when the yield rate in the secondary market is kept at 10 percent to 14 percent, the yield rate of T-bonds will drop significantly.

Although the yield for different issuances varied from one another because of fluctuations in market rates and the supply and demand profiles at the time of offering, the overall interest rates of the treasury bonds in 1996 maintained a downward trend (see Figure 6.3).

Since 1988, the treasury bond market in China has experienced continuous development, as witnessed by the increasing volume of transactions. The total volume of transactions in 1996 reached RMB171.3 billion, almost the total market trading volume of the previous years (see Table 6.7). Due to the negative impact of the Asian financial crisis, the trading volume of T-bonds dropped drastically during 1997 and 1998. After 1999, however, trading volume rebounded dramatically when the liquidity ratio was above 60 percent.

From 1999 to 2000, the investment in securities market by both institutional investors and retail investors were confined to stocks and treasury bonds. The ordinary retail investors (retired workers) focused on certificate treasury bonds (dominated by the saving bonds), while professional retail investors (those holding accounts at the exchange especially for the purchase of stocks and concurrently buying the T-bonds) purchased tradable treasury bonds.

Since the Chinese stock market was buoyant from time to time during 1990s, retail investors crowded into it, and T-bonds that targeted individual

TABLE 6.7 Issue Size and Trading Volume of Treasury Bonds in China, 1981 to 2001

Year	Issue Volume	Trading Volume	Float Ratio (%)
1981[a]	48.7		
1982	43.6		
1983	41.6		
1984	42.5		
1985	60.6		
1986	62.5		
1987	116.9		
1988[b]	188.8	Experiments conducted on OTC transactions of two issues of T-bonds of 1985 and 1986	
1989	223.9		
1990	197.2	93.28	47.30
1991	281.3	199	70.76
1992	432.3	302.79	70.04
1993	381	381	100.00
1994	1137	327.06	28.75
1995	1510	665.2	44.03
1996[c]	2126.2	1713	80.57
1997	2411.8	330.2	13.69
1998	3808.8	90	2.36
1999	4015	2426	60.42
2000	4657	3000	64.42
2001	4884	3084	63.14

[a]China resumed issuing treasury bonds in 1981.
[b]The year 1988 was the first year when China legitimized bond transfer over the bank counters.
[c]At the end of 1996, the outstanding tradable treasury bonds were RMB171.68 billion, out of which RMB126.835 billion was deposited with the Shanghai Stock Exchange, accounting for 74 percent of the total outstanding volume.

investors were not selling well. Corporate bonds, due to their small issue size, higher risk, and low yield rate, were not well received by investors. Since 1999 onward, due to the high fragmentation of the market, T-bonds and policy-related financial bonds were mainly issued in the inter-bank market, where banks were the primary investors. Since banks would not buy T-bonds unless their yields are higher than the interest rate for bank deposits, it is unlikely that the cost of issuing T-bonds would be lower than the interest rate of bank deposits if T-bonds target banks only.

After 2001, due to a sharp decline in the stock market, interest rate cuts, and abundant liquidity in banks, retail investors expressed great enthusiasm for investing in treasury bonds, which led to the recovery of the T-bond market. At the end of 2001, for the first time, yields on T-bonds dropped significantly below the interest rate on bank deposits. This meant that, if the bond market continued developing in the same direction, treasury bonds could be the investment product and market instrument with the lowest yield. However, it is believed that this will not happen unless interest rates for bank deposits and loans are liberalized. Therefore, to date, the interest rates of treasury bonds on average are still higher than the interest rates of bank deposits. For the time being, T-bonds cannot be the most cost-efficient financing instruments.

EVALUATING TREASURY BOND MARKET DEVELOPMENT: ESTABLISHING CRITERIA

In measuring the development of the treasury bond market, certain criteria must be established based on the targets of T-bond issuance, conditions of the national economy, and actual financial market.

Effective Primary Market: High Efficiency and Low Cost

The primary market is the most essential component of the treasury bond market. The two key objectives, high efficiency and low cost, are closely related to each other and must be well defined. The yardstick of the objectives is specified as:

- *Short offering process.* As a basic indicator of the issuing efficiency, the offering process refers to a span of time between the issuing date and the settlement date. To achieve this, market infrastructure, institutions, and modern technology are necessary.
- *High visibility and transparency.* The market shall have a predefined schedule for the issuance, through which the investors are well informed of issue date and size in advance. Based on this information, they can make fund arrangements as soon as possible.
- *Timely settlement*, which means the payment are fully funded in a timely manner and the investors are efficient in money transfer.

- *Efficient and effective services.* Debt service shall be timely and efficient to ensure that investors can get their money back and avoid delivery delay and payment calculation mistakes. In China, this has been achieved via the China Government Securities Depository Trust & Clearing Co, Ltd. (CGSDTC), which has greatly improved the issuing efficiency of T-bonds by electronic money transfer during the trading process. To this end, issuing scripless book-entry T-bonds is essential. By reducing the transfer and transportation time, scripless T-bonds lead to increased issuing efficiency and reduced issuing cost.
- The liberalization of interest rates on treasury bonds is a necessary step toward realizing these criteria. It has been recognized that T-bond auction selling is a key to achieve the intended objectives and would shorten the offering time frame as well.

Effective Secondary Market: High Liquidity

The vitality of the secondary treasury bond market depends on its liquidity, that is, the turnover rate in the market. Improvement in liquidity can be achieved in a number of ways:

- *Large trading volume.* High-volume buying and selling for each product means that a large number of treasury bonds can be bought or sold at any time without leading to significant price fluctuations.
- *Ability to absorb new issues.* The rate of absorption of a new issue in the secondary market reflects the liquidity of the bond market. In general, when treasury bonds have high liquidity, the secondary market will have stronger capability in absorbing the newly issued T-bond securities.
- *Diverse market instruments.* Diversification is a prerequisite for liquidity. More market instruments mean more choices for investors and other market participants and a corresponding increase in trading volume.

Effective Coordination with the Money Market

Without a developed money market, it is hard to imagine that there could be any well-developed treasury bond market. The money market provides market players with sufficient and efficient money transfer facility and benchmarks for pricing T-bonds.

Since 1998, the central bank has been promoting the development of the money market. As a result, the transaction volume of both inter-bank borrowing and bond repurchase has increased significantly. The bills issued by the central bank have become important money market instruments. The development of the bond repo market has directly facilitated the issuance of the treasury bonds and the financial bonds, which are two major instruments for repo transaction.

In 2004, the China Development Bank initiated floating-rate bonds issuance with the interest rate based on the seven-day repo rate, which effectively aligned the bond market with the money market. Obviously, a developed repo market is helpful in providing benchmarks of short-term money, which are sensitive to changes in the macroeconomic environment yet relatively stable.

Effective Financial Infrastructure

The term "financial infrastructure" refers to the facilities and institutions for settlement, clearing, and depository trust of treasury bonds. The more developed the financial infrastructure is, the better service it offers, the higher the issuing efficiency of treasury bonds, the lower issuing cost, and the higher market liquidity.

In recent years, China has instituted the use of scripless bonds, which is reflected in its ongoing efforts toward well-functioning registration, depository trust, settlement, and clearing systems. Not long ago, the Ministry of Finance promulgated *Regulations on the Registration and Depository Trust of the Treasury Bonds* and approved simultaneously the *Method of Treasury Administration* of the CGSDTC, which are of critical significance to the further market-oriented development of the treasury bonds.

Judging by these criteria, China's bond market has made great progress, insofar as the primary market is concerned. For example, the offering process has been shortened significantly, and settlement can be completed within one week. This would have been unimaginable before 1996. In addition, because bids are submitted electronically, the invisible auction has been realized. All the legal formalities relating to bond issues have been standardized, and the procedures have been made uniform. Trading volume and the settlement volume in the secondary market have been enhanced.

Despite all this, China still has far to go to reach its intended goals. For example, the fragmented market reduces its liquidity, the market instruments are still limited in number, and derivatives instruments are almost absent.

Emergence of
a Secondary Market

CHAPTER 7

History of China's Secondary Bond Market

The place where bonds trade, in financial jargon, is called the secondary market (in contrast to the primary market). The secondary market differs from the primary market in that the former reflects the relationship between investors and investors or between investors and intermediaries while the latter reflects the relationship between issuers and investors or intermediaries. In this chapter, we view China's secondary bond market from an historical perspective.

TREASURY BOND SECONDARY MARKET, 1988 TO 1990

Beginning in 1981, bonds were issued in consecutive years. As more bonds were issued, their lack of liquidity caused T-bond holders to feel inconvenienced and increasingly unhappy, which, in turn, made it increasingly difficult to execute T-bond issuance. To address the liquidity problem, in 1985, the People's Bank of China (PBOC) established a treasury bond discount procedure, but that did not solve the fundamental problem that the discount rate was not market based but instead was fixed for a certain period.

From that time on, it was imperative to establish a market for treasury bond trading to satisfy investors' liquidity requirements. The year 1988 witnessed the emergence of China's secondary bond market with the opening of the bond transfer window. This market made the circulation of T-bonds possible, helped ease the trading difficulties bondholders had experienced, and thereby gradually improved the reputation of treasury bonds. Although the rationale was to offer convenience to investors, in the mind of government the goal was to allow for the *circulation* (*Liu Tong* in Chinese) and *transfer* of treasury bonds. By "circulation," we mean the ability for bonds to change hands among investors (i.e., principal-to-principal exchange). "Transfer" means the ability to cash in the principal through over-the-counter (OTC) trading.[1]

Against this background, in the beginning of 1988, the state decided to launch an experiment to allow treasury bills issued in 1985 and 1986 to circulate and transfer. Initially, the experiment was limited to seven cities. During this experiment, relevant regulatory agencies representing the financial and banking authorities helped set up securities companies or Treasury Bond Service Departments to handle the actual transactions. In June 1988, 54 large and medium-size cities were approved to implement a pilot program for the circulation and transfer of treasury bonds.

After the service for circulation and transfer were formally provided, a number of problems emerged. The transfer service was only made available at bank counters to individual investors. Bank counters were responsible for withdrawals of paper securities at par value. Individual investors were eager to get their money back regardless of their legitimate return. In the first two months after the opening of the market, 70 to 80 percent of the OTC transactions handled by intermediaries were transferred to the redemption units, which resulted in a price decline. Especially in 1988, due to the overheated economic climate in China, serious inflation exacerbated a selling craze, which led to a price crash and soaring yields (higher than 20 percent) for secondary treasury bills.

In order to protect bondholders' interest, the Ministry of Finance decided that intermediaries should not be allowed to buy back bonds at a price below its face value and that the bid-offer spread should not be higher than 2 percent of the face value. These requirements helped prevent T-bond prices from declining further. During this period, efforts were also made to increase the number of bond instrument to 10 (it had been 2) and to shorten the bond maturity.

However, most new entrants refused to buy T-bonds or lower the purchase price since there was a great demand for capital. It follows that without a stable commission income, it was difficult for the intermediaries to continue in business. Since the scope of the experiment was limited, and the black market was rampant elsewhere, it was common for illegal sellers to take advantage of regional price gaps and scalp treasury bonds.

In 1990, the overheated economy was under control. Inflation decreased from the 18.5 percent in 1988 and 17.8 percent in 1989 to 2.1 percent in 1990. The PBOC adjusted the deposit interest rate twice in one year, and the easing monetary policy brought about a favorable environment for the T-bond market. The purchase price of treasury bills turned around from lower than face value to higher than face value while the yield decreased to below 20 percent. The regional price gap of treasury bills was narrowed to RMB1 to 2 from RMB3 to 6.

In December 1990, the opening of Shanghai Stock Exchange further boosted the development of interregional transactions of treasury bills. In the same year, the securities trading automatic quotation, or STAQ system of the Stock Exchange Executive Council (SEEC), was put online, which accelerated securities exchanges as well as the development of treasury bonds market. To meet the need for bond transactions, securities intermediaries emerged like bamboo shoots after a spring rain. With continued development of the market, trading volume of treasury bonds also increased. By the end of 1990, the trading volume in Chinese securities market reached RMB12 billion, of which treasury bonds were around RMB10 billion, accounting for 83 percent of the total market transaction volume.

TREASURY BOND SECONDARY MARKET, 1990 TO 1992

Between 1988 and 1990, the treasury bond market developed rapidly, but there were four problems:

1. *The bond transfer market existed only in certain areas.* Therefore, many profit-seeking sellers appeared to profit from regional price disparities. The control of bond prices in the initial stages of the T-bond market gave those selling illegally the opportunity to take advantage, and the black market was pervasive. Under these circumstances, the Ministry of Finance decided to push ahead with the experiment that had begun in 1991 to permit the circulation and transfer of T-bonds to 400 cities on the regional and municipal levels. With this, the preliminary stage of the secondary market started to take shape.
2. *Local market segmentation became an obstacle to the establishment of an integrated nationwide bond market.* To develop the local economy, many areas issued corporate bonds to finance local infrastructure projects. To secure the issuance of these bonds, some local governments took measures to block incoming T-bonds from entering into the local market. This was especially true after underwriting issuance was implemented. However, the T-bonds trading through the national market conflicted with local interests. This certainly slowed down momentum toward a uniform national T-bond market.
3. *The widening transaction gap in transaction prices in the OTC market encouraged speculation on price differences.* For example, the price gap in some securities companies reached as high as RMB8. In such a market, large number of potential individual investors had no enthusiasm for investing in treasury bonds, and securities companies were unable to make a profit on their intermediation business. The price difference

between the OTC market and the exchange market also provided loopholes for opportunists to arbitrage on price differences. The greatest problem was that the large number of potential investors who used to purchase T-bonds had no incentive to take part in the T-bond offerings. This was one of the primary reasons for the undesirable development of the Chinese OTC market.

4. *The small number of bond varieties led to market inactivity.* Tradable treasury bonds, as financial commodities, should be tailored to the preferences of heterogeneous investors. If the market does not supply new bond instruments, the market would definitely shrink, as off-the-run bonds would exit on maturity. This would undoubtedly be counterproductive to market development. Therefore, it is important to design a mature and diversified payment pattern to cater to the changing preferences of investors and keep the supply flowing continuously.

Due to these issues, the OTC market in China never developed in a meaningful way.

It is recognized that the primary market boosts secondary market and vice versa. The development of the secondary market and the increased number of bond intermediaries laid the foundation for the further development of the primary market of treasury bonds. At the same time (in 1991), the appearance of market-oriented underwriting further speeded up the development of the secondary market in T-bonds. For example, in 1991, trading volume of treasury bond reached RMB37 billion.

With the substitution of the underwriting issuing mode for administrative distribution, securities intermediaries were booming and mushrooming. In 1991, there were more than 2,000 securities intermediaries of various kinds all over the country. In order to strengthen management of the securities and treasury bond industries, the Government Bond Association of China and the Securities Association of China were founded, symbolizing the commencement of self-regulation of the market.

TREASURY BOND SECONDARY MARKET, 1992 TO 1993

In 1992, the treasury bond secondary market continued to develop, and trading volume kept increasing. The trading volume for the whole year reached RMB108.3 billion. However, the development of T-bonds was influenced by the prevailing economic environment. Due to the acceleration of economic growth, increased investment, the credit squeeze of the central bank, and the increased deposit interest rate, bond prices in the secondary market decreased, and the yield rate rose again.

In the first half year of 1992, when new issues commenced, securities intermediaries held a great amount of T-bonds, the majority of which were not resold to individual and institutional investors. At the same time, most securities intermediaries had little money of their own; most of the capital on hand was borrowed from banks. Therefore, with monetary tightening, those securities intermediaries had to sell off T-bonds, which created seller's market and a quick fall in bond prices. Although the market size had broadened, lack of transactions had a negative impact on the distribution of the Phase II T-bond (for which a contract had already been signed with underwriters in the first half of the year).

In the same year, the Wuhan Treasury Bond Exchange was founded as the first centralized transaction market exclusively for treasury bonds in China. This exchange promoted transactions of T-bonds in the central and southern China. At the same time, to satisfy the demand of bondholders for short-term bonds, some securities intermediaries in the finance sector adopted the method of dividing long-maturity bonds into short-maturity bonds. For example, they divided five-year and three-year bonds into shorter-term instruments, such as five or three pieces of one-year bonds. This long-to-short innovation was favorably received by investors and played an important role in activating the secondary market for treasury bonds. However, these long-to-short practices were later replaced by standard STRIP and synthetic bonds.

TREASURY BOND SECONDARY MARKET, 1993 TO 1994

In 1993, derivatives of treasury bonds began to emerge. Repurchase (repo) between securities intermediaries and banks as well as among the securities intermediaries was conducted widely and soon became an important financing instrument for short-term capital. Shanghai Haitong Securities employed a composite certificate to sell T-bonds, and some securities companies followed this practice. The securities underlying the composite certificate are actually secondhand treasury bills, which had higher yields than the primary issues; therefore, the composite certificate had a higher yield and was more attractive to investors.

The composite certificate was a financial innovation created by securities intermediaries for the benefit of investors and of course for their own benefit as well. Although at the time it had certain negative impacts on bond distribution due to its nonstandard operation and untimely launch at a time when the Ministry of Finance was in the process of offering of new treasury bonds, it played a positive role in activating the secondary T-bond market. Coincidentally, a treasury bond futures market, jointly established by the

Shanghai Stock Exchange (SSE) and the Ministry of Finance, opened on the SSE at the beginning of the year in a bid to boost the sluggish T-bond secondary market.

In 1994, treasury bonds repo was launched in several exchanges simultaneously to meet the demand of securities intermediaries for short-term financing. The development of the repo market was a positive step to facilitate short-term financing of financial intermediaries—mainly nonbank financial institutions. It played an important role in revitalizing the primary and secondary markets. Repo transactions also proved to be a powerful lever for the development of the financing function of the financial market.

TREASURY BOND SECONDARY MARKET, 1995

The diversification of market instruments also brought about speculative opportunities for market participants. In early 1995, the futures market for government securities had become increasingly speculative. Two groups of securities firms and investors would bet on whether the government would give an interest subsidy to the underlying T-bonds in the period between the issuing date and the time the government announced its interest subsidy policy. One group took the short position, assuming that the government would not give the subsidy in that time interval; the other group took the long position, based on their judgment that the government would give the subsidy in that time interval.

The futures price between Shanghai-based companies and those based elsewhere diverged widely in early 1995. The market shut the book when securities firm Shanghai International put the short orders to overturn those in long position on February 23, 1995. This was a violation of the order of limitation (prior to the government's announcement granting subsidy to the time interval). This incident is called 2.23 event.

The 2.23 event created a panic in the financial market. Many securities firms suffered substantial losses while others became wealthy overnight. The incident reinforced the government's perception that the futures market was speculative and needed to be shut down. It eventually caused the State Council to close the market.

Since serious short selling still was popular in the repo market, the state began to overhaul the repo markets in the Wuhan Securities Exchange, the Tianjin Securities Exchange, and the STAQ system, mainly because they were endorsed only by local governments. However, those in Shanghai and Shenzhen, which were officially approved by the central government and had the right to trade futures, were still very active.

In order to avoid short-sale activities in the market and to speed up paperless transactions, promote liquidity of T-bond market, and establish and develop financial infrastructure, in 1993, the Ministry of Finance began to seek ways to establish more effective clearing and settlement institutions. After a few years' efforts, the Ministry initiated and established the T-bond registration and depository company (the China Government Securities Depository Trust & Clearing Co., Ltd. [CGSDTC]) in 1996 in cooperation with the PBOC.

TREASURY BOND SECONDARY MARKET, 1996

In 1996, additional market-oriented reforms of the T-bond primary market improved the liquidity of the secondary market and revived trading in it. In the second half of the year, the average daily trading volume of treasury bonds hit record highs, thereby facilitating the coordinated development of the primary and secondary markets of treasury bonds.

After six years of development, the Chinese T-bond market had expanded from only some cities to the whole country, from OTC transactions to on-exchange transactions, from spot transactions to futures transactions. At the same time, the secondary bond market had been undergoing profound changes: Market capacity had been enhanced. Over-the-counter transactions of T-bonds had expanded to many cities throughout the country. With diversification efforts, the varieties of listed bonds were growing. After 1992, with the approval of the central government, treasury bills and special treasury notes held by state-owned enterprises and fiscal bonds held by banks and financial institutions came to market. In addition, with the growth of listed treasury bonds in exchanges, the trading volume increased rapidly (see Table 7.1).

TABLE 7.1　Turnover in China's T-Bond Secondary Market, 1988 to 1996 (Unit: RMB100 million)

Year	Turnover	Year	Turnover
1988	24.2085	1993	803.7113
1989	21.26	1994	1376.939
1990	115.9353	1995	775.2
1991	370.1728	1996	1087.37
1992	1082.57		

TREASURY BOND SECONDARY MARKET, 1997 TO 1999

The most important event during this time was the establishment of inter-bank bond market (IBBM) in 1996. The IBBM was an outgrowth of the earlier financing center, which regulated inter-bank borrowing (the mutual financing of short-term money [up to 120-day] among the financial institutions) through the interbank borrowing network.

In 1997, the State Council requested all banks to withdraw from the stock exchanges to break the linkage between the banking sector and the stock exchange, because of its concern over the overheated stock market. This gave rise to the emergence of the IBBM, since banks still held treasury bonds and other securities and needed to trade among themselves. In the meantime, the PBOC (the central bank) worked out rules for the interbank trading. Today the IBBM is a marketplace in which banks trade bonds they hold as well as bid for the new issues placed in the market. Thus, the creation of IBBM led to the coexistence of two separate marketplaces. Investors trade in the exchange market, while banks trade in the interbank bond market.

After the banks completely withdrew from the exchanges, government bonds and financial debentures (which were used to promote government policy initiatives) purchased and held by banks could no longer be traded in the stock exchange market. To maintain the liquidity of these instruments, CGSDTC took over the settlement of the transactions on the interbank market, while the Shanghai Foreign Exchange Center remained responsible for quotations of transactions. In the beginning of 1999, the central bank allowed some insurance companies to enter the IBBM but did not change the market segmentation. To improve the liquidity of the interbank market, the central bank began to permit some securities intermediaries to enter the IBBM. The IBBM's advantage is that it was an institutional market from the very beginning; its drawbacks, such as infrequent trading and undisclosed trading prices, soon became evident. As a trading platform for bonds, the IBBM has many flaws.

- The IBBM is a vague concept. Interbank market is a money market, while the bond market is a capital market, and therefore, the concept of the interbank bond market technically mixes up the functions of the money market and the capital market.
- There is an inherent liquidity problem for this market. Since all the bondholders are banks and, therefore, homogenous, their bond trading behavior will comply with monetary policies. Because their interests are similar, their reactions to the monetary policies will be similar. As a result, the transaction behavior of the major participants in this market, sell or buy, tends to be on the same side, and no transactions can

be made. Contrariwise, the major participants in the stock exchange market are a diverse group of investors who have different behaviors. Therefore, there are more transactions. Viewed in this light, the homogenous investor base is the major, continuing defect of the IBBM.

TREASURY BOND SECONDARY MARKET AFTER 1999

After 1999, there was a short period of time when circulation diminished and the secondary market shrank. Later, the number of participants in the IBBM began to increase. The newcomers were mainly insurance companies and securities firms. By this time, all the financial institutions were permitted to enter the interbank market directly or indirectly. Although the amount of bonds traded in the IBBM far exceeded that in the exchange market, its trading transactions were far less active than in the stock exchange market. The situation continued until after 2000, when the trading volume in the IBBM began to increase rapidly due to a growing number of principal participants and active short-term capital, especially the direct participation of the central bank.

In 2001, the total annual trading volume of Chinese bond market exceeded RMB7,000 trillion; the trading volume of the IBBM doubled and broke through RMB4 trillion, and the trading volume of the exchange market reached RMB2 trillion. In 2003, the total settlement of bond market transactions throughout the country exceeded RMB21 trillion; the IBBM market accounted for RMB15.13 trillion and the exchange market for RMB6.16 trillion.

The central bank's open market has gradually become the key window through which the monetary policy authority conveys its policy signals. It is also an important means by which central bank exercises indirect control over banks. Through the open market, the bond trading volume for the entire year exceeded RMB1 trillion. The bond repo rate in the interbank market has become the important benchmark interest rate for short-term financing.

After 1998, the major problems for the secondary market were the separation of the two marketplaces and the lack of market instruments. These problems were addressed in part by active market innovations.

FUTURE BOND MARKET DEVELOPMENT: LESSONS LEARNED

Although the ways to develop a sound bond market seem simply to be common sense, the lessons that we learned from our experience are very profound.

China has a long history of incurring debt, and for many years, most people in China thought of bonds as synonymous with debt. They did not even know that bonds were (or could be) tradable debt. Many people had no sense of a bond market. Therefore, bonds issued before 1988 were essentially debt instruments, and the secondary market was unknown. For example, the People's Victory Bonds issued in 1950 and the Economic Development Bonds issued from 1954 to 1958 did not come into the market, so there was no secondary market at all. During the first seven years after China resumed issuing T-bonds in 1981, there was no secondary market, since in a planned economy, treasury bonds held by residents and organizations were considered patriotic contributions and treated as a bank deposit; therefore, there was not much need to trade them.

Initially, the primary purpose for establishing the secondary market was to facilitate the execution of new issues in the primary market. Later, after the central bank's efforts significantly improved the secondary market, the advent of the secondary bond market paved the way for the development of the entire financial market, including the emergence of money markets, many of whose instruments and methods were designed and introduced with reference to bond market instruments. For example, such instruments as commercial paper and central bank notes arose, and the market infrastructure for trading money market instruments, which is the same as the bond market's, developed.

FUNDAMENTAL RELATIONSHIP BETWEEN PRIMARY AND SECONDARY BOND MARKETS

The importance of the secondary market is evident from both international and domestic experience. International practices provide ample evidence of the necessity and importance of a sound secondary market to the debt capital market as a whole and suggest that it is critical for government debt managers to establish a highly efficient secondary market in treasury bonds and to price new issues in line with the yield in the secondary market. In the past decade, many countries worldwide have been using their best efforts to develop the secondary market in treasury bonds.[2]

Analogous to the primary economic exchange and primary financial exchange, the primary treasury T-market is vital for the exchange between government and market participants where government debt managers (usually the Ministry of Finance) act as the issuer distributing bonds to banks, institutional investors, securities intermediaries, and individual investors so as to enable the state to meet its funding requirements. The secondary market for treasury bonds is for the transfer and trading of previously issued

T-bonds, so that bondholders can trade the bonds when they are in need of money and T-bond investors have opportunities to participate in the market. The primary and secondary markets are inseparable components of the whole T-bond market.

China has gradually realized the importance of secondary bond market. As we have seen, the development of the secondary market creates conditions necessary for the development of the primary market. As illustrated by the experiences in China in the early 1990s (see Chapter 3), it is extremely challenging to execute treasury distribution in the primary market when the secondary market is experiencing volatility and fluctuations; similarly, price stability and yield level in the secondary market is dependent on the development of whole market. Hence, an efficient secondary market is crucial to ensuring the government's funding requirements in the long run.

CRUCIAL ROLE OF FINANCIAL INTERMEDIARIES

After the secondary market gradually took shape, securities intermediaries began to emerge. The intermediaries were mainly securities firms and T-bond service departments promoted by the finance authorities, trust and investment companies, and securities companies or securities sales departments affiliated with the banking sector. Initially they were small in number, but soon they mushroomed throughout the country.

The advent of the financial intermediary industry provided the institutional base for the development of a market-based primary market, which had been unknown until then. All these laid the groundwork for the development of the issuance market (i.e., the primary market).

In 1991, the Ministry of Finance and the treasury bond underwriting syndicate signed an underwriting contract for a RMB10 billion bond transaction. This preceded the era of market-based bond offering. It is important to note that, without the participation of institutional investors and financial intermediaries, this underwriting syndication would have been impossible.

The changes in the primary market have helped stabilize the secondary market. Usually the terms of new issues have an impact on the rate of return of the secondary market. If the new issue has a high interest rate, then the yield of underlying bonds in the secondary market will increase correspondingly, as investors and market makers perceive this to be a signal of monetary movement.

If the transaction is not priced via the market, then the price distortion would mislead market participants. For example, before 1990, when T-bonds were issued by administrative assignment, there was no secondary market in modern sense. The vacancy was filled by underground market.

So the black market was rampant before 1991, and most bonds were sold below face value, which eroded investors' confidence in the bond market.

For this reason, the task of developing a treasury bond market should encompass both the primary and the secondary markets. The development of the primary market, as we saw, should be a phased process. This is actually the case in China. The Ministry of Finance abandoned administrative assignment and issued bonds first through consultation between the issuer and the underwriting syndicate in 1991; after the primary dealer system was established in 1993, then the issuer could solicit bids from primary dealers. Here, the evidence supports the institutional economic engineering (IEEN) framework. In our view, the primary bond exchange is essentially an internal exchange, which results in transaction cost savings.

In developing the secondary market, China shall, as far as possible, focus on establishing organizations of primary dealers, developing brokers among dealers, and improving the management and legal environment in which the securities intermediaries operate. In the meantime, developing derivative instruments such as futures, options, repo, and so on would give enomous benefit to those who manage the market risk. As long as the development of both markets is market based, the two markets will evolve in mutually beneficial ways.

Moreover, from the issuer's point of view, trading is different from redeeming a bond before maturity. As a matter of fact, in redeeming a bond before maturity, the issuer is obliged to pay the principal. Although the investors receive interest compensation, the funding program for the issuer is terminated prematurely as there is adverse money transfer to the investors. In the case of trading in the secondary market, only the bonds change hands; the issuer does not have to pay anything and can use proceeds for the full length of the bond's term. Therefore, it is in the issuers' interest to establish a secondary market for T-bond trading to secure their funding program.

This is contrary to conventional wisdom. Conventionally, the secondary market has been perceived as a trading platform for the benefit of investors. The IEEN framework captures the essentials of the relationship between the primary market and the secondary market. From the point of view of IEEN, the primary market is a place where investors and other market participants can achieve mutual benefits (i.e., a win-win outcome), through exchanges of their comparative advantages (here mostly information assets). It is secondary exchange, so to speak, the primary market the formal and informal primary exchange. When the Ministry of Finance acts as an issuer, it is both formal and informal as the Ministry can set the rules and regulations (e.g., auction rules) on the formal or external primary exchanges. At the same time, the Ministry, as a market participant, can also enter into contracts (e.g., syndication agreements) with other market participants; this is an informal or internal primary exchange. The primary market is a platform on which issuers and investors achieve their win-win outcome through the exchange. If the exchange can lead a win-win outcome as opposed to a win-lose outcome, as it often happen, the primary exchange will be conducive to the secondary exchange.

CHAPTER 8

Secondary Market: Operational Issues and Role of Participants and Financial Intermediaries

OPERATING PROCEDURE FOR SPOT TRANSACTIONS ON THE STOCK EXCHANGE

In developing a sound secondary market for treasury bonds, the standardization and establishment of the clearing and settlement system are fundamental. If treasury bond managers are interested in building an effective wholesale market and a framework in which T-bond market experts (i.e., the primary dealers) can play a role to develop a multifunctional derivatives market, it helps to promote a system of automated market transactions.

As was indicated, China experienced a period during which individuals were the primary bondholders and transactions were handled manually. It then shifted to an institution-based wholesale market utilizing electronic transmission systems to raise the efficiency of market transactions. The operational framework is discussed in this chapter.

Opening an Account

Investors who want to purchase or trade book-entry T-bonds issued by the Ministry of Finance through the Shanghai Securities Exchange and the Shenzhen Securities Exchange must open both a "securities account" in a branch of a securities business department (SBD) of securities firms and a clearing company's securities registration institution (SRI), both of which are members of the stock exchange.

Shenzhen Securities Exchange Account

Individual Investors Individual investors can apply through local SBDs or SRIs using a valid identification (ID) card (original and one copy); those entrusting others to apply for the account card must also provide the trustee's ID card (original and one copy).

Legal Person A legal person (any organizational body, including corporations, state-owned enterprises [SOEs] that can perform as a economic unit and enter an legal relationship with other entities, and have rights and obligations specified by law) can apply with a business license (and a copy), legal representative's power of attorney, corporate representative certificate, and ID card of the authorized person.

Securities Investment Fund, Insurance Company Both securities investment funds and insurance companies must open the account directly in the Shenzhen Securities Exchange.

Account Charges The charge is RMB50 per account for individual investors; RMB500 per account for institutional investors.

Shanghai Securities Exchange Account

Individual Investors Individual investors can apply through local account opening agencies of the Central Registration & Clearing Company of Shanghai Securities Exchange with a valid ID card (original and one copy).

Legal Person A legal person can apply with a business license (or a copy of it) or registration certificate (original and one copy) issued by the civil administration authorities or other competent departments; legal representative's power of attorney and ID card (original and one copy) of the authorized person.

Those entrusting others to apply for the account card must provide the trustee's ID card and a photocopy as well as the letter of attorney.

Account Charges The charges are RMB40 per account for an individual paper card; RMB40 per account for an individual magnetic card; RMB70 per account for individuals residing outside of Shanghai; RMB500 per account for institutional investors.

Issuing and Listing

According to the issuance bulletin for treasury bonds, bearer bonds (suspended) and registered bonds can be publicly issued through the electronic mainframe of the trading system of the exchanges. During the issuance, investors may go to designated securities dealers to handle the formalities and purchase the bonds directly through the trading system of the exchanges. Investors may also purchase treasury bonds from directly designated securities dealers.

The institutional framework of issuance and subscription of treasury bonds on the stock exchange differs from that applied for the stocks. (See Figure 8.1 for a flowchart illustrating how bonds are issued and Table 8.1 for the rules for purchasing the treasury bonds.)

Trading and Clearance

A transaction for the purchase or sale of a registered treasury bond is similar to that of stocks. The gain and loss of the bonds is registered in the owner's securities account after the transaction. Investors or traders must put their bearer bonds in custody and register them in book-entry form before they are traded. Buyers of bearer bonds are entitled to withdraw the paper securities from the securities intermediary who has custody of the bonds.

The spot transactions of treasury bonds use "board" as the unit of purchase. One board equals RMB1,000 of face value. The applied amount each time should not be more than 10,000 boards, and the valuation unit is 100.

T + 1 settlement is applied for spot transactions of treasury bonds. Investors and securities intermediaries complete the transaction on the second business day after the transaction is concluded.

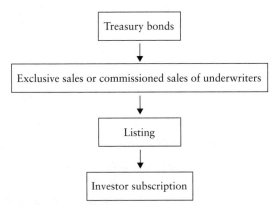

FIGURE 8.1 Flowchart of the Issuance of Treasury Bonds

TABLE 8.1 Rules for Purchasing Treasury Bonds

Issuing Mode	Listed distribution and contract distribution are adopted for the sale of the T-bond. "Listed distribution" means that the underwriters sell the bonds in the listed mode in the exchange market, and each institutional member makes the transaction for itself or purchases the bonds as the agent of investors through a seat on the exchange. "Contract distribution" means that the underwriters sign distribution contracts with other institutions or individual investors to execute distribution and purchase.
Subscription Account	Shenzhen securities account, Shanghai securities account or fund account
Subscription Code	Shenzhen Exchange: 1016** or 1017** Shanghai Exchange: 751***
Subscription Price	RMB100 for listed subscription (bond)
Subscription Institutions	The minimum applied number of sold bonds is one piece ("piece" is the unit of purchase; the RMB note with 100-yuan denomination is one piece). The minimum applied amount of purchased bonds and repurchased bonds is 10 pieces.
Subscription Fee	None.

1016** and 1017** are the transaction codes for Treasury Bond subscription and trading. Every single code consists of a six-digit number; the first four digits of the bonds code are assigned specifically to the Shenzhen Securities Exchange; every code is prefixed with 1016 of 1017. ** refers to the other two digits, which are assigned to each listed T-bond and could be any two numbers from 1 to 9. Each listed T-bond has an identical code.

Likewise, 751** is the transaction code for Treasury Bond subscription and trading. Every single code consists of a six-digit number; the first four digits of the bonds code are assigned specifically to the Shanghai Security Exchange; every code is prefixed with 751. ** refers to the other three digits, which are assigned to each T-bond and could be any three numbers from 1 to 9. Each listed T-bond has an identical code.

Safekeeping Depository and Redemption

As the legal custodian institution for treasury bond transactions, China Government Securities Depository Trust & Clearing Co., Ltd. (CGSDTC) established a centralized treasury bond custodian system. The spot transaction of the bonds is based on the custody-first-and-transaction-second principle. Before the bonds can be traded, they must be put in custody in the

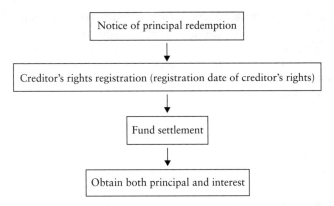

FIGURE 8.2 Redemption Procedure of Government Bonds

custodian account of Shenzhen Securities Exchange or Shanghai Securities Exchange of CGSDTC.

When the T-bonds reach maturity, investors can handle the transaction with designated securities dealers according to the bulletin on redemption of the maturing bonds.

Procedure for Redeeming Principal   Based on the Ministry of Finance bulletin on the redemption of maturing treasury bonds, the exchanges delist the maturing bonds one working day prior to the redemption date, and the principal and interest payment can be made to the investors in book-entry form. The redemption formalities are illustrated in Figure 8.2.

For the maturing T-bonds, the exchanges, after receiving the redemption funds from the Ministry, transfer the principal and interest due on the bonds into the cash account of the investors according to the balance owed to each dealer based on the registration of creditor. Investors receive their payment of principal and interest from their custodian or depository trust securities dealer.

Transaction Costs

Shenzhen Securities Exchange   Investors have to pay a commission to the securities firms when entrusting them to trade bonds. The commission must be less than 1 percent of the transaction value. Securities intermediaries engaged in spot transactions of T-bonds in Shenzhen Securities Exchange are obliged to pay a commission (0.05 percent of the transaction value) to the exchange.

Shanghai Securities Exchange Investors have to pay a commission to the securities firms that act as agents to perform spot transactions of treasury bonds on their behalf: RMB1 for those in Shanghai and RMB3 for those outside Shanghai. The commission is deductible from investors' accounts. The commission must be less than 1 percent of the transaction value.

Securities intermediaries engaged in spot transaction of T-bonds on the Shanghai Securities Exchange have to pay a commission (0.1 percent of the transaction value) to the exchange.

OPERATING PROCEDURE IN THE INTERBANK BOND MARKET

Transactions in the interbank bond market (IBBM) are performed neither through an exchange nor through brokers and dealers. They are negotiated and traded among the banks. Trading volume is huge but less frequent, so market records are hard to find. At present, the total volume of transactions of each bank comes from the bank's own reports.

Bond delivery and capital clearance in the national IBBM are two separate functions. The CGBDTC is responsible for the management of investors' bond accounts and the corresponding real-time bookkeeping and transfer. Money clearance is performed by investors through the Fund Payment System of the People's Bank of China (PBOC) or the bank in which they open an account.

There are three major means of settlement in the IBBM: Free of Payment (FOP), where payment is not against delivery; Payment after Delivery (PAD), where delivery is made before payment; and Delivery after Payment (DAP), where payment is made before delivery. The transaction can be completed only after via China National Advanced Payment System (CNAPS) and with the bank's bookkeeping system. Real-time settlement and delivery versus payment (RTS + DVP) was achieved in 2004.

The bond system of the CGBDTC has a central system—central bond book-entry system (CBBES)—and five subsystems—bond issuance system, open market operations (OMO) system, over-the-counter (OTC) central system, bond information statistics system, and customer inquiry system. Each of the five subsystems is connected to three external systems: state payment system, China's financial authentication system, and inter-bank central trading system.

The central bond book entry system's function is bond registration, custody, settlement, and clearance. By the end of 2005, total bonds in custody reached RMB7.3 trillion, issuance volume through the system amounted to RMB1 trillion, total transaction settlement volume came to

RMB40 trillion, and the redemptions reached RMB2 trillion. The frequency of issuance through the system was three per week.

The OMO system issues central bank notes, cash, and repo transactions and provides services such as on-the-line daily reports, statistics, and treasury agent cash management operations. All the transactions met the DVP standard since 2003.

The OTC center system is connected to the bank counters and provides services related to OTC transactions. There are two levels of custody: CBBES is the primary custodian responsible for trading and agent accounts. By the end of 2005, OTC had 30,000 bank counters for 900,000 individual customers.

Since 1998, all tradable government bonds in the IBBM are in book-entry form and, since 2003, central corporate bonds are registered in paperless book-entry form in CBBES. Beginning in 2004, certificate savings bonds were registered in CBBES.

The system also underpins such financial innovations as the STRIPS (separate trading of registered interest and principal of securities) and put-able bonds since 2002, sub-debt (or subordinate bond) and corporate bonds since 2004, and short-term paper. Asset-backed securities (ABS) and RMB bonds issued by international institutions are now eligible securities, and, in 2005, the services were extended to the settlement of bond forward transactions.

In addition, the settlement system in the CGBDTC has gradually connected with the national and international payment system. On November 8, 2004, the bond system was connected to the national payment system. As a result, DVP settlement was achieved, and there are 100 institutions engaged in DVP transactions through the CBBES.

DEVELOPMENT AND FUNCTIONS OF SECURITIES INTERMEDIARIES

The term "treasury bond market participants" refers to the institutions and individuals that participate in market activities and play a role in market functions. Government (usually the Ministry of Finance), the central bank, commercial banks, institutional investors, individual investors, and the securities intermediaries are the major participants in the government bond market.

From the point of view of market function, they can be divided into issuers, investors, and intermediaries. Generally, the Ministry of Finance is the issuer and agent of treasury bonds; the central bank provides services to the issuers; securities companies serve as the intermediaries; and banks and institutions are the investors.

The secondary market of treasury bonds is divided into three parts: market operators, market makers, and investors. The government usually does not get involved in the secondary market directly, but sometimes takes part in market operations as debt manager. The central bank participates through its open market operation. Therefore, both government and the central bank are the market operators. The primary dealers play the role of market makers, while the banks and institutional and individual investors are the major traders.

As a dominant player in the bond market, the primary dealer, or market maker, quotes bid and offer prices according to clients' demand. Clients execute the transactions directly with the market makers based on the quoted price. The market makers can also trade among themselves. The major participants in the bond market are institutional investors.

Securities intermediaries in China came into being in 1988 along with the secondary market in treasury bonds. To ensure an effective T-bond market, the Treasury Bond Service Department, which used to be in bond service agent for the issuance and redemption of treasury bonds, began to engage in T-bond circulation and transfer. Around the same time, banks also began to establish their affiliated securities companies. These securities firms, although in the preliminary stages, became the first T-bond intermediaries in China. By the end of 1990, there were nearly 100 securities intermediaries.

After 1990, some T-bond service departments began to evolve into treasury securities companies. In addition, the trust and investment companies that emerged after financial reform began to set up securities sales departments. After 1993, almost every specialized bank had its own trust and investment companies, and every trust and investment company had its own securities sales department. By 1995, there were nearly 1,000 securities intermediaries, treasury bond service departments, and trust and investment companies engaged in the stock exchange in China.

One of the most important advances in 1993 was the establishment of the primary dealer system of the treasury bonds. That year the Ministry of Finance and the China Securities Regulatory Commission ratified 19 institutions as the first group of primary dealers in T-bonds. The qualification requirement at that time was that the institution should possess over RMB30 million paid-in capital and have a sound record in underwriting T-bonds and handling T-bond transactions. The advent of primary dealers marked a new stage in the development of the securities intermediary sector.

In 1993, after the reform of the banks, all the specialized banks were required to hold a certain amount of the treasury bonds in order to conduct asset and liability management (ALM), and, since 1995, the specialized banks have gradually begun to enter the T-bond market. When the qualifications of the primary dealers of treasury bonds were reviewed in 1995, the major specialized banks and the commercial banks were also included among the primary dealers of T-bonds.

In 1994, the Ministry of Finance took the lead in issuing a short-term treasury bill underwritten by banks to cooperate with the OMO of the central bank. As a first step, banks were requested by the central bank to hold treasury bonds, which enabled the central bank to trade in T-bonds with commercial banks and specialized banks. After 1995, banks actively participated in the underwriting and the business of T-bonds, playing a significant role in the growth of the T-bond market.

At present, Chinese securities intermediaries are mainly nonbank financial institutions—the securities firms and securities departments in trust and investment companies, whose major business is as clients' agents. Banks are involved in the T-bond business as buyers and holders. They hold treasury bonds only for the purpose of ALM. In this sense, banks are not financial intermediaries of T-bonds. However, as some big banks are assigned the role of primary dealers of treasury bonds, they are very active in underwriting them. In fact, the major state-owned commercial banks, such as the Industrial and Commercial Bank of China (ICBC), Bank of China (BOC), China Construction Bank (CCB), and the Agricultural Bank of China (ABC) also play the part of treasury bond wholesalers. Thus, they are also financial intermediaries in the IBBM. Because of the managerial requirement to separate securities from banking, the trust and investment companies and securities sales departments affiliated with banks are separating this business from their banking business. Many of them have gradually become completely independent securities intermediaries.

In the late 1990s and early 2000s, as a result of a slowdown in the economy and a large number of non-performing loans, banks were less inclined to give loans to the industrial and commercial sectors; rather, they preferred to buy and hold T-bonds, which provide risk-free profits for them when the bank deposit interest rate is lower than the T-bond yield.

In China the securities intermediaries can be divided into four groups:

1. *Wholesalers.* As underwriters of treasury bonds, the securities intermediaries played an important role in the underwriting syndication program in early 1990s. Underwriters distribute the treasury bonds to investors, making their sale more efficient. As the primary dealers of T-bonds have the liability to underwrite new issues in the primary market, they also share the selling obligation. This is crucial to ensure a smooth sale of T-bonds.
2. *Trade agents.* The securities intermediaries offer agent services to investors for the trading of the T-bonds. Most individual investors

trade T-bonds and other bond securities through securities firms since they are not members of the stock exchanges.

3. *Brokers.* Brokers provide agent services to the small local intermediaries. Many big securities firms are assigned the brokerage function. They do business on behalf of other institutions, not as dealers on their own.

4. *Market makers.* Market makers facilitate the bid and ask (two-way quotation) system in the market. Although the market-making function is not performed very well in China, some primary dealers, including securities firms and banks, are required to make the market when trading is inactive.

Thus, Chinese securities intermediaries play a vital role in not only underwriting and distributing treasury bonds and facilitating the liquidity of the secondary market, but also in transforming the T-bond market from a retail market to a wholesale market and thereby driving the development of the entire securities market.

FINANCING CHANNELS OF SECURITIES INTERMEDIARIES

The financing channels of Chinese securities intermediaries are relatively one-dimensional. The paid-in capital of Chinese securities intermediaries is fairly slim, and their debt ratio is relatively high. In middle of the 1990s, market participants in the stock exchange market began the practice of repo spontaneously in their hope to alleviate short-term financing issues. Soon after, the Ministry of Finance issued a regulation on repo transactions. For a period, the repo market became the major source of financing for securities firms. As securities firms continued to feel financial pressure, they sought alternative sources of financing. In fact, as mentioned, there was a time when securities firms embezzled the deposits of clients for their own financial needs.

In 1993, when the stock market was overheating, securities firms were very active in the stock market. The lucrative stock trading business alleviated their financing difficulties. However, toward the turn of the twenty-first century, the stock market was fluctuating and even declining, and some firms suffered losses and went bankrupt. Since 2004, the market began sliding again, triggering a crises in the whole securities industry.

Against this background, in 2005, the People's Bank of China and the China Securities Regulatory Commission pursued a new initiative—to open the bond market to securities firms. Securities firms may now issue short-term paper as their financing instrument. In addition, the bail-out policy for the banks was also available to securities firms, and many firms get capital from Hui Jin Company, a state vehicle investing in ill-performing state financial institutions.

Role of Banks in the T-Bond Market

In the 1950s, banks were the underwriters of treasury bonds. Throughout the 1980s, banks mainly engaged in policy-based lending and were not interested in underwriting and trading T-bonds and other bond securities only for the commissions they might earn. However, at the end of 1980s, the government wanted to absorb excess liquidity in the banking system and encouraged banks to invest in treasury bonds.

The first step following this policy move was to target fiscal bond issuance only to banks. From 1987 to 1993, the Ministry of Finance issued fiscal bonds through private placement on a yearly basis that were subscribed by banks and financial institutions. In 1991, the banks, along with securities firms, participated in the subscription of T-bonds through an underwriting syndicate. In 1994, the banks subscribed six-month and one-year T-bills and underwrote all the three-year savings bonds before they were redistributed to individuals. It was the first time the banks rather than securities firms underwrote most treasury bonds.

Securities intermediaries were mainly securities departments affiliated with specialized banks and commercial banks, including securities companies and the securities departments of the trust and investment companies. The institutions with comparatively strong financial strength were, among others, Jiangsu Securities Company, Zhejiang Securities Company, Haitong Securities Company, and Shenyin Securities Company. By 1992, there were more than 1,000 securities intermediaries; however, most of them had little paid-in capital and were weak financially. To reinforce the strength of the securities intermediaries, three securities companies—Huaxia, China Southern, and Guotai—each with capital of RMB1 billion, were established by the ICBC, ABC, and CCB, respectively. In addition, there are some joint venture securities intermediaries. The companies with strength in this area are Shenyin Wanguo Securities Company and Jun'an Securities Company.

Toward the end of the twentieth century, many securities firms were reorganized, and many were annexed to each other. A number of mergers and acquisitions occurred. New companies, such as Guotai Jun'an, were established. This restructuring reflected the furious competition and the weakness of individual securities firms. This move marked a new era of consolidation.

Institutional Investors

The social insurance industry in China is composed of the government social security system and commercial insurance. The social security system is managed by the Ministry of Labor and Social Security. Commercial insurance can be divided into state-owned commercial insurance companies and joint venture insurance companies.

Early institutional investors in China fall into two categories: pension funds and unemployment funds, usually called "Two Funds." They are government-run funds.

The practice of purchasing the treasury bonds through "Two Funds" started in 1989. "Two Funds" used two different ways to invest in treasury bonds. One was to purchase the special bonds issued from 1989 to 1991, in the form of international bonds with a total amount of RMB3 billion or so; the other was to purchase treasury bills issued from 1992 to 1993, in the form of physical bonds (i.e., bearer bonds), which are the same as the treasury bills purchased by individuals. The issuing amount through this method was approximately RMB4 billion. They all traded in the market in the same way as other treasury bills did.

In 1992, the state stipulated explicitly that the balance of "Two Funds" should be used to purchase the treasury bills. In recent years, much of "Two Funds" assets have been used to pay for pension and unemployment relief, so the balance is limited. As a result, the amount of treasury bill assigned to "Two Funds" was decreasing gradually. From 1992 to 1997, the special T-bonds issue targeted to "Two Funds" was kept between RMB3 billion and RMB4 billion.

In 1998, the National Council of Social Security Fund (NCSSF) was set by the State Council to run the social security fund assigned by the central government. The NCSSF invested in government bonds from its establishment.

Commercial insurance companies, such as the People's Insurance Company of China (PICC), were founded as early as the 1950s. Toward the end of the twentieth century, there existed several life insurance companies and shareholding insurance companies, such as Huatai Insurance Company, Property and Casualty Company; Life Insurance of PICC; and Reinsurance of PICC. The registered capital of joint stock insurance companies includes three national insurance companies with capital of over RMB1 billion each: Ping An Insurance Company, China Pacific Insurance Company, and Huatai Insurance Company.

In addition, rural unemployment insurance exists. Commercial insurance companies did not invest in government bonds and other bond securities until very recently. Some insurance companies set up asset management companies to run their ever-increasing insurance assets. Huatai Assets Management Company, among others, is one of the most active investors in bond securities.

Currently the payment of premiums is calculated based on the present value of future anticipated payments discounted by the current interest rate. The discount rate should be based on the market rate, but, in practice, it is based on so-called estimated rate.

At present, the social security system holds RMB70 billion cash balance, which was mainly invested in special treasury bonds issued by the Ministry of Finance during early 1990s. Toward the end of the last century, commercial insurance companies in China developed rapidly. In 1997, the premium income of commercial insurance across China was RMB108 billion. It is predicted that the premium income will increase at the rate of 20 to 30 percent in the future.

Currently, the major institutional investors are banks and insurance companies. Before 1997, Chinese T-bonds were issued in the stock exchange market. In 1997, a large amount of money financed through repos flowed into the stock market from banks. This illegal action increased risk on the banking sector. For this reason, the central bank limited banks and non-bank financial institutions from investing in the inter-bank bond market. That is why the treasury bond market is divided into two separate markets: the Stock Exchange Market (SEM) and the IBBM.

This separation of marketplaces also reshaped the investor base. Obviously, banks remain the principal sources of money in the treasury bond market. However, due to the separate marketplaces, the major market participants in the T-bond market are segmented between the IBBM and the SEM, which is naturally counterproductive to the development and growth of the treasury bond market. As a result, the late 1990s saw a slowdown in the development of the T-bond market, which prior to that time had achieved rapid growth.

However, institutional investors as a whole developed very rapidly in the aftermath. From 1998 to the early 2000s, investors in the Chinese T-bond market expanded greatly. In addition, investment sophistication has substantially improved, and investment behavior became more rational. The organizational structure of institutional investors has also changed to cater to the needs of a changing market environment.

In the SEM, the investor base has been relatively diverse for some time. Nonbank financial institutions, individuals, and institutional investors can be involved. The market is quite energetic and more liquid than it once was.

As far as the IBBM is concerned, with the increased growth in national savings, the transformation of the corporate governance of the commercial banks, the narrowing spread in the interest rate differentials between deposits and loans, and the piling up of bad debts in banks, banks become more risk-averse, therefore T-bonds become the main investment instruments for them. It has been gradually understood that holding liquid bonds would enable banks to improve their assets and liabilities management, reducing nonperforming assets ratio and increasing profit (reclaimable profit, not book profit).

Amid rapid development of the OMO of the central bank, the institutional investors in the inter-bank treasury bond market has mushroomed from only a dozen institutional investors to over 800 financial institutions, including commercial banks.

In order to boost the advancement of the T-bond market and reshape the investor structure in the IBBM, the central bank and the Ministry of Finance wanted to bridge the gap between IBBM and OTC where individual investors buy T-bonds via bank counters. The idea was to encourage individual investors, rather than those who open accounts at stock exchanges and engage in frequent trading of both bonds and stocks, to access the book-entry securities. The two agencies jointly promulgated the management method for the OTC trading of book-entry-form treasury bonds on April 4, 2002. The government's pilot program in OTC transactions began on June 17, 2002, bringing middle and small investors, including individuals, into the IBBM. The PBOC approved 39 commercial banks, including the Industrial and Commercial Bank of China, to provide securities clearing services for nonfinancial institutions, which means that these enterprises, as the microeconomic mainstay of China's economy, can enter the IBBM through securities clearing agents. This move is not only favorable for the diversification of current institutional investor's behavior, which is characterized by homogeneity and common knowledge of market awareness in the inter-bank treasury bond market, but also for encouraging the market activity of institutional investors.

RATIONALE FOR DEVELOPING THE SECONDARY MARKET

In summary, the secondary market is important to a healthy debt capital market as well as the whole financial market for several reasons.

First, a sound secondary market can improve the liquidity of financial market, which can increase the daily turnover so that money can be more efficiently used. As the secondary market is a place where bond securities can be traded among investors, it reduces investors' transaction costs, thereby raising the efficiency of financial market.

Perhaps there are more peculiarities than commonplaces insofar as the secondary bond market is concerned. Different countries have different secondary markets with different structures for their T-bond transactions. In some countries, the tradable T-bonds are held mostly by individuals, while in others they are held by institutional investors.

Such differences in holding structure have major implications for the transaction mode. If the T-bond market is an OTC market focused on trading among individual investors, government debt managers do not have to get directly involved in the management of secondary market, as individual investors for the most part buy and hold the bonds (i.e., they do not trade much in the market). However, if institutional investors and experienced asset managers are the major participants, the T-bond secondary market tends to trade more frequently and create substantial market turnover. In such circumstances, government debt managers must consider establishing a highly efficient secondary market for treasury bonds to ensure a smooth selling of T-bonds in the primary market.

However, because institutions tend to be active in the market, a developed secondary market should be an institution-based one. Nowadays, most bond markets are institution-based markets or are transitioning to such markets. China recognized this important fact fairly early. As noted, when China began its secondary market in 1988, it was completely an individual-based market. The defects of individual-based market were soon realized, and China started to build an institution-based market.

Second, due to the close relationship between primary and secondary markets, the development of the secondary market will help to boost the primary market, and vice versa. The secondary market provides benchmarks for pricing in the primary market. Investors in the primary market always refer to the yield in the secondary market. The capital gains of "secondhand" treasury bonds refer to the income investors earned from bond transactions in the secondary market relative to their initial investment. This rate of return on T-bonds in the secondary market provides the basis for the pricing of new bond issuances and reference for bidders in auctions. Therefore, whatever selling technique is used, the offering price of new issues must be consistent with the rate of return in the secondary market to ensure a smooth execution of the transaction. Historical data show that new issues tend to encounter significant selling distress when the secondary market is volatile. The stability of price levels and yields in the secondary market depends on how deep the market is. This is also evident in China. For example, in 1992, China's primary market for T-bonds encountered significant downturns. One of the major reasons was the inversion of the interest rate of the new issues and the yield rate of old ones. In 2003, when the central bank raised the interest rate, as has happened before, there were several times when government securities failed to fulfill their issuance targets through auctions.

Third, an efficient secondary market is crucial in order to meet the government's requirement for long-term financing. Institutional investors are the only ones that prefer to hold long-term treasury bonds, as their liabilities are long term by nature (e.g., pension funds, insurance funds, and annuities all have long-term liabilities). Longer-term assets would therefore help the banks match their assets and liabilities. However, the longer they hold the bonds, the more risk they face. Therefore, they need a highly liquid market to manage their risk.

Fourth, the secondary market can help to smooth, and to ensure the continuity of, the selling process. This is especially true when treasury bonds are sold through public bidding or tap issue, because the new selling price should reflect the changing secondary market price. This means the secondary market can be imagined as a reservoir of market instruments, with the water always readily available whenever the tap is turned on.

Finally, the secondary market, as viewed from institutional economic engineering (IEEN) perspective, is a secondary exchange, where the market is built for the benefit of market participants.

Although this observation is now considered common sense, the essence of the secondary market has never been properly revealed. From the perspective of IEEN, the secondary market is an efficient way to carry out secondary exchange, that is, the social economic activities for the benefit of each market participants. Functions derived from secondary exchange boost the exchange via division of labor. Here, it is important to make a distinction between the *social* division of labor and the *economic* division of labor. The division of the market into retail and wholesale markets is a specialized process that reduces economic (both transaction and production) costs. However, this entails more transactions, for example, the transactions between primary dealers and investors and between financial intermediaries and retail investors. This is the so-called economic division of labor as opposed to the social division of labor, or institutional division of labor, which is the division of labor between the primary exchange and the secondary exchange.

As indicated, a primary exchange function to create rules exerts enforcement, and defines property right. But rules are not primary exchange per se. Rules are made as a result of the primary exchange. Primary bond exchange includes of all the interplay between government relative agency and the other market participants. As a government agency is entitled to make rules, but not laws, the primary bond exchange (similar to other primary exchanges) is not pursued on an equal footing. So the primary political exchanges (PPEs) enter the picture at higher levels of primary exchange. However, the primary bond exchange will eventually reach in equilibrium. This process tends to favor government agency at beginning and subsequently move back to a balance. The development of China's bond market reflects this process exactly. The primary bond market is the most efficient way to pursue the primary bond exchange.

CHAPTER 9

Treasury Bond Investment Fund

The fund industry in China includes venture capital funds, industry investment funds, joint venture funds, and securities investment funds. Along with the financial market development, the fund industry has increasingly become a more and more important component of the capital market. Funds step into the spotlight as active institutional investors; their holdings of bond securities are second only to those of the banks. In fact, it is anticipated that the fund industry will replace banks as the main institutional investors.

In 1995, there were only 21 venture capital funds in China, and total investment by the funds was RMB4.38 billion. However, by the end of 2004, the number of venture capital funds reached 217, and local governments were financed mainly by the venture capital fund industry. Local government direct investment amounted to RMB19.4 billion in 2004.[1] The development of the fund industry reflected the need to transform indirect financing to direct financing. It also reflects the fact that the local governments are dissatisfied with the slow progress in developing a corporate bond market, so that they have to rely on the fund industry.

Joint venture funds are created by the combined investments of foreign governments and a Chinese counterparty, such as the China Development Bank (CDB) and other financial institutions. The main objectives of these funds are to invest in joint venture companies and China-related small and medium enterprises (SMEs). Today, there are three joint venture funds in China: the Sino-ASEAN (Association of Southeast Asian Nations) fund, the Sino-Belgium fund, and the Sino-Swiss fund. The Sino-Swiss Partnership Fund (SSPF) was established in January 1998 based on a memorandum of understanding signed by the governments of the People's Republic of China and the State Secretariat for Economic Affairs (SECO). The Sino-Swiss Venture Capital Fund Management Company (SSVC) was formed in September 2001 by SECO and SSPF. The Sino-Belgium Direct Equity Investment Fund was established on November 18, 2004, with an investment of €100 million. Shareholders include the Chinese Ministry of Finance, Belgian

Public Telecommunications Operator Belgacom, China Haitong Securities Co. Ltd., Belgium-based Fortis Bank, China Development Bank, National Social Security Fund, China Banknotes Printing and Minting Corporation, State Development and Investment Corporation, and Guangdong Strong Group. Investments are confined to unlisted SMEs.

The China-ASEAN Investment Fund for Small and Medium-Sized Enterprises was established on May 15, 2003, with a total investment of $76 million. The shareholders are the Asian Development Bank, Swiss State Secretariat for Economic Affairs, China Development Bank, Venture Management Ltd. of Singapore-based United Overseas Bank (UOB), Japan-based Asian Investment Company, and France-based Economic Cooperation and Investment Promotion Company. The fund is designed to target SMEs based in China and ASEAN member countries.[2]

Although these funds do not invest in bonds, the development of the fund industry helped improve fund management in general and furthered the development of fund management institutions in China. That development is important for the securities investment fund industry. The securities investment funds are closely related to bond market development.

TREASURY BOND AND SECURITIES INVESTMENT FUNDS

The treasury bond investment fund, or the treasury bond fund, is designed to boost the institutional investor base, and the advent of T-bond fund is an important step in promoting the function of the secondary T-bond market. The fund will help to transform the original retail market into a wholesale market.

The proposal to establish a treasury bond investment fund was initiated by Ministry of Finance as early as 1993. The initial motivation was to facilitate the investment in treasury bonds by individuals in cities and in rural areas and remote areas who had difficulty accessing treasury bonds because the participation of institutional investors squeezed the individual investors. The Ministry discussed the possibility of developing a treasury bond fund and concluded that its development would help middle and small investors gain access to the bond market, so that their desire to purchase bonds could be satisfied. If individuals had no complaints regarding access to treasury bonds, then the program to boost the institution-based treasury bond market could be carried out without opposition.

However, to avoid increasing the financial chaos due to the illegal activities of financial institutions around middle 1990s, the Ministry of Finance decided not to proceed with the treasury bond fund program and postponed issuing a formal timetable. Some pilot programs were conducted, however. Seeing the positive role the fund program, the central bank expedited the process of drafting regulations for the fund's management.

Meanwhile, Huaxia Securities Company and Daiwa Securities Group of Japan, China Southern Securities Company and Yamaichi Securities Company of Japan, and Shanghai Finance Securities and Xinghui Financial Company of Hong Kong had begun to prepare for the establishment of a joint venture in treasury bond securities companies, and applied to the central bank for authorization to proceed.

The motivation to develop a T-bond fund also came from market participants. In fact, in the absence of a T-bond fund, many securities firms designed and sold composite certificates (CCs), a kind of derivative product based on a package of listed T-bonds, or long-term bonds broken down into short-term bonds. These practices were similar to selling a fund to individual investors. In late 1990s, the inactive stock market stimulated the idea of setting up a stock investment fund to encourage the individual's investment in stocks. This move overshadowed the Ministry of Finance's efforts to establish a T-bond fund, but, as a compromise, the stock investment funds were required to invest at least 20 percent in treasury bonds.

STOCK INVESTMENT FUND

Based on the regulations, securities firms launched the stock investment fund. The term of the fund was determined by the fund's initiator. With the approval of the China Securities Regulatory Commission (CSRC), the term can be extended one year, although it can be terminated earlier if the total shares of beneficial interest are less than the original shares or any irresistible natural forces occur.

The corporate governance of the fund is the same as that of other types of funds. The fund managers are legally ratified as fund management companies while the beneficiaries are the fund ticket holders (including individuals and institutions). The trustees are the institutions where stock and T-bond assets are put in custody; the operational institutions are banks and securities companies, assigned by the management companies and trusteeship companies, dealing in T-bond funds.

Targeted investors include any natural person or legal person with legal status at home and abroad. Every fund unit shares equal rights, including automatic reinvestment of beneficial interest, callability, distribution of surplus assets, and any other rights stipulated in the fund's contract.

The fund issuance and the subscription mode are confirmed by the sales institutions assigned by the fund managers and are promulgated in the Fund-Raising Directive. The beneficial voucher has two forms: bearer voucher and registered voucher. The bearer voucher is denominated, while the registered voucher can be either denominated or nondenominated. The beneficiaries can either hold the vouchers or entrust the sales companies to keep the vouchers for them, and hold them in trusteeship companies. The trusteeship companies are required to maintain a registry of holders, and the management companies keep the photocopy. The minimum amount subscribed is a designated fund unit, which increases by a multiple of the initial unit. The commission charge for raising funds usually is 1 percent of every fund unit. The fund cannot be legally established if it fails to reach the minimum.

FIXED INCOME FUNDS

At present, there are two types of fixed income funds: bond funds and money market funds.

Bond Funds

As their name implies, bond funds are funds specially invested in bonds. In China, the investment objectives of the bond funds are the treasury bonds, financial bonds, and enterprise bonds. Usually the fund offers investors a fixed return and repays the principal at maturity. As the risk of investment in a bond fund is lower than investing in stocks or a stock fund, bond funds offer stable income and lower risk, and, therefore, they are designed to attract risk-averse investors.

At present, the small individual investors can access only certificate savings bonds over the counter (OTC) of banks. However, the bonds are in limited supply; the bond's coupon rate, the simple interest, is going down gradually to close the bank deposit rate, and loss is incurred for early withdrawal.

Insofar as investment channels for marketable bonds are concerned, residents, ordinary enterprises, and institutions are not permitted to enter the interbank bond market (IBBM). Financial bonds and most enterprise bonds are not issued to ordinary investors. Moreover, the exchange market is volatile; ordinary investors do not have time, professional knowledge to invest directly in this market. Hence, the bond fund is an ideal channel through which ordinary investors can access these bonds. Management of the funds by professional experts can disperse risk and improve returns. Furthermore, the investment can be redeemed at any time and therefore has better liquidity.

Based on different forms of organization and legal status, the securities investment funds can be categorized into contract funds and corporate funds. At present, the securities investment funds in China are set up as contract funds. Depending on whether the issuing amount is fixed or not, the funds can be divided into closed-end funds and open funds. Most current securities funds are open funds.

The bond investment funds in China are usually invested in certificate savings bonds over the bank counters. Book-entry-form T-bonds and financial debentures are sold and traded in the IBBM. The book-entry-form T-bonds and enterprise bonds are sold and traded in the exchange market.

In China, bond fund development is just beginning. The first bond fund, China Southern Baoyuan, appeared in September 2002. Thereafter, numerous bond funds were established, with 12 bond funds set up in 2003 alone, accounting for 80 percent of total. The enthusiasm for setting up fund companies faded, and no new bond fund was set up in 2004 except Xingye transferable bond fund. The initial size of the 15 bond funds was 31.572 billion shares. By the third quarter of 2004, this had shrunk to 9.412 billion shares. The size of some funds was quite small. Jingshun Hengfeng has been less than 100 million shares, and the bond funds of Guotai, Jiashi, and Penghua have little more than 100 million shares for each.

So far the performance of security investment funds has been unsatisfactory for several reasons. Most funds in this category have invested their portfolios mostly in stocks. They cannot hedge their systematic risks. In addition, fund managers are not educated in fund management and are generally inexperienced. There are more restrictions on investment fund managers to limit alternative investments.

Bond funds have not been well received because of their unsatisfactory yield. From the establishment of the fund to early 2006, 6 out of 15 bond funds have had a negative growth rate in net value (the growth rate of net assets value of the Jiashi bond set up in July of 2005 was −5.4 percent). The net redemption rate of these six funds over the past year was around 80 percent, and some individual funds reached 90 percent.

However, even funds with higher growth in net value have suffered net redemptions. Baokang bond fund ranked first with 9.25 percent of the return. This fund was established on July 15, 2003, with satisfactory returns. China Southern Baoyuan, which has been operating for two years, has outstanding performance, with a net value growth rate of 9.92 percent since its establishment. Despite their good track records, Baokang and Baoyuan also suffered the redemption of large amounts from investors. China Southern Baoyuan dropped from 4.9 billion shares at the very beginning to 1.2 billion shares in the third quarter of 2005. Baokang bond dropped from 1.3 billion shares to 840 million shares.

However, the funds have not yet attracted sufficient attention from individual investors. Besides the fact that the initial offering size went beyond the approved size, which resulted in early redemption, another important reason for lack of active individual participation is that some investors who were seeking higher short-term returns did not realize that funds, which have lower risk than stocks, also have lower returns. China Southern Baoyuan is a good example; its annual return is around 5 percent, which is quite good for a bond fund, but investors are dissatisfied with this yield. The year 2006 witnessed a soaring increase of stock market index, which turned around the five-year decline trend. However, the market is mainly supported by individual investors rather than by institutional investors, especially by the funds.

Prospects for the success of a bond fund in the short term are not good. China has entered a period of interest fluctuation, and the underdeveloped bond market characterized by market segmentation, insufficient liquidity of IBBM, incomplete bond variety, lack of short-term bonds, and an underdeveloped enterprise bond market, has dragged down the development of bond funds, which require sophisticated fund management skill. These institutional-based issues restrict the development of bond funds.

Money Market Funds

From the birth in 2002 of the first Chinese money market fund—Hua'an Cash Fuli Fund under Hua'an Fund Management Company—to the present, seven money market funds have been founded one after the other. According to the Interim Provisional Regulations of the Money Market Fund Management, money market funds should be invested in these financial tools:

- Cash
- Time deposits and wholesale funds deposit receipts (up to and including one year)
- Bonds whose remainder term is up to 360 days
- Bond repurchases with a term of no more than one year
- Bills of the central bank with a term of no more than one year
- Other money market tools with good liquidity accredited by China Securities Regulatory Commission and the People's Bank of China

Currently, the investment scope of the money market fund is limited in the types of bonds, bills of central banks, and repurchase (repo) instruments it can purchase.

The money market fund is the investment fund invested in the money market (the average term is 120 days) and in short-term currency tools, such as T-bonds, wholesale transferable deposit receipts, commercial paper, and corporate bonds.

There are four main differences between money market funds and traditional funds.

1. The most obvious distinction is that the unit equity of the money market fund is fixed as RMB1 per unit of fund. After making an investment in money market funds, the investor can use the repayment to reinvest, increasing the number of shares in the fund, and investment payments continually accumulate.
2. In money market funds, the valuation standard for the fund is the return rate, which is different from other funds that gain incremental value and profit from net assets.
3. The money market fund is liquid and secure, as money market instruments are generally low risk and highly fluid.
4. The money market fund has a lower return as it has lower risk.

The maturity of money market tools is usually very short. The average term of combined investment of the money market fund is four to six months. Accordingly, the risk is quite low, and the price is only subject to the market rate. The money market fund usually does not charge a redemption fee, and the management expense is relatively low, about 0.25 to 1 percent of fund equity, much lower than the traditional annual management expense rate of 1 to 1.25 percent.

In addition to stable proceeds, strong liquidity, low purchase quota, and high capital security, the money market fund has other functions in the mature market. For example, the fund account can be used to sign and issue checks and pay consumption bills; it can temporarily serve in lieu of cash before making a new investment. The cash earns a higher rate than the current bank deposit rate and can be withdrawn at any time for other investments. Some investors initially purchase a large amount of money market funds and then redeem them gradually to invest in stocks, bonds, and other types of funds. Many investors even put their emergency money in money market funds. For the convenience of investors, some money market funds even allow investors to withdraw money directly through automated teller machines (ATMs).

As investment instruments for individual investors in China are confined to certificate savings bonds and the stock market, with little in between, the money market fund, among others, provides the most convenient investment instrument. In a market economy elsewhere, this type of deposit offers higher security and liquidity and certain profitability. Therefore, it serves individual investors well. The advent of the money market fund caused the outflow of money from the banks.

Chinese institutional investors are also interested in money market funds. More and more institutional investors regard such funds as a liquid reserve of capital, which can optimize cash management. At present, a good many domestic enterprises lack cash management tools. With higher liquidity and stable income, money market funds can serve as a cost-efficient management tool for both large-cap and small-cap institutions. For instance, among institutional investors, the not-for-profit asset management institutions, such as the Chinese Social Security Fund (including pension fund and unemployment insurance fund), possess a huge amount of capital. With the continuous improvement in the social security system, the amount of cash in the Social Security Fund is constantly increasing, and, therefore, the money market fund is an ideal choice for it.

The fund industry has been developing very rapidly to reflect the need for industry investment and private equity investment, as well as the needs of developing institutional investors and the increase in size of the social security system. From the point of view of bond market development, funds play a very important role in investing in government bonds and other bond securities.

However, a successful fund depends on the fund's management. Management companies are owned by either institutions (captives) or management themselves (independents) or a combination of the two. The source of their income is primarily management fees and a share of the net gains of a fund. Their survival depends on their ability to replace the funds under management as and when they are liquidated. Management companies that produce superior returns are able to raise more and larger sums.

It is important to recognize that the development of the securities investment industry will depend on the evolution of institutions with respect to fund management and that the lessons learned from joint venture funds can provide China with beneficial international experience.

CHAPTER 10

Treasury Bond Repurchase Market

Bond repurchase (repo) is one of the basic instruments in China's financial market. It serves not only as a short-term financing instrument for financial institutions, but also as one of the basic instruments with which the central bank can carry out its open market operation.

HISTORY OF TREASURY BONDS REPURCHASE

The treasury bond repo transaction in China includes on-exchange trading and over-the-counter (OTC) trading. Over-the-counter repurchase applies to the bearer form; that is, physical or treasury bond agent certificates, which are not currently standardized. On-exchange trading is carried out on various exchanges. In the 1990s, the institutions providing such repurchase transaction services included the Shanghai Stock Exchange, the Shenzhen Stock Exchange, the Wuhan Treasury Bonds Exchange Center, the stock trading automation quotation (STAQ) system, and the Tianjin Stock Exchange Center. These institutions have their own rules to regulate the term structure of T-bond repo transactions, eligible bonds for repurchase, as well as the amount and mode of transaction of the repurchase agreement target.

On December 25, 1993, the Shanghai Stock Exchange began its T-bond repurchase transaction. At that time, there were only three instruments: one-month, three-month, and six-month. The transaction size was relatively small, and repurchase transactions were based on the five underlying bond securities.

In September 1994, the repo products based on a specific underlying bond of a particular year were abandoned, and standardized repo products, which were converted at a specified ratio to the bond's face value regardless of how the specific bond was designed, were used for repo transactions. The annual return rate other than price was quoted for transactions.

On May 3, 1996, the method of ratio setting was adjusted, with the periodic announcement of the conversion ratio of the standard bond being applied. On May 6, a new instrument, the three-day repo, was added.

To encourage and standardize the T-bond repo business, simplify repo products, and promote convenient repurchase transactions, the Shanghai Stock Exchange, starting on September 12, 1994, abandoned the method of setting the price of repurchase products according to the specific year or terms of the underlying bond regardless of type. The exchange thereby created the standardized treasury bond repurchase product, which was converted based on the face value of different bond securities.

Throughout 1990s, the T-bond repo rapidly evolved into an important transaction instrument. In Shanghai, the total repurchase amount of the stock exchange reached RMB42 million and RMB6.31 billion in 1993 and 1994 respectively. According to incomplete statistics, the on-exchange transaction amount in 1994 had already reached RMB310 billion (amount of unilateral transaction), accounting for 12.4 percent of total T-bond transactions. Included were several T-bond transaction products, such as spot, futures, and repurchase. (See Table 10.1 for transaction amounts in various exchanges and their market shares.)

The repurchase business was conducted mainly by the Wuhan Stock Exchange Center, the Tianjin Stock Exchange Center, and the STAQ system. The minimum denomination for transactions was increased to cater to huge volume transactions. For instance, the Shanghai Stock Exchange and the Wuhan Stock Exchange Center requested that the minimum denomination of the bond repurchased be the standard one of RMB100,000. According to the regulation prescribed by the Shenzhen Stock Exchange, the minimum requirement of on-exchange repurchase agreement was about RMB20,000 and the amount of OTC transaction was increased to RMB500,000 and higher. The money market interest rate quotation replaced the yield of underlying treasury bonds for the repo market.

In the late 1990s, during the national campaign to rectify the financial problems, all exchanges other than the Shanghai Stock Exchange and the Shenzhen Stock Exchange were closed and the inter-bank bond market (IBBM) repo market emerged in parallel to the stock exchange. From then on, the repo market was limited to the stock exchange bond market (SEBM) and IBBM. However, the repo trading rules of each exchange and IBBM were yet to be unified or standardized, which was counterproductive to the further development of the repo market in China.

TABLE 10.1 Treasury Bond Transaction Amounts on Various Exchanges

Name of Exchange			Transaction Amount (RMB 100 million)	Accounting for Percentage of Total Transaction Amount of Treasury bonds
Bond Products	**Bond Code**	**Conversion Ratio**		
Five-year term of 1992	1925	1:1:6		
Five-year term of 1993	1935	1:1:6		
Three-year term of 1995	1953	1:1:1		
One-year term (1) of 1996	1961	1:0:9		
Three-year term (1) of 1996	1963	1:1		
One-year term (2) of 1996				
Ten-year term of 1996	1965	1:0:9		
Three-year term of 1996	1966	1:1		
	1967	1:1		
Shanghai Stock Exchange			107.9	0.96
Shenzhen Stock Exchange			15.73	3.12
Wuhan Stock Exchange Center			1500	45.59
SATQ system				
Tianjin Stock Exchange			900	80.00
Center			750	90.00

REPO MARKET OVERVIEW

Types of Repo Products

On September 9, 1994, the Shanghai Stock Exchange fixed five repo products corresponding to the underlying treasury bonds (see Table 10.2).

Repurchase Transaction Method   In the repurchase transaction method, both purchasers and sellers are participants in the repo market. The repo has two transactions but in one contract when the repo is maturing, the reverse transaction is carried out. The definition of buyers and sellers is based on their behavior in the second stage, the reverse transaction is opposite to the initial transaction. The repo is concluded as soon as reverse transaction is conducted. The one who pays to purchase bonds is the seller of the repurchase transaction while the one who receives money that paid for the bonds in such a transaction is the purchaser.

When market participants conduct a repurchase transaction, they entrust the securities intermediaries to conduct the trading on their behalf. As to the maturity repurchase price, annual capital yield return is applied.

Underlying Bond—Repurchase Mortgage Bonds or Pledged Bonds   In August 8, 1995, the Government Bond Management Department (GBMD) of the Ministry of Finance, the People's Bank of China (PBOC), and the China Securities Regulatory Commission issued documents requesting that only treasury bonds and financial debentures be designated as the underlying bonds for repurchase transactions. These are known as repurchase mortgage (or pledge) bonds.

At present, the exchanges carrying out repurchase transactions use mostly treasury bonds listed in the market. Since market participants hold different kinds of T-bonds, it is more practical to set a conversion ratio

TABLE 10.2   Types of Repo Products in the Shanghai Stock Exchange, 1994

National Repurchase Product	Name	Code
7 day	R007	201001
14 day	R014	201002
28 day	R028	201003
91 day	R091	201004
182 day	R0182	201005

based on the treasury bonds held in each account of the various securities firms to create a synthesized bond for repurchasing purposes (called 1990 synthesized bonds). The 1990 synthesized bond is a virtually universal repurchase bond composed of various converted bonds.

If securities intermediaries withdraw some of their money, the exchange automatically reregisters the 1990 synthesized bond of these securities firms. If the securities firms repurchase more mortgage bonds than the 1990 synthesized bonds they hold, they are considered dealers engaged in repurchase of a short sale, which is called "under mortgage" or in a "short position." Under such circumstances, the securities intermediaries immediately add mortgage bonds to increase the stock amount of 1900 synthesized bond, which is called "recovering the short position." Without recovering of mortgage bonds, the exchange reserves the right to freeze the repurchase capital of the account until the recover is completed.

Bond Conversion Ratio The exchanges use different methods to set the bond conversion ratio. To calculate the conversion ratio of on-exchange repurchase bonds, the Shenzhen Stock Exchange applies the theoretic market value of the mortgage bonds as the basis for calculating the mortgage amount. The exchanges are also in a position to adjust the conversion ratio based on the market value of underlying bonds (see Table 10.3).

Repurchase Bid and Quotation on the Market Quotation of repurchase trade applies to the annual yield. The settlement of a repurchase transaction involves the difference between the initial transaction price and the reversed transaction price. Therefore, the buyer of repo only bid for repurchase price

TABLE 10.3 Bond Conversion Ratio, 1992 to 1996

Bond Products	Bond Code	Conversion Ratio
5-year term of 1992	1925	1:1:6
5-year term of 1993	1935	1:1:6
3-year term of 1995	1953	1:1:1
1-year term (1) of 1996	1961	1:0:9
3-year term (1) of 1996		
1-year term (2) of 1996	1963	1:1
10-year term of 1996	1963	1:1
3-year term of 1996	1965	1:0.9
	1966	1:1
	1967	1:1

(yield return rate) at maturity since the initial repo prices are all converted into RMB100 to facilitate the calculation.

The quotation display in the Shenzhen Stock Exchange shows only the bidding result at the mature repurchase price (rate) of the transaction, the number of deals, shown in per 1,000 units, and money settled of the day.

Settlement of Transactions   Investors go through two steps when they conduct repo transactions. First, they must work through a securities firm to bid the transaction. If the transaction is successful, two records are created: the initial record of the sale at a price of RMB100 its buy-sell type is exactly opposite to that of the client's initial order, and the record of the biding price for the maturing repo, which is used only to report the result of any repurchase transaction. Its price is the repurchase-bidding price (quotation with interest rate), and its buy-sell type is consistent with the client's. Zero is the automatic default for the volume column.

Second, upon maturity, the exchange will automatically create one reverse transaction record as the return. The first digit of the number of each deal is 9. To distinguish from the return of the transaction, the buy-sell type remains the same and the sale price is equal to the result of the bidding.

Settlement of Repurchase   Bond repurchase is composed of one transaction and two settlements. On the same date as the transaction, the exchange uses the face value of RMB100 to calculate the initial settlement price for both parties in the transaction and freeze the relevant amount of the financing party's 1990 synthesized bond. It also registers the corresponding amount of the lender's 1990 synthesized bond and transfers the money for the transaction. Upon the maturity date, the exchange will refer to the final bidding price (return rate) to complete the transaction for both parties. The purchaser of the bond repurchase (i.e., the party who receives money in the initial transaction) will pay the principal and interest to the seller (i.e., the party who pays money in the initial transaction). The formula is:

$$\text{Principal} + \text{interest paid} = \text{repurchase amount} \times [1 + \text{repurchase rate}(\%) \times \text{repurchase term}(\text{number of days})/360]$$

The exchange releases the corresponding amount of frozen 1990 synthesized bonds to the financing party and reduces the amount of such bonds in the lender's account. Clearance of bond repurchase follows strictly the principle of centralized settlement. On the date the transaction is reversed, the exchange automatically pays the principal and interest to the seller (i.e., the lender), and the purchaser of the repo (i.e., the borrower) pays the relevant principal and interest to the exchange.

At the close of each trading day, the clearing company affiliated with the exchange transmits the data on the amount of money and the settlement to all securities intermediaries through the transaction network. At present, the Shenzhen Stock Exchange records the transactions of the securities intermediaries. It does not set up a subsidiary ledger for each investor. The securities intermediaries are responsible for the subsidiary ledgers.

Commissions The exchange charges fees for the repurchase transaction based on different products and pro rate (see Table 10.4). The commission charge is only charged upon initial transaction; the reverse transaction is free.

Calculation on Return Rate of Treasury Bonds Repo The yield of the treasury bonds repo is an indicator of the rate of return on investment. For the borrower, it is the cost of money. For the lender, it is the profit on that money. The next formula is used to calculate the financing cost to the borrower in selling treasury bond repo contracts:

$$\text{Annual repurchase yield rate} = (\text{spot offering price of bond} \div \text{long dated purchasing price} - 1) \times 360 \div \text{repurchase term}$$

Accounting for the Transaction and Settlement Parties involved in treasury bonds repo transactions are either lenders—banks, securities firms, enterprises, funds, and individuals—or borrowers—securities firms, enterprises, funds, and individuals.

The financing parties first verify their seats, representing its legal status, before they put in custody of tradable national bonds to the treasury bond's custodian bank, the Shanghai Stock Exchange's Central Depository Trust & Clearing Co., Ltd.

The book-entry T-bonds serve as the standard bond for repurchase mortgage only after receipt is confirmed by the clearing company. This is because the bond is currently deposited in the stock account instead of the securities firm's account as physical T-bonds are. Furthermore, in the repo

TABLE 10.4 Calculation on the Yield Rate of Treasury Bonds Repurchase

Term of Repurchase	7 Day	14 Day	28 Day	63 Day	91 Day	182 Day
Commission Charge (%)	0.001	0.002	0.004	0.005	0.006	0.01

business, the securities firms not only act as dealers, but also serve as agents of their clients, and therefore the book-entry T-bonds are deposited in the clients' own accounts.

The lender first confirms their transaction seat (representing the firm's legal status and identity) before depositing money in the settlement account of the seat for the transaction.

There are four forms of repurchase notice: the repurchase transaction form and the delivery form applicable for both the financing party and the lender.

Quotation   Quotes are made as annual rate of return on money loaned upon the maturity of repurchase. In the repo transaction, the lender is the seller (S) while the financing party is the buyer (B). The percent symbol is omitted in a quotation. No more than three-digits are needed after the decimal point. The minimum change shall be 0.005 or its integral multiple. Deal (D) is the unit of transaction. Each deal is RMB1000. Transaction volume shall not below 100 deals (i.e., the total amount of RMB100,000 or its integral multiple).

Stockholder Code   It is not necessary for securities firms to disclose the account number for transactions made on behalf of clients. Settlement and bond management, like bearer bond settlement and management, can be made in the dealer account of the firm's seat. The stockholder's code could be used to differentiate the dealer's account from clients' account.

Term of Transaction   In general, the settlement term of a repurchase transaction usually applies a basic term of seven days (i.e., 7 days for one week, 14 days for half a month, 28 days for one month, 91 days for one quarter, and 182 days for one year). However, the seventh article of Trading Methods of Treasury Bonds Repurchase in the Shanghai Stock Exchange prescribes that "if the repurchase maturity date is on a holiday, the settlement date may be postponed to the first working day after the maturity date." For transaction arrangements on holidays, see Table 10.5.

As shown in the table, the number of days between the repurchase settlement date and the purchase date of each week is different. A transaction on Monday and Thursday has three settlement days while a transaction on Tuesday, Wednesday, and Friday has a settlement date less than three days. There are five days for the settlement for Tuesday, four days for Wednesday, and one day for Friday. Because of this feature, the real repurchase price of various dates is different and constantly changes.

Features of Liquidation   The Shanghai Stock Exchange applies the method of one deal and two liquidations for each repurchase transaction.

TABLE 10.5 Holidays Arrangement on Repurchases Transactions

Serial Number	Monday	Tuesday	Wednesday	Thursday	Friday	Saturday	Sunday	Monday	Tuesday	Actual Days Spent
1	T	D		U	S					3 days
2		T	D		U			S		5 days
3			T	D		U		S		4 days
4				T	D		U	S		3 days
5					T			D/U	S	1 day

Note: T refers to trading date, D is the repurchase settlement date, U is the repurchase maturity date, and S is the reverse trading date. For example, if a repurchase transaction occurs on Tuesday, then Tuesday is trading date (T), the next day (namely Wednesday) is the repurchase date (D), two days later (namely) Friday is the repurchase maturity date (U), and the following day (namely Saturday) should be the reverse trading date, but Saturday and Sunday are holidays, according to the transaction rules, the reverse trading date was postponed to the next workday (namely next Monday), therefore this repurchase transaction has a span of five days instead of three days.

The first liquidation occurs upon transaction. On that day, the costs to both capital contributor and bond contributor are liquidated. Cost is calculated according to the standard face value (RMB100) upon which both parties could settle the accounts receivable and the amount of the bond contributor's mortgaged standard bond, the money paid as well as the incremental amount of the standard bond.

The second liquidation occurs upon the repurchase. The computer performs this liquidation upon the maturity date of the repurchase.

To calculate the repurchase price, first, refer to the transaction yield rate, then use this formula:

$$\text{Price of repurchase} = \text{RMB100} \times \text{Annual yield rate} \\ \times \text{Repurchase term} \div 360$$

The Shanghai Stock Exchange's Central Depository Trust & Clearing Company next refers to the repurchase price to return the capital to the capital contributor from the bond contributor.

Last, the bond contributor unfreezes a certain amount of standard bonds and deducts the corresponding mortgaged amount from the standard bond account of the capital contributor.

Since 1998, the IBBM has become the major marketplace for repo transactions.

TREASURY BOND REPURCHASE TODAY

At present, bond repurchase transactions are open in both China's interbank market and stock market. Such transactions mainly take two forms: closed-end repurchase (mortgage repurchase) and buy-out repurchase. According to the *Administrative Rules Governing Bond Transactions in the National Interbank Bond Market*, the closed-end repurchase is a short-term financing business carried out by both parties with bonds as a hypothecation (i.e., security or collateral for a debt without transfer of title or possession). Thus, both capital receiver (financing party) and capital contributor (lending party) agree that, on certain date in the future, the party selling the repo, the financing party or the repo party, shall repay the amount of money plus the interest to the party buying the repo, the lending party or the reverse repo party, and the latter shall return the bonds collateralized in its account to the former. The party of the reverse repo, the repo buyer, does not have ownership of the mortgaged bonds and shall not use them for other purposes during the repurchase period.

The buy-out repurchase is a kind of repo transaction that, when the repo seller (the financing party) sells the bond to the bond purchaser (the lending party), both parties agree that the party of the repo seller shall purchase an equal amount of the same bonds from the party of the reverse repo at an agreed-on price when repo is maturing.

The closed-end repurchase effectively avoids short sale and credit risk in the repurchase transaction, which allows institutional investors to raise short-term money and provides arbitrage opportunities to make profits by leveraging the repurchase rate. However, the only function of closed-end repurchase is financing and short purchasing; China's closed-end repurchase lacks the functionality of bond financing and short selling possessed by closed-end repurchase widely used in other countries.

China's T-bond market has a short-purchase mechanism but lacks the corresponding short-selling mechanism, which has had a negative influence on the balance between supply and demand. During the first half of 2002, because of the stagnant stock market, a great deal of capital rushed into the bond market through closed-end repurchase, which greatly boosted the price of treasury bonds. Since there is no short selling as a balancing mechanism, the yield of treasury bonds skyrocketed, and interest rate risk emerged.

During the second half of 2002, the PBOC began to withdraw money in circulation via open market operations, and the market expected that interest rates would continue to rise. As a result, the price of treasury bonds slumped, which had a negative impact on new issues (three issues fell short) that year. With expansion in the number and types of products available and the development of China's T-bond market, limitations on the closed-end repurchase have gradually appeared. In April 2003, the Ministry of Finance, the PBOC, and the China Securities Regulatory Commission jointly issued the Notice on Conducting Treasury Bond Buy-out Repurchase Transactions. On May 20, the PBOC issued *Administrative Rules Governing the Buy-out Repurchase Business of the National Interbank Bond Market*, which provided detailed regulations and marked the formal entry of buy-out repurchase into the IBBM.

At the same time, the buy-out repurchase business debuted on the exchanges. In contrast to the interbank market, repurchase transactions in the exchange market are solely of T-bonds. On November 24, 2003, the Shanghai Stock Exchange formally published *Shanghai Stock Exchange's Detailed Rules on Implementing Buy-out Treasury Bond Repurchase*. The formal entry of buy-out repurchase on the stock exchange had a significant impact on the diversification and improvement of repurchase transactions in the inter-bank market, setting up a bridge linking the two markets.

The buy-out repurchase provides the reverse purchaser with the proprietary right to the mortgaged bonds. Such a purchaser could dump the mortgaged bonds in the spot bond market within the term of repurchase or apply to sell repo for financing. The buy-out repurchase only requires that, upon the maturity date of repurchase, there shall be enough bonds for settlement. This new instrument offers greater flexibility, eliminating many of the disadvantages of the current closed-end repurchase. By the first half of 2005, outright (buy-out) repo traded 628 deals with a turnover of RMB90.661 billion yuan. The average daily turnover was RMB743 million yuan, up 100 percent year over year, although down 16.84 percent from the second half of 2004. (See Tables 10.6 and 10.7.)

Repurchase Transaction Method: Shenzhen Stock Exchange

Both the purchaser and seller of repo products are participants in the repo market. The respective role of each is set according to their position in the reverse transaction on the date of repurchase. In the initial transaction, the one paying money to buy the bonds is the seller of the repurchase transaction; the recipient of the money is the purchaser.

All bond dealers who have a seat or a special bond seat in the Shenzhen Stock Exchange may carry out repurchase transactions. Based on the regulation, other institutions participating in the repurchase transaction may delegate the bond dealer to carry out such transactions. The bond dealer bears the risk that may occur as a result of conflicts between clients.

Underlying Bond—Repurchase Mortgage Bond   At present, there are nine treasury bond repurchase products on the Shenzhen Stock Exchange: 3-day, 4-day, 7-day, 14-day, 28-day, 63-day, 91-day, 180-day, 273-day, and two enterprise bond repo products: 3-day and 7-day.

TABLE 10.6 Repurchase Products on the Shanghai Stock Exchange

R-003(131800)	R-007(131801)	R-014(131802)	R-028(131803)
R-063(131804)	R-091(131805)	R-182(131806)	R-273(131807)
R-004(131809)	RC-003(131900)	RC-007(131901)	

TABLE 10.7 Treasury Bonds Repurchase Products of the Shenzhen Stock Exchange

R-003(131800)	R-007(131801)	R-014(131802)	R-028(131803)
R-063(131804)	R-091(131805)	R-182(131806)	R-273(131807)
R-004(131809)	RC-003(131900)	RC-007(131901)	

Conversion Ratio   Exchanges calculate the conversion ratio of bonds in various ways. The Shenzhen Stock Exchange uses the theoretical market price of the mortgage bond as the mortgage amount to calculate the conversion ratio of the on-exchange repurchase bond. Exchanges also refer to the change in the market value of treasury bonds to adjust the conversion ratio. (See Table 10.8 for the current conversion ratio of T-bonds.)

Display Repo Bids and Quotes   The Shenzhen Stock Exchange uses computerized bidding for the annual rate of return of repurchase transaction. The principle of match bidding is the same as that of the spot bond trade (i.e., price priority and time priority). The maturity purchase price of a repurchase transaction equals the sum of the principal and interest. On the maturity date, the Shenzhen Stock Exchange automatically conducts the reverse transaction based on the maturity purchase price. The amount of maturity date transactions is not included in that day's volume.

Repo Settlement   There are two steps for settlement of repo transactions:

1. *Settlement of the initial repo transaction on the very day it occurs.* The settlement price is calculated by RMB100, and the bond with corresponding value is taken out of circulation (i.e., is frozen).
2. *Settlement of the repurchase maturity date.* Such settlement is based on the maturity repo price, which is set during the bidding; at settlement, the corresponding bonds are put back into circulation. If the maturity date is not a transaction day, settlement may be postponed to the next day.

In repo transactions, the net amount of capital borrowing by each bond dealer (total borrowing amount/minimum total offering amount) may not exceed the maximum repo amount ratified by the Shenzhen Stock Exchange, which verifies the sum in the bond account to calculate the conversion ratio (the quota is represented by the virtual synthesized 1990 bond).

Commission   The exchange refers to different products and rates to determine the fee for the repurchase transaction (see Table 10.9). The fee is charged only on the initial transaction; there is no fee on the reverse transaction.

Calculating the Rate of Return on Treasury Bond Repos   The formula to calculate the costs to the repurchaser, the financing party, in the sale of treasury

TABLE 10.8 Conversion Ratio of the Standard Bond Repurchased on the Shenzhen Stock Exchange

Shortened Form	Code	Maturity Date	Denomination of Spot Bond (RMB)	Ratio	Synthesized Bond (RMB)
T-bonds 966	101966	2006.06.14	100	1:1.16	116
T-bonds 973	101973	2007.09.05	100	1:1.15	115
T-bonds 995	101995	2007.08.20	100	1:0.96	96
T-bonds 998	101998	2009.09.23	100	1:0.93	93
T-bonds 904	101904	2010.05.23	100	1:0.93	93
T-bonds 905	101905	2007.11.14	100	1:0.99	99
T-bonds 903	101903	2008.04.24	100	1:0.96	96
T-bonds 917	101917	2021.07.31	100	1:0.93	93
T-bonds 918	101918	2011.09.25	100	1:0.92	92
T-bonds 912	101912	2011.10.30	100	1:0.88	88
T-bonds 0115	100115	2008.12.18	100	1:0.93	93
T-bonds 0203	100203	2012.04.18	100	1:0.85	85
T-bonds 0210	100210	2009.08.16	100	1:0.89	89
T-bonds 0213	100213	2017.09.20	100	1:0.76	76
T-bonds 0214	100214	2007.10.24	100	1:0.95	95
T-bonds 0215	100215	2009.12.06	100	1:0.91	91
T-bonds 0301	100301	2010.02.19	100	1:0.91	91
T-bonds 0303	100303	2023.04.17	100	1:0.80	80
T-bonds 0307	100307	2010.08.20	100	1:0.88	88
T-bonds 0308	100308	2013.09.17	100	1:0.85	85
T-bonds 0311	100311	2010.11.19	100	1:0.94	94
T-bonds 0401	100401	2005.03.15	100	1:0.97	97
T-bonds 0403	100403	2009.04.20	100	1:1.00	100
T-bonds 0404	100404	2011.05.25	100	1:1.01	101
T-bonds 0405	100405	2006.05.15	100	1:0.93	93
T-bonds 0407	100407	2011.08.25	100	1:0.98	98
01The Three Gorge 10	111015	2011.11.08	100	1:0.94	94
01Guangdong Nuclear Power	111016	2008.12.10	100	1:0.94	94
02 Power Grid 3	111017	2005.06.18	100	1:1.05	105
02 Power Grid 15	111018	2017.06.18	100	1:0.88	88
02 Guangdong Nuclear Power	111019	2017.11.10	100	1:0.83	83

TABLE 10.9 Products and Standard Quotations on Treasury Bond Repurchase Transactions

Days		Market		Charger
		Shanghai (%)	Shenzhen (%)	
3	Commission calculated on transaction volume	0.015	0.01	Securities firms
4			0.012	
7		0.025	0.02	
14		0.05	0.04	
28		0.1	0.08	
63			0.10	
91		0.15	0.12	
128			0.14	
182		0.15		
Transaction fee: 5% of standard commission				Securities Stock Exchange
Bond transactions are exempt from stamp tax				

bonds is:

$$\text{Annual repurchase yield} = (\text{Spot bond offering price} \div \text{forward purchasing price} - 1) \times 360 \div \text{repurchase term}$$

NEWLY EMERGED SWAP MARKET

Most commercial banks and economic entities have floating liability and fixed assets because the holding of fixed-rate government bonds and other bond securities gave rise to a severe mismatch between assets and liabilities in banks' financial statements. In addition, enterprises have fixed investments, but the loans they received from the banks were floating. They are all exposed to the interest rate risk in volatile market conditions.

Along with the process of market development and interest rate deregulation, enterprises and financial institutions, including banks, need assets and liabilities management (ALM). This is an important area of risk management. Since the China Development Bank (CDB) introduced floating-rate notes (FRNs) in China in 1999, market participants have urged the government to open the floating–fixed swap market.

In the meantime, the spontaneous fixed–floating swap with a forward option attached for fixed bond instruments was introduced by the CDB in 2003. Called symmetrical bonds, and peculiar to China, they were a very important financial innovation at the time. Symmetrical bonds are issued in two tranches, floating and fixed interest rate, in the same amount and with the same maturity, but investors have the option to swap fixed for floating, or vice versa, at a specified future time.

In 2004, the China Banking Regulatory Commission promulgated the interim regulation on the transactions of derivative instruments conducted by financial institutions. Over 10 financial institutions have been granted licenses to engage in derivative products transactions on their own or on behalf of their clients.

In 2005, a CDB initiative was under review by the PBOC. In 2006, the PBOC formally endorsed the RMB swap transaction on a trial basis. Soon afterward, the CDB and Ever-Bright Bank concluded the first swap contract in China.

This progress also provides fresh evidence that it is the interaction between the incentive structure and the constraint structure via the primary financial exchange that creates favorable conditions for the RMB swap market.

PART Four

Policy Issues

CHAPTER 11

Treasury Bond Market and Open Market Operations

China started to carry out its monetary policy through open market operations (OMOs) only after the bond market had developed in a meaningful way. For many years, even many years after reform, China managed its financial system and financial activities using the administrative approach. After 1994, the deposit-to-loan ratio was used to control commercial banks' lending activities. The administrative approach is easier and more cost-effective for government agencies, but it is ineffective for adjusting financial activities and counterproductive to developing a financial market.

Unlike China's other exchanges, the OMOs, according to institutional economic engineering (IEEN), is a market-oriented primary financial exchange. However, it will take some time before the market can be established. The bond market serves as the link between the primary economic exchange, mainly public financing, and the primary financial exchange, mainly the central bank's open market operation. The Ministry of Finance, the central bank, and market participants are the major players in the OMOs.

INSTITUTIONAL FRAMEWORK OF OPEN MARKET OPERATIONS

Agencies such as the Ministry of Finance and the People's Bank of China (PBOC) played a positive role in ensuring the success of the bond market reform program. The Ministry of Finance in the 1990s and the China Development Bank (CDB) in the 2000s led the way to the financial innovations that have facilitated market development. Technological progress, such as the introduction of the electronic transmission system, makes the book-entry form of bond securities and their trading possible.

Various government agencies have played a crucial role in the development of the bond market. Government debt managers (GDMs) are the representatives who pursue such policies. In the past, the Treasury Bond Management Department and today the Treasury Department, under the jurisdiction of the Ministry of Finance, were and are the GDMs.

One question that needs to be answered is why how to guarantee and promote the sale of treasury bonds and meet investor needs so appropriate market instruments can be designed. A sound bond market must meet the needs of both seller—in this case, the government—and buyer—the investor. As we will see, in China, this orientation is still in its early stages. In our view, market building serves as the basis for a sound financial system, which is crucial for economic development.

The special features of the institutional arrangement are best illustrated by examining two typical models: the American and the British. In the American model, treasury bonds are organized and issued by Department of the Treasury in the primary market; then the Federal Reserve Bank of New York conducts OMOs in the secondary market. In the British model, Her Majesty's Treasury delegates to the Bank of England authority to issue T-bonds. The Bank of England conducts OMOs in the secondary market (see Figures 11.1 and 11.2).

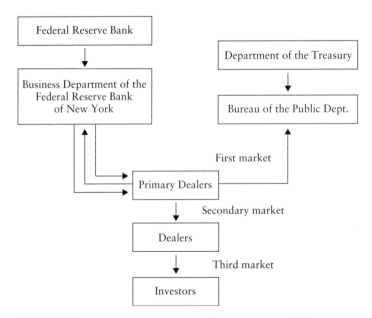

FIGURE 11.1 Institutional Framework: American Model

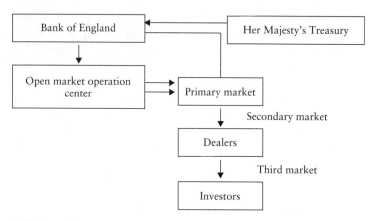

FIGURE 11.2 Institutional Framework: British Model

In the United States, the open market operations are carried out by the Business Department of the Federal Reserve Bank of New York. The general manager of the Business Department is responsible for arranging OMOs. Once the general manager decides on the specific program of OMOs, the Federal Reserve Bank of New York informs the primary dealers to quote on the treasury bills and the treasury bonds. As market makers in the secondary market, the primary dealers assume the responsibilities for quotation. After the primary dealers are informed, they quote prices based on the yield rates in the market. There are two forms of OMOs: the one-way transaction, such as public buying and selling, and buy-back. Public buying and selling is used when the general manager believes that the market development has long-term potential. This operation usually is carried out through public bidding (i.e., tender issue). When tender is conducted, the primary dealers make bids or offers on the securities prices. The bids are ranked according to price, from high to low when selling and from low to high when buying, until the required transaction volume is reached.

The bond products that are available to the public have been short-, medium-, and long-term treasury bonds. However, only short-term bond products are used often for OMO purposes. When the general manager of the OMO office is instructed to create a short-term effect on the market, the manager usually adopts the repurchase (repo), or buy-back transaction.

When repurchasing T-bonds, the central bank in China usually signs a repurchase agreement with those primary dealers willing to sell the bonds. Both parties agree that the underlying T-bonds will be repurchased at a predetermined price within a specified period. The terms of the repurchase agreement may vary from 1 to 15 days, but most of them are within

7 days. In the international capital market, for open-end repo, as a rule, primary dealers are entitled to terminate these agreements in a specified date whereas in China now termination of agreement prematurely is forbidden.

Institutional arrangements for OMO varies across countries. In the United Kingdom, both OMOs and treasury auctions are conducted by the central bank; it is easier for the central bank to coordinate the two market operations. In the United States, the two market operations are run by different agencies. It is therefore reasonable to suppose U.K. model is transaction cost effective. This transaction cost is related to the secondary administrative exchange (SAE; the exchange between agencies). In China, these agencies are the Ministry of Finance and the central bank. China has an institutional arrangement similar to United States insofar as the relationship between the Ministry and the central bank is concerned. (See Chapter 1 for more details.)

EARLY STAGE OF OPEN MARKET OPERATIONS IN CHINA

The People's Bank of China was founded in December 1, 1948. Since that time, it functioned as China's monetary authority, but it also engaged in commercial banking activities. In 1994, its central banking function began to be separated from its commercial banking function, and it became a real central bank.

In 1994, the PBOC began, for the first time, open market operations by trading on the foreign exchange market. Beginning in 1996, OMOs had become market-based instruments as opposed to instruments of a planned economy. OMOs allow the central bank, in accordance with monetary policy goals, to adjust commercial banks' excessive reserve positions through the public buying and selling of marketable securities and foreign exchange.

In order to hedge the sharp increase of RMB counterparts for the underlying foreign exchange (Forex) reserves that result from an increase of Forex reserves, it is necessary to withdraw funds from the commercial banks through OMOs. Nonbank financial institutions and the newly founded banks do not acquire reloans from the central bank, so OMOs are the only way the central bank can make necessary adjustments.

China has adopted some methods, for example, reserve requirements and rediscounts windows, to achieve its policy goals, but these are ineffective because interest is regulated. Therefore, OMOs have become the major method of readjustment. As there were fewer types of short-term treasury bonds circulating, from 2002 on, the central bank began to issue notes and to adjust the money supply through the buying and selling of these notes.

The first few years of the new century saw a rapid development of China's reserve position. Economic theory holds that if a country has a fixed exchange rate, monetary policy is passive. The monetary authority has to cleanse the system of its excess money supply. Therefore, the central bank reinforced its presence in the open market.

In 2004, the central bank issued paper to increase the short-term market instruments. Since then, OMOs of the central bank have become more frequent.

REFORM AND DEVELOPMENT OF THE TREASURY BOND MARKET PAVES THE WAY FOR THE CENTRAL BANK'S OPEN MARKET OPERATIONS

Since 1996, the development of the treasury bond market has created favorable conditions for open market operations by providing market infrastructure as well as instruments that the central bank uses frequently to implement its monetary policies.

Mode of Issue

In designing China's markets, both the issuers' and investors' perspectives were considered. However, since 1996, the Ministry of Finance has also considered the central bank's OMO requirements. As early as 1994, the Ministry issued short-term government securities, such as six-month- and one-year-maturity treasury bills, designed specifically for central bank OMOs.

The change from underwriting to tender issue was a decisive step in the market-oriented process. As we have seen, the tender issue method is used by almost all developed countries and in over half of the developing countries for issuing treasury bonds, particularly short-term T-bonds. One of the major advantages of tender issue is that it provides a competitive market-oriented price-setting mechanism. To date, China has used subscription quota bidding and settlement date bidding. Because China's money and capital markets are still being formed, the secondary market in treasury bonds remains under development, and due to lack of market benchmarks, the bidding price of the T-bond issuance is arbitrary. Therefore, the base price and the minimum price were designed and used to direct the bidding of primary dealers. At the same time, in order to secure a T-bond transaction, a certain number of primary dealers must participate in the bidding to ensure that there will be a market. It has been proven that the bidding method currently in use is suitable to the status quo in the primary market for China's treasury bonds. The development of the primary bond market, although preliminary and transitory, has paved the way for open market operations in China.

Fixed Issuing Schedule and Rollover Issue Method

Rollover selling increases the frequency of issuance. The well-arranged issues schedule and well-designed market instruments which based on with the market instruments can meet the budgetary demand for financing and also increase the capability of the market to absorb new bonds at the same time as it helps alleviate issuance pressure and saves on costs of issuance. This is crucial for investors and intermediaries because it allows them to arrange money and ensures the liquidity of the secondary market.

Short-term Bond Products

The increase in short-term bond products promotes the diversification of terms and varieties of the government debt. The increase in types of T-bond products and their terms expands the investors' basis and increases the alternatives for market transactions, which helps to invigorate secondary market trading and hence boost market liquidity.

Issuance of Zero-Coupon Treasury Bonds

The issuance of zero-coupon treasury bonds changes the payment format. Discounted treasury bills and mid-term treasury notes are kinds of zero-coupon bonds.

Coordinated Development of the Primary and Secondary Markets

Coordinated development of the primary and the secondary markets helps create continuity and promotes activity throughout the T-bond market. The trading price and the issuing price of the new issues in 1997 became close, something that had never happened since the establishment of the T-bond market.

Major Investors in Short-term Treasury Bonds

The specialized banks and the commercial banks participate in the primary market of the T-bonds and are major investors in short-term T-bonds. Toward the turn of the last century, banks became the main investors in bond securities.

Transparency of the Primary Market

Transparency of the primary market has increased and the principles of openness, justness, and fairness are well reflected. As a result, investors and underwriters are more enthusiastic about purchasing treasury bonds.

Primary Dealers of the Treasury Bonds

Primary dealers provide a ready-made institutional arrangement for the central bank's open market operations. The primary dealers are the major participants, and their role as market makers is essential in the central bank's OMOs.

Issuing Conditions and Product Design

The issuing terms and the product designs of the treasury bonds take into full consideration the central bank's requirements regarding OMOs. In addition, the short-term T-bond is designed to meet the needs of the banks by offering high liquidity. For this reason, it is the ideal financial asset for commercial banks.

Characteristics of Related Banks

The adoption of OMO tools by the central bank has significant implications. It greatly promotes the further development of the bond market. However, after 1998, the central bank decided to adopt the practice of the Hong Kong Monetary Authority and absorb the excess liquidity of the money market by issuing short-term notes and using the purchase and sale of T-bonds as one of its OMO instruments.

POLICY-RELATED FINANCIAL BONDS AND OPEN MARKET OPERATIONS

The central bank's OMOs require market instruments of high prestige and liquidity to meet its operational objectives. The central bank in China carries out its OMOs primarily in the interbank bond market (IBBM), where to date only treasury bonds and policy-related financial bonds are traded. The quantity of policy-related financial bonds is larger than that of treasury bonds in the IBBM. Therefore, in 1997 and 1998, the central bank chose policy-related financial bonds as the market instrument for its OMOs.

In 1998, the China Development Bank issued policy-related financial bonds in a market-oriented manner. Within the current regulatory framework, the CDB's offerings mainly target commercial banks. By increasing the bond securities holdings of commercial banks, the CDB provides a ready-made instrument for the central bank to pursue OMOs.

Single Clearinghouse for Open Market Operations

In 1995, the Ministry of Finance decided to set up an institution to accommodate the trading of book entry treasury bonds and prepare the organization structure. The Ministry later accepted the suggestion from the PBOC that the company would be based on the PBOC's National Electronic Trading System (NETS), which has a direct connection to the PBOC's settlement system. The institution is formally established in 1996 and named the China Government Securities Depository Trust & Clearing Co., Ltd. (CGSDTC), which was designed as a clearing, settlement, and depository trust for treasury bonds. The CGSDTC provides a ready-made settlement institution for the central bank's open market operations.

In addition, the financial debentures (i.e., financial bonds) issued by the CDB and other banks and financial institutions have been put in custody in book-entry form in CGSDTC, making it possible for the central bank to carry out its OMOs for both government securities and financial debentures without paper transactions. In 1997, the central bank set up its Open Market Operation Office at the CGSDTC, which has greatly improved the convenience and speed of its OMOs.

Impact of the Central Bank's Purchase and Sale of T-Bonds on Monetary Policy

The central bank buys treasury bonds from the commercial banks and savings institutions—excess compulsory legal reserves, which represent the increase of base money (M0) supply—and buys treasury bonds from other institutions, increasing both the excess legal reserves and deposits, so they have the same monetary implication.

The central bank sells treasury bonds to the commercial banks and savings institutions, reducing their excess legal reserve and deposits. By doing so, the central bank can contract money supply if that is its policy objective. This is also true if the central bank sells T-bonds to nonbank institutions and individuals, as this would reduce its reserves or deposits. Since deposits are a portion of the currency in circulation, reducing deposits means the reduction of money (M1). Since 2000, many non-bank financial institutions in China have had access to the IBBM as a part of the central bank's move to revitalize the IBBM. With the participation of nonbank financial institutions and state-owned enterprises, the strength of the central bank's monetary moves has improved substantially.

Impact of Government Debt on Money Supply

The impact of treasury bonds on the central bank's money supply depends on the targeting of issuance. When the government directly acquires loans from the central bank, the central bank increases the money supply by the same quantity. When the government carries out debt financing directly with the commercial banks, the impact on money supply depends on the money multiplier; the degree of impact is equal to the reciprocal of the money multiplier. The bigger the money multiplier is, the smaller the degree of impact is. When government debt is issued to individuals directly, it generally reduces their deposits and, therefore, affects the banking system's source of credit. Therefore, it is evident that the market-based OMOs enhance the central bank's monetary moves and, as a result, they have a more direct effect on aggregate demand and supply.

FUTURE OF OPEN MARKET OPERATIONS

The greatest achievement in the primary financial exchange, in our view, is the progress that has been made with respect to OMOs by the central bank. Although the central government still uses the credit ceiling and other administrative measures to control financial activities to a certain extent, OMOs are gradually replacing them.

As China changes its fixed exchange policy, its monetary policy will become more effective. In the recent economic cycle, China successfully cooled its economy down without slowing it down; this success can be attributed to the nation's monetary policy.

The financial market's institutional arrangements are handled primarily through exchanges other than the market. In this way, the government can help to set up legal and regulatory frameworks to reduce exogenous transaction costs.

In 2003, the China Bank Regulatory Commission (CBRC) was established to supervise bank and nonbank financial institutions. Although the CBRC has played an important role in the establishment of the legal framework and in the supervision of bank and nonbank financial institutions, some important issues were not very well addressed. For example, the primary exchange should ensure that banks and financial institutions compete on equal footing, but this is not the case. The fact that he tax levied on domestic banks is different from that levied on foreign banks is one example.

Although the merits and demerits of primary economic exchanges and financial exchanges can be compared in many different ways, arguably, only those social exchanges that result in a win-win outcome can drive institutional evolution forward. Even the regulatory framework, as an interaction between the incentive and constraint structure, has to evolve by various means to cater to changing financial market development.

Here again, government agencies should confine themselves to building the legal and enforcement system. Anything beyond that should be left to the market participants to work through by means of market-based win-win exchanges in their effort to reduce endogenous transaction costs.

CHAPTER 12

Government Debt Policy and Macroeconomics

The government's fiscal and debt policies are related to the primary economic exchange. Although this exchange cannot be valued by the market, its merits and demerits can be judged by cost-benefit analysis. The question of whether resources used by government or by the private sector are more effective has been greatly debated. Here we discuss several important issues relating to that debate.

"CROWDING-OUT" EFFECT OF GOVERNMENT DEBT

In market economies where the private sector plays a dominant role in the national economy, issuing government debt would have a crowding-out effect. This means public investment would reduce the investment from the private sector.

In China, the issuance of treasury bonds had an impact on the self-financing and investments of state-owned enterprises in the early 1980s, as bonds were targeted mainly to them and drain down their retain earnings. Because the terms of the bonds were long and some of the bonds were later rolled over into new bonds, they effectively scaled down the production expansion from state-owned enterprises. As the private sector accounted for only a small proportion in China's national economy, the crowding-out effect was insignificant in 1980s and even 1990s.

IMPACT OF GOVERNMENT DEBT ON EXPENDITURES

In the early 1990s, as the date to service the debt neared, an item called "debt repayment item" was added to the budgetary expenditures. When the government issues debt, the debt proceeds become part of the budgetary revenues and helps to make up the deficit. At that point, the debt has a positive effect on the balance between government revenues and expenditures. However, when the government pays principal and interest to the investors, the debt becomes a heavy burden on the government. Therefore, when government evaluates these two factors, it always pays great attention to net revenue from debt. Net revenue is the net amount of debt receipts minus debt repayments. If net revenue from debt is positive, debt revenue is greater than debt repayments; if net revenue from debt is negative, debt revenue is less than debt repayments. Obviously, when net revenue from debt is positive, debt has a positive impact on balancing the budget; otherwise, debt has a negative effect on the budget.

If debt issued by the government is operated on rollover basis (the government issues new debt to finance the maturing debt), as long as the government ensures its repayment of debt it can always borrow new debt to repay the old debt, and the debt principal is continuously renewed. In this sense, the debt is similar to tax revenues. What becomes a burden on government is the interest payments on the debt. To some extent, the debt burden is almost entirely the payments of accrued interest.

In analyzing the debt capacity of government debt service, people mainly focus on the government's ability to repay the interest. For this reason, most countries categorize the interest as a current government expenditure and categorize the expenditure on repayment of the principal as a capital account expenditure.

WHY COMMERCIAL BANKS, NOT THE CENTRAL BANK, SHOULD HOLD TREASURY BONDS

In many countries, central banks are forbidden by law to purchase treasury bonds directly. For example, Article 5 of the Banking Law of Japan stipulates that the Bank of Japan shall not purchase T-bonds in the primary bond market. In China, the Law on the People's Bank of China contains similar provisions. However, the buying and holding of T-bonds by commercial banks and the central bank's buying of T-bonds have different impacts on the monetary policy.

On one hand, the holding of treasury bonds by commercial banks can help to diversify their assets portfolio, and banks can manage their assets and liabilities by selling and buying securities; on the other hand, the holding of securities by banks is the precondition for the central bank's open market operations (OMOs). The commercial banks' purchase of treasury bonds will not cause the central bank to issue more money. Bond issuance by the government, regardless of whether the bonds are sold to individuals or to banks, reduces the banks' credit account by the same amount. Even if individuals buy T-bonds with cash, the result is the same.

Historically, when the liquidity of banks is strained, given the reserve ratio, they used to apply to the central bank for reloan (i.e., a loan directly from the central bank). Through such a loan, the central bank would inject base money (M0) into the banks; however, the increase in base money is only equal to the required refinancing divided by the money multiplier. For instance, the current money multiplier in China is five, and the actual base money is only one-fifth of the money required. Clearly the central bank's direct buying of T-bonds and the commercial banks' purchase of T-bonds have significantly different impacts on the amount of currency injected into the economy.

In fact, all of the commercial banks in the world participate in buying and selling T-bonds. Some countries have even enacted compulsory regulations requiring commercial banks to purchase and hold T-bonds. For instance, both India and Pakistan stipulate that a proportion of commercial banks' credit funds should be used to buy T-bonds.

RATIONALE FOR COUNTRIES TO ISSUE FOREIGN DEBT

China benefits from using foreign capital. For example, China uses World Bank loans and foreign government loans to gain access to preferential multilateral and bilateral loans and other forms of aid as well as technology. Commercial borrowing in the international capital market was a subject of controversy for many years after reform. Late in the 1980s, China decided to have a commercial presence in international capital market.

In China, per capita income gradually increased, and multilateral and bilateral loans lessened in absolute terms and became insignificant compared to foreign direct investment (FDI) and therefore to China's economy. However, sometimes the government may find it necessary to increase its official foreign exchange reserve or to finance its current balance of payments deficit. In such circumstances, the government can issue bonds in the international capital market. For that reason, China still maintains a conduit to borrow in the international capital market. The Chinese government has engaged in international borrowing since 1987.

The rationale to borrow is the interest differential between China and international capital market. In addition, China would like to maintain a long-term relationship with international financial communities. The U.S. government borrows from U.S. investors through the federal bond market at an interest rate of 6 percent (the investors receive 5.8 percent as interest income; 0.2 percent goes to market intermediaries). The Chinese government borrows from Chinese investors through China's T-bond market at an interest rate of 10 percent, out of which the Chinese investors receive 9.8 percent as interest income. Since the interest rate in China is higher than that in the United States, issuing foreign debt through the Yankee Bond Market, where U.S. investors buy bonds issued by foreign issuers, helps reduce the issuing cost. The U.S. investors buy Chinese treasury bonds at an interest rate of 7 percent, which is 1 percent (100 basis points) higher than buying U.S. T-bonds because the rating of the Chinese government is lower than the rating of its U.S. counterpart. American investors receive a higher return if they are willing to buy bonds issued by the Chinese government. The Chinese government issues bonds at an interest rate of 7.25 percent, out of which 0.25 percent goes toward the underwriting commission. Thus, the Chinese government may raise funds in the Yankee Bond Market by issuing external debt at a lower interest rate than in its domestic market (see Figure 12.1). However, this rationale is based on a fixed exchange rate regime. Since 2005, China liberalized its exchange rate regime in a controlled process, and the interest rate between China and the United States is narrowing.

In addition, for many years, China has had an outflow of savings. China's foreign exchange reserves piled up to over US$900 billion as of the middle 2006. Against this background, obviously, there is not much need to conduct international borrowings. Three high-profile issuers—the Ministry of Finance, the China Development Bank, and the Export-Import Bank—actually have maintained only a small volume of international funding for the last five years.

The balance between the budget deficit and the current account of international payment can be depicted as:

$$\text{Budget deficit} = (\text{private deposit} - \text{private investment}) + (\text{export} - \text{import})$$
$$= \text{currency issue} + \text{internal debt} + \text{external debt}$$

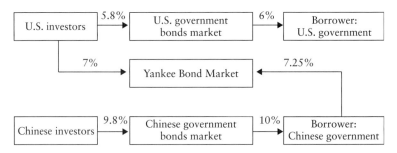

FIGURE 12.1 Balancing Internal and External Government Debt

Thus, the deficit (export-import) in the balance of international payments is also a factor increasing the budget deficit. If domestic savings are insufficient, then foreign savings (external debt) are needed in the form of capital inflow to the capital account.

These issues are related to the primary economic exchange and are usually not carried out through the market. However, their economic and financial implications can be judged by cost-benefit analysis.

Primary economic exchanges, as a means of institutional evolution, are driven by political exchanges. If they result in a win-win outcome rather than a win-lose outcome, social change will be stable and without social repercussions. Recognizing this, China always considers the interests of different social groups and tries to make the majority of its people happy. For example, when China started to build up its institutional investor base in the early 1990s, it considered the interests of individual investors. In 1994, China introduced the certificate savings bond targeting individual investors. In this way, the majority of debt securities could be issued through book-entry form in the market without incurring complaints from individuals. China has pursued this gradual approach in the process of reform.

REASONS FOR FINANCING AND DEVELOPING A SOUND BOND MARKET

The primary objective of issuing bonds is to meet the government's financing requirements. The funding demand may arise directly from the need to finance fiscal deficit or for investment in some specific construction projects. The requirement of government funding here includes new borrowing and borrowing to repay debt already incurred. Therefore, there are three basic objectives: (1) financing the deficit, (2) repaying the maturing debt, and (3) investments.

Government funding is not necessarily solely for financing fiscal deficit; government debt managers should consider many other factors. A very important factor is that treasury bond issuance should not cause an excessive increase of money supply. Direct loans to the government from the central bank will lead to an increase in the money supply. This phenomenon frequently occurs in centrally planned economies, which tend to achieve their funding objectives through the banking system.

However, this certainly does not mean that the government should not fund temporary, short-term capital from the banking system when tax revenues are not sufficiently available to ensure necessary disbursements. For example, the government may issue short-term T-bonds to make up a shortfall in the tax revenues (i.e., when a discrepancy between the increase in tax receipts and the increase in budgeted expenditure occurs in a given quarter or a given month, resulting in a temporary imbalance in the budget). In these circumstances, the government should make certain that the bonds thus issued are repaid within the fiscal year and, more important, do not result in an increased money supply.

The government should finance its budget deficit with its own cash when it is available. Only when the government does not have cash in its own account should it finance the deficit through the issuance of treasury bonds or bills.

In addition to its own financing considerations, the government should also have other objectives, such as supporting the monetary policy pursued by the central banks. Treasury bonds may absorb some excess liquidity (i.e., additional money in circulation) by selling medium- and long-term bonds to nonbank financial institutions. At this time, the amount of T-bonds issued may, at the requested of central government, exceed the amount needed for financing the government's fiscal deficit and refinancing maturing debt. It is common in many countries for the central bank to hold T-bonds and adjust money supply through OMOs (i.e., by central bank's purchase and sale of T-bonds to achieve its monetary objectives).

The government may issue securities for some alternative uses: for example, to support domestic organizations in their investments, such as investments by government policy organizations; to support the national social security fund, for the payments to the beneficiaries; to help state banks meet their deposit requirements; or to finance infrastructure projects. In addition, the government frequently takes proactive, expansionary fiscal policy to increase aggregate demand as a countercyclical measure.

Most developed countries have laws, regulations, or conventions, which form the basis of their debt policy, to regulate the funding objectives. China issues treasury bonds mainly to finance its deficit and refinance maturing debt, although in 1994, it did issue short-term treasury bills designed specifically to enable the central bank to carry out its OMOs. In the middle of 2006, China restarted to issue T-bills following a new rule on treasury cash management in which only outstanding bond is restricted. This gave the Ministry of Finance a mandate on treasury cash management and made T-bill issuance necessary and possible. China issued T-bills in 1994, but suspended them between 1995 and 2005.

In 1997 and 1999, banks transferred part of their nonperforming loans (NPLs) to asset management companies (AMCs), some of which were financed by treasury bonds issued by the Ministry of Finance. However, it was suggested that this should no longer be done.

By the end of the 1990s, China increased its issuance of treasury bonds for earmarked to projects selected by the National Development and

Reform Commission in its pursuit of a proactive fiscal policy. This policy was suspended in 2005 as increased demand made it unnecessary.

Government Objectives and Debt Management

Different countries may have different objectives in developing their treasury bond markets. The goals that follow are based on international experience and are believed to be important to government debt managers.

Ensure Continuous Government Access to the Financial Market   It is important to ensure continuous government access to the financial market, so that it may tap into the financial market to satisfy financing needs at any time.

To this end, the government needs to provide investors with an attractive rate of return and maintain its creditworthiness as a borrower. To do this, the government should abolish compulsory selling and provide no preferential tax treatment to treasury bonds. In essence, it should ensure that the government, as a borrower, has no privilege that any other borrower cannot enjoy. In this regard, China has learned a number of lessons. In the early 1990s, the Ministry of Finance forbade other issuers from setting their bond coupon rates higher than that of T-bonds in order to guarantee the sale of T-bonds. Even today, China's T-bonds enjoy preferential tax treatment, most of which is unnecessary.

To achieve creditworthiness, the government must guarantee the timely repayment of debt. Should the government have difficulty repaying the debt, it should take on new debt to repay the maturing debt rather than postpone repayment. The only time China postponed the repayment of T-bonds held by state-owned enterprises was in the early 1990s. Recognizing the importance of its reputation, the Ministry of Finance prioritized debt repayment in its budgetary arrangement. Never again has China failed to meet its obligations.

Reduce the Cost of Funding the Government   Cost reduction has three goals:

1. To get the government the funds it needs at the lowest cost possible in each issuance.
2. To reduce the cost of all public debt. In countries where debt service is burdensome, debt managers should pay special attention to pursuing systematic and effective debt management techniques (in particular risk management) to reduce the cost of the outstanding debt.
3. To reduce commissions as much as possible. In many countries (including China before the late 1990s, when T-bonds were sold over the counter through a network of banks, securities companies, and post

offices), commission fees for issuance and settlement tended to be high. Today, most countries have successfully reduced commission charges through the improved issuing technologies and the introduction of new issuing techniques. For example, issuing T-bonds via auction can substantially reduce commission charges, although some countries still pay commissions to banks and securities institutions for their assistance in collecting the bidding documents. In addition, most countries reduce settlement and redemption commissions through the central depository trust system.

Ensure Effective Government Control over Cost and Risk This is an extension of the traditional objective of reducing government's funding costs. According to modern asset management theory, government debt managers should try to achieve an overall reduction in total funding cost. This is an obvious step beyond merely paying attention to issuance cost. Effective control over cost and risk needs to take into consideration the cost and risk associated with internal debt, assets and liabilities management, and cash management.

Adjust Government Asset and Debt Structures At present, some countries have expanded their debt management functions to include the comprehensive management of assets and liabilities. To achieve this long-term objective, the currency composition and term structure of debt must be considered in line with asset and liability management. In this regard, the problem debt managers may encounter is how to forecast government assets and liabilities accurately. In addition, government debt managers must understand under what circumstances and to what extent the assets it manages will be affected by fluctuations in the foreign exchange rate and the interest rate. Most countries have streamlined their debt management through modern debt management techniques.

Reduce the Market Impact of Treasury Bond Operations In order to achieve this objective, the coupon rate of newly issued bonds in the primary market should be consistent with the yield of bonds with the same maturity in the secondary market. Sometimes people interpret this objective to mean the maintenance of orderly market conditions. This phrase means that the government, as the issuer, must frequently inform market participants of its borrowing plans, timetable for new debt issuance, and terms of issuance. Orderly market conditions are usually realized through the improvement of the salability of the T-bonds. In order not to distort orderly market conditions, government debt managers should intervene in secondary markets as little as possible and, if it is necessary, announce such intervention in advance to the major market participants.

As a matter of fact, new issue yield is usually referenced to the secondary market yield. Secondary market yield is indicated by on-the-run bonds. This does not mean that new issue yield should be exactly equal to the yield in the secondary market, as off-the-run issue lacks liquidity and would not serve as a benchmark. If there is no such bond, new issue will serve as reference of market yield. In such circumstance, new issue would add up on-the-run bond instrument to the market.

Increase the Varieties and Distribution of Government Debt Instruments If the issuing amount of T-bonds has increased gradually, then treasury bond managers should try to increase the variety and quantity of the debt instruments. As the amount of issuances increase, it is necessary to attract new investor groups and satisfy their requirements for T-bond investment vehicles. This can be accomplished, for example, by issuing fixed-rate T-bonds or floating-rate T-bonds of medium terms to meet the requirements of banks and some asset managers and fund managers, or by issuing tradable or nontradable short-term T-bonds to meet the requirements of risk-averse or risk-sensitive investors.

During periods of inflation, protecting the value of bonds is helpful to attract traditional investors. For example, price-indexed bonds encourage investment in long-term bonds. High-income investors prefer zero-coupon bonds, as they do not have to pay tax on the interest income.

The government should pay attention to two issues when choosing debt instruments:

1. *Flexibility.* It is important that debt instruments can be selected at any time to reflect changing issuance conditions.
2. *Objectives.* Different objectives require different debt instruments; it is therefore important to keep the objectives in mind and to maintain flexibility in selecting bond instruments. Thus, it is better not to fix the issuing technique too early so that the issuer can, if necessary, select an alternate issuing technique, should the market situation change. The development of T-bond instruments should go hand in hand with the development of the financial intermediary industry.

Ensure the Effective Operation of Treasury Bonds in the Secondary Market As indicated, maintaining an effective secondary market is important to the issuance of treasury bonds. An effective secondary market ensures reasonable pricing of new issues and makes pricing more synchronous with market conditions. Reference to the secondary market helps ensure that the newly created T-bond can be placed in the market at any time. Although it is highly recommended that governments do this as little as possible, an effective secondary market would allow a government to intervene in the market at any time in order to neutralize the negative impact of issuance and settlement on the secondary market.

The sine qua non of an effective secondary T-bond market is high liquidity. This means the secondary market must effectively disperse and digest the newly issued treasury debt in the primary market and speed up bond trading turnover and frequency among investors. Doing this requires more diversified government debt instruments and various financial derivatives, an effective bond depository trust and book-entry system, as well as an advanced clearing and settlement system, which would help promote active trading.

Create an Effective and Rational Term Structure for Treasury Bonds   An effective and rational debt structure refers to a maturity profile that comprises long-, medium- and short-term maturity to prevent, from the issuer's point of view, a debt principal and interest repayment peak, and to cater to the heterogeneous preference of investors. Such a structure helps establish orderly market conditions and reduces the negative impact of government operations on the market. It is also advantageous to integrate the government's fiscal policies with monetary policies, and with cash management policies, since cash flow is related to the repayment of the principal and interest on government debt and the refinancing of maturing debt.

Ensure the Successful Operation of Newly Issued Bonds   The realization of this objective depends mainly on the selection of the most effective selling methods. It is advisable to choose one or a combination of several different selling methods according to specific economic and market conditions of the country. When choosing the selling technique, it is important not to lose sight of other debt management objectives, such as reducing the negative effects and increasing the positive effects on the secondary market. The long-term objective of increasing government debt instruments should also be kept in mind to coordinate with the objectives of the monetary policy.

Relationship between Debt Management Objectives and Other Government Policy Objectives

As we have seen, the T-bond market does not operate in a vacuum, but interacts with other government policies as well as with other investment vehicles. In the institutional economic engineering (IEEN) framework, the financial exchange is superior to the bond exchange. Therefore, a healthy development of the financial market is essential to the bond market development.

Promote the Healthy Development of the Financial Market   The development of the financial market, the external environment in which the government bond market operates, is the foundation for and precondition of a T-bond market. For example, over the last decade, the establishment and development of the primary market and the rapid development of secondary market for Hong Kong's treasury bonds would not have been possible without its full-fledged financial market. Treasury bond management departments should work to promote the establishment and development of both the money market and the capital market in order to promote the financial environment of T-bond market.

Promote the Development of the Entire Bond Market   In the entire bond market, the treasury bond is in the dominant position. The T-bond serves as a benchmark for the pricing of the corporate bond, the financial debentures, the central government agency bond, and the municipal bond. Therefore, when the government considers the debt scale, the time to enter the market, the introduction of new market instruments, and so on, it should pay attention to how the treasury market would affect the entire bond market.

Promote Private Deposits, Especially Long-term Deposits   The treasury bond is the main financial asset held by individuals. Absorbing private deposits through attractive government debt instruments may effectively reduce private consumption and increase investment in key government construction projects. In many countries, issuing savings bonds to private investors is an effective way to attract private investment. Because the goal and purpose of the issuance of savings bonds are different from that of government, some countries make such issuance part of their national saving's plan.

Promote Rational Distribution of Income and Private Wealth   In order to prevent the loss of the financial assets held by individuals in case of inflation, some countries issue nontradable inflation-linked bonds or indexed bonds, which protect the interests of small investors and help avoid the negative impact of irrational income redistribution on private investors during a period of inflation.

However, in our view, the government should have alternative ways to achieve its policy objectives rather than via the bond market, as we believe frequent use of private placement would jeopardize the market. There were many occasions when some institutional investors requested the Ministry of Finance to offer them a private placement.

Promote Effective Cooperation between the Government and the Central Bank
Government debt can transfer private savings into public investment and

lead cash to flow into and out of the government's account. In either case, debt has a huge impact on the liquid assets of the entire economy and on the interest rate level. Therefore, it is important to coordinate the government's debt management policy and the central bank's monetary policy.

Coordination between the two authorities depends on the institutional structure and the historical evolution of and between the two organizations. The division of economic functions between the two authorities varies from country to county. Therefore, the way their activities are coordinated may differ as well. What is important here is whether and to what extent the central bank exercises the function of fiscal agent.

As indicated in Chapter 11, if the central bank in fact exercises the function of government debt management, then the coordination between the two authorities is a matter of coordination between two internal departments of the central bank. An advantage of this system is that the central bank has more contacts with participants in the securities market.

In most cases, the central bank is responsible only for the management of the government's cash and its payment activities or for part or all of the market operations of the newly issued bonds and repayment of principal and interest of debt due. Under such circumstances, it may be advisable for the debt management department of the Ministry of Finance or the debt management department under the jurisdiction of the government to coordinate the relationship between the two authorities. Here it is important to have a sound institutional and legal framework within which the coordination between the two authorities can be pursued and secured. It was noted that the slow process of bond market development during the early stage of primary market reform in China was attributable to the coordination between Ministry of Finance and the People's Bank of China (PBOC), China's central bank, as it was not legally a fiscal agent—although in the 1950s it was responsible for the sale of treasury bonds.

When dealing with concrete issues, it is important to be able to cite a principle on how the two different authorities should coordinate with each other on debt management and monetary policy. When formulating debt management policy, the debt management authority should consider the orientation of the monetary policy in a given period. At the same time, the T-bond operation should consider how its actions would affect the direction of interest rate movement, and the central bank needs to think about the impact of interest policy on T-bond issuance.

In 2004, there were several occasions in China when interest adjustment led to selling distress due to investors' uncertainty about future interest rates. Sometimes, when the amount of currency in circulation is excessive, government debt managers, or the central bank as their fiscal agent, may absorb currency in circulation by issuing new debt. When implementing a tightened economic policy, government debt managers, or the central bank as their fiscal agent, may issue long-term treasury bonds to nonbank financial institutions, so as to restrict the expansion of money held by these institutions. To coordinate with the open market operations of the central bank, the T-bond managers should try to maintain a highly liquid secondary market and diversify the bond instruments, thereby enabling the central bank to exercise its monetary policy effectively. These principles are usually stipulated by legislation on T-bond management policy or on the banking system, but depending on laws alone is not sufficient. Here again, in order to coordinate the T-bond management policy and the monetary policy, a sound institutional and legal framework has to be in place.

Although there is no special institutional arrangement in China for coordination between the central bank and the Ministry of Finance, they do try to collaborate. For example, the Ministry issued short-term T-bonds to the banks and the nonbank financial institutions in 1994 and 1996, mainly to coordinate with the open market operations being carried out by the central bank in April 1996.

Here again we see evidence that the secondary administrative exchange was affected by the primary administrative exchange.

Many countries have an institutionalized system, such as an economic policy committee or a monetary policy committee. In some countries, the government has created an advisory board to coordinate the activities of the two agencies. China, in a very positive step, set up a Committee on Open Market Operations in 2001 with members from the PBOC, the Ministry of Finance, and other agencies to coordinate the monetary policy among the different agencies, especially between the Ministry and the PBOC. In IEEN framework, this committee functions as an internal primary administrative exchange, which, as indicated in Chapter 1, is more transaction cost effective than an external primary administrative exchange, such as the legislative arrangement in the United Kingdom, where the central bank is an agent of Her Majesty's Treasury (also see Chapter 11).

DEFINING AND SETTING GOALS FOR THE TREASURY BOND MARKET

China gradually realized that defining and setting appropriate goals and objectives is of paramount importance for the government. To achieve the government's funding objectives, it is imperative for China to work energetically to develop a sound T-bond market, that is, a fully functional, well-configured, hierarchical, and structured market system with an efficient and cost-effective primary market, a highly liquid secondary market, and an advanced derivative market.

The primary and the secondary T-bond markets are inseparable parts of the entire bond market system. Within the market system, market participants should be diversified with respect to their preferences and polarized with respect to their market roles, such as buyer and seller; hedger and speculator; and buyer, seller, and intermediary. The system should interact with the other components of the financial and economic systems to generate economic efficiency.

First Steps

An efficient and cost-effective primary market can ensure a successful issue of bonds at any time at the lowest possible cost. From 1981 (when treasury bond issuance resumed) to 1990, China pursued the administrative allocation regime to carry out its funding program. This regime, rooted deeply in the planned economy, turned out to be inefficient, time consuming, and costly. During this time, the T-bond market was primarily a retail market targeting individuals, and it took half a year for bonds to be distributed to individual investors. The administrative allocation regime has these defects:

- *High interest rates.* Treasury bonds did not enjoy the creditworthiness they should have had as the bonds of a sovereign issuer.
- *High issuing expenses.* The selling fees, commissions, and printing expenses of the bonds as well as promotional expenses were higher than those associated with market-based issuance.
- *Weak liquidity.* In an underdeveloped market, individual investors mainly buy and hold. In addition, the interest rates on T-bonds were 1 to 2 percent higher than the bank deposit rates; therefore, there was little trading.

Given these facts, based on the defined goals and objectives described earlier, when the Ministry of Finance started its reform program in 1991, it set six goals:

1. *Market-based interest rate.* The interest rate should be directly determined by supply and demand in the market rather than administratively.
2. *Market configuration.* The market should have a clear division of functions and a hierarchical structure. The market had already developed from a two-tier market composed of investors and issuers to a three-tier market of investors, intermediaries, and issuers. In the future, the

intermediaries would be further divided into brokers and dealers, and the investors would be divided into institutional and individual investors. Towards this direction, underwriting syndication was perceived as the first and most important step. The development of underwriting syndication would boost the institutional investors, financial intermediary, market wholesalers, and market makers.

3. *Paperless book-entry securities.* Treasury bonds should be issued using a book-entry system to reduce printing, transportation, storage, transaction, and destruction costs.

4. *Electronic transactions.* Both on- and off-exchange transactions should be carried out through a computerized electronic transmission system, and the information related to transactions should be transferred electronically.

5. *Diversification of bond instruments.* There should be tradable and nontradable bonds; book-entry, bearer, and registered bonds; and varieties and series of long-, medium- and short-term bonds.

6. *Standardized procedures.* There should be a fixed-issuance timetable, and the issuing method should be stable.

A number of developments with respect to these goals occurred between 1991 and 1996. Among them were underwriting syndication in 1991 and the primary dealer system in 1993, which helped to build an institution-based market and facilitated the transformation from a retail to a wholesale market. Treasury bond trading in the stock exchange in 1993 made the electronic transmission system possible. The issuance of short-term treasury bills as well as the introduction of savings bonds greatly diversified of the number and types of bond instruments. It is recognized most goals are not readily achievable. But the reform program, as an ongoing process, has phased stages, of which the first step is more important. To select underwriting syndication as the first step is undoubtedly correct. Underwriting syndication can be pursued, to the extent possible, without changing the interest regime, yet it can help to build up institutional infrastructure on which an institution-based bond market can be developed.

Many of the initial objectives were gradually achieved. Although the bank deposit and loan interest rate remain to be decided by State Council, bond issuing interest rate, the coupon rate had been decided via auction since 1996 and therefore it had already subject to the market. With respect to market configuration, China proceeded from a retail market to a wholesale market, which is more efficient from the issuer's point view. However, this in no way implies that the retail market is not important; it helps distribute the bond securities to retail investors for their convenience in buying, trading, and redeeming bond securities.

With respect to paperless book-entry securities, the number of book-entry form securities increased from 10 percent in 1991 to 80 percent in 1996. Insofar as computerized electronic transactions are concerned, T-bond transactions at present are carried out mainly on the exchanges where the mainframe of the electronic transmission system is used for recording, data processing, and information display. As to diversification of varieties, new short- and long-term bonds have been introduced to the market. Last, the goal of standardized procedures was met with the rolling issue of treasury bills on a quarterly and monthly basis. The financial infrastructure, which includes the clearing and depository systems and the legal and institutional framework, provides backup facilities to the bond market.

Macroeconomic Policy Objectives

It is the key responsibility of government debt managers to ensure the coordination of bond development policy objectives with the macroeconomic policy objectives of the government. As the issuers of T-bonds are market players and policy makers, it is relatively easier for the managers to develop a strategy that can go hand in hand with the macroeconomic policy objectives. Therefore, they should work toward the following:

- *Promoting the well-being of the financial market.* It is difficult to achieve the objectives of the T-bond market without a healthy external environment. For example, the overheated stock, investment, and real estate markets in 1993 hindered the government's funding program.
- *Facilitating the development of the securities market.* The significance of establishing and developing the T-bond market goes far beyond the market itself and has great implications for the securities market as a whole. Just as in most countries around the world, the securities market in China is an outgrowth of its T-bond market, which is in a position to provide a channel for transforming deposits into investments. Moreover, the yield of the T-bond market provides a benchmark for the securities market.
- *Fostering thrift, especially long-term private savings.* Increasing private deposits and enhancing the savings rate would boost China's economic growth. Since 1994, savings bonds (certificate treasury bonds) have been issued to collect idle money from individuals. As a government policy, this encourages thrift.

In summary, based on conventional wisdom, goals set by government agencies are readily achievable. However, the real process is through what

I termed as secondary administrative exchange. This exchange between the Ministry of Finance and the PBOC—which has great bearing on primary bond exchange, the legal system and debt policy, secondary bond exchange, and free market transactions—is typically neglected in most literature on the issue in China.

Therefore, it is reasonable to suppose that the bond market should be a priority policy for China's government. However, what happened was the other way around: The stock market gained the support of government, and since financing is not a problem for the government, the goals of the T-bond market have not been pursued properly since 1997.

It should be especially noted, however, that these goals cannot be achieved solely by government efforts. The evolution and contribution of institutions is also crucial. The government's role is to provide a legal framework. For many years, people in China believed that national debt existed only in capitalist countries, whereas national debt was unnecessary in socialist countries. It was believed that if, for example, national debt was incurred to finance government investment, the instrument was irrelevant as long as the financing objective was achieved. Therefore, the government did not make the development of the T-bond market a government priority.

With the development of the market economy and an increased understanding of the nature of national debt, that debt is now regarded as a financial commodity. Therefore, it is necessary to establish a market for the circulation of this commodity. The establishment and development of the T-bond market is an important task for government debt managers.

As we have seen, one of the central bank's functions is the pursuit of open market operations through treasury bond trading. The central bank can carry out this function only through the participation of the commercial banks in the national debt transactions; therefore, the central bank should also care about the establishment and development of the national debt market.

Individual investors view treasury bonds as a kind of financial commodity, and they buy them not only as vehicles for saving but also for investment purposes.

Financial reform is the key to reforming the current economic system. The cultivation and development of the national debt market is an important component of this reform, especially in the establishment of a macroeconomic control system. China is currently facing the urgent task of positively promoting the development of the national debt market and integrating it with financial reform.

The objectives of bond market reform go far beyond the bond market itself. In our view, the bond market can help to build the infrastructure for the whole financial market. Some say the government built the bond market only to facilitate the sales mechanism; they do not mention the implications of bond market development on institutional movement. To our way of thinking, the exchanges in their various forms are the main catalysts of social progress.

CHAPTER 13

Government Policy on Debt Instruments and Term Structure

As international experience indicates, most planned economies have pursue their funding program through bank loans while market-based economies depend primarily on a variety of market instruments to finance their fiscal deficit. In 1994, the Ministry of Finance was not permitted to borrow from the central bank. Therefore, it had to rely on issuing securities to finance the growing government deficit. From 1994 onward, China has had to resort to the market-oriented approach. The China bond market's transition from administrative placement to auction selling and from single issuing format to diversified bond products has given market participants a lot of flexibility to select readily available instruments.

OBJECTIVES AND TYPES OF DEBT INSTRUMENTS IN AN ADVANCED BOND MARKET

The experience of advanced bond markets demonstrates that there are four primary market instruments:

1. *Short-term bonds,* which the government can use to satisfy seasonal demands for funds
2. *Tradable medium-term bonds (from 1 to 10 years),* which can be used to satisfy the needs of institutional and individual investors as well as banks and securities intermediaries
3. *Long-term bonds of more than 10 years' duration,* designed to meet the demands of institutional investors who prefer to hold long-maturity bonds to match their liabilities
4. *Nontradable savings bonds,* which satisfy the demands of individual investors who do not want to take market risks

Determining which market instrument to use depends on financing objectives, investor preferences, and the stage of the market development.

As China's budget includes the expenditures of infrastructure investment, it issues long-term bonds mainly for financing the construction account deficit; the short-term instruments are available only for central bank market operations. This is due to the fact that during the early stages of market development the Ministry of Finance did not have the function of cash management, so selling short-term treasury bills was unnecessary.

BRIEF HISTORY OF CHINA'S GOVERNMENT DEBT INSTRUMENTS

During the early bond market development, the brand-new instruments were designed just to deal with investors' needs, in order to facilitate selling, the needs of the issuers were not catered to. From 1981 to 1986, China had only one category of government debt: treasury bonds, which were targeted to state-owned enterprises and individuals through public offerings. Later, a series of new bond instruments was introduced. For example, the government issued the Key Construction Treasury Bond in 1987 and the Construction Bond in 1988, both of which were sold to individuals. In 1988, China issued fiscal bonds, which were subscribed by banks. In 1989, special bonds were issued, aimed at companies at first and then at the pension fund. In 1989, China also issued, for the first and only time, an inflation-linked treasury bond. The bonds issued in 1990 included the bearer form of treasury notes aimed at individuals, special treasury bonds targeted toward companies, and fiscal bonds for banks. In 1993, the book-entry form of T-bond was issued, which was an important step forward.

To facilitate the sale of bonds to individuals, China issued the savings bond (i.e., certificate savings bond) in 1994. In 1995 and 1996, China issued four kinds of T-bonds: bearer bonds, book-entry bonds, certificate bonds, and special bonds. In the first half of 1999, the China Development Bank (CDB) began issuing the floating-rate bond. Since that time, bonds issued in China can be divided into two types in terms of interest payment: fixed-rate bonds and floating-rate bonds.

Throughout 1980s and 1990s, the major financing requirements were for long-term bonds; medium-term bonds were issued only to satisfy investors' preferences. The instruments were selected for their ease of issuance regardless of developments in the bond market, until the Ministry of Finance provided a fixed timetable for issuance and the CDB created a reasonable plan for the arrangement of the term structure, or maturity profile, and interest payment format.

Term Structure and Yield Curve

In the early 1980s, China issued long-term T-bonds of 10- and 8-year durations; however, such terms have gradually been shortened. China did not have its own T-bond market until the late 1980s, and in its initial stages, there was no trading market. Therefore, individual investors could hardly accept long-term T-bonds due to lack of liquidity. In the late 1980s, 3-year and 5-year terms were the usual ones. By the early 1990s, their term was usually 3 years, and in 1994, China issued the bonds with five maturities: 6 months; 1, 2, 3, and 5 years, of which most were 2- and 3-year government securities. The major term in 1995 was 3 and 5 years.

Although China has been paying attention to diversifying the terms of its treasury bonds, it did not make real progress in this direction until 1994. By 1996, China had achieved diversification by successfully issuing coupon-bearing T-bonds with 7- and 10-year terms. It also issued the short-term T-bonds with a 3-month term. To date, that is the shortest term issued.

The term structure of the treasury bonds is an important aspect of the government debt and market structure. An appropriate term structure will boost issuance in the primary market and trading in the secondary market. A sound term structure is one with a combination of long, short, and medium terms and diverse types that together form serial bond products. Many factors affect the term structure of a country's T-bonds, such as national savings, consumption structure, the financial system, structure of investors, demands for government funds, and the liquidity of the secondary market.

The experience of countries with an advanced treasury bond market indicates that balanced and reasonable term structures help cater to the heterogeneous preferences of both investors and issuers. As the most developed market in the world, the U.S. T-bond market has most diverse structure, including super-long-term T-bonds as well as short- and medium-term bond products.

Our experiences indicate that a sound maturity profile depends on the development of diversified issuers and investors. Long-term marketable bonds were made possible in early 2000s because institutional investors developed in a meaningful way in the later 1990s. In 2002, the Ministry of Finance issued a 20-year bond and the CDB issued 20- and 30- year bonds. However, as market interest rates went up, the long bond issuances were suspended for three years. In late 2005, the CDB resumed issuing 20- and 30-year bonds. At present, there are three different term bonds issued in China: long term, medium term, and short term.

Selection of the Payment Structure

In some countries, debt managers prefer to issue bonds that have call options. For example, they may attach special clauses that permit "payback before maturity." In a market that changes constantly, such prepayment of treasury bonds enables debt managers to replace a bond that has a high coupon rate with one that has a lower coupon rate. However, if pricing is not market based, in order to promote T-bond distribution in difficult market conditions, it is advisable not to use such a prepayment device because it creates uncertainty about the exact term and interest payment of the bond.

Should debt managers find it necessary to incorporate such an article, certain subsidies, such as a preferential tax rate, should be given. Although these subsidies are not desirable, they help compensate investors. In recent years, developed market economies have gradually abandoned such articles. However, when a developing country is contemplating a long-term bond with a high coupon rate, it could apply this method to achieve flexibility.

International experience shows that when government debt managers want to satisfy the preference of investors for a particular term of treasury bond, they can achieve that flexibility by allowing investors themselves to select the terms. For example, debt managers could issue a bond with longer term (i.e., a 20-year bond) but that permitted the investor to request settlement in advance after a specified period (i.e., 5 or 10 years later). This kind of bond is called a contractive bond. The issuance of contractive bonds could be broken into longer- and shorter-term bonds. Government debt managers could do this by referring to the forecast of long-term market interest rates to pre-fix the coupon rate for the various durations.

Similarly, to guarantee the flexibility of the term and interest rate, debt managers could also issue a bond with a shorter term and permit bondholders to prolong the term; that is, investors could replace their current bonds with new ones with a term equal to the remaining term of the older one. Such bonds are called extensible bonds; the bond it is replaced with what is called a protractible bond. The protractible bond may also be considered a new issuance. However, the bondholder knows its conditions in advance. Such bonds could also serve as a new bond whose interest rate and term corresponds to the bonds listed. In 1994, the old-for-new policy—that is, the rollover policy—was initiated as a way to extend bond maturity.

To improve the liquidity of T-bonds in the secondary market, government debt managers could use the "reopening" technique; that is, reissue an existing bond but at the prevailing market price. Since 2002, the CDB has frequently used this technique to increase the stock of existing bonds in order to boost liquidity.

More selective bond instruments would help the government issue T-bonds during times of market uncertainty. If most bondholders extend their bonds, government debt managers may reduce the refinancing burden. However, such extension carries a higher cost than issuing new bonds.

Debt managers could also use the convertible method, which is cheaper than extending the original form. Sometimes, for reasons of cost, government debt managers do not want investors to settle in advance; nor do debt managers want to extend a bond's term or convert it. In general, as investors do not know the interest rate level in the future when the bond is settled, they would prefer to have a put option attached to the bonds. However, debt managers risk lack of investor interest in the new bond because the prospects for the interest rate are not clear.

The above-mentioned irregular practices were frequently used in China when the market was not yet fully built up. It is not advisable to follow such practices once the market condition has improved. Instead, issues should be priced based on the option pricing model. For this reason, the CDB issued a number of put-able and callable bonds. Although the option offered more flexibility to issuers and investors, it must be priced to ensure that the transaction is fair. Therefore, the CDB introduced the option pricing model to calculate the price of options. However, due to lack of data on bond volatilities, the model was used only as a reference. In order to create market stability, both issuer and investor must allow market forces to price the transaction. To this end, the instruments designed must be standardized so that they can be traded as frequently as possible to reflect the true market demand and supply.

Short-term Treasury Bonds

Generally, there are three main purposes for the government to issue a bond with a time frame of one year or less: (1) to make up the government's short-term budgetary shortfall; (2) to meet the government's seasonal requirements for cash; and (3) to help the central bank absorb excessive liquidity of banks or nonbanking financial institutions.

Before 2006, the Ministry of Finance rarely issued short-term T-bonds, because it can adjust the time of disbursement of budgeted expenditures and therefore does not need short-term bonds to finance its fiscal deficit.

One important role of short-term T-bonds is as an instrument the central bank can use to adjust the money supply in the economy. The goal of such issues is not raising funds for the government but rather managing the banking system or conducting a certain monetary policy by requiring, compulsorily or voluntarily, commercial banks to hold certain liquid assets. Sometimes, when the central bank does not have its own deposit receipts, it may expect government debt managers to issue short-term T-bonds in order to regulate liquidity. If the central bank lacks an effective interbank money market, introducing short-term T-bonds is preferable for the central bank to pursue monetary policy.

For these reasons, the Ministry of Finance issued treasury bills in 1994 solely to provide the central bank with instruments it could use carry out open market operations (OMOs), they were not issued for financing purposes. These issues did not become regular, and in 2003, the People's Bank of China (PBOC), began issuing central bank notes (CBNs) for financing purposes.

In countries that use the minimum legal reserve as a kind of monetary instrument, monetary administration departments may oppose nonbank institutions holding additional short-term T-bonds because this practice may weaken their role as the monetary authority. In China, the CBNs are targeted only at banks. Although the reserve rate is one of the monetary instruments used in China, nonbank financial institutions do not generally hold many short-term treasury bonds.

The term structure of the short-term T-bond is usually three, six, and nine months. In addition, debt managers can also match the issuance and settlement time of these bonds by issuing one special bond for cash management. Canada, France, Ireland, Japan, and the United States once issued such bonds, but China has not used this instrument. Before the PBOC issued CBNs, the CDB was the only issuer of short-term financial debentures to manage its cash needs. Three- and six-month debentures are popular. Moreover, the CDB also issues two-month futures rollovers.

Medium- and Long-term Tradable Treasury Bonds

When designing long- and medium-term treasury bonds, eight factors should be considered:

1. The government's current and future debt size
2. The interest rate structure of the financial system
3. The capital supply structure of the securities market
4. The diverse needs of investors
5. The status of the treasury bond's secondary market
6. The system and legal structure of the financial system
7. The flexibility of interest rates as well as taxation
8. Foreign exchange policies

In designing the tradable debt instrument, government debt managers need to consider the requirements of investors and the establishment of an effective secondary market in T-bonds through standardization of the bond. Standardization is necessary because it facilitates the transactions. The experience of developed market economies in developing medium- and long-term T-bonds over the past 20 years shows that it is necessary to have a wholesale issuing market and an active secondary market.

Based on China's experiences, however, if the institutional investor base is yet to be established, the retail market is necessary and can be complementary to the wholesale market. Nowadays, issuing T-bonds through administrative measures no longer works, but many countries are making efforts to improve and expand their retail T-bond markets. China has embarked on an institution-based wholesale market after a period of retail domination of the bond market. At present, the retail market is confined only to selling certificate savings bonds.

Financing through long-term instruments has always been the objective of the government in China, but the ability to issue a long-term bond depends on the extent to which the market is developing. For most of the 1980s, individuals were forced to buy long-term bonds, which, as mentioned earlier, were poorly received. In the early 1990s, when bonds started to enter the market, their time to maturity was decreasing, with most bonds being of three to five years' duration. In 1996, the Ministry of Finance was concerned about the increasing debt service burden and tried to extend the maturity. In June 1996, the Ministry resumed a 10-year bond issuance, which was very well received and ultimately became the benchmark instrument. These transactions were successfully placed due to improving market conditions, an institutional investor base had been created and trading in the secondary market created liquidity.

Flexibility of Term

Uncertainty and increasing fluctuation of interest rates could change investors' preference for the term of the tradable bond, which will result in a change in the structure of investors.

If government debt managers cannot fix the total issuance amount, they can refer to the interest rate level in the market to obtain a rough estimate of the yield of various terms as a group instead of fixing the issuance amount of each term group. In the end, the market decides the final issuance amount. In China, this is called a quantity auction; there is a fixed interest rate, and the total issuing amount is determined by the market. This method is occasionally used by the Ministry of Finance and the CDB, but not very often.

When selling treasury bonds through the tap method, government debt managers or the central bank, which acts as an agent of the government to issue the T-bonds, could issue one group of medium- and long-term bonds with different terms within a certain period. The interest rate could be fixed based on the yield of the secondary market and could be adjusted according to changes in the market. Such issuance may be done through the government's brokers, who would conduct the sale in the secondary market. This kind of bond could also be sold over the counters of financial institutions to guarantee the flexibility.

China had similar experiences in selling bearer-form bonds in the 1980s and early 1990s, but today tap selling is used only for certificate savings bonds because China's institutional framework changed rapidly and can accommodate the more advanced, institution-based bond market. Thus, this type of flexibility may be more applicable to those economies whose market infrastructure is not fully in place.

Taxation

The development and expansion of the T-bond market and the promotion of T-bond sales are very important jobs for government debt managers. As government debt managers, they could also realize their own goals by granting preferential tax policies to treasury bonds. For example, they could exempt T-bonds from either all taxes or one or several taxes, or they could apply a lower tax rate. Government debt managers might also want to deduct the cost of purchasing T-bonds from individual income tax. To avoid losing too much tax revenue, government debt managers often set an upper limit for such deductions.

Tax policy can also have negative effects on T-bond market development. Government debt managers could hold an ideal market share of treasury bonds in the whole bond market through tax policy. For instance, pension funds investing in T-bonds could enjoy income and corporate tax exemption, which would allow investors to ignore the tax impact; without this incentive, investors might prefer to invest in nontreasury bonds as long as the yield of the nontreasury bonds were higher than that of T-bonds. Similarly, foreign investors are not in a position to benefit from a preferential tax policy, since they have to pay taxes to their home country. In this case, implementing preferential tax treatment for T-bonds may have a negative influence on both the primary and the secondary markets.

China's treasury bonds are fully exempt from taxes; investors do not pay business tax and income tax.[1] Since the late 1990s, withholding taxes have been levied on interest payments on bank deposits; however, savings bonds, like other T-bonds, are exempt from such taxes. Since other bond investors do not enjoy preferential tax policies, as the demand for government securities goes up, the yield goes down. Therefore, a preferential tax policy should be used carefully, and investors should differentiate tax factors from credit factors in defining the spread between treasury bonds and other bonds.

CHAPTER 14

Impact of Government Policy on Term Structure of Interest Rates

In this chapter, we examine the importance of diversification of bond instruments from the perspective of the issuers, especially the government debt managers. The primary bond market exerts great influence on the secondary market, and it is usually the issuer, especially government debt managers, who are in a position to design the bond instrument. Just as primary economic exchange and primary financial exchange is superior to secondary economic exchange and secondary financial exchange, respectively, the same is true of the relationship of the primary and secondary bond markets. In China, the Ministry of Finance and the China Development Bank (CDB) are the two major issuers as well as the main designers of bond instruments; however, in designing debt instruments, they recognize that investors' preferences must be taken into account.

FORMS OF PAYMENT FOR MEDIUM- AND LONG-TERM TREASURY BONDS

As mentioned, bonds are a tradable debt. Like any commodity, bond varieties would help cater to the heterogeneous needs of buyers: in particular, the diverse needs of investors.

There are three ways to diversify bonds: (1) based on maturity, (2) based on cash flow, and (3) based on options. All three ways are related to risk management; for example, maturity-based diversification helps manage the assets and liabilities of different market participants.

Issuers are heterogeneous as well. In principle, China's Ministry of Finance and CDB are medium- and long-term issuers; corporate and commercial banks are short-term issuers. It is tempting to say that a one-to-one, identical borrower-to-investment match is the preferred mode. However, that is not necessarily true. For instance, short-term issuers are supposed to target short-term investors; long-term issuers are supposed to target long-term investors. However, long-term issuers usually have to manage their short-term cash, and therefore need to issue short-term financing and investment instruments. Conversely, short-term issuers can roll over their debt, thereby creating long-term debt.

Typically, banks and corporations are short-term investors and long-term borrowers, and generally have surplus money for short periods. Individuals are medium-term investors, depending on their savings pattern. Institutional investors, such as pension funds and insurance companies, tend to favor long-term investments.

In general, investors in medium- and long-term bonds should consider the way in which payment is made. There are two different forms of payment: zero-coupon bonds (payment on maturity) and installment payment. Since the payment policy for installment payment bonds is relatively complicated, investors may get confused about the real return of the bond. However, it may be to some investors' advantage to receive a yearly payment or periodic payment of principal, so that they can obtain the principal reinvestment profits within a short period. Others prefer to receive the principal payment within several years.

Obviously, the administrative cost of an annual principal payment is higher than a "bullet" payment. Therefore, some issuers prefer the "one-time" payment; zero-coupon bonds and discount bills fall into this category. From the point of view of government debt managers, if the government's goal is to balance the term structure of the bond, installment payments may improve the structure. In the 1980s, Chinese treasury bonds were paid in installments. After primary market reform in 1991, however, this method was suspended because it was considered too costly. Therefore, alternative products having varying maturities were issued to meet investors' needs.

However, when the primary offering is uncertain, debt managers can roll over maturing bonds and alleviate pressure of a new issue. This old-for-new primary issue was frequently used in China in 1993 and 1994. For example, in 1994, the government successfully implemented this policy for two-year treasury bonds. However, since that time, the practice has been discontinued.

INTEREST RATE STRUCTURE FOR MEDIUM- AND LONG-TERM TREASURY BONDS

In designing the interest rate structure of medium- and long-term T-bonds, debt managers can choose between a fixed rate and a floating rate. The former is the major type of medium- and long-term T-bonds and more frequently traded in the secondary market when the market is stable. However, when the market is volatile, the medium- and long-term fixed-rate T-bond price will fluctuate in a wide range. Conversely, floating-rate bonds can more easily withstand similar market shocks.

Floating-rate bonds give investors cash flow–based diversification. Investors or traders select floating or alterable payment terms according to their preferences and use these instruments to hedge their risk or to match their assets and liabilities. Among these bonds are floating-rate notes, fixed coupon rate bond, alterable coupon rate bonds, price-indexed bond, lottery bonds, and so on.

Although issuing bonds with floating rates expanded throughout the 1970s, in recent years, debt managers in various countries have been issuing bonds with fixed rates in order to develop the wholesale market for T-bonds. In particular, with the emergence of many derivative instruments, including futures, options, and swaps in the rising T-bond market, which can be used to hedge interest rate risk, issuing bonds with alterable rates seemed unnecessary.

In fact, beginning in the late 1990s, T-bonds and CDB financial debentures, the two primary bond instruments, have traded in the inter-bank bond market (IBBM), and investors in them are mainly banks. Therefore, issuers must consider the special feature of banks in the financial market. As banks' liabilities are, by nature, floating, they need to match them with floating assets. To assist banks in their asset and liability management, in 1999, the CDB began to issue floating-rate notes in the IBBM. These notes were very well received by banks.

As international experience indicates, if a treasury bond market has no derivative instruments, government debt managers need to focus on the design of the term structure of medium- and long-term T-bonds. This is particularly true when fixed-rate T-bonds are hard to sell due to volatile interest rate environments, and, for that reason, investors would rather subscribe to short-term T-bonds.

China's experience has also proved that when the market is in transition, market shocks can be a great threat to the new issues. Due to liquidity problems, banks prefer not to buy bonds when market interest fluctuates substantially, as they expect more downside risk. In such circumstances, issuers have to be flexible in designing the instrument for the new issue. For example, in 2003, when the PBOC tightened interest rates, there were a number of cases of new issue failures; the bidding price of most bidders was below the pre-set ceiling, so the successful bidding were not up to the targeted volume. To prevent this from happening again, the CDB designed twin-tranche bonds—10 billion fixed-rate bonds and 10 billion floating-rate bonds—and allowed the two tranches to be swapped with each other one year later. This new instrument gives investors an option for future swaps; it was essentially a swaption bond and therefore was very well received by the market. In fact, the issue became the only successful transaction at that time.

In general, the discount rate of the central bank, the yield curve of the bond, the consumer price index (CPI), and the exchange rate of a major currency act as reference points for pricing the short-term bond.

Whether government debt managers choose floating-rate bonds also depends on other factors. For example, if the floating-rate bond is very attractive to banks, debt managers should consider whether such bonds could affect the monetary policy of the central bank. Moreover, government debt managers should also consider the negative influence of the floating-rate bond (i.e., whether such a bond will further exacerbate instability of the interest rate system).

If government debt managers think that rate flexibility helps to sell treasury bonds, they could easily use floating-rate bonds, which would avoid excessive reliance on short-term T-bonds as well as the negative influence on liquid assets of banks.

One way to maintain the flexibility of the medium- and long-term T-bonds is to fix the coupon rate in advance at various specified periods throughout the bond's life span. Such bonds are called changeable coupon bonds and were designed to meet the need of some corporate issuers to borrow against their future incoming cash flow. The funding cost can be calculated as yield to maturity (YTM).

When the coupon rate is preset, whether the market yield of the bond changes at the time the transaction is launched depends on whether it is priced at a discount or at a premium. However, sometimes, to make payment convenient, issuers may prefer to issue discounted bond securities. For example, in China, one-year treasury bills are usually issued at a discount.

There are other bonds with special interest rate designs. The zero-coupon bond is one example. It has no coupon payment but its return is implied in the bond price, and its yield in the secondary market is calculated based on the difference between the purchase price and the selling price. Zero-coupon bonds were initially introduced for tax purposes. Because there was no interest payment per se, the gain is added to the principal, and investors can avoid paying withholding taxes. The other advantage of zero-coupon bonds is that there is no need to calculate accrued interest, and, therefore, such bonds are welcomed by some groups of investors in the secondary market.

Until 1993, bonds issued in China were basically zero-coupon bonds not for tax reasons but for reasons of cost. During that period, individuals were the main investors, and bonds were bearer securities in paper form. Yearly payments on such bonds are costly. Unlike coupon-bearing bonds, investors in zero-coupon bonds do not expect reinvestment income; instead, they see their payment only when they sell the bond or at maturity. It should be noted, however, that the real interest earning of zero-coupon bonds could not guarantee the appropriate return because investors do not know the rate of reinvestment from their coupon rate income in advance. In other words, the maturity yield calculated for the zero-coupon bond does not guarantee the real earnings of the bond because the formula used to calculate the bond's YTM assumes that each coupon rate could be reinvested at the same interest rate. If the market interest rate gradually declines after investors purchased the bond, investors may enjoy greater actual returns; if the rate picks up, the return would decrease.

The three- and five-year bearer treasury notes issued in China in the early 1990s were mainly zero-coupon bonds, where the coupon was paid in a lump sum at maturity. In 2002, China introduced STRIPs (separate trading of registered interest and principal of securities) to create zero-coupon bonds with different maturities. The zero coupon yields at different maturities could represent the spot yield curve, which otherwise would be derived by so-called booth stripping from coupon-bearing bonds at consecutive corresponding yearly maturities. This is possible only if all remaining maturity bonds are available. The merits and demerits of zero-coupon bonds depend on investors' particular preferences. However, if the taxes on bond earnings are taken into account, zero-coupon bonds offer a unique advantage to investors. For instance, there are no coupon payments, and they are free from interest withholding tax.

For government debt managers, the zero-coupon bond has many disadvantages. For example, although the issuance amount of the zero-coupon bond is calculated according to the settlement value, as it is sold at discount, its proceeds will be less than the total denomination issued, which reduces the amount of money raised for financing purposes, since the issuance size has already been legally fixed. Furthermore, the zero-coupon bond may cause problems with fiscal accounting, such as the calculation of underwriting fees.

An example of a bond with an uncertain interest payment is lottery bonds. Although lottery bonds are popular in the United Kingdom and Australia, they are not issued in China because of their similarity to gambling.[1] Lottery bonds would reinforce the irrationality of China's investors and would be counterproductive to healthy market development. However, China may introduce a lottery bond at some future time, when investors become more sophisticated.

Option-based diversification includes putable and callable bonds, or convertible bonds. In 2000, for the first time in China the CDB introduced putable and callable bonds in the IBBM market. Later these bonds became the main instruments in the corporate bond market. Callable bonds are frequently used by financial institutions for the issuance of subdebt. This format gives the issuer a right, but not an obligation, to terminate or continue the bonds. Usually, when the market rate goes down, the issuer calls back the bond, so that it can arrange refinancing at a relatively cheaper cost.

CHAPTER 15

Types of Bonds

NONTRADABLE BONDS: GOVERNMENT SAVINGS BONDS

As its name indicates, nontradable government debt instruments do not trade in the secondary market. This is considered a major advantage by some (the minority) investors who are not in a position to take on interest rate risk. The main type of nontradable bonds are government savings bonds.

Liquidity

The government savings bond is designed specifically for investors who are risk averse. However, as they are not tradable, savings bonds are not liquid. Therefore, government debt managers must provide liquidity in alternative ways. For instance, the bondholder could be allowed to return the bonds to the issuer during a certain period (i.e., premature redemption). When the market rate level is relatively stable, the liquidity of nontradable bonds hardly bothers government debt managers because most bondholders hold the bonds for their entire life span.

It is worth noting that if, upon issuance of a bond or for some time thereafter, holders of nontradable bonds wish to redeem the bond before maturity, it could be a disadvantage because issuers and their agents regard early redemption as extra work and charge investors for this service. For example, in China, the charge for early redemption of a certificate savings bonds would be 2 percent. In addition, early redemption may create refunding risk for the issuer. This is especially true if the market rate jumps, and bondholders who are sensitive to interest rates return their bonds to the issuer so that they will have money to buy newly issued treasury bonds or other bond securities with higher rates of return. Under such circumstances, government debt managers might have to increase the debt service budget.

Interest Rates

In designing the interest rate structure of the savings bond, debt managers often have two choices: fixed interest rate or floating interest rate. The floating interest varies, as, for example, in the progressive interest rate bond, where the interest rate for the first year is relatively low and rises year by year and interest payment is stepped up. The progressive bond is used primarily for callable subdebt. Moreover, when inflation occurs in the economy, inflation-protection subsidies could also be used. Sometimes the sales promotion can be linked to the relatively lower fixed interest rate instrument.

Interest can be paid in two ways: at specified times or reinvested as part of principal. These methods are related. As for the capitalized interest, the concept of "accrued interest" should apply. By calculating monthly or annual interest, investors can estimate the price that they are likely to get prior to the redemption time.

In choosing the form of the nontradable bond, government debt managers should also consider the mode of interest rate payment preferences of investors in savings bonds. Some of these investors prefer annual interest payments because they can use the annual earnings for further investment; other investors want to obtain all their interests on the maturity date. To meet both groups' needs, the debt manager could design two different nontradable bonds.

To promote sales of government savings bonds when the interest rate fluctuates greatly or increases, and to avoid preredemption of bonds, government debt managers should employ flexible policies as far as interest rates are concerned and refer to on-the-run issues or those already issued. To achieve this goal, tap issue is recommended (i.e., the issuance is a successive process or is carried out during a relatively short interval). Furthermore, debt managers should pursue more independent and flexible policies to adjust the forms of issuance at any moment to cater to the changed environment. From a technical point of view, it is relatively hard to achieve such flexibility if physical paper bonds are being used. In contrast, modern communication technology and non-bond book-entry systems facilitate such issuance. In China, savings bonds were all issued in certificate paper form until 2003, when book-entry form savings bond was introduced to increase government efficiency and give more convenience to investors. However, the book-entry savings bonds remain nontradable, and their redemption service is done manually; they are different from book-entry tradable bonds. In 2004, electronic savings bonds were introduced in China for the convenience of investors in buying, selling, and redeeming.

There are times when flexible interest rates of on-the-run issues are not high enough to keep investors holding bonds until maturity, if they find newer issues more attractive. In this event, there are three ways to solve the problem.

First, issuers should be allowed to replace such bonds with new ones if they find that the yield deviates from the market. To achieve this goal, on-the-run issues should provide greater flexibility and holders should be able to redeem old bonds or exchange them for new ones at any time during a certain period. The coupon rate of both new and old bonds should be interchangeable and could also be convertible according to market price; otherwise, it would be hard to avoid the preredemption of old bonds. A potential drawback is that the tap issue may result in relatively high costs if the government debt managers have to pay relatively high commissions to banks and their branches. Of course, government debt managers could make an agreement with banks and their subsidiary bodies to replace old bonds with new ones without paying additional commission charges.

The second method is the old-for-new format, where in addition to coupon interest, investors would also receive additional compensation and thus be rewarded by having all benefits equal to that of the market. However, this could create a problem if the new retroactive preferential policy resulted in a yield different from that for other treasury bonds. Moreover, for bondholders, the old-for-new method does not offer the flexibility of presettlement option unless the holders give up some compensation.

The third method applies the same interest rate to both new and old bonds. This method is usually used to compensate depositors. If the interest rate increases constantly, using this method could require the government to pay an incredibly high interest, but the reverse is also true: If the interest rate declines, the government could greatly reduce its interest costs. In pursuance of this method, government debt managers must consider other available choices.

If government debt managers do not want to employ flexible policies for the interest rate of the on-the-run issues and old bonds, they could strive to postpone the date of preredemption and limit preredemption by not paying interest on the bond for the first year. In 1994, China issued the three-year savings bond and did not pay interest on it within first six months, which effectively restricted preredemption. Increasing the annual interest rate may help to encourage investors to postpone payment of bonds. However, whether such solutions are effective depends on the interest rate compared with that of other treasury bonds and bank deposits at that time. For example, if the government wants a minimum term of three years, it should guarantee that the yield of the nontradable bond after three years would be equal to the interest rate of the time deposit with a term of three years. The yield of the nontradable bond usually can be a little bit lower than that of the tradable T-bond with same maturity because the latter bears certain market risks, although comments from agencies suggested that the yield of a nontradable bond should be higher than that of the tradable bond because the latter could result in capital gains if the interest rate declines.

Government debt managers could also attract money of risk-averse investors through preferential tax treatment instead of flexible and preferential interest rate policies of nontradable bonds. For instance, investors could enjoy full or partial exemption from taxation on savings bonds purchased. At the same time, debt managers must realize that, in general, investors with higher incomes will benefit most from such preferential tax treatment, and therefore it is necessary to restrict the maximum benefit of preferential policy.

Successfully achieving the goal of attracting investment through preferential taxation depends on whether other borrowers would increase the yield of their bonds to compete with the government's nontradable bonds. The investors in China are indifferent to the issuers regardless of their creditworthiness as long as they are state-owned enterprises. Even today, investors prefer higher-coupon-rate instruments irrespective of issuer type. Until very recently, the coupon rates on savings bonds were higher than the bank deposit rate. However, if tax treatments are taken into consideration, their real rate of return remains higher than the bank deposit rate for the same maturity.

Limitations on Ownership of Government Savings Bonds

In designing nontradable government debt instruments, debt managers must also consider how to deter other groups of investors (not the traditional savings bonds investor or active individual investor) from purchasing such debt instruments, because those investors are not entitled in our policy, to enjoy favorable terms (higher interest rate, premature redemption, etc.) and preferential tax treatment. In general, the government sells nontradable bonds only to individual investors and avoids selling them to banks and institutional investors. However, this restriction is subject to the sales performance of banks and other financial institutions. Since these institutions usually serve as agents, they could control the sales procedure of such bonds. To effectively avoid institutional purchases, the government usually sets limits on the maximum amount of nontradable T-bonds possessed by individuals. However, the government often faces a difficult choice when implementing this restriction. If the government wants to sell more nontradable T-bonds, it should not impose too many limitations on sales, but without such limitations, banks and institutional investors may easily access such bonds.

In addition, since interest rates could create conditions favorable to fair competition within the financial system, the government should not give excessive preferential interest rate treatment to the nontradable bond, because this is not only costly to issuers, but it may also crowd out private investment.

PRICE INDEX BONDS

The price index bond (PIB) is a new vibrant market instrument. All bonds linked with the price index are called price index bonds. They are issued for the benefit of investors in volatile market conditions. Most alterable cash-flow bonds are designed to allow investors to hedge market risk. However, the PIB is designed to protect investors from macroeconomic risk.

The most important feature of price index bonds is that, during the whole life cycle of the bond, both its coupon rate and principal will be adjusted according to the accumulative price index. Thus, during periods of inflation, if government debt managers want to issue medium- and long-term bonds linked to the price index, both the interest and the principal need to be considered.

Price index bonds, like other alterable cash-flow instruments, seem to be similar to floating-rate bonds, but there are significant differences. The floating-rate note (FRN) is based on future market changes, whereas the PIB is based on future economic performance. If the rate continues to increase in the coming years, issuing a floating- or alterable-rate bond will effectively attract more investors. However, whether or not performance of the PIB can be less venerable to interest rates risks depends on how the floating rate compares with the short-term rate (CHIBOR, one-year deposit rate, seven-day repo rate) can serve as index is related to the risk calculation of bondholders. For example, if the FRN is indexed to the one-year deposit rate and the money market rate is higher than the one-year deposit rate, the price of the FRN would go down.

Compared with the nominal coupon-bearing bond, the PIB has many advantages. The fixed-income bond cannot provide inflation-linked protection. Cash flow of the general nominal-rate bond is predetermined and does not change during the life cycle of bond. Therefore, when the price index goes up, the real value of the bond is reduced. The investor has to bear the risk of inflation, and the issuers would encounter weak demand. In fact, the traditional nominal government fixed-income bond only secures the nominal earning of investors while the price index bond protects the real benefits of investors.

The PIB also provides protection benefits to issuers in the event of deflation and reduces the risk premium shouldered by issuers by cutting down cost of issuance.

Major purchasers of the PIB include fund managers, hedge funds, and pension funds. Many fund managers consider the PIB as one component of price indexed mutual funds or asset portfolios. Hedge funds hold PIBs to protect themselves against future inflation, or to get relative value amid market change, or to hedge their position in fixed-income bonds. Pension funds invest in PIBs to hedge inflation-linked liability. Practices vary around the world. In many countries, insurance companies are major holders of PIBs. In other countries, such companies have yet to invest in PIBs and are only potential investors. In European countries, especially in Britain, insurance companies are the major investors in PIBs. However, in the United States, the law restricts insurance companies from investing in PIBs. Some corporate or fund investors have yet to invest in PIBs not because they are not interested in such bonds, but because their internal regulations restrict such investments.

For calculating interest, it is assumed that the issue date of the bond is December 20, 1996. After the bidding is completed, the coupon rate is fixed as 4 percent. Every six months, interest is paid. On December 24, 1996, the clean price was RMB101. It is assumed that the urban consumer price index (CPI-U) on December 1, 1996, and January 1, 1997, was 157.8 and 158.3, respectively. The index on any date in between can be calculated by linear interpolation. The formula is:

Initial index + (ultimate index − initial index) × (certain day in one month − 1)/(the number of all days of that month)

Therefore, the index value of December 24, 1996, was:

$$157.8 + (158.3 - 157.8) \times 23/31 = 158.17097$$

Similarly, the index value of December 20, 1996, was:

$$157.8 + (158.3 - 157.8) \times 19/31 = 158.10645$$

Ratio of inflation index : 158.17097/158.10645 = 1.00041

The added interest of the bond was:

(Coupon interest/times of interest payment) × (number of days with interest/number of days during the interest bearing period)
$$= (4/2) \times (4/182) = 0.044$$

Thus, the price of the bond should be:

$$101.44 \times 1.00041 = RMB101.085$$

International Experience with Price Index Bonds

North American and most European countries as well as Australia have issued price index bonds, and other countries are considering issuing them. In addition, PIBs are issued by central or local governments, municipal governments, and corporations.

Although PIBs have a relatively short history in the United States, the marketing mechanism is instructive especially because the American bond market is the most advanced in the world and the conditions are favorable for the development of PIBs.

Treasury Inflation Protection Securities (TIPS) is the oldest PIB in America. It was first issued on January 29, 1997, and is issued once every quarter. At first, the unified term was 10 years; since then bonds with other terms have been issued. Later some corporations issued Company Inflation-Protected Securities (CIPS). The guiding price index is the consumer price index of all CPI-U. If the issue date is in the middle of one month, the CPI is calculated through linear interpolation.

In general, the sale of bonds is achieved through one-price bidding with the real coupon rate as the objective. Selling the PIB could employ the STRIPS (separate trading of registered interest and principal of securities) mode; that is, it would be the same rate as the nominal rate bond. However, capital and interest of various bonds are not interchangeable.

There are two payment methods for CIPS. One is the same as TIPS and is called the TIPS structure; the other is called the REAL structure, where all interest paid is the sum of the coupon interest according to the face value and the increased interest resulting from rising inflation. In the United States, according to relevant tax laws, the government taxes both forms of interest.

In recent years, the issuance of American TIPS has increased constantly while that of nominal fixed income bonds has declined.

Price Index Bonds in China

China once issued a bond similar to the PIB: the inflation-linked bond issued by the Ministry of Finance in 1989. That bond belongs to the category of zero-coupon bond and had no cash flow, so investors could only enjoy benefits of the inflation-linked bond upon the maturity, and it protected only interest, not principal. Moreover, the bond was not directly linked to a price index, but rather to the inflation subsidy ratio of bank deposits. Since the inflation-linked subsidy ratio of bank deposits did not reflect real price changes, the bonds issued at that time could hardly protect investors from being negatively affected by the changes in price. Furthermore, the minimum inflation-linked subsidy ratio is zero, which guarantees only that the interest rate will not be negative. When the interest rate declines, the real inflation-linked subsidy ratio may be higher, but when the interest rate rises, investors may not enjoy the benefits of the inflation-linked subsidy. For these reasons, the government abandoned the inflation-linked subsidy in 1994.

In times of deflation, bonds offer relatively high real interest rates and lower nominal interest rates. Issuance of the PIB reduces the real rate and thus cuts down on the issuance cost. In an inflationary environment, although investors enjoy relatively high real interest rates, they tend to feel that the interest rate is too low and therefore do not want to deposit their money in banks or purchase bonds. Issuance of a PIB may help to solve this problem. In a deflationary environment, issuance of the PIB could help the issuer reduce issuance costs and make it possible to issue a long-term bond. For investors, since the PIB could protect them from the negative influence of inflation, it would be in their interest to invest in such a bond instrument. For issuers, the PIB would create some uncertainty about their future payments. To solve this problem, it is necessary to link the price index with both assets and liabilities and to fix the interest rate spread, which could make banks match its assets with its liabilities. Since the CDB has already issued the floating-rate bond, it would be easy for it to issue PIBs.

The only possible problem is that such bonds may be incompatible with the current interest rate system. However, in fact, with market-oriented reform of treasury bonds, the yield of T-bonds in the secondary market is different from that in the regulated interest rate system. Again, since the CDB now issues policy-based financial bonds through bidding, the interest rate is decided by the market. Actually, the price index adjustment can be added to both market-based instruments and instruments with government-set coupon rates.

Selection of the price index to act as the benchmark interest rate could depend on which group of investors is targeted. Currently these price indexes are available: retail price index (RPI), production material price index (PPI), and consumer price index (CPI). Since most investors in China are urban residents, the CPI-U of the CPI bears a closer relationship to the value of assets. Use of the CPI-U is recommended. As with all other marketable securities, auction selling is advisable. This formula for calculating interest payments is recommended:

> Term interest paid : capital × price index × coupon rate
> Maturity payment : capital price index × (1 + coupon rate)
>   Price index : apply CPI − U of last month
> Term interest paid : capital × index ratio
>   Index ratio : target purchase index + index on the issue date

If there is no index published on the purchase date and issue date, the index could be calculated through linear interpolation.

The method to calculate the index if there is no index published on the issue date is:

Initial index + (ultimate index − initial index) × (certain day in one month − 1)/(the number of all days in that month).

Since the introduction of the PIB is of great significance, it needs to be thoroughly studied before an appropriate plan can be worked out. However, it appears that the PIB can serve not only as a fundraising instrument for the Central Development Bank but can also provide the bond market with an investor-friendly instrument in China.

In China, the PIB is linked to the price index whereas the FRN is connected to certain interest rate indexes. Since the nominal interest rate is different from the real interest rate, the PIB provides more protection to investors.

In summary, bond instrument diversification represents the main trend in the bond market. There are three categories of bond instrument diversification, which are designed to satisfy the needs of market participants: maturity-based diversification, cash flow–based diversification, and option-based diversification. Each is related to risk management in the financial market.

Diversification of debt instruments is an important market function carried out by governments and issuers for the benefit of both issuers and investors. Since diversification of instruments can improve the relationship between issuers and investors, it is indeed a win-win outcome and therefore represents institutional progress in the debt capital market.

CHAPTER 16

Government Policy on the Holding Structure of Treasury Bonds

The change in the investor base was a milestone in the development of the market. It is important to understand the primary and secondary markets through the study of the holding structure of treasury bonds. When the primary market is a wholesale market, the holding structure is different from when a market is composed of underwriters, who subscribe the primary issue and sell to the market, or primary dealers.

In general, the underwriter may sell T-bonds directly to individual and institutional investors in the secondary market. Thus, the structure is equivalent to the final investors. Generally, the underwriter, including securities intermediaries and banks, who directly underwrites the T-bonds in the primary market is actually the primary dealer. Investors in T-bonds include individual investors in the secondary market, various pension and issuance funds, banks, and foreign investors. There is a close relationship between the structure of investors and various market participants.

HOLDERS OF T-BONDS IN CHINA

The structure of China's treasury bondholders relates to the issuing method along with the development of primary market. Before 1991, banks did not own treasury bonds. Funds only held a few T-bonds, which accounted for approximately 2 percent; T-bonds held by enterprises, such as state-owned enterprises (SOEs), and governmental institutions, held 31 percent; the financial institutions held 13 percent; and individuals held the rest. This is because prior to 1991, T-bonds were issued mainly through assigned subscription and were aimed at SOEs, public and governmental institutions, and individuals. In 1991, with the adoption of the underwriting syndication method, the structure of bondholders changed significantly. Treasury bonds held by the pension and insurance funds reached 3 percent while holdings by the financial institutions increased remarkably, reaching 65 percent; enterprises, such as public and governmental institutional holders, declined to 3 percent.

In 1992, when securities intermediaries rushed to purchase T-bonds, individual investors could hardly access the primary market; as a result, the securities intermediaries held approximately 95 percent of the T-bonds. In 1993, when administrative placement resumed in many places, individuals, corporations, and public institutions as well as governmental institutions gradually regained a larger share of the bonds. In 1994, banks underwrote short-term T-bonds and thus possessed around 13 percent, while individual investors held the rest. As institutional investors and financial intermediaries became more involved in the government securities primary market, it gradually became a wholesale market.

Characteristics of Market Participants and Holders of Treasury Bonds

From the point of view of economic theory, the structure of holders of treasury bonds should correlate with the fund flow and the distribution of financial assets. Since the business sector is always in a deficit financial position and has to depend heavily on debt financing, it could hardly spare much money to invest in government bonds. However, corporations may have short-term money to purchase short-term T-bonds. Since the budgets of various government departments and other non-productive agencies are mandated by the government, they are not in a position to buy medium- and long-term T-bonds, either. Therefore, corporations and government institutions could hardly become major holders of bonds. The financial institutions, especially securities companies, acting as securities intermediaries or market makers, function as distributors rather than treasury bond holders; they cannot hold T-bonds for long periods because they do not have sufficient capital to do so. Therefore, individuals and institutional investors are the mainstay of the market.

Traditionally, in China, individual investors were depositors, who bought and held government bonds for savings rather than investment. With relatively low per capita income, individuals could not be the major bondholders; therefore, the holding structure of bonds in the early 1990s was unsustainable. Beginning in the middle 1990s, with institutional investors at a preliminary stage of development, banks became the major bond investors during this transition phase.

Banks in China had surplus money due to the rapid increase in savings, which were mainly bank deposits. Bank loans were not growing as quickly as deposits because of concerns about loan safety. At the same time, the yield in the bond market was higher than the bank deposit rate (as it had been for many years). For this reason, banks were more than willing to buy and hold bonds, not only for safety reasons but also to get risk-free profits. Since the middle of the 1990s, banks had been piling up nonperforming loans. Against this background, after 1997, the central government encouraged banks to buy treasury bonds, so that they could get leave risky investments to the business sector. Gradually, banks became the overwhelming majority investors in bond securities (see Figure 16.1, which illustrates the structure of T-bond market participants).

Most of China's treasury bonds are held by individuals, banks, and financial institutions. Funds hold only a small percentage of the bonds, and foreign institutions barely subscribe to China's T-bonds. This structure could potentially hinder the further development of T-bond issuance.

For this reason, recently, while changing issuing methods, the government also has been paying much more attention to gradually broadening the distribution structure. The primary focus now is targeting T-bond issues at institutional investors instead of individuals, governmental departments, corporations, and institutions; the securities intermediaries then distribute the bonds to individual and institutional investors.

The goal of issuing T-bonds directly to financial institutions instead of individuals is mainly to increase efficiency in order to create an effective T-bond market. Issuing bonds only to institutions could reduce the cost of issuance and shorten the issuance period. In the early 1980s, the issuance of a treasury bond often took half a year mainly because it was targeted to individuals. During such a long period, the market rate level would most

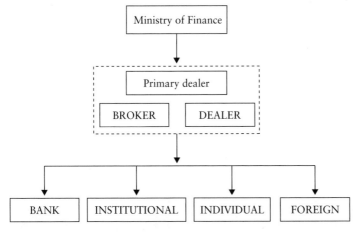

FIGURE 16.1 Primary Market and Bondholding Structure

certainly change. If the market rate increased, it was very difficult to sell the bond. China's experience proves that issuing bonds only to institutions leads to the creation of an interinstitutional market. Since institutions are market specialists, their participation is a necessary precondition for the development of a healthy T-bond market.

As for the estimated structure and changes in the holding structure of treasury bonds, see Table 16.1, which offers a historical perspective of the structure of China's bond market from 1981 to the present.

International Comparison: Lessons for China

An examination of real conditions in T-bond markets in various countries indicates that treasury bonds are held by all kinds of institutional investors: pension and insurance funds, hedge funds and banks, as well as individual and foreign investors. Most countries issue tradable treasury bonds to institutions, which helps create a special structure of bondholders (see Table 16.2).

As shown in Table 16.2, in each of the five countries, pension and insurance funds, banks, and foreign investment agencies are major bondholders. Businesses, securities intermediaries, and individuals hold the remaining share. Pension and insurance funds are always holders of long-term bonds. Banks hold T-bonds as current assets for their relatively high liquidity.

TABLE 16.1 Holding Structure of Treasury Bonds (percent)

Year	Individual	State-Run Enterprises	Non-Bank Financial Institutions	Pension and Insurance Funds	Bank
1981		100			
1982–1990	80	20			
1991–1993	75	10	10	5	
1994–1995	75	5	10	5	5
1996	30	15	20	15	20
1997	0	0	51	0	49
1998	0	2	12	1	85
1999	0	7.6	0.8	3.8	87.8
2000	0	1.2	7.4	6.4	85
2001	0	8	3	6	83
2002	0.07	7	20	5	68
2003	0.08	14.4	21	5	59.4
2004	2	13	21	7	57
2005	0.3	11.3	18.5	8.5	61

TABLE 16.2 Distribution of Investment in Treasury Bonds in Various Countries (percent)

Country	Banks	Pension Funds	Foreign Investment Agencies	Others
United States	10.4	20.2	19.3	50.1
United Kingdom	5.4	37.4	14.1	43.0
Japan	58.6	27.1		
Germany	41.0	10.0	17.0	21.0
Canada	709	19.8	25.8	46.5

This structure is an important sign of a sound T-bond market and offers four advantages:

1. Institutional ownership helps promote issuing techniques; for example, auction or underwriting.
2. Fund ownership over a long period helps stabilize the treasury bond market.
3. Bonds held by banks create conditions for the central bank to pursue open market operations (OMOs).
4. Institutional ownership simplifies marketing procedures and helps to reduce the cost of issuance.

To achieve a structure of holders composed mainly of institutional investors, China must develop not only its wholesale market but also various investment funds to create an institutional investor base and gradually set up a multilayer market structure.

In comparing China's bond market structure with those in developed countries, it is apparent that there are fewer institutional investors, less foreign participation, and more bank holding of T-bonds.

As banks in China embarked on commercialization programs and assets and liabilities management become important requirement of risk management by the Bank for International Settlements, banks have come to hold more treasury bonds, especially book-entry ones, so that they can buy and sell T-bonds to match their assets and liabilities (see Table 16.3 for the treasury bonds possessed by various banks in 1996).

Although book-entry treasury bonds are not convenient for individual investors, they have attracted more and more urban-dwelling individuals, who purchase them through their accounts in stock exchanges. For instance, for the two long-term T-bonds issued in 1996, there are 19,825 personal

TABLE 16.3　Amount of Book-Entry Treasury Bonds Held by Commercial Banks (Unit: RMB10,000)

Name of Bank	196	596	696	896	Total
ICBC (Industrial and Commercial Bank of China) Head Office	63216.4	43056.4	35130.2	18399.5	159802.5
Agricultural Bank of China Head Office	8897.8	0	0	20200	29097.8
China Construction Bank Head Office	3387.8	101098.1	190092.1	11486.4	306064.4
Bank of China Head Office	0	22509	16.5	18500	41025.5
Bank of Communications	7000	14998.6	3000	36700	61698.6
Shanghai Pudong Development Bank	15107.8	0	0	10109.5	25217.3
Investment Bank	29285	31356.7	105566.4	39954.9	206163
China Everbright Bank	12415.4	5000	0	0	17415.4
Industrial Bank	507.4	0	13199.1	0	13706.5
China Merchants Bank	21019.7	52	0	1200	22271.7
CITIC Bank	23242	4107.2	0	7187.6	34536.8
Shenzhen Development Bank	2069.7	4503.7	0	0	6573.4
Nanjing Cooperative Bank	0	17213.5	8808.9	0	26022.4
Shanghai Cooperative Bank	27129.5	94525.3	6023.9	19122.7	147801.4
Beijing Cooperative Bank	0	13000	10000	26900	49900
Total	214474.5	352016.5	372533.1	210656.6	1147297

accounts, accounting for 8.41 percent of the total amount issued (see Table 16.4).

For the percentage of different investors possessing long-term treasury bonds, see Figures 16.2 and 16.3.

CHINA'S BOND MARKET STRUCTURE AND INTERNATIONAL PRACTICES COMPARED

To develop an effective treasury bond market, four conditions must be met. They are:

1. Like the wholesale business of the foreign exchange market and the money market, the T-bond market requires a market maker system.

TABLE 16.4 Amount and Structure of the Treasury Bonds (696 and 896) Held (Unit: RMB100 million)

T-Bond Holder	696			896		
	Amount Possessed	Structure (%)	No. of Accounts	Amount Possessed	Structure (%)	No. of Accounts
Individual	24.16342	10.20	7519	14.63476	8.41	19825
Institution	98.1197	41.40	341	71.25137	40.95	398
Five major banks (including ICBC, Agricultural Bank of China, China Construction Bank, Bank of China, Bank of Communications)	22.89348	9.66	307	10.61819	6.00	409
Commercial Banks	14.35983	6.06		10.44747	6.00	
Securities Firms	77.46278	32.68		67.03821	38.53	
Total	236.9992		8167	173.99		20632

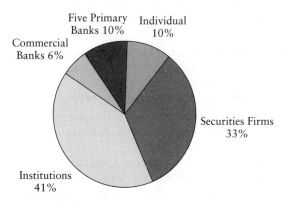

FIGURE 16.2 Proportion of 696 Holders

The market makers need to be able to make two-way quotations (i.e., to report instantly the purchase price and sale price for each transaction, so that market participants can find transaction counterparts at any moment and thereby make transactions possible). If there are more competing market makers, and their quotations are competitive, markets participants will benefit from transactions. If the

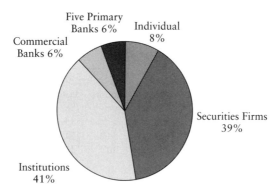

FIGURE 16.3 Proportion of 896 Holders

transactions themselves are conducted through financial intermediaries (i.e., brokers), transactions tend to be efficient because financial intermediaries save transaction costs.

2. All market participants must be able to obtain the most up-to-date market information. Investors should be aware of the market pricing process and real-time market movements. In order to improve the speed and efficiency of information transmission, an electronic network that would allow immediate access to real-time market information is essential.

3. The process for bid-offer matching and clearing pricing should be safe, quick, and accurate. Again, a modern computer system is the only way to realize these requirements.

4. The trading, clearing, and settlement process should be effectively supervised in order to guarantee the principles of fairness, justice, and openness and to reduce credit and liquidity risk.

The objective of establishing a highly efficient, cost-effective, and liquid market can be achieved only if it is an institution-based wholesale market with a diverse investor base, active financial intermediaries and market makers, book-entry instruments, diversified maturity profile, and an electronic transaction trading system.

Internal Consistency of Market Structure

International experience shows that selling and trading technology depends on the transaction volume and market structure classified according to market participants. In a market with a small transaction volume, the sequentially matching orders submitted by market participants in the exchange bond market can be used. Prices formed in the secondary market after each issuance would then be consistent with pricing in the primary market, and the secondary market price can serve as a benchmark for transactions of similar treasury bonds in other markets.

From the initial establishment of the primary market in China, the goal was set to keep price consistency by reconciling the price between primary market and secondary market. This could only be achieved by improvement of market-based selling techniques. China was trying to streamline its selling technique as early as 1991 when underwriting was introduced, and since then it has been a high priority. In fact, auction selling techniques were used more extensively than in the United Kingdom or the United States during 1996 and 1997. In addition, China uses auctions not only for T-bond offerings but also for selling financial debentures. As T-bonds were sold in both the inter-bank bond market (IBBM) and the stock exchange bond market (SEBM), the issue price in the IBBM serves as a reference of the SEBM, and vice versa.

When the T-bond market is liquid due to augmented turnover, or when institutional investors and fund managers are the active participants, the T-bond market may also be used as a ready-made marketplace for the central bank's OMOs. This is exactly the situation in China. The development of market infrastructure and the evolution of institutions in the second half of the 1990s helped to build up an institution-based market, where the central bank has been carrying out OMOs since 1997.

Dual System for Transition

In some countries, in an effort to create not only an effective T-bond wholesale market but also a retail market, treasury bond managers employ a dual system, each with different objectives.

In China, a dual system was deliberately designed to meet both the requirements of individual investors and to serve the objectives of government debt managers for market development. In 1994, China introduced certificate savings bonds to cater to the needs of individual investors; however, the purpose was not to set up a retail market; rather, it was to allow the majority of bonds to enter the wholesale market. Thus, although the savings bonds introduced in 1994 were perceived as a step back, they were actually intended to satisfy individuals' needs while at the same time boost the institutional market and wholesale trading. This win-win arrangement benefited both investors and issuers and helped to achieve a smooth transition to an institution-based bond market.

However, two problems may interfere with this dual objective:

1. If book-entry bonds are traded through primary dealers, it is necessary to define the minimum order quantity required to enter the mainframe of the electronic transmission system.
2. Due to different trading volumes, the transaction cost per unit may vary. Therefore, the standard transaction commission should be specified in advance.

The first problem can be solved by establishing two systematic pricing modes that are closely associated with each other. The wholesale market for transactions between large institutions should be performed mainly through the two-way quotations by market makers, whereas the retail market for transactions between institutional investors and individual investors, who have less financial strength, should be priced through the matching of orders based on the principle of price and time priority.

The second problem involves the commission charges for small orders. Clearly, it is hard for small investors to survive in the retail market where their per-unit cost is much larger than those who are able to buy or sell in large quantities and therefore have a lower per-unit cost. Therefore, treasury bond managers should develop a low-cost pricing technique to protect the retail market.

Where there are a large number of small investors in the market, wide price fluctuations may affect the yield of T-bonds, unless brokers in their capacity as brokers buy and sell sufficient quantities to stabilize the market. The standard commissions in different countries vary. Usually in China, the government formulates a uniform standard on commission fees; in some countries, commission fees are based on market convention. However, to maintain an active secondary market, intermediaries are encouraged to compete so that commission fees tend to be lower.

In China, small investors only participate in a separate over-the-counter market, and the savings bonds they hold are not tradable. Therefore, for the convenience of small investors, the government allowed savings bonds to be redeemable before maturity at a discount. However, in the SEBM, individual investors are often exempted from fees as long as they deposit money with the securities firms.

In cases where commercial banks broker the treasury bonds, the government and the banks should consider an agreement that allows the banks to withdraw part of the commission charges obtained from the wholesale transactions to subsidize the medium and small investors in the retail market, thereby reducing their commission expenses. In practice, to address this issue, many countries set an upper limit for retail commissions; thus, brokers can set their commission charges under the limit for small investors. The total trading volume of small orders can be increased through collection procedures designed for small-quantity orders in the retail market, whereby retail investors save commission charges as a result of mass-market transactions.

These international experiences are instructive to China, where the trading volume in the stock exchange market tends to be small. Commission fees tend to be higher when the SEBM is active; investors have requested that trading commissions be reduced when the stock market became sluggish. Today, as market convention is formulated, the Stock Exchange Market sets a relatively stable commission rate. However, the IBBM is composed mainly of banks, whose trading turnover tends to be huge, and, therefore, the transaction cost per unit is relative low.

Creating an Institutional Base

Unlike countries where it takes many years to build up a financial intermediary industry and it always occurs at a late stage in market development, China built up its financial intermediary system, though preliminary, as early as the late 1980s, when treasury bond service departments were established and banks set up security firms. In fact, this industry was built before the primary market was established; therefore, it is fair to say that from the very beginning, China foresaw the institutional implications of a financial intermediary system on a sound bond market.

When the development of an effective T-bond wholesale market becomes necessary, how the organizational structure of market participants is arranged is crucial. One way is to select several banks and securities firms with market experience and financial strength as the market experts for trading intermediation—that is, as the primary dealers. This structure can be formed through agreements concluded between the government debt managers and the primary dealers. The agreement would specify the functions, rights, and obligations of the primary dealers in the primary and secondary markets.

China set up a primary dealer system only two years after the introduction of underwriting syndication. Later on, this primary dealer system turned out to play important role in the bond market development. To date, both the Ministry of Finance and the China Development Bank (CDB) have their own primary dealer groups in their syndicate. In addition, since 2003, the People's Bank of China (PBOC) the central bank, established its primary dealer system for trading central bank notes. The primary dealers are entitled and obliged to bid in auctions. In 2005, the central bank had 52 primary dealers in its OMOs.

The primary dealers bear the obligation to underwrite treasury bonds as well as price and distribute the bonds to the final individual investors and institutional investors in the primary market. In the T-bond secondary market, primary dealers act as market markers by offering two-way quotations. It is clear from international experience that in the secondary market, primary dealers are also obliged improve market infrastructure—such things as screen display system, automated quotation system, and financial services, including depository trust, registration, and clearing and settlement through the book-entry method. Usually primary dealers advise government debt managers on how to design market infrastructure.

However, as the primary dealers in China were generally firms with only limited paid-in capital and a few years' experience in the bond market, they did not perform as well as it had been hoped. Thus, they did not contribute much to market efficiency.

It is hoped that inter-dealer brokers can be introduced as part of the market infrastructure and institutional arrangement in order to create a genuine over-the-counter market or revitalize the current IBBM. It is also expected that joint venture securities firms, which were set up between Chinese securities companies and foreign investment banks and are popular in China in the aftermath of its World Trade Organization commitment, will yield productive results insofar as market intermediation is concerned.

Support System for Primary Dealers

For market makers to be able to provide instant two-way quotations, it is necessary to provide them with refinancing instruments, such as the repurchase (repo) market for treasury bonds. Such a system would help market makers close and open the positions they take in order to make the market. Therefore, T-bond managers in many countries regard the financing system and repo market as important components of market infrastructure for the promotion of the secondary market of treasury bonds.

China set up its repo market in 1993 in order to finance the financial intermediaries. The repo market helped alleviate the pressure of short-term financing of insolvent securities firms. However, international experience shows that securities firms or investment banks tend to raise money by issuing stock or short-term paper. Currently most investment banks in the United States are listed on one or more stock exchange markets. Equity financing is conducted by issuing long bonds, including mortgage and financing bonds. Short-term financing or cash management refers primarily to repurchase and the issuance of commercial papers. The debt ratio of quite a number of giant American securities companies has reached over 90 percent.

In contrast, in China, only a few securities firms are listed on the stock exchange. For a long time in the past, securities firms in China were prohibited from accessing any financial resources except their own capital. This is part of the reason why many securities firms in China illegally embezzled customers' deposit until very recently. In 1997, when banks withdrew from the stock exchanges, securities firms were completely cut off from their connection to banks. Since that time, many have begun to speculate with the deposits in their customers' accounts. To address these financing issues faced by financial intermediaries, the PBOC recently permitted them to issue short-term paper in the IBBM. In 2006, the Ministry of Finance was contemplating open bond financing (borrowing bond securities as opposed borrowing money) in China as another concrete step toward bailing out firms with financial problems.

Standardization of the Treasury Bond Market

To secure the sale of treasury bonds, it is desirable to establish a highly efficient wholesale market. A highly efficient and cost-effective primary market requires relatively standardized commodities and a certain level of trading volume. For this reason, countries with T-bond markets still in the primary stage of development cannot develop their retail markets until the wholesale market is developed adequately and is able to provide sufficient tradable T-bonds. Still, it is very useful to maintain a high degree of standardization of government debt instruments, even in the preliminary stage of development of the wholesale market.

In the institutional economic engineering (IEEN) framework, standardized market instruments would facilitate transactions and thereby help institutional progress. In the debt capital market, standardization has five aspects:

1. Structured maturity profile of treasury bonds (i.e., maturity covers the whole spectrum so that all investors' needs can be satisfied).
2. New treasury bonds shall be designed to fill the vacancy of bond inventory, to replenish the maturing bonds, so that the market's capacity may be continually broadened.
3. Newly issued government bonds shall cover the off-the-run illiquid small-volume bonds in the secondary market. Schedules of issuance are designed to realize one-to-one correspondence of the newly issued treasury bonds with the maturing standardized bonds.
4. Standardization of T-bonds also includes standardized interest rates, settlement time, and issuing schedules.
5. Public offerings shall serve as the main selling format; private placement shall be used when market conditions are unfavorable or when they are unwilling to make information disclosure, as this is compulsory for public offerings

In some countries, a sound financial system was already in place when the treasury bond market was created. However, for historical reasons, China has two different marketplaces: the SEBM and the IBBM, each with its own supervisory system and under different jurisdictions. For this reason, standardization cannot be achieved as quickly as is desired.

However, some preliminary progress has been made. For example, both the Ministry of Finance and the CDB have arranged a fixed timetable for the issuance of treasury bonds and financial debentures. However, for market reasons, maturity dates are selected for expedience; a diversified maturity profile is not a priority. Throughout 2003, the Ministry kept issuing bonds with seven-year maturities, for example.

However, standardization must not conflict with the some degree of flexibility, especially when the market is in a preliminary stage of development. Government debt managers should be aware that, in establishing standardized policies for the secondary market, it is hard to satisfy the particular interest payment requirement for some investors unless some flexible special policies are taken. For example, issuing "bullet" bonds (i.e., bonds where interest, capital, and interest are not paid before maturity) will not work because it will cause inconvenience to those investors who hope to earn interest annually.

The Ministry of Finance paid a great deal of attention to standardized issuance at the beginning of reform; however, in early 1998, companies, especially insurance companies, demanded that the Ministry to offer private placements with higher-than-market return. The Ministry refused to do so, since private placement is not a standardized selling technique and is counterproductive to the effort to establish a standardized bond market.

The CDB has also made significant contributions to the standardization of the bond market. After leading a number of financial market innovations, it increased the volume of outstanding bonds in order to improve liquidity by reopening the existing bonds traded in the market. The CDB is also trying to make its maturity profile as diversified as possible. In 2001, it issued 20- and 30-year maturity bonds to make long bonds available to investors, especially institutional investors.

Unified Tax Policy

It is also recognized that taxation on government debt instruments should be as moderate as possible. For instance, how the interest withholding tax is applied should take into consideration the impact on the sale of T-bonds in the primary and the secondary markets, as well as how a tax-free policy for some T-bonds impacts other T-bonds and whether it is necessary to apply the same policy to all T-bonds.

Although current tax policy is the same for both the SEBM and the IBBM, a business tax is levied on Chinese banks that is not levied on foreign banks. Therefore, Chinese banks are at a tax disadvantage when competing with foreign banks.

Structure of the Secondary Treasury Bond Market

In a developed treasury bond market, the institutions comprise the secondary market and primary market, which is a desirable conduit for secondary bond exchange and primary bond market exchange. This arrangement ensures the healthy functioning of the market. Generally, the market includes issuers, investors, and financial intermediaries, collectively called market participants. The issuers are agencies and corporations. Investors include institutional investors, individual investors, and foreign investors. They can be securities firms, commercial banks, and non-banking financial institutions, such as insurance companies and pension funds. In China, financial intermediaries are mainly securities firms and banks.

Many countries separate the securities industry from the banking industry in order to secure a division of market function. To date, China has been following this model. Banks are not allowed to engage in the securities business. Commercial banks have great financing capacity, and, therefore, they are the leading investors in treasury bonds in China.

In the T-bond market, securities intermediaries are divided into different levels, and each plays a specified function. Primary dealers are found in the top level. They are the market makers and are obliged to offer a purchase price and a sale price in the primary market. Brokers are the go-betweens between securities intermediaries or between securities intermediaries and investors. Investors are those who hold bonds and often trade them in their own names in the market. These market structure and organization layouts are—in principle—in place.

For historical reasons, the form of the T-bond market varies in different countries. (Figure 16.4 illustrates the structure of the British T-bond market.) However, the structure of the secondary market in different countries has many features in common. One of the most important features, the structure of market participants, divides the market into different levels with diverse functions. Figure 16.5 illustrates a typical structure.

Generally, most intermediaries are securities institutions. With the development of the market, primary dealers gradually separate from dealers, allowing a multilayer wholesale system to develop for the issuance of treasury bonds. At the same time, in order to improve the functions of agent service and self-management, dealers specializing in proprietary businesses and brokers specializing in agent service emerge. The development stimulates

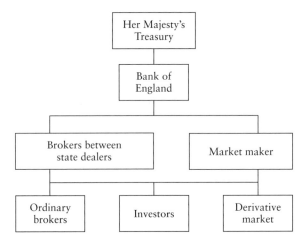

FIGURE 16.4 Structure of the British Treasury Bond Market

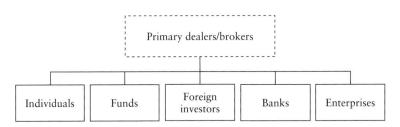

FIGURE 16.5 Structure of the U.S. Treasury Bond Market

a new division of labor, which not only improves market efficiency but also helps to diversify market risk.

The structure of investors also changes with government movement in economic policy and the market environment. The more developed the T-bond market becomes, the more T-bond investors there will be. Treasury bond markets in most countries have experienced the evolution from individual investors to institutional investors. This process also has happened in China. These changes not only enhance the efficiency of the market itself, but further improve the financial market and the entire national economy.

In summary, the structure of China's bond market is now similar to those of the advanced markets in the United Kingdom and the United States, but it is still developing. Two issues are not properly addressed: (1) a market-making function—market makers do not perform very well, and (2) lack of a sound derivative market. Although some progress has been made insofar as fixed-floating swaps are concerned, principle derivative markets such as financial futures and options are not open yet.

FUTURE OF CHINA'S BOND MARKET

The roadblocks to further development of the bond market, in our view, are the underdeveloped financial market, which is the institutional base of the bond market; unsophisticated investors; overlapping jurisdictions and an inadequate agency role in developing the bond market; and insufficient use of technology. At present, it is recognized that many problems remain in the Chinese treasury bond market. Nevertheless, China's bond market is an example of the successful pursuit of a deliberately designed reform program. From the beginning of market development, its institutional arrangement was deliberately considered and arranged sequentially. Although the international bond market development provided China with experience, models and rules are produced through the primary and secondary exchange of their own market participants. Models and rules can be introduced but exchanges cannot be introduced, to say nothing about the enforcements of rules.

It was this combination of international experience and China's specific social, economic, and financial systems that made it work. Going forward, the market has to be built on China's own institutional framework from which it can then evolve.

Five

Organization and Legal Structure

Organizational Structure and Institutional Arrangement of the Treasury Bond Market

ROLE OF GOVERNMENT: BUDGET, TREASURY, AND DEBT MANAGEMENT AGENCIES

As a major government funding conduit, the treasury bond market has been effectively managed in many economies. The objective is to boost the image of the government as a market participant and secure smooth selling of government bonds. To improve the T-bond's reputation, the government must ensure the fairness, openness, liquidity, and transparency of market transactions. In addition, it is necessary to establish a sound infrastructure (i.e., trading, depository trust, clearing, filing, and bookkeeping systems).

Debt financing is closely related to the government's treasury and budgetary functions; it is also part of the nation's institutional arrangement and legal systems. All in a way pertain to the primary economic and financial exchanges and, more specifically, the primary bond exchanges, which, in turn, are related to the political and administrative exchanges. Therefore, it is reasonable to suppose that government agencies, as agents of the government, would play a very important role in administrative exchange.

Budget System and National Budget Structure

China's fiscal year starts on January 1 and ends on December 31. Annual budget preparation begins on the last day in September. National and local governments prepare their budgets for the coming year according the budget instructions given by the Ministry of Finance. The Ministry collects and reviews these budgets, and summarizes them into a draft national budget for the State Council. Once approved, the draft is submitted to the National People's Congress (NPC) for discussion and approval before it comes into force.

According to the budget law of the People's Republic of China promulgated in 1994, the NPC is responsible each year for approving the central budget and its implementation report, and the local people's congresses are responsible for the examining and approving the draft general budgets of the relevant local governments and their implementation reports.

The financial resources at disposal of the Chinese government consist of budgetary and extrabudgetary revenues and expenditures. The national budget is made up of the central government budget and the local governments' budgets. The central budget consists of the budgets of the state departments, including the revenues turned in by the local governments to the central government. The local budgets consist of the consolidated budgets of the provinces, the autonomous regions, and the municipalities directly under the central government. Each of them is made up of the budget of the relevant government, the budget summary covering the governments at lower levels, and the amounts returned or subsidized to them by the central government. According to the budget law, the national budget is prepared in a double-entry form and divided into government revenues and expenditures. (In principle, when they are drafted, local government budgets carry no deficits.)

Along with the diversification of China's national economic structure, many revenue and expenditure items that once were included in the national budget are no longer in the budget and have become extrabudgetary items. However, the extrabudgetary revenue and expenditure is still, to varying degrees, subject to the management of the central government. In order to monitor extrabudgetary items, the Ministry of Finance gradually put most of them under budgetary management jurisdiction.

The current national budget includes the public budget and the construction budget. The public budget covers such expenditures as government administration, national defense, social development, and social security. Tax revenue and other general revenue support its expenditures. The revenue of construction budget is the remittance of profit from state-owned assets, while the expenditure of construction budget is earmarked construction outlay and the construction fund run by CDRC which are productive expenditures by nature. According to the budget law, the public budget of the central government may not incur deficits; and the financing gap in its construction budget must be made up by issuing treasury bonds at home and abroad; in addition, the debt must be kept in proper size and structure.

Before 1994, central government budget deficits were financed by overdrafts from the central bank and the issuance of treasury bonds. Concerning the risk of monetary expansion, the central government has taken firm measures to cope with government direct borrowing and overdrafts from the central bank. The Decision of the Central Committee of the Communist

Party of China on Issues regarding the Establishment of the Socialist Market Economic System promulgated in 1993 clearly stated that, starting from 1994, the Ministry of Finance could no longer overdraw from the central bank and all budget deficits had to be covered by government borrowing at home and abroad. The change of legal environment requires the Ministry to streamline its borrowing vehicles.

Government Oversight

Generally, the Ministry of Finance has three basic functions: budgetary management, treasury management, and finance management. Here we will focus on treasury management.

Treasury management is a basic function of the state financial management authority. It includes cash management, debt management, account management, and assets/liabilities management. Treasury management underpins budgetary management.

The aim of treasury management is to ensure the efficiency and safety of the budgetary account. In most market economies, government revenues are pooled into a bank account, called the treasury single account, which is opened with the central bank. An auxiliary account is opened for pension and social security funds managed by the government. These consolidated accounts facilitate control over the treasury's capital and provide up-to-date information so that the treasury's management function can be executed efficiently.

Treasury management is often the responsibility of the central bank, which acts as its agent. This is known as the treasury surrogate system. The tax and public debt account set up by the Federal Reserve System in Britain and the treasury bond stabilization fund and debt service fund set up by Japan are examples of this system.

Treasury management is not fully executed in China's treasury surrogate management. In particular, treasury cash management is not done by the state financial management authority. It is partly for this reason that short-term treasury bills are not well used as instruments of cash management.

As we have noted, there were few short-term T-bills in the market. This made the short end of the yield curve incomplete. A lack of short-term instrument is also counterproductive to the money market, which would hurt the ongoing development of the T-bond market. This situation changed in late 2005 when the NPC endorsed the Ministry of Finance's authority to manage outstanding treasury securities and opened the possibility for the Ministry to issue short-term treasury bills to pursue its cash management function. The Ministry resumed the long-awaited treasury bill transactions at the end of 2005 and has announced a timetable for issuing T-bills in 2006.

Role of Government Debt Management Agencies

Government debt management agencies and the Treasury Department (formerly the Government Debt Management Department) are key participants in the issuance and management of China's treasury bonds. Therefore, it is important to understand their institutional and organizational structure.

The GDMD in China's Ministry of Finance (now the Treasury Department) functions as the organizer of bond issuance and is engaged in the relationship between the government and the NPC with respect to government debt management, cash management as well as treasury management.

The institutional structure of government debt management includes the accounting management system, government debt service, and the system for managing certificate savings bonds. The organizational structure of primary and secondary market management includes the distribution channels and selling procedures for newly issued government bonds, the organization of the secondary market, and the organizational relationship between the financial market and the securities market.

As indicated, the treasury bond market is a key factor in ensuring the successful offering of T-bonds; thus, governments around the world are trying to manage these markets as efficiently and effectively as possible. The primary management functions of the Ministry of Finance are to:

- Prepare and execute the national budget
- Supervise the implementation of budgeted revenues and expenditures
- Draft and execute China's financial and taxation policy
- Manage the debts of the central government

The department in the Ministry responsible for these functions evolved over time: the Debt Office of the Comprehensive Planning Bureau (from 1981 to 1989); the Government Debt Management Department (from 1989 to 1999); and the Treasury Department since 1999. There are nine basic functions of the Ministry in T-bond management:

1. Devise policies governing government borrowing at home and abroad; work out related regulations based on the laws; set up the lending regime for government CBCR (collectively borrowed and collectively repaid) foreign debt; and institute accounting and budget management rules for the government's domestic and foreign debts.

2. Prepare an annual plan and medium- and long-term plans for borrowing and repaying the government's domestic and foreign debt. Also, prepare and examine the statistical reports, the budget, and the final accounts of the government's domestic and foreign debt. Provide the funds for repayment of government budgetary debts.

3. Study the performance of the domestic and foreign capital markets, work out domestic and international funding strategy, and institute the treasury bond reform program.
4. Deal with bond issuance and debt service. Unlike the United Kingdom and many other countries, where operational matters with respect to bond issuance and debt service are dealt with by the central bank, in China, the Ministry of Finance is very focused on the daily operational work of debt issuance and service.
5. Manage and supervise the secondary T-bond market. This function is not yet clearly defined; the People's Bank of China and the China Bank Regulatory Commission also get involved in supervising the trading of T-bonds.
6. Participate in drafting the policies and regulations governing the T-bond and securities market, and supervise the implementation of the relevant financial laws and regulations in collaboration with the related departments.
7. Supervise the use of domestic and foreign debt.
8. Raise funds in the international financial market on behalf of China, subject to the authorization of the State Council.
9. Approve and manage foreign debt–funded projects that are financed through proceeds borrowed and serviced by the Ministry.

Since 1999, the Finance Management Department has been responsible for raising capital in the international capital market; the Treasury Department is only in charge of domestic bond offering and management. Although the name and function of the government debt management department in the Ministry of Finance changes over time, the department will always be responsible for treasury bond management in China.

Debt management experience around the world indicates that the proper division of labor among the various government debt management agencies is essential for effectively carrying out the debt management function. How this is managed in China is illustrated in Table 17.1.

The debt management department is usually established under the jurisdiction of the Ministry of Finance. The status of the government debt management department in the Ministry and the relationship between this department and others are illustrated in Figure 17.1.

Throughout the 1980s, reform was at the top of the agenda of China's development program, and all government agencies were requested to push ahead with the reform program in their relevant fields. Each agency had a Reform Department that was under its leadership but instructed by the State Committee on Economic Restructuring (SCER). Therefore, the government debt management agencies in China not only had management functions

TABLE 17.1 Government Debt Management: Major Function and Division of Labor

Function	Description	Main Department(s)	Auxiliary Department(s)
Planning financing needs	Measure need for government borrowing. Keep debt at appropriate level. Coordinate debt policies with government, cabinet, and congress.	Ministry of Finance	Central bank and planning departments
Establishing debt policies	Set up targets and strategies for debt management. Determine issuing quantities, types, time, frequency and method. Develop benchmark debt structure.	Debt management department under the Ministry of Finance	Ministry of Finance or central bank
Organizing issuance of T-bonds	Determine issuing channels and distribution methods. Manage underwriting or bidding operation. Organize and arrange underwriting syndicate.	Debt management department under the Ministry of Finance	Ministry of Finance, central bank, and primary dealers
Organizing the secondary market	Manage T-bonds in circulation. Facilitate increase of market liquidity. Organize and arrange for market intervention and relations.	Debt management department under the Ministry of Finance	Primary dealers, brokers, and banks
Redeeming T-bonds	Arrange for redemption of T-bonds.	Debt management department under the Ministry of Finance	Primary dealers, brokers, and banks
Managing administration and accounting	Manage the debt operation accounting system. Manage the recordkeeping of debt holders. Account for T-bond debt service. Conduct registration and depository trust of T-bonds.	Debt management department under the Ministry of Finance	Central bank and chief accounting department
Clearing and settling T-bond transfer	Manage and develop the calculation and clearing systems of T-bonds.	Debt management department under the Ministry of Finance	Ministry of Finance and central bank

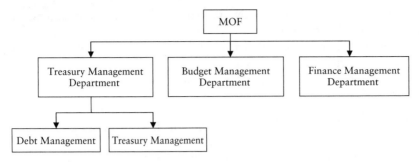

FIGURE 17.1 Status of the Government Debt Management Department in the Ministry of Finance

but also a reform function. Such arrangements of government functionaries are not common elsewhere in the world.

The reform function can be performed in many different ways. Reform, from the perspective of institutional economic engineering (IEEN), is an evolutionary institutional arrangement that, in our view, should achieve a win-win outcome as opposed to interest redistribution, which is a zero-sum game with a win-lose outcome. Therefore, any reform program, when pursued, should find the common ground of different market participants.

Earlier, we listed a number of functions that government performs that are important to economic development. They mainly had to do with building a sound institutional framework. The capital market per se is an institutional development that is path dependent (i.e., driven endogenously by market participants), but this in no way gainsays that government is not important. As already indicated, government is one party of primary exchange. In the debt capital market, the government's functions include setting up incentive apparatus, regulating issuers and financial intermediaries, protecting investors, and ensuring fair transactions. When market building is contemplated, it is important to consider where to start the reform program and a proper sequence of reform. In China, much of our efforts have been devoted to the exogenous institutional arrangement (i.e., primary bond exchange defined by secondary economic exchange, or SSE).

Relationship between Government Debt Management and Budget and Cash Management Departments

Before 1991, China's treasury bonds were issued via administrative allocation, and the allocation and transportation of paper bonds, the collection and transfer of the proceeds from investors, and the checking of issuance accounts were all delegated to the Treasury and Issuing Department, or TID, under the central bank.

Auditing the Treasury Department's bond accounts is an important aspect of government debt management. The auditor will check if the amount of printed bonds minus the issuing proceeds deposited in the treasury equals the amount of bonds to be destroyed. Since the term of the bonds is long, misallocation of bond proceeds and other treasury funds often occurs. The cross-year transfer of these proceeds leads to the accounting difficulties.

It was not until 1994, for example, that the audits of 1981, 1982, 1985, 1986, and 1987 were completed. The Ministry of Finance itself conducted the audit of the special T-bonds of 1989 to 1991 and the T-bills of 1993. Auditing of the bills and proceeds is the basic to scheduling debt service, and confusing accounts can hardly ensure that the debt service and the issuance amount will be identical. The same is true of bond redemption. The main problem lies in the imperfectness of the accounting system. In addition, redeemed and repealed bonds were destroyed at the same time, which was not in accordance with the rules of bond redemption management.

One of the outstanding problems is that the entry settings do not reflect the changes in the bond types. In the past, China issued treasury bonds once a year, and the entry was very simple. With the development of the T-bond market, the types of bonds increased, but the entry settings have not been modified accordingly.

There were four types of treasury bonds in 1994, and the proceeds from two were transferred via different channels, but there were only two entries, "current-year treasury bonds and previous-year treasury bonds," in the treasury accounts. Four types of bonds and two different means of transfer were incorporated in one entry, which could not reflect the actual proceeds transferred for each type of T-bond.

A second problem is that the treasury is designed in accordance with the tax collection system, which cannot reflect the need to transfer and allocate money for bond service. Tax revenues cannot be removed once they enter the treasury, but, due to the need for issuance and redemption, bond proceeds are sometimes used to redeem previous bonds. As a result, the original treasury management system cannot meet the need to transfer issuance proceeds smoothly.

The third problem is that the treasury entries are determined at the beginning of the year while the bond issuance plan is determined and ratified by the National People's Congress each March. Thus, the treasury entries can hardly comply with changes in proceeds transfer channels caused by changes in the issuance methods.

The above-mentioned problems have been gradually addressed; the establishment of the Treasury Department in 1999 represents part of these efforts.

Relationship between Government Debt Management and Budget Management Departments

Treasury bond management and budget management must be effectively coordinated. Since cash-basis accounting is employed in the issuance of the treasury's monthly and yearly redemption reports as well as the budget and the final accounts, and accrual-basis accounting is used in government debt management, the inconsistency between the issuance statistics and the budget amounts causes difficulties in the supervision and management of government debts. In practice in China, this results in:

- Actual current-year issuance is not reflected in the debt proceeds in the final accounts of that year. In some years, a negative amount appears in the treasury balance.
- Frequently, items are listed in the final accounts early or delayed against the budget management requirements when using cash-basis accounting. Conversely, when using accrual-basis accounting, it is difficult to keep government debt consistent with the budget and the final accounts figures. Both are counterproductive to the preparing and examining of the final accounts.
- The actual proceeds of short-term T-bills in the current year cannot be reflected at full face value in the budget, as they are issued at discount. However, as requested, both debt proceeds and debt service expenses related to short-term treasury bills issued during the year with less than one-year maturity should be incorporated in the budget.

Relationship between Foreign Debt Management and Budget Management

There are two major problems in this area:

1. Budget entry of foreign debt proceeds and debt service expenses
2. Preparation of the foreign debt budget

Regarding the budget entry of foreign debt proceeds and debt service expenses, the rules of China's foreign debt entry in the budget is made when most of the debt was collectively borrowed and collectively repaid (CBCR) by the Ministry of Finance in its capacity to run central public finance. When CBCR is discontinued (with the deepening of reform), the opening up of China's financial market and the continual enhancement of foreign debt management, the accounting related to foreign debt budget entry had following issues:

- *Actual proceeds from the foreign debts cannot be reflected.* In the past, the amount of foreign debt proceeds was entered in accordance with the principle of the set revenue plan based on the expenditure requirement. In practice, this means that an amount equivalent to the actual expenditure allocated to capital construction for the current year from the foreign debts becomes the foreign debt proceeds entry. The principle was designed to prevent the balance of the domestic finance revenue and expenditure from being influenced by the balance of foreign debt proceeds, expenditures (investment), and debt service expenses.

  In recent years, however, with the increase in the types of foreign debt, the principle can no longer adapt to the changes. This is primarily because the balance between the actual foreign debt and capital construction expenditure allocated in the current year and the foreign debts earmarked for other purposes cannot be reflected in the current year's foreign debt proceeds entry. The result is that the foreign debt figures in the final accounts of the Treasury Department are inconsistent with those of the foreign debt statistics.

- *Classification of expenditures allocated from foreign debt is unclear.* Expenditures allocated from the foreign debt proceeds in the capital expenditure item in the budget reflects amounts collectively borrowed and collectively repaid from the central government budgetary account only, which includes only capital construction. Foreign debt used for other purposes, such as expenditures from new foreign debts used to repay previous foreign debts, cannot be reflected in the budget entries.

  In addition, foreign debt collectively borrowed and collectively repaid through the central finance account has been carried in the national budget since 1986, but due to limitations of the foreign debt management system, it is difficult to clearly distinguish among the different categories of expenditures. For example, it is hard to clarify how much was spent on capital construction, technological transformation, expenditure for businesses, and administrative agency expenses relating to foreign debt collectively borrowed by the government and individually repaid (CBIR) by the fund's users. Clearly, it is not proper to incorporate the foreign debts repaid by fund users in the capital construction expenditure.

■ *Principal and interest cannot be reflected separately.* In recent years, the amount included in the debt expenditure entries of the central government budget includes not only debt service expenditures but also subsidized and advanced interest service on foreign debts CBCR by the central government budget. The principal and interest repaid in advance by fund user in the format of foreign debt CBIR would stay in the budget as debts. From the lender's point view, they were not yet mature and should be repaid in future years; therefore, if it is not separately reflected in the budget entries, future repayment could be affected.

The CBCR proceeds are treated as budgetary revenue, expenditure is arranged by the central government budget, and the debt service is arranged in the budget for the next year. This part of foreign debt proceeds are accounted for in the central government budget, and the accuracy, completeness and timeliness of the final account can be secured in the same way as other budgetary expenditures were.

CBIR is borrowed through the relevant agencies authorized by the state and on loan to the responsible authorities, the enterprises and the local governments. The authorized agencies are required to cooperate in its repayment. Since CBIR foreign debts are undertaken by different local finance departments, such departments are in a position to reinforce the financial management and supervision on the use of foreign debt.

In 1986, the CBIR foreign debts by the fund users were specified in the finance final accounts. In the 1990s, the main problem in preparing the budget and the final accounts of foreign debt was the lack of a correct and reliable channel to collect the proceeds and expenditure data of CBIR foreign debts. Therefore, the data from the foreign capital utilization plan of the State Development Planning and Reform Commission were occasionally used as a reference to prepare the revenue and expenditure budget of CBIR foreign debts; and the statistics of the national utilization of foreign funds from the Ministry of Foreign Trade and Economic Cooperation were used to prepare the final accounts.

Using this double-account budget will lead to two problems. First, according to the principle of double-entry budgeting, the national budget revenue and expenditure entries are classified first by their economic nature, then by their economic purpose. Such a budget also specifies the guidelines for foreign debt utilization. If there are no available channels from which to obtain CBIR data on foreign debt, it will be difficult to classify such debt by its economic nature or purpose; thus this requirement of double-entry budgeting cannot be satisfied.

Second, since the data of the CBIR foreign debts incurred by the users were carried in the national budget in 1986, such debts have been reflected in two different accounts (i.e., "proceeds revenue from foreign debts" and "expenditure on capital construction—the expenditure of capital construction through use of foreign debts") in order not to affect the fiscal balance. The debt service expenditure on such debt is not reflected in the national budget. Thus, the greater the borrowing reflected in the budget, the lower the repayment that is reflected; in fact, repayment corresponding to borrowing was not even reflected.

Thus, finance accounting related to the budget should be improved to reflect the foreign debt entries item by item and comply with the requirement that treasury bond revenue and expenditure shall be put into the construction budget in accordance with the principle of double-account budgeting. To reflect debt revenue and expenditure comprehensively in the national budget, the detailed items and subitems in the construction budget of the double-account budget shall be added up, and China can consider creating a separate debt budget in addition to the current budget and construction budget.

Insofar as CBIR foreign debt is concerned, the establishment of a management system for the foreign debt budget and the final accounts, by adopting the reporting procedures of the financial accounting statements used by industries and other sectors, has been suggested. In this way, China can establish both central and local finance systems for preparing the budget and the final accounts for the foreign debts borrowed by the government. It also can improve the long-term planning of the double-entry budget, so as to enhance the finance department's management and supervision of projects financed through foreign debt.

Additionally, all foreign debt of local governments should be incorporated in budget management. The foreign debt entries and the foreign debt–related entries of a local finance department include foreign debt borrowed by the local government itself, foreign debt used by the local government in the utilities and directly repaid by the finance department, and debt repayment funds established by the local government.

During the 1990s, there was no unified regulation on the source of repayment for foreign debts used by the administrative institutions. In the later 1990s, the number of projects using international financial organizations and foreign government loans for the development of education, public health, science and research, environmental protection, and the like increased continually. The users were mostly administrative institutions. The foreign debt repayment sources of such institutions come from the surplus of revenue of utilities, finance and administration expenses appropriated by the finance department at the same level, capital construction investment appropriation to the department, and other money transfers from the government. Repayment of foreign debts by these administrative institutions must be correctly accounted for in the debt budget.

HOW THE LAUNCH OF T-BONDS IS MANAGED

There are four institutional arrangements for structuring bond-issuing organizations:

1. The Ministry of Finance delegates responsibility for issuing bonds to the central bank, which determines the issuing terms and conditions by tender or through negotiations with the bank syndicates or members of the underwriting syndicate. This is the same procedure as is used in the United Kingdom.
2. The Ministry delegates the central bank to conduct the specific functions related to bond issuance, such as the organization of the bank syndicates or the underwriting syndicate. However, the issuing terms, such as the interest rate, debt instruments and terms, are determined by the Ministry.
3. The Ministry of Finance and the central bank divide the responsibilities for the primary issuance. In this scenario, the central bank is in charge of the auction to the banking system and the organization of the bank syndicates, and the Ministry is responsible for the distribution of T-bonds to institutional investors and the securities companies. The central bank organizes the issuance by tender and underwriting, and the Ministry directly organizes the tap method issue.
4. The Ministry directly organizes the issuance. It also deals directly with the primary transaction by either directly inviting syndicate members or conducting the auction itself. This is the primary format used in the United States.

China's organizational structure falls primarily into the U.S. model. The Ministry directly organizes the underwriting syndicates or invites the primary dealers to bid; it can also sell savings bonds to individuals using the tap method. The institutional arrangement for selling government securities varies due to different delegation costs. According to the new principal-agent theory, the principal delegates the power to the agent simply because it is more efficient to do so. The Ministry prefers to organize the primary issue rather than delegate the power to the central bank, because the auction method has made the sale of treasury bonds cheap, easy, and efficient, and, in fact, less expensive than the cost of delegating the function to other institutions.

HOW DEBT MANAGEMENT DEPARTMENTS SHOULD BE ORGANIZED

Efficient and effective government debt management needs a proper organizational and institutional structure. The decision-making process should be straightforward and transparent, with responsible departments performing their duties efficiently and decisions made based on legal procedures.

In many countries, debt management decisions are made by the Ministry of Finance, which authorizes debt managers to draft guidelines on debt management and determine government debt management policies. In its debt management function, the Ministry of Finance should be responsible for reporting to the government and Congress.

The responsibility for implementing debt policies is generally handled in one of two ways. As indicated, most countries have a debt management department under the jurisdiction of the Ministry of Finance, as exists in China; in a few countries, the central banks manage the government debts. If the central bank acts as the treasury agent of the government, the Ministry can also authorize the central bank to act as debt manager. This practice has two merits: (1) the central bank can cooperate better with the market participants in the market operation of debt management, and (2) the bond market and monetary policy can be better coordinated.

In many countries, there is a division of labor and cooperation between the Ministry of Finance and the central bank. For example, the central bank manages the negotiable treasury bonds, and the Ministry or an independent debt management department manages the non-negotiable ones. In some countries, a special independent debt management department under the jurisdiction of the Ministry employs high-caliber debt managers.

In order to manage the debt and bond market on a daily basis effectively and efficiently, the debt management department needs to cooperate closely with the budget and cash management departments, in order to be constantly informed about the government's revenues and expenditures, disbursement requirements, and the position of the cash account. For their part, government debt managers are required to keep the budget and cash management departments up to date on the issuance of new bonds and the implementation of debt service. The government debt management department can help the budget department arrange daily disbursements by issuing short-term treasury bills. In China, until 2005, there was no cash management function in the Ministry. Short-term treasury securities were issued only occasionally, for example, in 1994.

In conclusion, government agencies matter to the debt capital market. However, it is the primary administrative exchange that engenders rules and their enforcement. It is therefore advisable to establish a formal dialogue between the departments under the Ministry of Finance, or between the central bank and the Ministry, or between the Ministry and the independent debt management department. If the central bank is responsible for treasury management, effective coordination is required between the Ministry and the central bank. This issue will be further elaborated later.

Administrative Functions in Primary Market

Debt management departments need an effective accounting system in order to keep abreast of all financial activities relating to government debt. The traditional budget and debt accounting system was set up based on cash management principles. Thus, financial assets and debts were separated and only cash activities were accounted for. Effective debt management should be conducted on a commercial accrual accounting basis. This accounting method can be used for treasury bonds issued at a discount. Using cash-basis accounting, the interest cost of discounted bonds issued is usually presented in the principal paid on redemption; using accrual-basis accounting, the discount is treated as a cost, regardless of the actual payment date.

In the general accounting system, debt management departments should have their own debt service schedules in order to make payments in an accurate and timely way. Depending on the depository trust system, debt service is usually executed by transfer through a series of accounts: from the account of the government to that of the China Government Securities Depository Trust & Clearing Co., Ltd., and the clearing company affiliated to the stock exchanges, then to the account of the agencies holding the treasury bonds. The central bank, the commercial banks, and the depository trust companies usually do the administrative work involved in the transfer from the depository trust agencies to the bondholders' agents, such as securities firms.

The next administrative task concerns the registration, printing, and transportation of the treasury bonds. This job has been gradually replaced by the computerized bookkeeping systems.

The organization of the distribution channel for newly issued bonds is essential regardless of the selling techniques employed. Managers have to be in direct or indirect touch with the banks to negotiate proper selling procedures. If the T-bonds are issued through underwriting syndication, the government must be in contact with the important members of the syndicate. If bonds are issued via auction, the government may want to select the most powerful accepted bidder among all the participating financial institutions. Sometimes, in public offerings, the government directly sells nontradable bonds in the primary market or sells the bonds through authorized brokers or the banking system but will bear the consequent fees. If private placement is employed, government debt managers can establish direct relationships with individual banks or institutional investors, or sell the bonds using brokers as agents. The managers often maintain close contacts with the central bank to support the monetary policies. No matter what sales techniques are employed, however, government debt managers must keep in direct touch with the market to ensure a successful issue.

Administrative Functions in the Secondary Market

Liquidity is essential to the secondary market. Therefore, the government needs to set up cooperative relationships with the financial institutions and establish a sound legal system. International experience has shown that a sound financial infrastructure, including an online bookkeeping system for the treasury bonds and the bond depository trust, registration, clearing, and settlement systems and other financial infrastructure, is essential. China focused on establishing these systems at the beginning of bond market reform in 1991. By 1997, the systems had, for the most part, been put in place.

Insofar as the role of government in the secondary bond market is concerned, there has been much debate in both academic circles and among market participants in China about whether the government should get directly involved in stabilizing bond prices. Many suggest that, to ensure the stability of primary market issuance, the government must at times directly or indirectly interfere with the secondary market in order, for example, to alleviate the pressure caused by an imbalance between supply and demand or, even more important, to stabilize market prices or temporarily stabilize the secondary market for new issues (in particular, for the issuance of long-term bonds through underwriting syndication). Usually government debt managers establish their own special organization to intervene in the market or delegate that function to the central bank.

Although such functions were necessary in the early stage of China's bond market development, experience suggests that the less the government interference, the better. The government related to the market only insofar as its capacity to set rules and exert enforcement is concern. Government agencies, such as the Ministry of Finance and the People's Bank of China, perform as market participants only confined to the primary bond exchange. Anything beyond that, such as market entry restriction or administrative instruction, will be counterproductive to the market.

There are times when government agencies had a hands-on policy toward the market and, in some cases, even acted as a player in the bond market. Actually, in middle 1990s, the government required all agency and corporate issuers to set coupon rates no higher than that of government bonds to make government bonds the most attractive investment instrument.

This policy was abolished soon thereafter, however, because it actually made it impossible for other issuers to raise capital in the market.

Coordination between the Ministry of Finance and the Central Bank

Government debt managers should consider monetary policy needs in any debt-related activities; similarly, monetary policy makers, or the monetary authority, should consider debt management in implementing monetary policies. This can be done by coordinating the activities of the departments under the Ministry with the committee in charge of coordinating fiscal policies and monetary policies. In China, the central bank is the finance agent of the government and no longer acts as a lender to resolve fiscal problems.

Both China's debt management policies and monetary policies are determined by the State Council in its capacity as the top administrative body. Thus, the Ministry and the central bank could perform on a unified basis in line with the policies of the State Council. Until banking reform in 1994, the central bank acted as a department under the Ministry, and its monetary policies had to support the policy aims of the Ministry. Budget deficits were covered primarily through overdrafts from the central bank, and only part of the deficit was covered by issuing treasury bonds. When commercial banks hold more government bonds, they lack the liquidity to supply businesses with working capital. When banks run short of money and have a shortfall of liquidity, the central bank had to, as it usually did, lend money to them via so-called reloan facilities. This gave rise to an increase in the base money.

As a result, the policy targets of the central bank to control the money supply and stabilize the economy inevitably were affected by debt policy. Although the Ministry began to issue domestic treasury bonds to cover the fiscal deficit in 1981, the proceeds derived were counted as budgetary revenue and, since 1982, the real gap between revenues and expenditures, the so-called hard deficit, was still covered by overdrafts and loans from the central bank. This practice lasted until 1993, when the central government suspended overdrafting. As a result, the Ministry could no longer cover the fiscal deficit in this fashion. From the beginning of the reform movement until early 1993, the central bank never reduced the amount of loans in its credit capital arrangement with the Ministry in consideration of bond issuance and overdraft loans. In the second half of 1993, banking system reform laid the groundwork for the coordination of government debt management policies and monetary policies. As a result of reform, the Ministry could no longer overdraw or borrow from the central bank;

the central bank became more independent, and its primary responsibilities became maintaining an appropriate money supply and economic stability; the Ministry was directed to issue short-term bills to banks and nonbank financial institutions, allowing them to hold the treasury bonds as liquid financial assets, which allowed the central bank to carry out its open market function. In fact, however, due to the incentive structure, the Ministry was not a regular issuer of short-term treasury bills before 2006.

The central bank has been relatively independent in pursuing monetary policy since the 1994 banking system reform. As is common elsewhere, since the Ministry is more powerful than the central bank, cooperation between them is not always smooth, which has a negative impact on government debt management. For instance, the People's Bank of China was not fully committed to the primary market reform in the middle of the 1990s. However, after it began work on its open market operations program and recognized the importance of the bond market to that program, cooperation between the two agencies has greatly improved.

Our experience also suggests that institutional arrangements can better ensure the efficiency of the secondary bond market. For example, when the central bank acts as the government's finance agent, it should design and establish an institution that can coordinate debt management targets and monetary policies to perform such functions.

CHAPTER 18

Legal Framework
of the Capital Debt Market

(Part One)

LAWS AND REGULATIONS GOVERNING
TREASURY BONDS

The transition of the bond market, as it relates to the primary bond exchange (the exchange between bond market manager and bond market participants), reflects the shift from a constraint-oriented institutional arrangement to an incentive-oriented institutional arrangement.[1] The constraint-oriented institutional arrangement focuses on the constraint side of the institution, such as laws and regulations on bond market, whereas the incentive-oriented institutional arrangement focuses on the incentive side of the institution, such as government policy to encourage institution participation in the market and tax benefit to hold government bonds. As discussed in Chapter 1, the institution is driven by the interaction between constraint apparatus and incentive apparatus. Earlier, we discussed how the government policy helped establish incentive apparatus; here we focus on the constraint aspect of the institution. However, it is important not to lose sight of the incentive aspect, as they are virtually indispensable.

The current legal framework of China's bond market is similar to that of developed countries, but some special features reflect the characteristics of China's legal system and the stage of development of the country's financial system. In China, the National People's Congress functions as a lawmaker with respect to the capital market and legislates the securities laws governing it. The State Council is the administrative body that issues administrative regulations concerning the capital market, but other agencies also issue departmental regulations. In an effort to reinforce financial management, three regulatory agencies—China Securities Regulatory

Commission (CSRC), China Bank Regulatory Commission (CBRC), and China Insurance Regulatory Commission (CIRC)—were established in 2003 and were designed to regulate the securities industry, the banking system, and the insurance industry, respectively. Insofar as the securities and bond markets are concerned, some other agencies played important roles as well: the Ministry of Finance, which has many responsibilities relating to government securities and treasury bonds; the People's Bank of China (PBOC), which regulates the interbank bond market (IBBM), and the National Development and Reform Commission (NDRC), which regulates the corporate bond primary market.

The division of labor among these organizations is not function based, and therefore there are some overlapping jurisdictions. These institutional arrangements have evolved in a way that reflects the interests of the agencies themselves. For example, the PBOC wants to develop the IBBM because this market is under its jurisdiction. As indicated, the relationship among agencies (which we called the secondary administrative exchange) has direct bearing on the economic exchange, the financial exchange, and the bond exchange. It is the exchange among agencies, rather than an individual agency, that make economic rules such as laws and regulations governing economic activities.

The rule of game is perceived by economists such as Douglass North as an institution, whereas another group of economists, including Masahiko Aoki, perceived game play per se as an institution. In the institutional economic engineering (IEEN) framework, both are components of institutions, but game play is pursed via the secondary exchange. Its economic function is to save exogenous transaction costs. The rules of the game are engendered by the primary exchange, which is derived from and mandated by the secondary exchange for the purpose of saving endogenous transaction costs. This chapter explains how laws and regulations are created and enforced via the primary exchange.

LAWS AND REGULATIONS GOVERNING THE PRIMARY MARKET

At present, there are no special laws or acts governing the primary bond market. Separate State Council regulations define the status of financing institutions as issuers. The major bond issuers in China are the Ministry of Finance, China Development Bank, the Export-Import (EX-IM) Bank of China, and authorized state-owned enterprises (SOEs). In 2005, most financial institutions, including commercial banks and securities firms, could issue financial debentures after being examined and approved by the PBOC.

Their entry into the market is based on the regulations of various agencies or specified in related laws, such as budgetary laws.

The State Council promulgated treasury bond regulations of the People's Republic of China (PRC) each year from 1981 to 1992, based on the budget report approved by the National People's Congress (NPC). Regulations on Treasury Securities, an administrative decree issued in 1992, specified the issuance amount, the target, and the term of treasury bonds including maturities, coupon, issuance period, and settlement date. The regulations also prescribed the punishment for the counterfeiting of paper securities. In the event of a dispute over enforcement, the Ministry of Finance was assigned the responsibility of interpreting each clause. The regulations remain in effect today.

In the early 1990s, when treasury bond market reform began, the major relevant legal documents were the Regulations on Treasury Securities and the Accounting Procedures for Treasury Securities Stipulated by People's Bank of China.

As a fiscal agent of the Ministry, the PBOC operates the treasury and prescribes the accounting of the financial statement. Until 1996, the PBOC was also responsible for distributing paper securities, repaying principal and interest, settling the proceeds of the bonds issued through administrative placement, and issuing (a week prior to issuance) the bulletin announcing new bond issues, which provides information on the issuance, settlement, and delivery dates and the total issuance volume.

Since 1996, the terms of a public offering of government bonds are made public through a Ministry bulletin one week before the issuance date; this bulletin also contains the information on issuance and settlement dates and total issuance amount. Since 1998, the CDB and the EX-IM Bank also follow these market practices and routines.

The Ministry was also involved in the formulation of a series of laws and regulations relating to the management of the treasury bond market. The Regulations on Treasury Securities of 1992 was, in its original form, only a guideline, but after the infrastructure of the bond market-oriented bond reform program was put in place, the regulations provided ample latitude for the reform program generated by innovative ideas to carry out.

As the 1992 regulations was no longer applicable, though still legally valid, in 1995 the Ministry redrafted a new regulation in collaboration with the Legislative Affairs Office of the State Council. In the meantime, the Regulations on Treasury Bills of the People's Republic of China were submitted in 1995 to the Legislative Affairs Office of the State Council for approval. However, because the reform program had accelerated so rapidly, the draft was no longer in line with the changes in the T-bond market.

Therefore, the Ministry eventually asked the State Council to postpone the promulgation of the draft regulations.[2]

China Securities Regulatory Commission is responsible for regulating securities companies and dealers in the stock exchange bond market and the IBBM. The Ministry of Finance and CSRC are in charge of managing primary securities dealers. China's Association of Government Securities Dealers (CAGS), which is a self-regulatory institution founded in 1993, regulates the securities firms.

On behalf of the central government, the Ministry, in accordance with treasury bond regulations of the PRC, may freely choose various internal and external debt instruments and issuance techniques to achieve its financing objectives. Since the State Council only sets the ceiling for total issuance amount rather than the size of a single issuance, the Ministry may define the amount of a single issuance on its own. The amount of bonds to be issued is based on the budgetary expenditures and the requirements for refinancing of maturing debts.

Before 1994, the Ministry had only one account with the PBOC, to which all the revenues and expenditures of the government were credited and debited. This account facilitated overdrafts by the Ministry with no interest payments before 1994. In early 1994, the State Council decided to forbid the Ministry from borrowing money from or overdrafting its account with the central bank. Later this decision was incorporated into the Central Banking Law of 1994.

The Ministry of Finance issues treasury bonds only in the domestic market; for international transactions, another institution is also involved. Before 1987, the Bank of China (BOC) was the borrower on behalf of the central government in the international capital market.

The National People's Congress is responsible for ratifying the total financing program. It formally endorses the issuing amount when the state budget report is reviewed and approved, as the number of T-bonds to be issued as a financing item was contained in the budget report. As the NPC is usually in session in March, the legal procedure for the domestic issuance is confirmed at the end of the March each year.

Before the promulgation of the Central Banking Law and Budget Law (enacted on December 12, 1995), bonds issued by the Ministry often went beyond the approved or specified size. That was because not only were there often unexpected budgetary expenditures, such as emergency funds for drought-stricken or flooded areas, but also because the Ministry wanted to issue a larger quantity at a time when bonds could be issued smoothly.

Until 2005, short-, medium-, and long-term bonds were subject to the approval of the central government. In November 2005, the NPC session transferred management of outstanding bonds to the Ministry, which means the State Council only approves the size of the bond issue; the Ministry can select the bond instruments and decide whether to issue additional short-term bonds. This change opens the possibility of the Ministry carrying out cash management through the issuance of short-term treasury bills.

However, international borrowing has to be approved separately by the State Council, because it usually regards international borrowing as a foreign debt that should be balanced by State Administration of Foreign Exchange (SAFE). Thus, the Ministry reports directly to the State Council, which distributes its report to appropriate agencies, such as the National Development and Reform Commission (or SDRC) and SAFE for comments. The CDB and EX-IM Bank first report to the SDRC, which signs off jointly with SAFE and then reports to the State Council for final approval.

According to the Budget Law, which is still in effect, local governments are not in a position to incur debt, which means that the primary market is regulated jointly by the Ministry of Finance, the SDRC, and the PBOC. The Ministry oversees the issuance of government securities, while the SDRC regulates the primary placement of corporate bonds and the PBOC supervises the offering of financial debentures and central bank notes (CBNs). The CSRC oversees the secondary market for government and corporate bonds in the stock exchange.

The PBOC approves only the size of the annual issuance by the CDB, the EX-IM Bank, and other financial institutions; the CDB and EX-IM Bank and recently the Agricultural Development Bank (ADB) determine the timing and the issuance amount of each transaction. After the State Council decided in 2005 to control the outstanding debt rather than the issuance volume in each individual year, the CDB requested the same treatment, and this is currently being reviewed by the PBOC. Outstanding debt (the cumulative stock of outstanding debt volume) control is a way to govern the issuance size, so that the issuer does not go beyond the ceiling (the total outstanding cumulative debt since the first issuance less the amount of principal repaid). The advantage of outstanding debt control is that it gives the issuer the flexibility of issuing short-term bills in order to pursue cash management. The issuing amount may go beyond the outstanding amount that the government set during the year, but it is not against the regulations as long as the issuance is within the ceiling amount at the end of the year.

The CBRC is in a position to approve the issuance of subordinated bonds. In 2004, the CBRC promulgated the Regulation on the Management of Subordinated Bonds Issued by Commercial Banks. According to the regulation, commercial banks shall issue subordinated bonds in the IBBM through either auction or private placement. The regulation also prescribes the amount limit for the subordinated bonds issued by the commercial banks. Policy-related banks, such as the CDB and the EX-IM Bank, are permitted to issue subordinated bonds for capital purposes and must abide by the same regulation.

The SDRC shall review and approve the issuing amount of corporate bonds. As indicated before, the coupon rate for corporate bonds is still regulated; the SDRC and the PBOC jointly set the coupon rate for corporate bonds.

The qualification status of corporate bond issuers had been strictly controlled, but in 2005 agencies left the door open to allow corporate issuers access to the market; for example, the NDRC approve more local issuers while the PBOC opened the IBBM to the commercial banks for issuance of short-term bills. The move was an attempt by the central government to bail out poorly managed financial institutions, especially commercial banks and securities firms. However, the amount of issuance still has to be approved on case-by-case basis, by the CSRC in the case of securities firms and by the PBOC in the case of commercial banks.

LAWS AND REGULATIONS GOVERNING PUBLIC FINANCE

In China today, the only legal document governing public finance is the budget law, which stipulates, among other things, the amount of bond issuance. According to this law, the size of treasury bond issuance is subject to the ratification of the central government. The NPC examines the issuance because the financing requirement is an integral part of the budget report submitted by the Ministry of Finance and the social development report submitted by the SDRC.

The report submitted to the NPC for approval is based on the draft budget. In drafting the current budget account, the Budget Department of the Ministry proposes target revenues and expenditures. The difference between revenues and expenditures is supposed to be financed by the issuance of new treasury bonds.

With the repayment peak in the early 1990s,[3] debt service became a big burden. Some suggested that the size of T-bond issuances should be brought under control, and the Ministry was asked to study the appropriate volume of bond issuance and to take measures to control the new issue amount.

Before 1993, the Ministry tried to change the term structure of the new issuance in an attempt to circumvent the debt service peak. At that time, the outstanding debt accounted for less than 20 percent of the budgetary revenue.

Since 1997, when the central government started to pursue proactive fiscal policies, the government's policy has been to keep the budget deficit stable, so that the debt financing would not increase very rapidly.

At present, the size of new issuance in the capital account includes refinancing maturing debt and financing deficits in the capital account. Usually the Government Debt Management Department (GDMD) compiles the refinancing program and the Budget Department compiles the new issue program. The two programs combined into the total borrowing program.

Other agencies and investors frequently questioned the Ministry about how the proceeds of bond sales were being used and asked it to make its budgetary arrangements more transparent. In the early 1990s, the Ministry compiled both the unified account budget and double-account budget. The double account budget[4] improved transparency and helped to address two related issues:

1. Debt proceeds were originally treated as part of revenue; now they are a source of money to make up the capital account deficit.
2. Capital expenditure financed by foreign debt is moved from off-balance sheet ("below the line") to on-balance sheet (above the line). As a result, the revenues and expenditures in the budgetary account better reflect the relationship between the source of the revenues and their utilization.

Table 18.1 shows the construction budget revenues and expenditures in double-account budget form.

We can see that there are two types of expenditures for debt proceeds in this budget: capital expenditure (foreign debt is found in the item labeled "capital construction disbursement from foreign debt proceeds" and reflected in the productive capital expenditure) and debt service expenditure, which includes both domestic and foreign debts.

LAWS AND REGULATIONS GOVERNING THE SECONDARY MARKET

The laws and regulations focus mainly on primary debt issuance; however, insofar as the secondary market is concerned, there is no uniform law governing the trading of bonds. The regulation on bond trading in the secondary market is reflected in the Securities Act.

The first securities-related law was the Securities Act of the People's Republic of China, which was approved by the sixth session of the standing committee of the ninth NPC on December 29, 1998, and enacted on July 1, 1999. This act mainly regulates the stock market, but it also governs the secondary bond market. Article Two stipulates that the act is applicable to stocks, corporate bonds, and all issuance and trading of other securities and derivatives. However, unless otherwise specified, bond trading is subject

TABLE 18.1 Revenues and Expenditures in the National Budget Capital Account

Revenues	Expenditures
I. Capital account revenue	I. Capital expenditure
A. Current account budget surplus	A. Productive capital expenditure
B. Specialized capital revenue	1. Domestic capital construction expenditure
C. Profit remittances by SOEs	2. Capital construction disbursements
D. Loss subsidies to productive enterprises	financed by foreign debts
E. Funds turned in	B. Expenses for technological updates and transformation and for new product trial
II. Debt proceeds	production
A. Domestic debt proceeds	C. Disbursement increase in the production
1. Treasury bill proceeds	capital
2. Other T-bond proceeds	D. Geological prospecting expenses
B. Foreign debt proceeds	E. Agricultural production expenditure
C. Borrowings from banks	F. Urban maintenance and construction expenditure
	G. Development funds supporting the economically underdeveloped regions
	H. Warehouse expenditure for the commercial sector
	II. Debt service expenditure for the domestic and foreign debts
	A. Debt service expenditure for domestic debts
	1. Debt service expenditure for T-bills
	2. Interest paid for debts from PBOC
	B. Debt service expenditure for foreign debts

to other laws and administrative regulations (referring to the laws and regulations governing the primary bonds market). Passage of this act played an important role in regulating the issuance and trading of bond securities and safeguarding the legitimate rights of investors.

However, at the time it was enacted, the securities market was in a very preliminary stage of development. As the market progressed, the act no longer met the changing market conditions. For example, at the outset, there was no secondary market, and the primary market was based on administrative placement. In the late 1990s, the situation changed. In addition, the securities market, stock market, and bond market were originally designed for financing and bailing out poorly managed SOEs rather than for providing an investment channel for investors. The stock market is said to be a place where SOEs that cannot be saved by the state can survive by getting money free of charge from the market. There was no such notion as safeguarding the interest of investors. As a matter of fact, until recently, the interests of investors were not fully protected.

In 2005, the Act was amended. The Finance and Economic Committee of the sixteenth party congress drafted the new act in pursuance of its policy orientation, which was to develop sound capital and labor markets, encourage direct financing, increase the number and type of market instruments, and pursue the principles of fair trade. The draft highlights the necessity to protect the small individual investors and required the CSRC to set up a fund specifically to support investors when their legitimate interests are jeopardized; for instance, when investors who lost money because of unfair trading would be compensated via the fund.

Regarding the entry of foreigners to domestic markets, Article 138 of the act stipulates that investors who intend to set up an account for the purpose of securities trading shall identify themselves as a Chinese citizen and/or Chinese legal person unless otherwise specified by the regulations. This reflects the desire of the authorities to open the market to foreign participation only gradually.

Regarding the settlement of the primary bonds offering and secondary market trading, Article 159 of the act stipulates that the trading shall be based on the delivery versus payment (DVP) principle.

However, some overlapping jurisdictions among agencies remain, due partly to the lack of unified primary bond market regulations and partly to multiple oversight authority. For example, in the issuance of corporate bonds, coupon rates are decided by both the SDRC and the PBOC; treasury bonds traded in the stock exchange and IBBM are separately regulated by the CSRC and the PBOC. In addition, the ill-defined division of labor among regulatory agencies undoubtedly leaves vacancies in some areas of regulatory coverage.

Most of the institutions and institutional arrangements have gradually been put in place in China as a result of the transformation from a planned economy to a market-based economy. Here again, the convergence of the evolutionary process of institutional movement and technological progress makes this transformation possible. The development of the legal framework for the bond market and the evolution of institutional arrangements are miniature versions of the whole process of transforming China's economy.

International practices can serve as models for China to follow, but any model is formulated as a result exchange, primary or secondary, the models formulated from West would not work in China's context as exchange per se is not transferable. Therefore, China needs to be very careful when initiating a market reform program through the introduction of foreign models. Remember, as we indicated, institution is driven by the interaction between incentive apparatus and constraint apparatus (laws and regulations). The incentive apparatus in the West has been in place for some time; what need to be improved are the laws, regulations and regulatory framework. Building up a constraint apparatus has become the focus of their major policy efforts. However, when China was contemplating market-based reform, an incentive apparatus did not exist because the country experienced had a planned economy for many years. It is reasonable to suppose that introducing an outside legal system is not advisable before an incentive apparatus is established.

We believe the primary bond exchange is a necessary step toward building a constraint apparatus. The evolution of a constraint apparatus has to accompany changes in the incentive apparatus. The incentive apparatus has gradually been established in the bond market since the reform in the early 1990s. Thereafter, the interaction between the incentive apparatus and constraint apparatus has driven the development of the bond market in China.

In the early 1990s China gave more preferential policies, such as grant market maker status to primary dealers, higher commission fees, flexible settlement date, and preference tax policy, among others, as an incentives package to market participants. As a result, institutions such as institutional investors and financial intermediaries have developed. This, in turn, made auction selling possible and primary dealer distribution more active.

In contrast, the stock market has not yet developed a similar process so far.

LAWS AND REGULATIONS GOVERNING TAXATION POLICY

In order to encourage individual and institutional investors to invest in treasury bonds, the Ministry of Finance adopted some preferential tax policies, such as exemptions from withholding, income, and business taxes. In recent years, institutions have become active investors in treasury bonds due partly to the downturn in the stock market. The tax authorities have begun to levy taxes on capital gains and interest income that institutional investors earned from the secondary market.

This discrimination in tax policy between individuals and institutions on one hand and between the income from the primary market and secondary market on the other has caused much controversy. In our view, the policy of exempting T-bonds from taxation should be the same for individuals and institutions; so should the treatment of income from the primary market and the secondary market. It is common for governments elsewhere to grant special tax treatment to individuals so that they have an incentive to invest in T-bonds. We believe this is necessary only when the primary market is underdeveloped and that the government should give up its discriminatory policy as soon as a sound primary bond market is established. In our view, when the market is in place and there are no restrictions on market entry, the market will always be able to achieve equilibrium pricing, and therefore a special tax policy is unnecessary.

LAWS AND REGULATIONS GOVERNING BOND ISSUANCE

The laws governing the issuance of the treasury bonds varies across countries and changes over time. The following sections review the essential characteristics of the legal system vis-à-vis T-bonds in different countries.

Ratification Process and Purpose of Issuance

The use of the proceeds from treasury bonds usually is strictly regulated in developed countries. For example, Japan's public debt is requested by the government to invest in utilities and public investment. In addition, the use of the proceeds is subject to the approval of the Diet (Japan's Parliament). According to Grundgesetz (Basic Law) of the Federal Republic of Germany, the proceeds of bond issuance must be earmarked for investment expenditures, and the amount shall be restricted not more than the credit limit. The United States, United Kingdom, and France have no special regulations on the use of bond proceeds, but Britain requires that public debt be incorporated into the national loan fund and used as loans to public institutions, such as state-owned enterprises and local organizations, and for the payment of interest on treasury bonds.

As to the amount of issuance, the United States and France set clear limits. However, although the United States set a limit on borrowing, that limit has been raised many times. On May 26, 1983, the Congress set a "permanent ceiling" of US$1.389 trillion. In November 1989, it was raised to US$3.1227 trillion, and on May 31, 1990, the ceiling was lowered to US$3.029 trillion.[5] The United States also restricts the total amount to the federal common debts and government guaranteed debts. According to the Second Act on Free Public Debt, the total balance is limited to no more than US$2.300 trillion. As to long-term bonds issued by the government and guaranteed by the Federal Reserve Bank, the legal interest rate is set at 4.25 percent, but the rate could be higher if the issued amount is more than US$250 billion.

In France, the amount of issuance public debts of different maturities is determined by a joint conference of the minister for economics and finance and the civil administration minister.

Although the institutional and legal framework varies across countries, administrative control and restriction are commonly used insofar as the use of proceeds from T-bond funding and funding objective are concerned.

Role of the Central Bank

In general, in developed countries the central banks are not allowed to purchase treasury bonds directly from T-bond issuer. However, in special cases, the law allows the central bank to buy T-bonds within certain limit. For example, the central bank of Japan is allowed buy and hold T-bonds within the limit set by the Diet. Before 1981, the Federal Reserve Bank could purchase up to US$5 billion in common bonds and government-guaranteed bonds although now the law in the United States forbids the Federal Reserve Bank from directly purchasing T-bonds. According to the Gesetz über die Deutsche Bundesbank (German Federal Bank Law), the federal bank can act only as the broker and cannot directly buy treasury bonds, but it can provide up to DM6 billion in short-term credit to the federal government. Similarly, French banking law does not allow the Bank of France to buy T-bonds directly. The government, however, may borrow from the Bank of France with the agreement of the joint conference of the ministers of economy and finance and civil administration; however, the National Assembly must ratify the loan ceiling. Britain's policy is somewhat different. The Bank of England may buy a portion of the stock of publicly offered bonds in some cases and purchase all the issued bonds in others.

In summary, worldwide, central bank purchase of government debt is commonly restricted; this is an important institutional arrangement to secure an independent monetary policy of the central bank. The legally defined relationship between the central bank and Ministry of Finance would balance the objectives of government macroeconomic policies. In this regard, China needs to contemplate a legal arrangement to grant the central bank more independent status.

Security of Repayment

Debt service is the basic legal issue in bond issuance. Therefore, to ensure the government's credibility, many countries have made debt service part of an institutional arrangement that guarantees timely payment. An example is Japan's treasury bond repayment fund. The Finance Law requires that 1.6 percent of the previous year's bond balance and half the remaining capital in general accounting be added to the T-bond repayment fund. In France, the submission of bond proceeds and disbursement for bond redemption is through a special treasury fund outside the budget. According to the Budget Organization Law, each year's budget surplus must be added to the treasury repayment provision. In Britain and the United States, setting aside debt repayment funds was once regulated by the law, but that law was later abolished. Today, repayment is made through a national loan fund, the balance of which is used to repay the debts.

The second type of system for servicing public debt is the redemption system. In the United States, savings bonds held by individuals are paid as debt service or reinvested via the treasury direct book-entry system.

The legal systems and institutional arrangements in developed countries have a number of implications for China. First, incurring debt and the use of its proceeds are strictly regulated, which has much to do with the political system and the institutional environment. Second, the regulations change over time, as the system's financial soundness is improved. Third, gradually, treasury bonds are seen as important instruments of government macroeconomic policies, and controlling the size of issuance becomes less important.

The development of the debt capital market is achieved in the West, in the language of IEEN, via secondary exchanges (i.e., evolutionary development over time). China can shorten the distance to the West by facilitating the primary exchange, but it is important to note that the primary exchange should confine itself to creating a legal framework that reflects the nature of institutional movement (i.e., the interaction between incentive structure and constraint structure). The constraint structure should go hand in hand with the incentive structure. Neither too much restriction nor too little restriction is productive.

Admittedly, the policies and practices used to promote and sell government bonds were designed to accommodate the administrative placement method. Although they have gradually gone out of use since 1996, some of these practices still apply to over-the-counter sales of savings and local corporate bonds. Obviously, these practices ought to change along with the changed incentive structure.

Nonstandard Practises

The applications of IEEN framework sketched before are developed more extensively in the following section, which demonstrate how the system evolved from the administrative placement in the planned economy into our contemporary market-based primary dealer system for selling government securities. It is noted during this process, a number of nonstandard practices were frequently used in the transition period. This nonstandard practices is, in Oliver E. Willianson's words, "have the purpose of safeguarding transactions."[6]

Sale of Bonds/Trade-in Policy   The sale of bonds/trade-in policy, enacted when maturity dates were concentrated and lacked an effective yield curve, was designed to rectify the maturity profile so that a complete yield curve could be established. The Urgent Notice of the Ministry of Finance on the Work of "Trading-in" Treasury Bills stipulated that the state encouraged investors to redeem bonds before maturity and buy two-year treasury bills issued in the same year. A special interest rate with a yield 1 percent higher than the original bonds was offered.

On-site Sales Policy   To facilitate the sale of bonds to individuals, the Ministry requires banks, post offices, and bond service departments to visit factories and mines, enterprises and institutions, schools, the military, and the like to sell bonds to people working at these organizations. This policy has played an important role in bond sales since the early 1990s.

Long-to-Short Policy   To satisfy the need of the individuals for short-term bonds, some securities intermediaries break middle- and long-term bonds into short-term bonds and sell them to the individuals.

Investors' Option Policy   To provide flexibility and to promote the sale of Ministry-issued twin bonds with three- and five-year maturities, in May 1993, the Ministry allowed treasury bills with a five-year term to be converted to three-year bonds after they were held for three years.

Time and Interest Rate Priority Policy   In 1993, because of irregular fundraising, the prevalence of interbank borrowing, and the difficulties issuing treasury bonds, the state adopted the time and interest rate priority policy for bond issuance. "Time priority" means that T-bonds should be issued prior to other bonds and that the latter could not be issued until the issuance of the former is finished. "Interest rate priority" means that the interest rate of the T-bonds should be higher than that of the other bonds. Such a policy has played an important role in ensuring the issuance of T-bonds, but it has also hindered the issuance of other bonds.

Issuing Conditions Policy   Because the deposit interest rate was increased in 1993, in order to protect investors, the government decided to adjust the coupon rates of previously issued bonds to maintain the value of those bonds.

The first adjustment occurred on May 14, 1993, when the coupon rate of treasury bills that matured in March 1993 was raised from 10 to 12.52 percent and the coupon rate of five-year T-bills went from 11 to 14.06 percent.

The second adjustment was made on July 11, 1993, to increase the rate on three- and five-year treasury bills issued in 1993 from 12.52 and 14.06 percent to 13.96 and 15.86 percent, respectively, in order to ensure that the coupon rate was 1.72 and 2 percent, respectively, higher than that of savings deposits with the same term.

Along with changes in the deposit interest rate, the secondary market yield of T-bills went through years of market adjustment, reflecting the quick response of treasury bond yields to market changes consistent with the supply-demand relationship. This indicates that bond yields were becoming increasingly market based.

This policy flexibility was expedient but was not consistent with market principles. Although the government would like to assume the market risk itself, this kind of protection is obviously counterproductive to raising investors' financial awareness. Therefore, after 1996, all of these policies were abolished when the market was fully established.

Reporting System

The treasury promotion committees were responsible for reporting the progress of the T-bond issuance to the State Council. Progress included:

- *The progress of settlement.* The amount of money put into the treasury is reported at the beginning of each month during the issuance, and those data are checked against the treasury statistics; treasury reporting should be identical with the settlement amount, no inconsistency is allowed; the treasury departments of the branches of the PBOC should actively support the statistical and checking work.
- *The progress of issuance.* The statistics on the issuance are recorded and reported through the Internet system.
- *The analysis on the issuance and settlement progress.* The problems and issues related to the issuance progress are analyzed in each report.

Auction selling through primary dealers has been used since 1996, and, therefore, reporting is done mainly through settlement and clearance companies, such as those affiliated with the stock exchange and the China Government Securities Depository Trust & Clearing Co., Ltd. (CGSDTC). Nowadays all the information can be accessed through the Web site of Chinabond.com.

LAWS AND REGULATIONS GOVERNING THE PRIMARY DEALER SYSTEM

The primary dealers are the major players in the primary and secondary markets. They directly underwrite and bid for the T-bonds from the issuing entities and act as the first link between the issuing entities and the investors. They are the market makers in the secondary market and guarantee the smooth operations of the T-bond market. Most of the developed capital markets around the world have primary dealer systems.

China established its primary dealer system in 1993 when 19 securities firms became primary dealers; the number was increased to more than 40 in 1997 and to 52 by December 2004.

To improve the primary dealer system of China's T-bond market and regulate the behavior of primary dealers, the Ministry of Finance, the PBOC, and the CSRC drafted the Administrative Rules on Primary Dealers of the People's Republic of China. It covers five areas:

1. *Qualifications of primary dealers.* Primary dealers must be financial institutions approved by the competent authorities. They include banks other than policy banks, securities firms, and trust and investment companies that engage in related businesses; and other financial institutions that engage in the treasury bond underwriting as well as transaction agents and dealer firms that have complied with the qualification requirements.

   When qualified institutions apply for primary dealer status, they must meet certain financial standards; for example, their paid-up capital in currency must meet the established minimum requirement, they must have a sound credit reputation, and they must have experienced no operational irregularities for the past several years.

2. *Legal rights of primary dealers.* Primary dealers are entitled to participate in the underwriting syndicate organized by the issuing entities or by the institutions entrusted by such entities or to bid directly for bonds during the treasury auction. As members of a syndicate, primary dealers are also able to negotiate with the issuing entities the term of the issue (based on specified procedures) before each syndicated issuance. In addition, they are entitled to participate in the open market operations of the central bank and to repurchase treasury bonds as well as to invest in the treasury bonds investment fund.

   Primary dealers were active in stock trading in early 1990s, as engaging in stock trading was a profitable business at the time while bond market was snubbed by them. To motivate primary dealer to turn their attention to bond market, the regulations of 1993 and 1994 specified the liability to participate in the underwriting syndicate for corporate initial public offerings.

3. *Obligations of primary dealers.* For each issuance, the primary dealers are obliged to underwrite or bid for an amount no less than a certain percentage of the total issuance volume. The ratio was no less than 1 percent in 1994. The primary dealers must strictly honor their obligations written in the underwriting and outsourcing selling contracts of each issuance. After signing the underwriting syndicate contract, primary dealers should actively outsource selling and retail sales of the T-bonds via their respective marketing networks. Primary dealers are obliged to maintain the liquidity of the secondary market and actively engage in the agent and dealer businesses of bond transactions. It is the obligation of primary dealers to submit regular reports and information on the underwriting, outsource selling, retail sales, and transaction performance in the secondary bond market to the issuing entities and the supervisory authorities. It also is the obligation of primary dealers to provide redemption services for maturing T-bonds on behalf of the Ministry of Finance.

4. *Process for becoming a primary dealer.* Any financial institution qualified to be a primary dealer of treasury bonds may submit an application for related materials. The qualifications of primary dealers are subject to the examination of the Treasury Bond Management, the central bank, and other related supervisory authorities.

   In the United States, the Department of the Treasury and the Federal Reserve Board jointly examine the qualifications of primary dealers and confirm their status. As primary dealers in China are also engaged in stock underwriting and trading, the CSRC is also involved in the approval process. The rules require that a team made up of the members from the Ministry, the PBOC, and the CSRC examine and confirm the qualifications of primary dealers.

   If a primary dealer does not perform any of the specified obligations as requested, the Ministry, the PBOC, and the CSRC are entitled via joint ruling to suspend or permanently rescind its qualification as a primary dealer together with the related rights. At present, the short sale of the treasury bonds incurs severe punishments; for example, all the proceeds from short sales are confiscated and several times more than such proceeds are assessed as a fine.

5. *Annual examination of primary dealers.* The Ministry regularly examines the qualifications of primary dealers in accordance with the Administrative Rules and the Implementation Measures on the Examination and Confirmation of the Qualifications of the Treasury Bond Primary Dealers. The key documents examined are financial statements;

work summaries on T-bond transactions, including participation in the underwriting; the transaction performance in the secondary market; and violations of the Administrative Rules or other laws, policies, or regulations of China.

Relationship among the Ministry of Finance, the Central Bank, and the Primary Dealers

The reforms of 1991 to 1996 fundamentally changed the selling mechanism as the system shifted from administrative allocation to primary dealers. This institutional revolution had political ramifications that affected the division of labor among agencies.

The Ministry of Finance, the PBOC, and the CSRC are the managers and supervisors of the primary dealers. They draft the administrative measures, examine dealers' qualifications, discipline them for irregular activities, and so on. As the department that supervises the examination of financial institutions, the PBOC is responsible for examining the business aspects of primary dealers' operations. The CSRC is responsible for market transaction management of primary dealers. In addition to the management of the primary dealers, the Ministry, as the issuer, also signs the contracts with primary dealers. Such contracts define the legal status of issuer and underwriters.

At present, there are about 78 members of the registered bonds underwriting syndicate which are the principle members for syndicate of the Ministry of Finance, PBOC, CDB, and other major issuers.

Bond Issuance in the Inter-Bank Bond Market

As the primary bond market in the IBBM evolves from the original administrative placement to the current auction selling method, market-based development progresses gradually. Inspired by the successful treasury bond market reform, the China Development Bank held a debut auction using the electronic transmission system of the CGSDTC. Thereafter, other commercial banks started to issue securities through auction or underwriting syndicates in the IBBM. However, they became active only after 2003. Today, the traditional administrative placement method is no longer valid in the bond primary market.

By the end of June of 2000, 333 issues had been made in the IBBM with the total amount of RMB4.17913 trillion, of which 504.20 billion yuan were issued by the Ministry and RMB365 billion by the CDB. The issuing methods include tender, private placement, and a combination of competitive and noncompetitive bidding.

LAWS AND REGULATIONS GOVERNING
THE REDEMPTION OF TREASURY BONDS

Treasury bond redemption entails the monetary reimbursement by the government to the investors; the quality of redemption reflects the government's willingness and ability to honor its contracted liabilities. From issuance to trading and then to redemption, T-bonds undergo a complete cycle. Legally speaking, rights and obligations reflected in the redemption are defined in the original issuing contracts. Therefore, redemption is the final phase of the cycle. Whether the rights and obligations contained in the issuing contracts can be honored is subject to the timely accomplishment of the redemption. For this reason, redemption plays a special role in the operation cycle of treasury bonds.

Types of Redemption

The redemption structure is part of the legal document and is generally agreed by both issuer and investors at issue, and is arranged for the convenience of both issuer and investors. Although the diversified bond instrument allows extensive flexibility, any payment mode should result in an equilibrium price (i.e., the net present value should equal zero).

Redemption of Principal   There are six different ways to repay principal:

1. *Lump-sum repayment upon maturity.* Most governments adopt lump-sum redemption; it is the usual form of repayment.
2. *Repayment in installments.* In the past, China sometimes redeemed treasury bills of some years in installments determined by casting lots.
3. *Rolling principal.* Once China issued convertible treasury bills held by enterprises and convertible financial debentures held by banks and financial institutions; thus, the principal rolled forward and repayment was deferred.
4. *Investor-selected redemption.* Investors are offered the opportunity to select the form of repayment. For example, both three-year and five-year T-bills were issued in 1993; holders of the latter were entitled to redeem their bills at the end of the third year as if they held the former.
5. *Issuer-selected redemption.* In some countries, the government may, based on its assessment of market conditions, redeem the bonds prior to maturity, which gives it greater flexibility to take the advantage of favorable interest changes.
6. *Redemption before maturity.* In China, this type of redemption applies only to certificate savings bonds. For example, the three-year bonds

issued since 1994 by the Ministry can be redeemed at any time before maturity.

Payment of Interest   The interest can be paid in four ways:

1. *Lump-sum payment upon maturity.* China used this method in the redemption of its treasury bonds when administrative placement was the prevailing selling technique.
2. *Annual payment.* In most countries, the interest is paid annually.
3. *Semiannual payment.* The United States uses this payment format.
4. *Daily payment.* This is not used for bond repayment.

Redemption System

At one time, treasury bond redemption agencies in China were mainly bank outlets, which had been assigned for debt service on behalf of the Ministry of Finance. As a growing number of bonds matured, the amount of debt service work required increased substantially. As a result, the debt service conduit increased from one channel to multiple channels to satisfy the cumbersome manual work of repayment to individual investors.

1. *Bank outlets.* Until 1990, debt service was primarily executed over the counter at specialized banks (SBs; now State Owned Commercial Banks, or SOCBs). However, due to the limited number of bank outlets, investors still found access over the counter bond market inconvenient. This fact demonstrates that a single-channel debt service cannot satisfy the requirement of timely redemption.
2. *Multichannel redemption.* In 1990, the State Council decided that the redemption of treasury bills should be handled through multiple channels. In the same year, the Ministry delegated part of the debt service work to the Ministry of Posts and Telecommunications (MOPT). According to the agent agreement between the two ministries, the MOPT is entitled to provide the debt service in its post office savings outlets in the provincial capitals and the Separate Planning Cities (SPC) for treasury bills maturing from 1982 to 1985. At the same time, the Treasury Bond Service Department (GBSD) and the securities firms were responsible for the rest of the debt service work. Later, the work of redeeming treasury bonds and the treasury bills was conducted through multiple channels, including the securities companies, trust and investment companies, the GBSD, outlets of the post office saving offices, over the counters of the SBs and the commercial banks, and so on.

To alleviate investors' "redemption inconvenience," the government required that all the offices, branches, business offices, and savings offices with counter operations and the counters of the urban credit cooperatives, credit and trust cooperatives and securities departments, and post office savings offices, among others, should offer redemption services for T-bonds.

Forms of Redemption, Disbursement, and Settlement

The redemption period is divided into two major categories:

1. *Concentrated redemption.* The redemption period through Local Finance Departments (LFDs) is within four months after maturity. Post office departments, investment companies, and SBs redeem bonds within two months after maturity. Generally, concentrated redemption does not carry over to the next fiscal year.
2. *Year-round redemption.* Redemption begins at the end of the concentrated redemption period. It often lasts for half a year. The money transfer for redemption of this period is incorporated into the budget for the following year.

Money transferred for redemption is disbursed prior to the beginning of the redemption period. After receiving the redemption funds, the chief accountant of the LFD transfers them to the local GBMD, the Treasury Division of PBOC branches, and lower-level GBMD departments.

The operational procedure for the disbursement of redemption funds and paper bills was subject to changes in issuing formats. Figure 18.1 illustrates the procedure.

The operational procedure in 1990 for the redemption funds report and settlement of the specialized banks and their outlets with the PBOC is illustrated in Figure 18.2.

In 1991, the operational procedure for redeeming bonds was the same as it had been from 1986 to 1989, except that the redemption fund was held in the central general treasury.

In 1992, the Ministry disbursed a prepaid provision of RMB7 billion yuan before the redemption began and added supplementary funds based on the actual redemption requirement. The PBOC transferred RMB2 billion yuan to the county branches of the SBs (or their accounts in the PBOC's branches in the same counties) for the daily redemption service. The actual redemption payment was deducted from the provision in the central general treasury, and the withdrawn paper securities were sent to the branches of the PBOC at the prefecture and city levels for destruction.

The redemption funds for the LFD and post office savings departments were disbursed by the Budget Management Department (BMD) of the

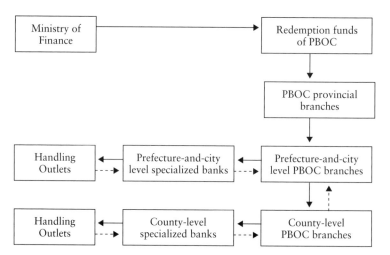

FIGURE 18.1   Working Procedures for Redemption Funds and Paper Bills[4]

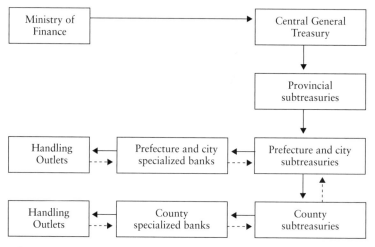

FIGURE 18.2   Working Procedure for Redemption Funds and Bills in the Banking System in 1990[5]

Ministry or the BMD on behalf of the GDMD of the Ministry to the provincial budget divisions of LFD. Then they were disbursed to the provincial comprehensive divisions and debt divisions of the provincial finance departments, followed by the prefecture and city comprehensive and debt divisions and county comprehensive offices of county finance departments, and finally to the redemption service outlets.

The GDMD of the Ministry of Finance shall make redemption plans for different regions and submit them to the budget department for the disbursement of redemption funds. The budget department transferred the redemption funds to the budget divisions in the provinces. Next, the money was transferred from the budget divisions to the provincial comprehensive divisions before being transferred to the different finance departments and debt service outlets. After the redemption period, the finance departments submitted the final report of redemption work up, level by level, to the head office. Upon the approval of the Government Debt Management Department, the redemption final accounts were compiled and submitted to the local chief accountants before reporting to the Ministry. The remaining redemption funds were returned to the local chief accountants and remain deposited there as a substitution of transfer payment from the central government to the local governments. The working procedure is illustrated in Figure 18.3.

Within 50 days after the redemption period, the Government Debt Management Department (GDMD) of the provinces, autonomous regions, and municipalities must clear the redemption accounts and transfer all the remaining redemption funds to the chief budget accountants at the provincial level. The settlement time at a level lower than the provincial level is determined by the provincial GDMD, but the provincial settlement must be made in accordance with the same timeline. The GDMD of the Ministry of Finance requires that the final account be based on the clearing reports submitted by the provincial chief accountants for the year. The local chief accountants deduct the appropriate amount from "the current account with the central public finance," according to the final account given by the Ministry.

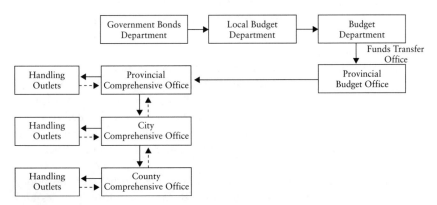

FIGURE 18.3 Working Procedure for Redemption Funds in the Finance and Post Departments

Initially (early 1980s), China's redemption fee for treasury bills was 0.15 percent of the notional principal; the fee increased gradually to 0.2 and 0.3 percent. In the later 1980s fees were a flat rate of 0.3 percent, plus 1 percent service charges paid directly to the redemption serve stuff.

The goal is to ensure that the grassroots units receive the major portion of the fees in compensation for their intensive work. According to Ministry provisions, all the redemption fees should be paid to the debt service units.

In 1989, the government decided to add 1 percent of the redemption principal as a redemption service charge in order to encourage the redemption outlets to participate actively in the debt service work. The added service charge is used mainly to pay for the labor costs of the organizations that directly redeem individually held bonds or bills. Such organizations include outlets of specialized banks, nonbank financial institutions and urban and township credit cooperatives, and others. The management departments in the finance and banking system do not share in the service charge. The Ministry appropriates the service charge to the local finance bureaus before the redemption period. Organizations that directly handle the redemption may draw the service charge at the local finance department with vouchers certifying their debt service work.

The work involved in redeeming treasury bonds is a kind of public service closely related to government policies. The fundamental requirement is openness, timeliness, and accuracy. The redemption policy is often set in the issuing terms before bond issuance, along with the interest rate and maturity. Before the redemption period, the Ministry would make a redemption announcement, disclosing the basic redemption policies to investors. At the same time, it drafts operational procedures of debt service for local debt service entities to follow. According to the issuance regulations and the relevant policies of the State Council and the Ministry, the names of the redeemable treasury bonds, the debt service methods, and the solutions to specific problems, among other things, are described in the Measures of Debt Service for Maturing Treasury Bonds.

The treasury bills promotion committees or the treasury bonds management committees organize the debt service work. Under their leadership, a group of the department, bureau, local finance departments, banks, post offices, and other departments work together to set up the detailed redemption network. The specialized banks must also establish their own teams and enhance the leadership of the nonbank financial institutions in cooperation with the committees.

Prior to the redemption period, the government organizes the bondholders and redemption workers to publicize the redemption policies and gives the publicity outline to the workers, especially those at the grassroots level. The outline lists the types or codes of the bonds to be redeemed in the current year, the interest calculation, the redemption period, redemption sites, redemption fees, solutions to specific problems, and so on.

Procedures for Treasury Bond Redemption

To ensure timely and accurate redemption and to avoid mistakes and errors, the government has devised strict redemption procedures. In 1988, the Ministry of Finance, the PBOC, the Industrial and Commercial Bank of China, the Agricultural Bank of China, the China Construction Bank, and the Bank of China jointly issued the *Several Rules on the Debt Service by the Banks for the Treasury Bills*, which strictly defined the redemption procedures.

As required by the government and the head offices of banks, when the treasury bonds held by individual investors are redeemed, the first inspector at an authorized redemption unit must carefully examine the amount, printing number, and denomination of the maturing bonds and bills and check if the numbers are lottery winners. When there are alterations, replacements, or fabrications in the face color, pattern, or number; and if the paper bonds are torn or dirty, redemption would not be made.

After the bonds are authenticated, the redemption units complete "the redemption list of treasury bills held by individuals (redemption list)," calculate the total amount of principal and interest, and enter the amount in the redemption list before stamping them and sending the redemption list with the paper bills to the reviewers.

After this second authentication, the reviewer adds a "Paid" stamp and a stamp with the reviewer's name to the paper bills, counts the redemption payment, and returns the bills and redemption list to the original inspector for another review. That inspector keeps the redemption list and pays the principal and interest to the bondholder. Upon redemption, the returned treasury bills are classified according to denomination and sorted, and every 100 pieces are bundled and attached with the name stamp of the handler. Torn or dirty bills are bundled separately. The bundled bills are put into the treasury for safekeeping before destruction.

When the bondholder is an institution, the redemption unit completes the "Redemption List of the Treasury Bills held by a Unit for the Year XXXX" in triplicate and gives the list to the original selling unit for examination. The original selling unit checks to make certain the bills were originally signed, the stamps are complete, no alterations have been made, the balance columns are correctly calculated, and so on. It then checks the counterfoil of the third form against the receipt copy to make certain they are identical.

The final work is validation. The first step is to calculate the principal to be repaid. If paid in installments, each payment should be equal to the total amount of the treasury bills bought by the unit multiplied by the redemption percentage. The second step is to calculate the accrual interest. It should be equal to the principal to be repaid multiplied by the annual interest rate and then multiplied by the remaining years. The calculated principal and interest should then be entered in the record columns of the stub and the receipt forms, and the staff of the redemption unit on duty should sign and stamp the forms. The redemption list and the receipt and stub forms are sent to the inspector who reviews them, then adds his or her name stamp and common stamp to the triplicate forms (one form is given to the counter for transfer, one returned to the purchasing unit, and one kept by the reviewer).

Redemption Report System

The main purpose of the redemption report system is to inform the Ministry of Finance of any issues related to redemption operations on a timely basis so that they can be addressed properly and in a timely manner. There are two kinds of redemption reports:

1. *Redemption progress report.* There are two basic reports on the redemption progress and on how the schedule of redemption is carried out: the 10-day report (first, middle, or last 10 days of a month) and the monthly report. During the redemption peak, the 10-day report is submitted within 5 days after the first, middle, or last 10 days of a month from the provinces, autonomous regions, and municipalities directly under the central government. During the concentrated redemption period and year-round redemption period, the monthly report is submitted within 3 days after a month ends.

2. *Redemption final report.* After the redemption period concluded, the treasury bond authorities (i.e., LFDs) of the provinces, autonomous regions, and municipalities directly under the central government complete the "Final Report on the Debt Service by the Finance Departments for Treasury Bonds for the Year XXXX" and the "Summary List of the Finance Department's Redemption of Treasury Bonds for the Year XXXX," and submit them to the Ministry of Finance by January 20 of the following year. The reports and the list provide the Ministry with the information required to review, check, and evaluate the debt service work. Based on the final redemption report, the Ministry shall deliver the notice to destroy the redeemed paper securities.

The debt service payment should be identical to the contracted principal and interest payments at the issue. The principal payment is equal to the number of bonds multiplied by denominations. The way to check if the redemption is correct, for the coupon-bearing bonds of annual payment, for example, is to see whether the paid interest is equal to the total face value multiplied by the interest rate and then multiplied by the maturities (payment times). The Ministry examines the results of the redemption work according to the "Summary List of the Finance Department's Redemption of Treasury Bonds for the Year XXXX." The formulas are:

Subtotal of Principal payment = the number of bonds × denomination
Interest Subtotal of Debt Service = Principal × Interest Rate × maturities
Total Principal and Interest = Principal Subtotal + Interest Subtotal

The destruction of the redeemed paper bonds is an indispensable part of the redemption work. The Ministry of Finance requires that the amount of principal in the "Summary List of the Finance Department's Redemption of Treasury Bonds for the Year XXXX" be equal to that of the destroyed bonds in the "Report on the Destruction of the Treasury Bonds by the Finance Department."

Issues Affecting Bond Redemption

At the end of the 1980s, to promote the selling of new issues, the bank counters and securities firms were assigned the debt service of maturing debt. The involvement of these institutions in debt service work undoubtedly ensured timely redemption of maturing bonds and also boosted the reputation of government bonds and therefore facilitated the issuance of new bonds. In accordance with the sales promotion policy, bondholders were encouraged to buy new bonds as soon as they redeemed maturing bonds. Until 1993, the banks and securities firms provided purchase, safekeeping, and redemption services. In practice, this "old for new" selling promotion offset the principal payment; money transfer related only to the interest payments. Therefore, this practice is convenient for investors, simplified the debt service formalities, and greatly facilitated the sale of new issues.

In 1993, the "old for new" policy also applied to the new two-year-maturity bonds. The holders of the maturing bonds enjoyed the preferential policy if they wanted to buy the new bonds (i.e., they received an interest rate 1 percent higher than the coupon rate and could redeem the bonds three months before maturity).

These issues were alleviated gradually after book entry bond was introduced in 1993. From 1996 onwards, with the advent of CGSDTC, redemption of marketable government securities was handled electronically, fundamentally erasing the redemption problems. However, remaining paper securities had been following the above-mentioned procedures until early

2000s. Paper certificate savings bonds were transferred into electronic savings bonds in 2006, which marked a conclusion of time-consuming manual redemption work.

Since 1996, marketable securities have been sold, traded and redeemed via electronic transmission system, which substantially economized the redemption fees. As of today, redemption fees are paid as a percentage of bond principal.

For marketable securities, fees are only paid to the underwriters or primary dealers. Currently, no redemption fees are paid for T-bonds below one year (one year maturity bill not included) maturity. For the T-bonds with one year to five year maturity (five year maturity bonds not included), 0.05 percent is paid; for the T-bond with five year maturity and above, 0.1 percent is paid.

As far as savings bonds are concerned, redemption fees are based on the type of savings bonds and to different redemption service systems. For certificate savings bonds, total 0.72 percent is paid, of which 0.7 percent goes to the underwriters, 0.017 percent goes to the banks and post saving offices, and 0.003 percent goes to the government bond service department affiliate to the Ministry of Finance. For electronic savings bonds, 0.43 percent is paid, of which 0.4 percent goes to the underwriters, 0.015 percent goes to the CGS-DTC, 0.0075 goes to banks and post saving offices, 0.0075 percent goes to the government bond service department affiliate to the Ministry of Finance.

Ad Hoc Policies Relating to the Redemption of Treasury Bonds

Redemption before Maturity Before 1988, bondholders were subject to a number of inconveniences. For example, treasury bonds were not tradable, which was inconvenient for investors who wanted to get their money back before maturity for contingency use. In addition, at that time, holders were unable to take their bonds abroad or redeem them before maturity if they left the country.

Therefore, the Ministry of Finance and the PBOC clarified in the "Notice on Redemption of Undue Treasury Bills" that redemption before maturity was allowed if one of these three conditions were met:

1. They were Chinese citizens whose entire family resettled abroad, had no domestic relatives to hold the bills on their behalf, and their purchase and departure were evidenced by their original serving units and the public security authorities at above the county level.
2. They were returned overseas Chinese, Hong Kong, or Macao residents who went abroad or returned to Hong Kong or Macao with their

entire family, and their purchase and departure were evidenced by their original serving units and the authorities in charge of overseas Chinese affairs.

3. They were foreigners working and residing in China who returned home with their entire family, and their purchase and departure were evidenced by the original serving units and the authorities in charge of foreign affairs.

Under any one of these circumstances, redemption prior to maturity could be handled at the local PBOC branch. The interest on the treasury bonds or bills redeemed before maturity was calculated based on the annual rate provided in the T-bill regulations. One year's interest would be paid if the bonds were held for no less than a year; six months' interest would be paid if the bonds had been held for more than half a year but less than a year, and no interest would be paid if the bonds were held for less than half a year. Redemption issues were, for the most part, resolved via the circulation and transfer market (the informal secondary market that opened in 1988). Therefore, the Ministry and the PBOC specified in the "Notice on Suspending Redemption of the Treasury Bonds before Maturity" that no redemption services would be offered before the maturity of T-bonds issued since 1988.

Deferred Repayment of Treasury Bonds   Debt service increased greatly at the end of the 1980s. To alleviate the debt service pressure, the Ministry and the PBOC in June 1990 published the "Notice on Temporarily Suspending Redemption Work on Treasury Bonds Maturing in 1990 and Held by Institutions." This notice stated that redemption would be deferred on treasury bonds issued to institutions between 1981 and 1985, on key construction project bonds issued to organizations in 1987, and on fiscal bonds issued to financial institutions in 1988 and held by enterprises, public institutions, armies, and financial institutions. In October 1990, the Ministry and the PBOC stated in the "Notice to Defer the Repayment of the Finance Bonds Maturing in 1990" that the redemption work would be deferred for three years. Interest rates were subsequently adjusted on treasury bonds on which repayment was deferred.

This deferment has happened only once since 1981. The idea was that the SOEs and other institutions are all state owned; therefore, repaying state institutions was the same as the government taking money out of one pocket and putting it into the other. However, these irregular practices were the subject of much criticism, and never happened again.

CHAPTER 19

Legal Framework
of the Capital Debt Market

(Part Two)

LAWS AND REGULATIONS GOVERNING TREASURY BOND
SUBSIDIES: A HISTORICAL PERSPECTIVE

Because of runaway inflation in the late 1980s, the government devised a value adjustment policy to prevent depositors from losing money. The value adjustment policy on bank deposits was based on the provision of the People's Bank of China (PBOC) that "the annual interest rate of the three-year savings plus the value adjustment subsidy rate [should be] equal to the inflation rate in the same period. The annual interest rate of the five- and eight-year savings plus the value maintaining subsidy rate [should] exceed the inflation rate in the same period."

Later this policy was extended to bondholders. The Ministry of Finance announced the interest subsidy policy in July 1993, stating: "The value adjustment should be executed beginning on July 11, 1993, for the treasury bills of 1992 and 1993 with reference to the Rules on the Value Adjustment of the RMB Savings Deposits of PBOC" and that "the subsidy rate of the value adjustment should be calculated in accordance with depositor subsidy rate announced by PBOC upon redemption."

All not-yet-matured bonds issued in 1988 were to be subsidized until 1991, when the subsidy was automatically suspended. Treasury bills subsidized from July 1993 were classified by type and included the third transaction in 1992, the fifth transaction in 1992, and the third and fifth transactions in 1993.

The value adjustment for 1988 bank deposits was based on the interest upon maturity. In July 1993, the base interest rate of the value-adjusted bonds was calculated in this way: The interest rates of three-, five- and eight-year notes were 13.14 percent, 14.94 percent, and 17.64 percent, respectively. After December 1, 1991, the bank interest rate after adjustment became the base interest rate.

The subsidy rate for bonds was to be determined with reference to the interest rate on bank deposits, but the question was how to determine the base interest rate of the bonds. Prior to the redemption of bonds maturing in 1995, there were three alternatives:

1. *Use the coupon rate as the benchmark.* Since treasury bills are a kind of fixed-rate bond, the coupon rate should act as the base once a rate was determined.
2. *Use the bank interest rate after adjustment as the base rate.* This option captures the idea that the same principle should be applied to both depositors and bondholders. Therefore, since the value adjustment of the bank deposits was based on the interest rate after adjustment, so should the subsidy rate of the treasury bills.
3. *Use a rate higher than the bank rate after the adjustment as the base rate.* Coupon rates on treasury bills were designed to be higher than the interest rate on bank deposits; therefore, the adjusted base rate of treasury bills should be increased commensurately.

The prevailing view at that time is that, since T-bonds are fixed-income market instruments, there is no reason for the base interest rate to vary with the yield changes of other financial instruments. Although there are bonds with floating interest rates in the international financial market, the fact that it is variable is clearly defined at the time of issue. At the time, all of China's treasury bonds were fixed-rate bonds; thus the first option seemed reasonable and was adopted.

The policy of subsidizing value began on September 10, 1988, when the interest rate on bank deposits with terms longer than three years was linked to the price index and fluctuated with anticipated inflation, causing assets and commodity prices to react. The policy was cancelled in 1991 and resumed on July 11, 1993, finally ending on April 1, 1996.

LAWS AND REGULATIONS GOVERNING THE TREASURY BOND CUSTODY SYSTEM

As agreed by the Ministry of Finance and the PBOC, all tradable treasury bonds could act as collateral for mortgage loans. In 1997, the Ministry and the PBOC allowed that the nontradable T-bonds issued by pension funds and unemployment insurance funds could be used as collateral for bank loans. In 1999, to encourage individual consumption, the Ministry and the PBOC allowed certificate savings bonds to be used as the collateral for bank loans.

LAWS AND REGULATIONS GOVERNING TRANSACTION FEES

The fees for the issuance of treasury bonds are remuneration to the underwriters or the sales agents and are part of the transaction costs. When administrative placement was the prevailing form of distribution, the Ministry required that the fees be paid mainly to the grassroots sales units and the underwriters. The fees were initially 3 percent and increased to 5 percent in 1994, and then decreased. They were 0.5 percent in 2005.

From 1995 until 1997, the issuing fees for coupon and certificate savings bonds remained at 1994 levels; in 1996, the issuing fees for registered bonds decreased. The issuing fees of certificate and bearer bonds in 1997 increased from 5 percent to 6.5 percent.

As shown in Figure 19.1, fees paid to the distribution network of the Ministry of Finance system (including local finance departments [LFDs]) reflect the single selling conduit of administrative placement.

However, as shown in Figures 19.2 and 19.3, in 1994, fees were paid to both the debt service departments under the Ministry and the banks, post saving offices affiliated with PBOC. However, more selling work had been accomplished through the Ministry's distribution network.

From 1995 until 1997, the issuing fees of coupon and certificate bonds were the same as in 1994. The issuing fees of the registered bonds decreased in 1996. The issuing fees of the certificate bonds and bearer bonds in 1997 increased from 5 to 6.5 percent (as shown in Tables 19.1 and 19.2). From 2003 until 2005, the issuing fees of certificate bonds increased from 0.2 to 0.42 percent, but there was a slight decrease in those of the book-entry (interbank) bonds (as shown in Tables 19.3 and 19.4). The issuing fees of these two bonds in 2005 were the same as in 2004.

LAWS AND REGULATIONS GOVERNING OPERATING MECHANISMS AND CLEARING AND TRUST SYSTEM

Overview of T-Bond Issues

In the 10 years between 1981 and 1990, treasury bonds were issued mainly through administrative allocation. The issuing targets were urban

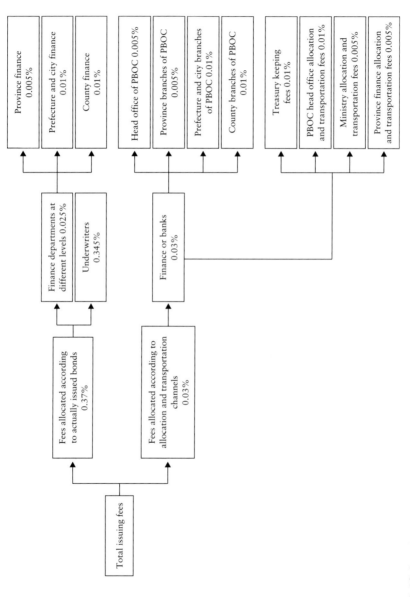

FIGURE 19.1 Allocation of T-Note Issuing Fees in 1993

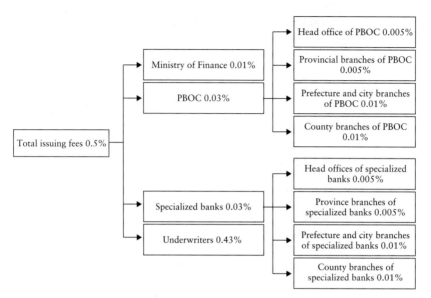

FIGURE 19.2 Allocation of Three-Year T-Note Issuing Fees in 1994

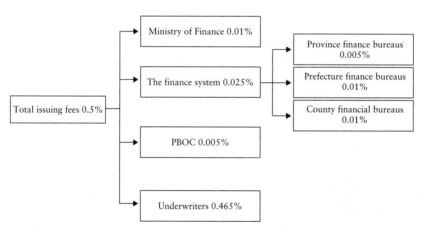

FIGURE 19.3 Allocation of Two-Year T-Note Issuing Fees in 1994

and rural residents and workers in factories, mines, businesses, public institutions, government agencies, schools, armies, and so on. The work flow is illustrated in Figure 19.4.

In 1991, some treasury bonds were issued via underwriting; the rest were issued over the counter and by assigned subscription. In 1992, all bonds were

TABLE 19.1   Selling Fee Rate in 1996

Bond Type	Issuing Rate (%)
Certificate bond	5
Bearer bond	5
Book-entry bond	4

TABLE 19.2   Selling Fee Rate in 1997

Bond Type	Issuing Rate (%)
Certificate bond	6.5
Bearer bond	6.5
Book-entry bond	4

TABLE 19.3   Selling Fee Rate in 2003

Bond Type	Issuing Rate (%)
Book-entry bond (interbank)	0.08–0.1
Certificate bond	0.1–0.2

issued via local underwriting, and the bills and proceeds channels remained unchanged. Figure 19.5 illustrates the bills and proceeds operation after the underwriting was tested in 1991 and 1992.

In 1993, T-bonds were issued in three forms: underwriting syndication, over-the-counter (OTC) sales, and organized subscription, each of which has its own system to channel paper securities and proceeds. Figure 19.6 illustrates the paper bills and proceeds operation of the treasury bills in 1993.

Treasury bonds issued in 1994 were divided into two categories: tradable and nontradable. Paper bills were still allocated and transported using the dual systems of the Finance Department and banks; the Ministry of Finance was not directly involved. Figure 19.7 illustrates the paper bills and proceeds operation of 1994 and 1995, while Figure 19.8 illustrated the operation of 1995 and 1996.

The auction system was used to sell T-bonds between 1995 and 1997. In 1995, this was only an experiment, and most of that year's bonds were issued as they had been in 1994. In 1996, T-bonds were issued mainly

TABLE 19.4　Selling Fee Rate in 2004

Bond Type	Issuing Rate (%)
Book-entry bond (interbank)	0.05–0.1
Certificate bond	0.42

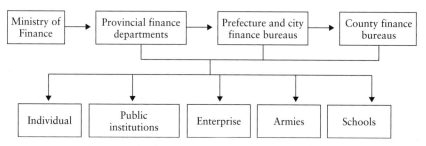

FIGURE 19.4　Issuance Work Flow of Bills and Proceeds, 1981 to 1990

via bidding processes; 53 percent of these were registered bonds. Since the bidding issuance was conducted on the two exchanges, the bills and proceeds operation was greatly changed. Treasury bond issuance via bidding on the exchanges was conducted in three ways: listed outsourcing selling, OTC agreement, and secondary market outsourcing selling. Individuals could open personal accounts if they wanted to buy the T-bonds on the exchanges. Thus, the exchanges and security firms became the key links in the paper securities and proceeds operation.

The measures of 1994 were again used in issuing certificate savings bonds to the individuals in 1998 and 1999. Since the issuance of the book-entry form bonds was transferred from the exchange market to the interbank bond market (IBBM), the bills and proceeds operation was conducted mainly via the banks and the China Government Securities Depository Trust & Clearing Co., Ltd. (CGSDTC).

Transformation of Paper Securities

In China, people today still refer to the interest rate on a bond as the "coupon" because, historically, paper bonds carried paper coupons that could be cut off and given back to the bank to get a payment. Bonds issued today no longer have coupons attached, but are represented by a certificate, similar to a stock certificate, with a brief description of the terms printed

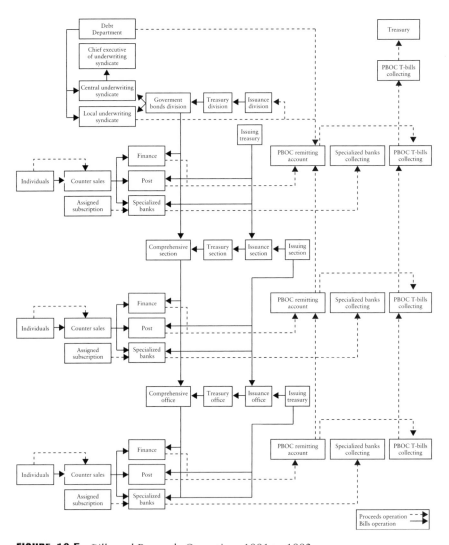

FIGURE 19.5 Bills and Proceeds Operation, 1991 to 1992

on both sides. In the United States, they are called registered bonds. In China, these paper securities are in bearer-bond form. The issuer does not keep a record on behalf of bondholders; therefore, its repayment is not claimable if the bonds get lost. China currently has two forms of registered bonds: savings bonds and book-entry bonds. If investors lose the certificate of savings bonds and the printed record for book-entry form securities, they

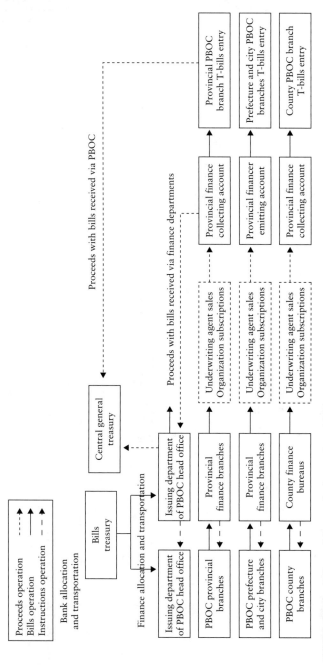

FIGURE 19.6 Bills and Proceeds Operation, 1993

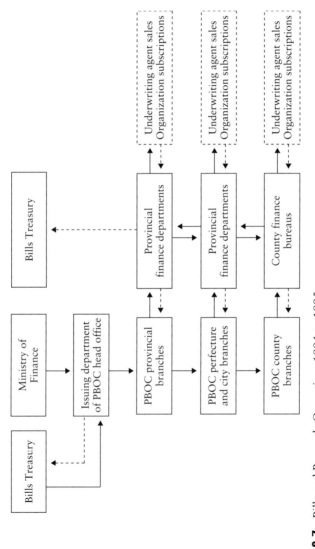

FIGURE 19.7 Bills and Proceeds Operation, 1994 to 1995

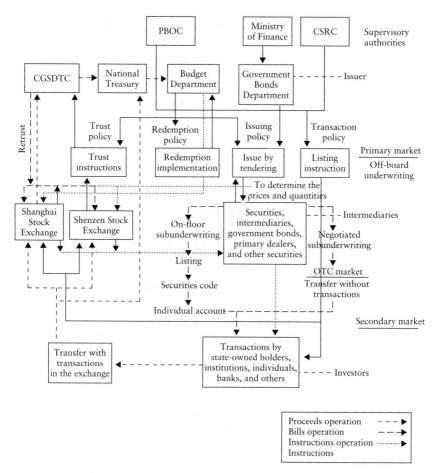

FIGURE 19.8 Bills and Proceeds Operation, 1995 to 1996

can still claim their right of payment because there is an electronic record of ownership. The principal amount of the bond is noted on the certificate, in addition to the name of the interest-paying agent or trustee.

Custodianship

The custodial business began in 1981 as a service provided by the government for the benefit of investors, to store and safeguard the paper securities since paper treasury bonds were inconvenient to carry and easy to lose. With the development of the repurchase (repo) business, security firms were first to take the initiative to establish custodial businesses. With the paper securities in their hands, they were able to conduct repo more efficiently. At the same time, some firms took advantage of the custody vouchers to sell treasury bills short to finance their money shortfall but in the name of government creditworthiness.[1] This illegal practice ruined the reputation of the of the T-bonds and affected the proper operation of the T-bond market.

As a result, in 1995, the Ministry of Finance devised a standard voucher for the custodianship of T-bonds in a bid mainly to facilitate the supervision and management of short selling in the bond market. According to the No. 4 Document in 1995, the standard voucher could be used only as evidence of custody of paper treasury bills already sold and could not be circulated or transferred in the secondary market; nor could it be resold, mortgaged, or repurchased. Using the custody voucher to sell puts or calls on the bonds was forbidden as well. Nevertheless, some institutions continued to use custody vouchers illegally to raise funds or to sell puts and calls. Therefore, the Ministry decided in 1997 to cancel all T-bond custodial businesses.

LAWS AND REGULATIONS GOVERNING CLEARANCE AND SETTLEMENT

Clearance and settlement is an integral part of the transaction process. They affect the whole process, from the verification and confirmation of the terms of the transaction to the completion of payment for and transfer of financial instruments.

"Clearing" means to confirm and examine the transaction conditions after the transaction is concluded; namely, the amount, time, purchaser, and so on. "Settlement" means the completion of the obligation on the part of either transaction party. In the bond market, for example, "clearing" means the buyer's payment of money and the transfer of financial instruments or, in legal term, the transfer of ownership of financial instruments to the buyer by the seller.

The transaction process varies greatly among different financial instruments, and clearing institutions are in place in many countries to deal with the specific issues related to clearance and settlement. In the United States, for example, there are many clearinghouses engaged in clearance and settlement; some specialize in certain kinds of financial instruments. In some countries (including the United States), many deposit and trust institutions focus on the custody of paper securities for the owners of stocks and bonds. They record the changes in the ownership of the stocks and bonds via book entry. In Europe, there are no special clearinghouses; instead, the related businesses are handled partly by the depository and trust institutions.

The methods of clearance and settlement of different countries vary greatly due to the economic, historical, and cultural factors.

LAWS AND REGULATIONS GOVERNING CLEARANCE AND SETTLEMENT

Risks Related to Clearance and Settlement

Two types of risk are generally associated with clearance and settlement in the financial markets:

1. *Market risk*, which occurs regardless of whether clearance and settlement were conducted in a timely manner
2. *Default risk*, which is directly related to the process

Default risk would occur when a party to a transaction does not execute the contract; it is, for example, the risk that the seller will not deliver the securities to the buyer although the buyer has paid for the securities or vice versa.

The basic function of clearance and settlement is to reduce the risks associated with securities transactions. The extent to which such risks can be managed is subject to market conditions. In the United States, the clearinghouses employ a series of systems to reduce the risks and protect investors; among them are supervision of the process of clearance and settlement and the implementation of the deposit system.

Custody and Settlement System

With modern technology, the custody and settlement of bond transactions could be conducted using the book-entry system, which rules out the possibility of the risk of theft or counterfeiting of paper bonds and eliminates the labor of physically counting the paper securities. It also eliminates the need for bondholders to clip coupons or submit the paper bills for redemption, thus reducing labor for both the investor and the issuer. This practice is widely used in most developed countries.

Usually the same system is used for custody and settlement. Bonds are delivered and money is transferred simultaneously. Most developed market economies have implemented or are in the process of implementing custody and settlement in paperless book-entry systems.

Securities Registration, Custody, and Settlement in the United States

The Department of the Treasury, the Fed, and the Federal International Institution have replaced most material treasury bills with a paperless bookkeeping system, which has greatly improved the safety of the federal treasury bonds. With custody and settlement institutions in place, the transfer and payment of the bonds has speeded up.

By the end of 1988, book-entry T-bonds amounted to US$1.8 million, or 98.7 percent of tradable treasury bonds. The bonds held by the trust institutions could be converted regardless of whether they were held on behalf of the institution or in trust for others.

There are four components of the U.S. custody and settlement system: (1) the Federal Reserve Bank's exchange system, (2) the U.S. Depository Trust Company, (3) the Treasury Direct Book-Entry System, and (4) the Clearinghouse for Inter-Bank Payments (CHIP). The treasury direct book-keeping system is used only for individuals who purchase T-bonds and do not participate in one of the systems. If individuals need to enter the transaction system, the commercial registration system is the only choice. The foreign exchange system is used only to connect the domestic and foreign systems. In fact, therefore, there are actually only two custody and settlement systems in the United States: the Fed's exchange system and the U.S. Depository Trust Company. The former is used to transfer the bonds issued by the federal government and its institutions, the latter for corporate and municipal bonds as well as stock, commercial paper, and the like.

Japan's Trust Institutions

The institutions performing the trust functions in Japan are mainly the securities companies. Their clients entrust their bonds to them, and they, in turn, deposit the bonds in trust to the Bank of Japan, which registers all the bonds in its trust according to the Article 2 of Ministerial Ordinance on the Unified Treasury Bonds Registration (see Figure 19.9).

Legally speaking, the bond trustee shares the common property rights with the bond holders. In 1971, the Tokyo Stock Exchange introduced the paperless bookkeeping system. The purpose at that time was to improve the efficiency of securities trust and transfer. Initially, trust measures were based on the previous Commerce Law. Because proper criteria were not established, the trust vouchers could be transferred with changes in owner-ship at the end of the accounting period. Later, the government trust system was continuously modified and supplemented. (The registration and trust system is illustrated in Figure 19.10.)

The Group of 30 (a private, nonprofit, international body composed of very senior representatives of the private and public sectors and academia) recognizes that every country should have an effective and developed central securities trust system and conduct proper organization and management, facilitating the participation of the relevant industries. In most countries,

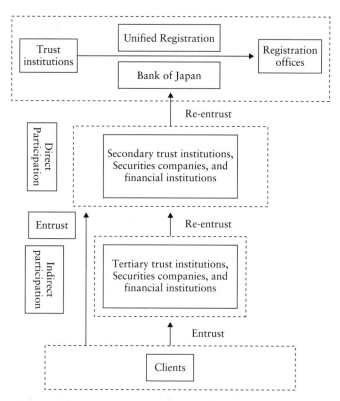

FIGURE 19.9 Trust Work Flow of Japan's Bonds

the capital market has developed the infrastructure necessary to support market transactions. At the core of this development is the establishment of a central securities trust system with defined clearance and delivery functions.

Clearance and Settlement in China Today

At present, the Shanghai Stock Exchange (SHSE) and Shenzhen Stock Exchange (SZSE) have their own central clearing companies.

Shanghai Securities Central Clearing and Registration Company The Shanghai Securities Central Clearing and Registration Company (SSCCRC) was established in 1993. Its clearance and settlement was initially handled at the counter; then an automated clearing system was put in place. The present mode of clearance and settlement is concentrated in the mainframe of the computerized transmission system of the SHSE.

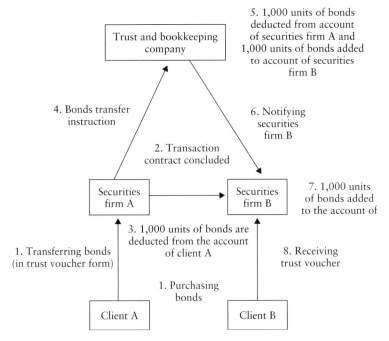

FIGURE 19.10 Registration and Trust System of Japan's Treasury Bonds

Shenzhen Securities Registration Company Limited Established in August 1993, the Shenzhen Securities Registration Company Limited (SSRCL) is not owned by but is affiliated with the stock exchange. After its establishment, clearance and settlement of securities shifted from the delivery of "a certificate per account" to standard delivery of "a certificate per board lot." At the end of 1991, concentrated stock custody was carried out in the Shenzhen securities exchange. Soon afterward, the securities central custodian and registration institution was established. Starting in June 1992, the SSRCL assisted the provinces, autonomous regions, and municipalities directly under the central government to establish local security registration institutions, which served as local depositories and money transfer agents. By 1994, there were over 60 such institutions. Toward the end of the 1990s, a central clearance and registration, the SSRCL, had been formed in SZSE systems.

China's Stock Exchange Executive Council Automated Quotation System The Securities Trading Automation Quotation system, or STAQ—the treasury bonds transfer and settlement center of China's Stock Exchange Executive Council (SEEC)—was established in 1991 on the base of SEEC's clearing department in order to accommodate the 1991 experiment of underwriting syndication to sell paperless T-bonds. The system went operational on July 1, 1991. SEEC operates and manages the new system. The settlement center operates on two levels. Registration and transfer operations are computerized, and clearance is handled in the standard manner; that is, the money is transferred at the specified delivery time and the securities are allocated and delivered according to the actual demand, through the communications devices and computer of the STAQ system. The settlement center has more than 310 members, including all STAQ members and dozens of institutions dealing in treasury bonds. The clearing members are from more than 20 provinces, autonomous regions, and municipalities directly under the central government and form a securities clearing network covering the whole country.

Settlement Center   The settlement center operates in accordance with its own "delivery and money transfer rules" and "business procedures." The basic operating mechanisms are discussed next.

Application and Open Account   Any financial institution approved by competent authorities to work on tradable securities can apply for membership in the settlement center; it does not have to be a member of STAQ. The applicant completes an account-opening card and submits its business certificate and a copy of the "Certificate of Engagement in a Financial Business" together with a signed and stamped application. The applicant shall undertake the obligations and agree to: (1) obey the clearing rules and business procedures and recognize the clearing rules and business procedures are part of the contracts between the applicant and the settlement center; (2) pay the fees and fines on behalf of its member to the settlement center according to the clearing rules and business procedures; and (3) accept the examination of the settlement center against its securities transaction account and accounting documents. The settlement center shall keep an account for the institution, open a money clearing account, and, finally, issue an "Account Opening Notice" to the applicant.

Delivery and Settlement   The settlement center works in a two-level system. Settlement among members is on the first level, and settlement between a member and its clients is on the second level. The member itself handles the second level of settlement, but it should be filed with the settlement center and subject to its examination and supervision. When there is plenty of money in the buyer's account and sufficient bonds in the seller's account on the delivery and settlement day, the settlement center will check the instructions from the two transaction parties, and, if there is no error in the instructions, the money will be transferred against the delivery of bonds. On the transaction termination day, the settlement center sends a confirmation letter via satellite communication to the members participating in the current day's transactions and concludes the transactions. The letter is kept as written evidence to prove that the settlement center has completed the transfer. Upon receipt of all such letters, and after it is verified that there are no mistakes in the letters, the members deal with the clearing work for their clients.

Delivery and settlement between the members is handled in two ways, "common delivery" and "promised delivery." "Common delivery" means that delivery and settlement are handled on the next business day after the transaction concluded; "promised delivery" means that delivery and settlement are handled on a mutually agreed day after the transaction concludes.

Account Management   On the transaction termination day, the balance of securities in the seller's account should be no less than the transaction volume of that day, and the balance of money in the buyer's account should be no less than that day's transaction amount.

Funds Management   Members should fax remittance vouchers to the settlement center after they remit the money to the settlement account. The settlement center transfers the money to the corresponding accounts.

Central Bond Custodial System   China Government Securities Depository Trust & Clearing Co., Ltd. was established on December 2, 1996, as a wholly state-owned and nonbank financial institution to serve the national bond market in the settlement, custody, transaction, and clearing, among other things, of treasury bonds, financial bonds, corporate bonds, and other fixed-income securities. It is the only institution authorized by the Ministry of Finance to manage the establishment and operation of the national T-bonds settlement and clearing system. It is also the bond settlement clearance and custodial institution assigned by the PBOC for the IBBM and the primary trustee designated by the PBOC for book-entry bond transactions at the counters of the commercial banks.

The operations of bond custody, registration, settlement, money transfer, and redemption works are described next.

Custody Account   The Administrative Rules of the Bond Custody and Opening Clearing Account classify custodian accounts in three ways:

1. Class A settlement member account—class A account. The accounts have these functions: custody of self-owned and entrusted bonds

(bonds put in custody on behalf of clients); transaction transfer of self-owned and entrusted bonds; nontransaction transfer of self-owned and entrusted bonds; principal and interest redemption of self-owned and entrusted bonds.

2. Class B settlement member account—class B account. Its functions are: custody of self-owned bonds; transaction transfer of self-owned bonds; non-transaction transfer of self-owned bonds; principal and interest redemption of self-owned bonds.

3. Indirect settlement member account—class C account. Functions: custody of self-owned bonds; transaction transfer of self-owned bonds; non-transaction transfer of self-owned bonds; principal and interest redemption of self-owned bonds.

The structure of the custody account system is shown in Figure 19.11.

The structure of class A account number (A/C No.) is shown in Figure 19.12.

Internal Structure and Content of a Custodial Account   Each custodial account indicates the type and purpose of the bonds in custody in the five account categories that follow. It reflects, through the sell-back sheet of the closed-end repurchase, the bonds to be sold back by the selling party in a closed-end repurchase through the sell-back sheet of the closed-end repurchase and reflects the initial transaction, maturity of the repurchase, and the custody amount. In cases of contract default, compensation is recorded in a client compensation account. Thus, the central final account and the client final accounts may be different in form, but the content is almost identical.

1. *Securities account.* The account in which the balance of bonds actually held by and available to the account holder, together with the information of transfer, is recorded.

2. *Payable account.* The transitional account in which the deducted but not-yet-transferred payment-on-sight bonds from the selling party is recorded.

3. *Repurchase account.* The account in which the bonds to be repurchased in a closed-end repurchasing transaction, and the information on the sale back, is recorded.

4. *Frozen account.* The account in which bonds frozen for special reasons are recorded; it also contains information on frozen bonds that are released for sale.

5. *Automated securities borrowing account.* The account in which bond information relating to automated mortgaged securities borrowing is recorded.

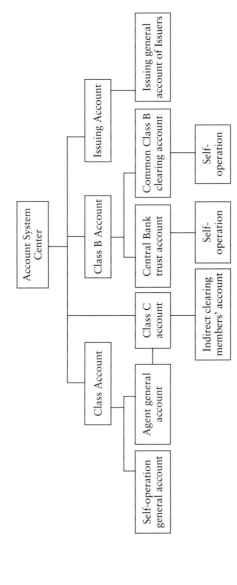

FIGURE 19.11 Structure of the Custody Account System

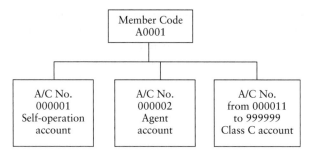

FIGURE 19.12   Structure of Class A Account Number

Bond Settlement   "Bond settlement" refers to the transfer of bond owner-ship or right pledged and the subsequent money transfer and delivery of bond securities from a bond transaction. In the IBBM, the settlement process starts with the transaction parties sending clearance custody instructions to the clearing agencies and ends with the delivery of the bond and money transfer. In some special cases, settlement may fail due to the default of one party.

Settlement is the key step in the bond transaction. The unified central bond custody mechanisms, sophisticated settlement system, and safe and efficient infrastructures supported by advanced technologies are critical to reducing the credit and liquidity risks in bond settlement.

The CGSDTC is an agency designated by the PBOC to handle bond registration, custody, and settlement, and it manages and operates the central bond bookkeeping system. The establishment of the central bond bookkeeping system ensures the quick completion of bond registration and custody, and property rights transfer, for the institutional participants within the specified time. The complete bond settlement operation, however, should be supported by the funds settlement operation. Therefore, the central bond bookkeeping system is linked to the national payment system in order to facilitate the future synchronization of bonds and money clearance, to improve efficiency, and to reduce risks to a minimum. The current money transfer of bond transactions is conducted by the clearing members themselves via banks.

The bond bookkeeping system of the CGSDTC can provide settlement services for many types of bond transactions, such as spot transactions, closed-end repurchase, open-end repurchase, pledges, and the like. The settlement services permitted at present are transaction clearing of interbank spot transactions and closed-end repurchase. A spot transaction is one in which the two parties exchange the ownership at the agreed price, namely, one-time buying and selling. A closed-end repurchase refers to a kind of short-term financing business in which the two parties use bonds as the pledged right. Thus, the borrowing party (or repurchasing party) pledges the bonds to the lending party (or reverse repurchasing party), and both parties agree that the repurchasing party will repay the other party on the agreed date the funds calculated on the basis of the agreed repurchase interest rate. Simultaneously, the reverse repurchasing party will return the pledged bonds.

Clearing Members All the financial institutions and other investors approved by the PBOC to participate in national inter-bank bond transactions could become clearing members of the CGSDTC after they open custody accounts in the CGSDTC. At present, the PBOC has designated three kinds of participants in the national IBBM: (1) commercial banks and their authorized branches with legal qualifications in China; (2) nonbank financial institutions and other institutions with legal qualifications in China; and (3) branches of foreign banks approved by the PBOC to run RMB businesses.

There are two types of clearing members: direct and indirect. Those who directly open bond custody accounts in the CGSDTC or directly delegate the CGSDTC to handle the bond clearing for them are direct clearing members; those who open class C custody accounts via the direct clearing members and delegate the direct clearing members to handle settlement operations for them are the indirect clearing members. The direct clearing members are divided into class A and class B members; those approved by the PBOC as qualified to run clearing member businesses as agents are class A members, and those who are not qualified to run clearing member businesses as agents are class B members.

Settlement Principles The principles governing the CGSDTC's handling of the settlement of bond transactions are real-time and full-amount settlement. The CGSDTCs control the accounts to ensure their confidentiality and that they are not overdrafted. "Real-time" means that transactions are settled instantly against the order of instructions (instead of being processed in batches or processed together at end of day). "Full-amount" means each transaction is handled separately and completely (rather than in parts due to insufficient bonds or money available). Full-amount settlement is different from net-amount settlement, which means that transactions of each participant are accumulated and cleared via net credit and debit.

Settlement Forms Different settlement forms are used in the process of transferring bond ownership or rights pledged and payment transfer. The settlement forms, which are designed by the central bond bookkeeping system, are free of payment, payment upon delivery, delivery upon payment, and delivery versus payment (DVP).

Work Flow of Bond Settlement Business In addition to the SZSE and the SHSE, in the second half of the 1990s, other exchange-based settlement and clearing systems were involved in the settlement of treasury bond transactions. They were Wuhan Transaction Center, Tianjin Securities Transaction Center, the STAQ system, the National Electronic Trading (NET) system, the IBBM, and others. During the late 1990s, both paper securities and paperless book-entry form securities were being used, and the relatively unified custody and national unified registration was established to accommodate transition period.

Problems in the Treasury Bond Custody and Settlement System and Prospects for the Unified Custody and Settlement System

Securities custody, settlement, and clearance are important parts of the modern securities market. In China, this infrastructure is not yet fully established. These issues need to be addressed:

- The custody and clearing centers remain segmented, and therefore the whole systems are separate. The policies, laws, and regulations are individually set and not yet unified. The bond clearance structure is characterized by the separation of bond and fund clearance, and is divided into three parts:
    - Bond clearance of the interbank market is handled at the CGSDTC. The final fund transfer is handled between the commercial banks and the PBOC.
    - Bond clearance of the stock exchanges is handled in the respective clearinghouses and finally concentrated in secondary accounts, and the money transfer is handled directly with the net balance.
    - Bond clearance of over-the-counter transactions in banks is handled in the respective banks, and the money transfer is handled between the PBOC and the commercial banks. No single custody, registration, and settlement system is complete. The custodial agencies of the exchanges set up their own systems, which do not connect to each other. Therefore, bonds cannot be traded across trading centers.
- The clearing company of the SZSE system is completely independent from the exchange, and the coordination between clearing company and the SZSE has not been optimum. This relationship is undoubtedly counterproductive to the development of a registration, custody, and settlement system. Shenzhen has two-level settlements: settlement between investors and securities firms and settlement between securities firms and clearing companies. The investors directly open

accounts in the securities companies. Investors can transfer bonds only within the corresponding companies without going through the clearing company.

- The SHSE exercises one-level settlement of registration; its custody and clearing mode facilitates easy coordination, simple procedures, and so on, but the volume of transactions in the central clearing center needs to be increased.

Clearing and settlement are important bond market infrastructure. Both have institutional and technological components. In China, only when institution-based markets have been put in place, can technology for bond clearing and settlement be applied. To further institutional development, the following steps are important:

1. *Establish a single settlement center or several national centers*. If the national unified settlement center were established, transactions would also be unified; if several centers are established, there will be separate markets and different prices. Clearly, the establishment of a national unified custody and settlement center would facilitate the formation and development of a unified national market.
2. *Establish a new separate national center or use clearing companies affiliated with the current exchanges to act as a national center*.
3. *Exercise two-level settlement*. This means there are a number of small clearing and settlement centers under the central clearing company. These small centers deal with small transactions. They can settle the net clearing among themselves through the central clearing company.

Need for Unified Nationwide Custody Centers

In my view, given the current institutional arrangement, it is advisable to have an exchange-based clearing system for trading in the exchanges and to have an over-the-counter clearing system for OTC transactions. The dual clearing system is consistent with the dual pattern of the bond market. The clearing function should cater to the specific needs generated by the different trading modes (i.e., the electronic transmission system in the exchanges, and the large number of telephone transactions between dealers and the many individual transactions in the OTC market). The transaction rules should be gradually unified among different trading centers. In addition, clearing and settlement member association shall be established to lay down a self-regulatory framework.

It is understandable that in the early stages of the development of China's treasury bond market, there was not much need for a national unified settlement and clearing system. As the national market grows, a national unified settlement center becomes necessary to facilitate supervision and increase liquidity. Considering China's immense size and far-flung institutions, as well as the current pattern of registration and custody system, a unified national central custody and settlement with a two-level system is recommended. There are a number of merits to establishing a unified national custody system in China:

- *It will help to change the current status quo of market separation and consolidate the national market.* It has been gradually realized that if national interexchange bond transactions are possible, unified securities custodians and unified custody vouchers are necessary. This unified custodian system would therefore pave the way for a unified, unsegmented national bond market.
- *It will help restrict and discourage short sales and other improper or illegal transactions.* A unified custody system would facilitate the examination and oversight of sales in a timely manner so that illegal short selling via custody vouchers cannot occur. In a consolidated system, custody information on the transaction parties in different marketplaces will be submitted to the mainframe of computerized electronic transmission system. Unified custody could help the authorities calculate the total bond securities in custody, which can provide information of the amount bond in custody so that any short selling through bond voucher can be supervised.
- *It will help reduce transaction costs and improve efficiency.* The transportation and delivery of large quantities of paper securities is costly and inefficient. Therefore, the larger the transaction volume, the heavier the burden and cost are on the transaction parties. Unification of custody will greatly reduce these transaction costs.
- *It will help to facilitate the establishment of the unified, safe, efficient and standard system of clearance and delivery.* Money transfer and security delivery are two aspects of the same transaction process. Computerized electronic transmission instead of the delivery of paper bonds helps payment and delivery to operate in synchronized manner. Thus, the transactions become more standardized, modernized, and, more important, internationalized, as in this way it is easier to connect with international system.
- *It will help to intensify the supervision and establish the regulatory framework of the treasury bond market.* Bond supervision is now under different authorities. With the consolidation of the settlement and custodian system, it would be easier to authorize one body to oversee the whole bond market.

Modes of Custody and Settlement   A well-functioning bookkeeping system of bond securities comprises two components: (1) a currency payment system and (2) a custody and clearing system. This system has to cover nationwide transactions and achieve an instant transfer of money between different regions and different accounts in the same city and instant delivery of treasury bonds between different regions and accounts. Such a system serves these important purposes: It establishes a speedy electronic transmission system connecting the whole country and sets up an accounting processing and book-entry system. It also creates a system of encryption for protection and an automated risk control system. At the same time, the money market payment system is required to ensure safe, fast, and reliable money transfers and payments.

China's current payment systems are the PBOC's national electronic interbank system and the cities' local paper clearance systems. The former is the special electronic interbank satellite transmission network supporting the PBOC's money market transactions. It connects the PBOC head office with primary and secondary branches in nearly 200 cities.

The local paper clearing system is operated manually and is not adapted to the centralized electronic transmission system in different regions. In addition, the paperwork is not up to the quality standards required by paperless electronic transmission.

To take advantage of technological progress and develop the bookkeeping system for paperless book entry securities, it is important to develop a computerized electronic transmission system for bond transactions. However, paper securities not maturing; they need to be dematerialized (become paperless) and demobilized (become frozen in where they are). Therefore, a custodian system is important. So far, the following suggestions have been made regarding the government custodian system:

- *Concentrated custody and multichannel transactions.* In this scenario, as a special agency under the Ministry of Finance or the PBOC, a treasury bond custody center would be established to record and manage the custody and transfer of T-bonds held in the names of the securities companies. Such an institution is similar to the U.S. Federal Reserve Bank or the national securities custody center of Japan's Ministry of Finance.

- *All the primary dealers could become members of the custody center.* In this scenario, members could open primary accounts whereas the securities companies could open secondary accounts. A dealer without a primary account could use the services of secondary accounts in the securities firms to carry out a transaction on behalf of customers. Upon bond issuance, the Ministry could receive the proceeds from the underwriters, and the securities would be delivered to the custody center for institutional investors or to the individual bondholders. If individual investors want to trade the bonds they hold, they could first deposit the bonds in a secondary custody account. The trading sites would clear transactions daily and send information on the net balance of the transactions to the T-bond custody center. The center would change the account balance according to the instructions sent by the trading site. When the account balance of a securities company is insufficient, the center would notify, in a timely fashion, the trading site or transaction center to treat the transaction as a short sale.

- *The instructions sent to the custody center by the trading sites would carry only the receivable net balance of the primary account dealers.* In this scenario, any market participants would assign a primary account dealer as its settlement agent. The primary account dealers only deliver the net receivable balance of bonds in custody at the custody center.
- *Dual system with national management and regional two-tier custody with paper and paperless bonds in circulation at the same time.* The laws and regulations governing the custody, safekeeping, and short sales should be promulgated as soon as possible. The plan for the establishment of a securities outlet system, computerized account management system, and storage data collection and distribution system should be made and executed upon approval. The elimination of paper bonds should be promoted, laying a foundation for opening up the domestic T-bond market.
- *Unified system with national concentrated custody and paperless book entry.* After the national registration, custody, and settlement institution for treasury bonds is established, all newly issued bonds could be placed in a central T-bond custody and settlement institution.

However, after much debate, only concentrated custody is recommended.

Concentrated Transactions and Concentrated Custody The current model, designed after the National Bond Custody and Settlement Company was established, envisaged concentrated transactions and concentrated custody. In this model, all T-bonds are held in the custody center, and all the related transactions are handled in the secondary account in the system.

To work in this model, all paper securities that still outstanding shall be replaced with paperless book-entry form securities. New issues shall all be in paperless form. Many countries have done this as they moved toward paperless book-entry form securities. Paper bonds should be taken out of circulation as they matured. New bonds should not be issued in paper form;

all new issues would be paperless throughout the country. The only paper bonds in the market would be not-yet-mature outstanding bonds.

Such a process goes hand in hand with the evolution of the T-bond market. In the 1990s, paper securities held by individuals accounted for the majority of outstanding bonds, and huge quantities existed in small- and midsize cities, townships, and even rural areas. Over-the-counter transactions once accounted for the majority of bond trading. Toward the end of the century, paper and paperless bonds were in circulation at the same time. Securities companies have issued large quantities of custody vouchers. However, nowadays, new issues of tradable government securities and CDB financial debentures are all in book-entry form. Only certificate savings bonds and some corporate bonds are still using paper securities.

In summary, the settlement, clearing, and custody are components of market infrastructure. The market infrastructure is essentially an institutional arrangement composed of four elements:

1. The institutional framework, such as the primary dealer system, institutional investors, and wholesale and retail market
2. The market structure, such as the primary market and secondary market
3. The regulatory structure, such as a unified regulatory system or a segmented regulatory system, as in China today
4. The operational system, such as selling, trading, and redemption operations

Settlement, clearing, and custody should be combined in a way to facilitate transactions that involve the entire process of selling, trading, and redeeming. However, they are not technology per se but rather institutional arrangements.

As indicated before, the existence of an active primary exchange and secondary exchange serves as a test of institutional progress. In the institutional economic engineering (IEEN) framework, the primary and secondary exchanges are achieved through social actions that are taken to save transaction costs, endogenous or exogenous. Technology, such as the book-entry form and computerized electronic transmission system, only helps to save transformation costs, which, in turn, would help to save exogenous transaction costs. Innovative ideas, however, help to save endogenous transaction costs of market participants. This is not to say that technological progress is not important. As a matter of fact, it is the other way around. As indicated in Chapter 1, when the efforts to save transaction costs are more difficult than those to save transformation costs, technological progress will drive social progress. When efforts to save transformation costs are more difficult than those to save transaction costs, institutional progress will drive social progress. It is noted, however, that institutional progress and technological progress are not mutually exclusive; rather they reinforce each other.

The practices in China provide fresh evidence of the relation of institutional and technological progress. China adopted up-to-date technology at an early stage of market development, due mainly to the slow institutional progress in early the 1980s. For example, China used paper shares in the stock market only for a few years and used paper bonds only for 15 years. Book-entry securities were introduced due to institutional progress, such as the development of the primary dealer system, the institutional investors' base, and improvement in selling techniques. Computer technology facilitates the use of book-entry securities and the electronic transmission system and therefore makes the modern settlement, clearing, and custody systems possible.

CHAPTER 20

Regulation and Deregulation Related to Bond Market Risk Management

Earlier, we described how important changes in the government's perception of debt and debt securities are to the development of the bond market. China gradually realized the importance of setting up a market for selling and trading securities. It also has come a long way in understanding the importance of debt management, which is a completely new issue for China.

In the 1980s, many countries had accumulated large amounts of debt, and government debt managers learned that the government's total liabilities were subject to the changes in the market as well as the outside financial environment; for example, debt may increase due to changes in the interest and exchange rates. As bonds stockpile, the greater the influence the market and financial environment exerts on the liabilities. Therefore, in recent years, many countries have attached great importance to the management of not only foreign assets and liabilities but also domestic government assets and liabilities.

The management of government debts is referred as "management of liabilities." It is a management system that adapts to the needs of government debt and risk management by utilizing the latest market techniques and instruments. Its purpose is to reduce the risk of the outstanding government debt. Since the assets and liabilities are closely related to each other, the government often combines the management of liabilities with the "management of assets"—not only domestic assets but foreign financial assets as well. With the increase of domestic assets such as cash and reserves, the government needs to consider how to manage foreign and domestic assets in an overall way. Management of government liabilities is important for four reasons:

1. To reduce the risk of government debt
2. To judge the government debt management policy and evaluate whether the policy is successful
3. To ensure that the terms or durations of liabilities match those of assets

To improve liability management techniques, the purpose and priorities of liabilities management should be clearly borne in mind, and the specific objectives should be defined. The objectives should be reflected by some indices, such as the definition of types of government liabilities and limitation of the risks of T-bonds. In addition, the standard structure benchmark of government debts should be established to measure the debt risks. New accounting systems must be employed to guarantee the effective evaluation of government assets and liabilities. Government debt managers should be able to convert the current debt structure into measurement and standard instruments to define debt management criteria.

OBJECTIVES OF LIABILITIES MANAGEMENT

The management of government liabilities must be conducted within a proper legal framework.

1. The authority of government debt managers must be defined.
   Related issues include: whether the government debt managers establish a relationship with one or several government departments; whether they oversee the management of all government debts, and whether they have the ability to manage all the assets and liabilities.
2. The relationship between government debt managers and the monetary authority must be delimited. The essence of this issue is whether the government managers are obliged to support the government's monetary policies.
3. The degree of responsibility has to be delineated. For example, the debt managers are authorized by the government or by the Congress to manage the risks of assets and liabilities and control the debt cost.
4. It must be specified if there is government and/or congressional authority over investors' credit ratings.

The management of government liability also must have clear-cut goals. Based on the experience of debt management around the world, there are two objectives of management of government liabilities:

1. *Reduce market risk.* The market is changing all the time. When interest rates are on the rise, the value of debt decreases. When interest rates move down, the value of debt increases. The change of debt value also depends on whether the debt liability is floating or fixed. For instance, when the interest rate goes up, the payments on floating-rate bonds would increase. The government must circumvent debt cost from increasing due to changes in the market and financial environment. The experience of the China Development Bank (CDB) is that when the yield curve is steep and the rate is not expected to go up as much as the market will, floating-rate liability is preferable. If the government is subsidizing interest in an inflationary environment, it has to take into account additional costs of the subsidy. This happened in China in the late 1980s and early 1990s. In addition, interest expenses increased due to early redemption (this occurred in 1994 from servicing the debt on nontradable savings bonds before maturity). In such circumstances, the government paid a 10 percent interest subsidy. For this reason, since the middle 1990s, the government has ruled out the possibility of giving such subsidies in inflationary environments.

2. *Reduce the risk arising from exchange rate fluctuations.* Exchange rate fluctuations often increase foreign debt denominated in domestic currency. On July 20, 2005, the government declared that China would shift from a fixed rate of exchange to a controlled floating rate pegged to a basket of currencies. This change will increase the amount of risk incurred because of exchange rate fluctuations. To manage that risk, China introduced a swap market and a foreign exchange futures market. However, for the market to operate, the debt manager has to set a benchmark, so that traders and liability managers can define their own goals and evaluate their liability management.

ASSETS AND LIABILITIES MANAGEMENT

In China's planned economy, assets and liabilities management (ALM) was utterly unnecessary. For example, bank interest rates were regulated. If the central bank moved the interest rate, it tended to move both the deposit rate and loan rate proportionally so that assets and liability were automatically matched. There was little foreign debt. Most managers knew little about what risk was and how to manage it. Only a few instruments were available to use for risk management. However, when the financial market was established, ALM becomes a very important instrument for banks' risk management.

ALM can help government debt managers to carry out overall risk management through hedges between both sides of balance sheet. As Lars Risbjerg and Anders Holmlund have said, "Assets and liabilities management (ALM) captures the idea that, as far as possible, the entire balance sheet (i.e., both assets and liabilities), should be included in the risk analysis so as to assess the overall risk exposure. This makes it possible in principle to limit the risk by matching the risk characteristics of respectively assets and liabilities. In the way, one side of the balance sheet hedges the other."[1]

Since 1970, technological progress facilitated market development. Deregulation was a hallmark of that period. As a result, the market became more volatile. Due to fierce competition, the financial institutions could no longer absorb deposits at a lower interest rate and provide loans at a higher rate to get wide spread and obtain desirable profits. Financial deregulation presents financial institutions with two types of challenges:

1. *The function of financial intermediaries has changed along with the change in borrowers' and investors' market behavior.* Deposits are no longer the only investment choice for investors, and loans are not the only source for borrowers. Both investors and borrowers want to enter the market directly. This changed financial environment requires financial intermediaries to help clients not only to enter the market but also to manage risk.

2. *The frequent fluctuations of interest rates and exchange rates greatly affect the capital value and profitability of the financial institutions.* Market participants are exposed to not only credit risks but also market risks. This change requires that risk management shift from the management of credit risk to management focused on market risk.

In reality, not all risk can be eliminated through the risk management. Therefore, the target of risk management is not to avoid all risks but to reduce risk as much as possible. However, risk can be transferred, diversified, and hedged. Although everyone wants to avoid risk, each person has a different perception of risk and a different preference for risks: risk neutral, risk averse, and risk loving. Risk is uncertainty, and therefore risk management is the work to access information and thereby reduce uncertainty. For example, due to information asymmetry, different market participants may face and undertake different risks. It is possible to exchange the assets of those who regard certain assets as risky with those who do not regard them as so risky. Considering the inverse relationship between risk and profit, some market participants are willing to take more risks in exchange for greater profits, while others prefer take less risk for less profit. Market participants may face different risks, or what is risky to one participant may not be to another; thus the same risk management measure may reduce the risk of both parties.

Financial institutions are risk takers by nature; they have to undertake risks that other market participants do not like to take. For example, individuals tend to be risk averse; therefore, someone shall take the risks so that the transaction can be carried out. However, professional institutional investors and financial intermediaries as market experts can use their profit to cover the risk. By and large, these institutions have set up sound risk management systems.

Portfolio managers tend to manage the risk by diversifying their asset mix. When the assets in the portfolio are less correlated to each other, risks can be more diversified. ALM is used to manage market risk as opposed to credit risk. The way to manage the risks is via hedge. The price of financial products can run toward the opposite direction against market movement. The hedge can be realized when negative correlated products are held in the same portfolio.

Earlier we indicated that exchanges can reduce transaction costs; one way to do so is to hedge. Risk can be reinterpreted as uncertainty due to information asymmetry. Therefore, the exchange of assets may lead to a win-win result because the asset seller has a different degree of uncertainty than the buyer of assets due to information asymmetry.

How to Manage Treasury Bond Risk

Financial intermediaries face three market risks: credit risk, interest rate and exchange rate risk, and operational risks. Interest rate risk has a common feature: the risk of one participant may be the potential profit of another; thus the exchange between the two participants may benefit both and help to reduce the risk of both parties.

There are three kinds of market participants: (1) the issuer borrowing money from the market; (2) the asset manager or investor buying bonds in the secondary market; and (3) the financial intermediaries operating between the issuer and investors. Each of them perceives and treats market risk differently.

The issuer and the investor see market risk differently. The issuer treats an increase in price as a risk, because the same funds could have been raised by issuing fewer bonds after the price increases. On the other side, fund managers or investors treat a decrease in market price as a risk, since they would rather buy bonds after the price had fallen. If the price rises, investors would take profit. Figure 20.1 illustrates the risks of different market participants.

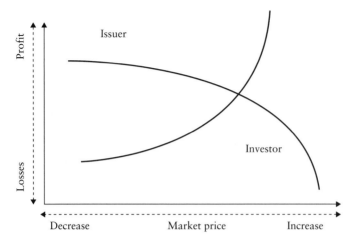

FIGURE 20.1   Risks of Different Market Participants

If the market is volatile, the risk manager may face potential market risks regardless of the market changing directions. As the market intermediary, market makers must take risks, but they can transfer, diversify, and hedge risks in its full capacity (i.e., intermediaries can sell or buy bonds instantly). If the market price decreases by a large margin, the intermediaries may buy more bonds, but, depending on the position of bond, the bonds they hold will also depreciate as a result of the drop in market price. If the market price rises by a large margin, the intermediaries may sell bonds, but their inventory of bonds will appreciate. These market activities are essentially a hedge strategy pursued by taking proper short and long positions. When the forward, futures, swaps, and option markets are developed and active, financial institutions can hedge their risks by taking opposite positions. Bond risk managers can also arrange their position, long or short, according to the bond price index. China Government Securities Depository Trust & Clearing Co., Ltd. (CGSDTC) published the first bond index in China in 2005, which provided conservative investors with a useful instrument. Most financial intermediaries prefer to take risk progressive strategy, such as take advantage of relative prices and the changing yield curve; these bond risk managers tend to use profit to cover the risk losses incurred. This practice is not advisable for individual investors.

However, in a underdeveloped securities market, it is difficult for participants to manage their risk when market instruments are not readily available or sufficient. In China, the financial market has developed gradually, and more market instruments have become available to risk managers. For example, the recently developed interest swap and currency swap market greatly facilitated market risk management. The fixed-floating swap helps the bondholder and risk manager to adjust their bond portfolio against interest movement. The People's Bank of China recently opened a currency swap market for the qualified risk manager market. Foreign currency bond-holders and risk managers also frequently use the offshore non-deliverable futures market.

The development of the derivatives market in China has been achieved through the recent financial deregulation, which makes the domestic regulatory framework more integrated with the rest of the world. This has far-reaching implications, especially on the eve of full implementation of World Trade Organization commitment.

Management of Liquidity Risk

Thus far, our discussion of risk has been based on the assumption that the instruments were available whenever needed. In fact, this is not always the case. If the financial market lacks liquidity and instruments, the need to manage risks cannot always be satisfied in a timely fashion.

With the development of the financial market and availability of more instruments, the interest risk, liquidity risk or market risk management can be carried out in more professional way and become more sophisticated. In recent years, many credit and debt vouchers, including mortgage vouchers, have been introduced into China's financial market. The current structure and market rules foster greater development of such instruments.

Credit Risk

Bonds are relatively safe instruments, especially government bonds, which are free from credit risk but not free from market risks. However, other bond securities—for example, corporate bonds—are subject credit risk. In the 1990s, the main problem for the corporate bond market was credit risk. There were many defaults. As a result, the National Development and Reform Commission resumed its case-by-case review of corporate bond issue applications. Credit ratings are important instruments through which investors can evaluate credit risk. However, the rating agencies in China have not yet established their reputations. Essentially, credit ratings are never an accurate science, but credit risk can be brought under control by appraisal of credit risk. Credit risk can be managed through sophisticated risk management tools. The main strategies are diversification, hedge, and transfer risks.

Economic cycles and the changing financial environment have important effects on the performance of bond securities. Inflation changes the real value of bond securities. Credit risks are subject to the type of contract, market conditions, and the credit status of the counterparty. If the contract is backed by strong legal force, credit risks are usually controllable. To encourage financial and nonfinancial institutions to manage risks and increase market liquidity, the government has reinforced its supervision of financial transactions. The establishment of the China Securities Regulatory Commission, the China Banking Regulatory Commission, and the China Insurance Regulatory Commission have strengthened the enforcement and supervision of financial activities under current legal framework. The improvement of the clearing and guaranty agreements also helps to reduce the credit risks.

In addition, a new regulatory framework needs to be established to cater to the changing financial environment and the trends of financial deregulation, so that, in IEEN's language, the constraints structure (reinforce regulation) can go hand in hand with the development of incentive structure (deregulation) and progress can be made insofar as financial institutional framework is concerned.

Legal and Institutional Risks

Legal and institutional risks are important parts of effective risk management. Financial intermediaries can control market risk, but they are not able to control legal and institutional risk. Therefore, some call such risks "taxes," because these risks are the price paid by market participants for the changing legal and regulatory environment. As China is in transition, bond risk managers will take such risk into consideration. Changes in tax policy and accounting policy also have a bearing on bond risk management. China's tax system and accounting system are becoming more integrated with the international one, so bond risk managers should be well aware of these possible changes.

Reducing Risks by Improving the Clearing and Settlement System

As mentioned, securities firms and investment banks are risk takers; international market practices and regulatory frameworks provide fresh experiences for successful debt management. Chapter 19 indicated that sophisticated delivery versus payment (DVP) for clearing and custody would greatly increase the safety of transactions. Recent suggestions to the Bank of International Settlement and the report of the Group of 30 on the settlement of the securities market pointed to solutions of problems related to the clearing and settlement of securities transactions. In China, the central bank could take the initiative in these endeavors. Technological progress in China made the book-entry form of securities and electronic transmission trading system possible. China's stock market experienced only a few years of paper stock trading. The system was replaced by the book-entry form in 1990. This newly established stock electronic transmission trading system provided a ready-made system for trading government bonds. Along with this process, institutions such as the custodial system and the clearance and settlement system were established. The creation of the CGSDTC, in particular, helped facilitate the smooth primary selling of jumbo-size bonds trading in the secondary market in China.

A perfect example of an institutional arrangement to hedge financial risk is the financial futures market, where participants can take a short position against market movement in any direction if they already hold a long position. By doing so, the risk can be hedged. Transaction cost can be hedged in the same way. Chapter 1 showed that the party who is in a better position to save transaction costs (e.g., the one that has lower information cost) has incentive to take the lead to reduce transaction costs, but the benefit engendered as a result transaction cost economizing and cost incurred for reduction of transaction cost (reducing transaction cost also incur cost) can be shared to achieve a win-win outcome. Alternatively, an institutional arrangement can also be made to offset the transaction cost if one party's information can be shared by its counterparty, which pays to be a party to the information. This is less costly to the counterparty than accessing the information on its own.

Regulation is important for risk management. However, this in no way means that deregulation is counterproductive to risk management. Quite the opposite. We believe that deregulation, if properly pursued, would facilitate the entry of more participants in the market and increase their access to available instruments, thereby enhancing their capability to manage risks.

Once again, in the institutional economic engineering framework, we stress that it is the interaction between the incentive structure, or deregulation, and the constraint structure, or regulation, that drives institutional progress related to the risk management. As indicated, institutions are made to save transaction costs. Risks and uncertainty are all typical transaction costs. Therefore, it is reasonable to suppose that risk management is an institutional arrangement.

PART SIX

The International Market

CHAPTER 21

Foreign Debt Issuance

Considerations Affecting Market Entry

China has incurred foreign debt several times since the Qing dynasty, usually during wartime. Between 1949 and 1979, China's policy was to rely on domestic financial resources rather than incur foreign debt. In 1968, the Chinese government announced that it was a country without debt, domestic or foreign. After reform, however, China resumed using foreign capital. In the 1980s, the foreign debts incurred in China were mainly World Bank and foreign government loans, referred to as multilateral and bilateral loans. Before 1987, China rarely tapped the international capital market. The Bank of China used to be the issuer, raising capital on behalf of the Chinese government.

Foreign debt through issuance of bonds in the international capital market is different from World Bank loans, foreign government loans, and foreign direct investment (FDI) in that bonds are standardized loans and tradable whereas loans are not tradable and therefore have no secondary market. However, international bonds are also different from domestic bonds because the secondary market is an international market and the primary market is a domestic market, and the two markets are under different jurisdictions. This special feature gives rise to a number of legal and market issues.

OBJECTIVES

The rationale for incurring foreign debt has been much debated, and it remains controversial because China has a surplus of savings. Since the late 1990s, it has been evident that China saves more and the United States consumes more. It therefore seemed absurd to suppose that China should

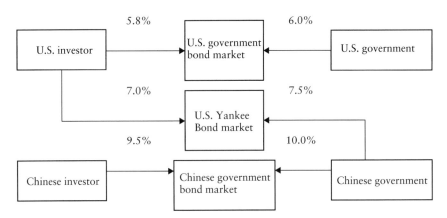

FIGURE 21.1   Rationale for International Funding

borrow from abroad. For this reason, many suggested that China should suspend international borrowing.

In addition, there is a commercial rationale for international funding (see Figure 21.1); that is, when domestic interest rates are high, the interest payment on foreign debt is low compared with domestic borrowing.

Thus, if there is a sufficient interest differential between China and the United States, it is always commercially advantageous to pursue international financing. However, when the interest rate in China is lower and close to U.S. rates, the advantage no longer exists and international borrowing is not justifiable.

However, there are objectives, beyond commercial advantages. These include long-term relationships in the international financial community for sovereign foreign debt issues. Sovereign issuers involved in international financing will help establish a long-term market position to secure long-term financing, set up a benchmark for other domestic issuers, expand the investor base, and obtain cost-efficient financing in the long run.

Long-term Market Position

Sovereign issuers are usually frequent-issuing entities. By establishing a long-term market status, foreign debt issuance not only familiarizes investors with the issuer but also helps market participants, including underwriters and other market participants, such as institutional investors, to understand the issuer's market performance. With an established long-term market position, issuers are able to have access to the market whenever necessary.

Market Benchmarks

The purpose of sovereign issuers *usually* is not only to raise funds but also to establish certain market benchmarks for other domestic issuers. With a well-established benchmark, other issuing entities in the country can price their transactions properly and reduce their financing costs accordingly. It just so happens that sometimes the government issues foreign bonds merely to establish a new benchmark.

Cost-Effective Funding

In most cases, issuers can save the funding cost by (1) reducing spread with the benchmark interest rates, choosing relatively low benchmark interest rates, and (2) reducing the issuing expenses as far as possible. A tight spread can be achieved mainly through boosting the issuer's credit rating, successful road shows, and appropriate marketing strategies.

Broad Investment Base

As a frequent issuer, the sovereign issuer should build up a broad investment base as well as a long-term cooperative relationship with investors. The continuous expansion of its investor base should be one of the sovereign issuer's offering objectives.

Like other issuers, a sovereign issuer should also consider its demand for currency, maturity, size, and so on. It is also important to consider other instruments (e.g., swaps) to hedge market risk, especially interest and currency-related risk and whether or not such instruments are available, which is often one of the criteria used to choose listing venues.

Unlike other issuers, a sovereign issuer should consider establishing benchmarks for other borrowers when defining the objectives of an international offering.

In addition to the sovereign issuer in China—the Ministry of Finance—there are two quasi-sovereign issuers: the China Development Bank (CDB) and the Export-Import (EX-IM) Bank. As a quasi-sovereign issuer that does not need to establish benchmarks for the country, the CDB and EX-IM Bank have three objectives in mind when contemplating an international funding program: (1) expanding their investor base, (2) raising funds at a relatively low cost, and (3) building up their own market position for the long term.

SOVEREIGN DEBT ISSUANCE IN THE INTERNATIONAL MARKET

Organizations of Sovereign Debt Issuance

The Ministry of Finance has raised capital in the international capital market on behalf of the Chinese government since 1987. It conducts the funding program, which is for financing the state budget deficit within a strict legal framework. The Ministry, based on the revenue-expenditure arrangement of the budget, shall define its financing requirement to make up the fiscal deficit and to repay the principal and interest on outstanding debts. Within the current legal framework, the Ministry submits its draft budget to the State Council for preliminary review. The National People's Congress approves the borrowing program along with the budget for both domestic currency and foreign exchange funding. The approved domestic funding serves as a guideline for the Government Debt Management Department (GDMD), under the Ministry of Finance, which works out its issuance plan. For foreign exchange funding, the Budget Management Department (BMD), also under the Ministry, will notify the GDMD of the amount to be borrowed. Next, the GDMD will work out a specific issuing plan and submit it to the State Council for approval. After obtaining this approval, the GDMD will execute the borrowing plan in its full capacity.

The CDB and the EX-IM Bank, as quasi-government issuers, have the quasi-sovereign issuer status as the Ministry of Finance. The international funding programs of the banks are based on their foreign exchange investment or loan plans. The legal procedures for the funding programs are complicated. Before submitting the plan for foreign debt issuance to the State Council for approval, the plan is submitted to and approved by the State Administration of Foreign Exchange (SAFE) and the National Development Reform Commission (NDRC). Moreover, the issuance amount of both banks is included in the foreign debt ceiling controlled by SAFE. After obtaining approval, both banks can execute foreign debt issues whenever they deem appropriate.

Legal Considerations

Sovereign Immunity   Sovereign immunity is the precondition for a sovereign foreign debt issuance. According to international law or convention, sovereign issuers waive their right of immunity when involved in commercial activities. In the first Deutsche Mark debt offering in 1987, with the prior consent of the Department of Treaty and Law of the Ministry of Foreign

Affairs, the Chinese government expressly waived its sovereign immunity. This statement was reflected in the prospectus for that transaction.

In the recent years, under the guaranty of the World Bank and the Asian Development Bank (ADB), the Chinese government has signed several joint financing agreements with foreign financial institutions. Due to the special status of the contracting parties (i.e., one party is a nation while the other party is a legal entity), the agreements can be categorized neither as state/governmental treaties nor as treaties between the state and international organizations. Furthermore, the Law of the People's Republic of China on the Procedures for Concluding of Treaties does not specify a definition for agreements of this category. Hence, it is important to define the treaty-conclusion procedures and certain major terms to avoid inconsistencies with relevant Chinese regulations or policies.

In principle, a sovereign state enjoys judicial immunity and is not subject to any foreign jurisdiction. However, by convention in the international financial market, most countries have stated that they would like to wave sovereign immunity and conditionally subject to foreign jurisdiction or foreign law governance when they are involved in commercial activities in the name of a nation or a government. However, practices varied widely in the early 1990s. For example, some financing agreements signed by the Chinese government expressly provided for a conditional waiver of sovereign immunity, which could have direct legal binding. As a consequence, should a dispute arise from such an agreement, China's state-owned properties or assets in other countries could be withheld or confiscated, which is unacceptable to China. In order to protect China's interests and more effectively manage financing agreements, these principles in addition to the relevant domestic laws and practices and international practice should be considered. As China becomes more integrated with the international financial market, it gradually is adapting international conventions.

Negative Pledge Clause   A loan agreement often contains a clause that constrains the borrower under certain circumstances. For example, if the principal and interest are not paid, the borrower shall not be allowed to take part in certain economic activities without the prior consent of the lender. Such clauses are called negative pledge clauses or non-commitment clauses. The purpose of such clauses is to ensure that the status of the lender is not damaged by changes in the borrower's business or by changes in the business of the borrower's subsidiaries (or affiliated units). The negative pledge clause forbids or restricts the borrower from engaging in mortgage-backed securities with its assets or earnings as collateral. The purpose is to prevent a mortgager from having priority over other creditors.

State-owned assets covered by negative pledge clauses in legal documents include fiscal revenue, foreign exchange reserves, state-owned enterprises (SOEs), mines, roads, land, and the like.

The concept of state-owned assets is defined in a broad sense in most countries. This is appropriate for countries with a large proportion of state-owned assets. However, for socialist countries where state-owned assets usually account for a relatively larger proportion of assets, a broad-based definition may cause many legal problems. At present, Russia's definition of state-owned asset is relatively narrow, covering only fiscal revenue and foreign exchange reserves.

The negative pledge clauses used by China's Ministry of Finance once covered a wide range of assets (e.g., the guaranty of assets covered in the legal documents relating to 1987's bond issuance). However, in 1994's global bond issuance, the Ministry's legal counsel began to narrow the assets covered, and they were further narrowed in the 1994 Deutsche Mark bond issuance. This means that a legal document of other government debt shall not carry terms equivalent to "including all assets." That is, the range of assets specified in other legal documents should not go beyond this narrow definition. By abstaining from unnecessary legal disputes, this redefinition is conducive to China's international borrowings in the future. China's current negative pledge clauses under World Bank loans cover all the state-owned assets, which is consistent with the legal clauses of World Bank loans provided to any other country.

Cross-Default   On July 1, 1997, the legal counsel of the Ministry of Finance provided a memo concerning cross-default facilities in which they recommended that due to the inflation in the economy since 1994, the total cross-default facility should be increased from US$25 million to US$30 million. In addition, in consideration of future inflation as well as the convenience of future debt financing, it might be appropriate to further increase the cross-default facility to US$35 million.

In April 1998, the CDB agreed to include these default conditions in its bond issuance documents: (1) if the stake held by the state is no more than 51 percent, or (2) if the central bank canceled liquidity support as specified by the No. 22 document of the State Council.

Legal Status of a Sovereign Issuer   According to U.S. laws, an issuer for 144A registration should satisfy three requirements:

1. It is completely funded by the government.
2. It can reflect the government functions.
3. It has obtained support from the government.

In addition to the Ministry, the policy banks of China also enjoy the status of sovereign issuers.

Use of Proceeds The proceeds of foreign debt issuance by the Ministry are to repay mature foreign obligations or to make up fiscal deficits. The proceeds of CDB issues in international capital market mainly are used for policy-related construction projects and refinancing.

PREPARATION OF GOVERNMENT BOND ISSUANCE IN THE INTERNATIONAL MARKET

The international debt market has long been dominated by some major markets. From the perspective of the investor, the bond markets can be grouped into the domestic market and offshore market. The offshore market is based on the domestic market but it is for foreign investors; the offshore market consists of such markets as the global bond market,[1] the Yankee bond market, the Euro dollar market and Euro market, the Dragon bond market (actually belonging to the European bond market), the Samurai bond market, the Maple bond market, Kangaroo bond market, and the Eurasian bond market. There have been some changes to these markets in recent years; for example, the Samurai bond market has declined and the Euro bond market has emerged.

Public Offering Market

Although each market has its dominant currency and different interest rate levels, theoretically, the offering cost should be the same due to existence of the swap market. However, whether the same funding cost can be achieved depends on whether the swap market is sufficiently liquid. For instance, in the Samurai bond market, a 20-year Japanese yen bond can be issued with a low cost; however, if the issuer wishes to receive the proceeds in U.S. dollars, it may have a higher-than-market funding cost because the yen/dollar swap market is illiquid. The advantage of a global bond market is the broad investor base. When the issuance amount is less than US$500 million (insufficient to maintain market liquidity), it is not recommended to launch in global bond market. The advantage of Yankee bonds is the comparatively long term and flexibility in issuing amount. However, less than US$500 million is not recommended either for liquidity reasons.

To understand the offering costs in different markets, it is important to compare the interest spread that borrowers have to pay among different currencies. Bond pricing is based on the yield of treasury bonds of the home country. The issuing yield is the treasury yield plus spread. To make the comparisons, first convert the fixed foreign exchange, or Forex, interest rate to a floating interest rate. This can be achieved using the swap rate between the fixed and floating rates. The interest spread added to the government bond basis less the swap interest rate represents the interest spread of the currency's floating interest rate. A basis interest spread can be set between one country's floating rate and another country's floating rate using the cost basis of currency swaps. Next, another currency's interest spread can be derived by swapping the floating interest rate into the fixed interest rate. This is another currency's ratio margin. If it deviates from the real price, arbitrage opportunities emerge.

The issuing fee for global bonds is comparatively low relative to Yankee bonds, which are as high as 0.875 percent.

Features of U.S. Private Placement Bond Market

As one of the leading private placement markets in the world, the U.S. private placement bond market is the market of choice for many sovereign issuers due to its large size. In 2004, the volume had reached US$515.5 billion. Approximately 100 U.S. institutional investors act as lenders for private placement offerings. The demand for each transaction is from US$5 million to US$150 million. Insurance companies are the major private placement investors, accounting for 85 percent of the total demand, while the federal social security fund takes a share of 5 percent. Private placement bond spread usually depends on internal credit analysis rather than external credit ratings. For the private placement offering, the major investors are the "buy-and-hold" institutional investors who pay more attention to the coupon return rather than the relative price. Issuers can benefit from simple legal procedures, lower information disclosure requirements, and stable prices.

Bond Selection

Fixed-Rate versus Floating-Rate Bonds   Fixed-rate bonds are usually designed for establishing benchmarks as they can better reflect the real interest rate and the credit spread. Fixed-rate bonds are usually issued when the market interest rate is low in order to lock in the interest rate risk. Therefore, sovereign issuers can establish issuance benchmarks by issuing fixed-rate bonds, which helps non-sovereign issuers establish their pricing base.

The U.S. market is focused on fixed-rate bonds while the floating-rate bond is dominant in the European and Asian markets. Since the U.S. capital market leads the international capital market, most issuers currently choose to issue fixed-rate bonds.

From the perspective of issuers, floating-rate bonds can be issued when the market interest rate is relatively high so that the issuer can benefit the declining interest payment in the future. The investor base for floating-rate bonds is different from that of fixed-rate bonds. The former are mainly banks while the latter are mainly institutional investors. In addition, banks pay more attention to the convenience in exchange of different currencies, while institutional investors pay much more attention to credit spreads. Therefore, floating-rate bonds issuance helps the issuer control credit spreads.

Plain Vanilla versus Structured Bonds   The term "plain vanilla bond" refers to the simplest and most basic type of bond whose interest is paid annually and principal is paid upon maturity. Structured bonds have additional conditions, such as additional repayment options (e.g., at the investors' or issuers' option) and additional currency options (e.g., dual currency bonds).

Plain vanilla bonds can be used to establish benchmarks; however, structured bonds are better for special purposes and controlling cost, but usually carry more risks than plain vanilla bonds.

Midterm Notes   Midterm notes (MTNs) are bond instruments that are continuously issued under predefined conditions and during a given period of time. A legal document could be prepared and used thereafter when issuing MTNs. If issuers prefer to have more flexibility, MTNs can be a good choice.

From the perspective of Chinese issuers, the funding objective should be taken into account. It is recommended that the Ministry of Finance, as a sovereign issuer, issue more plain vanilla bonds with fixed interest rates so that it can provide a benchmark for other China-related issuers. Other issuers, such as the CDB and EX-IM Bank, are advised to stay flexible to choose the type of bonds to cater to their customers' actual requirements (i.e., their customers' fund use duration, interest rates and currency preferences, etc.) in given market conditions.

SELECTING LEAD UNDERWRITERS AND LEGAL COUNSEL

Appointment of Lead Underwriters

Nowadays, issuers do not need to organize funding in person; instead, they give the mandate to underwriters. Therefore, the selection of qualified underwriters, especially the lead manager, is crucial to a successful transaction. A lead underwriter, or a lead manager, is appointed based on three criteria:

1. *Market position.* The ranking can clearly demonstrate an underwriter's market strength. Every year, the *International Financing Review(IFR)* publishes each underwriter's market position and rankings, which can be used as a reference in selecting underwriters.
2. *Commitments to the issuer.* A long-term cooperative relationship with the issuer can reflect the underwriter's commitment to the issuer.
3. *Marketing strategies.* To ensure the success of the offering, it is critical to know if the underwriter has developed effective and efficient marketing strategies.

Fee and Commission Proposal   How much commission fee the underwriter asks the issuer to pay, usually reflected in the fee proposal underwriter submit to the issuer, is a factor in choosing a lead manager. Underwriters sometimes prefer accept lower commission fees to get a mandate to participate in the transaction. However, fee requirement does not necessarily reflect an underwriter's market strength; the fee proposal often misleads issuers, as funding cost can be saved mainly by market strategy and pursuance a successful strategy relay on a lead underwriter's real strength in the market. Sometimes investment banks prefer to bid commissions or fees so that they can compete with other underwriters and win the mandate. Due to unfair competition, the proposed fee may not reflect the manager's true cost or the conventional commission ratio. A good underwriter may help make a transaction a success mainly through its marketing strategies and distribution capabilities. Therefore, it is recommended that the issuer does not select the lead manager based on the fee and commission proposal.

Ranking   The annual ranking, or league table, by the *IFR* can serve as a credible reference for selecting a lead underwriter. The issuer should pay attention to the underwriter's overall market position as well as its strength in the market selected by the issuer.

Marketing Strategies   Insofar as market strategy is concerned, four major factors should be considered in selecting a lead manager:

1. *Distribution capabilities.* A lead underwriter with strong distribution capabilities can help sell the bonds to the end investors, which is crucial to the success of an issuance, especially in a volatile market environment.
2. *Credibility and coverage of credit research.* In-depth research should be carried out in order to fully understand the issuer's credit conditions and effectively communicate with investors. A well-prepared credit research report on the issuer's real strength would give investors more up-to-date information and strengthen their confidence that the transaction could turn out to be better than its actual rating might indicate.

3. *Ability to stabilize the secondary market.* An underwriter's ability to stabilize in the secondary market is an important criterion. A stable secondary market protects investors and thus helps build their confidence in the issuer over the long term.
4. *Leadership ability.* A strong and capable lead manager will be able to bring every member of the syndicate into full play and make the issuance a success. Such leadership can be judged by the syndicate's position, reputation, and integrity in the market.

Derivative Capabilities Sometimes the proceeds of bonds are not issued in the required currency; swap transactions can help transfer the proceeds to the needed currency. In China, most of the projects are in U.S. dollars. If the issuer wants to take advantage of investor perception or receptiveness of the transaction in markets, such as the Samurai or Euro market, it has to swap the Japanese yen and euros into U.S. dollars. In addition to the currency swap, the issuer may wish to conduct an interest rate swap. For example, depending on market conditions, the issuer may want to swap floating-rate for fixed-rate bonds, or vice versa. If immediate swaps are needed, then the lead underwriter's ability to swap them at a relatively low cost must be considered.

Mandate Notice Usually the issuers, such as the Ministry of Finance, the CDB, and the EX-IM Bank, are in a position to give the mandate (it may be a formal written notice or an oral notice) to the investment banks and assign them as lead manager or underwriter, but only after the formal approval of relevant regulatory bodies can the issuers forward the mandate to selected lead managers and underwriters. In principle, the issuer selects a group of underwriters and from them assigns one lead manager. The lead manager sets a timetable for the transaction and convenes underwriter meetings, with representatives from issuer side present also, to discuss matters related to the upcoming transaction.

Appointment of Lawyers, Lead Trustee, and Law Firms

The issuer's underwriters may select lawyers to act as the legal counsel on their behalf. From the issuer's point view, the law firm selected should have extensive experience and a good reputation in the capital market. The law firm should also understand investors and market. It will help both issuer and investors to understand their rights and obligations so that the transaction can be performed within a proper legal framework or based on market conventions without incurring any legal proceedings or violating market conventions, which are both counterproductive to the issuer's long-term funding program. The law firm should be also familiar with the applicable laws in the local market, which will help it address relevant legal issues about market entry, in particular registration and issuance. In addition, it should have experience as an issuer's legal counsel.

It is advisable not to change lawyers frequently to ensure continuity and efficiency in drafting the legal documents.

In addition to the lawyers, the trustee and payment agents are also part of legal arrangement. A lead trustee applies only to the Samurai bond market, and is equivalent to the financial agent in the Yankee bond market. More often than not, two primary banks act as payment agents: JP Morgan Chase and Citigroup. Both, in turn, serve as payment agents for most of China's foreign debt offerings.

The number of lead underwriters relates to the size of the transaction and the target market.

Usually a transaction has one lead underwriter who, by and large, also "runs the book." This arrangement ensures that the lead manager will exert its best efforts in the offering process and save transaction costs. See

TABLE 21.1 Lead Underwriter Structure in Yankee Sovereign Debt Market, 1980 to 2005 YTD

No. of Lead Underwriters	No. of Bonds Issued	Total Volume (US$million)
1	113	32895.338
2	7	1485.00
2+	0	0
Total	120	34380.338

TABLE 21.2 Lead Underwriter Structure in Global Sovereign US$ Debt Market, 1980 to 2005 YTD

No. of Lead Underwriters	No. of Issued Bonds	Total volume (US$million)
1	53	18088.00
2	33	47562.67
3	6	6750.00
3+	0	0
Total	93	72400.67

Tables 21.1 and 21.2. For very large transactions, the joint lead manager and joint book runner format are used. Usually, for a jumbo transaction—US$2 billion, for example—a hierarchical structure consisting of managers and co-managers is used. However, rarely should there be more than three lead managers or/and book runners for any issue, because it has been proven that using several lead underwriters for one transaction leads to lack of accountability and buck passing.

LEGAL ISSUES AND PROCEDURES FOR MARKET ENTRY

U.S. Yankee Bond Issuance

There are various types of registration at the Securities and Exchange Commission (SEC), and foreign debt offerings registered with the SEC can be categorized as:

- Schedule A and Schedule B SEC registration procedure
- Rule 144A
- Private placement

Shelf Registration and One-Time Registration

Shelf registration allows the issuer to file one registration statement covering several issues of the same security; one-time registration allows the issuer to file one registration statement for a single issue. Shelf registration has five advantages:

1. It enables qualified issuers to quickly enter into Yankee bond market.
2. It enables the issuer to regularly register with the SEC. For one year following registration (which includes filing an annual report), the issuer can have direct access to Yankee bond market.
3. Regular reporting updates the latest information.
4. Once approved, shelf registration allows the issuer to execute an offering simply by taking out the tranches rather than waiting for the SEC's consent.
5. It only takes one day to take the required volume off the shelf.

In short, shelf registration has great flexibility. For this reason, it is used by frequent-issuing entities. Due to registration fees, infrequent issuers usually adopt one-time registration.

Information Disclosure

The requirement for disclosure is meant to protect the investors. All material information and some facts that are not as material must be disclosed. Usually SEC disclosure requirements are much broader than those of the European bond market. Table 21.3 is a comparison of disclosure requirements between SEC-registered and Rule 144A bonds.

Issuer's Obligation

The issuer's in-charge officer and the underwriter can be held liable for untruthful information relating to a material fact or material omissions in the legal documents.

Due Diligence

Due diligence is required in order to minimize the possibility of untrue statements or omissions and to reduce the underwriter's due diligence responsibility. Due diligence includes business and legal issues. In terms of scope, Yankee bond offerings require more due diligence than European offerings. Senior officials from relevant governmental agencies are required to conduct a due diligence defense. Legal due diligence should be carried

TABLE 21.3 Comparison of Disclosure Requirements between SEC-Registered and Rule 144A Bonds

	SEC Registration	144A
U.S. GAAP	Net income and equity shall be prepared in compliance with U.S. GAAP.	Compliance with U.S. GAAP not required, but the difference between U.S. GAAP and domestic GAAP requirements must be detailed.
Information disclosure	Ambiguous terms and all material information must be explained.	Only material information is required, although the range of the disclosure requirement is similar to that for bond registration with the SEC.
Regular reporting	Range of information disclosed in the annual report is similar to that required by offering.	Very limited regular reporting is required; the disclosure requirement in the issuer's home country is sufficient.

out at the same time. Usually the issuer's legal counsel participates in the due diligence process. The issuer should also assign an internal liaison organization (internal legal counsel or treasury department) specially mandated to address the legal issues.

Reporting Requirement

SEC-registered offerings are required to submit annual reports (six months after the end of each year). The information required for the annual report is identical to the information disclosure required upon debt issuance.

Publicity

U.S. laws restrict the issuer and underwriter from publicizing the issuance in the United States. At the kickoff meeting, the issuer's legal counsel shall clarify this issue to the relevant parties.

ROAD SHOW: DISSEMINATING INFORMATION ABOUT THE ISSUANCE

There are two ways to conduct road shows in an international issue: press conferences and one-on-one meetings with investors.

Types of Road Shows

Various investors as well as underwriters and media will attend a press conference for a new issue. Targeted at the wider investor community, those with influence, and for publicity effect, the press conference provides general information and usually includes an announcement by the issuer's representative of the offering intent and a brief on the basic conditions of the national economy. In the case of a Ministry of Finance issue, information about budget execution is also included. Policy banks should also provide information about their own business performance as well as their relationship with the government, and so on.

One-on-one meetings are often arranged to attract large potential investments. Such investors usually have some understanding of the issuer but may request more information at the meeting. At the same time, the meeting gives issuers the opportunity to introduce the more specific information. One-on-one meetings can generate better results than general press conferences.

Timing of the Road Show

The road show usually takes place one week prior to the issuance, so that the information presented via the road show can be directly reflected in the issuing price. If the price is not fixed soon after the road show, investors may believe the issue has either been postponed or cancelled.

OFFERING STRATEGIES

An offering strategy can either be cost-oriented or market position–oriented. Simply to maintain their market position, frequent issuers sometimes issue bonds even when they do not have a funding requirement to do so. However, for a sovereign issuer, the ultimate purpose is to establish a benchmark for the market. However, the CDB, as a commercial entity, should adopt the market position–oriented strategy. The CDB should be more flexible in selecting the marketplace and market instruments; for example, it should tap more diversified marketplaces in order to broaden its investor base; select callable bonds to take advantage of falling interest rates; or select putable bonds to give investors the option of early repayment should market interest go down.

Several factors are deemed important to ensure a successful issuance. Defining a sound target for the offer—for instance, selecting the target market and the target investor—is of paramount importance. Based on the target, a timetable of execution and working procedures are necessary to ensure a orderly and timely execution of the offer. As issuer does not present in person and directly face investors in most cases. Selecting a top-notch underwriter in the syndicate would greatly help marketing and leading a successful transaction. In the changing market environment, issuer must make sound judgments about the market's movement and take full advantage of optimal market windows.

Highlights of Successful Offering Strategies

Successful issuing strategies are based on market judgment and timing. Market research is the key to grabbing the best market windows. Seven steps are very important:

1. *Go through domestic legal procedures as quickly and as thoroughly as possible.* Then registration and documentation shall be kicked off, and market strategy shall be decided as soon as possible.

2. *Maintain flexibility and elasticity in timing the offering.* The timing of an international offering depends on the changes in the capital market and changes in the credit and interest spread markets. Given the right opportunities, these two factors can be locked up by market instruments.

3. *Structure the syndicate.* The optimal time for forming the syndicate is after the start of the road show, so that if there are changes in the market and/or the bond requirement, proper adjustments can be made.

4. *Conduct credit research and analysis.* Credit research and analysis aims at positioning the issuer in the credit market or the interest-spread market, thereby building a solid foundation for achieving the objectives and successful pricing.

5. *Analyze relative value.* It is crucial to compare the issue to those of the issuer's peers to gain an understanding of investors' preferences and position the issue in the market.

6. *Determine pre-deal strategies.* These strategies prepare the issuer for the transaction. The major objective is to understand investors' perception of the issuer in order to address their concerns.

7. *Maintain confidentiality.* Effective confidentiality is a necessary condition to a successful issuance. In addition, according to applicable U.S. laws, it is illegal to solicit investors before the registration's effective date.

The goal of market strategy is to achieve a win-win outcome among the issuer, underwriters, and investors. The efforts that the issuer made in collaboration with underwriters in information disclosure through documentation, rating, and the road show help reduce investor uncertainty that results from information asymmetry. Therefore, the issuer's goal is to reduce transaction costs and share the benefits.

Some international offerings by sovereign issuers or quasi-sovereign issuers in the international capital market have failed. The principal lesson to be learned from these failures is that inexperienced issuers tend to antagonize underwriters and investors by putting pressure on the underwriters to reduce the interest to below market levels. This is because they initially perceive the issuer-investor relationship as a win-lose relationship instead of a win-win relationship.

Role of the Underwriters

The underwriters essentially share the same goal as the issuers. In the jargon of investment bankers, "they are in the same boat" as soon as the syndication agreement is concluded. For example, underwriters attach great importance to their reputation in the market; therefore, their first objective is to conduct a successful transaction. The underwriters' four obligations to issuers are to:

1. Recommend offering strategies in line with the issuer's offering objectives and market conditions.
2. Report the progress of the offering and the market conditions on a timely basis.
3. Facilitate the issuer's participation in the decision-making process.
4. Help reduce transaction costs.

However, there are several considerations from the underwriter's point of view. For example, underwriters do not like to see dramatic unfavorable market changes due to economic shocks or monetary moves soon after the transaction is launched. Under such circumstances, they may suffer losses resulting from difficulty in placing the issue. However, there should be always a way whereby issuer and underwriters can achieve a win-win outcome—that is, for the issuer to achieve successful funding without incurring additional cost and risk to the underwriters.

Flexible Marketing Strategies

Due to the changing market environment, issuers should maintain sufficient flexibility in the secondary market, so that they can extend the schedule for the road show if necessary, make additional efforts to solicit important investors, and determine the demand and price range and the size of the "pot" (the methods the lead underwriter uses to control the allocation) based on distribution conditions. In addition, issuers can monitor the movement of the benchmark government bonds, pay close attention to other issuers' timetables, and leverage the issue based on the optimal market window based on the market trends. It is sometimes advisable to test the market with a comparatively small-scale offering and consider increasing the offer size with an oversubscription outcome.

EXECUTING MARKET STRATEGIES

Premarketing

Premarketing is the preparation for entering the market. It is intended to attract investors to the proposed offering by addressing their concerns.

The nondeal road show and the lead manager's sale conference are the major part of the premarketing efforts. Premarketing is even more important if the issuer is unfamiliar to investors.

Book-building

In the Yankee market, the special underwriting form—the pot—is used to control allocations. However, in the global bond market, the pot is used only in rare cases, such as a volatile market. The main purpose of the book-building process is to facilitate bond distribution. With the pot mechanism, the underwriter takes only limited responsibility, and the completion of the sale of the lead manager's own shares is sufficient. Without the pot, underwriters have to meet their own clients' demand by themselves.

In order to control the distribution process, the lead manager sometimes controls the absolute majority of shares. By doing this the lead manager takes more responsibility in a volatile market, which helps ensure a successful issuance. The disadvantage, however, is that other institutions may have little incentive to support the deal.

When market conditions are unfavorable, the lead manager's allocation will account for approximately 90 percent of the total volume. On one hand, this method enables the lead manager to effectively control the issuance and the secondary market performance; on the other, this may negatively affect other members' incentives.

Allocation Formula

The allocation is important to ensure a proper distribution to the investors and secure a stable secondary market. The considerations and allocation formulas.

To ensure balance between the primary and secondary markets when demand cannot be fully satisfied, the partial allocation formula is used. For example:

$$\text{Orders} \times 66\% = \text{allocated volume}$$

The remaining part will be kept in the hands of the lead manager and distributed to the secondary market rather than primary market.

Determine the proportion of buy-and-hold investors and intermediary underwriters; the former help stabilize the market while the latter help stimulate it. Usually allocation is arranged to make each group account for 50 percent of the issue.

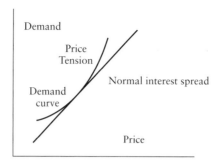

FIGURE 21.2   Price Tension

To ensure the proper operation of the secondary market, the lead underwriter should sell short, for example, about 12 percent of the allocated volume. This sales quota equals allocated volume.

$$\text{Orders} \times (1 + 12\%)$$

When the short-selling allocation format is executed, the lead manager has to buy back the bonds in the secondary market, thereby facilitating the stability of the secondary market, but the managert has to take the risk resulting in the market change.

Creating of "Price Tension"

When executing market strategy, market sentiment and investor psychology must be taken into account. Price tension is a market strategy to test and boost market demand. A successful issuing strategy is usually designed to create price tension, as illustrated in Figure 21.2.

As Figure 21.2 illustrates, if premarketing was successful, the demand curve moves to the right and the interest spread narrows. Therefore, because of price tension, increased demand dampens the spread.

As to the relationship between demand and duration, demand tension pushes the normal curve rightward, and, with the same demand, the duration is extended.

Pricing

Pricing is the price discovery process, and can be divided into three stages:

1. *Price guidance.* This is often a range of interest spreads. A very wide price range may mean the range will not narrow sufficiently, while a range that is too narrow will result in an undersubscribed issue.

2. *Price negotiation.* In this stage, the interest-spread range is further narrowed and the interest spread compared with U.S. treasury bonds can be directly obtained.
3. *Pricing and launch.* Here, the price, volume, terms, and conditions have all been determined.

Negotiation strategy is part of the issuing strategy. The lead manager proposes the price range after consultation with the issuer at the beginning of the road show. In setting the price range, consideration must be given to taking as many subscription orders as possible.

The price negotiation aims at increasing the demand and achieving oversubscription. In negotiating price, investors should be informed of the price range and should decide if it is acceptable. They will consider, of course, the overall demand at that time. The range should be wide enough in a volatile market so that if the market changes, most investors are still included within that range. A tight spread will cause some investors to exit, but as the launch date approaches, the range is narrowed and a single price is set for the transaction.

Launch and Pricing

The issuing size and the spread are set initially through price negotiations. As book building progresses, the market accepted spread for U.S. treasury bonds narrows and one spread is selected to clear the market. The determination of spread is called the launch. Once the spread is decided, the pricing process is concluded.

The next step is to calculate the total yield, which is the underlying U.S. treasury yield plus the spread decided by market. The issuing price is determined after the launch of the transaction.

After pricing, the total yield is determined. The issuing price is decided according to market convention. Since U.S. treasury securities are priced based on one-eighth of a unit, the coupon is not precisely equal to the total yield; therefore, the issuing price, or face value, is adjusted as a discount or premium so that the real yield is equal to the total yield decided via pricing.

Theoretical Rationale for Price Setting

In the United States, Yankee bonds belong to the corporate bond category. The pricing formula is:

US treasury yield + credit risk spread + options spread + liquidity spread + new issue premium

The pricing formula may vary depending on the types of investors. Most U.S. investors are spread traders, meaning they trade relative value; therefore, the spread is more important than the actual yield of the bond. In contrast, European and Asian investors are buy-and-holders, seeking actual yield.

Determining the Credit Spread Using a Sovereign Benchmark Theoretically, the interest spread between a quasi-sovereign issuer and a sovereign issuer depends on the quasi-sovereign issuer's legal status, economic status, and financial condition as well as its relationship with the government. The interest spread between CDB-issued bonds and Ministry of Finance–issued bonds was once reduced to 10 basis points. In the late 1990s, due to the Asian financial crisis and the change in ratings, the interest spread once increased to 70 to 90 basis points. According to U.S. rating agencies, a downgrade in sovereign ratings will weaken the government's support of quasi-sovereign issuers, which may lead to a wider spread. In 2005, Standard & Poor's upgraded China's rating from BBB to A-, and the spread narrowed again.

Determining Liquidity Spread Liquidity depends on the investor base and the size of the issuance. The more diversified the investor base, the more frequent the trading, the higher the liquidity will be. Furthermore, the larger volume may lead to a wider investor base, a more active transaction, and bigger trading volume, thereby improving liquidity. Since the issuing size of corporate issuers is usually smaller than that of U.S. treasury securities, their liquidity is therefore less than that of the U.S. treasury bills. As a result, investors require certain compensation from issuers, the so-called liquidity spread.

New Issue Premium A new issue premium occurs only when investors are anticipating an interest rate hike resulting from either an economic shock or a central bank monetary move and require that their investment be protected. U.S. investors have requested this new issue premium in the aftermath of the Asian financial crises. In addition, in the U.S. capital market, bonds from emerging markets belong to the category of corporate bonds. However, even with the same rating level, emerging market issuers and U.S. corporate bond issuers have very different, albeit changing, spreads. For example, the impact of a volatile economic movement on an issuer from an emerging market may deviate from U.S. corporate bond issuer with the same credit rating.

Although the market has witnessed a declining new issue premium and a narrowing differential between equally rated U.S. issuers and emerging market issuers, this unfair market treatment apparently reflects the lower degree of international financial market integration and the dominant position of the U.S. capital market. In particular, this domination of the U.S. capital market gives rise to a kind of market monopoly, which obviously favors U.S. investors over investors elsewhere. For example, knowing that Asian investors require a lower new issue premium or no premium at all, U.S. investors can take advantage of equal distribution of global bond transactions to get risk-free profits through direct sell-off to Asian investors. This can occur because there is no international primary exchange to establish governance of international transaction, due to the fact that the primary bond market has issuers who are subject to the domestic laws and regulations and underwriters and investors who are subject to the foreign laws and regulations. Here market convention plays an important role in maintaining the so-call primary exchange from an institutional economic engineering point of view.

Bond Allocation

Upon offering, it is also important to consider the bondholder's structure to ensure the bonds are smoothly transferred to the end investors. In the bond allocation process, the distribution proportion between long-term bond-holders and proprietary dealers must be carefully considered. Long-term bondholders usually are institutional investors who buy bonds and hold them until maturity. Such investors do not buy and sell in the market, which helps prevent price fluctuations. Acting as market intermediaries or market makers, dealers and brokers can earn relatively stable incomes, known as commissions, from issuers. Some institutional investors, such as hedge funds and investment funds, tend to be active in selling and buying bond securities to get relative value. This category of market participant helps maintain the market's liquidity. Therefore, the rational distribution of bonds among different category of investors will help to achieve a reasonable balance between market stability and liquidly.

Issuers should keep in mind the possible consequence of mispricing. If the issuer has tighter pricing in the price-setting period, secondary market trading may be substantially wider, which would definitely hurt the investors and substantially lessen their willingness to participate in the next trans-action. Therefore, regular issuers should not follow tight pricing strategy. However, if the pricing is tighter than market expected then the trading yield would be widen, and the issuer will fail to achieve a successful funding and set up a good benchmark.

Pricing a transaction is an art. Successful pricing can result in a secondary trading price several basis points tighter, so that a win-win outcome is achieved without any undesired consequence.

Pricing is also related to the allotment of bond securities in the primary market and distribution in the secondary market. If a wide price range is set, investors, who seek relative value, may prefer to buy more bonds in the primary market and sell them in the secondary market, which may lead to a price drop in the secondary market and subsequently exert a negative effect on the offering. Therefore, the allotment to such investors should be carefully handled.

DEBT MANAGEMENT

Usually the proceeds will be in place upon settlement of the issue. The use of the proceeds falls into the category of asset management. However, it is also crucial for issuers to manage their liabilities effectively in order to reduce risk. The major risks for issuers are currency and interest rate risks. At the time of foreign debt repayment, if domestic currency depreciates, issuers will have to spend more local currency to pay foreign currency. This uncertainty of exchange movement is the currency risk that issuers undertake.

Interest risk management is also important for liabilities management. If the interest rate goes up after a foreign bond issuance, then floating-rate bond issuers will have to pay more interest than fixed-rate issuers; however, if the interest rate goes down, fixed-rate bond issuers will have to pay more interest than floating-rate bond issuers. In both cases, the issuers face risks from interest rate fluctuation.

The most frequently used market instruments are currency swaps and interest rate swaps. Swaps can be divided into different categories, such as plain vanilla swaps and structured swaps. The former is a simple currency swap or interest rate swap, while the latter is usually associated with futures or options. Generally, a plain vanilla swap can help issuers hedge their risk rather than take more risk. The structured swap, though it offers the chance to make huge profits, also tends to have unlimited downside risk.

To manage their liabilities, issuers often enter into swap contracts with financial intermediaries, such as investment banks engaging in derivative transactions. The issuers are advised by these banks to engage in swap contracts; however, most risk-averse issuers in China advised by the department in charge or internal regulation not to enter into structured swaps.

Fees and Commissions

The issuer is liable for issuance-related expenses. Such expenses are paid according to market convention. These expenses usually include:

- *Legal counsel fees* can be either a fixed retainer or billed according to the amount of work and time spent. This figure usually amounts to US$150,000 to $200,000 for a US$1 billion transaction.
- *Credit rating fee* is a lump sum or paid in installments. It is about US$150,000 for a US$1 billion transaction.
- *SEC registration fee* for shelf registration is calculated as 0.3 percent of the total issued volume and paid in a lump sum. The payment is less for each subsequent registration. For non-shelf registration, fees are paid for each registration.
- *Accountant fees.* Issuers can use their own accountant to save the fees.
- *Printing expenses.* The printer is selected through competitive bidding. This expense is about US$50,000, but for last-minute or urgent services, the fee is relatively higher.
- *Road show expenses.* The issuer pays the road show expenses. The actual figure is subject to the number of cities visited and people involved. It is usually about US$200,000, and is either a charge for actual expenses or a fixed retainer. To control the cost, the latter is preferable.
- *Blue sky laws expenses.* Legal expenses in various cities in the United States can run about several thousand dollars.
- *Finance agent fee.* The payment agent is determined through competition, and the expense is fixed at several thousand dollars.
- *Listing expenses.* This is a fixed expense, normally US$2,000.
- *Translation and advertising fees* are paid by the issuer. They can be paid by the underwriter and then reimbursed.
- *Underwriters' legal counsel fees* can be paid by either the issuer or the underwriters, depending on the total underwriting expenses. If the issuer has made a large payment to the underwriter as the underwriting expense, then the legal fees can be paid by the underwriter.
- *Underwriting expenses.* According to market practice, Yankee bond issuance incurs a relatively high underwriting expense; global bond expenses are lower, and Euro bond expenses are the lowest. The underwriting expense is also subject to the issuer's credit ratings. The higher rating the issuer has, the lower the underwriting fee. The underwriting expense is also subject to the maturity of the bond issued. For instance, the underwriting expense for 10-year global bonds is around 45 basis points.

Fees and expenses are transaction costs that all issuers have to pay. However, in certain circumstances issuers can save these costs. One-time issuance and shelf registration issuance differ in many ways. One-time issuance will incur a higher expense than shelf registration issuance. Usually legal and accounting expenses must be paid by the job or by time spent. Fees can be reduced by reducing the comments from the SEC and modifying the registration application; printing expenses can be reduced by avoiding last-minute or urgent service expenses whenever possible.

Timetable for the Initial Issuance in the Yankee Bond Market

The whole process of the Yankee bond issuance consists of two phases: preparation of legal documents and investor-focused marketing. During the legal documentation period, the issuer is required to obtain both domestic and foreign regulatory approvals. During the marketing period, the issuers advertise and boost the issue's image to investors. The whole process can be further divided into six stages:

1. Decision-making period before financing (time to be defined)
2. Before submitting application (about four to six weeks)
3. SEC's confidential review period (about four to six weeks)
4. Marketing (one week)
5. Pricing (two days)
6. Closing (three business days)

The first three stages are deemed as the legal period, and the last three are perceived as the marketing period.

Legal Period The financing decision-making phase involves matters such as determining the time required for the issuing process and identifying the work required for the issuance. During this period, the financial data are reviewed to ensure it complies with the requirements of generally accepted accounting principles (GAAP); the issuance cost is estimated. There is no regulatory requirement in this phase. Prior to submitting the application, issuers must appoint the lead manager, select legal counsel, and get legal endorsement from the relevant domestic agencies. When informed of the legal endorsement, the issuer or the lead manager convenes a kickoff meeting. Meetings with rating agencies are arranged as well. Following the kickoff meeting, documentation work commences. Usually the syndicate structure can be decided at this time. Due diligence is conducted by the syndicate on behalf of investors and the syndicate.

The Ministry of Finance maintains frequent contact with the budget and finance departments. According to the relevant regulations, at this time, no indications (oral or written) or promotions are allowed in United States regarding the issue.

If the transaction is global or Yankee, SEC registration is requested. The SEC does a confidential review of the registration. The issuer must submit an issuance application to the SEC at least two weeks prior to the launch. After the SEC's confidential review, the comments are transferred from the SEC to the applicant by legal counsel. The SEC may make comments on the registration; if it does so, the issuer must reply to those comments and submit a revised application.

Again, legally during this phase, no indications (oral or written) or promotions are allowed in the United States, in case of Yankee and Global, regarding the issue.

Marketing Period During the marketing period, the issuer files a formal and open registration with the SEC, and the timetable for the effective date of registration is set. At the same time, a press release is issued. Marketing is very much focused on investors. The underwriters distribute the red herring prospectus to the sales force and investors and the road show begins. At this point, registration at the SEC is coming into effect and the credit rating is determined. Issuance indication, in oral but not in written form, is given, and promotion is allowed in the United States.

After pricing, the coupon rate and price is set based on the pricing yield and coupon convention (one-eighth differential) and the underwriting agreement is signed. Investors must send a confirmation letter (by accountant). At this time, the transaction is concluded through an announcement.

Oral issuing indication is allowed; written indication is confined only to red herring prospectuses. The final stage is closing. At this time, the final prospectus is printed and submitted to the SEC and the potential investors and the names of syndicate members are announced. At closing, the issuer can receive the proceeds and deliver the bonds simultaneously via the electronic transfer system, Centrale de Livraison de Valeurs Mobilieres (CEDEL), or the European Clearing House (Euroclear).

Timetable for Rule 144A Offering

Rule 144A issuance also consists of legal and market phases, but the legal phase is relatively simple. The process is divided into five stages. The first two stages relate to the legal issues while the last three stages concern marketing work.

1. *Decision-making period* (three to five weeks). In this period, funding requirement is worked out, the application is submitted, and formal approval is processed. After a funding program is endorsed, a lead manager and legal counsel are assigned to organize or advise on the

issuance. In this period, the timetable for the transaction is worked out and a kickoff syndicate meeting is convened where the work required for the issuance is identified and assigned to the underwriters. Financial indicators of the issuer are requested by the SEC for the issuance in the United States are identified and reviewed in line with GAAP requirements. Issuance costs are estimated as well. During this period, there is no regulatory requirement in the country where the market is located.

2. *Documentation preparation* (four to six weeks). In this period, the prospectus, the most important document of the issue, is prepared by legal counsel; therefore, the legal counsel must be assigned earlier. Road show material is prepared at this time as well. In addition, meetings with rating agencies and due diligence are arranged. As China's accounting standard is somewhat different from the international accounting system, from time to time discussions with the accountant regarding relevant financial issues may be necessary. According to the relevant regulations, no issuing indication (oral or written) is allowed in the United States at this stage.

3. *Marketing* (one week to 10 business days) is very much focused on investors. In this period, the red herring prospectus is distributed and the road show is under way. In order to improve the settlement of the transaction, the lead manager and underwriters shall identify the qualified clearing companies, such as (Euroclear) and Centrale de Livraison de Valeurs Mobilieres (CEDEL), depending on the listing stock exchange. During this time, oral issuing indication is allowed; written indication is confined only to red herring prospectuses.

4. *Pricing* (two days) is critical to the transaction; the market will be cleared and it can be determined whether the issue is a success. During this period, the final due diligence is made. The price and the coupon rate are decided; the purchase agreement is formally signed; and the comfort letter (a certificate from the accounting firm on the authenticity of financial statement of issuer, which is issued at the request of underwriters) from the accountant is sent. At this time, the legal restriction is lifted; promotion is allowed in the United States.

5. *Close* (three business days) marks the end of the transaction and the beginning of secondary market trading. At this stage, the final prospectus is printed and distributed, and the issuer receives the proceeds. Information is regularly disclosed. According to the written contracts, new foreign debt offerings are not allowed for a specified period.

HIGH-YIELD CORPORATE BONDS

The sovereign or quasi-sovereign issuers are classified by investment bankers as high-profile issuers to indicate the importance that they attach to the issuers and the implication for their reputations. Other categories of international borrowing are high-yield transactions as opposed to high-profile transactions.

Historically, several other issuers were active in the international capital market, such as Guandong International Trust and Investment Corporation (GITIC). GITIC was closed in 1997. Thereafter, local and nongovernmental organizations have been prohibited from entering international capital market.

Due to strict legal control, companies other than the government and governmental organizations are not allowed access to the international capital market. However, recently a high-yield market has been cultivated that has attracted many Chinese small and medium enterprises. In 2005, Asian high-yield issuance reached more than US$13.35 billion, of which China and Hong Kong accounted for 14.4 percent.

The qualified issuers are companies with offshore holding company structures. If they do not have this structure, companies must reorganize their corporate organizational structure in order to be qualified to solicit a high-yield transaction. In applying for the transaction, companies must demonstrate stable cash flow from operations and attractive business prospects; financial viability must be shown; and the company's financial statement will be audited by international standard auditors. As a rule of thumb, a company that can leverage its earnings before interest, taxes, depreciation, and amortization (EBITDA) three to five times is considered a potential candidate.

There are several major restrictive covenants on issuers. The major restrictions are limitations on incurring additional debt, restricted payments, distributions from restricted subsidiaries, and the issuance and sale of capital stock of restricted subsidiaries. The covenants also restrict issuers' ability to consolidate, merge, or sell all or substantially all of their assets.

ISSUES RELATED TO INTERNATIONAL OFFERINGS

The benefits that China and China's financial institutions gained from issuing securities in the international capital market are not confined to foreign capital, but also include knowledge of advanced market practices.

International funding also facilitated the integration of China's domestic market with the international capital market and the establishment of a relationship with the international financial community. China can still benefit from financial activities in collaboration with foreign financial institutions, for example, from syndicate loans, financial advisory, and derivative transactions. As long-term issuers, sovereign issuers can always benefit from increased integration with the rest of the world's markets.

However, as indicated earlier, the international capital market is characterized by incomplete international primary exchange (i.e., there is no universally recognized and representative international organization to set rules on the transactions related to the international funding). For this reason, pricing and trading are not considered to take place on a completely on fair, open basis. For example, the U.S. rating agencies use their own standards to judge the credit rating of foreign issuers. In addition, they tend to use different standards to evaluate the creditworthiness of developing countries vis-à-vis developed countries. More often than not, China was, and still is, in our view, underrated. It is also recognized that the U.S. investors' requirement for the new issue premiums from Asia issuers in the aftermath of Asia's financial crises is also against the market principle and this requirement (for new issue premium) it is indeed unjustifiable.

The Non-Government Securities Market

Structure
of the Non-Government
Bond Market

Non-government bonds (NGBs) are traded on the inter-bank bond market (IBBM), the Stock Exchange Markets (SEMs), and the over-the-counter (OTC) market. Financial debentures are traded mainly on the inter-bank market, and corporate bonds are mainly traded on the exchanges. The non-government bond market (NGBM) includes the primary market and secondary market. The primary market issuing volume is illustrated in Figure 22.1.

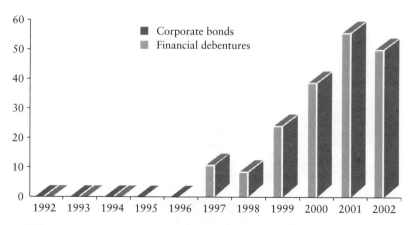

FIGURE 22.1 Transaction Volume of Corporate Bonds and Financial Debentures (100 million yuan)

MARKET STRUCTURE OF NON-GOVERNMENT BONDS IN THE INTER-BANK BOND MARKET

The NGBs traded in the IBBM include bonds issued by policy banks, commercial banks, and other financial institutions. The primary issuers are the China Development Bank (CDB), the Export-Import (EX-IM) Bank of China, and the Agricultural Development Bank of China. The qualifications of issuers of financial debentures must be approved by the State Council, and the People's Bank of China (PBOC) sets the total issuance quotas. The issuing method is primarily public auction.

The CDB is the leading market player. As the main issuer of policy-oriented financial debentures, the CDB issued RMB1.938 trillion financial debentures cumulatively from 1998, when the market mechanism was introduced into the process of the bond issuance, until the end of 2005.

Commercial banks are the principal investors in financial debentures. At present, the IBBM players include all the domestic financial institutions, a few nonfinancial credit unions, and other institutions. The structure of investors in the interbank market is shown in Figures 22.2 and 22.3.

The main investors in the NGB market are banks, insurance companies, and investment funds, and the financial intermediaries are securities companies. Banks tend to be investors rather than financial intermediaries. However, in China, the four big state-owned commercial banks (SOCBs) often act as financial intermediaries, partly because they already hold huge

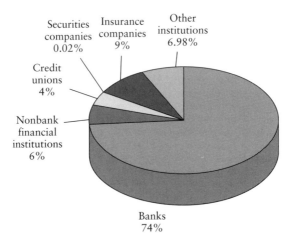

FIGURE 22.2 Financial Debentures Underwriting in Inter-Bank Bond Market in 2005 (100 million yuan)

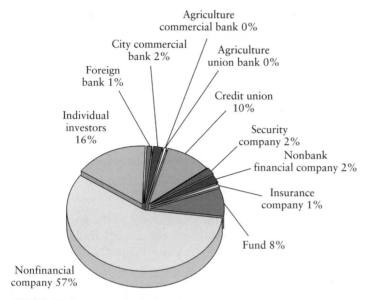

FIGURE 22.3 Breakdown of Inter-Bank Market Members as of December 31, 2005 (6574 IBBM members total)

amounts of bonds and partly because securities firms in China are relatively small and it is difficult for them to perform as functional financial intermediaries. The central bank would prefer SOCBs to perform as financial intermediaries, presumably due to expediency as banks are under the jurisdiction of central bank.

As the leading market player, the CDB has pioneered many financial innovations, including floating-rate bonds, zero-coupon bonds, super-long-term fixed-rate bonds, put-able bonds of investors, separately trading registered interest and principal bonds (STRIPs), forward bonds, interest rate swap option bonds, repurchase (repo) indexed floating-rate bonds, and many others.

Prices are set through auction in the market, book building, and negotiations, and prices in the secondary market are mainly decided through negotiations. Transactions in the IBBM are settled in the Shanghai Foreign Exchange Center. Since the establishment of the interbank bond market in 1997, the total volume of bond transactions has amounted to RMB2.300 trillion, of which bond repo transactions and bond transactions account for RMB2.135 trillion and RMB1.610 trillion respectively. In the first half of 2003, trading in the IBBM was unusually active. The trading volume topped RMB1.000 trillion in half a year, increasing by 302.42 percent

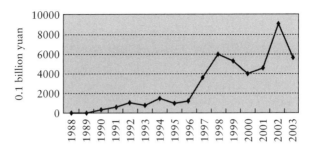

FIGURE 22.4 Trading Volume of National Debt Spots, 1988 to 2003

compared with the trading volume in the same period of the previous year. In the first year the market was established, the annual trading volume was less than RMB1 billion (see Figure 22.4 and Figure 22.5 for details). In 2003, the trading volume of financial debentures rapidly exceeded that of the government bonds: The trading volume of financial debentures was 74 percent, while the trading volume of government bonds accounted for the rest 26 percent; in November 2004, financial debentures had risen to 81 percent, while government bonds had fallen to 19 percent.

For all NGBs, including corporate bonds, settlements are made through the China Government Securities Depository Trust & Clearing Co., Ltd. However, trading of corporate bonds in the IBBM only began in 2004.

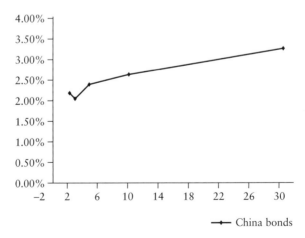

FIGURE 22.5 Yield Curve (vertical axis: yield in percentage; horizontal axis: number of years)

STRUCTURE OF THE EXCHANGE MARKET

The non-government bonds traded on the Shanghai Stock Exchange and Shenzhen Stock Exchange are mainly corporate bonds. By November 2004, 82 bond products were listed on the Shanghai Stock Exchange. These included 70 bond spots (27 financial debentures, 24 corporate bonds, and 19 convertible bonds) and 12 repurchase bonds (9 government bonds repurchase and 9 corporate bonds repurchase). As of November 2004, the trading volume of listed bond products was RMB4.585 trillion, among which bond spots were RMB302.024 billion (including RMB262.117 billion government bonds, RMB8.767 billion financial debentures and corporate bonds, and RMB31.14 billion convertible bonds), and RMB4.283 trillion bonds repurchase (including RMB4.049 trillion government bonds repo and RMB233.496 billion corporate bonds repo). See Table 22.1 and Table 22.2 for the names of companies on the stock exchanges.

When an issue is approved, the underwriters negotiate with the issuer on the terms of the transaction. To take advantage of its market position and its ability to create market innovation, as an underwriter of corporate bonds, the CDB helps corporate bonds issuers design the instruments that adapt to the preferences of investors. The China international capital corporation introduced the book-building technique to sell corporate bonds in 2001 in order to create competitiveness in pricing a transaction, but the final price is subject to the approval of National Development Reform Commission (NDRC). *Rules on Corporate Bonds* requires that each corporate bond issuance shall be guaranteed by qualified institutions (see the Guarantee Law for specific regulations). At present, there are three main ways to issue corporate bonds: mutual guarantee between enterprises; bank guarantee; and construction fund guarantee. Examples of the latter are Three Gorge Bonds and Railway Bonds.

INTER-BANK BOND MARKET VERSUS THE STOCK EXCHANGE BOND MARKET

The yields of bonds issued by the Ministry of Finance and the CDB in the IBBM tend to be similar. The average fixed interest rate of 10-year bonds issued by the Ministry at stock exchanges is 3.8 percent, and the fixed interest rate of 10-year bonds issued by the CDB at the IBBM was the same 3.8 percent as of the end of 2005; however, the yields of government bonds tend to be volatile in the SEMs vis-à-vis the IBBM.

There are obvious differences in transaction activities. Trading in the stock exchange bond market tends to be thriving. The fact that there are

TABLE 22.1 Corporate Bonds Listed on the
Shanghai Stock Exchange

Full Name	Maturity Date
99 Baoshan Steel	2005-08-10
01 China Mobile	2011-06-17
01 Three Gorge	2016-11-08
02 Three Gorge	2022-09-20
02 China Mobile (5)	2007-10-28
02 China Mobile (15)	2017-10-28
02 Jiangsu Transportation	2017-12-12
02 Chongqing Urban Investment	2012-12-09
02 Wuhan Steel (3)	2005-11-04
02 Wuhan Steel (7)	2009-11-04
02 Jinmao	2012-04-28
03 Shanghai Railway	2018-02-19
03 Suzhou Garden Construction	2013-07-17
03 Three Gorge	2033-07-31
03 State Grid	2013-12-31
03 State Grid	2013-12-31
03 China Power Investment	2018-12-07
04 General	2014-03-30
04 Sinopec	2014-02-23
98 Three Gorge (8)	2007-01-17
98 China Railway (3)	2009-10-12
99 Three Gorge	2010-07-25
98 CITIC (7)	2006-06-15
98 Petroleum	2007-09-08

different investors in the stock exchange bond market and the IBBM has resulted in differences in investment preferences. According to a rough estimate, the proportion of institutional investors to individual investors is approximately 6:1 in the SEM. Although few individual investors are registered in the SEM, they are active. (See Figure 22.6.)

The development of NGBs is attributable to the changing awareness and shift in focus of government policy. In the introduction, we indicated that the financial market would flourish when government policy makes it a priority. This is true not only of the government bond market, but also of the NGB market. The corporate bond market stepped into the spotlight in 2001 at a point when the stock market had been sluggish for five years, because of the SEM's inability to facilitate the financing of the state-owned enterprises (SOEs) and the reform of the corporate governance program.

TABLE 22.2 Corporate Bonds Listed on the Shenzhen Stock Exchange

Brief Name	Issuing Volume (0.1 billion yuan)	Listing Date	Interest Accrual Date	Maturity Date	Face Rate
01 Three Gorge 10	20	2002-04-19	2001-11-08	2011-11-08	0
01 Guangzhou Nuclear	25	2002-06-06	2001-12-11	2008-12-10	4.12
02 State Grid 3	5	2002-12-10	2002-06-19	2005-06-18	3.5
02 State Grid 15	35	2002-12-10	2002-06-19	2017-06-18	4.86
02 Guangzhou Nuclear	40	2003-08-18	2002-11-11	2017-11-10	4.5

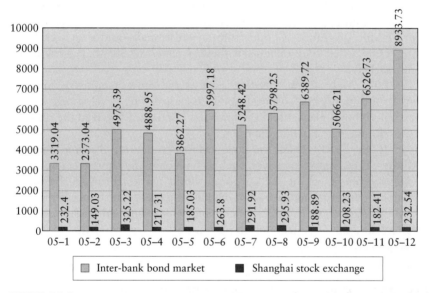

FIGURE 22.6 Comparison of Monthly Market Turnover of Circulating Bonds in the Inter-Bank Bond Market and the Stock Exchange Bond Market, January 2005 to December 2005

Initially, the government and business firms regarded corporate bonds only as financial instruments needed to carry out the government's investment policy. Therefore, the National Development and Reform Commission (NDRC) qualified the issuers, and the local planning commissions approved local enterprise bonds. They did not see the bond market from a financial perspective; instead, they saw it only from an investment perspective. This was also a reflection of the depressed nature of economic policy at that time.

Throughout the 1990s, many issues of company bonds were approved by local planning commissions. Since there was no secondary market, issuing firms were mostly substandard local firms, the issuing size tended to be small, and most issues were not listed on the stock exchange. There were a number of defaults. The investors claimed repayment from the securities firm that had underwritten the bonds, and the China Securities Regulatory Commission, concerned about their contiguous liabilities, would not allow the bonds to be listed on the stock exchange. Therefore, the real size of new corporate bond market actually declined.

For many years, government agencies were not been fully aware of the importance of the bond market to businesses. The government was not concerned about the bond market because there was little pressure on firms, which were financing through traditional ways. SOEs would first seek a government grant, then look to the stock market, which they thought of as another kind of grant—a grant from an individual—and then seek bank loans. Only when they exhausted these avenues would they turn to the bond market.

In 2001, only a few agencies, such as the railway ministry, and big firms could qualify for corporate bond issuance. The development of the government bond market and the financial bond market paved the way for the development of the bond market.

In 2004, the PBOC felt the time was ripe to develop the bond market, and carried out many initiatives, such as financing and short-term notes.

The development of the corporate bond market provides fresh evidence of the institutional economic engineering theory introduced earlier. It proves that government policy, the changing institutional framework, the ideology, and the organizations all play important roles in the bond market development.

ROLE OF UNDERWRITERS IN ISSUANCE OF CORPORATE BONDS

To date, the coupon rate of corporate bonds has been set administratively by the NDRC and the PBOC. However, recently underwriters have advised issuers on what price and coupon rate is appropriate for the transaction based on their judgment of the yield in the secondary market of compatible instruments. Government bonds that have closer maturity with traded corporate bonds in the secondary market can also provide a benchmark and reference for the pricing of corporate bonds. As a market expert and active market player, the CDB explored the possibility of setting up a price discovery mechanism for market-based pricing within the current legal framework. For example, when the CDB received the mandate to issue the 2001 Guangzhou Nuclear Power Bond, it sent a price inquiry to investors asking for and obtaining feedback on their views on the price. This feedback reflected an overall market view on the price, and the CDB presented it to the agencies as evidence of the market demand for the new issue. It convinced the agencies of the right price to set. This practice helps achieve a multiple win outcome among issuer, investors, and underwriters. Although this progress is confined to CDB related transactions, preliminary, it did lead the corporate bond market to develop towards market-oriented direction. The road show conducted by the lead manager, underwriters, and the issuer was effective and helped strengthen investors' confidence in the transaction.

Although this marketing method is commonly pursued and is conventional in the international capital market, the CDB was the first to introduce it in China. The CDB recommended the road show to promote the 2001 Guangzhou Nuclear Power Bond because some investors worried about the safety of nuclear power generators, fearing, for example, that radiation would lead to operational failure and eventually affect the payment of interest and principal. In addition, the bank did not follow the conventional international practice and conduct the road show in key cities; instead, it did it at factories in order to make investors feel comfortable about investing in the project.

Since the domestic underwriters were not familiar with the new issuing practice for introducing the Guangzhou Nuclear Power Bond, the CDB frequently communicated with them during the course of issuance, to familiarize them with the intended strategy. At the same time, the bank modified its commission in order to provide an incentive to syndicate members.

Because syndicate members are market experts and understand the market better than investors, especially individual investors, the CDB required syndicate members to distribute no less than 50 percent of the nominal underwriting amounts in book-building process to the individual investors. As noted, this investor-friendly marketing practice resulted in a positive response to the transaction.

FUTURE OF THE NON-GOVERNMENT BOND MARKET DEVELOPMENT

At present, investors in China can choose among only a limited number of investment instruments. For example, the alternative investment choices for corporate bond investors are government bonds and stocks. When the stock market was in recession, individual investors fled for safety and shifted their investments to government bonds. Between 2001 and 2005, the rapid increase of investment in government securities gave rise to a downward movement of the yields of government securities.

The development of the NGB market may favor China's investors who, due to their heterogeneous nature, would like the opportunity to invest in more diversified instruments. Corporate bonds and other instruments, which offer a risk/return that falls between government bonds and stocks, will attract those investors who prefer to take some risk in order to achieve a better return, such as insurance companies and investment funds.

The capital market is composed of the stock market and the bond market. The dividend yields of the stock market should be based on the yields of bond market. The volatility of the stock market in China is partly due to the volatile bond market. Therefore, it is essential for China to try to develop a spectrum of bond instruments that can provide reference for discovering the fair value of stocks and trace the stock market movement.

CHAPTER 23

Financial Debentures and the China Development Bank's Financial Innovation

A s financial instruments, bonds can be looked at in various ways. In China, there are government bonds, financial debentures, corporate bonds, and bonds issued in the international capital market. The term "non-government securities" refers to securities issued by government agencies, financial institutions, and corporations other than the central government or the Ministry of Finance. Fixed-income instruments in China are not identical to those of the United States. China does not issue municipal or other local government bonds, whereas the United States has not only municipal bonds but also bonds issued by the various state governments. China does issue a huge number of bonds that the United States does not have, which is a reflection of the special features of China's financial market.

China's bond market in the first five years of the new century has been eventful, and most conspicuous is the development of non-government securities markets (NGSMs). These developments are an outgrowth of the government's securities market reform.

In China, the non-government bond market is segmented, but its primary constituents are the inter-bank bond market (IBBM), the exchange market, and the over-the-counter (OTC) market. Financial debentures are traded mainly in the IBBM, and corporate bonds are traded mainly in the exchange markets.

FINANCIAL DEBENTURES

The term "financial debentures" refers to the securities issued by banks and non-bank financial institutions. In western countries, since most financial institutions are publicly owned companies, bonds or debentures issued by financial institutions are also classified as corporate bonds.

Classification of Financial Debentures

Debentures can be grouped in various ways: First they can be classified based on the way interest is paid:

- *Coupon-bearing financial debentures*. These types of bonds generally have a three- or five-year maturity. Their interest and principal payment methods are the same as those of common coupon bonds.
- *Discount financial debentures*. These are short-term financial debentures with a one-year term. Normally they are sold through auction at discount. Once approved, they can be traded OTC among the financial institutions.

Second, financial debentures in China can also be classified based on issuance conditions:

- *Common financial debentures*. These are certificates of deposit (CDs). Their term can be one, two, or three years. The principal together with interest is paid in a lump sum on maturity. They are issued at par value with simple interest rather than compound interest. Common financial debentures are similar to fixed-rate bank deposits, but the interest rate is normally higher than that of bank deposits.
- *Progressive interest financial debentures*. These are a type of floating-rate financial debenture. Their terms range from one to five years. Bondholders can redeem these debentures before maturity.

Like corporate bonds, financial debentures can be further classified as short-, medium-, and long-term instruments; registered bonds and nonregistered bonds; credit and secured bonds; callable and noncallable bonds; fixed-rate, floating-rate and progressive-rate bonds; option and nonoption bonds, and so on.

Issuance Expenses

The expenses related to issuance and payment of financial debentures include underwriting fees, debt service fees, and service fees for custodianship. The underwriting fees and debt service fees are the expenses that issuers, such as financial institutions (e.g., China Development Bank [CDB]), pay to the underwriters via the China Government Securities Depository Trust & Clearing CO., Ltd. (CGSDTC), which in turn receive the fees for clearing and settlement service.

Bond Underwriting Fees   Bond underwriting fees cover expenses, including labor and travel costs, as well as costs for other goods and services the underwriters incur. These expenses should proportionally relate to the size of the issue and the number of subscribers.

As the major issuer of financial debentures, the CDB pays a fixed amount of fees, or commissions, and expenses directly related to the underwriters' out-of-pocket expenses. When issuing bonds with terms over one year (not including one year), the CDB pays 0.05 percent of the face value of the financial debentures underwritten (see Supplementary Agreement of Financial Debentures Underwriting 2004 by China Development Bank for details) to the underwriters in addition to underwriting fees for bidding in every transaction. With respect to expenses related to the underwriters' out-of-pocket expenses, the CDB sets rates in the issuing documents of every bond based on such factors as the term and type of the bond issued. Rates are generally set in multiples of 0.05 percent. Payment of underwriting fees is the fourth workday after the proceeds are remitted to the CDB's account.

Custody Service Fees   Issuers pay custody service fees to the CGSDTC for custodianship of the issued financial debentures. At present, the rates are prescribed in the documents issued by the People's Bank of China (PBOC); and payment is made on the fourth workday after the proceeds are remitted to the CDB's account; the standard fee rates at present is 0.01 percent of the face amount of the financial debentures in custody.

Payment Service Fees   The payment service fees are prescribed at issuance agreement and paid at maturity to compensate underwriters for the expenses incurred when they provide redemption services on behalf of the issuer to the bondholders.

At present, the service fee rate (compared to market-based bond issues) of prescribed purchasing bonds is 0.001 percent. Payment service fees of market-based issuing bonds are set forth in the issuing documents of each transaction.

There is no payment service fee on newly issued short-term bonds (the payment service fee is set as 0 percent) because there are few expenses, if any, for underwriters when the maturity is short.

Principal Redemption Service Fees, Interest Redemption Service Fees   Principal and interest redemption service fees are paid by the CDB to the securities firms for the intermediary service of redeeming bonds (principal and interest) on behalf of the bank.

The principal payment service fee is paid once a month on the last workday of each month; the interest payment service fee is paid once a year on the last workday of each year. At present, the fee for principal and interest payment service is 0.00005 percent of the face amount.

FINANCIAL INNOVATIONS OF THE CHINA DEVELOPMENT BANK

The China Development Bank is not only the second largest issuer in the market; it is also a pioneer of financial innovations in the IBBM ever since the market was established in 1997. The CDB introduced the majority of market instruments in the market, such as short-term bills of 3 months and 6 months and 20-year and 30-year bonds in the aftermath government bond market reform in middle of 1990s, when the Ministry of Finance introduced the 1-year, 2-year, 3-year, 5-year, and 10-year treasury notes and bonds. The CDB also introduced floating-rate notes (FRNs), put-able and callable bonds, STRIPs (separate trading of registered interest and principal of securities), and forward and swaption bonds. Tenders, including interest rate tenders, price tenders, single-price bidding, and complex-pricing bidding are frequently utilized by the CDB. In terms of interest payment formats, there are zero-coupon bonds as well as coupon-bearing bonds that are paid annually and semiannually. These diverse instruments across the spectrum of the yield curve help to satisfy the needs of the investors and dealers. The instruments introduced by the CDB are shown in Figure 23.1.

A discussion of the main types of bonds issued by the CDB follows.

The China Development Bank issues different categories of short-term bonds of three and six months[1] in the IBBM with the objective of promoting the liquidity of interbank market, adjusting the structure of bonds held by investors, and facilitating the issuer's cash management. Short-term securities can also help the CDB manage its short-term position. When the Ministry of Finance suspended short-term transactions, the CDB's short-term instruments served as the benchmark for short-term bond funds.

The total short-term bond issuance since the end of 2002 by the CDB was RMB85 billion, and the balance by the end of 2005 was RMB20 billion. These short-term instruments were well received in the market.

Ten-year and 7-year medium- and long-term FRNs were first issued by the CDB in March 1999 with great success.

One of the important contributions of the CDB to the market was the introduction of 20-year and 30-year long-term fixed-rate bonds. These types of bonds were issued when interest rates in the market were relatively low and the yield curve was flat. The long bonds not only provided new instruments for institutional investors, such as insurance companies, pension

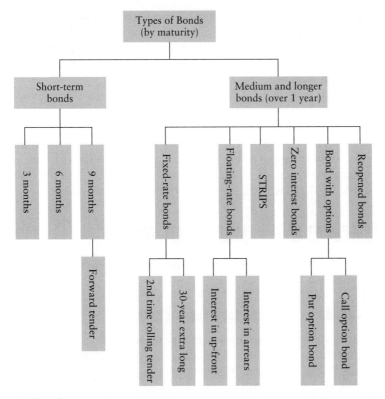

FIGURE 23.1 Financial Bond Innovations of the China Development Bank

funds, and various investment funds, and filled the vacancy on the long end yield curve, but also substantially secured the long-term funding costs of the CDB.

The CDB also designed the swaption bond, which is peculiar to China. In 2003, the market became nervous about the central bank's move to tighten the money supply, and new issues became very difficult to place. In order to achieve a successful transaction at this critical moment, the CDB issued twin bonds with 10 billion fixed-rate bonds and 10 billion FRNs—two tranches as a package with the same amount and same maturity—but allowed the holder to swap one for the other one year later. In China, this is also called a symmetrical bond. The idea behind the symmetrical bond is to give investors the flexibility to select a fixed- or floating-rate investment when the trend of interest movement has become clear. The symmetrical bond is issued only when the market changes suddenly, and the issuer wishes to protect the investor and itself.

On March 20, 2002, the CDB reopened the 30-year bonds that were issued in 2001. The purpose was to expand the volume of the 2001 issuance of RMB5 billion to RMB15 billion to improve the liquidity of off-the-run bonds that were not trading very actively. Reopening the bonds has been widely accepted and welcomed by market participants.

Put-able bonds were first issued in 2001, with a view to giving investors some flexibility to select early redemption. Put-able bonds facilitate investors' risk management and will stimulate bond trading activities.

On June 12, 2004, the CDB issued subdebt for the first time in China to increase its tier-two capital. This bond has a 10-year maturity but is callable in 5 years, with stepped-up interest payments after five years to give investors confidence that the bond is unlikely to be called five years later.

CHINA DEVELOPMENT BANK'S FLOATING-RATE BONDS

A detailed explanation of three products that marked milestones on the path to financial innovation follows.

Floating-Rate Bonds versus Statutory Deposit Rate

Floating-rate bonds are mid- and long-term instruments. Their interest rate usually correlates with a specific financial index, normally a reference interest rate index based on the short-term money market rate plus a spread, which is subject to periodic adjustment (in line with its semiannual or quarterly interest payments). The spread reflects the underlying risk, such as credit risk of the issuer compared to funding cost of the referenced issuer, and the risk premium of long-term debt compared with the short-term interest rate. In practice, the spread of the CDB transactions was, as for other fixed instruments, decided through a bidding process. The actual interest payment is the applicable one-year deposit rate plus the fixed spread.

There are several categories of floating-rate instruments, among them FRNs, variable-rate notes (VRNs), and inverse floating-rate notes (inverse FRNs).

In Europe, typical bond issues are euro-dollar FRNs, which are issued by government agencies, banks, corporations, savings institutions, and so on. A typical FRN usually has a 10- to 15-year maturity, a coupon of 3 million LIBOR (London Interbank Offer Rate) plus a spread that is subject to adjustment semiannually or quarterly. For such a transaction, the initial commission and expense is 0.30 to 0.50 percent. There may be some options granted to investors; for example, some FRNs can be redeemed before maturity.

Legally, FRNs contain four important elements.

1. *Reference index.* Generally, the reference index is the interest rate in a certain money market over a specified period. In theory, the reference index is selected based on four considerations:

   a. It is very well known to the market participants and is universally recognized as reliable.

   b. It is sensitive to market changes and sufficiently liquid.

   c. It is actively traded and based on real offers from multiple institutions with significant trading turnover, and, therefore, it is not subject to manipulation by market participants.

   d. It provides continuous quotation so that the observable data are available in the event the interest rate is reset.

      The most commonly used reference index in the world is LIBOR, which is published every business day. As the market rate for euro dollars, LIBOR is calculated by the British Banker's Association, which averages the inter-bank offer rates from selected banks in the London market. Generally, the LIBOR agreed in the Agreement of Financial Industry Loans is the average of the rates from several designated reference banks at the fixed time (normally 11:00 a.m. London Time). Currently the most widely used LIBORs are the three- and six-month.

      The movement of LIBOR depends mainly on monetary policies, and fluctuations are driven by the changes in supply and demand in the money market. The LIBOR is the most important and most frequently used market reference index. Besides the price information of LIBOR from major news agencies, historical information is available on the Web site of British Bankers Association (www.bba.org.uk).

      On January 1, 1999, 11 countries in Europe began to use the euro as a uniform currency. Although the older FRNs use the LIBOR as reference interest rates, these reference rates will be replaced by the new reference interest rate, European Interbank Offer Rate (EURIBOR), which will be in a leading position in the global monetary market to serve as the benchmark in pricing new FRNs.

      Other reference indices include the American 90-day treasury bill rate, Federal Fund Rate, most favored loan rate, commercial bills rate, and other three-month and six-month short-term rates, among others.

2. *Spread.* On each rate-resetting day, the spread is adjusted based on the reference index to determine the real interest rate for the forthcoming interest payment period. The spread should reflect the difference between the issuer's credit rating and its sovereign rating. The risk of default is subject to the creditworthiness of the issuer and the type of the security issued. The FRNs from some government-owned companies

have relatively narrow spreads. The CDB's FRN spread is now trading around 20 to 30 basis points over comparable treasury securities.

3. *Frequency of interest rate changes.* Normally, interest rates of FRNs are reset at the same frequency as interest is paid. Generally, the interest rate of a floating-rate bond is reset after three months, six months and one year. In the international bond market, a six-month interval is typical.

   Some FRNs, however, are reset more frequently. For example, the rate may be set once a month and the interest paid every three months. The interest payment date may be later than the date the interest rate is reset. For example, the rate may be reset bimonthly, and the interest paid on the last day of March, June, September, and December.

4. *Observable data.* In resetting a reference rate, it is necessary to define the time and specific location on which the rate is set in accordance with various rules. For example, three-month LIBOR is defined as the average rate of three-month euro-dollar deposit offered by the designated banks in London at noon on the two business days before the interest resetting date. If no LIBOR is available on that day, then the LIBOR at the same time on the preceding day is applied. If there is more than one designated LIBOR, the one with the highest value will serve as the benchmark rate.

History of China's Floating-Rate Bonds

The first floating-rate bond (99CDB1) in the history of the Chinese bond market was issued in March 1999 by the CDB. It had a maturity of 10 years, and the coupon rate was the one-year statutory deposit rate plus 116.5 basis points. This transaction, as it turned out, was well received. The introduction of floating instruments opened a new chapter in bond market development in China.

The FRN was introduced against the background of a turbulent financial market. After seven interest rate cuts from the second half of 1998 to the early part of 2000, consensus was the interest rate would reach bottom. After a series of interest rate cuts by the central bank, the absolute levels of the official interest rate and the market rate were greatly reduced, and investors became concerned with the excessively low bond yields and the anticipated rate increase. Under such market conditions, it was extremely difficult to issue of mid- and long-term fixed-rate bond transactions, with the offering price of three- and five-year fixed-rate bonds reaching 5.94 to 6.30 percent. By alleviating the financial institutions' interest rate concerns about subscribing to long-term bonds, the launch of floating-rate bonds allowed the CDB to raise cost-efficient long-term capital in a difficult market.

The key to designing FRNs in China was to select a reliable reference rate that was not only sensitive to market changes but also catered to the investors' desire to lock in their risk. The Chinese bond market was still in its infancy, and had neither a complete treasury bond yield curve nor a stable and mature inter-bank offering rate. Therefore, first and foremost, it was necessary to select an appropriate reference rate. The CDB proposed to use the statutory one-year deposit rate as the reference rate and, after consultation with the PBOC and other related authorities, the framework of the floating-rate bonds was finalized.

These new instruments are designed to cater to the need of commercial banks to manage their assets and liabilities. As banks lend money on a floating basis subject to the central bank's adjustment based on monetary considerations, they would like, when a bond investment is contemplated, to have floating-rate-based liabilities in order to match their floating-rate-based assets. Historically, when the central bank pursued any monetary move, it tended to adjust both deposit rates and loan rates simultaneously. Therefore, the FRN based on the one-year time deposit rate provides the perfect instrument for banks to hedge their interest risk.

At the current stage of market development, banks remain the main investors in government bonds and financial debentures. Therefore, banks' requirements have to be taken into account when designing floating instruments. An advantage of deposit-rate-based FRNs is that the major investors in the IBBM are banks, and banks' major liability item is the one-year deposit. Therefore, the one-year deposit rate as a reference rate helps banks manage their assets and liabilities. It also helps the issuer, the CDB, to achieve its assets and liability management (ALM).

The interest rate, benchmarked against the one-year term deposit rate by the PBOC plus a fixed spread determined through the auction method, will "float" with the interest rate adjustments as determined by the PBOC. As loan interest rates fluctuate in line with adjustments in the deposit rate, the duration of the outstanding bond should match the mid- and long-term loans of the CDB, which would effectively hedge the interest rate risk of the CDB's portfolio.

Since their introduction, floating-rate bonds have become a very important product in China's bonds market. A few months later, treasury and corporate bonds followed the CDB's FRN model for large-volume issuances. As an important innovation, floating-rate bonds had a major function of reducing interest rate risk. Despite further declines in statutory and market interest rates, floating-rate bonds have witnessed increasing investor demand. Although issuers expanded their issuances and the number of transactions, the market spread had tightened, and the spread for the CDB's floating-rate bond issuances narrowed from the original 1.165 percent to

0.49 percent in 2003, reflecting investors' preference for floating-rate products. As of May 31, 2006, the CDB had issued 47 floating-rate bonds with a volume of RMB604.5 billion (excluding fixed-rate bonds convertible into floating-rate bonds). Except for the three-year financial debenture issuance in September 2003, almost all floating-rate bonds are interest-bearing mid- and long-term instruments with a maturity of 7 years (10 issues) and 10 years (23 issues), among which 10 year bonds account for the largest amount.

Table 23.1 summarizes the differences among deposit rate-based floating-rate bonds and those popular in the international market.

Pricing China's Floating-Rate Bonds

The rationale behind bond pricing is to create as accurate a market-term structure curve (yield curve) as possible by employing real data from the same period and the same market (e.g., quotations, trading, clearing, etc.).

In calculating yields, the deposit-based floating-rate bond is quite different from its counterpart in the international market. The interest rate of the floating-rate bond is composed of the interest rate D and the spread S. In the international market, the reference interest rate is usually the relevant market interest rate and the credit spread of the issuer over the reference interest rate (the funding cost of reference issuer). In China's context, however, the reference interest rate is the one-year deposit rate, which has been regulated up to now.

Analysis of the pricing of floating-rate bonds should start with the factors behind the bond prices. In the international market, floating-rate bonds are usually treated as short-term (the remaining days of the corresponding interest payment period) bonds. Regarding cash flow, interest payments as an ongoing cash flow, although uncertain, will not lead to a price change as variable as fixed instruments but will stay in line with market interest going forward.

However, because the predefined spread is fixed, depending on its share of the total real interest (reference rate plus fixed spread), real interest payments will not change along with the market interest rate and therefore will deviate to some degree from the market interest rate. The bond price will also deviate from par value. Therefore, in the international market, the factor behind price changes of floating-rate bonds is the deviation between the fixed interest rate for the next interest payment period and the intraday market rate. If the interest payment cycle can be shortened to one day, the next real interest payment will be reset in line with the market on a daily basis, and the price of floating-rate bonds will remain at par value.

The factors behind price changes of floating-rate bonds in the domestic market are more complicated due to the market's special interest calculation

TABLE 23.1 Comparison between Chinese Floating-Rate Bonds and LIBOR-based Floating-Rate Bonds

	Chinese Floating-Rate Government Bonds	LIBOR-Indexed Floating Rate Bonds
Reference Rate	One-year bank term deposit rate.	Calculated from the rates of 3-month or 6-month loans and the average loan rate of the 16 major banks in London at 11:00 AM every business day.
Characteristics of Basic Rate	Policy rate issued by the central bank.	Market rate decided by commercial banks according to supply and demand.
Basic Rate (Dividend distribution spread)	Decided through tendering upon issuance. The rate remains unchanged before maturity date; the dividend distribution spread reflects anticipation of the trend of future interest rate at the date of issue.	Finalized upon issuance. The rate remains unchanged before maturity date; the dividend distribution spread reflects anticipation on the credit of the issuing institution in the market.
Yield Spread	Varies in line with market anticipation over future interest rate movement and reflects the difference between this anticipation and the initial anticipation (dividend distribution spread). Because it is an interest rate spread, it is connected closely to the trend of the interest rate. For the floating rate spread of non-government bonds, interest rate anticipation and credit anticipation coexist.	Changing constantly and reflecting the difference between the credit of potential issuers and that of the best commercial banks in the market. Individual issuing institutions are correlated, although insignificantly, with LIBOR spread.
Value of Yield Spread	As the floating rate bond has a longer-than-1-year maturity and the deposit interest as its base interest, the value of the spread (including basic spread and yield spread) is usually positive, unless the long-term rate is lower than the short-term rate.	As this value reflects a relative credit, it will be negative as long as the issuer has better credit than the best banks (e.g., U.S. treasury bonds and the bonds from GE, the best company in the United States. As the majority of issuers have worse credit than the best banks, they have a positive spread value.

method. The ongoing interest payment cash flow, as well as the cash flow for next interest payment period, cannot track changes in the market, which leads to price fluctuation. Therefore, in pricing the floating-rate bond in the Chinese market, we must consider not only the next period's interest payment but also every payment throughout the bond's entire life span. Hence, floating-rate bonds cannot be simply regarded as short-term bonds.

The bank's time deposit interest rate, as the present basis of floating-rate bond interest, is actually a policy index. From the point of view of monetary policy, the central bank, in the process of setting the time deposit interest rate, would consider macroeconomic conditions. Therefore, the time deposit interest rate changes are usually inconsistent with market movements.

From a legal point view, a bond is similar to a loan repayment agreement in which the repayment date and amount for each period are expressly defined (i.e., a kind of contract for future cash flow). Both fixed-rate and floating-rate bonds can be regarded as the contracts for the future cash flow. The difference is that fixed-rate bonds expressly define the amount of cash flow for each payment period, while floating-rate bonds only define the method for determining future cash flow without explicitly defining the real payment.

In terms of fixed-rate bond pricing, investors are concerned mainly with cash flow discount factors in every corresponding period. It is therefore necessary to create a market term structure in order to calculate the discount factor for each period. Floating-rate bonds are much more complicated; they not only demand the calculation of discounting factors Φ but also the occurrence of the cash flow C. The pricing formula is:

$$PV = \sum_{i=1}^{N}(\Phi_i \cdot C_i) + \Phi_N \cdot 100$$

The discount factor Φ can be calculated by using the market term structure curve. The bonds with the same credit ratings, whether fixed or floating rate, should enjoy the same returns. Hence, the discounting factor Φ in pricing the floating-rate bond has the same value as that used in the fixed-income market.

Therefore, pricing floating-rate bonds is ultimately an issue of forecasting the occurrence of C_i future cash flows, while C_i is composed of $C_i - D_i + S$.

D_i, the bank time deposit interest rate corresponding to the date the interest rate is set, is the same index for all bonds; S, the spread of a fixed rate bond, has a different value for different bonds. Again, the ultimate problem is the market forecast on D_i. Therefore, we can conclude that the prices of floating-rate bonds are subject to Φ_i and D_i.

In practice, short- and long-term floating-rate bonds differ in their sensitivities to D_i. Generally, long-term bonds will fluctuate more than short-term bonds, reflecting the fact that future cash flow of these bonds will affect bond prices at any given moment.

Floating-Rate Bonds Benchmarked against Seven-Day Repurchase Rate

The CDB made an effort to explore the possibility of using a more market-sensitive reference rate for China's FRNs. Attention focused on the seven-day repurchase (repo) rate. In comparison with other reference rates, the seven-day repo rate is actively traded and is the most liquid and market-sensitive instrument. Soon consensus was reached that an ideal reference for the FRN in China is the seven-day repo rate. However, there are repo rates in two different marketplaces, the inter-bank repo rate and stock exchange repo rate. The reference rate must have indisputable legal authority and not be subject to any manipulation by monopolists so that it can accurately reflect the demand and supply relationship. Only after these issues are properly addressed would the seven-day repo-based FRN be possible.

However, neither of the repo rates could fully comply with these conditions. Market participants in the stock exchange repo market were more diversified, but trading was not as active as in the IBBM. The PBOC favors using the IBBM market repo rate and would like work with CSRC to improve the legal authority of the repo rate as the reference index for FRNs in China. After two years of effort by the CDB in collaboration with the central bank, the conditions were ripe for the seven-day repo-based FRN.

On November 17, 2004, the CDB issued its landmark three-year floating-rate bond benchmarked against the seven-day repurchase rate in the inter-bank market, the first-ever market-oriented floating-rate bond in China. This issue has been the seventeenth financial debenture issued by the CDB since 2004, and its total size was RMB10 billion. The reference interest rate adopted the arithmetic mean of the seven-day weighted repurchase rate for the 10 days prior to November 15 (namely the two weeks benchmark repo, or B2-W data on November 15). This reference interest rate also was used as the benchmark for the bond's first interest payment. The reference interest rate for the second interest payment was the arithmetic mean of the seven-day weighted repurchase rate of the 10 days prior to the previous interest payment date (namely the B2-W data of the previous interest payment), with other reference interest rates calculated by analogy. In addition, the bondholders could choose to put the bonds wholly or in part to the issuer on November 25, 2005, and November 25, 2006, and the face value of the put bonds would be RMB10 million and its integral multiples. The put price was RMB99.8 for every RMB100 face value. The method for calculating interest remains unchanged; calculations were still based on a face value of RMB100.

The benchmark interest rate was the weighted seven-day repurchase interest rate announced by China Foreign Exchange Trading System & National Inter-bank Funding Center. The repo-rate-based FRN was designed to cater to the needs of non-bank financial institutions. Unlike deposit-rate-based FRN instruments, the new reference index is market based and therefore is beneficial to those whose assets are in money market instruments as opposed to loan-based instruments. Therefore, floating-rate bonds are suitable for money market funds and money market arbitragers but not for insurance companies and deposit banks.

This change in the benchmark interest rate partially overcame the weakness of the one-year time deposit interest rate–based FRN: its sensitivity to market changes. The repo rate–based FRN better reflects the issuer's true funding cost (the market interest rate plus a fixed credit spread). In cases where the issuer's credit had no significant changes, the bond price might fluctuate around the face value, which, at least in theory, might avoid the problem of sharp price fluctuations.

Based on the rules of China Securities Regulatory Commission (CSRC), the bond has a 90-day interest payment and rate-resetting period. This means it has a duration of only 45 days and a high yield (similar to that of one-year note from the central bank), and therefore bonds are especially adapted to money market funds with restricted durations. The bonds, as a tool of liquidity management, are also suitable for depository institutions and certain enterprises that are in need of short-term liquidity. As for long-term and short-term money market arbitragers, these bonds have two advantages: (1) they have a more stable trading price than fixed instrument have; and (2) their yield is comparable to the interest rate of one-year bills from the central bank. Theoretically, except for negligible transaction costs, the spread of the bonds is the risk-free income of arbitragers in one year.

However, there are a number of problems involved with the seven-day repo-based FRN.

- *The repurchase interest rate is not completely in line with the interest rate adjustment cycle.* The bonds use the seven-day average repurchase interest rate two weeks or 10 days before the setting date as the benchmark, but the interest rate adjustment cycle is three months; therefore, the two do not match. The benchmark interest rate cannot be secured to reappear in every investment cycle; therefore, investors cannot reset loan investments by investing in benchmark interest rate products, nor can they realize risk-free arbitrage between the bonds and the benchmark interest rate products. Therefore, in pricing the bond, one cannot refer to the interest rate of the three-month central bank note. The benchmark interest rate is directly relevant to the interest spread, but must consider the trend of the following seven-day repurchase rate. Hence, it is necessary to adjust the reference rate in accordance with the future benchmark interest rate.

■ *Historical data on the volatility of the put option is absent.* The transaction cannot be treated as a short-term bond due to the mismatch between the reference interest rate and the interest rate resetting cycle. Therefore, the CDB designed the put option at the end of each year to ensure that the bond's value would be no lower than the put price at year-end. However, the value of the put option involves the judgment regarding the levels of the forward repurchase rate and money market interest rates. The current market yield curve makes possible the calculation of the one-year forward interest rate of financial debentures for the following three years (roughly 3.50 percent, 4.35 percent, and 5.60 percent respectively) and even the quarterly forward interest rate for the next several years. However, because it is difficult to make sound judgments about the forward movement of the benchmark interest rate, it is hard to price the put option.

■ *Pricing should reflect uncertainty of market and institutional move-ment.* The holding period of the bonds can be regarded as one year, with the liquidity risks similar to the one-year central bank note, because of the put option, but as an investment, a higher yield is required. This is because a quarterly adjusted interest rate implies that, unlike fixed-rate bonds of the same maturity, a one-year floating-rate bond has an uncer-tain yield. It is essentially different from inflation-protected floating-rate bonds, which can secure a fixed return. Higher uncertainty may lead to greater downside risk and higher upside potential. In addition, the reference interest rate is sensitive to the reserve ratio and the interest rate on excess reserves. Over time, along with the development of market-oriented reform of interest rates, the excess reserve ratio will gradually diminish. Therefore, the reference interest rate may decline at some time later. Against this background, the bonds do not provide any protection. These policy-related risks must be reflected in the basis points of the floating-rate bonds.

■ *Arbitrage leverage strategy need to be taken into account.* Using arbi-trage, investors can raise funds through repo to buy the floating-rate bonds. Therefore, the difference between the reference interest rate and the financing cost is their profit. If the repo rate is close to the reference rate, as it usually is, then they offset each other, and spread becomes a stable income for the arbitrager. Furthermore, if the reference interest rate is expected to be the repo financing cost three months in the future, it is risk-free to arbitrage as long as the cash flow chain is not broken. The gross profits using the arbitrage can be represented by B2 W—the benchmark interest rate of the new bonds—minus B3 M—the lag time for three months (seven-day repurchasing weighted average interest rate of the past three months). According to historical data, gross profits have great volatility, from -97 basis points to -103 basis points, as the changes in the statutory reserve rate and interest rates of excess reserves led to sharp changes in the seven-day repo rate. This, in turn, prevents B2 W from accurately representing the financing cost three months in the future.

Whether the comparable benchmark in the reference market is the yield of the three-month or one-year central bank note is highly relevant to the business strategy of institutional investors. Because of the relatively poor liquidity, at present, the three-month central bank note is less viable than roll-over selling repo (or 2004 China Development Bank seventeenth issue) (i.e., requiring relatively higher liquidity compensation). The strategy generally adopted in the market is selling repos and buying central bank notes as a hedge. This is called *carry trade*. Therefore, it is natural that the final spread should be compared with the one-year central bank note. As the investors' major investment strategies are based mainly on allocation rather than on seven-day and three-month spread arbitrages, investors require a higher compensation premium for the mismatched risk between the reference interest rate's term and the resetting term. Meanwhile, investors tend to focus on the downside risk of the reference interest rate. Due to the transaction's annually exercisable put option, investors are more inclined to price the transaction against the one-year central bank note. As arbitrage investors focus more on the spread arbitrage opportunity between the short-term interest rate and the interest rate of the FRN, however, they tend to price the transaction against the three-month central bank note.

As most allocation investors are leading market players, it is critical to consider their pricing decisions when positioning a transaction in the primary market. However, the bid-winning results will show the investment opportunities in the shorter-term bonds. For example, suppose the liquidity of three-month central bank notes or short-term bonds can be boosted (e.g., if the CDB reopens or debuts shorter-term bonds); then the arbitrage strategy can be activated, and bonds will have greater investment potential. We believe that the investment opportunities, whether arbitrage- or allocation-based, will play an equally important role along with the development of more sophisticated investment models in the fixed-income market.

CHINA DEVELOPMENT BANK'S OPTION BONDS

The option bond is an important bond product in developed markets. The key to pricing option bonds is in pricing the option, commonly based on the option pricing model.

Introduction to Option Bonds

The right to buy the bond is a call option and the right to sell the bond is a put option. The issuer's option is equivalent to a call option, and the investor's option is equivalent to a put option. Correspondingly, option bonds are divided into callable bonds and put-able bonds. The former offers issuers the right to choose to sell back the bonds before maturity; the latter offers investors the right to choose to repay the bonds before maturity. Under uncertain market conditions, the options provide the issuers or investors with the flexibility of adjusting their investment strategy according to the market movement.

The CDB is a pioneer of option bonds in China. Since the advent of option bond, CDB has made an effort to pile up the stock of option bonds to a certain level in order to strengthen their liquidity by periodically issuance of the bonds. In addition, CDB has been an active market player in the option bond trading since then. Table 23.2 summarizes the issuing statistics of these bonds.

Pricing Methods

When an issuer issues a callable bond, the issuer has the right to redeem the bonds at face value either on a specified redemption date (European option) or on any business day (American option). If the actual term of the bond is uncertain, whether the issuer chooses to redeem the bond before maturity depends mainly on two factors: (1) the forward curve implied in the current

TABLE 23.2 Issuing Statistics for CDB Option Bonds, 2001 to 2005

Option Bonds	2001	2002	2003	2004	2005
Callable bonds of issuers		02 CDB 06th, 02 CDB 15th, 02 CDB 18th	03 CDB 02nd, 03 CDB 13th, 03 CDB 14th		05 CDB 10th, 05 CDB 13th
Put-able bonds of investors	01 CDB 20th	02 CDB 05th	03 CDB 15th, 03 CDB 16th	04 CDB 02nd, 04 CDB 11th	05 CDB 03th, 05 CDB 05th, 05 CDB 07th, 05 CDB 22th

yield curve (the yield to maturity [YTM] curve) in comparison with the forecasted future interest rate, and (2) the bond coupon rate in comparison with the market yield. If the bond coupon rate is higher than the market yield, the issuer will not exercise its call option, and vice versa.

Subdebt is commonly designed as a callable bond with a step-up structure; that is, the coupon is set higher some years in the future than it is in the first few years. This gives the issuer the right to exercise the option. However, if a step-up structure is attached, investors believe the possibility of a call by the issuer is slim; therefore, the price of the call option is lower, which benefits the issuer. The difference between forward yields and step-up coupon rates is perceived in the market as a key factor in pricing the option product. The same is true of the subordinated financial bonds issued by the Bank of China and the China Construction Bank; since the step-up coupon added 280 basis points, the issuer is unlikely to exercise its option after five years, and, therefore, the yields are closer to a five-year product.

Bonds with an issuer's call option and those with an investor's put option are similar in regard to pricing. An investor's put-able bond gives the investor the right to sell the bond to the issuer at the face value on a specified date. In practice, the decision to sell the bond is made based on the comparison between the forward interest rate and the coupon rate. Based on pricing in the issuing market, the issuing yield of the product is consistent with short-term fixed-rate products, which means that investors will exercise their option to sell, reflecting the fact that the intrinsic value of the put-able product is underestimated to a certain extent.

Modern financial theory provides more sophisticated tools for pricing options; the Black-Scholes model and the binomial model are commonly used. However, the undesired market liquidity and limited data for calculating volatility has restricted China's ability to use these models. Many research institutions affiliated with securities firms are using computerized option pricing models as a pricing reference.

For these reasons, unsophisticated investors, especially individual investors, tend to compare option bonds with fixed coupon-bearing bonds; for example, they compare 5-year put options with 10-year bonds and 5-year bonds. There are three different ways to see these comparisons.

1. Ten-year bonds with a 5-year put option are equivalent to 5-year bonds, and therefore the pricing should be the same as that of 5-year bonds.
2. Put-able bonds of 10-year maturity are priced lower than 5-year bonds, so the coupon rate should be higher than that of the 5-year bonds although lower than that of the 10-year bonds.
3. The coupon rate of put-able bonds should be lower than that of the 5-year bonds.

Obviously, the first two views are incorrect. Since the 10-year bonds can be repaid after 5 years, they are at least equivalent to the 5-year bonds. That is to say, the 10-year bonds with 5-year put option are no worse than the 5-year bonds. If the investors have the right to choose to be repaid after 5 years, the 10-year bonds with 5-year put option are equivalent to the 5-year bonds. We believe that the 10-year bonds with 5-year put option are better than the 5-year bonds because they are more flexible (i.e., the option has value). After 5years when the option is due, if the interest rate goes up, investors may choose to exercise the option and reinvest; if the interest rate goes down, then investors may choose to continue holding the bonds and keep the higher rate of return. Five-year bonds do not offer this flexibility.

REOPENING BOND AND ITS PRICING

A new issuance with a term identical to an outstanding bond is called a reopening bond. Reopening bonds are designed to boost the liquidity of an off-the-run bond (a bond that is not traded actively because the time remaining to maturity is short) in the secondary market by expanding the total stock of that bond. (It was gradually realized that the liquidity of bonds is valuable: The more liquid the bond, the higher the price, and the lower the yield.) The larger the issue, the better the liquidity, and the more confidence investors will have in the issue.

Introduction to Reopening Bonds in China

The CDB issued 10 billion yuan of 30-year fixed-rate bonds for the first time in March 2002. This was the first reopening bond in the interbank bond market in China. After reopening, the total volume of this instrument amounted to 15 billion yuan, and the liquidity of the secondary market was greatly improved. The terms of the newly issued bonds are identical to the terms of the previous bonds, and the price is set through auction. Because reopening boosted trading and enhanced liquidity, it made the new issuance costs cheaper and therefore benefited the issuers.

There were eight reopening transactions among the CDB's 31 issuances in 2003, with an issuance level of 90 billion yuan accounting for 24 percent of the total bond issuance of that year. When the market was exposed to fluctuations in the second half of 2003, the CDB reopened off-the-run bonds, which had shorter remaining maturities, thereby improving the liquidity of the bonds. Reopening bonds were well received in the market and helped to stabilize investors' confidence. In addition, reopening off-the-run instruments greatly strengthened the appeal of the CDB's debt financing.

TABLE 23.3 CDB's New Issuance of Bonds
(Unit: billion Yuan)

2002	2003	2004	2005	2006	Total
250	420	360	365	630	2025

Table 23.3 shows the rapid increase of CDB new issuance. In 2001, CDB new issue was only 250 billion yuan, but in 2006 the new issue increased to 680 billion yuan, close to the T-bond new issuance of the year. The total new issuance in the past five years is up to 2075 billion yuan.

Pricing New Issues

In theory, the value of bonds is the present value of future cash flows. Fixed-rate bonds and floating-rate bonds can be perceived as committed contracts of future cash flows. The difference between the two categories of bond instruments lies in the fact that fixed-rate bonds clearly define each cash flow, while floating-rate bonds only define the formula by which the future cash flows can be calculated.

As was indicated, the pricing formula of the fixed rate bond is:

$$PV = \sum_{i=1}^{N}(\Phi_i \cdot C) + \Phi_N \cdot 100$$

Where Φ_i represents the discount factors of every term and C represents the cash flow.

For a reopening bond, the term (i.e., coupon and maturity date) is identical to the existing bond. The unique difference between reopening bonds and the off-the-run bonds they relate to is that the spot rate curve, by which the discount factors are calculated, has changed; that is, Φ_i is no longer the same as when the off-the-run bond was issued. As discount factors have to be changed to be consistent with the current market spot rate curve, the reopening bonds are usually not sold at par. This is because when the bond is reopened at par value, $PV = 100$, the coupon rate C should change, and then the coupon rate would be different from the coupon rate of the off-the-run issue, which is counter to our assumption that the coupon rate should be identical. However, if the coupon rate remains unchanged, the reopening price would not be at par.

In practice, investors tend to use a straightforward pricing method, which is different from the theoretical method. When investors bid for the reopening bonds, they generally base their bids on the yield to maturity in the secondary market of bond issued and use it as a benchmark. At the same time, taking into consideration the increased liquidity of the existing bonds resulting from reopening, the real yield should be the yield to maturity in the secondary market less a certain liquidity premium. In this way, the yield is calculated.

In summary, financial debentures issued by financial institutions are the main fixed-income instruments in China; for example, the debentures issued by the CDB alone accounted for one-third of the total bond stock at the end of 2005. This special feature is due mostly to the dominance of the banking sector in China's financial system. In addition, the main investors in China are, at least to date, commercial banks. This unique feature has three implications for market development:

1. The primary bond exchange (i.e., the exchange between government and bond market participants) is very much influenced by the supervisory structure. Three agencies—China Bank Regulatory Commission (CBRC), CSRC, and China Insurance Regulatory Commission (CIRC)—oversee banking, the stock market, and insurance companies, respectively. The capital market is related to these three sectors, and many financial products, especially derivative products, are cross-sector products. However, no unified regulation covers the three sectors. As a result, overlapping jurisdictions and a lack of supervision are becoming problems. For example, one of the consequences is that IBBM disassociates from the stock exchange market. Financial debentures issued by banks are very much controlled by the CBRC; however, the CBRC's trading is confined to the IBBM, which is essentially based on the money market.
2. The banks' function as investors has two important preconditions: Bank loans are controlled by the central bank either via deposit/loan ratio or via quota, and the yields on government bonds and financial debentures are higher than the bank deposit rate. These two conditions would no longer exist if the central bank's control over the deposit rate is removed and loan interest regulation is liberalized.
3. Risks within the banking sector cannot be diversified through the capital market in the current institutional framework due to the segmentation of the IBBM from the SEM.

CHAPTER 24

Development of China's Corporate Bond Market

L egally, corporate bonds are certificates of a corporation's indebtedness. However, from a market point of view, corporate bonds are the principal market instruments. In the United States, most non-government bond instruments fall into the category of corporate bonds. For example, the Yankee bond, issued by issuers outside of the United States, is classified as a corporate bond. For many years, corporate bonds in China have been dubbed enterprise bonds to reflect the fact that the issuers were state-owned enterprises (SOEs), which are not corporations in terms of their organizational structure. According to the *Rules on Enterprise Bonds* promulgated by the State Council in 1993, enterprise bonds are securities issued by the businesses established in accordance with China's legal procedures as legal entities. However, since 2001, against the background of changing corporate governance of businesses in China, more and more non-SOE corporate companies have been authorized to issue securities in the market. Nowadays, the concept of corporate bond is generally accepted in China.

CORPORATE BOND MARKET DEVELOPMENT

There are two categories of corporate bonds in China—central corporate bonds and local corporate bonds—which reflect their relationship to the central and local governments. The bonds issued by government agencies and large enterprises directly under the central government are the central corporate bonds. Generally, they are approved by the State Council and listed on the stock exchanges.

Local corporate bonds were first issued in 1985. Their maturities were mainly between one and five years, and their interest rate was slightly higher than the banks' corresponding deposit rate. The issuing target was mainly the individual investor whose interest income from corporate bonds was subject to a 20 percent withholding tax. Local corporate bond issuance was suspended at the end of the 1990s because of the government's concern about default cases due to ill-performing corporations.

The standard local corporate bonds in China can be divided into three types:

1. *Coupon-bearing corporate bonds.* Similar to the coupon-bearing government bond, coupon-bearing corporate bonds have coupon attached to the paper bonds. The bearer form of the coupon-bearing corporate bond is not registered, and the issuer is not liable for its loss. The paper securities have at most five-year maturities and, generally, the interest is paid once a year. When the coupon payment is due, the underwriter, who worked as an intermediary to sell the bonds, detaches the coupon and pays the interest on behalf of the issuer. When the bonds are mature, the holders can redeem the principal with the underwriter. Today, most paper coupon-bearing corporate bonds are issued through private placement.

    Since 2000, most central corporate bonds have been issued in book-entry form, targeted at institutional investors and traded in the stock exchanges.

2. *Bearer-form zero-coupon corporate bonds.* This category of bonds was issued mostly by local corporations with paper-form securities. The term was between one to five years, the bonds were issued at par value, and the interest was paid in a lump sum on the maturity date. After issuance, the bonds can be transferred or held as collateral for other borrowing. The target investors include enterprises, public service units, and urban and rural residents.

3. *Structured corporate bonds.* Structured corporate bonds are corporate bonds with options, such as put-able or callable corporate bonds. These categories of corporate bonds are designed to attract banks and institutional investors and since the early 2000s have become very popular. Floating-rate notes, following the model of the China Development Bank (CDB), are also frequently issued by corporations to cater the investor's preference for these structures.

In addition, short-term corporate notes have been major corporate financing instruments, used to finance their short-term funding requirements. The short-term bill was first issued in Shanghai in 1987. In 1989 they were promoted nationwide to facilitate enterprises' short-term financing needs. The term was generally three months, six months, and nine months. The issuance target was enterprises and individuals, and the interest rate was higher than that of the corresponding deposit rate. Use of the proceeds was restricted to short-term financing rather than for investing in fixed assets or for long-term financing.

In the 1990s a number of special-purpose bonds were issued. Most notable were housing construction bonds (issuance has been suspended), which began in 1992, when RMB643 million were issued; the proceeds were used mainly for the construction of local residential housing. Internal bonds once were popular as well. The issuance of this type of bonds began in 1988; the issuance target was mainly employees in the enterprises. For the state-owned enterprises, the proceeds were used mainly for short-term liquidity while for the collectively run enterprises, they were used for start-up capital. Finally, bonds of local investment companies (issuance has been suspended as well) also were popular in the early 1990s. These new corporate bonds were first issued in 1992, with an offering volume of RMB437 million. The issuers were local investment companies, and the proceeds were used mainly for key local construction projects.

The early stage of corporate bond market development was characterized by loose and segmented supervision. A number of cases of corporate failure triggered defaults. Therefore, in the second half of 1990s, corporate bond issuance subsided.

Since 2000, China's corporate bond market has started to pick up and has developed rapidly in terms of issuance size and market structure. The issuance size of corporate bonds was 8.3 billion yuan in 2000, 14.7 billion yuan in 2001, 32.5 billion yuan in 2002, 35.8 billion yuan in 2003, and 32.7 billion yuan in 2004. At the same time, institutional investors (insurance institutions, fund institutions, and rural credit cooperative unions) became the mainstay of the investor base. Along with the financial market reform, the number of institutional investors continues to grow and the market infrastructure is improving constantly.

CORPORATE ISSUING STATUS

Corporate bond issuers must be qualified enterprises, and their qualifications are reviewed and approved by the National Development and Reform Commission (NDRC). Issuers in the corporate bond market must meet certain minimum requirements before they can issue corporate bonds. Several documents govern corporate bond market, such as *Corporation Law* and *Rules on Corporate Bonds*.

Corporation Law is the principal legal document governing the corporate bond market. According to this document, there are six requirements for a corporation to issue bonds:

1. The net assets of public companies may not be below 30 million yuan, and the net assets of limited liability companies may not be below 60 million yuan.
2. The total amount of bonds outstanding may not exceed 40 percent of the net assets of the company.
3. The average distributable profits over the previous three years must be sufficient to defray one year's interest payment on the company's bonds.
4. The proceeds raised through corporate bonds must be consistent with state industrial policy.
5. The coupon rate on corporate bonds must not exceed the levels set by the State Council.
6. The corporation must meet other requirements specified by the State Council elsewhere.

Rules on Corporate Bonds regulates corporate enterprises' bond issuance in China. Five requirements are specified:

1. The financial accounting system of the enterprise must comply with state regulations as established by the NDRC.
2. The enterprise should be rated and proved able to pay its own debts.
3. The enterprise should have made profits for three consecutive years before issuing corporate bonds.
4. The purpose of the funds raised should accord with the state industrial policy.
5. The proceeds should be proven to have social and economic benefit and that they will be used effectively. The total face value of the corporate bonds issued should not be greater than the net value of self-owned assets of the enterprise.

In addition, the funds raised by corporate bonds must be used for the purposes approved by the relevant authority and may not be used:

- To cover losses or for nonproductive expenditures
- In such risky investments as real estate transactions, transactions unrelated to the production and operation of the company

If the funds raised by corporate bonds are used to invest in fixed assets, the relevant authority must approve the transaction.

The NDRC sets priorities for the projects that it deems important to be financed, wholly or in part, by the issuance of corporate bonds. However, the total issuance is subject to the corporate bond quota, which is set by the State Council to control the amount of corporate bonds issuance. Central corporation enterprises can, based on their funding program, forward their application directly to the NDRC for their bond quota. The NDRC reviews the applications and provincial reports toward the end of the year and prepares an annual corporate bond-issuing plan for the State Council's approval. After the plan is approved, the NDRC allocates bond-issuing quotas to the central government affiliate enterprises and the provincial development and reform commissions.

After the enterprise obtains its bond-issuing quota, it applies to the administrative department according to the requirements of the bond-issuing application documents. If the bond is targeted to investors nationwide, it is up to the NDRC together with the People's Bank of China (PBOC) and the China Securities Regulatory Commission (CSRC) to jointly approve the issue. If the bond is targeted at local investors, the provincial development and reform commission must approve the issuance and file a report with the NDRC for approval.

The Shanghai Stock Exchange introduced one-, three-, and seven-day corporate bond repurchase products at the end of 2002, which has exerted a far-reaching influence on the corporate bonds market and its development as a financial derivative.

DEVELOPMENT OF REGULATORY FRAMEWORK

Securities Law, Corporation Law, and other codes regulate the issuing and underwriting of corporate bonds in China. The approval procedure of issuance is covered mainly in the *Rules on Corporate Bonds* issued in 1993, which regulate the issuance quota, targeted industry, interest rate, and so on. However, these rules are no longer applicable and enforceable because of changes in the market environment.

As the leading supervisory department, the NDRC is contemplating the drafting of new rules, and it is expected that these rules will relax to some extent restrictions on the approval procedure, issuer, interest rate, and information disclosure, among other things. In addition, the regulatory framework of secondary market trading is also due for a new round of reform. In 2003, the corporate bond repurchase (repo) was introduced, making trading in the secondary market more active. As a result, market liquidity has improved. The administrative approval authority for a listing corporate bond on the exchanges was transferred to the Board of Exchanges in 2004, substantially simplifying the approval procedures. In the same year, corporate bonds were introduced to the inter-bank bond market (IBBM) when the first China Railway Bond was issued. This marked a breakthrough in transmarket corporate bond trading.

The liberalized policy toward the corporate bonds market has improved the efficiency of listed corporate bonds and significantly enhanced the liquidity and investment value of all corporate bonds. The positive policy orientation also boosts the outlook of bond market development in the future.

This change in the regulatory framework of corporate bonds has provided more room for market participants to maneuver and paved the way for the further development of the corporate bond market. However, due to overlapping jurisdictions of the corporate bond market, it is unlikely that there will be a unified regulatory framework and general rules for the corporate bond market in the near future. Market innovation is therefore limited within the current legal framework. However, for there to be a fundamental change in the regulatory framework, further changes in institutional arrangements are necessary. For example, merging the three supervisory bodies that regulate banking, the stock market, and the insurance industry into one body and ruling out the possibility of government direct intervention in market activities would help create a sound, unified, market-oriented, powerful regulatory framework. Thus, the solution must go beyond the bond market itself.

Since 2003, the direction of the corporate bond market reform has been focused on deregulation, such as relaxing entry restrictions and diversifying instruments, reflecting the government's concern over corporate financing amid the recessionary stock market. However, the overlapping jurisdiction over bond markets constitute an insurmountable constraint and circumscribes fundamental changes in the corporate bond market.

Relaxation of Restrictions on Market Entry

The deluge of defaults in the 1990s led to strict regulations on corporate bond financing. With the shift in focus from SOEs to private companies and small and medium enterprises (SMEs), diversification of issuers has become the policy orientation of agencies involved in industrial development. Along with economic reform, private companies and SMEs became the mainstay of China's economy. However, these companies have long been excluded from bond financing and also are not able to access bank credit because of their lack of credit history and the cumbersome evaluation process.

Liberalization of the Policy Mix

Recognizing that the regulations related to corporate bond transactions contained too many constraints that stifled the innovative efforts of market participants and that unnecessary policy obstacles had to be removed in order to promote innovation in the corporate bond market, the agencies initiated a number of moves to liberalize financial regulations.

Since 2003, several constructive policies have been promulgated, relating to expanding the issuing size, broadening the investor base, and revitalizing trading in corporate bonds. These policies include mainly:

- *Regulations Governing Investment in Corporate Bonds by Insurance Companies*. These regulations were issued by the China Insurance Regulatory Commission, which encourages the insurance companies to expand their investments in corporate bonds in order to diversify their portfolios. The participation of insurance companies in the bond market has greatly broadened the investor base.
- *Rules of Registration and Depository Trust of Real-name Book-entry Corporate Bonds*. These rules were promulgated by the China Government Securities Depository Trust & Clearing Co. Ltd. (CGSDTC), which regulates corporate bonds with respect to registration, custody, and trading in the electronic transmission system.

    Both regulations help the market operate safely and effectively. The book-entry form clearance and settlement regulatory progress helps eliminate paper securities and improves the use of the electronic transmission system for trading corporate bonds. This not only increases the efficiency of the corporate bond market, but also broadens the investor base as more investors can access the local corporate bonds.
- *Rules of Interbank Transaction of Corporate Bonds*. These rules, issued by the PBOC, cover trading in the IBBM. They allow corporate bonds to be traded in both IBBM and the stock exchange market.

MARKET INNOVATIONS

Since 2003, the bond market has become increasingly volatile amid the changes in the macroeconomic environment. Corporations that wished to shake off the financial distress were under pressure of new financing. Orthodox corporate financing through bank loans was difficult, as banks tended to lend money to the corporations or enterprises with sound financial positions and records. Thus, corporate bonds were only available to small number of good firms who had financial strength. The financial institutions were stimulated by the financial distress to initiate a new round of market innovation.

Market participants wanted to reduce uncertainty via market instruments that would hedge their risks. Financial innovations emerged and were put into practice. According to monetary theory, if the demand for money is greater than the money supply, then the supply of bonds will outnumber the demand for bonds. When bonds are in short supply amid monetary expansion, then investors tend to be defensive. When bonds are in good supply amid monetary tightening, the opposite is true, and issuers will be defensive. In both cases, market participants have an incentive to manage their risks via innovative activities.

Issuer-driven Innovations

Innovations driven by market participants relate to designing new instruments and working out innovative selling methods. In 2004, numerous newly designed instruments and selling techniques were introduced to cater to the changes in investors' behavior as a result of changes in the bond market environment. The financial intermediaries played an important part in these innovations. However, most of the market innovations were led by the CDB, although they were extensively used by financial institutions. Some successful examples, as indicated, are the introduction of floating-rate notes (FRNs) and callable and put-able bonds. In 2003, long-term bonds were introduced in the corporate market. Three Gorges Company issued the 30-year super-long-term fixed-rate 03 Three Gorges Corporate Bond, advised by the CDB, captured the market and was very well received. The coupon rate was only 4.86 percent compared to the 5.76 percent of a bank loan.

Intermediary-driven Innovations

Financial intermediaries are the main contributors to market efficiency. As a result of their efforts, the selling period was cut from 20 workdays to 5 workdays (from the day of launch to the time when the bond was sold to the end investor), and the time horizon between launch day and closing day was shortened to 6 days.

The interaction between issuers and investors is the main driver of bond market innovation. For example, market innovations make the issuer pay more attention to negotiating with institutional investors and give more benefits to investors when they design the issuing format. Instruments were diversified to cater to the needs of both issuers and investors. For example, the put-able bonds, callable bonds, convertible bonds, bonds with minimum rate guarantees, and others were designed to meet the needs of risk-averse investors. In this way, China's corporate bonds became more investor-friendly. In addition, professional price negotiation alliances, composed of professional institutional investors and some insurance companies, have been formed to take the advantage of the collective power of investors and negotiate bond prices with corporate bond issuers.

The financial intermediary industry has evolved to accommodate the changing market environment. First, joint lead managers emerged to strengthen the intermediation function of syndicate. For example, the joint lead underwriters of the 2003 China Railway Bond were the CDB and the China International Trust and Investment Company (CITIC) Securities Co. Ltd.; the joint lead underwriters of the 2003 Shanghai Rail Transportation Construction Bond were the CDB and China Galaxy Securities Co. Ltd.; and the joint lead underwriters of the 2004 Chinese Railway Bond were CITIC Securities Co. Ltd., China Galaxy Securities Co. Ltd., and China Securities Co., Ltd.

At the same time, underwriters devoted a great deal of work, material resources, and financial resources to bond transactions, and the financing size of a single bond transaction has expanded substantially. Years ago, a bond issuing size over RMB2 billion was rare; today, many transactions are over RMB8 to 10 billion. There is more competition among the securities firms to become bond transaction lead managers. Financial institutions need to demonstrate their financial strength before they can be chosen as lead managers of underwriting syndicate.

The credit rating became a legal requirement for corporate bond issuance. To meet this requirement, rating institutions were enhanced, and the double-rating mechanism was introduced to give investors greater confidence. For instance, 2003 High and New Technology Bond was independently rated by China Lianhe Credit Rating Co. Ltd. and China Chengxin International Credit Rating Co., Ltd.; 2003 China Railway Bond was independently rated by China Lianhe Credit Rating Co. Ltd. and Dagong Global Credit Rating Co., Ltd. For many years, the market convention was that investors would accept only triple-A-rated bonds, a reflection of the risk-averse nature of investors. However, with the rapid development of the institutional investor industry, some institutional investors, such as investment funds, looking for higher yields, were willing to invest in lower-rated bonds, such as the 2003 High and New Technology Bond, which was rated grade-AA by two credit rating institutions.

This important step demonstrates that investors already have accepted the idea of higher risk/higher yield in their investment philosophy. In addition, credit rating companies are paying more attention to improving investor services and have strengthened their follow-up work after bond transactions.

Commercial banks became the main guarantors of corporate bonds. Among the 15 corporate bonds issued in 2003, 11 corporate bonds, containing irrevocable joint and several liability clauses, were guaranteed by commercial banks, substantially reducing the bonds' credit risk and boosting the confidence of investors. Until 2006, corporate bonds issuance had to be guaranteed by qualified institutions; however, this rule has been abolished. In May 2006, Three Gorges Company placed its corporate bond transaction after approval by the NDRC. This is the first transaction since 1998 without an explicit guarantee. This new practice signifies a policy move that investors have to take responsibility for the risk of their investment decision.

Market-driven Innovations

The rapid development of the financial debenture market opened a conduit for other financial institutions to access the bond market. The innovations of the CDB stimulated the idea that financial institutions can manage their risk and diversify their asset portfolio through the corporate bond market. In 2003, a short-term financing bill was introduced by the CSRC to ease the financing pressure on securities firms. At the same time, subordinated bonds, which were designed to enable commercial banks to increase tier two capital, were introduced by the PBOC in an effort to satisfy the capital adequacy ratio requirement. By 2004, the total amount of public offerings of subordinated bonds by commercial banks exceeded 65 billion yuan, while short-term financing bonds of securities companies (over 6 billion yuan) were mostly done by private placement due to the issuers' substandard credit ratings.

There are certain similarities between the subordinated bonds of commercial banks and short-term financing bonds of securities companies on one hand and corporate bonds on the other. Therefore, the experience gained from issuing corporate bonds was referred to extensively in designing and selecting the selling format of these instruments. Investors' preferences are the major consideration in designing the bond instrument and selling format. As more and more new faces enter the market, investors become selective; pricing favors investors due to competition among issuers; and more investors and financial institutions shift their focus from the stock market to the bond market.

The CDB made a great effort to open the corporate bond market to private companies and SMEs via so-called credit enhancement and package issuance. In 2004, the issuance of 2003 High and New Technology Bond was lead-managed by the CDB and underwritten by an underwriting syndicate. The bond issuer was a package issuers group; members are technology-related SMEs, similar to the collectively borrowed by the government and individually repaid by borrowing institutions (CBIR) format (see Chapter 17), which was credit-enhanced by the Ministry of Natural Science and Technology.

Similar to the securitization program, the package issuing structure was characterized by combined issuance, individual repayment, and government credit enhancement. Package issuance was new to the corporate bond market and provided a fresh solution to the financing problems of private companies and SMEs. Reguarantees committed by local finance departments boosted the creditworthiness of the technology-related SMEs. The CDB not only served as the guarantor of corporate bond it underwrote, but also gave investors enough confidence to invest in the bond because of its own financial strength and quasi-sovereign rating by international rating agencies, such as Standard & Poor's and Moody's.

This credit enhancement, while necessary, provides the opportunity for substandard companies to enter to the corporate bond market. However, with heterogeneous credit of issuers, investors have to be educated, trained, and advised to evaluate each investment on their own.

UNDERWRITING CORPORATE BONDS

As indicated, the capital market in China only began in the early 1990s. Indirect financing remains the major conduit for business firms. Banks accumulated risks amid economic cycles, but there is no way for them to diversify their risks without a sound capital market.

The CDB has been engaged in policy-related lending, the proceeds of which are invested in long-term projects. Although the duration of liabilities matches its long-term assets, it is in the CDB's own interest to diversify its assets portfolio. Therefore, the CDB is not only reinforcing its securitization program but would like also to bring some qualified firms into the bond market in order to reduce the financing costs of these firm and to diversify the bank's own risks. The CDB can play a role in this area by underwriting corporate bonds.

Early Period, August 2000 to May 2001

After the rectification period from 1993 to 1995, the corporate bond market entered a new period of development. The total number of new issues increased gradually. At the end of 1999, there were changes to the supervisory system of corporate bonds. The State Council delegated examination and approval authority to the NDRC, which now is responsible for work related to corporate bond issuance and the approval procedure for issuers whose project is a state priority. At the same time, the *Rules on Corporate Bonds* was revised. During this period, such key customers of the CDB as the Ministry of Railways and China Yangtze Three Gorges Development Corporation obtained issuance quotas and issued several bonds in succession. In order to provide improved service to these key customers and take advantage of the market opportunity to broaden its business line, the CDB participated in the underwriting of the 1999 Chinese Railway Bond and the 1999 Jiangsu Expressway Bond. These bonds were sold mainly to individual investors through commercial banks or sold to the bank's depositors via the bank's branches.

To help its customers diversify their financing resources, the CDB applied to the NDRC and the PBOC for qualification as a bond underwriter. In August 2000, the CDB was licensed to underwrite corporate bonds for its loan customers. In May 2001, the 2001 China Mobile Bonds were lead-managed by the CDB. After being approved as the only banking financial institution allowed to engage in underwriting business in China, the CDB gradually gained underwriting experience and since then has been an active market player.

Period of the Intermediaries, May 2001 to December 2002

This period began with the issuance of the China Mobile Bond in May 2001 to complete the issuance of the Jiangsu Transportation Bond in December 2002. It marked rapid development of the financial intermediation industry.

In December 2001, the 2001 Guangzhou Nuclear Power Bond was lead-managed by the CDB with a great success, proving that the CDB had become an important underwriter in the corporate bond market. Thereafter, the CDB lead-managed 2002's Shenhua Bond, Guangzhou Nuclear Power Bond, and Jiangsu Transportation Bond, becoming a leading underwriter in the corporate bond market.

Due to fierce competition, only those underwriters that can provide the best service and have a strong position in the market can get the mandate from the issuers. Pressures from both issuers and investors lead underwriters to become more sophisticated. As a result, underwriters' services have been improved substantially. The China Mobile Bond of 2001 was the first bond transaction priced through book building. This new selling technique was successfully introduced by the CDB and the China International Capital Corporation (CICC). The CDB also jointly lead-managed the transaction with a 850 million yuan share. Since the underwriting amount in this transaction was the biggest ever, the CDB took advantage of joint efforts between its head office and the branches to accomplish the selling. Soon it established connections with main institutional investors in the bond market, including insurance companies, fund companies, rural credit cooperative unions, big enterprises, and others, and thereby set up its own network of institutional investor bases. The CDB has extensively used the market technique and selling techniques, such as price tension, achieving oversubscription in each transaction.

Period of Rapid Development, 2003 to the Present

The corporate bonds market fluctuated substantially in 2003 due to the upward economic cycle and the central bank's monetary moves. During the first three quarters, there was unprecedented growth in the market; issuances in the primary market and transactions in the secondary market were all very active. Prices in the secondary bond market went down because of the central bank's monetary tightening. In October, the market feared further interest hikes as after the PBOC raised the reserve ratio.

As a result, the long end of the corporate bond yield curve moved upward, and the price of most bonds in the secondary market dropped below face value. This made selling corporate bonds in the primary market very difficult, especially because the administratively set coupon rate cannot match the changing secondary market yield. Under such circumstances, the CDB introduces new instruments to help market participants manage their risks. This effort related to a number of financial innovations, such as FRNs and put-able bonds. The underwriting performance of the CDB in 2003 was gratifying as well. It lead-managed six bond issues: Pudong Development Bank Bond, Shanghai Rail Transportation Construction Bond, Suzhou Gardens Bond, Science and Technology Bond, Railway Bond, and China Netcom Bond. The total amount underwritten was 4.672 billion yuan, and the CDB was recognized as the best underwriter of the year in terms of the number of bond transactions lead-managed and joint-lead-managed as well as the amount underwritten in the securities industry. The CDB withstood the test of market fluctuation. Moreover, unlike other securities firms, which had to hold a certain amount of unsold bonds, the CDB sold all the bonds it had subscribed and distributed to end investors.

The corporate bond markets in 2004 and 2005 were characterized by a number of developments. The most remarkable was the increase in the number of local corporate bond issuers. These issuers are mainly local infrastructure developers; most have some kind of implicit guarantee by the local governments. Due to the depressed stock market during this period, corporate bonds, as an instrument with a relatively higher yield vis-à-vis government bonds and relatively less risk vis-à-vis stocks, attracted most of the institutional investors and individual investors. Most securities firms shifted their attention to the corporate bond market. In addition, during this time, the NDRC accelerated the process of drafting corporate bond regulations. Today the corporate bond market is believed to be on the verge of new era of development.

CHINA DEVELOPMENT BANK'S MARKET PROMOTION EFFORTS

Financial institutions are market participants whose financial innovation efforts are believed to be only for their own benefit. This is not true of the CDB in China. The CDB, as a policy-related financial institution, has not only positioned itself as a market pioneer and an innovative player but also wants to be an institution builder. To do this, the CDB first had to boost its reputation as a successful market player.

The CDB achieved this market position by becoming the *only* bank-related underwriter. By the end of 2003, it had underwritten 26 corporate bonds and was the lead underwriter for 10 corporate bonds with cumulative sales of 11.727 billion yuan. It led the market in sales, operations, and innovation, and was one of the most active and powerful participants in the corporate bond market.

Since 2001, the CDB has established a professional customer service system providing financial advisory services and initial project training, assisting customers applying for bond quota issuance, selling, and listing. The CDB's services cover the entire process of corporate bond issuance, providing customers with a one-stop route to direct financing. As a syndicate member, the CDB brings its customers to the market, provides overall credit enhancement, and helps establish market infrastructure to the corporate bond market, which, in turn, helped create a prosperous corporate bond market.

Client Development

At present, the issuers of corporate bonds are mainly the large-scale state-owned enterprises engaged in building the nation's infrastructure and backbone industries, such as energy, transportation, and infrastructure construction. Many of these enterprises are long-term lending customers of the CDB. Compared to the other bond underwriters, the CDB has the natural advantage of having an extensive customer base. While offering loan financing to large-scale projects, the credit departments of both the head office and branches of the CDB are in a position to help customers with their overall financing arrangements, which gives them firsthand information regarding their customers' demands and preferences.

Characteristics of the CDB's customer relationships are (1) early and active client cultivation; (2) better service and professional advice; and (3) overall financing arrangements. Although the underwriting business in corporate bonds has become more and more competitive, the CDB has taken the advantage of its extensive customer base and network, and won the confidence and satisfaction of its customers with high-quality and professional service.

In the process of developing a potential a bond issuer or bond project, the CDB evaluates the customer's financial condition based on the *Rules on Corporate Bonds* and *Corporation Law*, advising them on how to meet the legal requirements based on their actual circumstances and on how to develop a sound strategy. For those projects that at first cannot meet the requirements of bond issuance conditions, the CDB offers positive guidance and relevant advisory services.

The application period for some projects may last several years. For instance, the CDB started assisting Yangzhou Mining Group in applying for the bond issuance quota of a 2004 corporate bond project in 2000, when the bank started to explore the possibility of bond financing. Yangzhou Mining Group, as a provincial coal enterprise, was not up to the standards of a qualified issuer and, in the initial stage, could not meet the financial requirements. For this reason, the NDRC was unlikely to grant the application for the bond-issuing quota. The CDB created a working team to consult with the relevant departments inside the company. It also acted as a liaison institution and a communications conduit to departments in appropriate agencies so that a solution to the problem could be found.

Yangzhou Mining Group was first advised to issue RMB bonds to replace yen debt incurred from a Japanese energy loan. The purpose of the bond issuance was later adjusted to encompass three projects: a "new-type of gasifier with 1000-ton-coal capacity and auxiliary projects," a "0.2-million-ton acetic acid project," and a "low-heat fuel power plant for Jinxing coal mine No. Three." After repeated coordination by the CDB with the administrative institutions, Yangzhou's financial arrangements met legal requirements and policy guidance for bond issuance.

The CDB also evaluated the financial accountability of Yangzhou and committed to providing a guarantee for its bond issuance. After four years of cultivation, the bond-issuing conditions of Yangzhou Mining Group gradually matured, and it obtained its bond issuance quota in 2004, as a result of the CDB's persistent efforts and effective customer service.

For those projects with relatively mature conditions or those that have obtained their bond issuance quota, the competition for lead manager is often fierce. The CDB takes full professional advantage of its position as a bond-financing bank, providing market analysis reports, program proposals, and working schedules. It also adopts flexible loan rates for large customers as part of the overall financing arrangement.

Project Planning: From Initiation to Issuance

The first stage of underwriting corporate bonds requires preparing application documents, designing the issuance program, and organizing the underwriting syndicate, among other things. The CDB's guiding principle is to give priority to customers' interests at every step. One of the important objectives of the CDB's customer service is to obtain the most cost-effective funding. As an underwriter, the CDB works to make the issuing period as short as possible to ensure the proceeds arrive in the issuers' accounts before the project gets underway.

At the early stages of corporate bond market development, the issuing period tended to be long. When bond issuance was conducted through administrative placement, the process could take months. Obviously, if bond issuance was not completed on time, the project would be delayed. Therefore, underwriters must devise a schedule to take advantage of market opportunities for the transaction. In principle, the lead manager would, in consultation with the issuer, prepare the issuance schedule based on the issuer's funding objectives, the market environment, the specific requirements of maturity, and funding cost.

As a lead manager, the underwriter needs to monitor the market closely so that a proper market strategy can be established. When the CDB is the lead manager of a bond transaction, it put its finger on the pulse of the market and studies interest rate movements, so that the schedule can be synchronized with market movement and can be adjusted to accommodate the changing market environment. As corporate bond issuers tend to be heterogeneous, the CDB designs each bond-issuing schedule according to the particular circumstances of each customer through careful and comprehensive analysis of the operational, financial, and cost status of the customer and market movement. The CDB also pays attention to investors' demands and preferences. When the issuance schedule and program are prepared, the CDB gets feedback from investors through a bond demand questionnaire, which it distributes to all kinds of institutional investors. This helps ensure that the issuing program will be well received by both issuer and investors.

As an application process assistor, the CDB coordinates and expedites approvals. Under the current legal framework, the corporate bond approval procedure remains complicated. As indicated, the NDRC must approve the issuance of corporate bonds. The interest rates of the bonds and underwriters' qualifications must be countersigned by the PBOC and the CSRC. To make the approval process as short as possible, early preparation of the application documents is crucial. Since the staff of the relevant agencies are not necessarily market experts, the CDB must communicate with the administrative institutions at all times, to reply to any questions they may have and clarify any confusion that might arise, and to explain details of debt payment, bond products, interest rates, and the composition of the underwriting syndicate. This requires a great deal of skillful coordination and professional advice. The CDB has institutionalized working procedures whereby the team involved in a project can track the whole approval process, keep strict checks on the quality of the financial statements before the issuance application documents are submitted, keep close contact with the agency staff after reporting, and solve problems in a timely fashion. In addition, the bank modifies the documents to update data and market strategy.

While paying close attention to the approval process, the CDB has revised its market strategy and prepare marketing and promotion strategies. The active market innovation and the synergy of its teamwork helps the CDB to gain momentum and market strength. For example, it launched the 2002 Guangzhou Nuclear Power Bond and 2002 Jiangsu Transportation Bond transactions only two days after receiving formal approval from the authorities; this unprecedented speed greatly satisfied the issuer.

Marketing a Bond Issue Marketing a bond issue includes preparing the road show and educating investors. With several years experience, the CDB has formed a sales organization system that includes such things as product design, the investor road show, and negotiating subselling agreements with other financial institutions. The contents of various related legal documents, such as product questionnaires, bond information materials, and agreement samples, are prepared at the head office and disseminated to the branches and distributed throughout the country through the CDB's national sales network. Well-designed institutional arrangements prepared in advance of issuance are a prerequisite to successful selling.

The working team for corporate bond selling requires a business staff with professional skills, which the CDB has achieved by continuous education and training. In the process of building up its underwriting business, the bank set up a corporate bond business operations system throughout its national network in order to strengthen the training of its branch staff in the corporate bond business. It issued a "Corporate Bond Underwriting Business Manual" to guide its staff. In addition, an incentive system constantly reinforces the employees' own efforts to improve their professional skills.

Listing the Bonds In addition to actively promoting large-scale SOEs to issue bonds in the primary market, the CDB also lists corporate bonds in the stock exchange. By doing so, the CDB can boost its active trading in the secondary market in order to lay the groundwork for a continuous financing channels. The CDB was qualified to recommend listings on the

Shenzhen Stock Exchange and the Shanghai Stock Exchange in 2001. By the end of 2005, 45 corporate bonds were listed in the stock exchange by the CDB's recommendation. After a successful issuance led by the CDB, 2001 Guangzhou Nuclear Power Bond and 2002 Guangzhou Nuclear Power Bond became benchmark products due to their outstanding performance. The first local corporate bond listed in recent years, the 2002 Jiangsu Transportation Bond, rebuilt investor confidence in local corporate bonds. The success of the 2003 Suzhou Gardens Bond stimulates the idea of establishing rollover issuance programs (finance maturing debt via new issue), so that long-term financing requirements could be met.

It is worth noting that the strict regulatory framework and complicated procedures add transaction costs to corporate bond issuance. However, it is unlikely that the agencies involved in the approval process will take the initiative to liberalize or simplify the procedure, since it is the source of their power. Reform is a public good, but it does not benefit the agencies involved, and therefore they have no incentive to change the system. The financial institutions, especially financial intermediaries, however, do have an incentive to reduce transaction costs within the current legal framework because they can share profit with issuers and investors. Both issuers and investors can also benefit from the intermediation of financial intermediaries, which save their transaction costs.

For many years, financial intermediaries were thought of as merchants, in the derogatory sense, meaning that they took advantage of both seller and buyer without contributing to value added. As we indicated earlier, the function of intermediaries is to reduce endogenous transaction costs, which helps to achieve a win-win outcome between the issuer and the intermediaries on one hand and a win-win outcome between the intermediaries and investors on the other.

The CDB's market promotion efforts have numerous implications. The bond market is underdeveloped, not because of market participants' behavior or the investors' irrational behavior, but because the primary economic exchange—the primary financial exchange—which, as an institutional arrangement, should provide rules of the game for the secondary exchange and thereby reduce transaction costs—is not fully developed.

Theoretically, the function of institutions is confined to market participation. As indicated, the primary economic exchange is the exchange between government and market. Market participants cannot present their views and requirements to the government agencies through dialogue. However, market participants can form a kind of *pressure group*[1] to make a strong argument and gain the attention of the government. Market participants are game players, and the rules of game are set by government agencies through the so-called primary economic exchange. If the market, which is where secondary economic exchange occurs, is imperfect, it is because the primary economic exchange is not fully realized. In the language of institutional economic engineering, this is called incomplete primary exchange.

RECENT PBOC INITIATIVES

To boost the IBBM and promote the corporate bond secondary market, the PBOC has taken a number of initiatives since 2004.

In August 2004, the PBOC permitted the China Railway Bond issued in 2001 to trade in the IBBM. Since then corporate bonds gradually have entered IBBM and become cross-market trading products. In December 2004, the PBOC promulgated the *Regulation on Examination on Bond Trading in the IBBM*, which defines the requirements and procedures of bonds traded in the IBBM. The regulation requires full information disclosure and rating by qualified rating institutions. After this regulation was published, another six corporate bonds were formally endorsed to trade in the IBBM.

To further enhance corporate bonds trading, one year later, the PBOC published a bulletin on corporate bond trading in the IBBM, which changed the case-by-case entry examination to the file system and allowed all IBBM investors to invest and trade in corporate bonds. The bulletin encourages the market maker system to extend to the corporate bonds that trade in the IBBM. In addition, the PBOC assigned the CGSDTC and the Interbank Lending Center to work out the operating rules on corporate bonds entry and trading in the IBBM. By 2006, the legal framework of interbank corporate bond market for primary issue and bond trading had been basically established.

The PBOC initiatives have greatly boosted corporate trading in the IBBM. By the end of June 2006, there were 132 corporate bonds traded in the IBBM. State-owned commercial banks remain the major corporate bond investors in the IBBM.

CORPORATE BOND DEVELOPMENT: PROBLEMS AND SOLUTIONS

Although progress has been made in the corporate bond market, many issues remain and need to be addressed.

Size Compared with Other Bond Markets

The size of the corporate bond market is relatively insignificant vis-à-vis the government bond market and the financial debenture market.

At the end of 2005, the stock of corporate bonds amounted to about 1 trillion RMB, compared with 3 trillion in government bonds and 2.5 trillion in financial debentures. Outstanding corporate bonds only accounted for less than 2 percent of gross domestic product (GDP), although the new issues had increased substantially. Compared to other countries, the corporate bond market in China is small by every measure. For example, in the United States, where the corporate bond market is fully developed and highly efficient, the corporate bond stock as a share of GDP was about 23.62 percent in the early 1990s and increased steadily to 39.08 percent by March 2006.

Lack of Diversification

Because of the restricted number of issuers, the bond supply is limited to those of SOEs, financial institutions, and some qualified companies. As of mid-2006, there were no municipal bonds or local government bonds. Within the non-government bond category, financial debentures are the main instrument; at present, more than 90 percent of corporate bonds are debentures and convertible bonds. All corporate bonds issued through May 2006 were secured debentures; there were no unsecured debentures or mortgage bonds. Due to this restriction, many feasible projects cannot access finance facilities because only certain institutions are eligible to provide such insurances. In fact, unsecured bonds are popular in mature bond markets abroad. In the United States, unsecured debentures have become an important corporate bond instrument due to diverse investor preferences and information disclosure requirements.

China has made a breakthrough in this respect. The first unsecured corporate bond, Three Gorges Company bond, was approved by the NDRC in early 2006, and the transaction was concluded in May 2006.

It is evident that investors in China have gradually increased their financial awareness and now understand how to evaluate the price of an investment based on judgment regarding its potential risk. However, the current investor base is very much polarized: risk loving and risk averse. China needs to cultivate an investor base whose investment focus is on the intermediate rate of return and intermediate risk while leaving the high risk/high-return products to professional institutional investors and specialized financial intermediaries. However, insurance companies and investment funds, which are in a position to take some risk to get reasonable returns, are now mostly regulated by supervisory institutions and are not able to purchase low-rated bonds, such as buy-and-hold subdebt and bottom-tier asset-backed securities.

Regulated Pricing and Some Nonstandard Practices

The pricing of corporate bond remains a problem. Corporate bonds are issued through an underwriting syndicate after the issuance is approved. The price of corporate bonds is not set through auction, as the prices of government bonds and financial debentures are. Within the current legal framework, the NDRC and the PBOC jointly determine the coupon rate. According to regulations, the coupon rate shall be set at no more than 140 percent of the statutory bank deposit rate of the same maturity. Although this requirement has not been followed for some time, the regulation still remains valid.

Settlement and clearing in the securities trading are carried out through clearing companies. Trading is mainly electronic; paper securities are no longer available, except for some local issues. The National Development and Reform Commission together with the related departments oversee corporate bonds issuance insofar as quotas, qualifications, and case-by-case examinations are concerned. The CSRC and the stock exchange are entitled to approve and exert supervision over corporate bond listing. However, in recent initiatives the PBOC resumed its authority regarding corporate bond trading in the IBBM.

The legal framework has gradually been put in place for trading corporate bonds in the stock exchange market. *Securities Law*, *Corporation Law*, and *Rules on Corporate Bonds* spell out the regulations for issuing and listing corporate bonds. At present, the NDRC is in the process of revising the *Rules on Corporate Bonds*, which was last revised in 1993. In the past, the separate jurisdiction of the primary market and the secondary market gave rise to a number of problems. First, primary examination focused on the project a priori rather than on the soundness of the issuers while the market is more concerned with the issuers' quality and financial soundness. Second, because the issuance and listing are approved by different departments, there is a gray market (between primary issue and open trading, the bond may trade privately, this is called gray market). Third, market supervision, though reinforced, remains weak due to the leakage in jurisdiction.

Inactive Secondary Market Trading and Relatively Low Liquidity

By December 2006, there were 84 corporate bonds listed on the Shenzhen Stock Exchange and the Shanghai Stock Exchange (see Table 24.1 and 24.2). As can be seen from the statistics on the number of transactions for listed

TABLE 24.1 Listed Corporate Bonds on the
Shanghai Stock Exchange

Year	Number of listed corporate bonds	Trading Volume (100 million)
1999	8	24
2000	8	39
2001	11	56
2002	11	51
2003	19	315
2004	24	96
2005	47	125
2006	62	125

Source: www.sse.com.cn

corporate bonds in Shenzhen Stock Exchange shown in Table 24.3, the turnover rates (bond trading volume to GDP ratio) were around 2 percent, which is much lower than the average turnover rate of 200 percent in the United States. Compared with other financial debentures and central bank paper in China, the turnover rate of corporate bonds is obviously lower as well. The daily turnover of corporate bonds listed in both stock exchanges is less than 50 million yuan, while the daily turnover of government bonds on these exchanges is over 1 billion yuan.

TABLE 24.2 Listed Corporate Bonds on the
Shenzhen Stock Exchange

Year	Number of listed corporate bonds	Trading Volume (100 million)
1999	3	21.5
2000	2	13.6
2001	1	8.4
2002	4	19.3
2003	9	47.6
2004	13	17.5
2005	16	29.8
2006	22	—

Note: "—" refers to the data couldn't be calculated
by now.
Source: www.sse.org.cn.

TABLE 24.3 Trading Volume and Turnover Rates for the Listed Corporate Bonds

Year	Trading Volume (100 million)	Turnover Rates (percent)
1999	45.5	0.06
2000	52.6	0.06
2001	64.4	0.07
2002	70.3	0.07
2003	362.6	0.31
2004	113.5	0.08
2005	154.8	0.08
2006	—	—

Note: "—" refers to the data couldn't be calculated by now.
Source: www.sse.com.cn, www.sse.org.cn, China Statistical Yearbook, 2006.

Many issues related to the corporate bond market are the same as issues with other bond securities, but some are specific to corporate bonds. The changes listed in the following sections are recommended.

Reform the Regulatory System   Clearly, the current regulatory framework hampers bond market development. Too much government intervention is not only a sign of financial repression, but also demonstrates the overlapping jurisdictions within the legal framework. Thus, there is more constraint than incentive in the corporate bond market. Therefore, creating an incentive structure for the corporate bond market is crucial. To this end, we would suggest, first, that regulations on market entry be relaxed.

It becomes more and more evident that the administrative approval system, or case-by-case approval, is time-consuming, less efficient, and mostly unnecessary. Many suggest that this system should be replaced with a qualified approval system or file system. The file system would give the issuer more flexibility in selecting timing and marketplaces. In this way, enterprises that are more qualified will have the opportunity to access financial resources via the bond market. Under the file system, every company would be able to access the bond market; however, the company's credit condition and performance would be reflected in its funding cost.

The shift from case-by-case approval to a filing system would allow investors to change their investment philosophy from investing only in high-quality bonds to investing in high-yield bonds. Investors would develop a new way of thinking (i.e., high risk and high yield are symbiotic) and learn how to make the trade-off between the two based on their own risk preferences.

The purpose of corporate bond financing is to support key national construction projects; however, at present, more attention is paid to examining the construction project and less to examining the performance of the enterprise. Recently it has been suggested that any enterprise that meets basic financial requirements should be permitted to access the bond market.

There have also been suggestions that when the market environment is not perfect and the behavior of market participants is not well disciplined, the government should retain a certain degree of control. Some argue that since the corporate bond market in China is at a preliminary stage of development, it is premature to move to a qualification examination system. We believe these arguments are groundless. Our view is that issuer and investor would, in a given incentive structure, formulate constraints on each other in their efforts to reduce endogenous transaction costs. This endogenous constraint structure can better serve the healthy development of the bond market.

With respect to the relaxation of investment regulations, efforts should be made to set up a proper incentive structure. It is counterproductive to restrict the use of proceeds raised through bond issues. Recently, some progress has been made. For example, the 10-year corporate bonds of 1 billion yuan issued by China Jinmen Group Co., Ltd. from April to May 2003 were partly used to repay previous debts, which broke through the original regulation that "the funds raised should be earmarked to the projects." an indication that the policy is gradually changing. The management of the company supports this positive change.

Liberalize Interest Rates   Regulation of the coupon rate of corporate bond remains a roadblock to corporate bond market development. Therefore, it is imperative to relax the coupon rate approval scheme.

The bond coupon rate, or yield, is the rate of return that investors are entitled to receive. It should reflect the supply-demand relationship and credit rating of issuers. To establish a market-based pricing regime, it is important to implement the market-based selling method and pricing mechanism; improve the credit rating system; manage operational risks, such as settlement and clearing risks; and improve the market infrastructure.

We propose a change in the current restrictive provisions of the *Rules on Corporate Bonds* on interest rates setting to encourage innovations in the corporate bond selling technique and allow the market to set corresponding interest rates based on the demand-supply relationship and credit ratings. In this way, the linkage between interest rate levels and risks can be established.

At present, a corporate bond must be approved by the State Council to obtain an issuing quota, by the National Development and Reform Commission for project approval and issuance, by the People's Bank of China for the interest rate setting, by China Securities Regulatory Commission for the underwriting qualification, and by China Securities Regulatory Commission and the Exchange (or Central National Debt Registration Co.) for listing on an exchange. The whole application period can be as long as one year, sometimes even two or three years. This gives rise to a mismatch between the funding schedule and investment schedule and between debt repayment cash flow and corporate profit cash flow. Because of the time-consuming application period, many able companies eventually give up their application for funding through the corporate bond market and turn to other markets.

How far we should go to liberalize the interest rate remains controversial. Some suggest that it may be difficult to totally abolish restrictions on interest rates and to have a single agency in control of the issuance of corporate bonds. A feasible approach would be to further relax the upper and lower limits of interest rates.

The way financial debentures are sold provides a successful example of market-based pricing for non-government bonds in China. Unlike in the United States, financial debentures as non-government bond instruments are priced through competitive bidding rather than book building. This is due mainly to the lack of an effective government bond yield curve to serve as a benchmark for pricing other market instruments.

In fact, both auction selling and book building are available for corporate bond sales because the market infrastructure is already in place. If the corporate bond interest rate is liberalized, the market can provide a ready-made facility for pricing corporate bonds. For example, corporate bonds can use the same auction system in the CGSDTC or use the book-building system, by which the underwriting syndicates can actively affect market sentiment and control the pricing process. Although book building is extensively used in the United States for pricing corporate bonds, and has the advantage of creating price tension in favor of issuers, whether it is more effective or not remains inconclusive. Auction selling has proved more efficient and appropriate in China's specific context, presumably because China's investors, even institutional ones, tend to be small and not price sensitive.

Consolidate the Regulatory Framework The current regulatory framework is characterized by overlapping jurisdictions, which is counterproductive to the development of the corporate bond market. For example, the NDRC regulates primary issues of corporate bonds, and the CSRC regulates the listing and trading of corporate bonds. This irrational division of labor leads to a disconnection between the selling and trading of corporate bonds. It sometimes takes six months to receive trading and listing approval from the CSRC; during this time, there is a so-called gray market for private trading.

Multiple supervision weakens regulatory authority, as the agencies supervise the bond market from different perspectives and tend to have different interpretations of the same regulations. At the same time, in a system where every department performs its own function, corporate bond market development is beyond their reach. This institutional arrangement is obviously unfavorable to the long-term development of the market. In addition, multiple supervision stifles the incentive structure of corporate bond market participants, who are the drivers of market movement.

Consequently, corporate bonds, as an essential part of the capital market and direct financing instruments, should be supervised by a single department in order to improve supervisory efficiency. To this end, a unified regulatory framework is necessary and helpful.

Develop an Independent Credit Rating System   Investors in China gradually learned how to judge credit risk on their own. Unlike government bonds and financial debentures, which receive sovereign or quasi-sovereign rating, corporate bonds have weaker and heterogeneous financial and business status, and their credit risk must be professionally evaluated through credit ratings. Therefore, when investors contemplate buying corporate bonds, the decision is based on their own judgment on the trade-off between risk and return, therefore, the ratings which indicating the degree of risk, are more important to investors, especially to individual investors.

Today, credit rating is one of the principal requirements for entry into the corporate bond market. It is increasingly recognized that the credit rating is an important tool for investors who are eager to ascertain credit risks. Although the quality of the ratings so far made by domestic rating agencies remains questionable, great progress has been made with respect to rating techniques. Rating agencies, such as Dagong and Chengyin, have established joint ventures with U.S. rating agencies (Moody's and Fetch, respectively).

More effort needs to be made to encourage the development of independent credit rating institutions, reform the rating system, improve the rating techniques, strengthen supervision of the rating institutions, allow rating institutions to provide rating materials and information to large-scale institutional investors, and encourage competition among rating agencies to eliminate bribery in return for a good rating. It is also important to create a credit curve as a reference for pricing.

Develop Information-Gathering and Processing Services   Since the second half of the 1990s, as the securities market developed, information-gathering and processing research institutions, as investor service institutions, have developed rapidly. Their purpose is to provide prompt, accurate, and complete issuing information and financial indications as well as continuous real-time information disclosure and financial indexing after bond issuance. The research institutions also provide standard analysis procedures and analysis reports prepared by professional analysts on risk return. Information gathering and processing aims to protect investors' interests, rate objectively and justly, gather true and accurate information, and standardize supervision and control. All bond issuers (except the government) must be subject to regular and irregular supervision and information disclosure by their financial intermediaries; otherwise they should not be allowed to access to the bond market.

Promote Financial Innovation   Innovation is the engine of financial market development. The government should encourage financial intermediaries, such as securities firms, to diversify instruments and improve selling techniques through innovation. Innovation of bond instruments includes designing internationally accepted and popular corporate bond products, such as mortgage bonds (the issuer agrees to specify some tangible assets as collateral, and the bondholders have the right to hold the mortgage assets in case of default) and unsecured debentures, among others.

Innovations with respect to bond issuance include all the selling techniques used by issuers such as the Ministry of Finance and the CDB, stimulated by the innovative ideas. Pricing has shifted from negotiation between issuers and underwriters, a process now used only for local corporate bonds, to a market-based pricing method, such as tender or book building. The method of distribution to the investors has also shifted from the underwriter distribution method to price-competitive distribution via the electronic transmission system on the stock exchange network. Although these changes took place years ago in the stock exchange trading system, this transformation has not yet been accomplished in the IBBM.

Improve the Market Infrastructure   Corporate bonds are traded mainly on the stock exchange market. As late as 2003, the PBOC began to encourage corporate issuers to issue and trade corporate bonds in the IBBM. However, the main marketplace for trading corporate bonds remains in the stock exchange markets because they have a more diversified investor base than IBBMs and investors in IBBMs are more risk averse than in stock exchange markets. It is interesting to note that the corporate bond market shares the same problems as the government bond market and the financial debenture market; that is, the stock exchange markets and the IBBMs are currently separate markets.

In our view, as a first step, the two marketplaces should be unified, and then an independent OTC market should be established. At this moment, it is necessary to continue developing the secondary market of corporate bonds on the exchange. However, an OTC market has the advantage of trading large volumes and offers convenience to those investors who prefer to keep their market motivation confidential. Compared with price matching based on price and time priority on the exchange, OTC trading can accommodate the trading of professional institutional investors, such as investment funds and insurance/ pension funds. However, the exchange market has the advantage of information disclosure, accommodating small trading volume, and therefore is more efficient for corporate bond trading, which tends to be small in volume. The overall aim for the corporate bond market should be to establish the exchange market as the primary marketplace and the OTC secondary market as the accessory market, thereby reducing transaction costs and facilitating trading. The CGSDTC should be the unified depository and clearing institution for issuance and circulation of corporate bonds in the exchanges and in the OTC market to facilitate unified management.

Finally, it is noteworthy that the corporate bond market was developed based on the government securities market. Thus, an evolutionary change of institutions, not technological progress, paved the way for the corporate bond market.

Establish an Investors' Association, Investors' Club, and Investors' Conference

Investors can make their voices heard and demonstrate their collective power through investors' conferences. Such organizations exist elsewhere around the world. The creditors' conferences in Japan, Hong Kong, and Taiwan are good examples. An investors' conference for corporate bonds is not a business firm; it is organized by the investors' association or club to discuss problems relating to the safety of their investment, in order to safeguard the creditors' interests in conformity with the laws. A creditors' conference, as the representative of the interests of all corporate bond creditors', has the right to make decisions on important investment issues and negotiate with government agencies and corporate bond issuers. The conference may discuss issues such as liability exemption, debt rescheduling, reconciliation with issuers for late payment, and liquidation in case of default; and, in compliance with the judicial act, it may pursue solutions related to the bankruptcy or reorganization of debt incurred by corporate bonds. Investors' conferences may entrust agents to implement or enforce the decisions of creditors' conferences; they may also implement administrative matters on behalf of investors based on conference decisions in accordance with laws. When the creditors' interests in corporate bonds are contrary to the agents' interests, the investors' conference has the right to dismiss the agents or trustees and appoint new executors to exercise the decisions.

With respect to the relationship between investors' conferences and issuers, the laws regulate that the bond issuer have the duty not only to convene investors' conferences but also to bear the expenses both for the conferences and for executing the decisions.

The primary exchange can help to rebate exogenous transaction costs while leaving endogenous transaction costs to be saved via the secondary exchange. As indicated before, in the secondary exchange market participants can realize the exchange only after they can economize their transaction cost, such as find counterparty, get information, negotiation, etc. This category is an endogenous transaction cost. Insofar as the primary bond exchange is concerned, however, the exchange between government and bond market participants is subject to the theory of public choice because this exchange is characterized by collective action. Investor conferences, or associations, are pressure groups that can help make the primary exchange more effective and achieve a win-win result. This not only improves market development, but also helps to establish a more just and fair trade in the secondary exchange.

Investor conferences and creditor conferences are internal exchanges created *directly* by the secondary exchange, such as norms and conventions, as opposed to external exchange, which is created *outside of* secondary exchange, such as laws and regulations.[2] The internal exchange is more transaction cost effective than the external exchange.

CHAPTER 25

Asset Securitization
of the China Development Bank

The theory of institutional economic engineering regards exchange as a way to realize comparative advantage; the market is essentially a place where the exchange of commodities is realized. Commodities can be best exchanged when they are standardized and specified. By analogy, a financial commodity can be best traded when it is standardized and has a spectrum of specifications. Securitization is the transformation of assets into standardized and tradable securities.

NEED FOR SECURITIZATION OF CREDIT ASSETS
AND THE ROLE OF THE CHINA DEVELOPMENT BANK

There are many different categories of securitizations, such as mortgage-backed securities (MBS) and asset-backed securities (ABS). Essentially, all kinds of assets can be securitized.

ABS can help banks diversify their assets portfolio to reduce systematic risks, transfer credit risks to the capital market participants, and improve the allocation efficiency of their financial resources.

Introduction to Asset Securitization in China

China started to realize that financial risks were very much concentrated in the banking sector when the bank nonperforming loan (NPL) ratio was on the rise in late 1990s. In particular, banks that engaged in policy-related investment were exposed to the systematic risk caused by economic movement and shocks. This has been especially true for banks such as the China Development Bank (CDB), which focused its investment in the infrastructure sector.

The efforts to introduce a securitization program date from the late 1990s. There were a number of seminars and conferences on this subject at that time. Concrete programs were discussed and designed. However, these efforts were suspended because they did not attract the attention of major government agencies, such as PBOC, NDRC and CSRC. In January 2004, the CDB submitted a formal recommendation to introduce ABS to China and suggested that it be the first issuer of these securities. This recommendation received a positive response from the People's Bank of China (PBOC), which forwarded a proposal, after consultation with the different agencies concerned, on experiments with MBS and ABS to the State Council. A working group and a documents drafting group were established thereafter.

Most bond market reform programs have been initiated by market participants; the initiation of the bond market reform program by the Ministry of Finance was an exception. The securitization program was initiated by the CDB and other banks, but this time, the central government supported the proposal, and the relevant agencies were urged to make efforts to clear the legal, tax, and accounting hurdles relating to securitization programs.

As Premier Wen Jiabao pointed out at the National Conference on Banking, Securities and Insurance held on February 10, 2004: "China Development Bank should bring into full play its role in developing financing, take advantage of and reinforce the strategic readjustment of the economic structure, and avoid random, low-value added investments; it should also reinforce internal management and strengthen risk control, and attach importance to the prevention of long-term credit risks."

Then Vice Premier Huang Ju gave instructions in the *2004 Working Report of China Development Bank*: "This year [2004] China Development Bank should continue to expand policy-oriented finance, control the targets of lending, focus on lending to infrastructure projects in the energy and transportation industries, prevent long-term credit risks, and improve its operational performance."

It was recognized that securitization would help to meet the requirement to implement the state's industrial policies; guide social capital to financing the construction of the national infrastructure, basic industries, pillar industries, and high-tech industries; increase the liquidity of the CDB's credit assets; and put development financing theory into practice using its capital guiding function.

According to the minutes of the China Banking Regulatory Commission's meeting on February 4, 2004:

China Development Bank should cope with the relationship between policy-oriented finance and commercial finance appropriately, and make further efforts to guide social capital investments. When loan-funded projects are put into commission and generate cash flows, China Development Bank could transfer these projects to commercial financial institutions to operate in due course through such market-based methods as syndicate loan, sale, and securitization in order to realize the guiding function and to support more policy-oriented projects.

The instructions from state leaders support and encourage the CDB to carry out the ABS program, among others. It is fair to say that both government support and the CDB initiative underpin the ABS program.

Comparative Advantages of the China Development Bank

The ABS market has to be cultivated to accommodate the ABS transactions. When introducing ABS, originators and regulatory authorities have to take into account market receptiveness; therefore, only the best market performers were selected as originators during the period when ABS transactions were permitted on a trial basis.

The CDB's strong internal risk management system and excellent asset quality are fundamental to the success of its securitization program. The CDB has a solid performance record and a professional team with expertise in macroeconomic policy, industrial development, and technological engineering. In addition, the CDB is dedicated to bringing innovative ideas in the financial sector. All of these factors illustrate the CDB's qualifications as the originator of the ABS program.

At the end of 2003, the CDB's loan assets amounted to RMB1.1381 trillion with 2,332 lending projects; its NPLs stood at RMB14.3 billion, or only 1.34 percent of the total loan portfolio, achieving a "double reduction" in the NPL ratio and NPL volume consecutively year to year. Meanwhile, its cumulative recovery rate of loan principal and interest reached 99 percent, with the current-period recovery rate above 98 percent for 16 consecutive quarters, which is comparable to the performance of world-class banks. It is in the CDB's best interests to select high-quality credit assets for the initial securitization program. The healthy asset quality and operational performance can significantly enhance investors' confidence and thereby secure a successful ABS transaction.

Market reputation is an important factor in selecting a qualified originator. The CDB enjoys the highest rating of Chinese banks. Moody's and Standard & Poor's rated the CDB as A2 and BBB-, respectively, equivalent to sovereignty ratings (i.e., it has the same rating as China's Ministry of Finance).

As the CDB has more diversified bond instruments and is an active market player, its bond transactions usually attract diverse investors with different risk preferences. By the end of 2005, the cumulative amount of financial bonds issued by the CDB hit RMB2.4322 trillion; its bond in custody reached RMB1.502 trillion, accounting for 20.81 percent of the national bond market, second only to that of government bonds; and its underwriting amount of corporate bonds ranked first domestically for five consecutive years.

Essentially, both performing and nonperforming assets may be selected as underlying assets for securitization. Not only does the CDB have high-quality credit assets (with only 0.80 percent NPL ratio at the end of 2005), but it is also in a better position to provide asset management service. The bank has most extensive custom service network via its nation-wide branches. This is important as the CDB would continue to manage the assets after ABS is issued.

Integrating these advantages could make CDB in a better position as originator of ABS. In addition, the ABS program, as was indicated, can be carried out for the benefit of the CDB as well, thereby achieving a win-win result for all of the parties.

The advantages of its quasi-sovereignty credit rating and its long-term experience with market-based bond issuance have laid a sound market and technological foundation for the CDB's successful asset-backed securitization program.

DEAL STRUCTURE DESIGN OF CREDIT ASSETS SECURITIZATION

The aim of asset-backed securitization is to transform loan assets into tradable securities through certain legal arrangements, for example, through special-purpose vehicles (SPVs). It is important to specify the legal status, risks, rights, and liabilities of each party involved in the securitization before the transaction can be made.

Requirements for Asset-Backed Securities

To ensure a successful transaction, the transaction structure design of asset-backed securities must meet these requirements:

- Legal Requirements.
  Limited recourse. The recourse of investors in ABS is limited to the securitized assets or their associated rights, and has nothing to do with the sponsor (CDB) or the issuer (trust company).

Risk separation. The risks of securitized assets should be separated from risks of other assets of the sponsor (CDB) and the issuer (trust company).

- Accounting Requirements.
  Off-balance-sheet securitization. In compliance with the requirements of International Accounting Standard (IAS) 39 concerning the principles for derecognizing assets, the securitized credit assets shall meet the requirements of substantive transfer, or material transfer, of all the risks and rewards from the securitized assets, and the assets shall be removed from the balance sheet of the sponsor (CDB).
- Market Requirements.
  Public offering and listing of ABS. It shall comply with laws and regulatory requirements for the public offering and listing of ABS. Investors' interests shall be protected.

Rationale for Deal Structuring

At a seminar on asset-backed securities in China on May 20, 2004, the CDB put forward a preliminary proposal concerning a pilot securitization model. Later, after extensive study of the international asset securitization experiences and China's legal and investment environment, the CDB modified the model based on the comments from experts and related authorities. Figure 25.1 illustrates the rationale.

The SPV model could not be used within current legal framework, although the CDB designed a special-purpose trust (SPT) model and set up a beneficial trust. In this way, the risk and benefit of assets were truly removed from the CDB's balance sheet while it adhered to IAS 39 principles.

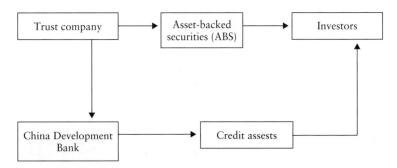

FIGURE 25.1 Basic Design of Securitization Deal Structure

Execution Framework   Based on this structure, a detailed execution framework was designed. The legal relationships among the parties involved are illustrated in Figure 25.2.

Cash Flow   As shown in Figure 25.3, the CDB, as the originator of the deal, shall transfer the underlying assets to the trust company (which is designed to function as trustee). The trust company shall set up a third-party beneficial trust fund, which shall pursue the ABS issuance. The holders of ABS are the corresponding beneficiaries under the trust.

ABS redemption is related only to the securitized assets, without recourse to the originator (sponsor; CDB) or the issuer (trust company). Therefore,

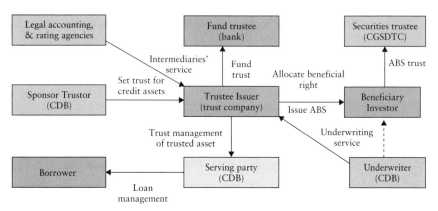

FIGURE 25.2   Legal Relationship among the Parties to the Transaction

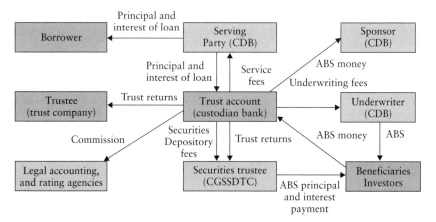

FIGURE 25.3   Cash Flow among the Parties to the Transaction

the repayment of ABS only relates to the cash flow generated by securitized assets; it would not lead to the bankruptcy of the sponsor or the issuer. The sponsor (original beneficiary of credit assets, i.e., CDB) of this deal and the issuer (trust company) of ABS are not obligated to repay principal or expected investment returns to investors in the ABS. Payment to investors come from the trusted assets (securitized credit assets) and their trust incomes.

As mandated by the trust company, the CDB will manage the credit assets under the trust fund as a service provider, responsible for collecting principal and interest from the borrower and performing other relevant management functions.

The custody of the trust fund will be an independent fund custodian (bank). The trust company would open a trust account with the custodian bank to carry out trust-related payments. The trust company (trustee) is responsible for reinvesting the incoming cash flows in the trust account.

As mandated by the trust company (the issuer), the CDB shall be responsible for selling ABS to the institutional investors. During the pilot period, ABS will trade in the interbank bond market (IBBM). The China Government Securities Depository Trust & Clearing Co., Ltd. (CGS-DTC) shall be responsible for the registration and custody of ABS. It is expected that in the future, this security can be traded in the exchange market.

To sum up, as the ABS sponsor, the CDB plays three roles in securitization transactions: (1) trustor of property trust, (2) service provider of loan assets, and (3) underwriter of ABS. All of these roles are clearly defined legally and do not conflict with one another. The trust company functions as the trustee, and the ABS issuer has the right to change an incompetent service provider and ask the sponsor to redeem or replace unqualified loan assets in accordance with the agreed-upon quality requirement. In addition, the function of the independent third-party bank as the trustee of the trust fund account is to minimize the possibility of trust fund embezzlement by the trust company. By such arrangements, risk can be minimized. In order to protect investors' interests and build a good-profile ABS in the market, it is crucial to choose trustworthy companies with commonly recognized qualities as trustee and issuer.

In international practice, an SPT usually functions as the issuer of ABS. However, given China's regulation on trust certificates, an SPT can issue trust certificates only through private placement, and the certificates are not tradable. Within the current legal framework, an SPT is not in a position to issue the ABS, as a trust property is not an economic entity according to Chinese laws and regulations. Therefore, the trust company is not allowed to issue the ABS on behalf of the trust properties, and, for the same reason, the trust company itself is not responsible for the redemption of ABS.

The new regulation gives trust companies issuer status for ABS. However, because trust companies currently are not market experts and most of them do not have any experience in issuing bonds, the trust company selected by the CDB, in turn, chose the CDB as the underwriter of the ABS transactions. With its outstanding reputation and extensive bond distribution network, the CDB is recognized as bond market elite who is in a position to secure ABS offerings.

Based on generally accepted SPTs in the international market, this model, as a pilot plan for credit asset securitization and tailor-made for the Chinese market, offers financial innovation and a high degree of functionality.

SPLITTING THE MATURITY OF ASSET-BACKED SECURITIES

Based on prevailing investor preferences and the bond market yield curve, it is advisable that the maturity of the ABS be set at three to five years. However, the loan assets of the CDB are mostly medium and long term (10 years on average). In addition, loan assets put in the pool may have different remaining maturities. However, the maturity of an ABS designed shall have unified maturity, longer or shorter than the remaining duration of the yet securitized loan assets; therefore, how to reconcile the discrepancy needs to be addressed.

Essentially, in the ABS, the securitized assets are priced based on the same pricing model, the present values of all future cash flows (i.e., the expected future cash flow discounted by the current interest rate). As cash flows can be segmented, the maturity of the ABS can be standardized by calculate the cash flows of the assets within a designated time frame. The loan assets can be arranged in two different ways:

1. *Establish a closed-end loan to back up the ABS.* The loan assets can be sold for a shorter time horizon than their real maturity. In this case, principal may not be sold. The originator, such as the CDB, would take back the loan assets when the ABS matures.

2. *Split the trust beneficial rights of the loan assets.* All cash flow from the assets shall be transferred to the trust company, which then sets up an assets trust fund. The trust company can then divide the trust beneficial rights under this trust fund into two categories of rights:

a. Rights related to the principal and accrued interest payments of the loan borrower during the life of the ABS; thereafter, the right is returned to the originator.
b. Rights related to the principal and accrued interest that the borrower is entitled to repay after the ABS expires.

In cases where the maturity of loan assets needs to be split, the legal framework of asset-backed securitization is subject to adjustment (see Figure 25.4; the corresponding cash flow is illustrated in Figure 25.5).

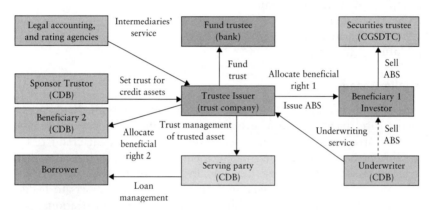

FIGURE 25.4 Legal Framework of Credit Assets Securitization

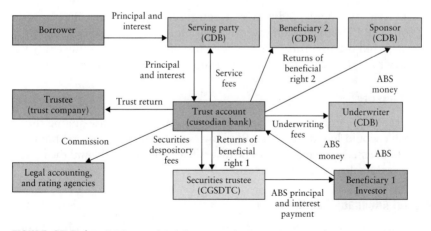

FIGURE 25.5 Cash Flows of Credit Assets Securitization Deal

STANDARDS FOR SELECTING SECURITIZED ASSETS POOL

In principle, all loan assets of a bank can be securitized as long as they generate foreseeable steady cash inflow. In selecting loan assets for securitization, seven points must be kept in mind:

1. Portfolio management
2. Industry distribution
3. Asset quality
4. Capital adequacy requirement
5. Quota requirement
6. Size of securitized assets
7. Maturity structure

Portfolio Management

Loan portfolio management needs to be taken into account. Banks need to make sure that the loan assets in their portfolio have less, preferably negative, correlation with each other in order to hedge their credit risks. This concept is based on asset management theory, which indicates that systematic risk can be hedged through diversification. Banks must scale down the volume of some assets and add up some other assets to hedge systematic risks. Oversized assets should be selected for securitization.

Industry Distribution

In selecting asset pools, industry concentration shall be taken into consideration. The CDB focuses on several major industries: electricity, highways, railways, and urban infrastructure. Therefore, from the view of diversifying industry risks, loans to these industries should be securitized first.

Asset Quality

From the originator's point of view, nonperforming assets are among those the bank would like to sell via ABS. However, from the investors' point of view, loan assets selected need to be diversified to reduce risk, and the better the assets' quality, the better investors like it.

Capital Adequacy Requirement

Bank originators have to consider the total size of the portfolio. Many banks wish to keep their assets at certain level to meet the capital adequacy requirement.

Quota Requirement

Banks in China, such as the CDB, have to consider the loan quota requirement, which is set by the central bank, the PBOC.

Size of Securitized Assets

The preferred issuing size for an ABS transaction is RMB10 billion to maintain liquidity.

Maturity Structure

The maturity of an ABS should match the underlying assets' cash flow. It is advisable to select loan assets with remaining life spans in line with the maturity of the proposed ABS.

PRICING ASSET-BACKED SECURITIES

Theoretically, the ABS is the securitization of cash flows from the underlying loan assets. The notional volume of securitization is the present value of discounted future cash flows. These future cash flows include both principal and interest payments, as shown in the equation.

$$PV = \frac{CF}{(1+d)^1} + \frac{CF}{(1+d)^2} + \frac{CF}{(1+d)^3} \cdots \frac{M+CF}{(1+d)^n}$$

Where PV = present value
CF = cash flow of coupon interest payments
M = cash flow of principal payment
d = discount rate
n = number of payments

Therefore, as indicated, it is reasonable to suppose that the future cash flow can be sold separately. The loan assets selected have different interest payment dates; in addition, these interest payment dates may differ from the interest payment date of the ABS. This can be worked through with index calculation. For example, if the settlement of ABS to payment date of loan assets is 25 days, then the present value can be calculated using this formula:

$$PV = \frac{CF}{(1+d)^{25/360}} + \frac{CF}{(1+d)^{1+25/360}} + \frac{CF}{(1+d)^{2+25/360}} \cdots \frac{M+CF}{(1+d)^{n+25/360}}$$

The pricing of the ABS essentially relies on the calculation of the discount rate d. It should be equal to the market-based rate of return for corporate bonds with the same rating plus the fees and commissions to the trust company and asset managers.

ASSET-BACKED SECURITIZATION STRUCTURE AND OFFER

Typically, ABS can be structured into different tranches (A, B, C...tranche). The coupon rate is set on the benchmark interest rates of one- to five-year financial debentures that the CDB issued between April and July 2005. The interest rates were 3.4 percent, 3.81 percent, and 4.2 percent for one-, two-, and five-year financial debentures, respectively. Based on our calculations, the senior ABS products should enjoy a 15 to 25 basis point spread over financial debentures of the same maturities. Therefore, the coupon rates for Tranche A and Tranche B would be 3.55 percent and 3.85 percent, respectively, with the 7.61 percent nominal interest rate for Tranche C.

The tranches were finally structured as 70, 30, and 10 percent, respectively, while the corresponding yields (i.e., the real interest rate) were set at 3.60, 3.90, and 4.24 percent, respectively.

The first ABS transaction by the CDB offered a floating rate, the same as the loan assets in the pool, which helps to hedge against the interest rate risk; the weighted average maturities of the three tranches is 0.88 year, 2.21 years, and 2.39 years, respectively; however, the official maturities for all three is three years.

Legal Framework for Issuing and Underwriting

Through PBOC and CDB initiatives, and efforts from different government agencies, the legal framework for issuing and underwriting asset-backed securities has been established. The next sections describe the basic procedures and content of ABS issuing.

Obtain Approvals from Applicable Authorities Like corporate bonds, where the issuer needs approval on a case-by-case basis, the bank originator needs to obtain written approval from the State Council or PBOC before making an ABS bond offer. However, many of the comments suggest formal approval can be shifted to the file scheme to give the originator convenience and flexibility to access the market.

Create Offering Prospectus In order to effectively convey the information on loan assets underlying ABS products to investors and make the transaction more transparent, the originator must prepare a prospectus that includes: component description, fact sheet describing asset pools, terms and conditions, loan assets' cash flow management, debt-servicing procedure, disclosures concerning asset pool project management, and auditing report.

Negotiate and Sign "Agreement Concerning Credit Issuance System and Bond Depository." This agreement, signed with the CGSDTC, specifies the rights and obligations of each party, including software and hardware support, service, listing, transaction procedure, depository fees, and information service.

Form an Underwriting Syndicate for the Asset-Backed Securities Transaction The underwriting syndicate formed in the inter-bank market should be composed of current members of the syndicate that underwrites the bank's financial debenture, and additional qualified institutions, such as insurance companies, investment funds, and securities firms. Depending on the ABS asset structure and issuance format, the CDB, as an issuer, may organize two syndications for the ABS: one syndicate for Tranche A and Tranche B via auction selling, and one syndicate for Tranche C via book-building distribution.

Design the Selling Method in the Inter-Bank Bond Market A selling documents must contain the description of bond products, issuing and bidding methods, syndicate members, both parties' rights and obligations, issuing venue, payment method, bond depository, and listing and transaction markets.

Bidding Methods and Bidding Document Design

Auction Method It is proposed that Tranche A and Tranche B are sold via auction and Tranche C by book-building issuance. At the same time, a contingency plan must be developed based on the evaluation of market reception.

The rate of return of ABS is determined by the incoming future cash flows. Normally, the coupon rate of ABS compounded shall not be more than the highest loan assets yield. The interest rate of Tranche A, which has the highest rating, should be no more than the average rate of return of the loan asset pool.

Unlike financial debentures, ABS interest rate has an inherent ceiling (i.e., yield of loan pool), so the upper limit of each tranche should be determined in advance. This also allows the bank originator to determine in advance what it will do should the ABS be undersubscribed within the upper limit and to consider whether it will terminate the issuance or launch the transaction through alternative methods to sell the unsold securities. However, even under such circumstances, the successful bidding remains valid. There are two alternative tender formats:

1. *Simultaneous bids for Tranche A and Tranche B.* The theoretical upper limit and total bids for Tranche A and B should be determined beforehand, and then bids should be invited for both tranches at the same time. If one tranche is not fully subscribed, adopt a contingency plan for issuance. This method requires accurate calculation of the theoretical upper limits of Tranche A and B.
2. *Consecutive bids for Tranche A and Tranche B.* Invite bids for Tranche A first, and determine the upper limit of Tranche B based on the bidding results for Tranche A. Then invite bids for Tranche B. The advantage of this method is that it is much closer to the real market yield and, to some degree, reduces the difference between the theoretical yield and actual market yield.

Book-Building Method   Book building is universally used for pricing non-government bond securities. In the United States, securitized transactions are normally priced through book building. In 2005, the China Construction Bank (CCB) launched a mortgage-backed securities (MBS) transaction via book building. Book building was also used by the CDB to underwrite the Tranche C of the ABS transaction.

Upon the completion of tender for Tranche A and Tranche B, syndicate members are asked to forward orders for Tranche C. The orders have to be obtained before a predetermined deadline. The book is built by underwriter (the CDB is both originator and underwriter for its ABS transactions) as incoming orders are collected. The bank underwriter could require its branches to cooperate in selling the bond when necessary.

As an underwriter in the two transactions done on trial basis in late 2005 and early 2006, the CDB also arranged the deposit registration, fee payment, and information disclosures: Tranche C bond will also be deposited in the CGSDTC. After the underwriters complete the payment before the deadline, the CDB transfers the underwriting fees to other underwriters through the CGSDTC and pays the depository trust fees to the CGSDTC. The lead manager of the underwriting must regularly disclose to investors cash flow and other information concerning the bonds.

Contingency Issuance Plan In the 2005 transaction, the CDB assigned three institutions as the final subscribers based on their financial capability. In order to ensure the success of the initial public offering of the ABS in case of an insufficient number of effective bids, the CDB had two contingency plans to complete the sale of Tranche A and Tranche B: (1) start quantity bidding at a preset interest rate with the total bidding amount equal to the unsubscribed portion; and (2) terminate the bidding and turn to various institutions for private placement. If Tranche C was undersubscribed, the underwriter may decide to cancel book-building issuance and turn to strategic investors for the entire issuance, according to the agreed-upon terms and conditions. Alternatively, the originator can retain Tranche C. Although this would make the loan assets stay on the balance sheet from an accounting perspective, it might have a credit enhancement effect on the whole transaction.

INFORMATION DISCLOSURE

The general principles for information disclosure are authenticity, accuracy, integrity, fairness, and timeliness.

Responsibilities of Each Party

Issuer The issuer shall be responsible for authenticity, accuracy, and integrity of the information disclosed. The issuer must ensure that there are no fraudulent or misleading statements or significant omissions in the information and undertaking of individual liability and joint and several liabilities. The issuer should take effective measures to ensure that qualified investors participating in subscribing and transferring bonds can obtain information related to the bonds on an equal basis.

Lead Managers, Law Firms, Accounting Firms, and Rating Agencies These institutions should be responsible for the professional legal opinion, auditing and rating reports, and comments and market strategy.

Securities Investors Qualified investors participating in subscribing and transferring bonds shall make independent analysis of authenticity, accuracy, and integrity of the information disclosed, independently judge the investment value of the bonds in accordance with the analysis, and be responsible for any investment risk.

Procedure for Information Disclosure

The institutions involved in the ABS transaction shall carefully check the information disclosure to ensure there are no fraudulent records, misleading statements, or significant omissions in the information, and guarantee to undertake corresponding liabilities.

Figure 25.6 illustrates the steps in the information disclosure process from announcement through postsale reporting requirements.

Disclosure mainly concerns the "Prospectus of Securities Offering." In line with disclosure requirements and practices insofar as corporate bonds and bank subdebt in China domestic market is concerned and the securitization practices in the international market, ABS disclosure materials in China should include information in 10 areas:

1. *Risk factors.* ABS risk exposure involves the asset pool's liquidity, country, regional economy, industry, regulatory framework, uncertainties about market interest rates, investors' preferences, and the investor base for the ABS market and subordinated securities. The originator's specific risks are also important risk factors.
2. *Terms and conditions.* This area includes general information on face value, maturity, principal and interest, bookkeeping, replacement,

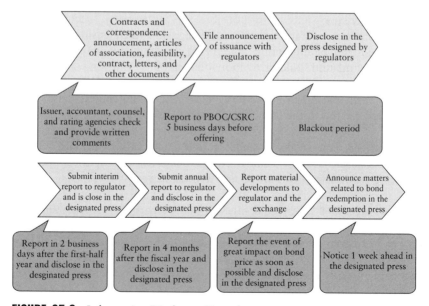

FIGURE 25.6 Information Disclosure Procedure

trading and transferring, payment date and payment agent, ABS redemption clause, description of defaults, and the like.

3. *Use of proceeds.* Normally, the use of proceeds of ABS transactions is not restricted or bound. However, sometimes there are regulatory requirements as to how the proceeds can be used.

4. *Description of participants.* This section identifies the issuer, guarantors, originator/management service providers, securities trustees, and payment agents. The originator/management service providers shall disclose their financial statement, including the capital and ownership structure, major businesses, internal risk management and credit evaluation, and legal/control framework. General information disclosure is required regarding the issuer's directors, management team and shareholders, issuer's financial positions, the financial position and profit distributions for the past three years and in the current fiscal period, and the like.

5. *Payment structure.* Legal arrangements for the cash flow payment and settlement must be specified.

6. *Assets in the pool.* When select the assets that to be securitized, the following information need to be taken into account: the loan's initial balance, current balance, type of interest and interest rate, initial clause and expiry clause; historical performance of asset pool portfolio (e.g., poor performance, default, and early redemption ratio); geographical distribution of the loans in the asset pool; concentration degree and type of borrowers; and so on.

7. *Guarantor's financial profile.* It includes the financial position and profit distributions in the past three years and in the current fiscal period.

8. *Tax consequences.* It includes the rates and preferential treatment of business tax and income tax vis-à-vis the sale of asset pools and securities interest income.

9. *Securities transfer clauses.* These clauses include some restrictive transfer clauses established for the initial public offering of the ABS.

10. *Distribution plans.* The distribution plans for lead underwriters and syndicate members, as well as listing arrangement after the offering, must be specified.

These are the major ABS documents currently required. They are subject to change in accordance with the proposed transaction structure and relevant legal requirements, which mainly include the following:

- Offering prospectus/announcement/articles of association
- Rating report

- Legal opinion letters and accounting and auditing reports
- Trustee arrangement
- Securities underwriting agreement and syndicate agreement
- Service providers' agreement
- Supporting service agreement
- Transaction management agreement
- Securities custody agreement
- Intermediaries' contracts (including contracts between the issuer and law firm, investment bank, accounting firm, credit rating agency, and property assessment agency)
- Security documents (i.e., the arrangement for bank account, pledge, etc.)

ISSUES AFFECTING FUTURE DEVELOPMENT

As an important financial innovation and financing product, ABS can facilitate the link between the capital market and the bank credit market. At present, the banking system is exposed to excessive risk due to highly concentrated and illiquid loan assets in the banking sector. In the United States and many western countries, asset securitization helps diversify the risk in the banking sector to capital market participants.

China still has a long way to go in developing a sound asset securitization market. However, the experiments carried out by the China Development Bank and the China Construction Bank mark a milestone of debt capital market development. They also prove that China does not necessarily have to follow the market practice in the developed countries to build up its own capital market. China can develop its debt capital market via financial innovation guided by up-to-date ideas.

Risk Control and Investor Protection

The risks involved in ABS can be manageable and unmanageable: manageable risks should be strictly controlled to the minimum level, while unmanageable risks should be fully disclosed. Credit risks, operational risks, and market risks specified by Basel II Accord can be addressed through internal rating and market-based risk management. The originator can boost the investors' confidence through so-called credit enhancement. In the second ABS transaction, the CDB deliberately held part of Tranche C of the transaction, which is considered riskier than Tranche A and Tranche B, to ensure investors that the CDB would not only share the risk but even bear more of it. This credit enhancement gave investors greater incentive to participate in the transaction.

Supporting Laws and Policies

During the trial phase, the CDB is mainly applying laws and regulations such as "Trust Law," "Administrative Regulation on the Trust and Investment Companies," "Securities Law," "Contract Law," "Guarantee Law," and "General Rules of Civil Law." In the current regulatory framework, there are still restrictions on entry to the ABS market. However, the PBOC is expected to lift the restriction as soon as the trial period is over.

In the long term, the government will gradually improve the legal system along with the development of the ABS market. Deregulation and enhancing the legal framework go hand in hand with improving the legal environment. It is anticipated that the amendment of corporate law will lead to the legalization of special-purpose vehicles, including special-purpose companies and special-purpose trusts.

The Debt Capital Market

Debt Capital Market and the Macroeconomy

NATIONAL SAVINGS AS A FINANCING INSTRUMENT

Before the reform and opening up of China, the net household income after consumption was far from sufficient for citizens to invest in real estate and securities. Although the savings rate was relatively high, savings were confined to bank deposits only.

The reform and opening-up policies increased enterprises' revenue and individual income. As a result of the government's preferential policies toward individually owned, collectively owned, and township enterprises, some people quickly became wealthy, especially in the eastern part of China and the coastal provinces, which led to significant changes in the distribution and consumption patterns of national income.

CHANGES IN THE PATTERN OF NATIONAL SAVINGS

Historically, in most countries, savings, both domestic and foreign, are the source of funding for domestic government bonds. A country's investment equals the total of its domestic and foreign savings. Bank deposits, stocks, and bonds are all forms of investment translated from savings. If there is no foreign investment, a country's financial resources are capped by the total amount of its savings.

China has always been one of the highest-saving nations in the world, with a continuous savings rate of over 30 percent.[1] By March 2004, the private savings deposit balance had reached to RMB11.2 trillion. In the past five years, the balance of private savings deposits has grown annually at the rate of about 18 percent, resulting in an increase of almost RMB1 trillion every year.

The continuous increase in private savings deposits is attributable to China's rapid economic growth. Since the reform and opening up, China's economy has gained momentum. The ensuing economic growth boosted the national income, in particular, the income of individuals. In recent years, China has implemented a series of policies to amplify individuals' income, which has led to the steadily rising living standard. Private savings deposits also grew steadily. A high savings rate underpins China's economic growth and paves the way for the development of the domestic treasury bonds market.

CHANGING CHARACTERISTICS OF PRIVATE SAVINGS OBJECTIVES AND INVESTMENT DIRECTION

Private savings is the main engine of China's economic growth. However, growth also generates income and additional savings. Along with economic development and increasing household incomes, individuals' consumption and savings behavior has also changed.

Before reform, and even in 1980s, private savings were used mainly to support parents and raise children, and for retirement and contingencies; there was no money for luxury consumption, to say nothing about investment. Since the 1990s, private deposits areere no longer the only conduit of savings. As early as 1994, the Beijing City Socioeconomic Survey Team carried out a survey of Beijing residents' financial assets, savings psychology, and investment plans. According to the results of the survey, individuals' use of surplus income had undergone profound changes. The major purpose of individual savings was to support children or elderly family members (23.8 percent of the surveyed households). Another major purpose of savings was for retirement (16.9 percent). Saving for children's marriages or unforeseen accidents was ranked third (15.6 percent) by individuals. Saving to buy a house accounted for 12.9 percent while purchasing high-quality consumer goods and gaining interest income accounted for 11.8 percent and 8 percent, respectively. The first three items essentially were for mid- and long-term consumption (56.3 percent). Against this background, the Ministry of Finance introduced certificate savings bonds to cater to the rising demand for government securities.

In addition to the changes in consumer behavior, with rising income, people started to think about how they could secure their futures with th the surplus income. As the reform program unfolded, individuals could no longer rely solely on the government for their retirement and medical care; instead, they had to arrange for their own savings for future expenditures on retirement, medical care, and their children's education expenses. As a result, the number of people who put money in banks only for interest income decreased whereas those who wished to buy insurance and investments increased. However, until the mid-1990s, mid- and long-term private savings deposits, rather than corporate savings and government savings, remained dominant and highly stable sources of deposits.

Individual investment in real estate, bonds, and businesses became popular as economic development created more business opportunities. Individuals who invest in bonds belong to a different social class. Ordinary workers remain depositors; they prefer to buy savings bonds; conversely, some wealthy people became professional investors who tend to buy stocks, tradable treasury, and other bonds.

By the end of 1996, the financial assets owned by urban and rural individuals in China amounted to more than RMB4.5 trillion. Because the central bank lowered the deposit and loan rates twice, the deposit growth rate slowed. As a result, the marginal propensity for consumption increased, and the intention to invest in financial assets other than deposits was enhanced. Consumers' awareness underwent three significant changes:

1. Consumers gradually become investors.
2. Since 1996, due to the increase in bond products in the Chinese securities market and their diversified maturity profile, there were more options available to investors.
3. The expectation for return on investment in the securities market is relatively high.

In 1997, as more securities instruments available to the consumers, securities investment became consumers' important option as opposed to their traditional choice which only confined to the bank deposit. Among those contemplating to invest in the securities market, treasury securities accounted for the lion's share.

In 1998, due to the anticipated increase in future expenses caused by the social security system, education, and medical care and medical reform, savings rates rose despite repeated interest rate cuts. Individuals' marginal propensity to save increased by 70 percent in 1999 from around 50 percent in previous years. Under the circumstances of depressed consumption and disincentives to invest, the demand for money also dropped; consequently, bank loans grew only slowly. With the increase in deposits, the loan-to-deposit ratio in the banking system declined. Risk-free treasury bonds and low-risk policy-related financial bonds became the primary investment option for the banks, which led to the relatively smooth issuances of T-bonds and policy-related financial debenture at lower interest rates. At the same time, there were consecutive cuts in the interest rate of bank deposits. The anticipation of further interest rate cuts made T-bonds the preferred investment option. Although the stock market began to heat up in early 1999 and attracted individual investment, the majority of individual investors still preferred to invest in T-bonds for reasons of safety. Since 1999, individual savings has experienced steady growth, mainly driven by four factors:

1. The steady growth of individual income in China
2. The accumulation of financial assets in the form of savings due to the limited investment channels for individual investors
3. The increasing potential risk
4. The comparatively low rate of return and high risk in the capital market or the lack of profitable investment opportunities

Bank deposits, stocks, and various kinds of bonds are all instruments that transform savings into investment. A country's maximum funding sources for investment are its domestic savings and incoming foreign savings. Therefore, the higher the national savings rate is, the greater is the availability of financial resources that can be mobilized through the market for investment. It is recognized that higher savings rate is one of China comparative advantages, vis-à-vis many other countries around the world, for China's economic growth. The savings rate of major countries in the world is illustrated in Table 26.1.

TABLE 26.1 Saving Rates of Major Countries (in percent)

Countries	Proportion of Gross Saving in GDP						
	1999	2000	2001	2002	2003	2004	2005
United States	19	17	15.2	14.1	13.4	13.4	13.5
Japan	28.4	27.6	26.2	—	—	—	—
Germany	24.1	22.3	21.5	22	19.5	20.4	—
France	22.5	22.1	21.5	21.3	12.9	12.6	12.6
United Kingdom	16.8	15.4	14.5	13.9	14.8	14.8	14.2
Italy	23.4	21.2	21.1	21	19.8	20.3	19.8
Russia	27.5	38.7	34.8	31.8	—	—	—
Republic of Korea	32	31.3	29.1	27.5	—	—	—
China	39.5	39	40.9	43.4	34.9	—	—

Note: "—"refers to the figure can't be calculated.
Source: International Financial Statistics, June 2006. *China Statistical Yearbook*, 2006.

The turn of the twenty-first century and the first few years of the new century witnessed an even more rapid growth in savings in China, although the reasons for it remain mysterious. China's saving rate, at about 40 percent, is perhaps the highest in the world. It is much higher than that in developed countries and in most developing countries (see Table 26.1).

ANALYSIS OF SAVING AND INVESTMENT

Although the high savings rate bolsters the engine of economic growth and the development of the bond market, it may be the main reason for the deflation that occurred toward the end of the twentieth century.

Savings were not used effectively, according to James Reidel, Jin Jing, and Gao Jian. They examined the savings-investment nexus in China and concluded that although investment is the main source of China's growth, it was also a weakness and a threat to the sustainability of the country's growth.[2] Nicholas K. Lardy argues, "Reform has done little to improve the allocation and use of China's capital. For the past two decades state-owned banks have channeled a large share of the sharply rising household savings into unreformed, money-losing enterprises, resulting in a dramatic rise in the debt of enterprises to banks."[3]

Today, we understand that higher savings rates give rise to so-called dynamic inefficiency and therefore need to be adjusted. Many economic policies have been taken to encourage domestic consumption. However, without a sound social security system, boosting domestic consumption in China remains a difficult task. In addition, using savings effectively is conducive to maintaining economic momentum. Direct financing substantially reduces transaction costs, and China is now in transition from indirect financing to direct financing. This trend is undoubtedly positive.

The corporate bond market is relatively small. Arguably, if more savings were channeled to the corporate bond market, financing costs would be lower. However, the structural issues remain, such as interest distortion and market segmentation. Therefore, designing and putting an incentive structure in place in the financial market is most important. However, doing this requires a liberalized legal environment and innovative ideas to stimulate financial innovation by institutions and organizations, such as the policy bank.

In our view, the higher savings rate may have to do with macroeconomic policies, such as regulated interest rate, exchange rate regime, and fiscal and monetary policies. Our interpretation of this phenomenon is based on the recursive model of dynamic economics by Thomas J. Sargent:[4]

$$c_t = (1 - \beta) \left[A_t + y_t \left(\frac{1}{1 - \lambda R^{-1}} \right) \right]$$

Where c_t = consumption at time t
 A_t = *nonlabor* wealth at the beginning of time t
 y_t = labor income at time t, β = discount factor
 λ = gross income growth rate
 R = gross observed interest rate

If the interest rate over the long term is below the growth rate, then consumption will be depressed. The statistics support this view. In the United States and the United Kingdom, the interest rate in terms of government bond yield is in principle higher than gross domestic product (GDP) growth rate; in China, it is the other way around (see Table 26.1).

It is reasonable to suppose that higher savings rates may have much to do with the lower interest rate, although this seems counterintuitive.

Following Phelps's framework, we can draw some conclusions based on three reduced-form first-differential equations:

$$(1) \ dS = c_{01} dM + c_{02} dF$$

$$(2) \ dP = c_{11} dM + c_{12} dF$$

$$(3) \ dY = c_{21} dM + c_{22} dF$$

Where S = national savings rate,
 P = price level,
 Y = level of economic activities;
 F = the degree of fiscal stimulus,
 M = the degree of monetary stimulus.

The macroeconomic policy parameters, F and M, determine the savings rate, price level, and level of economic activities in a given institutional arrangement and economic structure. The outcome of regressions is:

$$(1) \ dS = 1.071145 dM - 0.012152 dF$$

$$(2) \ dP = 0.046332 dM - 0.003317 dF$$

$$(3) \ dY = 1.81724 dM - 0.152168 dF$$

which means $c_{12}/c_{11} > c_{22}/c_{21}$ as all the coefficients are negative. Therefore, the optimal price level curve and the curve of level of economic activities is downward sloping.

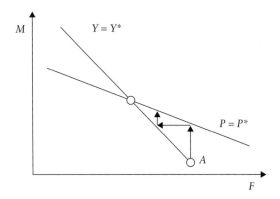

FIGURE 26.1 Fiscal and Monetary Policy
Reaction Function

The two curves intersect at the point where both fiscal policy and monetary policy are optimal. The macroeconomic policy orientation depends on the initial position. China is on the southeastern side of the optimal point, where more fiscal policy and less monetary policy was being used as the country pursued a proactive fiscal policy and a contractionary monetary policy toward the end of the century. If A represents the starting point in Figure 26.1, the trajectory of policy mix is, as the arrows illustrate, an expansionary monetary policy and a less proactive fiscal policy, which is the preferable policy mix.

Note, however, that the coefficients of F, which reflect the institutional arrangement and economic structure peculiar to China, are all negative. This is due to the negative effects of the expenditure-based fiscal policy. Therefore, it is reasonable to suppose that the institutional arrangement is a crucial factor in selecting the policy mix. The negative coefficient of F also provides further evidence of the failure of the trilemma theory applied in China.[5] (A more detailed discussion of this subject goes beyond the scope of this book.)

FINANCIAL SOURCES FOR INVESTMENT IN BONDS

The deposits of urban and rural individuals and cash held outside of the banking system by individuals are the main sources of money that individuals have to invest in government securities. When China adopted the administrative allocation method for government bond distribution, the subscription task in the provinces depended mainly on the total amount of deposits and total wages in those areas. Although the available financial assets have increased in recent years, these indicators do not completely reflect individuals' capacity to invest in treasury bonds and other bond securities. After the 1990s, although there was a significant increase in the amount of T-bonds held by individuals, there was also a sizable increase in individual income, which sustains the demand for bonds securities.

INSTITUTIONAL CHANGES AND THEIR IMPACT ON THE BOND MARKET

Deregulation

The increase in bond investment is also attributable to the financial deregulation that occurred toward the end of the twentieth century. In 1998, China shifted its original policy of not allowing commercial banks to hold T-bonds to encouraging them to invest in bond securities. In order to minimize non-performing assets and to diversify bank assets, the State Council permitted commercial banks to buy treasury bonds. Since 1998, the commercial banks have become the leading investors in T-bonds and other bond securities. The source of funds for the commercial banks to invest in treasury and financial debenture is private savings deposits, which is in fact a transfer from private investment to government investment.

Rate of Return

As the rate of return on treasury and financial bonds was in practice higher than the deposit rate, banks could get risk-free profits by investing in them. By 2004, the proportion of bonds as a share of the banks' total assets increased to 20 percent from 4.98 percent in 1997. Some commercial banks, especially the city commercial banks, have become savings banks as they invest solely in bond securities.

New Sources of Funds

The development of the insurance industry in recent years provides a long-term stable fund source for investment in bonds. By the end of 2004, the premium income of insurance institutions amounted to RMB1.3 trillion. The bonds bought by insurance companies amounted to RMB224 billion. The liabilities of insurance companies are generally long term by nature, and the development of insurance institutions supports the issuance of long bonds.

Since 2003, postal savings deposits have been used more efficiently, and they have become a major source of bond investment. The Post Saving Department (PSD) used to be an administrative organization that submitted post deposits to the central bank; it has now become an economic entity and is authorized, as a primary dealer, to bid government bonds in the auction process.

In 2004, the growth rate of all types of deposits in national financial institutions dropped; the growth rate of the private savings deposits dropped for seven consecutive months. Even though the savings deposit balance reached RMB11.4 trillion, the rate of growth of savings deposits had dropped from 20.5 percent at the end of January to 15.3 percent by the end of August and the amount of savings deposits declined RMB42.8 billion on a year-to-year basis. When reviewing individual consumption during this period, we find that, deducting a year-to-year increase of 3.8 percent in the consumer price index (CPI) from January to August, the total amount of consumer goods actually increased by 8.8 percent on a year-to-year basis, which was lower than the average growth rate of total retail sales of consumer goods from 2000 to 2002. Moreover, the overall price level continuously fell in that period. Therefore, the view that the decline in the growth rate of private savings deposits represented enhanced propensity to consume proved to be incorrect; the expansion of consumption expenditures was caused by price inflation, and the negative interest rate did not stimulate individuals' consumption behaviors. In August, the growth rate of total retail sales of consumer goods was low compared with the same period in the previous year, and the growth rate of private savings deposits continued to drop, further verifying this conclusion.

If consumption was not the major cause for the accelerated decline in private savings deposits and the fund outflow from the banking systems, then a more rational explanation is that individuals had turned to other investment options. With an interest rate of only 1.98 percent, or 1.58 percent after taxes, the one-year term deposit had a real interest rate of −3.72 percent deducting 5.3 percent year-on-year CPI growth rate in August 2004. Therefore, individuals were urgently in need of investment opportunities for preserving and increasing the value of the large amount of idle funds. On October 29, 2004, the central bank raised interest rates, for the first time in nine years, by 27 basis points, which still did not change the negative real interest rate.

To date, three main channels have been identified as investment options for the individual savings: (1) investment in financial assets such as funds and treasury bonds, (2) investment in real estate, and (3) investment in the credit market.

Although the anticipated price of long-term bonds dropped after the interest rate hike, the public's judgment about treasury bonds as their main investment instrument remained unchanged, and investment in them continued to appreciate rapidly.

CHANGING INVESTOR BASE

As we have seen, the main form of savings in China is deposits, especially private deposits. Since the reform and opening up, an increasing amount of savings is being used by the government. Individuals for the most part are savers, not investors. In China, for many years deposits were seen as a preventive measure rather than an investment. At present, expected future expenses are the main impetus for saving.

Due to the limited number of available investment channels, savings deposits were the primary repository for an individual's financial assets. Since 1998, banks have been the main investors in treasury and other bonds. Although institutional investors, such as insurance companies, pensions, and investment funds, have become important long-term investors, banks remain the mainstay of T-bond investment. For this reason, long-term bonds account for only a small share of the total outstanding bonds. In addition, cyclical deposit changes are likely to cause fluctuations in the bond market. It is now understood that it is counterproductive for the government and state banks to use the majority of personal savings because of the crowding-out effect that results.[6]

As a consequence of social security reform, payments into the system became an important source of government and corporate funding. Due to the increase of personal income, private investment increased as well.

FINANCING BEFORE 1994

Before reform and the opening up in China in 1979, there were deficits approximately 50 percent of the time, and all were financed by borrowing from the central bank. Thereafter, the government ran hard deficits every year (except 1985). Treasury bonds issued in 1981 were for financing the deficits of 1979 and 1980; the proceeds from the 1981 T-bonds were not incorporated in budgetary revenue of the same year. In addition, beginning in 1989, fiscal bonds issued were not reported as budget revenue but were used to make up deficits incurred as a result of unexpected expenditures.

The initial reason that it was decided to resume T-bond issuance was because T-bonds can be used as a substitute for overdrafts and borrowing from the central bank. However, until 1994, the deficit incurred during budget implementation continued to be financed through overdrafts and loans from the central bank in addition to T-bonds.

By the end of 1992, the national soft fiscal deficit came to RMB422.3 billion, of which RMB114.5 billion was financed by the issuance of treasury bonds, RMB132.9 billion by foreign debts, RMB5.4 billion by the issuance of construction bonds, RMB28.1 billion by the issuance of fiscal bonds, and RMB44.9 billion by the issuance of other bonds. There were still hard deficits of RMB132 billion, of which RMB4.9 billion was financed by the issuance of treasury bills, RMB12.5 billion by public debt (inflation-linked subsidy), and RMB82.6 billion by overdrafts and loans from the central bank. Fiscal bonds and foreign debt financed a small part of the hard deficit.

In China, collectively borrowed and collectively repaid (CBCR) loans represent borrowing and repayment in the name of the central government, and the proceeds are earmarked to specific projects. For this reason, CBCR loans are listed as both revenue and expenditures in the national budget. CBCR is accounted as a financing item in the budget, although the proceeds of these loans usually are used directly for construction projects.

In the second half of 1993, China twice issued bonds in the international capital market to repay the maturing foreign debt. Actually, this new issue had already been incorporated in the budget. As the fiscal deficit expanded during the budget execution process, foreign debt, in fact, was used to finance the deficit rather than being earmarked to projects.

Beginning in 1994, the State Council started to circumscribe the ability of the Ministry of Finance to finance deficits through overdrafts from the central bank, and all fiscal deficits were to be made up through bond issuance.

FISCAL DEFICIT IN CHINA

The term "fiscal deficit" has different connotations. For historical reasons, various practices and forms of deficit have evolved in China.

Public Sector Deficits

Public sector deficits include government deficits as well as net balance of payments of all the state-owned enterprises (SOEs) affiliated with the central government. In China, besides hard and soft budgetary deficits, there are deficits incurred by local governments and financed by extrabudgetary funds and bank loans of SOEs. Based on this definition, the revenue from treasury bonds issued by the Ministry of Finance, the subsidies that the state pays to SOEs as well as the loans provided by banks are public debt. According to current statistical definition, the loans that banks provide to SOEs are not included in the public-sector fiscal deficit. However, since a portion of these loans are policy loans, it makes sense to include them.[7] Policy-based lending of the central bank, policy banks, and state-owned commercial banks includes, among other things:

- Investment and loans to infrastructure projects such as power plants, transportation, communications, and so on
- Loans for technological upgrades of state-owned enterprises
- Rural development loans, loans for purchasing agricultural products (short-term), loans for supporting underdeveloped regions, and rural economy credit (long-term)
- Development loans from the central bank

Since the banking system reform in 1994, the central bank no longer directly provides policy-based reloan facility; instead, these funds come from the newly founded policy banks, such as the China Development Bank, the Export-Import Bank of China, and the Agricultural Development Bank of China. Although the state-owned commercial banks have already become, at least legally, market-based entities, they still provide part of the policy-based lending. In evaluating the overall impact of fiscal deficit on the national economy of China, the World Bank used the broader concept of public-sector deficit.

National Fiscal Deficit

The national fiscal deficit includes the deficits of both the central and local governments, including the deficits financed by bond issuance and alternative borrowing, as well as planned but not yet realized expenditures. Based on prevailing statistical standards in China, such unrealized disbursements are not calculated in the national fiscal deficit.

Central Government Fiscal Deficit

The budgetary deficits of the central government include the imbalance between revenues and expenditures; bond issuances, if bond financing is calculated as revenue, from the central government; and budgetary appropriations payable to local governments or central departments.

Central Government's Soft Fiscal Deficit The soft deficit is a concept applied to the central government's bond issuance, overdraft, and loans from the central bank. It is used when China implements a dual budget (i.e., a current account and a capital account budget). The dual budget concept is used by the International Monetary Fund for government finance statistics.

Central Government's Hard Fiscal Deficit Before 1993, deficits financed by overdrafts or loans from the central bank, known as hard fiscal deficits, were not calculated and incorporated into the budget deficit in the annual budget report.

Deficits classified in different ways have different implications for the national economy. Before 1992, China's budget report was based on the definition of hard fiscal deficits; in 1993, when dual budgets were temporarily implemented, hard and soft fiscal deficits were simultaneously reported. Since 1994, when dual budgets were formally executed, the soft fiscal deficit has also been used in China's budget report.

Budget Deficits and Principal Deficits

The budget deficit is the sum of government expenditures plus refinancing costs for maturing principal and interest repayment minus tax revenues. The principal deficit is the sum of government expenditures minus tax revenues (see Table 26.2). There is no significant increase in China's principal budget deficit. Part of the budgetary expenditure is used to repay the bond interests.

TABLE 26.2 Budget Deficit and Principal Deficit

Revenue	Plus/Minus	Expenditure	Equals
Tax revenue	Minus	▪ Government current account expenditure ▪ Government production expenditure ▪ Interest payment to the bondholder	Principal deficit
Principal deficit	Plus	Financing deficit by foreign and domestic debt issuance and/or Financing deficit by overdrafts and loans from the central bank	Budget deficit

NATIONAL DEBT AS A FINANCING ITEM IN THE BUDGET

Comparison between Debt Revenue and Tax Revenue

Generally, the main sources of fiscal revenue are tax revenue, revenue from the state-owned enterprises, social security revenue, and so on. Debt is incurred only to finance the fiscal deficit. There are significant differences between debt revenue and other fiscal revenues. Tax revenue is based on economic performance, the tax base and structure, and the tax collection system; therefore, tax revenue is stable and collection is enforceable. Unlike tax revenue, debt revenue is subject to the conditions of the financial market and the financing scale and therefore faces uncertainty. If market conditions are favorable, the government, in accordance with its funding requirements, can raise capital through bond issuance at any time. The most important difference, however, is that tax revenue does not need to be repaid, but debt must be repaid in the future.

As sources of fiscal revenue, both tax revenue and debt revenue have some features in common, and as long as the government continuously renews its debts, there is no difference between the proceeds of debt and tax revenue. Therefore, when the government is considering how to increase its fiscal revenues, both the common nature and the different characteristics of tax revenue and debt need to be kept in mind. It is especially important that the characteristics of debt financing be taken into account when the government is contemplating debt issuance to finance its budgetary shortfall.

Pros and Cons of Various Debt Instruments

Tax income and debt proceeds have different effects in enhancing fiscal revenue (see Table 26.3). As illustrated, different fiscal revenue instruments have different features. Therefore, to increase fiscal revenue, it is important for the government to select different instruments in accordance with its specific objectives.

Generally, the government chooses debt as a financing instrument when tax revenue increase is constrained, or when the government is facing a period budgetary shortfall due to either reduced revenues or increased expenditures As we have seen, China increased debt financing in the later 1990s because of declining tax to gross domestic product ratio, which was an outcome of decentralization since the early 1980s, and increased expenditures due to a proactive fiscal policy toward the end of the last century.

TABLE 26.3 Pros and Cons of Various Financial Tools

Tool	Pros	Cons
Tax revenue	Low cost	Increases burden on enterprises and individuals
Banknote issuance	Low cost	Inflation exposure
Internal borrowing	Convenient, no inflationary pressure	Depreciation exposure
Foreign borrowing	Taps into other markets	Forex risk (faced by the government)
Commercial paper	Accesses markets with high liquidity	No Forex risk; legal requirements (e.g., registration); interest rate risk; short-term volatility; poor visibility of long-term borrowing cost

FISCAL DEFICIT, GOVERNMENT BOND ISSUANCE, AND FOREIGN EXCHANGE RESERVES

Fiscal deficit, government bond issuance, and foreign exchange (Forex) reserves in a country are closely related. The fiscal deficit $(G - T)$ means an increase in debt stock. The increased debt stock includes bonds held by both the private sector (ΔDPS) and the central bank (ΔDCB), as shown in this formula:

$$G - T = \Delta DCB$$

According to the definitions, the sum of the current account (CA), the capital account (CP), and the official reserve (OR) equal 0:

$$CA + CP + OR = 0$$

Therefore, the surplus of the current account is equal to the reduction of net foreign assets (ΔF), while the increase in the government's Forex reserves equals the reduction in Forex reserves held by the central bank (ΔR), namely:

$$CA = -\Delta F$$
$$OR = -\Delta R$$

Therefore, net exports $(EX - IM)$ are equal to the increases in net foreign assets and Forex reserves of the central bank:

$$EX - IM = \Delta F = \Delta R$$

As money (M) equals bonds held by the central bank plus reserves, namely

$$M = DCB + R,$$

therefore

$$\Delta M = \Delta DCB + \Delta R$$

This demonstrates that there are two ways for the central bank to increase base money: by purchasing domestic bonds and by increasing Forex in its reserves. Both are components of open market operations.

These equations reveal important economic relationships and the role the central bank can play. In the early 2000s, the central bank reinforced its OMOs by selling bills in the market in an attempt to neutralize the effect of stockpiling reserves. However, as indicated, OMO is possible only if a bond market is already in place.

INSTRUMENTS TO FINANCE FISCAL DEFICIT AND THEIR ECONOMIC CONSEQUENCES

Theoretically, there are four main instruments to offset fiscal deficit: currency input, use of Forex reserves, internal debt issuance, and external debt issuance. The formula is:

Fiscal deficit = currency issue + use of Forex reserve + external debt
+ internal debt

If measured according to domestic currency and foreign currency:

Fiscal deficit = (currency issue + internal debt) + (use of Forex reserve
+ foreign debt

The first two items on the right side of the formula represent the proportion financed by domestic sources, while the second two represent the proportion financed by external sources. If measured in terms of their implication to the monetary policy, the formula is:

Fiscal deficit = (currency issue + use of Forex reserve) + (internal debt

+ foreign debt

The first two items at the right side of the formula represent the proportion financed by the central bank, while the second two represent the proportion financed by debt financing.

To further explain the factors that offset deficit, we use the next formula to present fiscal deficit and the sources of funds to offset the deficit:

$$D = B + B * E + DCG$$

Where D = fiscal deficit
             B = internal government debt
       $B * E$ = external government debt
      DCG = treasury overdraft

The left side represents the balance between government revenues and expenditures in a given year, namely, the fiscal deficit. The overdraft is a simple method to offset fiscal deficit, but it increases base money and directly causes inflation. The use of the foreign reserve means imposing taxes on banks or levying seigniorage. The remaining approaches are domestic and foreign debt issuance.

Several major factors affect base money (M): the Ministry of Finance's overdraft on its account at the central bank and the central bank's reloan to the commercial banks and to SOEs. The increase of foreign assets and the RMB counterparts of the Forex reserve mean either a reduction or an increase in the base money supply; however, the increase in cash held outside of the banking system by residents and the reserve held by the central bank mean either an increase or a decrease in the base money supply.

CHAPTER 27

Size of Government Debt

There is a great deal of literature devoted to government debt management and government bond market development. However, government debt is not necessarily the same as the government bond market, although they are closely related and often identical. Government debt management is perceived from a macroeconomic point of view while government bond market management is seen from the point of view of the financial market. In our view, there are five criteria for judging the appropriateness of the size of government debt.

1. Debt-absorption capacity; that is, whether the society has sufficient funds to absorb the debt.
2. Debt-raising capacity, or whether the government has sufficient capacity to repay its future accumulated debt.
3. The impact of government debt on the central bank's money supply; that is, to what extent will the government debt affect the general price levels?
4. The impact of government debt on private investment, or the so-called crowding-out effect.
5. The capacity of the securities market. The outstanding government debt shall be accommodated by the securities market.

CURRENT CONDITIONS: REVENUES AND EXPENDITURES

Indicators of Budgetary Revenue

Since 1993, as a result of tax system reform and stable economic growth, the budgetary revenues have witnessed a rapid growth with an annual increase of tax revenue RMB50 to100 billion and, after 2000, over RMB200 billion, a record level since the opening up and reforms in 1979 (see Table 27.1 and Table 27.2).

TABLE 27.1 Budget Revenues by Item (Unit: RMB 100 million)

Year	Total Revenue	Total Taxes	Revenue from Enterprises	Subsidies to Loss-making Enterprises	Revenue Raised from Funds for Key Construction Projects in Energy and Transportation	Revenue Raised from Budget Adjustment Fund	Revenue from Extra-charges for Education	Other Revenues
1950	62.17	48.98	8.69					4.5
1951	124.96	81.13	30.54					13.29
1952	173.94	97.69	57.27					18.98
1953	213.24	119.67	76.69					16.88
1954	245.17	132.18	99.61					13.38
1955	249.27	127.45	111.94					9.88
1956	280.19	140.88	134.26					5.05
1957	303.2	154.89	144.18					4.13
1958	379.62	187.36	189.19					3.07
1959	487.12	204.71	279.1					3.31
1960	572.29	203.65	365.84					2.8
1961	356.06	158.76	191.31					5.99
1962	313.55	162.07	146.22					5.26
1963	342.25	164.31	172.68					5.26
1964	399.54	182	212.93					4.61
1965	473.32	204.3	264.27					4.75
1966	558.71	221.96	333.32					3.43

Year						
1967	419.36	196.63	218.47			4.26
1968	361.25	191.56	166.73			2.96
1969	526.76	235.44	286.74			4.58
1970	662.9	281.2	378.97			2.73
1971	744.73	312.56	428.4			3.77
1972	766.56	317.02	445.69			3.58
1973	809.67	348.95	457.02			3.7
1974	783.14	360.4	407.26			15.48
1975	815.61	402.77	400.2			12.64
1976	776.58	407.96	338.06			30.56
1977	874.46	468.27	402.35			3.84
1978	1132.26	519.28	571.99			40.99
1979	1146.38	537.82	495.03			113.53
1980	1159.93	571.7	435.24			152.99
1981	1175.79	629.89	353.68			192.22
1982	1212.33	700.02	296.47			215.84
1983	1366.95	775.59	240.52	93		257.84
1984	1642.86	947.35	276.77	122.45		296.29
1985	2004.82	2040.79	43.75	−507.02	146.79	280.51
1986	2122.01	2090.73	42.04	−324.78	157.07	156.95
1987	2199.35	2140.36	42.86	−376.43	180.18	212.38
1988	2357.24	2390.47	51.12	−446.46	185.93	176.18
1989	2664.9	2727.4	63.06	−598.88	202.18	91.19	179.41
1990	2937.1	2821.86	78.3	−578.88	185.08	131.21	299.53

(continued)

TABLE 27.1 (Continued)

Year	Total Revenue	Total Taxes	Revenue from Enterprises	Subsidies to Loss-making Enterprises	Revenue Raised from Funds for Key Construction Projects in Energy and Transportation	Revenue Raised from Budget Adjustment Fund	Revenue from Extra-charges for Education	Other Revenues
1991	3149.48	2990.17	74.69	−510.24	188.22	138.53	28.01	240.1
1992	3483.37	3296.91	59.97	−444.96	157.11	117.47	31.72	265.15
1993	4348.95	4255.3	49.49	−411.29	117.72	102.46	44.23	191.04
1994	5218.1	5126.88		−366.22	53.96	59.1	64.2	280.18
1995	6242.2	6038.04		−327.77	17.42	34.92	83.4	396.19
1996	7407.99	6909.82		−337.4	3.78	11.09	96.04	724.66
1997	8651.14	8234.04		−368.49			103.29	682.3
1998	9875.95	9262.8		−333.49			113.34	833.3
1999	11444.08	10682.58		−290.03			126.1	925.43
2000	13395.23	12581.51		−278.78			147.52	944.98
2001	16386.04	15301.38		−300.04			166.6	1218.1
2002	18903.64	17636.45		−259.6			198.05	1328.74
2003	21715.25	20017.31		−226.38			232.39	1691.93
2004	26396.47	24165.68		−217.93			300.40	2148.32
2005	31649.29	28778.54		−193.26			356.18	2707.83

Note: The budgetary revenue excludes domestic and foreign debts.
Source: Finance Yearbook of China 2005, China Statistical Yearbook 2006.

TABLE 27.2 Government Expenditures by Functional Categories (Unit: RMB100 million)

Year	Total Expenditure	Economic Construction Fund	Culture and Education Fund	National Defense Fund	Administration Fund	Other Expenditures
1950	68.05	17.36	7.55	28.01	13.13	2
1951	122.07	35.11	13.44	52.64	17.45	3.43
1952	172.07	73.23	21.11	57.84	15.49	4.4
1953	219.21	87.43	32.44	75.38	19.72	4.24
1954	244.11	123.58	34.61	58.13	21.62	6.17
1955	262.73	137.62	31.89	65.00	21.54	6.68
1956	298.52	159.14	45.96	61.17	26.6	5.65
1957	295.95	163.04	46.42	55.11	22.7	8.68
1958	400.36	278.86	43.54	50.00	22.72	5.24
1959	543.17	389.33	58.6	58.00	30	7.24
1960	643.68	460.71	86.95	58.00	31.39	6.63
1961	356.09	210.01	61.25	50.00	27.14	7.69
1962	294.88	152.64	51.73	56.94	21.91	11.66
1963	332.05	174.12	51.45	66.42	23.86	16.2
1964	393.79	209.99	66.09	72.86	26.22	18.63
1965	459.97	254.11	62.7	86.76	26.34	30.06
1966	537.65	309.43	67.06	101.01	26.59	33.56
1967	439.84	244.03	60.83	83.02	22.95	29.01
1968	357.84	166.03	47.88	94.09	22.91	26.93
1969	525.86	295.52	49.77	126.18	29.82	24.57
1970	649.41	392.61	52.22	145.26	32	27.32
1971	732.17	418.3	63.8	169.47	37.62	42.98
1972	765.86	431.96	75.31	159.39	38.93	60.27
1973	808.78	468.27	88.57	154.39	38.59	67.96
1974	790.25	460.93	95.02	133.39	39.76	61.15
1975	820.88	481.66	103.55	142.46	41.81	51.4
1976	806.2	466.22	120.06	134.45	43.38	42.09
1977	843.53	493.73	119.43	149.04	45.18	36.15
1978	1122.09	718.98	146.96	167.84	52.9	35.41
1979	1281.79	769.89	175.18	222.64	63.07	51.01
1980	1228.83	715.46	199.01	193.84	75.53	44.99
1981	1138.41	630.76	211.46	167.97	82.63	45.59
1982	1229.98	675.37	242.98	176.35	90.84	44.44
1983	1409.52	794.75	282.51	177.13	103.08	52.05
1984	1701.02	968.18	332.06	180.76	139.8	80.22
1985	2004.25	1127.55	408.43	191.53	171.06	105.68
1986	2204.91	1158.97	485.09	200.75	220.04	140.06
1987	2262.18	1153.47	505.83	209.62	228.2	165.06

(*continued*)

TABLE 27.2 *(Continued)*

Year	Total Expenditure	Economic Construction Fund	Culture and Education Fund	National Defense Fund	Administration Fund	Other Expenditures
1988	2491.21	1258.39	581.18	218.00	271.6	162.04
1989	2823.78	1291.19	668.44	251.47	386.26	226.42
1990	3083.59	1368.01	737.61	290.31	414.56	273.1
1991	3386.62	1428.47	849.65	333.31	414.01	364.18
1992	3742.2	1612.81	970.12	377.86	463.41	3.8
1993	4642.3	1834.79	1178.27	425.80	634.26	569.18
1994	5792.62	2393.69	1501.53	550.71	847.68	499.01
1995	6823.72	2855.78	1756.72	636.72	996.54	577.96
1996	7937.55	3233.78	2080.56	720.06	1185.28	717.87
1997	9233.56	3647.33	2469.38	812.57	1358.85	945.43
1998	10798.18	4179.51	2930.78	934.70	1600.27	1152.92
1999	13187.67	5061.46	3638.74	1076.40	2020.6	1390.47
2000	15886.5	5748.36	4384.51	1207.54	2768.22	1777.87
2001	18902.58	6472.56	5213.23	1442.04	3512.49	2262.26
2002	22053.15	6673.7	5924.58	1707.78	4101.32	3645.77
2003	24649.95	7410.87	6469.37	1907.87	4691.26	4170.58
2004	28486.89	7933.25	7490.51	2200.01	5521.98	5341.14
2005	33930.28	9316.96	8953.36	2474.96	6512.34	6672.66

Note: The figures in this table exclude the principal and interest expenses of internal and external debts as well as expenditures for capital construction with foreign loans.
Source: Finance Yearbook of China 2005, China Statistical Yearbook 2006.

Budgetary Revenue to Gross Domestic Product Ratio

Budgetary revenue increased significantly toward the end of last century due to reform of the tax-sharing system beginning in 1994. As a result, the budgetary revenues and expenditures as a gross domestic product (GDP) ratio demonstrate steady increases after a period of decline. Table 27.3 shows the government tax revenue to gross national product (GNP) ratio from 1995 to 2003.

In fact, the budgetary revenue to GDP ratio had been declining until the mid-1990s. It began to increase steadily beginning in 1995 (see Table 27.4).

Compared with other countries, China's budgetary revenue to GDP ratio is relatively low (see Table 27.5).

TABLE 27.3　Budgetary Revenues and Expenditures to GNP (Percent)

Year	1995	1996	1997	1998	1999	2000	2001	2002	2003	2004	2005
Central government revenue to GNP (%)	5.7	5.5	5.8	6.4	7.3	7.9	8.97	10.00	7.92	9.07	9.04
Central government expenditure to GNP (%)	3.5	3.2	3.5	4.1	5.2	6.3	6.03	6.52	6.25	4.94	4.79
Central and local government revenue to GNP (%)	10.9	11.1	11.8	12.8	14.2	15.2	17.12	18.19	15.18	16.51	17.27
Central and local government expenditure to GNP (%)	11.9	11.9	12.6	14	16.4	18	19.75	21.22	18.00	17.82	18.53

Source: China Statistical Yearbook 2006, Finance Yearbook of China 2005.

Many studies have commented on the low level of China's budgetary revenue to GDP ratio. According to the World Bank, this ratio is related to per capita income.[1]

Budgetary Revenue of the Central Government to the National Budgetary Revenues Ratio

The ratio of budgetary revenues of the central government to the national budgetary revenues also declined as a result of the decentralization policy[2] in the early 1980s. By the mid-1990s, the central government's budgetary revenue to the national budgetary revenue ratio fell to less than 30 percent. The ratio then began to turn around in 1995. By 1998, it had increased to about 50 percent (see Table 27.6).

The expenditures of the central government have been on the rise continually since a proactive fiscal policy was pursued. As a result, the fiscal deficit has widened, and the government's dependence on the debt ratio also increased. (Table 27.7 illustrates the central government's budget deficit and debt.)

TABLE 27.4 Budgetary Revenue to GDP Ratio

Year	Financial Revenue (RMB 100 million)	GDP (RMB 100 100 million)	Budgetary Revenue to GDP (%)
1950	62.17		
1951	124.96		
1952	173.94	679	25.6
1953	213.24	824	25.9
1954	245.17	859	28.5
1955	249.27	910	27.4
1956	280.19	1028	27.3
1957	303.2	1068	28.4
1958	379.62	1307	29
1959	487.12	1439	33.9
1960	572.29	1457	39.3
1961	356.06	1220	29.2
1962	313.55	1149.3	27.3
1963	342.25	1233.3	27.8
1964	399.54	1454	27.5
1965	473.32	1716.1	27.6
1966	558.71	1868	29.9
1967	419.36	1773.9	23.6
1968	361.25	1723.1	21
1969	526.76	1937.9	27.2
1970	662.9	2252.7	29.4
1971	744.73	2426.4	30.7
1972	766.56	2518.1	30.4
1973	809.67	2720.9	29.8
1974	783.14	2789.9	28.1
1975	815.61	2997.3	27.2
1976	776.58	2943.7	26.4
1977	874.46	3201.9	27.3
1978	1132.26	3624.1	31.2
1980	1159.93	4517.8	25.7
1985	2004.82	8964.4	22.4
1990	2937.1	18547.9	15.8
1991	3149.48	21617.8	14.6
1992	3483.37	26638.1	13.1
1993	4348.95	34634.4	12.6
1994	5218.1	46759.4	11.2
1995	6242.2	58478.1	10.7
1996	7407.99	67884.6	10.9
1997	8651.14	74462.6	11.6
1998	9875.95	78345.2	12.6

TABLE 27.4 (*Continued*)

Year	Financial Revenue (RMB 100 million)	GDP (RMB 100 100 million)	Budgetary Revenue to GDP (%)
1999	11444.08	82067.5	13.9
2000	13395.23	89468.1	15
2001	16386.04	97314.8	16.8
2002	18903.64	105172.3	18.0
2003	21715.25	117251.9	18.5
2004	26396.47	159878.3	16.5
2005	31649.29	183084.8	17.3

Note: The budgetary revenue excludes domestic and foreign debts.
Source: China Statistical Yearbook 2004, 2006.

TABLE 27.5 Budgetary Revenue to GDP Ratio in Some Countries (Percent)

Country	1979	1985	1992	1993
United States	32.0	33.7	34.5	34.3
France	41.4	46.7	47.1	48.3
Germany	43.8	47.1	55.1	54.8
United Kingdom	38.1	43.4	39.8	39.5
Australia	31.0	35.6	36.7	36.9
Sweden	54.0	57.8	61.0	58.4
China	28.4	22.4	13.1	12.6
Singapore	23.9	38.1	32.6	35.1
Malaysia	28.4	35.0	31.5	31.4
Thailand	14.9	17.3	20.1	20.1

GOVERNMENT BOND ISSUANCE AND DEBT SERVICE

The increased tax revenue did not totally alleviate the government's expenditure requirement. As more debt was maturing, the refinancing pressure became intense. Table 27.8 summarizes domestic treasury bonds issuance and debt service as well as collective borrowed and collective repaid (CBCR) of foreign debts.

INDICATORS OF GOVERNMENT DEBT SCALE

At present, there are two general approaches to evaluate the size of government debt. One is the index approach or econometric model, which is

TABLE 27.6   Budgetary Revenue of the Central Government[a] to National Budgetary Revenue (Percent)

Year	Revenue from Central Government to National Consolidated Revenue	Total Net Central Government Revenue to National Consolidated Revenue
1990	33.8	30.3
1991	29.8	27.7
1992	28.1	27
1993	22	23.3
1994	55.7	20.8
1995	52.2	21.3
1996	49.4	20.8
1997	48.9	22.8
1998	49.5	21.9
1999	51.1	20.6
2000	52.2	21.8
2001	52.38	19.4
2002	54.96	19.4
2003	54.64	19.4
2004	54.9	17.8
2005	52.3	—[b]

Notes:
[a]The term "central government total net revenue" refers to the sum of the central government's revenue plus net contribution from local governments. "Net contribution from local governments" refers to the revenues from local governments minus rebates and subsidies the central government paid to local governments.
[b]"—"refers to the data can't be received.
Source: China Statistical Yearbook 2006, Finance Yearbook of China 2005.

based on statistics, empirical data, and fixed formulas of calculating ratios as indicators of debt management. The other is the factor approach, which, as the name suggests, is based on factor analyses.

Multinational institutions, such as the World Bank and International Monetary Fund, and domestic debt managers frequently use the index approach to compare a country's indicators against benchmark ratios to evaluate how well the debt is managed. Among other things, they look at the country's degree of dependence on debt and its debt service ratio. The factor approach is used only as a complementary analysis to the index approach when empirical data cannot provide convincing evidence.

TABLE 27.7 Central Government Balance of Payments and Debt, Unit: RMB100 million

| Year | Fiscal Deficit of the Central Government | Total Debt Incurred | Among Them | | |
			Domestic Debt	Foreign Debt	Other Domestic Debt
1950		3.02	3.02		
1951		8.18	0.01	5.49	2.68
1952		9.78		9.78	
1953		9.62		9.62	
1954		17.2	8.36	8.84	
1955		22.76	6.19	16.57	
1956		7.24	6.07	1.17	
1957		6.99	6.84	0.15	
1958		7.98	7.98		
1979	98.07	35.31		35.31	
1980	86.9	43.01		43.01	
1981	51.02	121.74	48.66	73.08	
1982	34.59	83.86	43.83	40.03	
1983	83.07	79.41	41.58	37.83	
1984	43.62	77.34	42.53	34.81	
1985	20.22	89.85	60.61	29.24	
1986	106.53	138.25	62.51	75.74	
1987	80.02	223.55	63.07	106.48	54
1988	161.93	270.78	92.17	138.61	40
1989	176.41	407.97	56.07	144.06	207.84
1990	115.14	375.45	93.46	178.21	103.78
1991	217.01	461.4	199.3	180.13	81.97
1992	228.79	669.68	395.64	208.91	65.13
1993	298.87	739.22	314.78	357.9	66.54
1994	666.97	1175.25	1028.57	146.68	
1995	662.82	1549.76	1510.86	38.9	
1996	610	1967.28	1847.77	119.51	
1997	558.45	2476.82	2412.03	64.79	
1998	958.01	3310.93	3228.77	82.16	
1999	1791.6	3715.03	3702.13		12.9
2000	2596.87	4180.1	4153.59	23.1	3.41
2001	2596.30	4604	4483.53	120.47	
2002	3690.90	5679	5660		19
2003	3197.70	6153.53	6029.24	120.68	3.61
2004	3191.80	6879.34	6726.28	145.07	7.99
2005	2999.60	6922.87	6922.87		

Source: Finance Yearbook of China 2005, China Statistical Yearbook 2006.

TABLE 27.8 Issuance and Repayment of Government Bonds (Unit: RMB100 million)

Year	Government Debt — Total Issuance	Among Which — Internal Debt	Among Which — Foreign Debt	Among Which — Other Internal Debt	Government Payment — Total Payment	Government Payment — Payment for Domestic Debts	Among Which — Payment for Foreign Debts	Among Which — Payment for Debts from Central Bank
1980	43.01		43.01		28.58		24.4	4.18
1981	121.74	48.66	73.08		62.89		57.89	5
1982	83.86	43.83	40.03		55.52		49.62	5.9
1983	79.41	41.58	37.83		42.47		36.56	5.91
1984	77.34	42.53	34.83		28.9		22.73	6.17
1985	89.85	60.61	29.24		39.56		32.59	6.97
1986	138.25	62.51	75.74		50.17	7.98	34.5	7.69
1987	223.55	63.07	106.48	54	79.83	23.18	51.96	4.69
1988	270.78	92.17	138.61	40	76.76	28.44	42.59	5.73
1989	407.97	56.07	144.06	207.84	72.37	19.3	45.84	7.23
1990	375.45	93.46	178.21	103.78	190.07	113.42	68.21	8.44
1991	461.4	199.3	180.13	81.97	246.8	156.69	80.22	9.89

1992	669.68	395.64	208.91	65.13	438.57	342.42	80.26	15.89
1993	739.22	314.78	257.9	66.54	336.22	224.3	89.22	22.7
1994	1175.25	1028.57	146.68		499.36	364.96	107.17	27.23
1995	1549.76	1510.86	38.9		882.96	784.06	71.69	27.21
1996	1967.28	1847.77	119.51		1355.03	1266.29	60.76	27.98
1997	2476.82	2412.03	64.79		1918.37	1820.4	70.76	27.21
1998	3310.93	3228.77	82.16		2352.92	2245.79	76.6	30.53
1999	3715.03	3702.13		12.99	1910.53	1792.53	90.99	27.21
2000	4180.1	4153.59	23.1	3.41	1579.82	1552.21	27.61	
2001	4604	4483.53	120.47		2007.73	1923.42	84.31	
2002	5679	5660		19	2563.13	2467.71	95.42	
2003	6153.53	6029.24	120.68	3.61	2952.24	2876.58	75.66	
2004	6879.34	6726.28	145.07	7.99	3671.59	3542.42	129.17	
2005	6922.87	6922.87			3923.37	3878.51	44.86	

Source: *Finance Yearbook of China 2005, China Statistical Yearbook 2006.*

Degree of Dependence

Debt dependency ratio is the indicator of how large the debt burden is on the consolidated central government budget. The consolidated central government budget has to include the net transfer between central and local government (because the central government deficit is offset by the bond issuance). The formula for determining debt dependency ration is:

Government debt dependency ratio

= the central government bond issuance (deficit)/the central government

  expenditures + net transfer between central

  and local government × 100%

Table 27.9 illustrates the three phases of the government debt dependency ratio. The first phase (1981 to 1993) occurred before the tax system reform in China, when the government debt dependency ratio declined gradually.

The second phase was from 1994 to 1997, when the government debt dependency ratio was greater than that in the first phase. That is mainly due to the tax system reform in 1994. Then, local government financial conditions became worse, the central government expenditure for allocation to local government increased greatly, which resulted in the great increase of the central government deficit. The size of transfer payment to local governments increased from RMB 54.5 billon in 1993 to RMB 238.9 billion in 1994. In 1997 the transfer payment amounted to 285.6 billion. However, the reform also boosted the central government revenue, which overran the transfer payment to the local governments. For this reason, the government debt dependency ratio declined gradually, though it was still higher than that during the first phase.

The third phase was after 1998, when the government debt dependency ratio increased greatly, which is due to a proactive fiscal policy in China from 1998 besides the tax system reform in 1994. When the proactive fiscal policy increased the number of long-term treasury bonds to finance infrastructure projects, the central government expenditure increased greatly besides the allocation to local government. In the meantime, the central government revenue also increased greatly, but the degree of increase was smaller than that of the expenditure. Consequently, the government debt

TABLE 27.9 Central Government Bond Issues and Debt Dependency Ratio

Years	Central Government Expenditure (RMB 100 million)	Central Government Bond Issuance (RMB 100 million)	Debt Dependency Ratio (percent)
1981	625.65	314.58	50.3
1982	651.81	304.97	46.8
1983	759.6	269.59	35.5
1984	893.33	227.86	25.5
1985	795.25	25.62	3.2
1986	836.36	57.94	6.9
1987	845.63	109.34	12.9
1988	845.04	70.28	8.3
1989	888.77	66.25	7.5
1990	1589.75	115.14	7.2
1991	1645.56	217.01	13.2
1992	1766.94	228.79	12.9
1993	1956.69	398.87	20.4
1994	4143.52	666.97	16.1
1995	4529.45	662.82	14.6
1996	4873.79	608.84	12.5
1997	5389.17	558.45	10.4
1998	6447.14	958.01	14.9
1999	8238.94	1791.6	21.7
2000	10185.16	2596.87	25.5
2001	11769.97	2596.27	22.1
2002	14123.47	3096.87	21.9
2003	15681.51	3197.68	20.4
2004	18302.04	3191.77	17.4

Note: Central Government Expenditure and Bond Issuance in 1981–1989 refer to the central level government figures, and those of 1990–2004 are the central government figures after reallocation between central and local government.
Source: Based on *Finance Yearbook of China, 2005*.

dependency ratio increased from 10.4 percent in 1997 to 14.9 percent in 1998 and to 25.5 in 2000. Then, the central government's revenue increased greater than its expenditure, causing the government debt dependency ratio declined gradually, from 25.5 percent in 2000 to 17.4 percent in 2004.

TABLE 27.10 Relationship between Government Debt (outstanding) and GDP (Unit: RMB100 million, US$100 million)

Years	Domestic Debt	Foreign Debt[a]	Central Government Debt[b]	GDP	Debt/GDP Ratio (percent)
1994	2282	545	2827	48197.9	5.9
1995	3084	528	3612	60793.7	5.9
1996	4339	582	4921	71176.6	6.9
1997	5539	563	6102	78973	7.7
1998	12420	604	13024	84402.3	15.4
1999	13109	681	13790	89677.1	15.4
2000	17592	672	18264	99214.6	18.4
2001	20806	712	21518	109655.2	19.6
2002	25621	617	26238	120332.7	21.8
2003	28806	789	29595	135822.8	21.8
2004	31849	828	32677	159878.3	20.4
2005	32072	766	32838	183084.8	17.9

Notes:
[a]The unit of external debt is the U.S. dollar. "Total debt incurred" refers to the total sum of external debt converted into RMB according to that year's exchange rates and the outstanding internal debt.
[b]The debt figures represent the year-end balance, and "total debt incurred" refers to the total sum of internal debt and external debt.
Source: Finance Yearbook of China, 2005. China Statistical Yearbook, 2006.

Central Government Debt Ratio

As an indicator of the burden of government debt on the whole nation, the government debt to GDP ratio is calculated by the following formula:

> Government debt to GDP ratio
>
> = government debt outstanding/gross domestic product

Table 27.10 gives the indicator of government debt to GDP ratio in China. The central government debt to GDP ratio rose from 5.9 percent in 1994 to 17.9 percent in 2005 (see Table 27.10).

Debt Service Ratio

Debt service ratio equals expenditures on debt servicing/total budgetary revenue. Table 27.11 shows the relationship between debt revenue and

TABLE 27.11 Relationship between Government Debt Revenue and Budgetary Revenue (percent)

Year	Domestic Debt Revenue/ Budgetary Revenue	Domestic and Foreign Debt Revenue/ Budgetary Revenue
1981	3.75%	9.38%
1982	3.38%	6.47%
1983	2.87%	5.49%
1984	2.47%	4.50%
1985	2.89%	4.29%
1986	2.77%	6.12%
1987	2.60%	9.23%
1988	3.51%	10.30%
1989	1.82%	13.28%
1990	2.82%	11.33%
1991	5.52%	12.78%
1992	9.53%	16.13%
1993	6.19%	14.53%
1994	16.09%	18.38%
1995	19.39%	19.89%
1996	19.71%	20.98%
1997	21.68%	22.26%
1998	24.48%	25.11%
1999	24.42%	24.51%
2000	23.63%	23.78%
2001	21.36%	21.93%
2002	23.89%	23.89%
2003	22.62%	23.09%
2004	22.03%	22.57%
2005	21.87%	21.87%

Source: Based on *China Statistical Yearbook 2006.*

budgetary revenue. We can see that the internal debt revenue to total budgetary revenue ratio increased gradually. The changes in the debt service ratio are reflected in three phases. The first phase was from 1981 to 1987, when the internal debt revenue to total budgetary revenue ratio accounted for approximately 4 to 5 percent. The second phase was from 1988 to 1993, when the internal debt revenue to total budgetary revenue ratio accounted for approximately 7 to 8 percent. The third phase was after 1994, when the ratio was up to 16 percent. This was the result of the suspension of financing through overdrafts and loans from the central bank, which significantly increased internal debt issuance. The internal and external debt to budgetary revenues ratio had the same characteristics. The ratio was

TABLE 27.12 Relationship between Government Debt Expenditures and Budgetary Expenditures (percent)

Year	Expenditures on Internal Debt/Budgetary Expenditures of the Central Government	Expenditures on Debt/Budgetary Expenditures of the Central Government	Expenditures on Debt/Consolidated Expenditures
1981	0.00%	10.05%	5.52%
1982	0.00%	8.52%	4.51%
1983	0.00%	5.59%	3.01%
1984	0.00%	3.24%	1.70%
1985	0.00%	4.97%	1.97%
1986	0.95%	6.00%	2.28%
1987	2.75%	9.44%	3.53%
1988	3.38%	9.08%	3.08%
1989	2.17%	8.14%	2.56%
1990	11.29%	18.92%	6.16%
1991	14.36%	22.63%	7.29%
1992	29.26%	37.47%	11.72%
1993	17.10%	25.63%	7.24%
1994	20.80%	28.46%	8.62%
1995	39.29%	44.25%	12.94%
1996	58.86%	62.99%	17.07%
1997	71.88%	75.75%	20.78%
1998	71.85%	75.28%	21.79%
1999	43.16%	46.01%	14.49%
2000	28.12%	28.62%	9.94%
2001	33.35%	34.81%	10.62%
2002	36.44%	37.85%	11.62%
2003	38.77%	39.79%	11.98%
2004	44.87%	46.51%	12.89%
2005	44.19%	44.71%	11.56%

Notes: The internal debt service began in 1986, so the expenditure on debt between 1981 and 1985 was zero.
Source: China Statistical Yearbook 2006.

about 6 to 7 percent from 1981 and 1987 and 10 to 13 percent from 1988 to 1993. The ratio after 1994 increased substantially.

Table 27.12 shows the debt service to budgetary expenditures of the central government ratio and debt service to consolidated expenditures ratio. As we can see, after a drop in the 1980s and a steady increase in the

1990s, the ratio of debt service to consolidated expenditures has declined since the beginning of twenty-first century. Therefore, the overall increase in this ratio was not too significant, but as local governments may not shoulder the debt service burden, the debt service to central government expenditures ratio is the real indicator of the ability of the government to service debt.

The figures in Table 27.12 indicate that the debt service to central government expenditures ratio has been similar to the debt service to consolidated expenditure ratio, which has been rising since 2000 after a decline in the 1990s. However, the absolute value of domestic central government debt service is much larger than the relative debt service to consolidated expenditure ratio. We may infer that the bigger the debt service to central government expenditure ratio is, the greater the debt service to the consolidated budget ratio for a nation will be.

While at a relatively low level in terms of the overall debt ratio, China's debt has been growing rapidly in comparison with the debt of other developed economies. China's debt indicators have four features:

1. All of China's foreign debt is public debt, including the debt of the central government, local governments, central government departments, financial institutions, banks, and state-owned enterprises. The private sector may not incur foreign debt due to foreign debt regulations.
2. The central government is the major borrower in the domestic debt market. At present, local governments may not issue bonds or carry out debt financing.
3. Compared with other countries, the debt of central government agencies is relatively large and should be included in the central government debt.
4. The central government is responsible for debt service, both internal and external, as well as CBCP debts utilized by the local governments and relevant departments. Although the debt service to consolidated expenditure ratio remains within acceptable levels, the debt service to central government expenditures ratio is much higher than that of many other countries. Therefore, it is advisable to reduce government expenditures and the deficit so as to minimize new debts in the future.

Government direct investment in specific projects has proven to be unnecessary in most cases. Since 2003, the central government in China has reduced direct investment in projects via fund-from-national-debt (FND, which is run by NDRC). The direct investment function has been gradually transferred to loans of policy-related banks and commercial banks. Also, part of commercial bank loans have shifted to the capital market instruments. As a result of this movement, the financial market is undergoing a change from indirect financing to direct financing. In recognition of this, the Chinese government started to pursue a small-government, balanced-budget policy. In fact, after 2003, new issues of government bonds have been scaled down.

China is not unique in having alarming debt issues. Both Britain and the United States experienced similar debt problems. In 1790, "the British national debt amounted to £272 Million, a sum roughly as awesome in the economic universe of the late eighteenth century as the $5 trillion debt of the United States is in the late twentieth. After all, at that time £500 a year was a handsome income, allowing its recipient to live a life of relative comfort; £10,000 in capital made a man rich in the eyes of his contemporaries."[3]

This issue brought to the attention to the British people, "certainly the example of Spain was fresh in the minds of British political and economic thinkers."[4] There is no one way to say whether a specific debt scale is right or wrong:

> "It is not that the size of the debt itself is the problem. A country as rich and productive as the United States can easily afford to service its present debt, just as Britain could afford its debt in 1819."[5] The key is whether the proceeds of bonds issued are being used effectively. In addition, investors' confidence is the cornerstone of the government's funding program. Debt can be a positive factor to the economy as long as it is fairly priced and timely serviced. Clearly Britain's experience in the eighteenth century proves that the size of a country's national debt is not necessarily inversely correlated with its power and prosperity. Far from it. Instead, the British experience demonstrates that a national debt, properly funded and serviced, can be a potent instrument of national policy.... The secret, of course, is in the funding and servicing. Spain's debt had been in both form and substance a personal debt of the king, mostly owed to foreign bankers, who lent short-term. More, the tax system of Spain and the other major European countries was chaotic, arbitrary, and wildly inefficient, making timely payment of interest on the debt doubtful. It is estimated that less than half the taxes

being paid by the French people in the 1780s, at the end of the ancient regime, ever reached the French treasury. The rest went into the pockets of the independent tax farmers who gathered them.[6]

This summary of international and historical experience is undoubtedly applicable to China.

CHAPTER 28

Debt Capital Market as a Stage of Financial Revolution

The stock of treasury bonds issued represents the indebtedness of a nation. However, the concept of debt is very different from the concept of bonds. In principle, debt is seen from legal perspective and bonds are viewed from a market perspective. Thus, debt to the borrower is a liability concept, while bond issuance is a financing concept and bond trading is a market concept. Bonds are issued not only for financing purposes but also to provide market instruments and thereby to facilitate market activities where transactions can be made by the exchange of market instruments.

The bond market is part of the financial market, the key institutional arrangement of a market economy. Similarly, national debt is not only a liability of the issuer, such as the Ministry of Finance in China, but also an important factor in economic stability and a lever of market development.

As debt and credit are same thing but from the opposite perspective, to understand the essence of debt, it is important to trace the origin of credit.

ORIGIN OF CREDIT

Until very recently, Chinese and foreign scholars and experts have debated the nature of the socialist market economy.[1] The Chinese people have come a long way in their understanding the functions of credit and finance, pillars of a market economy. When China embarked on the road toward a market economy, people's awareness of credit was deeply rooted in education in planned economic theory and a planned economy, in which credit was defined by Marx in his famous work *Das Kapital*.

Definition of Credit

"Credit" refers to the ability to obtain goods and services in the present time against the payment in the future. Credit is given based on the creditor's trust in the debtor's repayment capacity, within a mutually agreed time frame.

Credit contains two important elements: trust (i.e., the creditor's judgment of the trustworthiness of the debtor) and time (i.e., the time limit for repayment). From the creditor's perspective, two factors are essential: the debtor's ability to execute the contract and his or her willingness to abide by the contract. "Ability to execute the contract" refers to the debtor's economic ability to repay the debt within a predetermined time limit. This factor is closely related to the debtor's economic status. "Willingness to abide by the contract" refers to the debtor's subjective motivation to make efforts to ensure payment in a mutually agreed time and is directly related to the debtor's moral character. Therefore, "breaking faith" means the debtor's breach of credit trust.[2] To deliberately evade or welsh or be unprepared or willing to pay are common occurrences when constraints are not in place. Economists call these phenomena moral hazards.

Credit is a multidimensional and multifaceted concept. It varies in form, subject to usage. In its simplest sense, credit is a bank loan. For example, the central bank controls the credit ceiling, meaning that it controls the total loan amount. In a way, credit is both a transactional relationship between people and an institutional arrangement between debtor and creditor or a contract on delivery of goods, services, and assets, all based on trust and conditioned on future repayment.

Development of Credit

The concept of credit is rooted in ancient times. Although the word was first introduced in China when the Chinese began to learn about Western civilizations, similar concepts can be found in the traditional Chinese word "Xin" or "Xin Yong," meaning "trustworthiness."

Credit originates from trust, but trust depends on value judgments. What is trust? In what ways does it function, when we come to agreements with others or have expectations about their future behavior? What are the implications of a clear understanding of the mutuality of trust to our notions of social justice, love, or even the value of human life? Clearly, attempts to formulate policy on issues like these can be greatly assisted by a clear and coherent analysis of the underlying values of life and respect that they each involve (see also Chapter 1).[3]

Credit differs from trust in that trust is related to people's daily person-to-person relationships and is based on culture and values while credit is associated with the creditor-debtor relationship and is based on the creditor's judgment of the debtor's historical performance.

Historically, the debit-credit relationship was established with the emergence of private property. With the development of private property rights and the social division of labor came improved productivity and surplus production (i.e., product volume that went beyond the laborer's own consumption needs), which in turn created the need for the exchange of goods and services among members of society. With the development of production and the exchange of goods, a merchant class came into being. Merchants specialized in the exchange of goods and services. These transactions focused economic activity on payment rather than on the delivery of goods and services. This form of exchange restricts successful transactions.[4] For example, purchasers might not have money to buy goods at the time the producers were selling them because their own goods had not yet been sold. As a result, "tally trade," where sellers sold products based on their trust in the buyers' promise to pay in the future, came into being. The term also itself implies that transferring goods and realizing value are two separate activities exercised at different points in time. In the early stages of a market economy, most participants provide mutual credit in the form of deferred payment. In this way, in addition to the trading relationship, buyers and sellers formed a relationship based on their legal rights and liabilities, which is known as commercial credit. As tally trade matured, purchasers repaid the loans in a unilateral transfer of value, where currency began to function as a means of future payment rather than current circulation, and the goods could realize their value independently after they had been physically delivered.

In essence, the entire process was a credit transaction, which is different from a barter trade or cash transaction (i.e., commodity transactions). As a result, the credit-debt relationship had been formulated and led to new concepts of "lending" and "finance."

The modern financial industry is traceable to the development of the culture of trust and the credit-debt relationship. In a developed market economy, along with the emergence of modern banking, bank credit gradually replaced business credit and became the most important form of credit in modern economic activities.

Ultimately, the credit system and credit-based transactions were established as a result of the continuous development of commodities and the money economy. The appearance of credit transactions and the establishment of a credit system promoted the development of commodity transactions. Finally, the modern market economy transformed into a credit economy based on these sophisticated credit-debt relationships.

FUNCTION AND FORMS OF CREDIT AND DEBT

Credit in financial transactions is based on the creditors' judgment of debtors' ability to repay the debt and the probability that they will do so.

Role of Credit in the Economy

The market modes of exchange went through three phases: barter trade, currency exchange, and credit transaction. This evolution has substantially increased economic efficiency and reduced costs. In the modern economy, credit transactions are superior to currency exchange, and currency exchange is superior to barter trade because of the gradual reductions in transaction costs. The principle functions of credit are to:

- *Facilitate fund reallocation and improve utilization efficiency.* Credit is the most flexible way to promote fund reallocation. By using credit, money can be mobilized efficiently. Through competition, credit can transfer funds from low-efficiency sectors to higher-efficiency sectors. It can promote the equalization of profits among different sectors through competition and concurrently improve the efficiency of the economy as a whole.
- *Minimize transaction cost.* Different credit facilities can be used to minimize transaction costs and maximize output.
  - Using credit instruments in place of cash reduces expenses related to circulating cash and thereby eases direct payment pressure.
  - With a developed credit system, money is concentrated in banks and other financial institutions that are the experts in the credit market. This can reduce the expenses incurred in storing, moving, and accounting for cash.
  - Credit can accelerate transactions and facilitate the realization of commodity value. In addition, using credit facilitates noncash settlement of all types of exchanges and transactions.
- *To facilitate capital concentration.* As a powerful tool to leverage capital concentration, credit serves as a conduit for capital accumulation and concentration, which can bolster the development of large-scale industry, improve social production, promote economic growth, and translate short-term financial resources into long-term investments, thereby expanding mass production and saving unit costs.
- *To adjust the economic structure.* Using the currency and credit system, the state formulates various financial policies and financial regulations and applies various credit leverages to adjust the money supply. With respect to credit's regulatory functions, the state not only can curb

inflation but also can stimulate the economy when it is in recession and deflation, revitalize effective demand, and promote the steady development of the capital market. By using its credit leverage, the state can also direct the flow of funds, shape and adjust the economic structure by directing the capital flow, and sustain economic development.

Credit and the Exchange of Financial Products

In rhombus theory (see Chapter 1), we demonstrated that comparative advantages can be realized via two different stages of reduction of transaction costs: the first stage, called primary exchange, is for saving exogenous transaction costs while the next stage, called secondary exchange, is for reducing endogenous transaction costs. When finance emerged as an industry, credit and debt was made tradable, and both became important financial products. At this time the rules of trading, defining property rights, and the enforcement of rules became important issues. The effort to reduce the transaction costs of both creditors and debtors entailed the establishment of rule-making associations or institutions, which serve as a constraint apparatus by regulating transactions to ensure fair exchange and manage risks. Later, the government stepped in to set civil laws to regulate commercial activities. The exchange between government or rule-making institutions and market participants is what we call primary economic exchange.

In terms of time sequence, we can divide the development of credit risk into three phases: negotiation, risk taking, and credit testing. At different developmental stages of exchange, institutional building plays different roles.

The negotiation phase, in which lender and debtor negotiate the transaction contract, happens before the credit transaction. The negotiation may include an exhaustive review of the debtor's credit status for the lender's information and security.

The risk-taking phase occurs in the period after the parties have signed a contract and the lender provides the loan to the debtor. If the debtor returns the money within the time frame specified in the contract, the credit transaction is concluded. If the payment is not made before the deadline, the debtor is in default. This is true even if the payment is made after the time limit. The lender bears the direct economic loss.

To manage the credit risk due to possible default, creditors want to set up an institutional arrangement to secure their repayment, but this institutional arrangement has to be achieved after paying transaction costs related to the information and setting up institutions. These institutions or institutional arrangements are formulated as a result of exchanges between market participants, on one hand, and the associations and government on the other. As indicated in Chapter 1, this exchange can be seen as an realization of comparative advantages of parties in question, or an equilibrium state of game play between players (agents, or persons in question), or the outcome of the interaction between incentive apparatus and constraint apparatus. The game theoretic equilibrium state has been modeled by modern incentive theorists and information theorists, such as Laffont.[5]

Risk Disclosure Mechanism in the Negotiation Phase   Negotiation includes consulting on the terms and conditions of the contract between the parties. More important, the creditor must determine whether to grant credit to the debtor, whether to use guarantees and insurance, and how much credit is appropriate.

Information asymmetry causes endogenous transaction costs. Information disclosure is an established legal arrangement to facilitate information flow from debtors to creditors or investors (the public). The costs incurred insofar as information disclosure is concerned are information costs, an important transaction cost. The information collected by creditors is used to analyze debtors' credit status; creditors need to fully understand debtors' economic status and then conduct a credit evaluation of them based on the acquired information by using credit rating technology. Finally, the credit decision and transaction are made in accordance with the evaluation results.

Information disclosure makes the transaction more transparent and helps the creditor to identify nonsystemic risks, such as the true performance, financial strength, past records of debtors. Debtors can therefore be ranked based on rating and transaction price, the interest rate can be decided based on rating and anticipated performance of debtor.

Initially, information disclosure was embodied in the contracts between creditors and debtors and was therefore a secondary financial exchange. As it became recognized that protecting creditors and investors was important, it gradually became a legal arrangement and, therefore, a part of the primary financial exchange that today is regulated by governments. For example, information disclosure is now a legal requirement of China's Securities Act and banking regulations. The People's Bank of China (PBOC) established a nationwide corporate and individual credit record database.

Risk Management System in the Risk Phase   Creditors should actively follow up and supervise debtors within the terms of the contract to guarantee the safety of the granted credit (receivables, loans, and investments, etc.). Creditors are also entitled to recall an overdue loan and sometimes to require premature redemption to minimize the loss. This is due to changes in performance environments. In China's banking practice, this is post-lending risk management.

The ways to manage credit risk are identical to those used to reduce transaction costs in exchange: hedging, diversification, and high risk, high profit. Against the background of a changing financial environment, enterprises, financial institutions, and banks reinforce credit risk management through internal rating or by outsourcing the task to professional credit management companies. Credit risk management ultimately reinforces the discipline of the market economy.

Penalty Mechanism in the Credit-testing Phase   The penalty mechanism is part of the incentive apparatus. It helps reduce moral hazard behavior by various forms of punishment, such as termination of the business relationship and increased interest rates.

There also are informal rules that can help improve the social ethos, since creditworthiness is essentially a social virtue. Therefore, the Chinese government has recently advocated education about the importance of keeping faith in financial dealings and has achieved positive results.

In addition, making credit information available to the public through the market helps reduce information asymmetry in the process of exchange by disclosing the credit status of bad-faith enterprises and individuals and praising those who honor credit and their promise. Accordingly, dishonest parties are "blacklisted" and isolated by other market players, while reputable parties greatly benefit by being widely recognized by the market. Gradually, economic and social order, discipline, and ethics evolve.

Classification and Forms of Credit

Credit and debt are classified by time frame, geographical distribution, and credit position. In terms of time frame, credit can be divided into long- and short-term credit; geographically, it can be divided into domestic and international credit. By credit position, it can be divided into public (governmental) credit, corporate (including industrial and commercial enterprises and banks), and consumer credit.

In China, credit was synonymous with trustworthiness, while the credit rating was the evaluation of trustworthiness. This narrow perception of credit is changing. The true nature of credit has been revealed gradually to the market participants.

Public Credit   The phrase "public credit," also known as government or state credit, refers to the overall debt financing and repayment capabilities at the state level. The government needs a large amount of tax revenue to provide public goods and services, such as national defense, education, communications, healthcare, and social welfare. However, the increase of government-levied taxes generally cannot keep up with growing annual expenditures, so it is common nowadays for governments around the world to accrue huge deficits every year. In order to make up for the fiscal deficits, the governments release or sell various types of credit instruments. The credit is reflected in the legal status of the governments, especially the security of tax revenue. For this reason it is called "public credit," which includes treasury bonds and loans from central bank.

Take the United States as an example. There are three levels of government: the federal government (central government), the state government, and the local government (including municipal and county governments). The government at all levels needs to borrow money every year in order to handle its huge expenditures. To accomplish this, the federal government sells these credit instruments for debt financing and fund raising: treasury bills, with a maturity of no more than 1 year; treasury notes, with a maturity between 1 and 10 years; and treasury bonds, with a maturity of over 10 years. Since the federal government has a reputable economic and credit record, foreigners and foreign governments—in addition to American citizens—are willing to purchase the securities. Most state government constitutions, however, do not allow state budgets to operate at a deficit. In special situations, though, when the state government cannot handle its expenditures within the budget, it has to raise funds by issuing public debt. Since state governments have limited financial resources and higher credit risk, the public debt they issue is not sold as easily as the debt of the federal government.

As indicated before, China's local and municipal governments are not entitled to incur debt or issue securities in their names. However, some local governments and municipal governments are sound financially and have good reputations. For this reason their public credit—their credit rating—if properly judged, should be higher than most corporate credit.

Corporate Credit   "Corporate credit" generally refers to the credit of corporate borrowers. It also refers to the credit granted by one corporate entity to another corporate entity. In essence, it is a currency loan from the products seller to the products buyer. It includes manufacturing enterprises' credit sales (i.e., product credit sales to corporate clients). In a product credit sale, the sellers are typically materials providers, products manufacturers, and wholesalers. The buyers—the beneficiary parties of the sale—include all types of corporate clients or agents. This category of credit is commonly perceived as commercial credit.

Corporate credit also involves credit granted by commercial banks, finance companies, and other financial institutions to the enterprises and the credit that emerges from other modes of exchange except for spot remittance, spot cash, and advance payments.

A bank is also a type of enterprise, and it operates on credit. Commercial banks or other financial institutions grant bank credit to enterprises or individual consumers. In the process of a product credit sale, banks and other financial institutions provide financial support for buyers and help sellers expand sales. Commercial banks and other financial institutions lend money to enterprises, with the loan and repayment modes based on the credit ratings of the enterprises. Enterprises that do not meet the credit standard are required to provide mortgages and surety for the commercial banks or to ask guarantors to provide guarantees on their behalf. The guarantee is virtually a special form of credit; the guarantors' credit is usually incorporated into the credit rating of the enterprises that apply for loans.

Consumer Credit Consumer credit is a relationship for the exchange of commodities and services, contingent upon consumers' promise of future payment. In fact, consumer credit as a transaction tool has a long history in the market economy. After World War II, science and technology advanced rapidly, and social productivity improved greatly. In order to sell commodities, businesspeople designed many innovative sales promotion methods, such as installment paying, credit-buying tickets, and credit cards. The emergence of consumer credit expanded the size of the market and allowed consumers to enjoy the goods or services before paying for them. The basic characteristics of consumer credit are a relatively higher interest rate and higher risk. Generally, the robustness of personal credit is directly related to the stage of development of financial services in a given country or region. Consumer credit in China has developed very rapidly in the early 2000s. Right now consumer credit is very much confined to mortgage home loans. But as statistics indicate, consumer credit with respect to mortgage home loans is less risky than corporate credit.

It is recognized that the legal framework and government policy can play an important role in enhancing the credit at different levels. For example, government can boost the rating of state-owned enterprises (SOEs) through government guarantees—implicit or explicit—and supply paid-in capital to SOEs as well as resumes high risks in investment projects. This is called credit enhancement.

ECONOMIC PRINCIPLES OF CREDIT

The development of modern economic theories provides an explanation for the emergence and development of credit. Fisher perceived credit as a conduit to transfer current savings to future consumption; the credit market would facilitate the effective distribution of consumption over time.[6] Hodgman indicated two factors that trigger the credit risks: external factors and internal factors. External factors are those that cannot be controlled by the firm or the individual in question per se, such as economic cycles and shocks. Internal factors relate to the moral hazard and reverse selections.[7]

These economic theories include information asymmetry theory, transaction cost theory, and game theory.

Information Asymmetry Theory and Credit

"Information asymmetry" refers to the uneven distribution of information (i.e., different participants possess different information due to their ability to access information, and, thus, some know more than others do). Information asymmetry is said to be the main reason for opportunistic behavior and the cause of faith-breaking behavior by enterprises or individuals. The more transparent and smooth the transaction is, the less frequently the faith-breaking behavior will occur. When all market participants have enough information to properly judge the credit status of their transaction counterparts, they can make better decisions. However, one has to pay transaction cost, here referred to information cost, to get sufficient information.

The legal system helps with the dissemination of information. According to the information dissymmetry theory, the solution to the faith-breaking problem is greater transparency in transaction behavior and improvements in the information transmission system. Experiences around the world show that the information disclosure system is essential to solve the problem of faith-breaking. For example, to protect investors' interests, listed companies are required to disclose information appropriately in order to provide investors with an indication of their true performance.

Transaction Cost Theory and Credit

From the point of view of transaction cost theory, the behavior of market participants will be affected by the existence of transaction cost. According to the theory, if a breach of faith or default will bring an entity more economic benefit than the cost it pays, such behavior will occur. To constrain the agent, the creditor (as a principal in the principal-agent relationship) has to pay the cost, such as rating, investigation, or legal proceeding cost to prevent the debtor (the agent) from moral hazard and adverse selection behavior, which may otherwise occur.

Again, this transaction cost can be saved when government makes clear rules—such as civil law, corporate law, and banking law—and when the laws are properly enforced. If the government directly participates in market transactions and benefit from its legal status, or if government policies favor of one group of market participants against another, then the transaction cost will not be saved; rather, it will augmented. Therefore, it is counterproductive for the government to give its affiliated enterprises preferential policies. Moral hazards behaviors were seen commonly from SOEs in 1980s and 1990s. This was partly due to the government's subsidy and bail-out policy regarding SOEs, such as debt-to-equity swap and tax exemption, which make them to perceive the loan from state banks as a kind of grant from the government.

Transaction cost theory also explains the economic reasons for the emergence and development of internal and external credit service institutions, such as internal rating departments and outside rating agencies. The costs incurred to the internal rating departments and paid to the rating agencies are transaction costs. Although these transaction costs are inevitable, the social division of labor can help to reduce them.

Game Theory and Credit

From the perspective of game theory, market participants achieve equilibrium via game play. A transaction can be made through the interplay between market participants. In a good credit environment with convenient access to information and perfect market supervision, if a person does not honor his commitment, then he or she cannot find any other counterparties to work with or to carry out a new transaction; his record has already been transmitted to market participants and supervisors. Other market participants will quickly learn about the information and refuse to work with the enterprise in subsequent transactions. Those who have morally hazardous behavior would be isolated and pay an expensive price for their faith-breaking behavior. Therefore, in the social environment with a perfect information transmission and supervision system, moral hazards rarely happen. Gradually, it is understood, the optimal strategy is maintaining a good reputation.

In a poor credit environment, however, moral hazards and adverse selection would be common as faith-breaking behavior cannot easily be discovered on a timely basis due to slow information transmission. And due to ineffective enforcement, violators are not punished. Therefore, in a society lacking a sophisticated credit supervision system, faith-breaking will inevitably become the best strategy. This has a snowball effect. When another enterprise realizes that a faith-breaking enterprise has reaped extra benefits in the short term, for example, the enterprise will likely also choose to break faith as a strategy. If breaking faith is seen as the best strategy by most enterprises, dishonesty will be encouraged and, in turn, will lead to a deteriorating credit environment.

According to game theory, if an enterprise focuses on the short-term rather than on the long-term game, it will lose the trust of others. Only through severe punishment that increases the cost of faith-breaking can market participants eventually focus on establishing long-term relationships and refrain from faith-breaking activities.

CHARACTERISTICS OF CREDIT

According to planned economic theory, credit, like other economic categories such as commodities and capital, exists only in a capitalist system. Credit is no longer necessary in a socialist economic system. After reform in China in the 1980s, the theoretical community recognized that credit can be used in a socialist system, but only on the condition that it will not lead to a situation of one person exploiting another.

For a long time, the old perception of credit restricted the expansion of financial activities in China. In the early 1990s, inspired by Deng Xiaoping's saying "Everything can be practiced on a trial basis as long as it can promote economic development," the capital market began to perceive that credit could be helpful in the developing socialist economy. It is now recognized that old perception of credit hindered the development of financial market, especially the movement from plan-based financial market to market-based financial market.

Institutional economic engineering (IEEN) helps us understand the essence of credit. Credit is essentially an exchange of comparative advantages of the parties in question. As credit makes the exchange of endowments and comparative advantages possible, it thereby helps achieve a win-win outcome and reduce endogenous transaction costs. Credit promotes economic transactions and activities and thereby improves economic development. It is also reasonable to suppose, based on the definition of the word "institution," that credit, as an institutional arrangement, is created as a result of the interaction between the incentive structure and the constraints structure.

Credit is also an evaluation of the debtor's ability and willingness to repay the debt. The main function of credit is to make the exchange possible. It also represents the risk that creditors take if their judgment is incorrect.

Credit and finance, as institutional arrangements, emerged along with declining exogenous and endogenous transaction costs due to technological progress and social developments. Without these institutional arrangements, many transactions would not have been possible.

Generally, value movement is realized through the buy-sell relationship, by which sellers receive money by forgoing their consumption and the buyer does the opposite. The equal-value exchange formed by this type of buy-sell relationship is complete when the seller and buyer finish the transaction (i.e., the parties get equal value at the same time).

However, the value derived from a credit relationship is realized through a debit and credit accounting, delivery and payment process. Money or goods may be physically retained, but only the right to use the goods changes hands. The lender temporarily releases the ownership of goods or money, but the ownership is unchanged. In the credit relationship, the focus of equal-value exchange is the right to use goods or money.

Credit is different from trust. Trust is based on philosophy, culture, and value while credit is based on the past performance of the person or legal entities in question. It is easy to see that both trust and credit are constraints. As North has said, "Institutions are the rules of the game in a society or, more formally, are the humanly devised constraints that shape human interaction."[8] (However, they are informal rules. Civil laws, such as Roman law, are formal rules insofar as the credit-debtor relationship is concerned.) Informal rules, such as those related to the tradition and culture, take longer, sometimes even generations, to form and become established. Therefore, credit marks institutional progress.

As mentioned, credit can be differentiated and classified as state credit, commercial credit, corporate credit, bank credit, and consumer credit. Credit can be rated on different scales, so that investors can evaluate the reasonable return to cover the risk they are taking. Credit can also be traded in the market to create a credit curve, which can serve as a good reference for the market's understanding of the underlying credit over time. This differentiation helps make credit per se measurable and tradable.

As indicated, credit and debt are two concepts that are related to each other. Essentially, they are the same thing but seen from opposite perspectives. Debt represents the legal liabilities of debtors to creditors and the financial debit-credit relationship of the two parties. National debt is an economic concept that represents the government's liability. The bond itself is a market instrument. When we refer to the obligations or national debt, we normally are referring to both the legal and the economic meaning of national debt.

Origin and Essence of National Debt

National debt first appeared in the commodity economies of ancient Rome and Greece. Wars led to a fiscal government shortfall. A debt-credit relationship between the national government and the newly emerged merchant class soon developed as well. Initially, public debt came in the form of royal loans and annual fees. Thus, it differed from the modern public debt system. According to Karl Marx,

The system of public credit, i.e. of national debt, whose origin we discover in Genoa and Venice as early as the Middle Ages, took possession of Europe in whole during the handcraft industry period. The colonial system with its maritime trade and commercial wars served as a greenhouse for it. Thus, it first took root in Holland. National debt, i.e., the alienation of the state—whether an autocratic, constitutional or republican system—marked the capitalist era.[9]

Marx believed that the fiscal deficits resulting from the colonial system, maritime trade, and commercial wars caused the emergence of national debt: "Public debt is just a new way of increasing taxes and meeting the bourgeois' new need for seizing state power."[10]

During the early development of capitalism, classical economists argued that the government should not incur debt, but by the first half of the twentieth century—the monopoly phase of capitalism—Keynesians were trying to convince the public that because of wage rigidity, aggregate demand and aggregate supply would not be in equilibrium, whereas in classical economics they are supposed to be. Therefore, they argued, increased government deficit would help boost aggregate demand. Many countries followed Keynesian economic theory in the post–World War II era, and, as a result, increasing government debt was common.

According to modern economic theory, governments may incur debt and invest in the areas where individuals are reluctant to involve themselves as long as the proceeds are used effectively and government debt is productive.

In pre-reform socialist economic theory, national debt was used mainly for economic construction—from the people, for the people. If used for public facilities—for example, infrastructure—money borrowed from the people would be used for the benefit of the people, and taxes levied would be used for debt repayment. However, before 1949 it was common for borrowed money to be alternatively used for nonproductive projects or purposes, such as wars or ill selected projects (for example, during the Qing dynasty, national debt was incurred mainly for wars).

The Ricardo theorem on the relationship between tax revenue and debt has experienced a resurgence in modern economic analysis. It reflects two issues with which governments are concerned: (1) the impact on the current macroeconomy if governments finance deficits though debts, and (2) the impact on the future social security system. If public expenditure is covered by issuing government bonds rather than by increasing tax revenue, what is its implication to the national economy? How will it influence the distribution of income? Increasing public expenditure by issuing national debt rather than tax revenues is virtually using future tax revenue for current investments. The present value of future tax revenue should be equal to the amount of planned future debt. In such a case, issuing national debt would not have a negative impact on a country's gross national wealth.

However, the vertical use of future tax revenue will lead to horizontal changes in income reallocation. If government expenditure relied on absorbing private savings, and overtaxation, it would give rise to decreases private investment and result in a "crowding-out" effect. In this respect, Ricardian equivalence theorem is impeccable.

David Ricardo's equilibrium theory is also applicable to the analysis of private consumption. The people who borrow money to buy cars are not necessarily poorer than the people who buy cars with cash. The borrowers do not have to change their current consumption patterns, but their future consumption will be reduced, especially when the debt matures.

Characteristics of Bonds

As standardized debt, bonds have three basic characteristics—credibility, profitability, and liquidity—which are highly correlated with one another.

Credibility, or assured or reliable repayment, means that after issuance, the interest will be paid regularly with the principal paid on maturity; or the interest and principal will be serviced on a lump-sum basis upon maturity. In contrast, stockholders can receive dividends but are unable to withdraw their equity investment.

Profitability means a certain amount of interest income in addition to the recoverable principal. Interest is the gain from principal. Unlike deposits, which are indirect investments, bonds are a form of direct investment and therefore require higher yields than deposits.

Liquidity in the market means the ability to convert the asset into cash. Bonds enjoy higher liquidity as their large issuing volume and standardized certificates make trading and settlement easy.

Differences among Bonds, Stocks, and Bank Deposits

Bonds can be further identified by way of comparison with other financial market instruments. Stocks and bonds, which are both securities, differ in a number of ways:

- *Stocks are the symbol of corporate ownership and a form of capital contribution to a company.* Stockholders become shareholders of the company with a right to share the company's profits and participate in the company's operation and management according to the proportion of their capital contributions. Bondholders regularly earn interest and receive repayment of the principal when it matures, but they have no right to share profit and participate in the operation and management of the company.

- *Stockholders can regularly earn dividends*, but they cannot take back their equity investment, even if the company goes bankrupt. Bond-holders regularly receive fixed interest income since there is no direct relationship between the performance of the company and the interest payment to them. However, once issued and traded in the market, bond yield is influenced by market fluctuations.
- *Stocks have no maturity.* Once shareholders purchase stock, they cannot withdraw their equity money from the company but can sell them to other investors. By contrast, bonds have maturities, and the issuer must service the debt when it matures.
- *Creditors have priority to claim repayment over shareholders.* When a company is in bankruptcy, it has to pay its bondholders before any payment is made to its shareholders.
- *Stock price is more volatile than bond price.* Both stock and bond prices are determined by market interest and the performance of the company (issuer) in question, but the stock price depends on the performance of the company, while the bond price depends on market interest rates in general.
- *Legally (in China), interest on bonds is paid before income tax* whereas dividends are paid after tax to reflect that shareholders are stakeholders in the company.

Bonds also differ from bank deposits in a number of ways:

- Corporate bonds are direct financing tools with relatively higher funding costs, because their credit is lower than banks. In turn, the interest rates for bank deposits are relatively low.
- Bank deposits can have different time limits and interest rates, while the same bond can have only one set of terms and conditions for all investors.
- Fundraising through bank deposits is far slower than through the issuance of bonds.[11]

Changing Perceptions toward Credit and Debt in China

Debt has both positive and negative economical implications. The negative aspect is that national debt reflects the weakness and vulnerability of the economy because it (1) is a liability that will have to be undertaken by later generations; (2) may lead to inflation; and (3) crowds out private investment. Historically, the negative connotation of debt prevailed. After World War II, however, the perception of debt has changed substantially. Its positive implication—that it can play an important role in economic development—has been gradually recognized. As securitized national debt, government bonds are perceived by market participants as financial commodities, a means of payment and a tool for open market operations (OMOs) by the central banks.

By the end of 1996, the total bond balance of public offerings in the 23 major bond markets in the world totaled US$21.5 trillion. Treasury bonds accounted for 40.6 percent, government agency bonds for 14.8 percent, local treasury bonds for 6.5 percent, corporate bonds for 13 percent, and other bonds of public offerings for 13.6 percent. Bonds released by foreign issuers accounted for 11.5 percent. By the end of 2000, the total stock of the world bonds market had reached $31.4 trillion, approximately equal to the world's total gross domestic product that year.

The changing perception of debt and national debt can be divided into five general phases. In phase 1, debt was seen as completely negative, as a means for one class to exploit another class of people. In phase 2, national debt gained a positive meaning; it was considered productive, because it was intended for economic construction rather than consumption. Then, in phase 3, national debt was defined as a kind of tax revenue that would place the burden of repayment on future generations. In phase 4, national debt was perceived as a tool of modern financial markets and macroeconomic management. Finally, in phase 5, debt and national debt were put into a new perspective and considered an institutional arrangement. Table 28.1 illustrates varying attitudes toward national debt throughout history.

Initially, China's understanding of national debt was somewhat shallow, superficial, and even negative. From 1958 to 1981, China did not incur government debt, as classical economic theories do not favor incurring national debt. However, new theories developed later to favor debt under specific circumstances, such as the so-called posterity repayment theory, which approves issuance of national debt. Whatever the theories are in favor of, modern governments in countries around the globe, as it turned out to be, frequently issue government securities for financing, creating market instruments, and fiscal policy. In general, the amount of government bonds issued in each country has never decreased but has only increased.

After reform in China, for many years, the incurrence of national debt was seen as a way to finance the fiscal deficit. Therefore, it always related to the phenomenon of a fiscal deficit, and related to excessive banknote issuance, and gives rise to inflation. Nowadays people in China realize that treasury bonds (one way to incur national debt) are not merely a way

TABLE 28.1   Attitudes toward National Debt throughout History

Time and economic school	Prevailing view of national debt
Ancient Greece and Rome	A means for the ruling class to expand consumption, a tumor on the economy
Since 18th century, when capitalism was taking shape; Marx's view	Lever for social development, and a vehicle for the primitive accumulation of capital
Socialist planned economy	A means for developing the economy
Socialist market economy	A way of financing deficits other than through overdrafts or loans from the central bank, also a means to reduce inflation pressure
Socialist market economy	A beneficial way to transform consumption funds into accumulation funds
Neoclassical economic theory	A way to use future tax revenue in the present; since later generations will benefit from this current investment, it is reasonable to pass the obligation for repaying the debt onto them
Neoclassical economic theory	An indispensable financial commodity in the securities market
Neoclassical economic theory	A driving force for economic growth

to finance fiscal deficit but also an instrument for government investment. As long as the proceeds of treasury bonds are being used effectively, the return generated will be more than sufficient to repay the maturing debt as evidenced by some successful examples around the world. Therefore, debt can be treated positively.

The perception of debt-related issues in China has evolved over time. China suspended incurring debt during the 1960s and 1970s; it resumed issuing debt in 1981. Given the Chinese antipathy to debt, the move took a lot of effort.

Throughout the 1980s, China benefited from continuously receiving debt proceeds from the issuance of bonds, and there was little concern about the establishment of bond market. In early 1990s, debt service became a burden for the government, which, in turn, intensified its reliance on refinancing through issuance of bonds. Note that when no real bond market exists, the market function of bonds cannot be understood and realized.

In the 1980s, there was no such true concept of a bond market. The placement of bonds was considered *"fenpei,"* or distribution, and was known as administrative placement; the trading of bonds was thought of as *"liutong"* or *"zhuanrang,"* circulation or transfer. In the later 1980s, redemption and trading difficulties emerged, and there were a number of complaints from individuals, which also triggered further issuance distress. As issuance became more and more difficult in the late 1980s, China gradually realized that debt issue would no longer possible without a sound primary market. In the 1990s, underwriting syndication was conducted, and bonds started to be traded on the Stock Exchange Bond Market (SEBM). This important step changed people's awareness of the bond market. They began to understand that bonds are not only debt certificates but also serve as market instruments. Although the public gradually accepted the concept of a bond market, the market was understood to be only a way to assist individual investors in the buying and selling of bonds.

As the market developed, the general perception of debt went to the other extreme. People saw the positive side of debt, and many regarded holding government bonds as a kind of welfare as the return of government bonds were higher than their alternative use of their savings, for instance, put in bank deposit. As a result, many individual investors complained that bonds were supplied via institution based market as opposed to individual based market is inconvenience to individual investors, another word, they wished to return to administrative placement regime. This is different from when investors felt that trading and redeeming bonds was an inconvenience. Some people complained that they could not access government securities; that, in the past, when they did not want to buy them, the government forced them to buy, but when they wanted to buy, they do not know where to find them. As a result, the Ministry of Finance had to increase the retail, investor-targeted issuance.

Because government bonds, as certificates of standardized national debt, are among the safest investments available in China, banks and, since the middle 1990s, securities intermediaries frequently used treasury bonds as mortgages or collateral for other borrowing. In such cases, T-bonds are similar to credit instruments.

In 1996, the 10-year bond was issued, the price in the aftermarket quickly rose to RMB137 because of the central bank's interest rate cut and market expectation. One institution even drafted a report on increasing the issuance exclusively targeted to the retailing market. In 1997, an insurance company wanted the government to have a private placement targeted only to that company.

Until the middle 1990s, only the securities firms and banks understood such concepts as yield and capital gain. Even the agencies still regarded financial intermediaries as merchants ("merchants" have a negative connotation in Chinese society; they are not considered productive members of society), their daily work of trading bonds was considered speculation, and the futures market introduced by the Ministry and the Shanghai Stock Exchange was considered a speculative market.

However, three important events, which began in the second half of 1990s and continued into the twenty-first century, stimulated the government to rethink the bond market.

1. In the early 1990s, the Ministry pursued a series of market-based reforms to alleviate the pressures relating to bond redemption, trading, and issuance.
2. In the late 1990s, the government started to deal with nonperforming loans (NPLs). One move was to establish asset management companies (AMCs), special vehicles to receive NPLs from banks, which are then resold through an open bidding process. Since the number of bidders was limited, the selling price was usually unfavorable, and, therefore, there was no financial incentive. At that time the AMCs could not price these assets properly because there was no active corporate bond market to serve as a benchmark. Many people have suggested that the price of bank assets should receive the same rating as corporate bonds and securitized bank assets.
3. In later 1990s, the PBOC accelerated reform, reducing the number of administrative measures, such as the reloan facility, and increasing the number of market-based instruments, especially OMOs. Therefore, it was in the central bank's own interest to build up a liquid bond market. In addition, as the foreign exchange reserve started to build up, sterilization[13] became a priority of the central bank.

Since 2000 onward, the PBOC took a number of initiatives to boost the bond market. As China gradually established the framework of a modern debt capital market, people's awareness of debt also changed. This revolutionary change in China's perception of the true nature of debt and national debt is of great significance to the country's bond market development. Gradually people came to differentiate between debt and bonds. With the development of the government bond market, they gradually discovered that the national debt could be bought and sold in the market. It was a kind of financial commodity and had the same characteristics as any other commodity. This further improved China's perception of the nature of national debt, which is close to the idea that government securities, such as bonds, are a standardized and specified national debt.

Government bonds are also the most liquid financial asset held by banks. The central bank adjusts the money supply by buying and selling government securities in a process known as open market operations. The central bank's OMO is a macroeconomic control method, with T-bonds serving as macroeconomic instruments.

Thus, national debt has both positive and negative implications to the national economy. To take full advantage of its positive aspects, it is important not only to use the debt proceeds productively, but also to set up a cost-effective and highly efficient bond market, which is the mission of the government and government agencies, especially government debt managers.

GOVERNMENT POLICY AND DEBT CAPITAL MARKET

It is noted that at the early stage, reform programs were characterized by a decentralized fiscal relationship between different levels of governments and the relationship between state and state-owned enterprises. This means more money retained in the local governments and SOEs. The decentralization was, in fact, achieved by decreased revenues and increased expenditures; as a result, government deficit increased, which had to be financed by issuing government bonds and, before 1994, borrowing from central bank.

Decentralization helped to build up the incentive structure, which benefited local governments, state-owned enterprises, and farmers and helped the economy develop. This institutional arrangement is of great significance as it enabled the government to achieve its goal of improving economic growth by providing incentives, which led to a win-win result for all parties. The current debt incurred will be paid through growing future tax revenues generated by the booming economy. However, while national debt provided the fulcrum for the economic reform of the early 1980s, accumulated debt must be kept at an appropriate level.

Institutional Framework of the Credit Debt Relationship and Debt Capital Market

Generally, securities markets are divided into two categories: an equity market and a bond market. As a kind of debt instrument, fixed-income securities fall into both categories and represent a credit-debt relationship; a bond is a certificate issued by government institutions, local public bodies, financial institutions, enterprises, and other entities. Bonds carry a basic legal clause stating the face value, interest rate, maturity date, and guarantee terms, and thereby bonds specify the rights and obligations that exist between issuers and investors. Usually the issuer agrees to pay a certain amount or a percentage of the principal value to the bondholders either periodically before maturity or in a lump sum on the bond's maturity.[14]

This explanation may be oversimplified, since it does not mention the establishment of institutions, laws, and regulations, which is by no means an easy task. Bonds can function correctly only when the proper institutional framework is in place. Therefore, bonds are also a type of security, a legal document representing certain property rights, which must be set forth in the securities in scrip form or in the legal documents for book-entry securities. The rights and obligations represented by the bonds may change hands, and their transfer should take place simultaneously. The property right may be legally transferred to another party against the delivery of physical securities.

From a legal perspective, a bond is a certificate of debt, and represents a specific right-obligation relationship between two or more parties according to the agreement or contract or the provisions of law. In this rights-obligation relationship, the people with rights are called creditors and those with obligations are debtors. Creditors can claim the right by requiring debtors to fulfill their obligation as prescribed by the contract or law. This rights-obligation relationship between creditors and debtors is called debt. However, not all loan agreements are bonds.

Bonds are specific, standardized borrowing agreements; they are not money-borrowing certificates in the common sense. They differ from money-borrowing certificates in two ways:

1. The total bond amount can be divided into small units, and such units can be held by many investors at the same time under the same terms and conditions.
2. A bond can be transferred to a third party at a price corresponding to the prevailing market rate.

A bond coupon is the periodic interest payment made to the bondholder during the life of the bond. The coupon rate is stated, along with maturity, in any quotation of a bond's price. The coupon can be in any number with two decimal places.[15]

However, the bond market can operate only within a legal or institutional framework. From the IEEN perspective, this is not sufficient.

IEEN Perspective on Economic Revolutions

As indicated earlier, from the point view of IEEN, people engaged in economic activities can benefit through an exchange of their endowments and comparative advantages. Because the exchanges are made among market participants, this is known as secondary economic exchange as opposed to primary economic exchange. From the perspective of economic managers, the purpose of primary economic exchanges is to set up rules so that secondary economic exchanges can be made on the principle of fairness, openness, and competition. Therefore, the function of the primary financial exchange is essentially to reduce exogenous transaction costs vis-à-vis the secondary financial exchange, which is realized via economizing endogenous transaction costs.

The first revolution in the secondary financial exchange was the standardization of commodities and specialization of business, or division of labor. As a result, the merchant class came into being. From the perspective of IEEN, production can increase comparative advantages, but it is exchange that can improve competitive advantages.

The second revolution in the secondary financial exchange was the emergence of money, which greatly facilitates transactions because exchange is more efficient if commodities are standardized and specialized. It is therefore reasonable to suppose that money is a standardized and specialized commodity. Money first appeared in the secondary financial exchange when market participants were trying to reduce their endogenous transaction costs and discovered that money could smooth transactions. As a standardized and specialized commodity, it must be dividable and measurable; therefore, commodities such as shells, gold, and silver became the first group of proxy of currencies.

The third revolution was the emergence of credit. The marketplace helps save transaction costs that result from space constraints. Credit helps save transaction costs that result from time constraints. Credit therefore marked a new era of secondary financial exchange development.

The mismatch in time between commodity delivery and money payment created tremendous uncertainties and risks. Most credit instruments, such as loans extended by banks, and debt instruments, such as corporate bonds, involve several types of risk. For example, a corporate bondholder bears interest risk, if the bonds pay fixed interest at some time in the future. This is because market interest changes over time. Holders of bonds are also exposed to credit risk, as the borrowers may default on their obligations.

The fourth revolution in the secondary financial exchange is the commoditization of money and the emergence of the banking industry and money market, which made the use of money more efficient.

The fifth revolution is the emergence of the capital market, where credit and debt become tradable. To facilitate the exchange, both credit and debt are commoditized and standardized so that more transactions can be made possible. As was indicated, social and economic development relies on the exchange of endowments and comparative advantages. There are many ways to make the exchange possible. Commoditization, marketization, specialization, specification, standardization, securitization and conglomeration are forces that reduce endogenous transaction costs. Nowadays, credit has two meanings: bank loans, or loan facilities, and the measurement of trustworthiness, or the degree of default risk. Bonds, for example, are standardized loans; credit derivatives are the specification and commoditization of credit risks. By analogy, stocks are standardized property rights, securitization is standardized assets, and futures are standardized forward contracts. In each case, the characteristics of the asset are clearly specified. The financial market is tending toward increased standardization and specificity. Capital concentration and accumulation can achieve a conglomeration effect. Therefore, mergers and acquisitions are used not only to reduce transaction costs, but also for achieving conglomeration effects.

The primary financial exchange goes hand in hand with the secondary financial exchange. When the secondary financial exchange developed as a result of the emergence of currency, the primary financial exchange developed laws and rules on the secondary exchange. The first revolution in the primary financial exchange was the advent of Roman law and civil laws. The parallel movement was the formalization of financial contracts from contracts based on oral commitments to those based on the written agreements. Gradually, contracts become tradable and even standardized and commoditized (e.g., loan transfer to bond, forward transfers to futures).

IEEN provides an explanation for the trajectory of financial market development from a historical perspective. It also heralds the development of the financial market in the future.

In summary, the debt-credit relationship is an equilibrium state based on the exchange of comparative advantages between debtors and creditors in an institutional arrangement, which is designed to achieve a win-win outcome for the benefit of both parties. Debt can be standardized and specified, and become a market instrument (i.e., bonds) through which all market operations can be carried out. Debt also can serve as collateral for guaranty. The standardized national debt is government bonds, which are treated as a benchmark for pricing other securities and are an important component of portfolio investment. All of these bond market developments are based on creative and innovative ideas that are realized through market participants' endeavors to save endogenous transaction costs through the so-called secondary exchange. However, the institutions and institutional framework for the bond market have been established via the so-called primary exchange, the exchange between government agencies and market participants.

CHAPTER 29

Development of the Chinese Government Bond Market

As an institutional arrangement, the financial market has two basic functions: finance and investment. The evolution of institutions is very much driven by the market participants' desire to reduce transaction costs and maximize their competitive advantage through exchange. In order to reduce transaction costs, the bond market creates diversified instruments readily available to trade in the exchanges. The diversification of market instruments is pursed for the heterogeneous preferences of market participants. Therefore, diversification helps to save endogenous transaction costs via exchange and thereby raise market efficiency. Market efficiency can also be improved by the division of labor, or specialization, whereby exogenous transaction costs can be saved. Through the division of labor, market function ramification takes place. For example, financial intermediaries are specialized in jobs which used to be done by borrowers or investors. Eventually, the financial system evolved into a contemporary market configuration.

Financial market movement is a combined process of evolution and revolution, driven by both endogenous and exogenous forces that motivate government and market participants to create institutions and design new instruments. In Chapter 1, we specified two different exchanges: the primary exchange and the secondary exchange. The former is the exchange between government and market participants; its function is to reduce exogenous transaction costs by establishing rules and enforcement systems. The latter is the exchange between market participants, and its function is to reduce endogenous transaction costs so that the exchange can be carried out more effectively and efficiently. These two exchanges go hand in hand. However, institutional evolution has to occur in an ad hoc legal framework where the government plays a very important role. International experiences shed light on the institutional economic engineering framework.

INTERNATIONAL EXPERIENCES AND THEIR IMPLICATIONS FOR THE DEVELOPMENT OF CHINA'S TREASURY BOND MARKET

Generally, the development of the bond market requires six conditions:

1. Rapidly growing investment in bond securities, with bond assets outpacing equity and other financial assets
2. An institution-based market
3. Diverse bond instruments
4. Structural institutional arrangements
5. Derivative bond instruments that can add value for market participants
6. Continued standardization and specification of existing credit and debt instruments

At present, the U.S. treasury bond market is the largest and most active government bond market in the world. By the end of 2003, the balance of the American T-bonds reached approximately $7 trillion, with negotiable treasury bonds accounting for $3.6 trillion. Table 29.1 shows the changes in American bond deposits from 1985 to the second quarter of 2004.

Funding-driven Market

In the United States, as early as the Revolutionary War, the government issued short- and medium-term bonds to finance its huge war expenditures. In 1770, the first American stock exchange was founded in Philadelphia (Philadelphia Stock Exchange), and bonds traded there as well at that time. In the 1930s, because of the Great Depression from 1929 to 1933, income taxes, on both the individual and the corporate level, fell to their lowest

TABLE 29.1   Auction Issue of 30-Year Treasury Bond

This is an addition to the 30-year term treasury bond issued on February 15, 2000.

Interest rate:	6.25%	Issue date:	August 15, 2000
		Value date:	May 15, 2000
CUSIP number:	912810 FM5	Maturity date:	May 15, 2030
Minimum sum of STRIP	$32,000		
Highest yield:	5.697%	Price per:	107.86

All competitive and non-competitive bidders will obtain the highest yield.

point. As a result, the average annual fiscal revenue at the federal level fell from $4 billion in 1929 to 1930 to $2 billion in 1932 and 1933, while fiscal expenditures during the same period rose dramatically. In order to alleviate the impact of the economic crisis, the U.S. government adopted a policy of deficit financing to stimulate economic recovery. Consequently, government debt increased and, in 1933, reached $23 billion. Since that time, U.S. government debt has expanded continuously. By the end of 1945, the American government debt totaled $51 billion. During World War II, 57 percent of the U.S. military expenditure was funded by government debt. Seven war bonds and one victory bond were issued at that time. By the end of the war, U.S. government debt reached $258.7 billion, accounting for 122 percent of the gross national product at that time.

After the 1950s, U.S. government debt expanded more quickly due to the Cold War with the former Soviet Union and the Korean War. In 1954, government bonds amounted to $294 billion. During the Kennedy and Johnson administrations, government deficits grew rapidly to fund federal social welfare programs as well as the Vietnam War. By 1969, U.S. government debt totaled $352.9 billion.

With the oil crisis and ensuing inflation of the 1970s, the American economy experienced sharp declines. The federal government resorted to government debt issuance to make up for the fiscal deficits. By 1980, government debt had increased to $936.7 billion. In the 1980s, the Reagan administration pursued a supply-side macroeconomic policy to stimulate growth by reducing taxes and expanding budgetary expenditures, which led to increased government debts. By the end of 1993, U.S. government debts reached about $4.410 trillion. After Bill Clinton came to power, the U.S. government began to curb the growth of government debt by increasing taxes and cutting fiscal expenditures, with the objective of eliminating the heavy debt burden. Beginning in the late 1990s, the issuance scale of government debt began to decline as a result of budgetary surpluses. After becoming president, George W. Bush has vigorously pursued a tax reduction plan, which has led to great fiscal deficits. U.S. government debt has once again achieved record levels.

The U.S. bond market was developed only for financing purposes. Gradually, it has been recognized that without a sound bond capital market, its financing purpose cannot be achieved, and this is where the government has a role.

Diversification and Standardization

Diversification and standardization, two important features of an advanced bond market, are driven by the needs of market participants. U.S. government bonds are not only large in scale but also diverse. At present,

50 to 60 different types of products are traded in the U.S. treasury bond market, ranging from spot, futures and options trading, to repurchase (repo) transactions.

Types of U.S. Government Bonds

Treasury Bills   Treasury bills have the shortest term of all U.S. government securities. There are three main types: three months, six months, and one year. T-bills do not have coupon rate and are generally issued at discount. In the 1970s and early 1980s, T-bills became one of the most attractive securities in the market due to their high liquidity and yield relative to the interest rate of most current bank savings and checking accounts.

Because of their large scale, T-bills can absorb new issues without significant impact on the market price. At the same time, due to their high liquidity, the T-bill market is affected by large fund outflows. If the stability of the U.S. political situation can be measured by value, then prudent investors are longing for a place to protect their property free of such menaces as confiscation of assets and threatened nationalization. Due to the scale and liquidity of the government bond market, government securities, especially T-bills, have become the choice of sophisticated investors, both domestic and foreign. By December 30, 2003, there were about $958.2 billion of T-bills in trade, accounting for 26 percent of total government securities.

Treasury Notes   Fifty-four percent of the traded U.S. government securities are treasury notes with a maturity between 2 and 10 years. This type of government security is appropriate for medium-term investors. Treasury notes cannot be redeemed before maturity. Like most treasury securities, the returns are fixed. The interest on the treasury notes are paid every six months by check or through the electronic transmission system. The treasury notes are issued at par, at premium, or at discount. Due to super large issue volume, the market is very liquid; therefore, although a $100,000 deal is insignificant compared to the more typical several-million-dollar deals, yet it still has a very small bid-ask spread.

Treasury Bonds   Treasury bonds, with a maturity of usually 20 to 30 years, are issued to meet the need for long-term financing. Nowadays, treasury bonds have become the benchmark for long-term financing in the United States. They also serve as an indicator of changes in the world interest rate. Bond yield and price change in opposite directions. Long bond prices tend to be volatile and are even more sensitive than short-term bonds to interest rate fluctuations. For this reason, investors are extremely cautious when investing in treasury bonds. Since 1994, the Federal Reserve Board's consecutive interest rate hikes resulted in the decline of T-bond prices. Unlike treasury notes, some treasury bonds are callable before maturity. In 1997, there were 17 callable T-bonds, all of which were issued when the interest rate was high. Bonds issued after 1985 did not carry these high rates. Thus, for example, a 13 percent callable bond is due in 2014, but the Department of the Treasury (Treasury) has an option to call it at any time between 2009 and 2014, so its maturity is not defined at issue. If the market interest rate at that time is relatively lower, the Treasury will call the bond before its maturity and refinance it at a lower interest rate. Treasury bonds accounted for only 15 percent of market share as of December 30, 2003.

Treasury Inflation-Protected Securities In 1997, in order to compensate investors for losses due to inflation, the Treasury issued a new type of fixed-rate coupon bonds, with a maturity of 10 years and 30 years. The value of principles can be adjusted in line with the consumer price index. As a new type of bond, Treasury inflation-protected securities (TIPS) have developed very quickly. As of December 30, 2003, they had reached $187.5 billion. With their relatively safer and more stable yields, TIPS are very attractive to long-term investors. Hence, compared with other fixed-income bonds, the price of TIPS changes little.

A breakdown of tradable U.S. government bonds is presented in Figure 29.1. It can be seen from the chart that treasury notes accounted for over 50 percent of the issue.

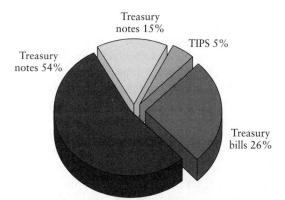

FIGURE 29.1 Classifications of Tradable U.S.
Government Bonds at the End of 2003
Source: www.publicdebt.treas.gov

U.S. treasury bonds cover all phases of the yield curve, from less than one-year treasury bills to 30-year treasury bonds. The Treasury constantly adjusts the bidding plans for bond issuance in line with the changing market demands. In 1986 and 1990, for example, it stopped the 20-year treasury bond and 4-year treasury note, while in 1991, it changed the 5-year treasury note from monthly issuance to quarterly issuance. In 1993, 1998, and 2002, 7-year and 3-year treasury notes and 30-year treasury bonds were discontinued. Due to this flexibility, the overall liquidity in the treasury bond market has been kept at a very high level.

INSTITUTIONAL DEVELOPMENT AND THE FORMATION OF AN INSTITUTION-BASED MARKET

Institutional development, in our view, is the prerequisite of bond market development. This is best illustrated by examining the U.S. market, which is not well designed, but rather the result of an evolution of institutions.

Configuration of the Market Structure

Changes in the bond market are characterized by configuration and specialization. For this reason, the bond market is structured into primary and secondary markets; cash and derivative markets; and an institutional superstructure and technological infrastructure. Stratification, displacement, and specialization are stages in a continuous process of financial market restructuring and institutional movement. Stratification is a means of differentiating the current performance function that results when added value is created. Displacement is the stage in which the government prepares for specialization. This process has been seen as two parallel movements. One movement is from a credit and debt relationship to a loan and bond market, and from a loan market and bond market to a credit market and credit derivatives market. The other movement is from a cash market to forward and options contracts, and from forwards and option contracts to a futures and options market. Specialization is based on detachment, and detachment is based on differentiation of functions. In the early stage of market development, the bond market's only function is financing. Soon after, the need for a risk management function emerges, and this new function is differentiated from the financing function. In the same way, the derivative market is differentiated from the cash market. As these processes develop, the market becomes more stratified and specialized. Over time, its configuration becomes evident. Take the U.S. government bond market as an example. After more than 200 years' development, the spot market is a sophisticated market system with an established and efficient institutional structure. In addition to the primary issuing and secondary trading markets, the U.S. treasury market also has when-issued, STRIPS (separate trading of registered interest and principal of securities), and a repo transaction market. Furthermore, there are also forward transactions, government bond futures, and options trading markets as well as other derivatives markets. The entire market system interacts extensively, meeting different demands of all kinds of investors (see Figure 29.2).

The primary market is the place where bonds are issued. Government bond issuance takes two primary forms: subscription and tender issue. Subscription is adopted mainly for nontradable government bond issuance, with the interest rate, maturity, purchase price, and redemption all determined by the Treasury prior to issuance. Investors need to supply only their subscription volume. Tender issue is used mainly for tradable government bonds, and the price and return are determined through auction.

The American when-issued market is a market where government bonds are traded before the transaction. In order to improve market liquidity, the Treasury carries out the auction based on a regular timetable. In principle, the Treasury announces the detailed information about the proposed government bonds, including the issuance volume and term, several days before the auction. After the conditions are announced, investors begin to buy and sell the bonds on the point of issuance in the when-issued market. The transaction parties agree to price bonds on the issuing day and deliver the proceeds on settlement date, but usually most positions of the financial institutions are hedged before issuance. The when-issued bonds market reduces operational risk as primary dealers can presell the bonds and provide reference information on auction prices for bidders. Hence, it has the function of price discovery. As an important supplement to the

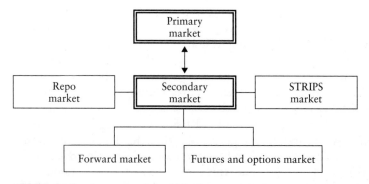

FIGURE 29.2   Structure of the U.S. Treasury Market

primary market, the when-issued market effectively facilitates the smooth execution of government bond transactions.

In comparison, although the pricing of primary issues in China's wholesale market are in principle via auction, the bidders have no clear idea of what price is safe to bid due to lack price references, the benchmark issues. A when-issued market can help issuers access information about investor demand and make the bid price more closely reflect true market demand. For these reasons, China is expected to introduce the when-issued market the first half of 2007.

The secondary market for government securities in the United States consists of financial institutions with large trading volume, such as commercial banks or insurance companies. The minimum trading volume is $1 million for each transaction. The average daily trading volume in the secondary market is over $50 billion. As the market makers in the secondary market, lead underwriters usually are required to maintain liquidity of government securities by providing bid and asked prices in the secondary market. Therefore, their activities are the core of the secondary market. The Federal Reserve Bank (Fed) implements monetary policies in the secondary market mainly through trading government securities. When the Fed wants to ease the money supply, it buys bonds in the market; if it wishes to tighten the supply, it sells bonds. Due to the high correlation with the monetary policy, the Fed's activities in the secondary market are closely watched by market participants and are always taken as the deciding factor for changes in market price and conditions. Currently, the processing of most U.S. government securities transactions is through the book-entry mode, that is, securities transactions are reflected by the changes in the Fed's account. The Fed has set up a department specifically for clearing securities, which greatly reduces their physical transfer costs. Most institutional investors choose one U.S. commercial bank as the depository bank and clearing agent for their government securities. Generally the transaction is conducted on the following business day after the trading, implying a T + 1 trading mode.

As coupon government bonds are exposed to interest rate uncertainties, some investors prefer to hold the bonds until maturity to avoid market risk, or to hold zero-coupon bonds to maturity when the principal and interest are paid on a lump-sum basis. (Note that zero-coupon bonds are issued at a discount.) Since 1985, the Treasury has permitted investors to buy and sell 10-year treasury notes and 30-year treasury bonds in the form of STRIPS. In September 1997, the size of STRIPS was expanded to all treasury notes: 2-year, 3-year, and 5-year notes. In 1987, the Treasury permitted a reorganization of these bonds, where the reorganized principal became the capital of the new bond, and the coupon could be separated from the original bonds. Due to their simple operation and low cost, STRIPS were very active as an arbitrage instrument. The prices of STRIPS and non-STRIPS are highly interrelated.

On the sophisticated U.S. repo market, most transactions are related to government securities, and their interest rate (called general-collateral repo rate) is the benchmark for the repo market. The dealers and other investors often build up short positions of government securities as part of their hedge or portfolio strategy. They purchase the bonds by reverse repo on the repo market and short sell them on the government securities market to build up their short positions. At the same time, dealers also raise funds to buy and hold long positions by selling repo. As of February 19, 2003, the total volume of repo positions held by U.S. primary dealers was $1.4 trillion, and the total volume of reverse repo positions was $2.1 trillion. As a supplement to the secondary market, the repo market enhances the liquidity of government securities by increasing market demand and supply. In addition, the repo market has established a short-selling system for government securities, which enables investors to hedge and arbitrage against interest rate risk of other bonds, thus promoting the development of other bond markets, such as the corporate bond market.

Major Participants in the Primary Market

On the open market, the federal government operates directly only with primary or licensed dealers. Appendix B presents the most recent list of the primary government securities dealers. The main rights and obligations of the primary dealers are conducting direct transactions with the Fed, participating in open market operations and auctions of government securities, market making, and providing liquidity.

A bank or a broker/dealer wishing to become a primary dealer must inform The Federal Reserve Bank of New York (FRBNY) in writing. As part of that notification, a prospective dealer must also provide appropriate financial data demonstrating that it meets the capital standards outlined above. The FRBNY consults with the applicable supervisory body to ensure that the firm in question is in compliance with the appropriate capital standards. When new firms are accepted as primary dealers, the nature and extent of the Bank's trading relationship with the firm will, as under current practices, evolve over time. As a result of this change and the elimination of the 1 percent market share criterion, there will no longer be any need for individual firms to be considered by the market as "aspiring dealers."

All primary dealers will be expected to (1) make reasonably good markets in their trading relationships with the Fed's trading desk; (2) participate meaningfully in Treasury auctions and; (3) provide the trading desk with market information and analysis that may be useful to the Federal Reserve in the formulation and implementation of monetary policy. Primary dealers that fail to meet these standards in a meaningful way over time will have their designation as a primary dealer discontinued by the FRBNY. Each dealer firm's performance relative to these requirements is reviewed on an ongoing basis and evaluated annually, beginning in June 1993.

Major Participants in the Secondary Market

Generally, the major participants in the secondary market include the Department of the Treasury, the Federal Reserve, institutional investors (commercial banks, securities companies, funds, etc.), and individual investors. The Treasury carries out debt financing in public on behalf of the federal government and makes policy decisions on government securities issuance. In addition to the management of the auction bookkeeping system for government securities, the Fed is also responsible for supervising the market and open market operations. The commercial banks and the securities companies can either trade bonds by themselves as institutional investors or for their clients as agents. Some commercial banks and securities companies are selected by the Fed as primary dealers, and are required to submit daily reports to the Fed on their trading positions and activities. If the Fed wants to trade bonds in the market, it usually does so through the primary dealers.

The primary dealers also act as market makers. They are the professional players, and their activities are the driving force of secondary market. Transactions among primary dealers, retail investors, and other market makers are carried out through brokers. The brokers show the maximum buying price and the minimum selling price on the computer network and terminals connected to each trading mainframe. The market makers respond to the reported bid and offer prices by "click" or "select," and all the market makers can immediately see the size and prices of these transactions. Six brokerage firms—Cantor, Fitzgerald Inc.; Garban Ltd.; Liberty Brokerage Inc.; RMJ Securities Corp.; Hilliard Farber (which deals only in government securities); and Tullett and Tokyo Securities Inc.—handle a great deal of daily transactions and provide services to a large number of market makers. The market makers use brokers to improve trading speed and efficiency. Except for Cantor, Fitzgerald, the market makers' brokers cannot trade for their own accounts, and they maintain the confidentiality of the names of the market makers engaged in their transactions.

The spot market for U.S. government securities is dominated by institutional investors. Government securities held by all kinds of institutional investors (excluding government securities dealers) exceed 30 percent of all tradable government securities. Foreign investors—mainly central banks and private investors—account for 30 percent of all the tradable government securities. In addition, the Fed holds a large amount of government securities as instruments for implementing monetary policy. State governments (18 percent) and local governments (5 percent) also purchase government securities as their asset management vehicles. Tradable government securities held by individual investors account for only a very small percentage of all tradable government securities (see Figure 29.3).

The spot market for government securities in the United States is highly internationalized. In the 1960s, U.S. government securities held by foreign investors was less than 5 percent of total government securities held by individuals. During the 1970s, this proportion increased to 15 percent. That number held until the middle of the 1980s, when it increased steadily to its current rate of 40 percent. Compared with other developed countries, foreign investors are more engaged in the spot market for U.S. government securities because of the leading role dollar assets play in the international market. Investors from different countries view U.S. government securities

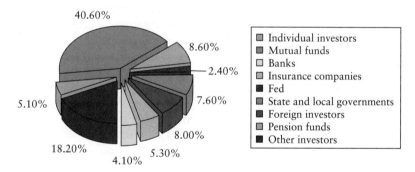

FIGURE 29.3 Breakdown of Investors in U.S. Government Securities (December 30, 2003)

1. Excludes the $2.6 trillion government securities in government accounts, most of which are nontradable treasury bonds.
2. Government securities held by individuals include $400 billion nontradable bonds.
3. Deposit-taking institutions include commercial banks, savings institutions, and credit unions.
4. Mutual funds include money market mutual funds, ordinary mutual funds, and closed-end investment companies.
5. Other investors include individual investors, state-owned enterprises, brokers, dealers, individual trusts, and real estate accounts in banks, companies, non-company commercial organizations, and other investment entities.

Source: www.publicdebt.treas.gov

as an important financial instrument for hedging risk and for mortgage and asset portfolio management.

The diversified structure dominated by institutional investors enables the spot market in U.S. government securities to operate smoothly and efficiently. Because of the well-informed and sophisticated investors in this market, market prices fully reflect real changes in capital supply and demand, laying a solid foundation for the efficient and smooth operation of the U.S. financial system.

Government's Role in Developing the Bond Market

The U.S. government bond market plays an indispensable role in the American economy. In addition to financing fiscal deficits and its macro role as the central bank's instrument for open market operations, it also plays significant microeconomic roles, such as financial asset pricing and hedging interest rate risk, among others.

Financing the Fiscal Deficit   Traditionally, U.S. government bonds are used to finance fiscal deficits during wartime and expansionary fiscal policies to minimize inflation brought about by the government's overdrafts from the central bank, which is beneficial to sustainable and stable economic development.

Instrument of Monetary Policy   Open market operations, the major method for the Fed to regulate the money supply, are fulfilled through one major instrument, treasury bond issuance. By directly trading treasuries and making repo transactions in the bond market, the Fed stabilizes the federal funds rate around the target rate level and achieves its monetary policy objectives.

Providing the Benchmark Interest Rate for Financial Assets Pricing   The yield curve formed on the spot market of U.S. treasury bonds is an important reference for pricing other bonds, such as federal agency bonds, municipal bonds, corporate bonds, and the like. Moreover, the treasury bonds' risk-free repo rates are always the benchmark for pricing more extensive financial derivatives and other financial assets.

Hedging Interest Rate Risk   Treasury bonds and corporate bonds with similar maturity are highly interrelated in terms of interest rates and yield rates, which implies that treasury bonds and their derivatives can be effective tools for hedging interest rate risks. For example, to hedge the declining risk of corporate bonds, investors can reverse repo and then sell treasury bonds short. As the government bond market enjoys great liquidity, these hedges can be completed at very low cost.

Financing Mortgages. The repo market in government bonds provides convenient facilities for the short-term financing by investors. In the United States, treasury bonds enjoy a far more active repo market than those for federal agency bonds, mortgage bonds, and corporate bonds. Due to their low credit risk relative to the interbank offer, the repo rate of the treasury-secured repo transactions is generally lower than the federal funds rate, with a much lower repo financing cost.

Managing Liquidity. In the United States, institutional investors often use treasury bonds as instruments for asset management. As short-term T-bonds are issued regularly and have great liquidity and low interest rate risk, they are the first instrument for short-term funds management. More often than not, they are seen as the equivalent of cash.

Managing an Investment Portfolio. With the lowest credit risk and low market risk, treasury bonds are relatively secure long-term investment instruments for pension funds, insurance funds, and other institutional investors to manage their asset investment portfolio in order to minimize the overall risk levels for their asset portfolios.

Arbitraging and Speculating. In the treasury bond market and its liquid repo and derivatives markets, investors can take profits by leveraging on speculation or arbitrage opportunities and quickly selling out their holdings.

Protecting against Financial Crisis. In a volatile financial market, the demand for a safe haven always exceeds the demand for profits. Investors usually transfer funds from the high-risk market to the treasury bond market, a shelter for these funds.

In addition, due to America's leading position in the global economy, U.S. T-bonds play an important role in the international financial market. Their yield rate is the benchmark for the market as well as an important component of global bond indexes. Nowadays, U.S. treasury bonds are an important part of the foreign exchange reserves of many economies as well as an important risk hedging and asset management instrument for many foreign investors.

Although many of the functions just discussed originate in the market, the U.S. government makes rules and regulates the market so that these functions work more effectively and efficiently.

MARKET INFRASTRUCTURE

The United States has established an integrated national depository and settlement system, in which the securities account system is completely integrated with the money account system. The system can be divided into the Federal Reserve exchange system and the system for the depository trust companies. U.S. government bonds are traded mainly through the exchange system of the Fed. The institutional users of the exchange system are banks and their branches, the federal government, the Department of the Treasury, other government agencies, and 116,000 securities depository agencies. They open their primary accounts on this exchange system, and other investors, such as the securities brokers and institutional investors, indirectly enter the central depository system. In addition, the special Treasury Direct System for individual investors and the government bonds bookkeeping system are managed by the Bureau of the Public Debt of the Department of the Treasury and operated by the Philadelphia office of the Federal Reserve Bank. The settlement and clearing systems for U.S. government bonds are separate, with the Government Securities Clearing Corporation (GSCC) responsible for clearing the government bonds.

Developed countries such as the United States have implemented whole-sale funds transfer of Real-Time Gross Settlement (RTGS), combined it with the settlement system for debt instruments, and created the delivery versus payment (DVP)–based RTGS, to transfer bonds to the depository account or to pay or replace funds when they are withdrawn from the depository account. By using this mode of settlement, trading is efficient.

Standardization of Calculation Method

In France, the secondary market for government bonds is the market maker system. At present, 18 market makers make quotations through Reuters. The quantity of each quotation is around 50 million to 200 million, with a market price gap of about 0.05 to 0.15 percent and yield spread of 0.01 to 0.03 percent. Transactions of mid- (BTAN) and short-term government bonds (BTF) are settled daily, while long-term government bonds (OAT) are settled in three to seven days.

Different bond varieties and settlement modes are calculated differently in terms of coupon rate and yields. Usually the domestic coupon rate is calculated by the date of transaction, while the international coupon rate is calculated according to the date of settlement. However, in domestic transactions, the mid-term government bond rate is calculated according to the date of settlement.

The short-term government bond yield is calculated according to the formula of 360/60 on maturity, while mid- and long-term government bond yields are calculated based on the actual number of days/360 on maturity.

In France, the BTE settlement is carried out through the payment system of the Bank of France; international payment is performed through European clearing companies and the Centrale de Livraison de Valeurs Mobilieres.

Selling Techniques

Before the 1970s, the U.S. Department of the Treasury issued bonds via the subscription offering method (preset interest rates and fixed priced); later it implemented the exchange offering method (investors exchange mature bonds for new bond issues at fixed prices) and advance refunding (substituting immature old bonds for the new bond issues). In 1970, the Treasury adopted the price tendering regime, in which the coupon rate was determined beforehand and investors were required to bid to determine the price. After 1974, the Treasury frequently used interest rate bidding. Since 1974, the Treasury has used the multiprice sealed tender method for issuing treasury bills and treasury notes. The issue date is announced well in advance, while the issuance amount was usually announced one week prior to the actual issuance.

There are two auction methods: the uniform-price auction (Dutch auction method) for two- and five-year treasury notes and the multiple-price auction (American method) for other government bonds. In the uniform-price auction, all the bidders get the bonds at the highest acceptable yield (i.e., the "stop-out yield"; see below). In the multiple-price auction, bidders who offer a serially rising yield will acquire the bonds at their respective offers. Since 1999, the uniform-price auction has been used for issuing all U.S. government bonds, and the multiple-price auction method is gradually being phased out. However, it is not yet certain whether the uniform-price auction is superior to the multiple-price auction. The Treasury determines a noncompetitive bidding limit for every bidder. Within this limitation, it permits bidders to buy bonds at the average successful bidding price, and the part that exceeds the limit is issued through competitive bidding.

The Treasury accepts two types of bids: competitive and non-competitive. In competitive bidding, the primary dealers and major institutional investors bid the price and amount simultaneously. All competitive bidders are allowed to offer multiple bid prices, although they may not succeed in every bid. The noncompetitive bidding amount from the public cannot exceed $5 million. The Treasury decides the interest rate to make the supply and demand for the competitive bids even. Using this method, the bid amount of the noncompetitive bidders is secured. As the Treasury restricts the noncompetitive tendering amount to less than $5 million, only individual and small institutional investors participate in the noncompetitive tender. The Treasury restricts the maximum amount that each bidder can acquire, known as the 35 percent rule (i.e., no bidder's net position in one bid issue can exceed 35 percent of the whole issuance, including the net position of futures, forwards, and when-issued markets). Once the issue ends, the 35 percent rule expires.

Table 29.1 and Table 29.2 illustrate an auction issue and result for a 30-year treasury bond.

From Table 29.2, we can see that the Department of the Treasury sold about $5 billion of 30-year (to be more specific, $29\frac{3}{4}$ years) T-bonds. Since they were reopened bonds, the coupon rate was fixed at 6.25 percent.

Liquidity in the Secondary Market

Most of the secondary market transactions of U.S. bonds (government securities, corporate bonds and municipal bonds, etc.) are carried out in the over-the-counter (OTC) market. Government securities transactions are carried out among the primary dealers, nonprimary dealers, and clients. Many primary dealers quote on particular tradable bonds, and their clients include all kinds of financial institutions, non-financial institutions, and individual investors. As illustrated in Table 29.3, the average daily trading volume of U.S. government securities had reached $433.5 billion in 2003.

The U.S. government securities spot market enjoys high liquidity. The primary dealers are the most active participants in the secondary market. In 2003, the average daily trading volume of primary dealers was $433.5 billion, of which transactions between primary dealers accounted for $200.8 billion and those between primary dealers and other investors amounted to $232.7 billion. Meanwhile, the secondary market is highly concentrated, with the trading volume of the top five primary dealers accounting

TABLE 29.2 Auction Results of $29\frac{3}{4}$-Year Treasury Bond

Total Bidding and Successful Bidding (1,000 US$)

Types of Bidding	Bidding Amount	Successful Bidding Amount
Competitive	$18,550,664	$4,985,464
Noncompetitive	$ 15,182	$ 15,182
Total Public Bidding	$18,565,846	$5,000,646
Federal Reserve	$ 723,700	$ 723,700
Foreign Government Agencies	$ 50,000	$ 50,000
Total	$19,339,546	$5,774,346

Note: Median yield: 5.688%

$$\text{Overbidding multiple} = 19,339,546/5,774,346 = 3.71$$

Source: www.publicdebt.treas.gov

TABLE 29.3 Average Daily Trading Volume of U.S. Government Securities (US$1 Billion)

Year	Transactions with Brokers	Transactions with Others	Total
1980	11.4	6.9	18.3
1981	13.3	11.2	24.5
1982	17.4	14.8	32.2
1983	23.3	18.8	42.1
1984	28.5	24.3	52.8
1985	39.6	35.8	75.4
1986	53.3	42.3	95.6
1987	64.6	45.6	110.2
1988	63.0	39.2	102.2
1989	69.8	43.1	112.9
1990	68.7	42.5	111.2
1991	78.5	49.0	127.5
1992	95.7	56.4	152.1
1993	107.7	65.9	173.6
1994	116.1	75.2	191.3
1995	112.7	80.5	193.2
1996	117.3	86.4	203.7
1997	120.9	91.2	212.1
1998	126.5	100.1	226.6
1999	101.3	85.3	186.5
2000	98.6	108.0	206.6
2001	138.8	159.1	297.9
2002	170.8	195.6	366.4
2003	200.8	232.7	433.5
2004*	230.4	270.8	501.2

*As of June 30, 2004
Note: "Transactions with brokers and others" respectively refer to transactions between the primary dealers and brokers and those between the primary dealers and other people.
Source: The Federal Reserve Bank of New York.

for 44.15 percent of all primary dealer transactions (see Table 29.4). The trading volume among primary dealers could circulate all the tradable government securities once every eight trading days. Thus, investors can quickly buy and sell a large amount of government securities with minimum impact on market prices. Due to the huge trading volume, competition,

TABLE 29.4   Average Daily Trading Volume of Primary Dealers in the First Three Quarters of 2004

Types	Transactions among Dealers (100 million US$)	Transactions with Clients (100 million US$)	Total Trading Volume (100 million US$)	Top 5 Dealers (%)
T-bills	177.468	276.123	19428.5	44.15
1–3-year treasury notes	667.505	660.281	1327.786	50.67
3–6-year treasury notes	466.630	512.971	979.601	52.32
6–11-year treasury notes and bonds	357.181	438.023	795.204	50.08
>11-year treasury bonds	77.392	118.046	195.438	46.68
TIPS	6.431	18.292	24.723	68.03

Source: The Federal Reserves of New York.

and transparency, the difference between the market makers' bid and offer prices is very small.

Government securities issued at different times have different liquidities. New bond issues (the most recently issued securities of the same type on the same terms) enjoy the highest liquidity. Other bonds of the same type are called old bonds. There are significant differences between new and old bond issues in terms of trading volumes. During recent years, although the stock of old bonds has been over 20 times greater than newly issued bonds, more than half of the government securities transactions between the primary dealers have been new issued bonds. Because new bond issues have greater liquidity, their returns are a bit lower than those of older bonds.

Other Advanced Bond Markets

The German government bond market had a large capacity of DEM2.742 trillion by the end of June 1993, following Japan and the United States. Since the German reunification in 1987, the balance of public debt has tripled to DEM957 billion, mainly due to the huge investment in the revival of the eastern region. In 1992, the net sales volume of public debt reached DEM187 billion, an increase of 115 percent over the previous year and triple the 1987 volume. The federal government is the major borrower in the market.

In Germany, all public debt and bank debentures are listed in the secondary market. Bond transactions are conducted via the OTC system (orders are made by telephone) and via exchanges through the electronic transmission system.

Due to the rapid growth of government bond issuance since 1983, the transaction volume of government bonds in the market has increased greatly, accounting for 93 percent of the total trading volume. Beginning in June 1984, banks were allowed to participate in government bond transactions. In 1989, trading volume increased dramatically due to the expected interest rate decline. The trading volume hit euro 8095.5 billion in 2005.

The Japanese government bond market is divided into the over-the-counter market and the exchange market. In 1990, trading volume in the OTC market accounted for 96.1 percent. The major dealers in the OTC market are securities companies and banks approved to conduct securities business. (Table 29.5 demonstrates the trading volume of government bonds in the Japanese OTC market and its proportion to total bond trading volume.)

There are securities exchanges in Tokyo, Osaka, and Nagoya. According to Article 120 of the Japanese Securities Exchange Law, the approval of the Japanese Ministry of Finance is not required for listing government bonds, government-secured bonds, and local government bonds.

In summary, it is worth noting that the United States and other advanced bond markets share some common features. The U.S. example demonstrates that the development of the bond market is an institutional evolution, a gradual process to establish an institutional arrangement for the contemporary debt capital market. In the United States, market participants were originally savers and investors; eventually the market became specialized, and financial intermediaries came into being. Gradually, market instruments were diversified and financial activities were standardized, so that they could

TABLE 29.5 Annual Trading volume of Government Bonds and Proportion to the Total Japanese OTC Market (Unit: ¥100 million)

Year	Government Bond	OTC Bond Volume	Government Bonds in OTC Market (%)
1983	1839054	2,478,921	74.2
1984	4733845	5,437,668	87.1
1985	18537388	19,130,923	96.9
1986	19355359	20,290,735	95.4
1987	42287514	43,275,011	97.7
1988	27567035	28,608,449	96.4
1989	24177227	24,995,232	96.7

be traded in the market. This process took over 200 years after the Revolutionary War. For the contemporary U.S. capital market, organizations have played a very important role in financial innovations.

Innovations have resulted from the liberalized legal environment, technological progress, and the development of finance theory, which facilitated the pricing of financial assets. As Robert Merton put it: "Those financial innovations came about in part because of a wide array of new security designs, in part because of the advances in computer and telecommunications technology, and in part because of important advances in the theory of finance."[1]

In most developed economies, debt capital markets have been driven mainly by market participants. As a matter of fact, governments in these countries have not presented in person frequently. However, they all play an important role in making laws, regulating the operation of the market, and setting up the regulatory framework and thereby saving exogenous transaction costs. Governments are issuers in the market and therefore market participants. As market players themselves, governments comply with the rules of fair exchange. They also take initiatives to facilitate specialization of market functions and diversification of market instruments. Governments can do this by directly organizing the primary dealer system, setting fixed issuing timetables, diversifying issuing instruments, and encouraging market innovation and technology application in the debt capital market via financial deregulation and economic policies. As we have seen, these experiences are reflected in the development of China's debt capital market.

Postscript

The 1990s witnessed a period of rapid financial market development in China; in particular, China's debt capital market made great progress, which stands in contrast to the slow development of the rest of the country's financial market. Although the achievements made in China's domestic bond market are conspicuous and remarkable, its bond market development remains at a preliminary stage compared with bond markets in many developed countries and has increasingly become a major impediment to economic development. Remaining issues, such as market segmentation, overlapping oversight jurisdictions, and a regulated corporate bond coupon rate, cannot be corrected overnight. Concern over the segmentation of marketplaces is also a problem. In addition, the underdeveloped corporate bond market is likely to drag down corporate financing.

CHALLENGES TO FUTURE DEBT CAPITAL MARKET DEVELOPMENT

As indicated, China's financial reform should lead to a liquid and cost-effective debt capital market. Many things will shape the postreform landscape of the financial market and dominate the future development of the bond market. However, many positive factors will help to drive the market forward.

Size of New Issuance

Ever since China pursued a proactive fiscal policy in 1997, the size of new issuances has expanded to finance a widening central government deficit and maturing debt. Even if the deficit remains unchanged or decreases, new issues will remain high, as maturing debt will not fall below RMB600 billion ($700 billion) in the foreseeable future.

Although China announced a neutral fiscal policy in 2005, given the continued income disparity, the central government is unlikely to reduce its expenditures for social development programs, which place a heavy burden on the nation's financial resources. The most costly burden is the anticipated bailout of China's banks. The forecast is that China's deficit will not be significantly reduced in the coming years. This is especially true of 2006, when, as of this writing, China's domestic banks must prepare for competition after the market opens to foreign banks, as required under the World Trade Organization (WTO) accession protocol.

Shift from Indirect to Direct Financing

Corporate finance in most developed countries is characterized by direct financing. However, corporations in China tend to raise money from bank loans, which account for 90 percent of the total corporate financing. This is not only because it is difficult for them to access other financial resources, but also because corporations are the traditional bank customers in China.

Equity and debt financing are the principal financing channels for corporations in developed countries. However, between 1996 and 2005, with slight fluctuations, the ratio of direct financing in China was relatively low: 10 percent in 2000, 4.8 percent in 2003, and 1.5 percent in 2004. Debt financing, as a percentage of gross domestic product, was only 0.9 percent in 2005, compared with 15 to 20 percent in most developed countries.

Development of the Corporate Bond Market

Debt financing is a major channel for most enterprises. It has three advantages: It reduces financing cost, reinforces hard constraints on enterprises (a weakness of China's corporate governance), and creates new market instruments for a market in which corporate instruments are limited.

When enterprises enter the corporate bond market, they have to establish a well-defined legal relationship with investors. The timely payment of interest and principal is their obligation. This is especially important in China where, for many years, state-owned enterprises financed their investments through bank loans and the credit-debt relationship was not clearly defined. It will take time for enterprises and corporations to adjust to the new environment.

Local Government Financing

According to China's constitution, each level of government has its own budget. Currently there are five levels of government: central, provisional (or autonomous region), prefecture level, county, and township government. Local governments are not entitled to incur debt, according to the Budget Law promulgated in 1992. However, they do incur deficits that result from unexpected expenditures and reduced revenue caused by natural disasters and undesirable economic performance. These deficits are financed mainly by extrabudgetary funds. In addition, local governments have to shoulder the expense of urban maintenance programs and city infrastructure construction, which require large pools of capital.

The demand by local governments for the introduction of local government and municipal bonds is stronger then ever and has gained ground recently. As in many socialist countries, local government in China has so-called soft budgetary constraints. The central government was very concerned about local government discretionary borrowing, a fact that was reflected in laws and regulations. Legally, local governments are not allowed to incur debt. This was stipulated in the Budgetary Law, which was promulgated in 1992 to reflect the central government's concern over any potential liability on the central government because a revenue sharing regime prevailed at that time. The problem that is built into the current institutional framework is that borrowing by local governments is delegated to institutions that are affiliated with the government, so that the borrower is the institution rather than the government itself. This misunderstanding about the true nature of the borrower has led to many legal issues, and there is increasing consensus that major cities should be allowed to issue local or municipal bonds.

For many years, local governments borrowed through international trust and investment corporations (ITICs). However, the identity of ITICs was not well defined, either in practice or in law. This necessitated the advent of local government bonds (i.e., borrowing on the credit and in the name of the local government). Local governments that went directly to the market reduced costs, as their reputations are normally better than that of companies; therefore, local government bonds and municipal bonds are better received than corporate bonds. Currently these shortfalls are financed by policy-related banks, such as the China Development Bank (CDB).

Securitization

Securitization has developed very rapidly in Asian countries, although it is still new in China. Corporations that engage in mergers and acquisitions and initial public offerings need bond market instruments in order to price assets in their transactions; therefore, they attach great importance to the underlying bond market. The asset management companies (AMCs), established several years ago, are targeting a securitization program to sell the assets they possess. Therefore, expanded corporate business requires a sound, liquid, and efficient bond market, in addition to a stock market. The recent asset-backed securities (ABS) program carried out by the CDB faced a problem selling the last tranches, as at the time there were no qualified investors to subscribe to them. Therefore, it is necessary to cultivate the ABS investor base in China.

Liquidity Issues

The development of the bond market would alleviate banks' liquidity risk. Currently banks in China have about RMB2 trillion in nonperforming loans. As long as deposits keep coming, banks remain solvent and can still operate as if there were no liquidity problem.

However, after China has fully committed to WTO requirements, foreign banks will enjoy resident treatment and can compete with their Chinese counterparts on an equal footing. As foreign banks are generally more efficient and can provide better service than domestic banks, they can offer more attractive deposit rates to compete with domestic banks. If domestic banks lose deposits, they are likely to have payment problems, especially if depositors also withdraw their money.

This is exactly what happened in Japan when, during the early stages of its financial reform, the Japanese government abolished deposit insurance. Domestic depositors shifted their deposits to foreign banks, which triggered payment problems and resulted in the bankruptcy of certain small banks. China is definitely in a position to set up a bank loan insurance system before its financial market is opened completely to the outside world, in order to prevent deposits moving from domestic banks to international ones. Alternatively, banks can sell their assets, such as bonds they hold, to repay the depositors; however, this is possible only if a sound bond capital market is in place. Since the majority of participants in the inter-bank bond market (IBBM) are banks, which tend toward homogenous behavior, should a liquidity problem arise, it is likely that they will all want to sell at the same time and that nobody will want to buy. For this reason, diversifying the investor base is crucial to the IBBM. Fortunately, progress has been made by the People's Bank of China (PBOC) initiatives in these areas.

Liquidity risks arise when banks hold long assets and their liabilities, such as deposits, are mainly short-term instruments. This happened in China in the late 1990s. Currently approximately 11 percent of banks' assets are bond assets, not a very high proportion compared with developed countries, where banks tend to hold short-term securities or liquid long instruments, such as treasury bills.

Banks and financial institutions that belong to the IBBM tend to have similar responses to the central bank's monetary moves. If, for example, the central bank tightens the money supply, all banks want to sell the securities they hold, and there is no one willing to buy; similarly, if the central bank expands the money supply, all banks want to buy securities from other banks, and there is no one willing to sell. This is due to the fact that IBBM has a homogenous investor base—mainly banks and financial institutions. In addition, the interbank market is a money market rather than a capital market. Therefore, it cannot function well as a capital market.

Although efforts have been made by the central bank to improve the liquidity of the IBBM—for example, by opening the market to individuals, securities firms, insurance companies, and investment and pension funds—the investor base remains confined to financial institutions because, until 2004, only nonbank financial institutions have been permitted to participate in the IBBM. Individual investors have been restricted to the stock exchange market and the bank over-the-counter (OTC) market, where they can buy bonds traded in the IBBM from banks and sell them to the banks. As indicated, some corporate bonds have been permitted to enter and trade in the IBBM since 2004.

There are many advantages to trading bond securities in the OTC market; among them are sizable trading and confidential trading, which substantially raises the possibility of trading among institutional investors. In many developed countries, government bonds are traded mainly in the OTC market. However, an OTC market for institutional investors, such as the one in the United States, does not exist in China. Although the IBBM market is perceived as a nonexchange market, it is not yet an OTC market for institutional investors.

Whether China needs to set up an institutional OTC market remains debatable. At present, the institutional investment is booming amid the development of the fund and the insurance industry. However, the institutional investor base remains dominated by the banking sector.

Individual investors in China include risk-taking investors and risk-averse investors. Risk-taking investors are confined to trading on the stock exchange market, where, although they are active traders, the volume tends to be small. Therefore, the exchange market, due to its trading and settlement procedures, is efficient and provides a comfortable environment for these investors. To meet the trading needs of the individual and small institutional investors, a stock exchange market is preferable to an OTC market because it is more efficient and transparent. In the future, when institutional investors become the mainstay of the investor base, a parallel OTC market will be necessary.

Investment Benchmark

China has a chronic problem with overinvestment. The central government controls investment by establishing credit ceilings and endorsing projects on a case-by-case basis. Some argue that if China's government bonds serve as a benchmark for investments, then overinvestment can be curbed. For example, when the marginal rate of return on investment falls below the government bond yield, investment would slow down dramatically, as in investors would prefer to buy government bonds. Therefore, a sound government bond market would act as a built-in stabilizer.

FUTURE DIRECTION AND RECENT DEVELOPMENTS

Institutional economic engineering provides a fresh way of thinking about the trajectory of future bond market development. The challenges of the current financial system, the vision and perception of the regulatory authorities on the challenges, the innovative ideas of market participants to drive the institutional development will shape the postreform landscape through the interaction of the primary financial exchange and the secondary financial exchange. The vision, courage, and awareness of government and government agencies to address these issues and challenges are essential. Note also that deregulation to encourage financial innovation of market participants is a key policy initiative.

The Asian financial crisis revealed the weakness and vulnerability of China's financial market. Although the financial impact on China's economy was less severe, the nation faces issues identical to many that were faced by other Asia countries. Central government agencies believe that China escaped the crisis only because its financial market was not completely open when the Asian financial crises took place. It is against this background that the Chinese government has stepped up its efforts to improve its debt capital market.

Recently, the impetus to develop a sound bond market has gained momentum. There are real grounds for hope that these issues will be put high on the agenda and be addressed properly in the future as policy initiatives are beginning to take shape in China.

The State Council issued a circular (Guozhi No. 9) on the promotion of China's capital market in 2004. The document contained measures to improve the then sluggish stock market and placed increased emphasis on primary market reform for corporate bonds.

After experiments in 2005 and 2006, the securitization program will be carried out more frequently in the debt capital market. At the beginning of 2005, the government approved the proposal on the securitization program by the CDB and the China Construction Bank (CCB) on an experimental basis. The CDB will pursue the asset-backed securities, and the CCB will be responsible for mortgage-backed securities.

The National Development and Reform Commission has recently explored the possibility of deregulating the primary corporate bond market and is likely to suspend the decade-long practice of administrative corporate bond placement.

In addition, the Monetary Policy Department of the PBOC, the central bank, recognized the importance of the bond market to monetary policy and started to trade government bonds on behalf of the PBOC in the China Government Securities Depository Trust & Clearing Co., Ltd. in pursuit of open market operations. In the first half of 2005, the PBOC reinforced its efforts to improve the IBBM by introducing short-term commercial paper. The door is open for forward trading, which was forbidden after the suspension of the government futures market in 1995. The central bank is currently considering forward trading in an effort to improve the liquidity of secondary market trading in the IBBM.

In October 2005, China unveiled rules for funds to protect securities investors. The much-anticipated emergency fund could amass as much as 50 billion and will be managed jointly by three government agencies. It is part of a long-standing project to reform China's unprofitable brokerage sector.[1]

Thus, China has gradually come to understand that the capital market, if it is not developed along with nation's economic development, would place a strain on the economy. It is fair to say that the impetus to develop a sound bond market has gained ground. China's debt capital market is preparing for rapid development in the future.

The introduction of new market instruments created by the CDB is still a major pillar of China's bond market, and demonstrates the innovation and forward-looking approach that the CDB has taken in this financial endeavor.

In the short term, a seismic shift toward a more deregulated primary corporate bonds market is unlikely. The only safe bet for now is that China will take a leap toward improving its debt capital market as soon as its financial reform program has been finalized. However, the timetable is not fixed yet. The behavior of market participants is also an important factor of market development. Education can help to change investors' mentality and market awareness in order to establish rational behavior. However, old habits and ways of thinking die hard, and China's bond market is no different.

Finally, it is important to note that revolution and evolution in the financial market go hand in hand, as they are driven by the primary exchange (exchange between government and market participants) and the secondary exchange (exchange among market participants), respectively. Outsiders see the formation of the bond market in China as a top-down process. In their view, the central government initiated the reform program, and, as a result, the bond market was born and started to develop. The real process was far less simple, however. The bond market was driven by the interaction between the primary exchange and the secondary exchange. Both the primary exchange and the secondary exchange are crucial to the development of the bond market.

Thus, market participants have an incentive to drive the market forward by way of financial innovations. As a matter of fact, market participants in China introduce many market instruments and selling techniques.

The key here is that government needs to encourage institutional and technological innovations by market players and to confine its role to rule making and enforcement.

Laws and Regulations Governing Financial Debentures

LAWS, STATUTES, REGULATIONS, AND POLICIES ISSUED BY THE PEOPLE'S BANK OF CHINA

1. Measures on the Administration of Bonds Trading on the Nationwide Inter-bank Bond Market (Decree No. 2 [2000] of the People's Bank of China)
2. Notice of Relevant Problems of Interbank Bond Repurchasing Business (Decree No. 242 [1997] of the People's Bank of China)
3. Notice of Interbank Government bond Transaction (Decree No. 44 [1997] of the People's Bank of China)
4. Announcement of the People's Bank of China (Matters Related to Participation of Financial Institutions in Interbank Bond Market) [2002] No. 5
5. Notice of printing and distributing Regulation on Fund Management Company Entering the Interbank Market and Regulation on Securities Company Entering the Interbank Market (Decree No. 288 [1999] of the People's Bank of China)
6. Notice of printing and distributing Regulation on Financial Company Entering the Interbank Market and Bond Market (Decree No. 194 [2000] of the People's Bank of China)
7. Provisional Regulation on Policy Bank Issuing in Financial Bond Market (Decree No. 576 [1998] of the People's Bank of China)
8. Notice of printing and distributing Rule of Operation Management of Issuing in the Interbank Bond Market (Decree No. 199 [2002] of the People's Bank of China)
9. Notice of Matters Related to Adopting unified Computing Method of Bond Yields (Decree No. 51 [2001] of the Department of Monetary Policy, People's Bank of China)

10. Notice of Relevant Problems of Bond Clearing Intermediary Business (Decree No. 325 [2000] of the People's Bank of China)
11. Notice of Matters Related to Implementing Net Price Trading of Bonds (Decree No. 27 [2001] of the Department of Monetary Policy, People's Bank of China)
12. Notice of Bond Listing Transaction in the National Interbank Bond Market (Decree No. 71 [2003] of the People's Bank of China)
13. Notice of Matters Related to Computing Bond Mature Yields in the National Interbank Bond Market (Decree No. 116 [2004] of the People's Bank of China)
14. Regulation on Buyout Repurchasing Business in the National Interbank Bond Market (Decree No. one [2004] of the People's Bank of China)
15. Administrative Measures on Issuance of Subordinate Bonds by Commercial Banks (Decree No. 4 [2004] of the Department of Monetary Policy, People's Bank of China)

LAWS, REGULATIONS, RULES AND POLICIES RELEASED BY THE MINISTRY OF FINANCE

1. Notice of Matters Related to Net Price Trading of Government bonds (Decree No. 12 [2001] of the Ministry of Finance, the People's Bank of China, and China Securities Regulatory Commission)
2. Notice of Interest of Government bonds Exempt from Corporate Income Tax after Trial Net Price Trading (Decree No. 48 [2002] of the Ministry of Finance and State Administration of Taxation)
3. Individual Income Tax Law of the People's Republic of China (Revised on August 30, 1999) (extract)

REGULATIONS AND POLICIES RELEASED BY CHINA GOVERNMENT SECURITIES DEPOSITORY TRUST & CLEARING CO., LTD.

1. Notice of Using Authentication in Bond Sub-underwriting Business by Underwriters
2. Notice of Matters Related to Bond Sub-underwriting and Transferring in the National Inter-bank Bond Market (Decree No. 028 [2002] of China Government Securities Depository Trust & Clearing Co., Ltd.)
3. Main Agreement of Bond Repurchase in the National Interbank Bond Market
4. Rules of Interbank Bond Transaction Clearing (revised)

5. Announcement of Computing Formula of Present Value of Bond
6. Authentication Using Procedure of Emergency Business (trial)
7. Business Operational Procedure of Separate and Reductive Trading Registered Interest and Principal Financial Debentures
8. Business Operational Procedure of Bond Swap and Combination

OTHER

Notice of Bonds Issued by Policy Banks Such as CDB Being Government Bonds (Notice No. 01[2004] Fund Department, China Securities Regulatory Commission)

Primary Government Securities Dealers Updated by the Federal Reserve of New York on August 3, 2004

ABN AMRO Bank, N.V., New York Branch
BNP Paribas Securities Corp.
Banc of America Securities LLC
Barclays Capital Inc.
Bear, Stearns & Co., Inc.
CIBC World Markets Corp.
Citigroup Global Markets Inc.
Countrywide Securities Corporation
Credit Suisse First Boston LLC
Daiwa Securities America Inc.
Deutsche Bank Securities Inc.
Dresdner Kleinwort Wasserstein Securities LLC.
Goldman, Sachs & Co.
Greenwich Capital Markets, Inc.
HSBC Securities (USA) Inc.
J. P. Morgan Securities Inc.
Lehman Brothers Inc.
Merrill Lynch Government Securities Inc.
Mizuho Securities USA Inc.
Morgan Stanley & Co. Incorporated
Nomura Securities International, Inc.
UBS Securities LLC

Source: The American Bond Market Association

Endnotes

Preface

1. Norman Chan, UNESCO roundtable conference, April 2000.

Introduction

1. These articles were collected in *Selected Articles by Gao Jian*, (Beijing: China Economic Publishing House, 2002).
2. James Riedel, Jin Jing, and Gao Jian, "Investment, Financing Investment, and Growth in China," working paper, August, 2004.

Chapter 1

1. New institutional economics focuses its research on institution issues and its relationship with economic development. New institutional economics is a newly emerged economic school; it differs from neo-institutionalism in that neo-institutional economics conceives institution is evolutionary while neo-institutionalism consider institution revolutionary.
2. My early research on game theory and institutional economics owes much to Jean Laffont. The profession of economics is richer for having had him in our midst during the last century and poorer for his passing in 2004. I hope this book will be a small tribute to him.
3. Douglass C. North, Institutions, *Institutional Change and Economic Performance* (Cambridge: Cambridge University Press, 1990), p. 3.
4. Eugene Kelly, *The Basics of Western Philosophy* (Westport, CT: Greenwood Press, 2004), p. 250.
5. Richard Swedberg: *Essays in Economic Sociology* (Princeton: Princeton University Press, 1999), p. 698.
6. Eugene Kelly, *The Basics of Western Philosophy* (Westport, CT: Greenwood Press, 2004), p. 250.
7. Richard Swedberg: *Essays in economic sociology* (Princeton: Princeton University Press, 1999), p. 17.
8. Ibid, pp. 18–19.
9. Mark Gertler and Andrew Rose: *Banking on financial reform?* in *Financial Reform, Theory and Experience*, ed. Caprio et al. (Cambridge: Cambridge University Press, 1994), p. 49.
10. Richard Swedberg: *Essays in economic sociology* (Princeton: Princeton University Press, 1999), Introduction, p. 3.

11. Mark Granovetter and Richard Swedburg (eds.), *The Sociology of Economic Life* (New York: Westview Press, 2001), p. 37. see also Weber: *Economy and Society*, 1922 (Berkeley: University of California Press, 1978), Fig. 6. pp. 1–24, 63–69.

12. Ibid.

13. Robert D. Putnam, *Making Democracy Work: Civic Traditions in Modern Italy* (Princeton: Princeton University Press, 1993), pp. 163–186.

14. Richard Swedberg: *Essays in economic sociology* (Princeton: Princeton University Press, 1999), Introduction, p. 15.

15. Douglass C. North: *Institutions, Institutional Change and Economic Performance* (Cambridge: Cambridge University Press, 1990), p. 6.

16. Ibid, p. 118.

17. Although North stated many times that incentives are embedded in the institutional framework—"The incentives that are built into the institutional framework play the decisive role in shaping the kinds of skills and knowledge that pay off" (ibid., p. 78 and "The agent of change is the individual entrepreneur responding to the incentives embodied in the institutional framework" (p. 83)—he nevertheless perceived institutional constraint as the rule of game and therefore did not view incentive as an element of institutions, although he does view incentive as an important facet of the institutional framework. North is navigating through murky waters. From time to time he implies that incentive is part of institution: "The incentive-embedded in intuitional constraints" (p. 74) and "Both the neoclassical and exploitation models are driven by wealth maximizing players and hence shaped by the institutional incentive structure." (p. 134).

    North seems aware that the lack of incentive is one of the defects of his theory. He discusses the incentive structure at the end of his book. Here again he refers to incentives as something built into the institution: "They are implicit in the theories we have employed and assumed to have a particular form and effect" (p. 135); however, he fails to mention the interaction between incentive and constraint.

18. Greif, Avner, *Historical and Comparative Institutional Analysis*, American Economic Review 88, 1998, pp. 80–89.

19. Douglass C. North, *Institutions, Institutional Change and Economic Performance* (Cambridge:Cambridge University Press, 1990), p. 7.

20. Rodrik, Dani (ed.) *In Search of Prosperity: Analytical Narratives on Economic Growth*, (Princeton: Princeton University Press, 2003), pp. 10–16.

21. Schotter, Andrew, *The economic theory of social institutions* (Cambridge: Cambridge University Press, 1981), p.11.

22. Calvert....Masahiko Anouki: *Toward a Comparative Institutional Analysis* (Cambridge, MA: The MIT Press), p. 2.

23. R. H. Coase, *The Firm, the Market, and the Law* (Chicago: University of Chicago Press, 1998), p. 12.

24. Douglass C. North, *Institutions, Institutional Change and Economic Performance* (Cambridge: Cambridge University Press, 1990), p. 135.

25. Jean-Jacques Laffont and David Martimort, *The Theory of Incentives* (Princeton: Princeton University Press, 2002), pp. 4–5.

26. Ibid.

27. Here, the equilibrium and exchange is not necessarily confined to economics but covers all social exchange and equilibrium reached through exchange.

28. Rugman, Alan M., and Joseph R. D'Cruz, "The 'Double Diamond' Model of International Competitiveness: The Canadian Experience," *Management International Review, Special Issue*, 1993(2).

29. Here it is important to differentiate four different concepts: exchange, transaction, market, and trading. Exchange is to give in return for something received; market is the place for exchange; transaction is the action for exchange; trade is the commodity exchange. The exchange is a sociological term; the other three are economic terms. The economic categories are contained by the sociological categories.

30. Douglass C. North, *Institutions, Institutional Change and Economic Performance* (Cambridge: Cambridge University Press, 1990), p. 111.

31. Oliver E., Williamson, *Markets and Hierarchies: Analysis and Antitrust Implications*, (New York: Free Press, 1975).

32. See President Hu Jintao's speech to the National Scientific and Technological Conference in Jan. 9, 2006.

33. Eugene Kelly, *The Basics of Western Philosophy* (Westport, CT : Greenwood Press, 2004), p. 34.

34. The incentive requirement ideology is in the tradition of Greek philosophy, whereas the constraint requirement ideology follows the tradition of Hebrew philosophy. The movement of these two lines of thinking and their interaction runs through all human ideological history.

35. John Maynard Keynes was undoubtedly the most influential thinker of the postwar decades. His views, formed in Britain during the Depression, were elaborated and formalized into a theoretical structure by his American followers.

36. Graham Romp, *Game Theory: Introduction and Applications* (Oxford University Press, 1997), p. 18. According to Romp: "The concept of Nash equilibrium is motivated by the question 'What properties must an equilibrium have?' The answer to this question from John Nash (1951), based on much earlier work by Cournot (1838), was that in equilibrium each player's chosen strategy is optimal given that every other player chooses the equilibrium strategy."

37. Jean-Jacques Laffont and David Martimort, *The Theory of Incentives* (Princeton: Princeton University Press, 2002), pp. 52–53.

38. Buchanan, 1981, p. 4. See also, Economics: Public or Private Choice (11th ed.), James Gwatney, Richard L. Stroup, Russell Sobel, and David MacPherson (Southwestern College Publication, 2005).

39. R. H. Coase: *The Firm, the Market, and the Law* (Chicago: The University of Chicago Press, 1998), p. 31.

40. Oliver E. Williamson: *The Economic Institutions of Capitalism, Firms, Markets, Relational Contracting* (Beijing: China Social Sciences Publishing

House, Chengcheng Books Ltd. Reprinted from the English Edition by The Free Press, a Division of Macmillan, Inc. 1985), p. 42.

41. Avinash K. Dixit: *Lawlessness and Economics, Alternative Modes of Governance* (Princeton: Princeton University Press, 2003), p. 27.

42. Here it is important to differentiate four different concepts: exchange, transaction, market and trading. Exchange is to give in return for something received; market is the place for exchange; transaction is the action for exchange; trade is the commodity exchange. The exchange is a sociological term while the other three are economic terms. The economic categories are contained by the sociological categories.

43. Bertrand Russell: *Political Ideals. Five Essays on the Individual and Society.* (New York: Simon and Schuster, 1964), p. 50.

44. John G. Cullis and Philip R. Jones (2000) summarized the public choice theory on the subjects, see their article: *Public Choice: Outrageous Theory and Enraging Tests?* in *Public Choice Analysis of Economic Policy.* ed. K. Alec Chrystal and Rupert Pennant-Rea, Proceedings of the British Association for the Advancement of Science, Section F (Economics), pp. 59–87.

45. John G. Cullis and Philip R. Jones (2000): *Public Choice: Outrageous Theory and Enraging Tests?* in *Public Choice Analysis of Economic Policy, Proceedings of the British Association for the Advancement of Science, Section F (Economics).* ed. K. Alec Chrystal et al., p. 59.

46. Oliver E. Williamson: *The Economic Institutions of Capitalism, Firms, Markets, Relational Contracting* (Beijing: China Social Sciences Publishing House, Chengcheng Books Ltd., Copyright 1985 by Oliver E. Williamson, Reprinted from the English Edition by The Free Press, a Division of Macmillan, Inc. 1985), pp. 22–32.

47. Rupert Pennant-Rea (2000), "Public Choice and Public Policy," in *Public Choice Analysis of Economic Policy. Proceedings of the British Association for the Advancement of Science, Section F (Economics)*, ed. K. Alec Chrystal et al., p. 18.

48. Charles K. Rowley (2000): "Budget Deficits and the Size of Government in the UK and US: A Public Choice Perspective on the Thatcher and Reagan Years" in *Public Choice Analysis of Economic Policy, Proceedings of the British Association for the Advancement of Science, Section F (Economics)*, ed. K. Alec Chrystal et al., p. 28.

49. Peter M. Jackson and Dean Garratt (2000): "Public Policy and Public Choice," in *Public Choice Analysis of Economic Policy, Proceedings of the British Association for the Advancement of Science, Section F (Economics)*, ed. K. Alec Chrystal et al., p. 138.

50. Ibid.

51. Rupert Pennant-Rea (2000): "Public Choice and Public Policy," in *Public Choice Analysis of Economic Policy. Proceedings of the British Association for the Advancement of Science, Section F (Economics)*, ed. K. Alec Chrystal et al., pp. 18–19.

52. Charles K. Rowley (2000): "Budget Deficits and the Size of Government in the UK and US: A Public Choice Perspective on the Thatcher and Reagan

Years." in *Public Choice Analysis of Economic Policy, Proceedings of the British Association for the Advancement of Science, Section F (Economics)*, ed. K. Alec Chrystal et al., p. 20.

53. Mancur Olson: *The Logic of Collective Action, Public Goods and the Theory of Groups* (Cambridge: Harvard University Press, 1971), p. 116.

54. Jean-Jacques Laffont and David Martimort: *The Theory Of Incentives* (Princeton: Princeton University Press, 2002), pp. 101–105.

55. As a reference, we cite Jean-Jacques Laffont interpretation on adverse selection as below, "Incentive problems arise when a principal wants to delegate a task to an agent. Delegation can be motivated either by the possibility of benefiting from some increasing returns associated with the division of tasks, which is at the root of economic progress, or by the principal's lack of time or lack of any ability to perform the task himself, or by any other form of the principal's bounded rationality when facing complex problems. However, by the mere fact of this delegation, the agent may get access to *information* that is not available to the principal. The exact opportunity cost of this task, the precise technology used, and how god the matching is between the agent's intrinsic ability and this technology are all examples of prices of information that may become *private knowledge* of the agent. In such cases, we will say that there is *adverse selection*." See Jean-Jacques Laffont and David Martimort, *The Theory of Incentives* (Princeton, NJ: Princeton University Press, 2002), p. 28.

56. Ibid., pp. 266–268.

57. Martin Ricketts (2000): "Housing Policy and Public Choice," in *Public Choice Analysis of Economic Policy, Proceedings of the British Association for the Advancement of Science, Section F (Economics)*, ed. K. Alec Chrystal et al., pp. 172–173.

58. North, *Institutions, Institutional Change, and Economic Performance*, p. 59.

59. Alan S. Blinder: *The Quiet Revolution, Central Banking Goes Modern, Forwarded by Robert J. Shiller* (New Haven, London: Yale University Press, 2004), pp. 14–30.

60. Caprio et al., "Policy Issues in Reforming Finance," in *Financial Reform, Theory and Experience*, ed. Caprio et al. (Cambridge: Cambridge University Press, 1994), p. 416.

61. Douglass C. North, *Institutions, Institutional Change and Economic Performance* (Cambridge: Cambridge University Press, 1990), p. vii.

62. Eugene Kelly, *The Basics of Western Philosophy* (Westport, CT: Greenwood Press, 2004), p. 7.

63. Herrnstein, R. J. "Relative and absolute strength of response as a function of frequency of reinforcement," *Journal of the Experimental Analysis of Behavior*, 1961(4), pp. 563–573.

64. Rachlin, H. et al., "Economic demand theory and psychological studies of choice," in *The psychology of learning and motivation*, ed. G. H. Bower (New York: Academic Press, 1976), vol. 10, pp. 129–154.

65. Herrnstein, R. J. et al., "Melioration and behavioral allocation," in *Limits to action: The allocation of individual behavior*, ed. J. E. R. Staddon (New York: Academic, 1980), pp. 143–176.

66. Kahnemann, D., Slovic, p. & Tversky, A., (1973): "On the psychology of prediction." *Psychological Review*, 80, pp. 237– 251.

67. Von Neumann and O. Morgenstern, *The Theory of Games and Economic Behavior*, (Princeton: Princeton University Press, 1947), 2nd edition.

68. As a reference, we cite Roger Guesenerie on Arrow-Debreu framework as below: "The rigorous and general reformulation of neoclassical ideas concerning competition and welfare has been a important achievement of postwar economic theory. This achievement is associated it the names of many outstanding researchers—Allais, Arrow, Debreu, Samuelson, to mention only those who have received the Nobel Prize. A most elaborate synthesis of this work has been provided within an integrated framework. This framework is associated with the names of two of its key contributors, Arrow and Debreu. The Arrow-Debreu model is a central construct of economic theory and an unavoidable reference for economists." Roger Guesnerie: The Arrow-Debreu Paradigm Faced with Modern Theories of Contracting: a Discussion of Selected Issues Involving Infrmation and Time. See *Contract Economics*, ed. Lars Werin and Hans wijkander(Cambridge:Basil Blackwell,1992), p. 12.

69. Alec Chrystal (2000): "Public Choice Analysis of Economic Policy," in *Public Choice Analysis of Economic Policy. Proceedings of the British Association for the Advancement of Science, Section F (Economics)*, ed. K. Alec Chrystal et al., p. 1.

70. Gerard Caprio, Jr. "Banking on Financial Reform? A Case of Sensitive Dependence on Initial Conditions," in *Financial Reform, Theory and Experience*, ed. Caprio et al. (Cambridge: Cambridge University Press, 1996), p. 49.

71. James Riedel, Jin. Jing. and Gao. Jian(2004), *Investment, Financing Investment and Growth in China*, a working paper, p. 54.

72. Lawrence H, Summers, *Financial Reform, Theory and Experience*, Ed. Gerard Caprio, Jr., Izak Atiyas, and James A. Hanson (Cambridge: Cambridge University Press,1996), p. xiii.

73. Two examples: 1994 exchange reform expanded consumer demand from outside China. Its strong diplomatic ties secured its supply of natural resources.

74. Rondo Cameron, Larry Neal: *A Concise Economic History of the World, From Paleolithic Times to the Present*, 4th ed. (New York: Oxford University Press, 2003), p. 17.

75. Ibid.

76. Richard Sylla, "Financial Systems and Economic Modernization," *The Journal of Economic History*, Volume 62 (June 2002), Number 2, p. 288, 280.

77. Robert C. Merton, Financial Innovation And The Management And Regulation Of Financial Institutions, NBER Working Paper No. 5096, National Bureau Of Economic Research, 1050, Massachusetts Avenue, Cambridge, MA 02138, April 1995. p. 4.

78. Mark Gertler and Andrew Rose, "Finance, Public Policy, and Growth," in *Financial Reform, Theory and Experience*, Ed. Gerard Caprio, Jr., Izak Atiyas, and James A. Hanson (Cambridge: Cambridge University Press, 1994), p. 45.

79. Mancur Olson, *The Logic of Collective Action, Public Goods and the Theory of Groups* (Cambridge: Harvard University Press, 1971), pp. 1–3.

80. R. H. Coase, *The Problem of Social Cost*. In *Economics of the Environment: Selected Readings* (3rd ed), ed. Robert Dorfman, and Nancy S. Dorfman. (New York: W. W. Norton & Company, 1993). pp. 109–138.

81. Gerard Caprio Jr. "Introduction," in *Financial Reform, Theory and Experience*, ed. Caprio et al. (Cambridge: Cambridge University Press, 1996), p. 1.

82. Modigliani and Miller (1958, 1963) assumed that all projects within the firm had the same business of operating risk. But M-M theorem is based many assumptions. See Copeland/Weston, *Financial Theory and Corporate Policy*, 3rd ed. (Addison-Wesley, 1992), pp. 439, 455–456.

83. Gerard Caprio, Jr. "Introduction," in *Financial Reform, Theory and Experience*, ed. Caprio et al. (Cambridge: Cambridge University Press,1996), p. 1.

84. Ross Levine, *Finance and Growth: Theory, Evidence, and Mechanisms*, March 18, 2003, University of Minnesota and National Bureau of Economic Research, working paper, pp. 20–22,

85. Greenwood, J., and B. Smith, "Financial Markets in Development, and the Development of Financial Markets," *Journal of Economic Dynamics and Control*, 1996(21), pp. 145–181.

86. Ross Levine, "Financial Development and Economic Growth: Views and Agenda," *Journal of Economic Literature*, Vol. 35, No.2 (June 1997), pp. 688–726

87. Ross Levine: *Finance and Growth: Theory, Evidence, and Mechanisms*, University of Minnesota and NBER, working paper, March 18, 2003. p. 21

88. Study Group established by the Central Bank of the Group of Ten Countries, *"Recent Innovations in International Banking,"* April 1986, p. 1.

89. Douglass C. North: *Institutions, Institutional Change and Economic Performance* (Cambridge: Cambridge University Press, 1990), p. 63.

90. Robert C. Merton, *Financial Innovation and the Management and Regulation of Financial Institutions*, National Bureau of Economic Research Working Paper Series No. 5096, April 1995, Cambridge, MA, p. 4.

91. Gertler and Rose, "Finance, Public Policy, and Growth," in *Financial Reform, Theory and Experience*, ed. Caprio et al. (Cambridge: Cambridge University Press, 1994), pp. 18–19.

92. Deborah Ray, *Development Economics* (Princeton: Princeton University Press, 1998), p. 147.

93. Richard Sylla, "Financial Systems and Economic Modernization," *Journal of Economic History*, Vol. 62 (June 2002), p. 280.

94. Caprio, Jr.: *Banking and Financial Reform? A Case of Sensitive Dependence on Initial Conditions*, in *Financial Reform, Theory and Experience*, ed. Caprio et al. (Cambridge: Cambridge University Press, 1996), p. 49.

95. James M. Buchanan and Gordon Tulllock, *The Calculus of Consent* (Ann Arbor: University of Michigan Press, 1962), pp. 43–62.

96. Ross Levine, *Bank-Based or Market-Based Financial Systems: Which Is Better?* NBER Working Paper No. 138, September 2002, JEL No. G0, K2, O4.

97. Richard Sylla, "Financial Systems and Economic Modernization. "*Journal of Economic History*, Volume 62, (June 2002), p. 280.

98. Adalbert Winkler, *Financial Development, Economic Growth and Corporate Governance*, International Center for Economic Growth, Near East Program, Feb. 1998.
99. Roger Martin, *Validity vs. Reliability, Implication for Management*, ed. Rotman, *The Alumni Magazine of the Rotman School of Management* (Toronto) (Winter 2005), p. 5.
100. Ibid., p. 6.
101. Douglass C. North, *Institutions, Institutional Change and Economic Performance* (Cambridge: Cambridge University Press, 1990), p. 34.
102. Caprio, Jr., *Banking and Financial Reform? A Case of Sensitive Dependence on Initial Conditions* in *Financial Reform, Theory and Experience*, ed. Caprio et al. (Cambridge: Cambridge University Press, 1996), p. 50.
103. Mark Gertler and Andrew Rose: "Finance, Public Policy and Growth," in *Financial Reform, Theory and Experience*, ed. Gerard Caprio et al. (Cambridge: Cambridge University Press, 1994), p. 16.
104. Douglass C., North, *Institutions, Institutional Change, and Economic Performance*. (Cambridge: Cambridge University Press, 1990), p. 59.
105. Adam Smith: *An Inquiry Into The Nature And Causes Of The Wealth Of Nations* (Beijing: China Social Sciences Publishing House, Chengcheng Books Ltd.,1999.reprinted from the English Edition by Methuen & Co. Ltd. 1930), Volume I, p. 421.
106. R. H. Coase: *The Firm, the Market, and the Law* (Chicago: The University of Chicago Press, 1998), p. 8.
107. Douglass C. North, *Institutions, Institutional Change, and Economic Performance*, (Cambridge: Cambridge University Press, 1990), p. 13.
108. Ibid., p. 133.
109. Ibid., p. 134.
110. Ibid., p. 3.

Chapter 2

1. Giovanni Sabatini, "The Role of Regulations in the Development of Government Securities Markets: An Overview," in OECD, Bond Market Development in Asia, Finance and Investment (OECD Press, 2001), pp. 47–48.
2. Ibid., p. 48.

Chapter 3

1. After studying how savings bonds were issued to individuals in the United States, I discussed the issue of individual losses in the secondary government bond market with Wu Xiaoling, then director general of the Policy Planning Department and currently vice governor of the People's Bank of China, proposing that savings bonds should be issued to individuals. Wu supported the idea. We then agreed that the specific method for savings bonds execution should be jointly worked out by the finance and the banking authorities, which led to the creation of

certificate treasury bonds. It is worth noting that the original intention of the certificate bonds issuance was to introduce a bulk T-bond transaction to the market rather than to gradually transform tradable T-bonds into nontradable certificate T-bonds.

2. In the beginning of 1996, Liu Zhongli, then minister of the Ministry of Finance, told me that he and Xie Xuren, then director general of the General Office of the Ministry, believed that the debt repayment peak was looming and that, should long-term T-bonds be issued, the debt service pressure could be eased. I told him that the issuance of long-term T-bonds depended on two preconditions: institutional investors and bonds' high liquidity. The developments of the government bond market in recent years had provided these two preconditions, and the issue of 10-year T-bonds could be attempted within the year of 1996. The issue-by-tender method was then conducted in Beijing, and Minister Liu Zhongli and Vice Minister Liu Jibin were both present. The issue of 10-year T-bonds solved a big problem for the Ministry of Finance.

3. The Ministry of Finance and China Development Bank issued ultra-long-term bonds (20-year and 30-year T-bonds and financial bonds) in succession in 2001 and 2002; however, the issuance of different types of bonds was based on particular market conditions and specific requirements of the issuers. Therefore, because the market anticipated higher interest rates in 2003 and the steep yield curve, long-term bond transactions encountered some difficulties, and issuing ultra-long-term bonds has been halted for now.

Chapter 4

1. The British do not call this an English auction; they call it an American auction.

Chapter 6

1. Bidders return is implicitly reflected in the difference between successful bidding price and their funding costs.
2. Due highest security, treasury yield should be lower, other thing being equal.

Chapter 9

1. Fang Han Ting et al., "Report on Venture Capital and Industry Investment Funds," April 2006 (Chinese version).
2. From the China Development Bank, introduction of its private equity investment, on April 2006 (Chinese version).

Chapter 13

1. In comparison, U.S. government bonds are exempted from federal government taxes but are subject to local government taxes.

Chapter 18

1. Please notice, as the primary bond market is only one component of primary exchange, it also includes the dialogue between bond market manager and bond market participants. I use the word " primary bond exchange in the primary-secondary exchange framework to draw the reader's attention to the fact that dialogue, among others, between bond market participants and bond market manager also matters to the bond market transition in China.

2. Please refer to Chapter 1, where it has been discussed that institution is driven by the interaction between constraint apparatus and incentive apparatus.

3. Oliver E. Williamson: *The Economic Institutions of Capitalism, Firms, Markets, Relational Contracting*, China Social Sciences Publishing House Chengcheng Books Ltd. Copyright 1985 by Oliver E. Williamson, Reprinted from the English Edition by The Free Press, a Division of Macmillian, Inc. 1985. p. 39.

4. Notes:

   - The "redemption funds" entry was set by the PBOC in the central treasury. Before the redemption work began, the Ministry of Finance would appropriate redemption funds in installments. The specialized banks and their outlets prepared the Report on the Paid Principal and Interest for the Treasury Bills for the Year XXXX at the end of each business day and sent it with the declaration forms to the local branches of the PBOC level by level up to the head office. The PBOC cleared the Upward Transfer Report on the Paid Principal and Interest for the Treasury Bills for the Year XXXX prepared by its branches with the specialized banks via the "linked banks current account" entry, transferred the account to the head office level by level, and deducted the "redemption funds" entry at the end.
   - The withdrawn paper securities were sent to the prefecture- and city-level branches of the PBOC for destruction.

5. Notes:

   - The working procedure for reporting and settling between the specialized banks and their debt service outlets and the PBOC is unchanged.
   - After receiving the redemption reports on the treasury bills, the PBOC's branches in the counties or prefectures combined the reports into a Daily Report on Central Budgetary Revenue (deducted from treasury revenue) and transferred them together with the budgetary revenue funds to their superior department. The central general treasury was responsible for the preparation of the redemption date report and submitted the report to the Ministry.
   - The withdrawn redeemed treasury bills were sent to the prefecture and city branches of the PBOC for destruction.

6. Oliver E. Williamson: *The Economic Institutions of Capitalism, Firms, Markets, Relational Contracting*, China Social Sciences Publishing House Chengcheng Books Ltd. Copyright 1985 by Oliver E. Williamson. Reprinted from the English Edition by The Free Press, a Division of Macmillian, Inc. 1985. p. 39.

Chapter 19

1. For safekeeping reason, individual investors tend to keep the custody voucher rather than paper bonds. The custody voucher is the certificate of bond that signed by the firm against the bond in custody in its warehouse, the amount of which should be identical to the total bond in custody. However, some firms sell short government bonds by bring forth more custody voucher to the investors, the proceeds excess the bonds in custody went to the firm. In this way, the firms achieved financing but in the cost equivalent to government financing.

Chapter 20

1. Lars Risbjerg and Anders Holmlund, "Analytical Framework for Debt and Risk Management," in *Advances in Risk Management of Government Debt* (Paris: OECD Press, 2005), p. 42.

Chapter 21

1. The global bond market has investor base around the world, but basically in U.S., Europe, and Asia, the bonds can be listed in several marketplaces.

Chapter 23

1. The Ministry of Finance resumed issuing the short-term bills in 2005.

Chapter 24

1. "Pressure group" is a term used in public choice theory. A pressure group is a group of lobbyists who persuade the government to do something and thereby are able to achieve their group objective.
2. Norms and conventions are created by the market participants themselves whereas laws and regulations are made by those who are outside of the exchange between market participants.

Chapter 26

1. It was up to 48 percent in 2004.
2. James Riedel, Jin Jing, and Gao Jian, "Investment, Financing Investment, and Growth in China," working paper, August 2004.
3. Nicholas R. Lardy, *China's Unfinished Economic Revolution* (Washington, DC: Brookings Institution Press, 1998), p. vii.
4. Thomas J. Sargent, *Dynamic Macroeconomic Theory* (Cambridge, MA: Harvard University Press, 1997), p. 24.
5. E. S. Phelps, *Seven Schools of Macroeconomic Thought* (Oxford: Clarendon Press, 1990), p. 71.

6. James Riedel, Jin Jing, and Gao Jian, "Investment, Financing Investment, and Growth in China," working paper, August 2004.
7. A recent study by Yi Heng and Ye Haiyun, based on a new data, provides evidence and theoretical proof that government debt crowds out private investment. The higher the government debt–GDP ratio is, the lower the private investment rate is. This negative effect of government debt may come from the fluctuation of government debt–GDP ratio. There is enough attrition in the real world to cause the Ricardian equivalence proposition to fail temporarily. See Yi Heng and Ye Haiyun, *The Crowding Out of Private Investment by Government, An International Experience*, in *Statistical Research*, 2005(10).

Chapter 27

1. World Development Report, *The State in a Changing World* (Oxford: Oxford University Press, 1997).
2. "Decentralization" refers to the central government's revenue-sharing policy vis-à-vis the intergovernmental fiscal relationship with local governments to replace the planned economy where all revenue goes to and expenditure comes from central government.
3. John Steele Gordon, *Hamilton's Blessing: The Extraordinary Life and Times of Our National Debt* (New York: Walker and Company, 1997), p. 1.
4. Ibid., p. 2.
5. Ibid., p. 5.
6. Ibid., pp. 3–4.

Chapter 28

1. See the discussion in the seminar held by UBS and SDRC on July 12, 2005.
2. We will see later that a failure to honor commitments resulted from information asymmetry, which is the main reason for the debtor's moral hazard.
3. Eugene Kelly, *The Basics of Western Philosophy, Basics of the Social Sciences* (Westport, CT: Greenwood Press, 2004), p. 29.
4. In the language of neoinstitutionalism, this is a transaction cost.
5. See Jean-Jacques Laffont and David Martimort, The Theory of Incentives (Princeton, NJ: Princeton University Press, 2002). Here again, we emphasize that IEEN and neoclassical economics are not mutually exclusive but complementary.
6. I. Fisher, *The Theory of Interest* (New York: Macmillan, 1930), p. 137.
7. D. R. Hodgman, "Credit Risks and Credit Rationing," Quarterly Journal of Economics 74, no. 2 (May 1960): 258–278.
8. Douglass C. North, *Institutions, Institutional Change and Economic Performance, Political Economy of Institutions and Decisions* (Cambridge: Cambridge University Press, 1990), p. 3.
9. Karl Marx, Capital (Dutton: Everyman's Library, 1972), p. 836.
10. Marx and Engels, *Collections of Marx and Engels (Chinese Version)*, People's Publishing House, 1972, Volume 27, p. 481.

11. Although the differences between bonds and deposits for investors and savers are obvious, it is important to point out that many investors in China confuse the bond instrument with the deposit facility. They regard bonds as saving instruments. This is, in part, why China's Ministry of Finance introduced savings bonds in 1994 to cater the needs of individual investors-savers.

12. Frank J. Fabozzi et al., *Handbook of Fixed Income Securities, 4th ed.* (Burr Ridge, IL: Irwin Professional Publishing, 1995), p. 207.

13. As exporting firms exchange their foreign currencies earnings with central bank via State Administration of Foreign Exchange (SAFE) for domestic currency, central bank has to increase domestic currency to buy the foreign exchange generated by exporting firms; this will increase money supply in excess of money demand, which is expansionary. In order to offset the negative impact of building up reserve to the economy, central bank has to issue central bank notes or bills to withdraw money in circulation and thereby reduce money supply. The central banks' passive action against rising money supply due to build up reserve is called sterilization.

14. Frank J. Fabozzi et al., *Handbook of Fixed Income Securities, 4th ed.* (Burr Ridge, IL: Irwin Professional Publishing, 1995), p. 203.

15. In the United States, investors always talk about ATT $5\frac{1}{8}$ due in 2008; and in China, investors say 5.5 percent is due 2008.

Chapter 29

1. Robert C. Merton, *Financial Innovation and the Management and Regulation of Financial Institutions*, National Bureau of Economic Research Working Paper Series No. 5096, April 1995, Cambridge, MA, p. 4.

Postscript

1. A Wall Street Journal News Roundup, China unveils rules for funds to protect securities investors, in the Asia *Wall Street Journal*, September 30–October 2, 2005, M2.

Index